Qualitative Sociology

QUALITATIVE SOCIOLOGY

A Method to the Madness

HOWARD SCHWARTZ

JERRY JACOBS

THE FREE PRESS
A Division of Macmillan Publishing Co., Inc.
NEW YORK

Collier Macmillan Publishers
LONDON

The Free Press
A Division of Macmillan Publishing Co., Inc.
866 Third Avenue, New York, N.Y. 10022

Collier Macmillan Canada, Ltd.

Library of Congress Catalog Card Number: 78–58915

Printed in the United States of America

printing number

    4 5 6 7 8 9 10

Library of Congress Cataloging in Publication Data

Schwartz, Howard
  Qualitative sociology.

  Bibliography: p.
  Includes index.
  1. Sociology--Methodology. 2. Knowledge, Sociology
of. I. Jacobs, Jerry, joint author. II. Title.
HM24.S376   301'.01'8   78–58915
ISBN 0-02-928170-9
ISBN 0-02-928160-1 pbk.

Epigraph from *The Everything and The Nothing* by Meher Baba, p. 20. Copyright © 1963 by Meher
House Publications, Beacon Hill N.S.W., Australia. Reprinted by permission.

To Alicia
who needs no "methods" to
understand another

In the beginning the seeker of Truth is like a man who, having heard that a priceless pearl is to be got from the depths of the ocean, goes down to the seashore and first admires the vastness of the ocean and then paddles and splashes about in the shallows and, intoxicated with this new excitement, forgets about the pearl.

Out of many who do this, one after a while, remembers his quest and learns to swim and starts to swim out.

Out of many who do this, one masters swimming and reaches the open sea; the others perish in the waves.

Out of many who master swimming, one begins to dive; the others in their enjoyment of mastery, again forget about the pearl.

Out of many who practice diving, one reaches the ocean bed and grasps the pearl. . . .

Meher Baba

Contents

Preface and Acknowledgments   xiii

BOOK ONE: THE REALITY RECONSTRUCTION BUSINESS

Part I. Reality Reconstruction: What Is It and Why Do It?
  Introduction   2

1. Qualitative and Quantitative Methods: Two Approaches to Sociology 3
   *Qualitative and Quantitative Data: What's the Difference? / Data
   and the Positivists / Data and the Symbolic Interactionists / The
   Case for Qualitative Sociology / The Case for Positivist Science /
   Summary*

2. The Sociology of the "Inside"   17
   *Max Weber / George Herbert Mead / Herbert Blumer / Barney
   Glaser and Anselm Strauss: Grounded Theory / Latter-Day Followers*

Part II. Reality Reconstruction: How to Do It
  Introduction   36

3. Participant Observation and Interviewing: Reconstructing the Reality of
   Social Groups   37
   Interviewing / Participant Observation

4. Personal Accounts and Life Histories: Reconstructing the Individual's
   Reality   61
   Analyzing Personal Accounts / Life Histories

5. Nonreactive Techniques for Studying Groups or Individuals   75
   Unobtrusive Measures / Audio-Visual Techniques

ix

Part III. Reality Reconstruction: What's Wrong with It?
    Introduction   106

  6. The Reality Reconstruction Business Reconsidered   107
    Subjective Phenomena and Reactive Techniques / Methods of Studying Subjectivity: An Evaluation / The Social Scientific Legitimation of Accounts: Deciding Between Competing Versions of Reality

Illustrative Case Studies for Book One
    Introduction   132

A. "Burp-Seltzer? I Never Use It": An In-depth Look at Market Research   133

B. Symbolic Bureaucracy: A Case Study of a Social Welfare Agency   143

C. A Phenomenological Study of Suicide Notes   156

D. The Clinical Organization of "Sub-Normality": A Case of Mistaken Identity   168

BOOK TWO: FORMAL SOCIOLOGY

Part IV. Formal Sociology: What Is It and Why Do It?
    Introduction   180

  7. The Sociology of Everyday Life: Nothing Unusual (or Otherwise) Is Happening   183
    Georg Simmel and Formal Sociology / Erving Goffman and "Finding Everyday Life" / Alfred Schutz: The Problem of Common Sense

  8. The World of Everday Life: Reconstructing Sociological Knowledge   209
    Harold Garfinkel and Ethnomethodology / Aaron Cicourel and Cognitive Sociology / Latter-Day Followers

Part V. Making Everyday Life Visible: How to Do It
    Introduction: The Problem of Visibility   240

  9. Participant Observation in Formal Sociology   247
    The Stranger / The Novice / Instructions / Multiple Observers / Cultural Misfits / Cultural Troublemakers

  10. Reification and Reactive Measures as Research Strategies   266
    Producing Multiple Realities / Making Methods / Manipulating Social Situations / Disrupting Social Settings

11. Hunt-and-Peck Ethnography: Studying Topics, Not People   289
    *Getting Started: Single-Case Analysis / The Method of
    Examples / The Use of Models, Paradigms, and Frameworks / The
    "What's New?" Problem / Natural versus Contrived Settings*

Part VI. Analyzing Everyday Life: How to Do It
    Introduction: Sight versus Thought in Formal Sociology   306

12. Making Patterns I: General Orientations   311
    *Type I versus Type II Errors / The "What If" Mentality and Its
    Alternative / Discovered Topics / The Traditional View of
    Hypotheses / Conceptual Laws / The Place of Rigorous Theory in
    Formal Sociology*

13. Making Patterns II: Two Exemplary Procedures   340
    Conversational Analysis / Classical Phenomenology

**Part VII. Formal Sociology and Reality Reconstruction: What's Wrong with
    Them?**
    Introduction   368

14. Patterns? What Patterns?   369
    *The Problem of Social Order / Socialization and the Problem of Social
    Order / Qualitative Sociologists: Do They Make Better
    Patterns? / A Word to Anyone Rarely Suffices*

Illustrative Case Studies for Book Two
    Introduction   380

E. The World of the Congenitally Deaf-Blind: Toward the Grounds for
    Achieving Human Understanding   381

F. Imitation and Competence: A Study of Retarded Adults   397

G. On Recognizing Mistakes: A Case of Practical Reasoning in
    Psychotherapy   405

H. On the Art of Talking About the World   418

Bibliography   429

Index   439

Preface and Acknowledgments

One fateful morning early in the summer of 1975, while having breakfast at the House of Pancakes, we hit upon what seemed like a good idea at the time, writing a short descriptive book on qualitative sociology. Several hours and innumerable cups of coffee later, we had written a preliminary outline on a table napkin. The idea was to make the book as comprehensive and simple as possible without being simplistic.

By comprehensive we meant we wanted the book to deal with all forms of qualitative sociology—for example, ethnomethodology, phenomenological sociology, conversational analysis, and formal sociology—not only with field studies. We also intended it to be more than a "cookbook"—that is, it was to be theoretically based, conceptually sound, *and* methodologically useful. Such a book, of the scope we envisioned, we felt was not currently available.

A year and some eight hundred painfully typewritten pages later, we had begun to recognize the error in our reckoning. Such a book was not easy to produce. Topics seemed to generate topics, and the book was growing like Topsy. Not only were there more things to consider than we had anticipated in order not to be "simplistic," but many topics we had planned to cover proved more difficult to put into readily comprehensible language than we had imagined. Anyone who has gone window shopping at an ethnomethodology or phenomenology emporium will be able to relate to that problem. However, perseverence won out, and the finished text is before you. As for the authors, we are both better and wiser for the experience. Having written and read the text several dozen times, we thought it might be well to share our understanding of it with our readers, in order to orient them to what they are in store for and how they might best deal with it, given each reader's particular purposes.

The book is really two books in one. Chapters 1 to 6 deal in one way or another with what we have dubbed "the reality reconstruction business." This topic is usually covered in books on field studies, ethnography, and symbolic interaction. Our treatment is in some ways similar to that found elsewhere in the literature and in many other regards radically different from other presentations. We will not attempt a detailed itemization here. The reader will have to take the usual with the unusual in order to find where the one begins and the other ends. Those concerned primarily with the "ethnographic experience" and methods and problems of pursuing it can restrict their inquiry to the first six chapters.

Those who seek to step into the great beyond can press on to chapters 7 to 14. There they will find a discussion of a series of methodological and theoretical topics we refer to as "formal sociology." This rubric encompasses formal sociology, ethnomethodology, phenomenology, and conversational analysis.

The format of each of these two major sections is the same. Both treat (but not necessarily in this order) the following questions: What is it? Who did it? How can it be done? Why do it? and What's wrong with it? Each section begins with a theoretical statement of what the topic is about by discussing a series of major figures who either founded or have practiced the kind of sociology being considered. There follows an exposition of the research methods this kind of sociology employs. Finally, there is, in each case, a summary evaluation of the major methodological, theoretical, and philosophical problems generated by the topic. We have also supplemented the text with a collection of case studies which illustrate the kind of substantive work qualitative research can produce.

One of the reasons this book was difficult to write has to do with the nature of qualitative sociology itself. While quantitative sociologists have achieved a certain standardization of their techniques, many qualitative sociologists find it necessary to avoid standardization because of the kinds of topics they study. For them research is an art form that requires the use of a large variety of very different research tools. More important, it requires that the researcher be able to improvise his own concepts and research methods in order to deal effectively with the novel situations that invariably arise in this kind of undertaking.

We attempt to deal with this problem by abandoning the customary format of a sociology text in favor of an approach more akin to a manual on some skill. Certain core concepts and techniques are spelled out in detail. But accompanying these main themes is a diverse assortment of additional ideas, procedures, and theories that are not spelled out. Rather, we "expose" the reader to them in a variety of ways. There is constant use of illustrations to anchor abstract ideas to concrete incidents and applications.

The illustrations also introduce the reader to the incredible variety of phenomena and situations which are dealt with in qualitative sociology, and to many concrete research problems that could otherwise not be discussed. Whenever it is not too confusing to do so, we introduce the semitechnical terminologies of various sociologists in order to make their styles of thought more accessible and familiar. In fact, in the pursuit of this goal, entire sections (such as the section on conversational analysis in chapter 6) employ a writing style that is distinctive to the topic being discussed. Finally, to try to keep the book alive and to give the reader access to some of the more difficult material, a variety of organizing formats and presentational styles are used. These range from the theatrical and tongue-in-cheek to the formal and philosophically grand. We apologize to our women readers on this score for our frequent use of masculine pronouns. Given currently available terminologies, we found no easy middle-ground between nonsexist wording and awkward, unreadable grammatical con-structions.

With these considerations out of the way, we invite the reader to read on.

We wish to express our thanks to our editor, Gladys Topkis, who, in the course of editing our manuscript, displayed greater sociological understanding and imagi-nation than many sociologists. This coupled with her tolerance for both the authors and their ideas leaves us doubly indebted.

BOOK ONE

The Reality
Reconstruction Business

Part I

Reality Reconstruction: What Is It and Why Do It?

... a recent Gallup poll (*Newsweek*, January 25, 1971, p. 52) indicated that approximately half of American college students have tried marijuana, and a large number of them use it fairly regularly. They do this at the risk of having their careers ruined and going to jail for several years. Why? Conventional research on the nature of marijuana intoxication tells us that the primary effects are a slight increase in heart rate, reddening of the eyes, some difficulty with memory, and small decrements in performance on complex psychomotor tests.

Would you risk going to jail to experience these?

A young marijuana smoker who hears a scientist or physician talk about these findings as the basic nature of marijuana intoxication will simply sneer and have his antiscientific attitude further reinforced. It is clear to him that the scientist has no real understanding of what marijuana intoxication is all about.[1]

To get a quick intuitive grasp of what reality reconstruction is all about, there is perhaps nothing better than the image created by a quote such as this. By reality reconstruction we mean the messy, tortuous business of learning to see the world of an individual or group from the inside. This is quite a different goal from that of discovering and verifying scientific hypotheses. There is often no way to do it scientifically nor any rigorous way to prove that it has been done. Yet many sociologists would agree that the scientists referred to in the quote do not understand "what marijuana intoxication is all about." To them there is something vital that one does not know if one has no access to the inside—that is, if he is unable to reconstruct the world as it looks, sounds, and smells to those within it. Many, if not most, of the techniques in qualitative sociology are designed to make this reconstruction possible.

In the next two chapters we examine the nature of insider's knowledge in detail, whether it can be obtained in some practical way, and why it is important for sociology.

Notes

1. Charles T. Tart, "States of Consciousness and State-Specific Sciences," *Science* 176 (June 16, 1972): 1203–1210.

CHAPTER 1

Qualitative and Quantitative Methods: Two Approaches to Sociology

Qualitative and Quantitative Data: What's the Difference?

Imagine an anthropologist from the starship *Enterprise*. For him, sociologists would constitute one of the many groups of persons whose business it is to construct belief systems about their society. An interesting question he might ask about them would be how they go about legitimizing these beliefs. One answer is that they do it by recourse to certain artifacts—i.e., that is by the production and display of "data." They interact with their fellows in various ways: They take notes, make counts, examine documents, ride in police cars, make films and tapes, and hang around and "keep their eyes open." They then take the products of these actions and organize, tabulate, graph, summarize, transcribe, code, and symbolize them. Finally, the "data" appear, usually in written form, in standardized notation systems as a special part of a text with its own unique format, labels, and explanations.

Various kinds of such artifacts are brought to mind by terms like *tables, path diagrams, regression graphs, transcripts, vignettes, exemplary stories, pictures,* and *excerpts*. Sociologists read and understand the objects in such texts as being partially capable of legitimizing their beliefs. These objects constitute highly stylized descriptions of the *particulars* of our social world—of who voted for whom, what was seen, what was said, how many were born, how much money was made. These particulars serve as examples of and evidence for hypotheses

3

about the nature of social life in our society. As an activity, gathering data represents, for sociologists, a mode of being in, and displaying, the world in the course of doing their job. As artifacts, data represent procedures of justification.

Understandably, sociologists as a professional group are interested in imposing normative standards on the collection, display, and use of data. However, this area of praxis is a source of continued controversy. For particular research, types of research, or research in general, there is simply no consensus on what constitutes legitimate data. In particular, individuals, groups, and exponents of various types of sociology take principled stands on what data should be and how they should be gathered. Further, these stands are blatantly competitive; partisans see themselves as advocating not additive but different procedures.

The descriptions of reality that sociologists call data are actually inventories of the real world—lists of the things to be found in societies, subcultures, institutions, bowling leagues, and so on. Thus, before we can consider any questions about how to analyze and explain things, we must deal with the question "What is it that I am going to explain?" and "What should I describe in the world and how should I go about describing it?"

Sociologists produce data by translating their observations and inquiries into written notation systems. The difference between qualitative and quantitative sociology can be stated quite simply in terms of the notation systems used to describe the world. Quantitative sociologists assign numbers to qualitative observations. In this sense, they produce data by counting and "measuring" things. The things measured can be individual persons, groups, whole societies, speech acts, and so on. Qualitative sociologists, on the other hand, report observations in the natural language at large. They seldom make counts or assign numbers to these observations. In this sense, qualitative sociologists report on the social world much as the daily newspaper does. This simple difference in commitment to notation systems corresponds to vast differences in values, goals, and procedures for doing sociological research.

There are two broad goals for sociology which are most important in this connection. For some it is intrinsically important for sociology to develop ways of gaining access to the life-world of other individuals. In this view, it is crucial to discover the daily activities, the motives and meanings, and the actions and reactions of the individual "actor," in the context of his daily life. In contrast, others take sociology's most important task to be developing itself into a full-fledged science. As we will see later, there are many, in both qualitative and quantitative sociology, who advocate and bask in the value of "science." It turns out that everybody is doing "science," although when one looks at what each individual investigator is doing, radically different activities are revealed. At the moment we are using the word *science* to mean the particular ways of discovering and verifying things usually identified as "positivist science."

We are now armed with two variables of sorts—namely, positive science versus the actor's point of view, and the use of numbers versus the use of natural language. From these we can produce that famous sociological resource, the fourfold table:

Goals of Sociology

Data	Positive science	Actor's point of view
Use of numbers		
Use of natural language		

It turns out, for reasons that will be explained in later chapters, that qualitative methods, which use natural language, are best at gaining access to the life-world of other individuals in a short time. On the other hand, quantitative methods are best for conducting a "positive science"; that is, they allow for the clear, rigorous, and reliable collection of data and permit the testing of empirical hypotheses in a logically consistent manner.

We should be clear about what we mean by the life-world of other individuals. This includes motives, meanings, emotions, and other subjective aspects of the lives of individuals and groups. It also includes their daily actions and behavior in ordinary settings and situations, the structure of those actions, and the objective conditions that accompany and influence them. Now, some of these items are directly observable and are in this sense "objective." However, in one way or another, it is usually necessary to have access to meanings and other inner phenomena in order to see and describe daily behavior in any detail. For instance, without knowledge of chess as a game, together with the strategies, reasons, and "moves" that go with it, one might describe the actions of chess players as two people moving pieces of wood around a board. Thus, in one way or another, the actor's subjective point of view is central to qualitative sociology.

Data and the Positivists

Positivists hold that whatever else science might turn out to be, it usually involves the sharpening up of an otherwise fuzzy picture of "what's really going on out there." The picture is fuzzy because lay persons have their own practical ways of describing the particulars of the world they inhabit. In fact, since they are not doing science but are doing the laundry or some similarly practical task, their descriptive apparatus is not particularly designed for scientific service. That is, it displays inconsistency, vagueness, multiple meanings, and other characteristics that contribute to a blurred and sketchy picture. It is therefore understood that one of positivistic sociology's services to society is to provide more accurate information. A familiar procedure is to take a lay concept, such as crime or suicide, and repair it or "clean it up" by precise definition and the development of measurement procedures in the hope that it will become capable of being used in a scientific theory. With its new definition and new use, the altered concept can be presented to colleagues and the society at large as contributing to a clearer, more valid picture of the world than its lay counterpart.

However, one is not limited to the use of overhauled lay concepts. A second preoccupation of those attempting to do science is the uncovering of empirical structures—laws, patterns, rules, or principles—that have hitherto been hidden in some sense. Therefore, any data that, first, present a sharp picture and, second, are helpful in finding these structures are, in principle, acceptable.

These two preoccupations combine to give a position that may be summarized thus: data are always to be some form of knowable, retrievable fact. The concern for facts, defined in this way, places constraints upon the procedures used to collect and display data. One illustration of such a constraint is based upon the sociological convention that "facts" must be external to the individual.[1] The individual may not consider himself to be a source of data, that is, sociologists may not study themselves directly. In contrast, phenomenologists and psychoanalysts consider themselves to be prime sources of data.

A second constraint is one of content. In a recent book on medicine, Freidson[2] characterized a profession as a group with autonomous control over the nature of its technical praxis. That is to say, in the practice of medicine, the patient hardly ever participates in decision making about his own treatment. If one takes the stand that "what's going on around here is science," a similar prescription tends to follow for positivistic sociology. As noted above, sociologists as a group are in the business of producing authoritative descriptions of the lay person's world. Here, as in medicine, lay persons have no business participating in decision making as to what these descriptions of their world are to be. Their business is to sit still and be measured—to answer the questions, push the buttons, or otherwise provide sociologists with what they need to describe them in ways that the sociologists, and their methodologies, determine to be correct. Any characteristics or actions which inhibit this function become nuisances. There are a variety of technical names for such nuisances, such as "response bias," "intervening variables," and "nonresponse error." The categorical imperative—the answer to "What's going on out there?"—becomes "What's going on out there is whatever we, the well-trained sociologists, say is going on out there." Given our value-laden description, this position sounds elitist and undemocratic, does it not?

Data and the Symbolic Interactionists

The second position is of the form "What's going on out there is what the actors say is going on out there." Advocates of this subjective point of view wish to make the lay person the expert about his world. He lives there; he knows better than we do what it is like and how best to describe it. Instead of choosing what to observe and describe merely on the basis of its scientific interest, a new criterion is introduced. The goal is precisely opposite to that of scientific sociology. Instead of trying to discover things about a social world that those within it do not know, the reverse is sought. We want to know what the actors know, see what they see, understand what they understand. As a result our data attempt to describe their vocabularies, their ways of looking, their sense of the important and unimportant, and so on. Science is replaced by access to meanings or "understanding"[3] as the most important preoccupation for sociology.

These goals can be justified metaphysically by the argument that the only "real" social reality is the reality from within. They can be justified politically by arguing that people have to live in the world that sociologists define for them, and that such definitions of their world will affect their lives in practical ways because of the political, social, and psychological consequences of research. Finally, they can be justified scientifically by taking the really deep questions in sociology to be social-psychological; ones such as how is communication possible; how do meaning systems mutually affect each other; or what is the origin of values?

In short, the reasons for concern with the actor's point of view seem to fall into two basic categories:

1. There may be goals that are more important than science.
2. In order to create a social science, it is *necessary* to learn the actor's point of view.

Proponents of the latter position came to be known as symbolic interactionists. It is to their perspective that we now turn.

The Case for Qualitative Sociology

Efforts to reconstruct the reality of a social scene have evolved numerous methodological strategies. For example, researchers have done participant-observation studies, conducted interviews, analyzed personal accounts, and reconstructed life histories. Many, if not most, of these attempts at reality reconstruction have been cast within the theoretical framework of symbolic interaction. This approach has its roots in the early work of George Herbert Mead, John Horton Cooley, and Herbert Blumer and the later works of Anselm Strauss and Howard Becker, to mention but a few.

The basic position of this orientation is that in order to understand social phenomena, the researcher needs to discover the actor's "definition of the situation"[4]—that is, his perception and interpretation of reality and how these relate to his behavior. Further, the actor's perception of reality turns on his ongoing interpretation of the social interactions that he and others participate in, which, in turn, pivots on his use of symbols in general and language in particular. Finally, in order for the researcher to come to such an understanding he must be able (albeit imperfectly) to put himself in the other person's shoes.

From this perspective, social meanings (which direct human behavior) do not inhere in activities, institutions, or social objects themselves. Rather, meanings are conferred upon social events by interacting individuals, who must first interpret what is going on from the social context in which these events occur. This emerging gestalt (the "definition of the situation") is seen to result from the interplay of biography, situation, nonverbal communication, and linguistic exchange that characterizes all social interaction.

In order to understand this process and the forms of social interaction that result from it, the researcher invoking, for example, a participant-observational strategy usually seeks to interact with the actors, to observe and partake of their activities, to conduct informal interviews with them and others who are or were party to the social environment under study, and, through these involvements, to reconstruct their reality. If successful, the researcher acquires "member's knowledge"[5] and consequently understands from the participants' point of view what motivated the participants to do what the researcher had observed them doing and what these acts meant to them at the time.

These efforts, it is hoped, lead to a kind and level of insight that Max Weber referred to as "Verstehen,"[6] a feature of the research process that he felt could be extremely useful in acquiring true sociological understanding.

However, a large number of American sociologists did not pursue the search for Verstehen but were concerned with what Emile Durkheim called "social facts." These are characteristics of groups that are viewed as external to the individual and constraining upon him:

> We thus arrive at the point where we can formulate and delimit in a precise way the domain of sociology. It comprises only a limited group of phenomena. A social fact is to be recognized by the power of external coercion which it exercises or is capable of exercising over individuals.[7]

Examples of such facts include the monetary system of nation-states, religious beliefs and practices, and the system of symbols we call language.

Sociologists of this school sought as data characteristics of groups which could be scientifically ascertained and verified. Since it was further stipulated that social facts could be explained only by other social facts ("The determining cause of a social fact should be sought among the social facts preceding it and not among the states of the individual consciousness"[8]), such facts constituted both the problems to be explained in sociology and the elements of explanations. It followed that, insofar as one adhered to this conception of explanation in sociology, one did not concern himself in any direct way with the individual, his interpretations, or their effects upon his behavior. Thus, this school came to regard detailed, natural observation of individuals in their everyday settings and situations as an unscientific or prescientific endeavor.

As a result, until very recently, the sociological literature has contained relatively few good descriptive accounts of the everyday life of persons in their natural settings based on unobtrusive observation of their activities over time. Not only was there a lack of material dealing with what people did in various social settings, but there was even less to indicate what these activities meant to them at the time and in the settings in which they occurred.

Proponents of the symbolic-interactionist approach were not surprised to find that, while there was a plethora of sociological theory, none proved capable of achieving the positivists' dream of explanation, prediction, and control. If social theory is seen to result (within a scientific framework) from observation, description, categorization, and synthesis of social actions and the meaning of social actions, then the absence of proven theories is in no way enigmatic. As things now stand, the descriptive data needed to take the first step in such a theory-building process are almost completely absent.

In order to rectify this state of affairs, those who recommend reality reconstruction within a symbolic-interactionist framework suggest the proliferation of descriptive studies. While these ethnographic case studies do not provide all the answers to the questions they generate, they do provide some. For example, it has been increasingly recognized that such studies are not necessarily parochial and can be applied to larger theoretical issues.

What has not been sufficiently recognized, either by those seeking the etiology of "social facts" or by those doing ethnographic studies, is that it may be more fruitful to spend less time considering the kinds of social setting and more time considering the forms of interaction *within* these settings. Ultimately it is the form and extent of interaction, not the settings per se, that are of greatest interest. Similar social settings often produce very different patterns of interaction, while patterns produced by different settings may be very similar.[9] This is best understood not only with reference to the kind of setting, but with respect to the unique characteristics of the individuals comprising it. Patterns of interaction, while they are partially influenced by the constraints of the immediate setting and the society at large, are also influenced by the acts of individuals. Indeed, this influence is sometimes so radical as to change the patterns of interaction not only within the subsetting but within the society at large as well.

Sociology continues to pay insufficient attention to the individuals who comprise social settings and to put undue emphasis on the effects of the "system" and its capacity to "shape" behavior. It is abundantly clear that the acts of individuals have had a good deal to do with shaping the system and that bureaucracy, despite its every effort, has not yet succeeded in ending the powerful influence of the "charismatic man."[10] Contemporary history is replete with examples. In light of this it is unfortunate (perhaps ironic) that sociology has prematurely abandoned not only the search for Verstehen but the effects of influential and/or charismatic leaders.

These recommendations constitute an important and neglected perspective from which to study the reciprocal effects of social settings upon individuals and of individuals upon social settings, and the relationship of the resulting interac-

tions to "social structure." Allowing that it is not always easy to explain the differences and similarities one finds between or within social settings, it is of prime importance to recognize and acknowledge these differences. Many hold that the lack of pat explanations for such idiosyncratic findings tends to muddy the waters. However, it is essential that the social sciences come to recognize and admit the complexity of social interactions and the fact that systematic and parsimonious explanations are not easy to come by. Those who have undertaken the search are painfully aware of this, despite the many "social theories" to be found in the literature. The move toward a social science would probably proceed with greater dispatch if more researchers recognized and openly acknowledged this problem. It might also be well for the discipline to begin at the beginning and do as so many have repeatedly recommended—that is, first observe, describe, and categorize social events, then construct theories that are consistent with the data. The current "fit" between theories and data leaves much to be desired. It is ironic that those who most strongly recommend the pursuit of such a program, in the name of social science, have been least likely to abide by it and are the first to chide those who have. Such studies should be encouraged and require no apology to those who contend that field studies offer "only descriptions." Without descriptive data to build upon, theories of social behavior are likely to continue to prove to be "only theories."

The Case for Positivist Science

In order to give the reader some idea of why many sociologists are not impressed with the actor's point of view, let us look at something that is, on its face, an eminently subjective phenomenon.

For a long time sociologists have been interested in occupational prestige— the degree of esteem, status, and general worth which people believe inhere in different occupations. Could one imagine anything better suited to a symbolic-interactionist perspective? The very topic itself consists of subjective evaluations of occupations. If we wanted to understand the source of such evaluations, we would need access to the life-world of the individual, would we not? After all, different people have personally occupied different jobs; they have different information and reports about the jobs they have not occupied; they differ in their politics, ethical values, and personalities, and they have had different experiences in their business dealings with people of other professions. Further, even their linguistic understandings of questions about occupational prestige should vary with age, ethnicity, subculture, and so forth. In short, morals, meanings, and motives should certainly underlie the amount of esteem someone accords to a given occupation.

While all this is very plausible, occupational prestige was studied by survey researchers in a very different way from the methods recommended by symbolic

interactionists: it was studied as a social fact. If all of the foregoing were true, this way of studying occupational prestige should have flopped. Instead, it succeeded brilliantly. Let us explain how.

In 1947 the National Opinion Research Center (NORC) undertook a pioneering survey of the prestige of ninety American occupations.[11] Respondents were instructed as follows:

> For each job mentioned please pick out the statement that best gives your own personal opinion of the general standing that such a job has:
> 1. Chemist
>   (a) excellent (b) good (c) average (d) somewhat below average (e) poor (f) don't know
> 2. Carpenter...

One way of evaluating these responses is to give each occupation a "score" consisting of the percentage of respondents who rated it as either excellent or good. All ninety occupations could then be ranked by arranging their scores in ascending order. We can interpret such a ranking, roughly speaking, as indicating the relative esteem people attributed to each occupation. Essentially we are conducting an election in which everybody votes on all candidates.

When one obtains an ordered list of occupations by this method, one discovers something spectacular and puzzling about this list. It behaves as if it were an external fact, not subject to the vicissitudes of individual subjective evaluations and interpretations. It is almost as if people are reporting on some preexisting ordered list in the sky, which is known to all of them. For example, as a country's occupational structure, political orientation, and particular population changed over time, one might expect these developments to change people's "heads" and thus their occupational ratings. However, the study was replicated 16 years later, when the country was populated literally by a different group of people than in 1947, not to mention the dramatic changes in life style, attitudes, and so on that had taken place. Guess what? The rankings of the occupations were almost identical. Even more dramatically, Hodge and his associates examined occupational rankings obtained by other studies prior to 1947 and concluded that this ranking of occupations had not changed substantially since 1925![12]

It might be supposed that if political, economic, and population shifts over time did not affect occupational rankings, subcultural differences would. However, studies of ethnic subcultures within our society reveal that this is not true. For example, it is known that blacks form a subculture within our society, that they are dispersed differently in jobs than is the population at large, that they are discriminated against in jobs, and that many of them know this. One would therefore expect that they would have different feelings about occupations than others. Yet, when the evaluations of occupations made by black Americans were examined, they were basically similar to rankings made by the general population. To see if he could find some way to argue that blacks were telling us about the occupational world they lived in, Siegel looked at income discrimination.[13]

One would expect that blacks would downgrade jobs in which they received less income than whites. That is to say, one would expect them not to look kindly on professions that discriminated against them. Yet blacks did not downgrade such professions; they evaluated them as others did. In fact, all sorts of subgroups of Americans seemed to rank occupations in about the same way.

The previous example deals only with political, economic, and cultural differences within the same society. It might be argued that these differences are not great. Yet when occupations were ranked in a number of other countries (India, Chile, Russia, and others), the same basic list of occupations yielded pretty much the same orderings.[14]

As the final blow, all of these stable response patterns allow us literally to eliminate the people. The scores for each occupation which were obtained by the survey can be obtained instead, by a simple equation. The original equation was this:

SES (socioeconomic status) = .59 (% of men in an occupation with a 1949 income equal to or over $3,500) + .55 (% of men in the occupation with four years of high school or college) − 6.[15]

This equation estimates the prestige score of an occupation by using the income and educational level of its incumbents in 1949. When we compare these scores with the ones obtained by the NORC survey, the correlation is .91 (1.00 is a perfect correlation). Thus we have finally converted occupational prestige into a social fact of the first order. We do not even have to ask the people to rank occupations anymore. We can estimate their responses directly, using the above equation.

To further elaborate the problem, consider just one occupation. Suppose we found that 49 percent of the American population rated the job of taxi driver excellent or good. Come rain or come shine, as time passed by, as people were born and died, 49 percent still rated taxi drivers in this way. If one person changed his mind against the occupation, somewhere, somehow, there was another person who changed his mind the other way, leaving the figure at 49 percent. Why in the world would something like this happen? The fact is, no one knows.

However, the discovery of facts like these initially caused great excitement. Such facts were never known in this way before. Even simple but important things like how many babies were being born each year, or whether the population was increasing or decreasing, were matters that no one knew about until very recently in history. Each person in daily life would just vaguely notice that the streets were getting much more crowded than they seemed to have been before, without actually keeping count.

It was discoveries like these that led positivists to believe there could be a real science of sociology. Societies, economic systems, networks of relationships, and flows of populations each appeared as a "thing" with a life and structure of its own. In fact, they seemed to "exist" somewhat independently of the individuals comprising them. A way of thinking and talking about all of this arose in sociology which came to be known as "structuralism."

Structuralists used a simple physical analogy. People were treated as social "atoms" (or molecules), while the social system was seen as the matter composed of these atoms. On the atomic or molecular level, there were only collections of particles moving in any and all directions. But if one looked at the whole instead of at its millions of parts, an entirely new world and its order appeared. Thus, just as simple laws governing the behavior of gases could be found without reference to the behavior of the individual molecules that made them up, why could the same not be done for society as well? This was the vision of some of sociology's founders, men such as Emile Durkheim[16] and Auguste Comte.[17] Indeed, Comte, the founder of sociology, sought as his goal the establishment of a "social physics."

Given a commitment to this perspective, it is easy to understand why structuralists were less than enthusiastic about "the actor's point of view." Indeed, they extended the physical metaphor described above to argue cogently against mixing a concern for the actor's point of view with the study of social facts.

First, if sociology was the study of social facts, then the actor's point of view was none of sociology's business. It was better left to psychologists, philosophers, phenomenologists—in fact, anybody but sociologists. Second, understanding the morals, meanings, and motives of individuals would not help to explain social facts. Durkheim gave an example of this. If it was the personal circumstances of individuals that disposed them to suicide, surely the poor had greater motive than the rich; yet the rich killed themselves more often.[18] Those who commit suicide vary widely in their biographies, psyches, morals, and motives.[19] Yet suicide rates remain substantially the same within certain groups.

Indeed, the very essence of a social fact is that particular individuals can change their assessments of jobs, or can decide or undecide to kill themselves, while the pattern for the group remains unchanged. The basic problem in explaining a social fact is to account for the persistence of general social patterns even though individuals change their minds and behavior.[20]

But what if individual circumstances are found *not* to vary? What if the 49 percent of the population who hold taxi drivers in high esteem are all people who regularly use taxis? What if virtually every successful suicide attempter turns out to be a manic-depressive? There would still be a problem. From a structural perspective, the very presence of a common individual circumstance in a group of people would itself be a social fact that needed explaining. That is, if we found manic-depression to be a common state of mind among suicide attempters, we might understand that manic-depression could lead a person to kill himself. But now the problem of explaining a stable suicide rate has merely been shifted to the problem of explaining a stable rate of manic-depression. One might argue that a certain percentage of people every year just happen to get to be manic-depressives. But structuralists would contend that there must be some social reason for such a pattern. As a result, persistent social patterns would always have to be explained by reference to social processes that transcend individuals and their personal circumstances.

If all this indicts the actor's point of view as not explaining the patterns of behavior and ideas found in groups, there is a further indictment. What about explaining the behavior of particular individuals? Many social scientists claim that even individual behavior is not adequately explained by reference to the actor's point of view. B. F. Skinner, perhaps the most eloquent proponent of such a view,[21] notes that personality, reaction to authority, and other actions can often be explained better by such embarrassing variables as diet or amount of sleep than by motives, emotions, values, and similar notions. From a behaviorist perspective, one can predict and understand even individual suicides without reference to subjectivity. One merely considers humans to be organisms which act and react to a complex environment over time in ways governed by knowable, behavioral laws.

Finally, even if there were some hope for the actor's point of view as an explanatory orientation, there are a number of overwhelming practical problems. The reader can appreciate the sheer quantitative impossibility of gaining detailed access to the life-world of thousands of individuals in order to understand how and why they assess the prestige of occupations the way they do. In particular, it is held that at this time there is simply no scientific or even credible way to ascertain what is in other people's heads while they go about the business of leading their everyday lives. Durkheim pointed out some of these difficulties when he discussed the problems of ascertaining the personal motives of suicides. After all, one cannot conveniently communicate with the dead.

Summary

Some of the major problems formulated above relate to the question of reality reconstruction: that is, how to retrieve the world of the individual. This problem has, in some ways, been dealth with best by philosophers, novelists, and playwrights. It may be, as Pirandello proposes, that there is no way to accurately reconstruct the "truth" or "reality" of one's (or another's) social existence in the "theater of the absurd."[22] In that case the intentions, motives, and perceptions of interacting individuals are destined to be at best problematic and at worst random. Indeed, if there is no satisfactory way to proceed in the enterprise of reality reconstruction, then qualitative sociology, anthropology, and psychology may be out of business. Upon careful examination this may prove to be true.

It should be noted at this point, however, that not everyone is convinced a problem exists. There are those who are happy with existing methods of reconstructing reality, and there are those who are optimistic about the future. As succeeding chapters unfold, the reader will have a chance to decide whether this optimism is justified.

Notes

1. Emile Durkheim, *The Rules of Sociological Method*, New York: Free Press, 1967, p. 10.

2. Eliot Freidson, *The Profession of Medicine: A Study of the Sociology of Applied Knowledge*, New York: Dodd, Mead, 1970.

3. "Understanding" is a translation of Max Weber's term *Verstehen*. For a description of the latter, see note 6.

4. W. I. Thomas, *The Child in America*, New York: Knopf, 1928, p. 584.

5. The term *member* is used in ethnomethodology and elsewhere to signify someone who is competent in the interpretations and behaviors appropriate to a particular social group, world, or environment. Thus a "member of society" can roughly be understood as a socialized adult.

6. Verstehen as this term is now commonly used refers to the observation and interpretation of the subjective states of mind of other people. This concept is discussed in greater detail in chapter 2.

7. Durkheim, *The Rules of Sociological Method*, p. 10.

8. Ibid., p. 110.

9. Jerry Jacobs, *Older Persons and Retirement Communities: Case Studies in Social Gerontology*, Springfield, Ill.: Charles C. Thomas, 1975.

10. Max Weber, *The Theory of Social and Economic Organization*, ed. by Talcott Parsons, New York: Free Press, 1964, pp. 358–359.

11. National Opinion Research Center, "Jobs and Occupations: A Popular Evaluation," *Public Opinion News* 9 (1947): 3–13.

12. Robert Hodge et al., "Occupational Prestige in the United States: 1925–1963," in Reinhard Bendix and Seymour Martin Lipset (eds.), *Class, Status and Power*, New York: Free Press, 1966, pp. 322–334.

13. Paul Siegel, "Occupational Prestige in the Negro Subculture," *Sociological Inquiry* 40 (Spring 1970): 156–171.

14. Bendix and Lipset (eds.), *Class, Status and Power*, pp. 309–321. Although this article and others report high correlations in prestige ratings between countries, recent work has cast methodological doubt on these findings. In some cases the "real" correlation between the prestige rankings of two countries has been determined to be as low as .52.

15. For an explanation of this index, see Otis Dudley Duncan, "A Socio-Economic Index for All Occupations," in *Occupations and Social Status*, ed. by Albert J. Reiss, Jr., New York: Free Press, 1961.

16. Durkheim, *The Rules of Sociological Method*.

17. Auguste Comte, *The Positive Philosophy of Auguste Comte*, trans. and ed. by Harriet Martineau, London: J. Chapman, 1853.

18. Emile Durkheim, *Suicide*, trans. by John A. Spaulding and George Simpson, New York: Free Press, 1951, pp. 297–298.

19. Ibid., p. 298

20. Ibid., pp. 297–298.
21. B. F. Skinner, *Science and Human Behavior*, New York: Macmillan, 1953.
22. See Luigi Pirandello, *Naked Masks: Five Plays by Luigi Pirandello*, ed. by Eric Bentley, New York: Dutton, 1952.

CHAPTER 2

The Sociology of the "Inside"

In chapter 1 we discussed some of the major needs and nettles of qualitative and quantitative sociology. On the one hand is qualitative sociology's insistence that the individual and his interpretive process should be included in the social equation, since no real understanding can emerge without it. On the other hand is quantitative sociology's contention that there is no scientific way to include the individual, his daily intentions, motives, or experience, nor is there any consuming need to do so, since one cannot account for society by means of the individuals comprising it. Rather, the individual is best understood by reference to his place in society.

In this chapter we shall be concerned primarily with formulations of what qualitative sociology is, why do it, and who does it. We begin by discussing the theoretical foundations of qualitative sociology from the perspective of some of its major spokesmen. It was their view(s) of social structure, the individual, and the relation of structure to the individual that inspired the development of the reality reconstruction as a research orientation.

Max Weber

Max Weber (1864–1920) is one of the few major figures of sociology whose ideas permeate the work of both quantitative and qualitative sociologists. In light of this, one would expect that his definition of the discipline would have been very influential. That it was not[1] reflects the fact that it contained "something for everybody." A major thrust of Weber's methodology was to link the scientific concepts of general laws and causal analysis with the purportedly unique subject

17

matter of social science—human beings. His definition of sociology reflected this:

> Sociology (in the sense in which this highly ambiguous word is used here) is a science which attempts the interpretive understanding of social action in order thereby to arrive at a causal explanation of its course and effects. In "action" is included all human behaviour when and in so far as the acting individual attaches a subjective meaning to it. . . .
>
> Action is social in so far as, by virtue of the subjective meaning attached to it by the acting individual (or individuals), it takes account of the behaviour of others and is thereby oriented in its course. . . .[2]
>
> Action in the sense of a subjectively understandable orientation of behaviour exists only as the behaviour of one or more *individual* human beings.[3]

As we can see, Weber's conception of sociology combines a concern for the individual (in particular, for his motives and meanings) with the goal of causal scientific explanation. His position was basically this: Any difference between the social and natural sciences comes from the basic fact that a social scientist is an object of the same type he is studying—a human. The fact that humans are interpretive animals—that they create meanings and work with symbolic and abstract representations—is what makes it possible for them to develop a science of any sort. But in the social sciences we have an additional advantage. In the case of inanimate objects and lower forms of life, we can only observe and describe them and, by interpretive understanding, detect patterns and general laws which they seem to obey. However, with humans we have an advance clue—we know about subjectivity. We have more or less directly experienced and observed our own motives, reactions, emotions, and meanings as they are connected to our social actions. Our fellows have communicated similar experiences to us in ordinary language. All this occurred before any science of human action began. Thus, the generic possibility that subjective elements determine actions is known to us.

Assuming that rocks or plants actually had motives, for their "behavior," it would be unclear that we could ever discover them. For, in order to find some things, one has to suspect in advance that they are there. Given that, as humans, we are aware of the general possibility of specific subjective states of others, there remains the question of how to go about gaining access to these states. Weber singled out three types of subjectivity, or "meanings," which were of special interest to the social scientist:

1. The concrete purposes, motives, and meanings of another person which accompany his specific social actions.
2. The average, common, or approximate meaning of something given to it by a group of people (the meaning of a word in a language is of this type).
3. The meaning(s) attributed to a hypothetical ideal actor in a symbolic model of action which is constructed by the social scientist.

Having discovered the meanings of types 1 and 2, their primary use for Weber was to incorporate them in theoretical models of type 3. But how does one discover meanings of types 1 and 2? Weber mentioned several human resources that could be used for this:

1. The capacity for "empathy" or "artistic appreciation": We can imaginatively place ourselves in another's shoes and grasp (or at least imagine) the emotional context of his actions.
2. The capacity for "rational" understanding (which Weber further divided into logical and mathematical understanding): This consists in the ability to grasp intellectually the intended context of meaning for certain actions. Examples of such actions are proving a theorem and using the Pythagorean theorem within a geometric argument. We can do this because we are familiar with the conventional symbolic meanings and intended purposes of such acts.
3. The capacity to formulate and test causal models: We can attribute motives, emotions, and meanings to a hypothetical actor in a theoretical model and use this model to derive expected courses of action. We can then check out our expectations with what is actually done by concrete actors, to see if and how they correspond.

Weber was especially interested in the motives of others as they related to the performance of social actions, because he was interested in how people went about acting rationally (or irrationally). In particular he was interested in what Schutz called "in-order-to motives"—goals and purposes.[4] In order to achieve certain goals and objectives, actors choose particular lines of actions as means.

In Weber's definition of sociology quoted earlier, the German word *Verstehen* has been translated as "understanding." Many American sociologists have associated the term *Verstehen* with Weber and have taken it to stand for a form of sociological analysis that emphasizes the achievement of empathetic appreciation as a goal. However, for Weber this was a secondary goal, the primary one being the acquisition of a causal explanation of social action. Empathetic understanding of the subjective elements of action was but one means, and not always a necessary one at that.[5]

In fact, Weber's goals and methods were quite peculiar to the nature of the questions that he dealt with. He did little or no direct observation of human actions. His intellectual problems were derived from broad historical situations such as the historical interplay of Protestantism and capitalism. As a result, he used various indirect and historical sources to put together "what had been going on out there." Indeed, since Weber was predominantly dealing with past events, there was no possibility for direct observation, or for anything but imaginative mental experiments.

His methodology reflects this as well as his definition of understanding. Although Weber claimed that sociological understanding must ultimately take as its topic the actions of one or several concrete individuals, he employed an intellectual shorthand by treating institutions, countries, and similar nonhuman totalities as real entities, with ethics, purposes, and so on, just like individual people. Second, his analysis proceeded by the construction of theoretical "ideal types."[6] These were hypothetical constructs put together on the basis of general laws and concepts, assumed to be relevant to a given problem. An example is his ideal type of a perfect bureaucracy, or of perfect rational action (*Zweckrational*). Such types incorporated idealizations similar to the assumption of a perfect vacuum in physics. These models were used to interpret historical events and actions, and to create causal explanations for them.

Thus we see Weber's major use of Verstehen: the observation and interpretation of the subjective states of mind of other people.[7] Verstehen generates hypotheses concerning the connections between subjective states and human action but does not validate them. These hypotheses and/or concepts were then put in theoretical models of social action, used to predict and understand courses of action. These predictions and understandings were then checked out against actual courses of action for adequacy. Thus the final test of adequacy for a subjective concept (such as a motive) attributed to others was its function in a theoretical causal model of action. Verstehen, for Weber, was a necessary tool in coming up with hypotheses and concepts that could be used in this way.

Finally, Weber's treatment of the subjectivity of the analyst should be mentioned. Again, he notes some consequences of the fact that in sociology it is humans who are studying other humans. For one thing, we have more than a generic interest in other humans. We find ourselves interested not merely in "women" but in our own wife or girlfriend, not only in "authority figures" but in our boss. As a result, sociology, as the understanding of general human behavior, may be used to understand particular individuals and particular behavior. Secondly, social science and its results are implicated in human values. Therefore, what a social scientist studies, how he studies it, and what he does with the results will be related to his ethical and social values. In this sense there can be no universal conceptual scheme or methodology for studying social action which is acceptable to all social scientists. This is so because different values imply the need to employ different conceptual schemes and methods. Lastly, Weber was virtually alone among the major theorists in continually emphasizing the subjectivity of his own interpretations of human conduct, independently of (indeed, precisely because of) the scientific nature of such interpretations. He held that what we do when we interpret is to select, abstract, and *purposely distort* concrete reality for the purposes of certain kinds of understandings. Thus he emphasized again and again that his theories were pragmatic devices and intentional distortions, not accurate or real pictures of the concrete things to which they referred.

THE SELF TRANSCENDING THE SELF: SOME IMPLICATIONS

As one can see from the foregoing, Weber explored in several ways the implications of sociologists being creatures of the same type that they studied. The reader might have wondered about this idea. For example, insofar as we are physical matter, are we not also objects of the same type as we study in physics? Clearly, any two distinct phenomena are similar in some ways and different in others. One can choose the similarities and claim that such objects are of the same type as easily as one can seize upon the differences in order to claim that they are qualitatively different. Either side of such an argument seems hopelessly equivocal. Quite true. But we invite the reader to consider the implications of an ancient observation. The presence of consciousness seems to result in one part of creation being able to be aware of other parts. When we consider what it is that the part that is aware has in common with the part that is the object of awareness, many fascinating logical problems present themselves: Can a characteristic of one's own seeing apparatus be seen with that same apparatus? Can a creature subject to certain natural laws discover those laws, or do the laws themselves prevent this discovery? How does the universe change itself when it becomes aware of itself? These are ancient questions, but they take on very practical and even urgent significance, as we shall see later, in the area of qualitative research.

In pointing to the importance of meanings, to the use of human empathy in ascertaining meanings, and to the fact that sociological theory itself created specialized human meanings, Weber gave qualitative sociology some of its key topics—and some of its nastiest problems.

George Herbert Mead

Many consider George Herbert Mead (1863–1931) the founder of social psychology, although only a small portion of modern social psychology stems from his work. Mead was primarily a theorist and philosopher. Although he did little research, he was friendly with many of the outstanding researchers of his day. What reserves for Mead a front-row seat in the theater of both social psychology and qualitative sociology is this: He was one of the first theoreticians to solder together the individual and his society. They became entwined in a new way, no longer two separate things one of which affected the other, but one thing showing itself in two ways (individual personality and social structure).

Perhaps the key idea that accomplished this fusion was Mead's conception of the "self." It arises from an ancient paradox: How is it possible for someone to deceive himself—for the one who knows the truth is identical to the one who must believe the lie? Most psychologies solve this dilemma by postulating several "selves" within the same personality, each with knowledge and motives that are unavailable to the others. Perhaps the most famous one is Freud's trinity of the id, ego, and superego. But all of these selves have something in common: They all exist objectively within the psyche, just as social structures exist objectively in society as social facts.

Mead goes about solving this paradox in quite a different way. He starts from the initial observation that we are explicitly aware of our own personal "selves."

We speak of such things as being "self-conscious" or of "not being myself today." In this sense, humans know of their "selves" as one of the phenomena in their life-world. Where does this self come from or, more pointedly, what is it that we are aware of when we are aware of our "selves"? One would think (as did Mead) that I, who am currently aware of myself cannot be identical to the "me" that I am aware of. This "I," the knower in the present, cannot be experienced as the known. It can, at best, be a hypothesis. The self which I can know is a "me" that can be reconstructed in memory and imagination as an objective person who has certain characteristics, who did and said this and that, and who plays a fair game of tennis but gets nervous at parties. Yet this is the kind of knowledge we have about other people. Surely we are aware of ourselves as active subjects as well as objects; we are also aware of ourselves as "I." Mead explains that this "I" is not the basic "I" that is involved in any and all acts of knowledge in the present. We can recall and imagine, among other things, our inner dialogues:

A: I need to get a good grade on that test; I need to cheat.

A: But if you cheat to get a good grade, you'll cheat on your friends or even on yourself.

A: Not so—I believe in myself and my friends but I don't believe in that school and its tests.

Here we can remember in the present an inner dialogue which took place in the past. In this, one person seems to talk and reason with another who listens and responds. There seems to be two kinds of people—"I," the subject with his own personal desires, reactions, and purposeful projects and "me," the moralizer, judge, and evaluator of "I."

At this point Mead makes a crucial observation. What enables us to separate the talk, listening, and interpretation in an inner dialogue into two halves, each belonging to a different person? Why is there the sense of two "people" talking to each other in such an exchange? Inner dialogues have a social counterpart. The counterpart is one of the simplest forms of social interaction, the two-party conversation. When you and another talk there is this same structure of an "I" who says things to a "you" who listens and responds—each taking alternate turns at talk. In fact the format of criticism and defense is a common one in conversations with others. But we can go further; this "me" who makes sundry approvals, judgments, and pronouncements—all in line with the morality and conventions of our culture—is not an unfamiliar character. He or she is a social stereotype set before us by parents, teachers, and authority figures. It may be their teachings that allow us to "package" a collection of subjective evaluations, pronouncements, and sayings into a type of "person." In fact, are there not other aspects of the self—other "me's"—that correspond to social stereotypes? There is the selfish hedonist, the coward, the egotist, and so on. This observation is not limited to the lay persons' experience. If one looks more closely at Freud's id, ego, and superego, at Fritz Perl's "top dog" and "underdog," or other such concepts, one finds the social again. These "inner people" in almost every case are stereotyped caricatures of people found in society. One comes to wonder if the theories of psychologists in other societies reflect their prototypical people as well.

What was said about inner people can be said, as well, about the relationships between these people. The concept of deception, for instance, is first acquired and used in connection with one's dealings with *others*. It is perfectly sensible that one person would deceive and hurt another, in order to spare embarrassment to himself. What then is to be made of something that one "did not know about oneself," that was embarrassing or degrading, and that was the apparent cause of a painful ulcer? *Self*-deception perhaps?

The upshot of all of this is a distinctively sociological conception of the self and, therefore, the possibility of a social psychology. The self is no longer some structure of inner people which exists in all human psyches. It is the internalization of the social processes by which groups of people mutually interact. Learning to participate in group action gives one a self and vice versa.

In particular, a developmental and eminently social conception of personality emerges. "In the beginning" there is, perhaps, the infant's primitive but developing awareness of "I-ness," an ability to distinguish oneself (one's body, actions, thoughts) from the world and tell which is which. Mead was skeptical about the existence and nature of such awareness. However, we do have certain experiments and observations about mental disorder which give some evidence for its existence. For instance, Hall reports encountering schizophrenics who experience events that occur within a certain area of their personal space as if these events were literally happening inside of them.[8]

Next, the child learns to experience others as "you's," as persons with thoughts, feelings, and motives. Even as adults, we find it hard to detect from the movement of rocks, ants, bees, or trees their motives, opinions, or emotional reactions. But with fellow humans, it becomes possible at some point to imaginatively experience them as beings with an inner life like ours, without being able to hear their thoughts or experience their emotions. In fact we do this while only observing their outward behavior.

The final stage is the crowning one for Mead and symbolic interactionism in general. We learn to experience ourselves as "me." We can imaginatively look at ourselves, our acts, and our inner dialogue from the standpoint of a "generalized other." Perhaps one of the simplest ways to experience this feeling is to notice what happens when one practices a music piece or works up a rough draft of a paper. There is the distinct feeling of "being heard" or "being read" by another. In seeing how the piece sounds to other ears, or observing what some general reader might or might not understand in the draft, one can improve or reorganize one's projects. This feeling of the other is distinctly different psychologically from the feeling that is present when one simply plays music unself-consciously or writes a memo to one's secretary. With the general ability to see oneself and one's acts from the standpoint of another human observer, it becomes possible to construct more specific generalized others. It becomes possible to see what a Communist, a senior citizen, or a professor would make of one's actions and talk.

All of this has a crucial implication for social action. Since a person can anticipate (really "see") other's reactions to his own actions before these reactions occur, he can adjust his actions accordingly. In this sense social action takes other people into account by incorporating an imaginative view of their interests and reactions in the original plan for such actions. To see how important this is, consider what happens to those who lack the ability to plan action in terms of others. For example, there is a type of schizophrenia called depersonalization that seems to consist of an inability to construct generalized others. People with this affliction seem to be completely amoral. They cannot anticipate the way an action will please or displease another until the pleasure or displeasure is actually expressed. Thus they continue to do things that bother their significant others intensely without learning to realign their activities.

As can now be seen, individual selves and social actions are united in Mead's philosophy and mutually influence each other. One learns to construct one's own self and those of others through social actions, and these very social actions, in turn, progressively alter the nature of one's "selves" and imagined other "selves." This makes individual action nonmechanical and creative. It also makes social structures the result of groups of "interacting selves" mutually adjusting their conduct with respect to one another in the light of who and what they know one another (and themselves) to be. As a result, social structure and self are constantly defining each other.

In summary, Mead has come up with a conception of individual identity and action, on the one hand, and society and social structure, on the other, that makes the two virtually inseparable. It fell to the researchers in the symbolic-interactionist tradition to put this perspective into practice. By inventing methods and carrying out investigations that put empirical meat on these theoretical bones, they set the stage for the development of qualitative methodology.

Herbert Blumer

An early proponent and major theoretician of the symbolic interaction school (indeed, he invented the term) is Herbert Blumer. Blumer, in numerous books and articles, has perhaps better than anyone else, set forth the basic tenets of this approach. According to him, symbolic interaction rests upon three major premises:

1. Human beings act toward things on the basis of the meanings the things have for them.
2. The meaning of such things is derived from, or arises out of, the social interaction one has with others.
3. These meanings are handled in, and modified through, an interpretive process used by the person in dealing with the things he encounters.

A good summary of what Blumer feels symbolic interaction is and how it operates is as follows:

There are two well-known . . . ways of accounting for the origin of meaning. One of them is to regard meaning as being intrinsic to the thing that has it. . . . The other major view regards meaning as a psychical accretion brought to the thing by the person for whom the thing has meaning. This psychical accretion is treated as being an expression of the constituent elements of the person's psyche, mind, or psychological organization.

Symbolic interactionism views meaning as having a different source than those held by the two dominant views just considered. It does not regard meaning as emanating from the intrinsic makeup of the thing, nor does it see meaning as arising through psychological elements between people. The meaning of a thing for a person grows out of the ways in which other persons act toward the person with regard to the thing. Their actions operate to define the thing for the person; thus, symbolic interactionism sees meanings as social products formed through activities of people interacting.[9]

As can be seen from Blumer's definition, symbolic interaction makes meanings a distinctively sociological phenomenon. Instead of the traditional question "Is a tree there if there is no individual to see and experience it as a 'tree'?" Blumer asks, "Do trees exist as such without social groups who invent, teach, and use the concept of 'tree' in diverse social situations?" From groups of interacting individuals come the social processes that produce meanings. In turn, from meanings are produced the realities that constitute the "real world" within which individuals of the group spend their lives. Finally, it is this socially constituted "real world" that serves as the basis of an individual's actions—that is, the world he lives in and continually comes to terms with on a daily basis. It was this orientation that led W. I. Thomas to note: "It is not important whether or not the interpretation is correct—if men define situations as real, they are real in their consequences."[10]

Apart from the question of what symbolic interaction is, as a theoretical orientation of sociologists, there is the problem of how to study it as a process taking place within social groups. In this regard Blumer notes: "Symbolic interactionism holds that social action must be studied in terms of how it is formed; its formation is a very different matter from the antecedent conditions that are taken as the 'cause' of social action."[11] In short, while social action possesses antecedent causes and consequences that enter into and influence it, these causes and consequences do not constitute such actions. Understanding the process of a social action consists in exploring the process by which several individuals, or "selves," mutually adjust various lines of action on the basis of their ongoing interpretations of the world. In order to do this one must necessarily get into what we have called the reality reconstruction business:

> On the methodological or research side the study of action would have to be made from the position of the actor. Since action is forged by the actor out of what he perceives, interprets, and judges, one would have to see the operating situation as the actor sees it, perceive objects as the actor perceives them, ascertain their meaning in terms of the meaning they have for the actor, and follow the actor's line of conduct as

the actor organizes it—in short, one would have to take the role of the actor and see his world from his standpoint.[12]

The principal tool for doing this was participant observation of two major types: (1) exploration and (2) inspection. There was no doubt in Blumer's mind that this was the best way to go about doing (qualitative) sociology. The question that remains is "Are there practical ways of carrying Blumer's program out?"

Barney Glaser and Anselm Strauss: Grounded Theory

So far Weber, Mead, and Blumer have provided us with a relatively coherent picture of the nature of social action, the origin of society, and the need to gain access to the life-world of individuals. But none of these men was involved to any extent in making firsthand observations in everyday situations. Mead and Blumer were basically theorists. Weber provided a list of human abilities that can be used to understand the motives, emotions, and meanings of other humans, but his systematic method of ideal-type construction, although a useful device, was basically designed to handle broad historical problems. Indeed, a pressing query of other kinds of sociologists has been "How do you do it?" Is qualitative sociology an art form, or does it really have systematic methods? Barney Glaser and Anselm Strauss, in their grounded-theory approach, have developed a systematic answer to this question.

They accept the basic symbolic-interactionist position as described by Mead and Blumer. They accept the pressing need to gain access to the life-world of individuals in order to do sociology. They also accept the views of scientists—in particular, Weber—that sociology should not be merely a rich description of other people but rather should be directed toward abstract theories which explain social action. The question before us now is "Is there any more efficient way of achieving these goals than by 'hanging around, keeping your eyes open, and using good common sense'?"

GETTING STARTED: RESEARCHER BIAS AND SENSITIZING CONCEPTS

When beginning a field project, sociologists (especially participant observers) face a problem that has an analogy in everyday life. In meeting a stranger, we are confronted with a person we have never seen before. Often we know virtually nothing about him, and he knows little or nothing about us. Nevertheless, we immediately have to do something with him. We have to have a conversation. But what does one have to talk about with someone one knows nothing about and shares no history with? When we have no advance knowledge of his point of view, it is difficult to tell how he will interpret something we might say. What will be offensive, what boring, what interesting? Clearly, what is needed is a procedure that will do two things simultaneously: It should be able to give us appropriate things to say immediately and independently of who the other person is; at the same time, the very things we say should get us back a lot of information about the life and personality of this particular individual. After that, it will be possible to act as Mead would want us to—to take the other into account while adjusting our behavior and talk.

There is a characteristic solution to this problem, one that is widely looked down upon but that may be indispensable. What we do is press into service stereotypes and clichés—that is, sets of things to say, concepts, and assumptions about "types of people" that are commonly known and that are floating around in the culture. They provide us with first things to say to anyone, which are at worst banal: "What do you do for a living? . . . Oh, you're a physicist, you must be very smart." As conversational items, they legitimately come in pairs. That is, given that we ask such things of another, he can ask them of us in return. In that way, the things we ask of him provide him immediately with things to ask us.

Second, unlike other first things to say, such as greetings, the content of these first things is informational. Thus we and the other, with the first things we say to each other, are providing large amounts of information about each of us, as people.

As long as these clichés and stereotypes are used merely as places to start and first approximations, they do valuable service as conversational items under rather delicate circumstances. Only if they are rigidly adhered to as the important matters to be dealt with do they constitute serious impediments to discovering the details of another's personality and life. In this sense, initial clichés are used *in order to* be abandoned.

There are several analogies between this commonsense procedure and the approach of grounded theory. In other styles of qualitative research, one is admonished to prepare oneself with a review of sociological literature before entering the field. One then comes into the presence of others with concepts, issues, and hypotheses about them obtained from sociologists. This is one way to proceed if you want to be systematic from the outset, not fool around, and go directly to the phenomena that you are interested in. An example of this is a recent study by Kristin Luker.[13] Her major question was this: Why do well-educated, middle-class women, who obviously know about birth-control methods, take risks that often lead to therapeutic abortions? She explored the question by intensive interviews with women who found their way to therapeutic abortion centers. A clearly defined problem such as this informs one where to go, whom to ask, and what to ask them, rather parsimoniously. However, this is unusual. More often than not, the situation is closer to that of being confronted by a stranger. The things one does not know and would ordinarily not ask about are likely to prove to be the very things that are most important to find out.

This is often the case when a sociologist enters the life-world of others. At such times sociological literature and ideas about what's important or "what's so" concerning a group of people can be an impediment. To counteract this prospect, an alternate strategy recommended by some qualitative researchers is to *minimize* explicit preconceptions—for example, by *not* familiarizing yourself with the literature in advance, and just "hanging out" in the field for a while. Field notes are to be as literal as possible, avoiding, at this stage, interpretations and theories. Of course, all this means is that your preconceptions will be implicit, guiding your observations in largely unknown ways.

Grounded theory rejects both of these poles and adopts, instead, the procedure of "getting to know the stranger." In sociological terms, this amounts to using preconceptions as "sensitizing concepts," in the manner outlined first by Blumer. Your preconceptions give you things to do and ask immediately. On the other hand, they are not firm research orientations. They are used in order to be abandoned and are invoked only to help find aspects of others' lives that confirm, deny, or transcend your initial preconceptions.

Conversely, if you are known to your subjects as a researcher, then initial "sociological concerns" can be seen by them as the understandable interests of a certain kind of outsider. In fact, such concerns, if visible to those you are studying, might quickly get back the kinds of correctives that lead to more relevant ideas about the group. The time this takes may be much shorter than would have been the case if you hung around and did not make your ignorance of "what's going on" visible to others.

There is another analogy between the commonsense strategy with the stranger and the Glaser-Strauss use of sensitizing concepts. The latter assume that standard sociological concepts are probably (if not certainly) not the appropriate ones to use in understanding a new field situation. Such a position is sociological heresy. Many sociologists are rather firmly convinced that understanding any group of humans, doing pretty much anything they might be doing together, requires that at some point one pay attention to existing standard sociological concepts—such as "sex ratios," "roles," "stratification," "age differences," "norms and sanctions." It is heretical to suggest that the sociology of law may look completely different, theoretically, than the sociology of stamp collection, or the sociology of chess playing. Of course, whether one can actually achieve this "assume things in order to abandon assumptions" attitude in practice is another matter.

CODING

In grounded theory, data collection, observation, coding and categorizing the data, and developing theories all tend to go on simultaneously and to mutually support one another. In this way, several levels of analysis are constantly feeding back into one another.

Rather quickly, one wants to come up with descriptive categories with which to screen, sort, and, in general, play around with data. Grounded theory has some guidelines for the selection of these categories. A prevailing concept is that of "process"—that is, patterned actions and interactions of individuals over time, which create and sustain what passes for social structure.

A helpful example can be found in ordinary natural conversation. It is a process in that it is a series of turns of talk, over a finite period of time. The process has several levels of patterned organization. There is an overall structure, with beginnings, endings, and topical sections. Each section, in turn, has its own organization. For example, in "beginnings" are found "greetings," "identifications," and so on. Each segment is related to the next in certain rule-governed ways; for example, a first topic must be "finished" or "changed" before the conversation can proceed to the next topic. There are other levels of organization, such as the relationships between a current remark and the next one, or the order and timing of turns at talk. Also, the meanings and interpretations of actions affect each individual's talk, on the one hand, and therefore the general nature and course of the process (the ongoing conversation), on the other. Structurally, diverse people with diverse things to say find themselves encountering similar problems, actions, and experiences because of standard features of "conversations" as a structural form. Structurally, roles, identities, social setting, and other nonconversational variables influence and create conditions for the course of the conversation itself.

The foregoing example includes many of the properties of social processes that Glaser and Strauss have a more technical nomenclature for and use as guiding ideas in research. The "symbolic interaction" comes into this preoccupation in the form of two assumptions: (1) social worlds are created and sustained by temporal patterned processes of human interaction and (2) individuals' interpretations of meanings, and their taking others into account imaginatively, determine their individual actions and thus the course of patterned group interactions.

SAMPLING

In selecting what to look for, what to count, and what to compare with what in one's observations, a procedure which Glaser and Strauss call "theoretical sampling" is employed. In quantitative research, objects (including people) are selected for observation on the basis of how representative they are of the objects of some larger collection. In grounded theory, one selects what to observe in a different way. One's initial coding provides a first stab at "what's going on" in semi-abstract form. The idea is to use this analytic framework (well, it really is not one yet) to select observations. One wants to look at things that clarify and validate "what's going on," that resolve anomalies and contradictions in the coding scheme, or that fill in parts of the process that have not yet been observed. All of these observational needs are indicated by the coding scheme.

What occurs, of course, is that coding, inventing codes, and observing proceed together, each amplifying the other. A strategy which Glaser recommends to help this feedback process along is the method of "constant comparisons." If one has a fairly good descriptive grasp of the process of "getting a driver's license" or "becoming a mental patient," obtained from watching a single licensing bureau or mental hospital, then one takes a look at some other ones. By comparing entirely different groups undergoing the same process, one can easily get ideas about where one is right and wrong concerning structural uniformities. Differences and similarities are highlighted. Verification of the descriptive scheme is made possible in this way. There are other advantages as well. In so-called deviant case analysis, one looks for particular individuals who have careers deviant from those of others within the same social world, and one does the same kind of things mentioned above. Comparing entire groups has advantages over deviant case analysis in that it offers better access to structural differences and similarities.

ANALYTIC MEMOS

While one is developing a descriptive coding scheme, one writes memos which describe the analytic properties of one's developing code. Since this is done while coding, the memos and the coding, again, mutually affect each other. The idea here is to get into the theorizing business rather quickly, so that one ends up with substantive theory instead of a good novel about a group of people. The memos are concerned with the logical relationships among one's coding categories. By "logical" we do not mean just deductive relationships. Using the example of the natural conversation, one might notice and write about the necessary order of the various segments of a conversation, the way in which who talks next affects a developing topic, or the conditions under which several people can negotiate an end to a conversation. In short, one is starting to build up a theory of the process in question, a theory which not only describes the process but "explains" it.

Multiple copies of these memos are made and filed using a system of categories to index the memos. Some might be filed under "endings," some under "incompetent talkers," some under "topic changing," and so forth. These categories help to organize one's developing theory and integrate ideas into coherent models and general explanations. Further, the categories help one to rework the memos in the light of the developing issues that need to be elaborated. The categorized memos provide a sort of card catalogue of ideas, sorted with respect to various subject headings.

INTEGRATING THE ANALYSIS

The goal of this kind of analysis is to put together an integrated, substantive theory of the process one has been studying. The whole grounded-theory approach aims at making substantive theory "grow," more or less naturally, out of observed data in daily situations. In this integration, Glaser and Strauss suggest a helpful strategy: Outline the relationships among the categories used in cataloguing the memos. This can help to put the whole thing into some general perspective suggesting a general theory (or two). Sometimes the phenomena and the original memos are such that a natural integrated theory suggests itself. But often enough, this integration escapes the eye unless one plays around with the organization of one's card catalogue and its contents in a lot of ways. Although we will not go into it here, grounded theory offers additional hints and advice on how to do this playing around.

CONSTANT FEEDBACK AND LEVELS OF ABSTRACTION

There are two main ideas behind the details of grounded theory. The idea of constant feedback has been repeatedly illustrated: Do research so that the various levels of analysis can mutually affect and validate one another over time. In formalizing this idea as a research strategy, grounded theory meshes itself with some of the characteristics of social meanings. For example, if one wants to gain access to another culture quickly, efficiently, and accurately, to learn the language, and to acquire the right habits, it would be best to proceed in this flexible ad hoc fashion rather than by adhering to a preconceived and fixed learning program. It is clear that people who immerse themselves in a culture learn its language more quickly and efficiently than those using a classroom approach with texts and lists of words. This seems to be so because of the very properties of meanings themselves.

The second idea and/or goal is that of obtaining a high level of abstraction in one's final theory. The reader may have noted that grounded theory is so arranged that it virtually forces a person to become more and more abstract in his understanding of his field situation. First, there are observations. The coding is about the observations. The analytic memos are about the coding. The descriptive catalogue is about the analytic memos. The integrated outline is about the descriptive categories. This is one way in which one progressively, by necessity, climbs higher and higher on the ladder of abstraction. Glaser and Strauss note other ways, which we will not go into here.

CONCLUDING REMARKS

Although we have devoted considerable space to grounded theory, we have not even begun to give the details of the approach. These may be found in the works of its authors.[14] Our attention to this theory is warranted by the fact that Glaser and Strauss are almost alone in spelling out a systematic, qualitative field *method* for research and relating it to goals of theory and verification. Their theory and method, in our view, has many virtues and integrates much of what is known about the nature of social interaction into its directives.

One final question may have occurred to the reader. Since observation, data collection, theory building, and theory testing are not separate operations, done in stages, how does one know how to stop the feedback process set up in grounded theory? One reply that Glaser and Strauss give is more a prediction than an answer. One hopes that there will come a point when the process will become repetitive, monotonous, and redundant. Nothing new will be coming through. Clearly, this would be a good place to stop. However, there is a danger. There is often a first plateau of redundancy where it seems that one has pretty well figured out "what's going on." However, after a period of time, perhaps months, there may be breakthroughs where crucial observations put a different light on what has previously been observed. An outstanding example of this kind of thing is Carlos Castaneda's work with Don Juan.[15] In the final analysis, there is really no certain way to establish whether one has stopped the process prematurely, this side of an insight, or gone on too long and come up on the other side of a redundancy.

Latter-Day Followers

There are certain American sociologists, and some anthropologists, whose work was founded primarily upon participant observation, depth interviews, or a combination of the two. These research strategies were in turn firmly rooted within the tradition of symbolic interaction. Among these groups are sociologists who either founded or worked within labeling theory, analytic induction models, ethnographic field studies, or grounded theory. Most of these men and women were sociologists in the tradition of the "Chicago school" and were concerned primarily with deviant behavior as an outgrowth of their preoccupation with social disorganizatiqn. The reason this work was done primarily by sociologists, even though anthropologists were steeped in the tradition of field studies, was that until recently the latter confined their efforts to studying other cultures.

It is beyond the scope of this chapter to deal in detail with all of these studies or their methods and findings. However, we list below some of the sociologists associated with the various approaches so that the reader can easily retrieve and consider their works, as his interests dictate.

Labeling theory: Howard Becker, Kai Erikson, David Matza
Analytic induction: Florian Znaniecki, Donald Cressey, Alfred Lindesmith, Edwin Sutherland
Grounded theory: Barney Glaser, Anselm Strauss, Cathy Charmez
Basic ethnography: Fred Davis, Howard Becker, Edwin Lemert, Sherri Cavan, Julius Roth, John Lofland, William Foote Whyte, Robert Emerson
These categories are in no way mutually exclusive. For example, descriptive

ethnographies may incorporate the notions of labeling and/or roles and be cast within a framework of grounded theory. The categories are meaningful and help to characterize the authors only with respect to their emphases but are not intended to suggest their exclusive use of the indicated conceptual orientations or methodological strategies. In fact, these categories refer more to groups of people taking off in different directions on some common themes than to consistent research perspectives. With this in mind, let us now consider some of the ways in which sociologists have sought to reconstruct the reality of others.

Notes

1. This claim is a controversial one, but we agree with it.
2. Max Weber, *The Theory of Social and Economic Organization*, ed. by Talcott Parsons, New York: Free Press, 1964, p. 88.
3. Ibid., p. 101.
4. Alfred Schutz, *Collected Papers I*, ed. by Maurice Nathanson, The Hague: Martinus Nijhoff, 1971, pp. 69–72.
5. The reader is again reminded that empathetic understanding is not the same as Verstehen, which is more general.
6. Weber, *The Theory of Social and Economic Organization*, p. 89.
7. Ibid., p. 87. Our definition of Verstehen is a paraphrase of the one used by Parsons in the reference given. Ours is inferior to Parsons's in several ways. When we construct an "ideal type" of theoretical person and impute to him states of mind and motives, *we* are engaging in an interpretive act, an act which by Weber's definition is therefore a social one. However, this theoretical puppet need not correspond to any real person (or persons) who has the states of mind and motives our puppet does. Yet we construct this puppet in part to help us grasp the motives and meanings in the heads of real people.
8. Edward T. Hall, *The Hidden Dimension*, Garden City, N. Y.: Doubleday Anchor, 1969, pp. 11–12.
9. Herbert Blumer, *Symbolic Interactionism: Perspective and Method*, Englewood Cliffs, N.J.: Prentice-Hall, 1969, pp. 4–5.
10. W. I. Thomas, *The Child in America*, New York: Knopf, 1928, p. 572.
11. Blumer, *Symbolic Interactionism*, p. 4.
12. Herbert Blumer, "Sociological Implications of the Thought of George Herbert Mead," in Clinton Joyce Jesser, *Social Theory Revisited*, Hinsdale, Ill.: Dryden Press, 1975, p. 325.
13. Kristin Luker, *Taking Chances*, Berkeley: University of California Press, 1976.
14. See, for example, Barney G. Glaser and Anselm Strauss, *The Discovery of Grounded Theory: Strategies for Qualitative Research*, Chicago: Aldine, 1967.
15. Carlos Castaneda, *The Teachings of Don Juan: A Yaqui Way of Knowledge*, New York: Ballantine Books, 1968.

Part II

Reality Reconstruction: How to Do It

The research strategies discussed in this section are basically ways of obtaining information. They are the principal means used to gain access to "the inside" and to insiders. For some, this access is an end in itself. They seek not to analyze and predict but to understand. If they can successfully reconstruct the reality of another human being, group, or way of life, this is accepted as satisfactory sociological knowledge in itself.

However, intimate knowledge of the insider's perspective may be used in other ways to form the basis for more technical forms of qualitative sociology. These forms, to be discussed in later chapters, also employ the methods of obtaining information that we are about to explore.

CHAPTER 3

Participant Observation and Interviewing: Reconstructing the Reality of Social Groups

Assuming that a goal (or the goal) of sociological research is to gain access to the "member's point of view," the question arises: What do we mean by the "member's point of view"? Different research problems and conceptual orientations result in quite different responses.

We will deal first with strategies that are best for getting at what might be called group life. The problem is similar to the problem faced by a foreigner entering a new culture without knowing the language, the customs, the ways of acting and reasoning, and so on. What are some practical and effective ways of understanding the world that individuals construct and maintain within a given society, subculture, institution, job site, or other "natural" social group? Such strategies must allow access to others' meanings in a reasonable amount of time. Obviously, hypothesis testing, controlled experiments, and extensive computer analysis are out of the question. Indeed, it would take an army of researchers to get at the meanings of a culture in a reasonable amount of time with such techniques.

Participant observation and interviewing are for the most part variants and extensions of the practical methods any intelligent lay person would use to get at the consensual meanings of a group of people with whom he was not familiar. A tacit assumption of any and all such methods is that some sort of consensus or common knowledge about meaning exists in groups and is sustained over time by social processes. For example, the researcher counts on a group's having some conception of "outsider" and some way of socializing outsiders so that they can

37

gain "insider's knowledge" about the group. Without this, there would be no practical way for the researcher to study the group. The way in which the researcher seeks access to this knowledge and the problems he encounters in such an undertaking will now be considered with respect to his use of participant observation and interviewing techniques.

Interviewing

When interviewing is used to reconstruct the reality of a social group, individual respondents are treated as sources of "general" information. That is, they are asked to speak on behalf of people other than themselves and to give information about social processes and cultural conventions that transcend their own personal lives. In an interview setting, the respondent is called upon to assume the identity of a member of his group in formulating replies—to "become" a woman, an old person, a prison inmate. Either the researcher asks directly about general issues or he interprets individuals' responses in such a way as to throw light on general attitudes, situations, and patterns.

SAMPLING

Survey researchers ordinarily select respondents by taking a statistical (random) sample from the population under study. Members of the sample "represent" the whole group, not in terms of the group's structure, but in terms of their mathematical relationship to the totality of which they are a part.

Qualitative researchers are usually less conservative. They count on the group's own patterns of interaction to ensure the validity of their "sampling logic"—their method of selecting whom to talk to. For example, in a study of a sociology department, the department secretaries may become the target of intensive interviewing. In contrast to individual faculty members, they are present every work day, interact with virtually every faculty member, and process most of the paper work involved in hiring, teaching, research, and other department business. Yet, paradoxically, to know which people are likely to possess what general information, one must be familiar with the group's internal processes to begin with. This is why interviewing is best undertaken in conjunction with a strategy like participant observation, which can indicate whom to interview, when, and about what and can act as an independent check on the information obtained.

STRUCTURED INTERVIEWS

Interviews usually take one of two basic forms, structured or unstructured. The former assumes, to one extent or another, that the researcher already knows the very thing the interview is designed to uncover. This is also true of those quantitative sociologists who use questionnaires. That is, the interviewer assumes that the questions contained in his "structured questionnaire" or "interview schedule" are relevant to the topic he hopes to learn about, that the questions are phrased unambiguously, that the "interviewee" (the respondent) will understand the questions and find them unintimidating, that the questions will not call forth answers from the respondent that the respondent feels are appropriate to the question but otherwise bear little relationship to what the respondent believes, that the forced choices provided in the schedule in the name of easy future statistical processing and analysis will not exclude more valid answers which the respondent might have been able to give were his answers not forced, and that the interviewer will present a neutral stance toward the respondent so as not to bias the answer he receives and thereby invalidate the group data.

Structured interviews are frequently organized so as to elicit, through a set of pretested, predetermined questions, what the respondent thinks about or what he thinks he would do about a variety of hypothetical questions or situations. However, few researchers are interested in attitudes per se; most believe, rather, that attitudes are indicative of future group behavior. That is, these surveys usually assume that a positive relationship exists between words and deeds.

A typical structured interview schedule is as follows:

NOW A LITTLE BIT ABOUT RELIGION . . . [1]

45. Before now, have you ever been an active member of any church or religious group other than the one you were brought up in?
no ___   yes ___
→ Describe them _____
_____
_____

46. How do you feel about Christ? (Interviewer watch for love and emotion vs. disbelief and rejection) _____

47. Have you ever gone through a ceremony in which you accepted Christ as your savior?
yes ___   no ___

48. Have you a reading knowledge of Eastern religions besides the writings of Baba?
no ___   yes ___ → Describe _____
_____

49. Have you ever practiced Yoga?
no ___   yes ___

50. Have you ever undertaken macrobiotic or other diets?
no ___   yes ___ → Describe, and why? _____
_____
_____

51. Have you ever experienced any of the following: (COMMENTS)
    (a) spirit visitations   yes ___   no ___   _____
    (b) unexplained
        unconsciousness   yes ___   no ___   _____
    (c) visions   yes ___   no ___   _____
    (d) experiences through
        mediums   yes ___   no ___   _____
    (e) ESP   yes ___   no ___   _____
    (f) premonitions   yes ___   no ___   _____
    (g) sudden insights   yes ___   no ___   _____

    (h) any other? _____

52. Have you ever sought insight or religious experience by any means other
    than the use of drugs?
    no ___   yes ___
                       ↘Describe _____
                                    _____
                                    _____

UNSTRUCTURED INTERVIEWS

Those who utilize unstructured interviewing techniques usually hold different sets of assumptions. Here it is assumed that the interviewer does not know in advance which questions are appropriate to ask, how they should be worded so as to be nonthreatening or unambiguous, which questions to include or exclude to best learn about the topic under study, or what constitutes an answer (what the range of answers to any question might be). The answers to these problems are seen to emerge from the interviews themselves, the social context in which they occurred, and the degree of rapport that the interviewer was able to establish during the interview. In short, appropriate or relevant questions are seen to emerge from the process of interaction that occurs between the interviewer and interviewees. Through this informal process of give and take the investigator becomes "sensitized"[2] to which questions constitute relevant and meaningful issues to the respondent (and others like him). At a later point these are incorporated into the "interview guide." Not only does a range of meaningful questions emerge in this way, but also, from the respondent's perspective, a range of meaningful answers.

The success of this undertaking is ultimately contingent upon the skill and sensitivity of the interviewer, who must ask the "right" questions at the right time, refrain from questioning at the right time, and generally be a nonthreatening, understanding, and empathetic listener. One's ability to succeed in this undertaking may rest more upon his preexisting social competence than upon learned skills in interviewing. Lofland notes:

> I would say that successful interviewing is not unlike carrying on unthreatening, self-controlled, supportive, polite, and cordial interaction in everyday life. If one can do that, one already has the main interpersonal skills necessary to interviewing.
>
> It is my personal impression, however, that interactants who practice these skills (even if they possess them) are not overly numerous in our society.[3]

While we are in part sympathetic to this view, we would take issue with Lofland on this count: He attributes the ability to achieve the kind of interaction described above exclusively to the interpersonal skills of the interviewer. This we take to be a necessary but not sufficient condition. We believe that the interviewer's ability to achieve this kind of interaction is specific to particular populations of interviewees.

In some cases the reasons for this are obvious. The interviewer's knowledge of and familiarity with the respondents' life style, subculture, and ethnic customs, or his co-membership with the respondent in certain social categories, such as race, sex, or personality type, all affect his ability to establish rapport. In other cases, the reasons for rapport (or the lack of it) are more elusive. For instance, in a study of mental health institutions, one author found that he could easily and successfully communicate with a given population of respondents. However, there were a few of these people, substantially the same as the others with respect to personality, background and social position, whom the author "just could not talk to." It is an awkward fact that there is no way to ensure in advance that a particular interview will go well.

In any kind of interviewing there is a possibility that there will be a discrepancy between what people say and what they mean. This may be explained in many ways, some of which are considered later in this chapter. If it is true that people do not always say what they mean or mean what they say, then it can be argued that the researcher in a face-to-face informal interview may be as easily deceived as the survey researcher employing structured interviews or questionnaires. There is, however, one crucial difference: The informal interviewer in a face-to-face interaction has a greater degress of feedback than those using structured interviews or mailed questionnaires. This feedback can be used as a way of evaluating the status of respondents' accounts. In addition, the social organization of this kind of interview situation allows it to alter its own ongoing course. As information flows from the respondent to interviewer, the interviewer is free to alter his line of questioning accordingly. The interviewer may of course be mistaken in his evaluation and may draw faulty conclusions on the basis of his emerging "definition of the situation." However, when all is said and done, this is the only method available for evaluating the current intentions and behavior of others (as well as making projections about their future intentions and behavior). While one may be mistaken in his total assessment on the basis of interpretation and reinterpretation of what others say, how they say it, and nonverbal cues, the grounds for such an assessment are much stronger in face-to-face interactions than in survey research, where there is no direct basis for weighing and evaluating the words of others.

THE ETHNOGRAPHIC CONTEXT OF AN INTERVIEW

Even with all we have said, the reader may seriously question the previous claim. Exactly how does face-to-face unstructured interviewing provide a stronger basis for assessing the goals, intentions, purposes, and behavior of another than structured interviewing and/or questionnaires? One answer to this is emphasized by Cicourel. He points to a key difference between researcher and respondent in an interview situation. The respondent, knowing his own life history, the ins and outs of the cultural milieu of which he is a part, and his own self-concept and practical purposes within the interview, has an "ethnographic context"[4] in which he decides both what to say to the interviewer and the precise meaning and significance of what he is saying (as seen by an insider). Unless provision is made for it, the interviewer does not have such an ethnographic context within which to interpret what the respondent means (as opposed to what he says) and decide how to follow up leads, what is important or unimportant, or when he is getting the official, versus the actual, version of the information sought. As a result, he is condemned to interpret the respondent's talk in whatever way he is accustomed to understanding English sentences, without access to the meanings and nuances that are distinctive to the social phenomena and class of respondents being studied.

In this connection, Cicourel recommends that during an interview a respondent be asked a series of detailed ethnographic questions about the main issues covered in an interview, in a manner similar to a lawyer cross-examining a witness and evoking details from him. In this way, the interviewer may acquire this elusive "ethnographic context" and be better able to interpret the significance of a respondent's remarks. Obviously, it is even better to be familiar with this ethnographic context before the interview starts, through some kind of prior observation of (and participation in) the subject's life-world. In this connection there is an important question: Should the participant-observer himself conduct systematic interviews, or should somebody else do it? In the latter case, the participant-observer would, as best he could, communicate the ethnographic context to another, who serves as interviewer. A different person serving as interviewer might combine the advantages of being "in the know" (through communication with the participant-observer) with those of being a "Martian" to the situation (so that he is able to think of new issues which those too close to a phenomenon would be unable to notice). On the other hand, the participant-observer, through his familiarity with the subjects and his skill in interacting with them, may be able to handle the interview situation better than an outsider. We cannot deal with all of the details here. However, it should be noted that whatever is decided in the above regard is likely to have a serious bearing upon the study.

THE RETENTION AND RETRIEVAL OF INTERVIEW DATA

Retaining and retrieving the information that the interview provides are essential in order to acquire a set of meaningful questions for future use and also for discovering the proper "sensitizing concepts" for use in organizing the data. There are two basic procedures for doing this. One can take notes during the interview or (if this is considered disruptive) as soon after its conclusion as possible, or one can tape-record and later transcribe the interview.

Tape recording allows the investigator to concentrate on the interview without distracting the respondent (or himself) by taking notes and still retain all that the respondent related. However, the tape recorder may be intimidating to the respondent (and the interviewer, for that matter) and may bias his account. There is the added hazard in taping that the interviewer, knowing that he has a spoken record of all that transpired for future analysis, may become lax and fail to pay sufficient attention to what is being said.

Those who prefer taping contend that the retention of vital information and the lack of distortion that taping provides more than outweigh these potential drawbacks. However, there are some less obvious disadvantages in tape recording. For one thing, a tape recording of an interaction is usually taken to be a complete record of what was said. In this view, if something is recorded on magnetic tape it is, in principle, always available to the researcher, and he does not run the risk of being without data that are later found to be relevant and sometimes crucial. But this position can be attacked in two ways. A tape recording contains an enormous amount of information which, in certain ways, is similar to a large library of uncatalogued books. The mere fact that something is on a tape (perhaps one of dozens of tapes made during a particular study) does not mean that it can be readily retrieved. Many scholars encounter this problem when taking field notes. They write down any and all of their thoughts on a problem, so that nothing will be lost. A large mass of heterogeneous material is thus amassed, which turns out to be all but useless. There is simply no practical way to review all the accumulated notes in order to find items that bear upon a given topic that has, at some point in the research, become a focus of interest. An item buried in a mass of unindexed material is just as unavailable as something that is not there at all.

Second, "what is said" consists not only of a series of sounds but of a complex of meanings. Numerous studies have shown that persons' memories and their reconstructions of what was said during an interaction alter radically with time.[5] When people hear a conversation at later times and in different social situations, they simply do not interpret its meaning in the same way they did during the original exchange. The very words and sentences that were uttered may seem to change over time. To illustrate, consider the following excerpt from a tape-recorded group-therapy session:

> "I don't know whether the medication's botherin' me or not. It's just that uh— following along—the way *he (you)* feels—think. An' whether the medication has anything tuh do with it—at the moment."

This tape was transcribed by someone who had been transcribing natural conversations for many years. Upon hearing this excerpt on tape while simultaneously reading the transcript, the author heard "he" on the tape, corresponding to the "he" on the accompanying transcript. However, the author was present when the taping took place and knew the people involved in the conversation. After listening to the tape a few times, he began to recover the "ethnographic context" of the session—i.e., he began to remember meanings. It occurred to him that the pronoun "he" was strange in this context and should have been "you." He listened to the tape again. Incredibly, he now heard "you" instead of "he." He played the tape over at least a dozen times. Each time, "you" was heard, now quite unambiguously. Yet it was undeniable that on the first hearing, he actually *heard* "he."

Clearly, words uttered during a conversation will not stand still on a tape so that they can be recovered in the same way at each listening, independent of time lapse, the particular listener, or the social situation in which the listening is done. Background assumptions about "what's going on," "who is who," or "what this is all about" run so deep that they can literally affect one's hearing. Here, as in most other instances in the doing of social science, "nothing is that simple."

One way to counteract these problems, is to index meanings as soon after the interview as possible, by talking into the tape recorder at the conclusion of every interview about what emerged as being meaningful and why.

In the final analysis, whether one resorts to taping, note taking, or some combination of the two will be contingent upon the researcher's style, memory, and immediate situation.

RECURSIVELY DEFINED QUESTIONS

Actually, dichotomizing interviewing into structured and unstructured forms was something of an oversimplification. We have thus far mentioned several types of questions that might be employed in an interview:

1. Questions decided upon in advance with fixed choices for answers.
2. Questions decided upon in advance which are "open ended" with respect to answers.
    a. Questions of this type with provisions for future questioning or "probes" depending on the initial answer to the main question.
3. Questions which are not decided upon in advance but which are asked

spontaneously during the interview because they appear relevant or important.

An actual interview may consist of only one of these types of questions or may employ some combination of them. The main difference among these questions is in the extent to which they are "recursively defined," in a phrase used by mathematicians. That is, to what extent is what has already been said in a given interview being used to determine or define the next question to be asked? When a researcher decides how "recursive" he wants his interviewing process to be, he must do so on at least two levels: (1) to what extent should prior interaction in a particular interview be allowed to determine what is asked next during that same interview? and (2) to what extent should the experiences and information of past interviews be allowed to determine the structure and content of current interviews?

It should be clear that making interviewing recursive allows the researcher to treat people and situations as unique and to alter the research technique in the light of information fed back during the research process itself. This is in principle consistent with the position of symbolic interaction. On the other hand, the more the order, nature, and content of an interviewer's questions vary from interview to interview (or during the course of a particular interview), the fewer are his opportunities to obtain "scientific data." If his questions are not standardized, then the answers of his respondents cannot easily be counted, categorized, or compared with each other.

However, allowing feedback and flexibility is not always antithetical to reaching general conclusions. Instead of interviewing people one at a time, the sociologist can talk to them in groups. As they talk to each other they can provide detailed feedback which allows them to discover points of agreement and common experiences—feedback that would be impossible for the interviewer to provide. This strategy is especially provocative when studying groups such as waiters or students, who may have individual ways of dealing with common problems but have never talked about this among themselves. Of course, the consensus reached in such discussions may come about because of the dynamics of the discussion and thus may be unreal. Here, as elsewhere, one does not obtain new resources without getting new problems.

Case Study A (page 133) is somewhat unusual in that it is a study about structured interviewing which utilizes tape-recorded, unstructured interviewing to get information. In it, Jacobs talks to market researchers about their techniques for learning the public's reaction to a nationally advertised product.

Participant Observation

Many people in the reality reconstruction business hold that interviewing (in whatever form) ought not to be used exclusively but should be used in combination with participant observation. The latter term means being in the presence of others on an ongoing basis and having some nominal status for them as someone who is part of their daily lives.

By becoming a participant-observer one is in a position to see if people "say what they mean and mean what they say." Participant observation, when used in combination with interviews, offers a potentially powerful way to call into question the relationship between words and deeds. Indeed, there is considerable evidence to support the contention that this relationship does not exist. Deutscher, in a now classic article, catalogues a number of studies that show no relationship, or inverse relationships, between expressed attitudes and behaviors.[6] Notwithstanding this, most survey research (market research is a subset) continue to take a positive relationship between words and deeds as given. Faith in this relationship is not in danger of being shaken since, as Deutscher and others have noted, few sociologists have combined participant observation with survey-type interviewing or questionaire studies. In one sense this is no surprise. Sociologists, like others in a variety of undertakings who hold legitimated work models, wish to maintain these models and not to undercut or transcend them. C. Wright Mills has noted how difficult it is, having adapted a "vocabulary of motives", to relate to competing vocabularies or transcend one's own.[7]

THE PROBLEM OF CONTRADICTORY EVIDENCE

But there is a less obvious reason why participant observation is not habitually combined with survey-type interviewing. Having discovered, through participant observation that words and deeds to not match, what do you do then? Participant observation often gives information that contradicts that obtained through interviews, questionnaires, or other research methods. Yet the information obtained using each method is internally consistent. Thus the resolution of these contradictions poses some extremely perplexing problems for a researcher. Such problems never become visible if one simply sticks to a single method of obtaining information.

Let's take an example. One research study in psychology undertook to study the dynamics of a particular family by using several methods simultaneously.[8] A participant-observer lived with the family for a period of time, expert psychological examiners administered the Minnesota Multiphasic Personality Inventory (MMPI) and the Thematic Apperception Test (TAT) to the family, and, finally, a clinical psychologist interviewed the family on a therapeutic basis. The rationale for the uses of these various methods was that they would yield different, but additive, information, which would give a more complete picture of the family's psychodynamics than could any one method used alone. The results? The different methods produced contradictory information in several areas. The examiners who administered the psychological tests (especially the TAT) found the father to be a dangerous, potentially violent, psychopathic personality. On the other hand, the clinical psychologist and the participant-observer (who had a chance to observe the father in potentially violent situations such as in bars when he was angry and drunk) found the father to be a basically normal, slightly neurotic person. In particular they characterized him as meek and "henpecked" in his father role.

What happens in such cases of contradictory evidence? As we noted earlier, each method of getting at "what's going on out there" may be internally consistent. For example, devices employed in interviewing to detect dishonesty (such as asking the same question in different ways) may reveal that the subjects are trying to be honest and are not consciously attempting deception. Further, many different subjects might agree when they report on what they "do" in some situation, indicating consensus.

On the other hand, by simply watching what people do in many different situations, the participant-observer might observe again and again that they are doing precisely the opposite of what they reported. This situation represents what Pollner has called a "reality disjuncture."[9] Two methods of obtaining the same "factual" information are each competently applied but somehow come up with two contradictory answers. What should be done in such a situation?

One answer lies in a more sophisticated appreciation of the significance of "accounts."[10] These should not be regarded in advance as "information," which is either "true" or "false," depending on how it compares to some "referent" "out there." Instead, an effort must be made to ascertain the purposes, understandings, and activities which the *members* associate with the accounts they give. That is, one must find out not only what questions to ask but also the *procedures* that respondents use, and that the researcher will use, to translate an answer into its intended meaning. That meaning may be a much more complicated thing than the truthful conveyance of "information."

As a case in point, one of the authors asked a noted survey researcher what he did in his profession. His first reply was that he constructed quantitative models of such phenomena as social mobility and occupational achievement in various societies. Considering the question from another vantage point, he decided that what he really did while he worked was "gossip." That is, very little of his actual time and energy on the job was spent examining data or figuring out equations. Mostly he talked to students and faculty about other people, their careers, and their work, "talked shop," and engaged in similar verbal activities that might loosely be labeled "gossip." Both answers were "right," in a specific sense. Each was addressed to a different sense of "what he did." In the first case, he gave a definition of his sociological specialty as it might be understood within the profession. In the second, he reflected on his activities during an average day on the job, including such activities as getting coffee, going to the restroom, and gossiping. In both cases his understanding of the question and our correct understanding of his answer involve intimate ethnographic knowledge, consisting of the different ways in which insiders (sociologists) think about their job. Ideally, the researcher should have a good grasp of the ethnographic context before trying to assess the relationship between words and deeds. Which words ought to be compared with which deeds might not be nearly so obvious as it appears.

We have considered some of the ways in which participant observation offers another, and more powerful, check than face-to-face interviewing on the question of the relationship between words and deeds. Let us now consider the various forms this research strategy has taken and some of the problems associated with it.

INVOLVEMENT VERSUS DETACHMENT

A basic problem in doing participant-observational research revolves around the delicate balance it is assumed the researcher needs to maintain between "involvement," in the search for "members' knowledge" (the need to acquire an insider's perspective), and the threat of "going native" (the danger that "too much" involvement may cause the researcher to lose his "objective," dispassionate, scientific orientation).

The latter threat assumes that the researcher has multiple goals. First, he wants to learn the actors' "definition of the situation"—to see what the actor sees, know what he knows, and think as he thinks. Second, having accomplished this reconstruction of the other's reality, the researcher hopes to transcend this view, to see what the actor does *not* see—the formal features, process, patterns, or common denominators that characterize the actor's view and situation. This, it is hoped, will allow the investigator to generalize his findings by allowing him to see what the actor and others in similar or different situations, holding similar or different definitions of the situations, have in common.

The extent to which one is committed to studying scientifically, as opposed to "becoming," the object of study will influence the degree to which he is prepared to play off "involvement" against the threat of "going native" in the search for member's knowledge. Those who are more concerned with more accurate descriptions of what's going on in the actor's head than with the scientific legitimization and generalization of these descriptions will not be overconcerned about "going native." On the other hand, those concerned with scientific legitimization will seek to maintain a "marginal man"[11] position, to be involved (but not too involved) while maintaining a certain degree of objectivity.

AN EXAMPLE: STUDYING RELIGIOUS CULTS

Perhaps nowhere is the conflict between these strategies and their accompanying research emphases more acute than in the study of religion. A poignant case of this conflict was reported by Robbins, Anthony, and Curtis in their study of a sect of "Jesus freaks."[12] Robert Bellah has proposed an epistemological orientation toward religious beliefs called "symbolic realism" which asserts the existential reality of these beliefs without necessarily accepting their empirical reality.[13] In research, one attempts to understand a sect's religious beliefs empathetically while not internalizing them to the point of becoming a convert, and while still translating these beliefs (with their causes and functions) into a scientific theory of religion.

Can this be done? Robbins and his associates report the following dilemma: The members of the sect of Jesus freaks did not understand their beliefs to be "existentially true," as did the researcher, but "empirically true." In addition, they regarded competing beliefs as empirically false. Finally, they believed that anyone who truly understood and appreciated their beliefs would naturally convert to their sect. This posed an agonizing dilemma for the researcher. He was indeed able to understand and demonstrate his understanding of their beliefs to the "natives." He did this partly through his experiences with, and commitment to, a similar but different religious faith. But he did not convert! This posed the following puzzle for the sect: Either their beliefs about understanding and its relation to conversion were wrong, or the researcher did not "really" understand their beliefs. But there was every indication that he really understood, and yet did not convert. How was this possible?

> Either (1) the researcher was not as nice as he had seemed and was somehow willfully opposing Christ; or (2) they were not true Christians and the Holy Spirit had not been speaking through them to the researcher; or (3) something was wrong with their sectarian ideology and possibly there were good persons who were not Christians or there were many paths to salvation, etc.[14]

As a result of this dilemma, members of the sect made frequent attempts to convert the researcher. Because of these attempts tensions escalated, interactions between the researcher and sect members were reduced, and the researcher lost his empathetic appreciation of the sect, replacing it with antagonism and bad feelings.

Here we see in a nutshell some of the major problems of participant observation. How can one empathetically understand others while maintaining a commitment to scientific understanding and theorizing? The authors of this study note that the problem here was how to accept and empathize with a group whose own belief system directly contradicted the researchers' and their "scientific," "tolerant" conception of the group. In attempting to be empathetic and still be scientific and detached, the researchers posed a dilemma to their subjects that could have radically changed the very people and practices they were studying. A "scientific," systematic attempt to achieve empathy, in the end, produced the very opposite. As the researchers noted:

> The degree of such tolerance, like the degree of other religious virtues which an individual actually practices, seems more dependent upon the character of his inner "spiritual" life than upon his commitment to a tolerant belief system.[15]

It may well be that society and people are so organized that the goals of scientific and empathetic understanding (access to meanings) are competitive in *principle*. It may not be possible to be a participant *and* a scientist simultaneously.

THE RESEARCHER: SELECTING A SOCIAL IDENTITY

The study cited above illustrates a few twists and turns to an old sociological saw. If the people who make up a social world are its "parts," then this world shows itself differently to its different parts. Who you are and where you are within such a world have a role in creating that world and in fashioning the colored glasses through which you see it and it sees you.

As a way to gather information, participant observation is almost alone in being able to take this old saw seriously. It can do this because the participant-observer can actually select one of many identities from which to learn about the cultural world. He can literally choose who he will be in that world. And he can make this choice with an eye to different types and amounts of knowledge that go with different identities.

By choosing an identity we have in mind such things as:

1. Learning, or pressing into service, sets of social skills for dealing with others and acting appropriately in different cultural situations.
2. Obtaining and fulfilling legitimate social roles, such as jobs or group memberships.
3. Cultivating and embedding oneself in networks of social relationships.
4. Psychologically identifying with types of people, certain self-images, moral values, and ways of life.

All these and more are involved in a social identity. These aspects of identity can to some extent be deliberately cultivated. We shall first illustrate some consequences of one aspect of social identity, social role. Then we shall take up some classical issues that have traditionally concerned sociologists when they undertake to select an identity for purposes of doing research.

THE EFFECTS OF THE RESEARCHER'S SOCIAL ROLE

The media have recently been carrying advertisements for two books, one about men, one about women. The book about women, it is claimed, contains valuable information for men who wish to meet and get to know the "women of their dreams." The authors selected twenty or so women who were deemed unusually attractive on a number of criteria, such as intelligence, appearance, personality, and professional status. They interviewed these women and asked such questions as: Where do people find someone like you? (that is, what public and recreational establishments do you frequent?). What would a stranger say to you that would catch your interest? What sort of dress and appearance do you find attractive in a man? What places do you enjoy going to? What activities do you enjoy? The results of these interviews were tabulated and are presented in the book as general information for men wishing to meet and get to know such women. The book about men simply reversed this procedure.

Why would people spend money for such a book? Clearly because of the belief that it contained information that they did not have and could not otherwise obtain. Why not? The main difference between the authors and the potential readers was their social role. The role of the authors allowed them to approach various people, arbitrarily chosen, who were total strangers to them, and have these people give them fairly intimate information about themselves and their activities. For most others, this information would have been unavailable, for a number of reasons.

THE PRINCIPLE OF REFLEXIVITY

Many of these reasons can be summarized by a principle Garfinkel has emphasized: the principle of reflexivity.[16] This states that descriptions about some aspect of the social world are simultaneously within (part of) the very world that they describe. As a result, as one sociologist put it, there is no room in the social world *merely* to describe anything. Descriptions in the social world, since they are within that world, simultaneously affect social relationships, execute moral evaluations, produce political, moral, and social consequences, and so on. Descriptions are almost always "doing" many more things in a social situation than simply "reporting" a set of facts.

Let's apply this principle to some of the questions asked in the book described above. A question such as "Do you like to dance?" has a massively different significance when asked by someone who has just met one of the women interviewed in the book than it might have if asked by one of the authors of the book. Such a query will undoubtedly be heard as "pre-invitation." If the woman says yes, the man might ask her for a date. Thus her answer will not merely report a personal preference, it will indicate her interest in the man and/or her willingness to pursue a relationship. From the woman's perspective, her reply may be chosen to reflect these delicacies. If she wishes to avoid a future meeting, she might be found to "not enjoy" any activity the man cares to mention.

Persons engaged in such a conversation, in such a social context, in such an initial relationship, will find that they cannot "simply" ask another for information about such things as what activities they enjoy.

The point is general. Social science researchers tend to want to treat their interactions with others as occasions where information about social life is given and received. However, for both the asker and the answerer, the roles involved, the social relationship, and the social context of the interaction often make this impossible. In our example, even so innocuous a query as "What time is it?" may be understood as constituting more than a request for information. As a consequence, one may find that the time is unobtainable from a whole population of opposite-sex persons at certain public places.

In the case of our researchers, approaching a stranger with the story that one is writing a book on "getting to know others" may itself prove to be the best opening "pick-up" line in the book. It allows the eliciting of information that is ordinarily politically charged and can be used subsequently to further the relationship. As one can see, the issue of the social context of information transfer is an exceedingly delicate one.

The previous remarks suggest another major point. Probably very few people in our society would think of using the pretext of writing a book as a pick-up strategy, although it is an elegant one in several ways. In fact, *only* in the role of the author of such a book would one think of asking a collection of others the sorts of questions we have mentioned. To most others, including the author when out of this role, such a project would never come to mind. Thus, it is not only that one's social role gains one access to persons, situations, and kinds of information that other social roles make unavailable. The mere embodiment of a given social role will cause one to have concerns and questions and to adopt methods of inquiry that the same person in other social roles would never consider.

This issue poses a delicate problem for the participant-observer. Whatever his role, it will automatically produce in him a set of concerns, ways of obtaining and believing information, and preoccupations, that another role would not have produced. The issue assumes greater importance when it is noticed that the initial social role (and/or status) adopted by the participant-observer usually remains fixed throughout his study. It will define for him and others the way in which he is part of the social world which he is studying. In turn, this will persistently affect his and others' definition of where he can go, whom he can talk to and about what, the significance of his actions, and many other such contingencies. In fact, a consideration of many participant-observer studies suggests that the particular social role adopted might be the determining factor in the general picture a researcher obtains of the group he studies.

The types of social roles a social scientist might adopt are catalogued in a few simple ways in methods books. This catalogue is designed to permit a discussion of traditional research issues and thus to give some guidance in the selection of roles. These traditional issues usually embody an "old-fashioned" point of view: that the social world is a "real" world that has a distinctive organization and structure. The main question is, how does a social scientist mesh himself into that world so that he finds out the things he is interested in while simultaneously avoiding the danger that his "enmeshment" will become a source of distorted information? The view is old-fashioned in that it does not consider the possibility that the number of "real" social worlds corresponds to the number of social identities within it. That is, social structure *consists* of the commonsense constructions of those within it. As we will see, it is this latter view that constitutes the underpinning of "formal sociology," discussed in chapters 7 to 12.

For now, let us review the traditional forms of participation as they relate to research roles and their accompanying joys and sorrows.

PARTICIPANT OBSERVATION: THE UNKNOWN
OBSERVER

In some forms of participant observation, the sociologist "goes native" in several senses of the word. He adapts an identity and a way of dealing with others that are normal, natural parts of some social-cultural world. Since he will not be a special kind of person, doing and thinking atypical things, his effect on this world, he hopes, will be minimized.

The "unknown observer" may be a spy or a naive member. In the latter case, he undertakes to study a social situation that he is (or is becoming) an integral part of—for example, his place of work, his home, a bowling league.

Among the natural advantages accruing to those who study the settings they are a part of is one which turns on the notion of "gatekeepers." The idea here is that there is in every setting certain persons from whom one needs acceptance in order to gain access to the setting and its participants. This is usually done by "going through channels" in the hope of winning official approval and thereby legitimizing one's presence. A less formal, more direct method is to make an approach through a friend or accomplice whose presence has already been legitimized. In any case, studying a scene one is already a part of is a way of gaining access to a setting without actually dealing with gatekeepers.

The problem of gatekeepers is only one aspect of the problem of "social territories" faced by the participant observer.[17] Some of the most impressive examples of modern research have been concerned with how access to physical, auditory, and visual space is tightly controlled—that is, how cultural rules and social groups control who can be where and what they can hear or see. Complementary to this research is the crying need for sociologists to observe areas of social life that have hitherto been merely the objects of speculation or inferences based on indirect information. In such a pursuit, it is safe to say, the unknown observer has access to persons and situations that the known researcher does not, and this can profoundly influence the research.

However, this strategy creates certain problems. When the researcher is already familiar with, and a part of, the scene he is studying, he need not worry about "going native"; he is by definition already native—that is, one of those he hopes to study. Scientific sociology, in its concern with objectivity, assumes that such a researcher lacks the "distance" and "objectivity" to see the forest for the trees. That is, it is assumed that his involvement will not allow him to transcend his member's understanding of the situation, so as to see "scientifically" the formal features or processes of the situation and how these relate to other social phenomena. As one researcher put it, the person who "goes native" knows too much about his phenomena; he takes so many things for granted that he no longer knows that he knows them. We have all probably had the experience of having to teach another some familiar skill such as driving a car. We find ourselves so familiar with the "how to" of driving that we literally do not know what we are doing for purposes of telling another. In fact, forgetting what we were doing, in terms of being explicitly aware of it, was virtually a precondition of becoming a good driver. Apparently, such a precondition also holds for becoming a good native.

In short, the unknown observer who is himself a member is not only in a position to get close to the phenomenon he seeks to study, he becomes it. Insofar as one seeks to understand the feelings and intentions of those in a setting, this would seem to be a definite advantage. On the other hand, to the extent that one seeks to transcend the data, it is taken to be a distinct disadvantage.

A second form of unknown observer is the classic spy. Here, as in the novice or naive member status, the researcher gets around the problem of gatekeepers by "passing" as one of those he seeks to study. However, passing and actually being or becoming a real member are two very different enterprises, involving different social skills and competencies, different moral commitments, and different self-images.

Both successful spies and those who are already members of the group they study are capable of performing as competent members of the group. Neither looks nor acts like a "cultural dope."[18] However, the member is known to others and himself as a member, while the spy is known to others as a member but to himself as an outsider.

The spy has the moral problem of pretending to be what he is not and using the information he gathers in ways that members are unaware of and have not sanctioned. There is the further danger for the spy that he may convert. This is a remote possibility, however; in the case previously noted, it is unlikely that a sociological spy passing as a Jesus freak would convert and literally become a Jesus freak. One reason is that if one sets out deliberately to enter and participate in a set of social situations *knowing* that he intends to study them, he becomes something more than a mere participant. There is every reason to believe that his interpretations and reactions will be colored by this orientation to research. He will not end up with the same view of the situation that he would have obtained if he was a true novice or naive member—that is, held the same reasons, goals, and purposes for being there as someone who was merely, and thus totally, a participant. While this might seem an advantage with respect to avoiding psychological identification, it may be trouble if one aims at a true insider's view. For the spy brings and leaves with concepts, concerns, evaluations, and interpretations which are foreign to the setting itself and its genuine members.

It is true that both the spy and the naive member may be incapable of seeing the forest for the trees, insofar as both are very much part of what they study. The spy is perhaps less subject to this complaint than the bona fide member. The question arises: What of the *known observer*? Is he more likely to be objective than the unknown observer, and if so, why? Intuitively it would seem that he has greater potential for distance and objectivity but lower potential for knowing or understanding. In practice this is often not the case.

PARTICIPANT OBSERVATION: THE KNOWN OBSERVER

The known observer seeks objectivity through distance and limited involvement. Those being observed know that the researcher is among them and who he is. This strategy is designed to ensure that the investigator does not "go native" and is able to transcend the data and construct general scientific categories. Those evoking this strategy hold a kind of scientific variation on the artistic homily "Distance lends enchantment to the view."

While the spy and the naive member are able to pass and gain access only by performing as competent members of the group, this is not true for the known observer. He gains access and acceptance by virtue of his status as a certain kind of outsider. Since he is not passing and does not have to know how to behave appropriately, he does not have to perform the duties or jobs of a member, nor is his incompetence or ignorance usually ground for sanction or exclusion. Quite the contrary. The known observer has the inestimable advantage of being a *known incompetent*. Insiders will theorize for him, teach him things, and tell him things they would not tell one another. For all of these reasons, he is less likely to take members' knowledge for granted and thus avoids the "forest for the trees" problem.

Since he does not have to live their life, he is less likely to identify with that life and the beliefs and actions that go with it. Then, too, since others consider him to be an outsider and act accordingly, he is less subject to the pull of group solidarity and its accompanying moral commitments.

However, known observers have other problems. They must deal with, or find ways around, gatekeepers in order to gain access to the setting. They are usually subject to greater constraints as well, with respect to what outsiders might be privy to. Additionally, the whole world of a group might transfigure itself when it presents itself to a person who has the status of known observer. Even if some of these constraints are overcome, the general problem remains that one will be introducing inquiries, concerns, and activities into a social world that are foreign to that world. In effect, the researcher himself becomes an intervening variable whose effects remain unknown. Insofar as he is not "doing what comes naturally" in such a world, these effects might be much more pronounced than would be the case in the unknown-observer situation.

Finally, if involvement is limited in the cause of objectivity, another question arises. From a symbolic-interaction perspective, one must have some involvement in order to understand the behavior one has described. It is, after all, the meanings that the actors attribute to their actions, not the acts per se, that the researcher seeks to uncover. These can emerge only through the process of interaction itself. Leaving out the interpretive process that interaction involves produces a description of the world much closer in form to B. F. Skinner's,[19] than to Howard Becker's.[20] Why is this so? The reader might voice the classic objection "I don't have to be able to lay an egg to tell a good one from a bad one." But it appears that this maxim does not hold for group life. Often you *do* have to be able to lay a social egg to be able to tell what to make of that egg from a member's point of view. In interpreting the actions of others and assigning morals, meanings, and motives to them, a person uses extremely complex skills of reasoning and perception. Psychologists still cannot explain how people translate sounds into words and sentences when they converse with each other.[21] No computer can duplicate this simple interpretive task, not to mention more complex ones. Further, those who use such interpretive skills cannot tell you how they do it, for the simple reason that they do not know. Sometimes they have ideas about how they do it, but these ideas, these interpretations of their own interpretations, are usually sketchy and inadequate.

So how can a person see what others see, hear what they hear, and understand what they understand, if it is not known how others are doing these things? The answer is that these skills are part of social activities in a definitional sense. Part of repairing a car is noticing "What is wrong?" "Is it working?" "Are the plugs dirty," "Are the valves sticking?" and so on. Part of playing chess is assessing "the safety of my king," "whether I have control of the center," and so on. In learning such activities and doing them, these interpretations and interpretive skills will naturally arise and be used. Without doing the activities, one will interpret things differently than those who do them. This will occur because he will not "know how" to interpret them naturally, as insiders do, nor will he be able to find out, explicitly, just what these interpretive skills consist of.

WHAT FORM OF PARTICIPATION?

In our discussion of known and unknown observers, we have been dealing with the implications of only two questions: How should I make myself known to others; who should they (and I) think I am? But there is an equally important matter to consider: What will I actually be doing while among others? What will be the activities I will be required or allowed to engage in?

For conceptual convenience, let's divide the social scientist's activities while doing participant observation into two categories—(1) making observations, such as "hanging around," "keeping your eyes and ears open," making tape recordings, or looking at documents, and (2) normal, natural participation, such as fulfilling the duties of a job or engaging in group ceremonies and rituals. Then we can treat who others think he is, and what he actually does while among them as two dichotomous variables, giving four pure types of participant observation, as indicated in the diagram on page 57.

Although the reader can interpret the table and its consequences for himself, it might pay to spell out the meaning of the four boxes a little more clearly:

How the researcher participates
in the setting(s):

		By making observations	By normal, natural participation
Who others think the researcher is:	A scientist	1	2
	A bona fide member	3	4

1. The investigator is known to others as a social scientist and confines his activities while among them to gathering information and observing.
2. The social scientist makes his identity as such known to all from the outset. However, he adopts the role of a bona fide member, such as a patient in a hospital or an employee in a factory. Others know him to be playing at being a member for purposes of getting an insider's point of view.
3. The researcher conceals his identity but adopts a social role which is naturally defined by the group as someone who gathers information about other people. For example, he becomes a ship's recreation director, a town gossip, or a plant psychologist.
4. Unknown to others as a social scientist, the researcher adopts some role such as factory worker and simply lives the life of that worker while letting nature take its course. He learns by being a factory worker, without any explicit attempt to observe or gather information about others.

Boxes 1 and 2 show two ways to be a known observer, while boxes 3 and 4 show two ways to be an unknown observer. With four kinds of social roles instead of two, new ways to plan for and assess old issues, such as detachment and involvement, emerge. The reader can figure out these elaborations for himself, as well as invent new variables and even more complicated roles to select from.

All of this should suffice to emphasize that the selection of who you are (to yourself and others) and where you are in a social world is worthy of being treated as a very delicate matter. Careful attention to this issue can perhaps bring more of a payoff in this kind of research than almost any other consideration.

The actual mechanics of gathering and analyzing data in participant observation involve many secretarial tasks: keeping and using notebooks, making and transcribing tapes, compiling journals, writing summaries and memos, duplicating and cataloguing them with some filing system. Much of this involves common sense, coupled with a sensitivity toward the situation and your own work habits.[22]

However, there is a final task to perform after working out an analysis and writing it up. Studies using participant observation often include a special sort of methodological appendix. The following is a presentation of what it typically contains.

THE METHOD OF TRUE CONFESSIONS

There is a procedure that is often recommended and used in qualitative (and quantitative) research to solve or alleviate many of the problems noted in the previous section. Many qualitative studies devote a good deal of space to relating in autobiographical fashion how and why the author conducted his research as he did. Such methodological appendixes describe the initial biases, values, and theories of the research and give a blow-by-blow description of how and why things progressed as they did. They describe the process of gaining entry, the people contacted initially, the process of following up leads, how and when notes were taken, the changing perspectives and reactions of the researcher to situations, people, and events as the study progressed, and the way in which notes, tapes, and anecdotes were translated into research findings. They describe as well the mistakes, failures, troubles, and insanities that a callous world imposed on the hapless social scientist in his innocent attempt to obtain accurate information about a social phenomenon.

The value of such a narrative is supposed to be, first, that it tells the reader what the process was that produced the researcher's data and, second, that it provides a crude reconstruction of the research endeavor which is helpful in sorting out fact from interpretation and general patterns from idiosyncratic incidents.

There is an astounding aspect to this methodological procedure. Reading such an appendix, one quickly comes to the conclusion that the various mishaps and conditions under which the research was done have made objective, unbiased sociology impossible. However, the appendix is often preceded by an apparently factual description of the structure and organization of a social community! In this sense, what might be called the real use of the methodological appendix is similar to that of absolution in the Catholic Church. One can commit (or be forced by the social world to commit) various methodological and scientific "sins" during research. However, if the researcher confesses these sins to his sociological "priests," he may do penance and be absolved. This saving cycle allows him to go on as if his sins had never happened. That is, he can devote the rest of the book to a recitation of the knowledge he obtained using a rhetoric of "fact," as if reporting what "really happened."

In making these comments we are by no means condemning methodological appendixes. They often present more interesting data than are offered within the study itself. What we are insisting upon is that the material in methodological appendixes do not solve the problem that our methods of observation and analysis may simply *not work in the social world*. There may be no solution to this problem, which is equivalent to saying that the social world may be so organized that certain things about it cannot be known in a systematic way. Some of the reasons that this may be true have been dealt with earlier. Still others will be considered in the sections that follow.

Now that we have outlined the "why do," "how to do," and "problems of doing" participant observation, the reader may wish to consider case study B (see page 143), a participant-observation study by Jerry Jacobs of a social-welfare agency, conducted from an unknown-observer perspective. It illustrates not only this strategy but the way in which participant-observational studies may overcome the charge of "parochialism."

Notes

1. The interview schedule was taken from an unpublished research study by Michael H. McGee: "Social Organization Study: Meher Baba," Department of Sociology, University of North Carolina at Chapel Hill, 1968.
2. The notion of "sensitizing concept" was invented by Herbert Blumer. We discussed the idea extensively in chapter 2, in the section on grounded theory. For more details see Herbert Blumer, *Symbolic Interactionism: Perspective and Method*, Englewood Cliffs, N.J.: Prentice-Hall, 1969.
3. John Lofland, *Analyzing Social Settings*, Belmont, Calif.: Wadsworth, 1971, p. 90.
4. For a discussion of ethnographic context, see Aaron V. Cicourel, *Cognitive Sociology: Language and Meaning in Social Interaction*, New York: Free Press, 1974, pp. 150–154.
5. Ibid., p. 124.
6. Irwin Deutscher, "Words and Deeds," *Social Problems* 13 (1966): 235–254.
7. See C. Wright Mills, "Situated Actions and Vocabularies of Motive," *American Sociological Review* 5 (December 1940): 904–913.
8. Unpublished senior honors thesis at Harvard University, spring 1971.
9. Melvin Pollner, "The Very Coinage of Your Brain: The Resolution of Reality Disjunctures," *The Philosophy of the Social Sciences* 5 (1975): 411–430.
10. Marvin B. Scott and Stanford M. Lyman, "Accounts, Deviance, and Social Order," in *Deviance and Respectability: The Social Construction of Moral Meanings*, ed. by Jack Douglas, New York: Basic Books, 1970, pp. 89–119.
11. Everett V. Stonequist, *The Marginal Man*, New York: Scribner, 1937.
12. Thomas Robbins et al., "The Limits of Symbolic Realism: Problems of Empathetic Field Observation in a Sectarian Context," *Journal for the Scientific Study of Religion* 12, no. 3 (September 1973): 259–271.
13. Robert Bellah, "Christianity and Symbolic Realism," *Journal for the Scientific Study of Religion* 9 (Summer 1970): 89–96.
14. Robbins, et al., "The Limits of Symbolic Realism," p. 267.
15. Dick Anthony et al., "Reply to Bellah," *Journal for the Scientific Study of Religion* 13 (December 1974): 491–495.

16. The nature and importance of reflexivity were first emphasized by Garfinkel. See Harold Garfinkel, *Studies in Ethnomethodology*, Englewood Cliffs, N.J.: Prentice-Hall, 1967, pp. 7–9.

17. For one account of some of the problems and topics inherent in social territories, see Robert Sommer, *Personal Space: The Behavioral Basis of Design*, Englewood Cliffs, N.J.: Prentice-Hall, 1969.

18. Garfinkel, *Studies in Ethnomethodology*, pp. 67–68.

19. B. F. Skinner, *Science and Human Behavior*, New York: MacMillan, 1953.

20. Howard Becker (ed.), *The Other Side: Perspectives on Deviance*, New York: Free Press, 1964.

21. For a review of this problem in experimental psychology, see Donald A. Norman, *Memory and Attention: An Introduction to Human Information Processing*, New York: Wiley, 1969.

22. Among the good treatments of this subject are: Howard Becker, "Problems of Inference and Proof in Participant Observation," *American Sociological Review* 23 (1958): 652–660; John Lofland, *Analyzing Social Settings*, Belmont, Calif.: Wadsworth, 1971; and L. Schatzman and A. Strauss, *Field Research: Strategies for a Natural Sociology*, Englewood Cliffs, N.J.: Prentice-Hall, 1973.

CHAPTER 4

Personal Accounts and Life Histories: Reconstructing the Individual's Reality

For some problems the researcher will find himself studying individuals who are a group only in the sense that they are collected together in his mind because of how they bear on some sociological problem. Such groups include suicide attempters, schizophrenics, and certain other kinds of deviants. In no natural way do these people share some common social world. They need not be regularly in one other's physical presence, need not be in any kind of communication with one another, and need not mutually affect one another's lives in any direct way.

Under such circumstances, the "member's point of view" refers to the subjective interpretations of individuals about the events, objects, and circumstances that they are confronted with over time. There is the "objective" world on the ground floor and the individual's experience of that world on the second floor. It is the latter that we seek to understand here, person by person, without assuming that a group consensus exists.

Analyzing Personal Accounts

There are many important aspects of people's lives that cannot be duplicated experimentally, or easily or morally observed in a direct way—for instance, sexual relations, suicide attempts, planning and carrying out crimes. Analyzing personal accounts is often the best way (perhaps the only way) to gain access to such phenomena. This strategy confronts the researcher with many of the same problems as do interviewing techniques, especially if the personal accounts are presented orally and in face-to-face interaction. He must rely upon the internal consistency and "integrity" of the account, the extent of the "rapport" he feels exists between himself and the one offering the account, the possible ulterior motives of the account giver, and why he might wish to engage in deception.

Having decided on the extent of the account giver's good faith with respect to some part or all of the account, the researcher may seek to analyze not only where the account giver "is coming from" but also how he got there. In short, he seeks to establish the process whereby the personal circumstances recounted in the account were interpreted by the respondent, so as to produce the actions related in the account. Here particular attention is paid to the temporal sequences of events, the social contexts in which they occurred, their interpretation by the individual, and how all this led him to believe and behave as he did. An underlying assumption of this strategy is that an analysis of the individual's personal circumstances is necessary to reconstruct the reality of a social scene as it existed for him at some point in time.

Apart from the face-to-face form of accounts, there are written documents of persons unknown to the researcher. Here, only the document serves as data, and the researcher's assessment of the account giver's intentions must be established without benefit of the feedback characterizing face-to-face interactions. Written accounts may be in the form of a diary, a letter, an autobiography, a suicide note, and so forth.

In light of the foregoing, it may seem somewhat awkward to call the analysis of personal accounts a research "strategy." After all, it typically employs techniques that have been or will be described in other contexts. What distinguishes this strategy from others is the kind of information sought and, therefore, the very special uses of other research tools required to obtain such information. What is sought is information about another's "personal life" in the world. This is the kind of news usually shared only with relatives, friends, and close consociates in the course of daily living. In particular, the researcher wants to reconstruct the unique personal experiences, history, and problems of each individual he interviews, without regard to how general or typical such information might be. One wants to know what happened to *him*, whom *she* knows, etc. For example, in studying the experience that mothers of retarded children had with the medical profession, Jacobs first sought to discover through interviewing, the events, circumstances, and problems encountered by each particular mother with particular doctors as she sought help for her particular child.[1] It was only after these individual accounts had been gathered that the search for patterns began.

If one is interested in this kind of information, the existence of the social form called "interview" is a boon. Common understandings about interviews endorse the relative importance of information transfer as compared with other forms of verbal exchanges, such as joking or greetings. Further, the interview is a semiformal social occasion with two known-in-common social roles, those of interviewer and interviewee. Generally, the role of interviewer grants its occupant certain rights in determining the course of a face-to-face conversation, rights which are ordinarily unavailable for other kinds of conversations. Here one party is seen as asking the questions and the other as giving the answers. The interviewer has the right to determine topics, to decide when "enough has been said" when to go on to something else, and so on.

The interview situation bears upon the retrieval of personal information in a very important way. There are certain kinds of personal information that are ordinarily unavailable to almost everyone. There are things that strangers do not have a right to know, while intimates (who do have this right) frequently cannot be told because of the practical consequences that may ensue from telling them. A husband would ordinarily not tell a stranger that in addition to a wife he had a mistress on the side, and certainly he would not tell his wife. However, the "interviewer" constitutes a special kind of stranger in our society, one who can ask about many personal matters without being perceived as breaching another's right to privacy. This is especially true if a person perceives the interviewer to be someone who is socially unconnected to the information that he or she is seeking. In such cases, personal information can be given for two reasons. As an interviewer he or she has the right to ask; and because the interviewer is a socially irrelevant person, the interviewee does not face the personal consequences of telling this information to a significant other. As a result the interviewer, at least in some contexts, can ask almost anything, and, in turn, can be told almost anything he or she wants to know.

Face-to-face interviewing would, therefore, seem to be the perfect medium to use if one hoped to elicit personal accounts. It allows access to private information and gives the researcher some nominal control over the kind and amount of information he gets. Such control is notably absent when letters, diaries, or similar materials are relied upon exclusively. However, there are some major drawbacks that render the social occasion of the interview problematic for eliciting personal information.

One of these drawbacks has been dealt with earlier: in interview settings, one of the key tacit understandings of the respondent is that the interviewer seeks *generic, not specific* information. This can lead to serious, and consistent, misunderstandings, as the following scenario amply illustrates.

WHO ARE "WE"?

Suppose that a person tells you something like "We do X," where X is some activity and "we" refers to some group of which that person is a member. Taking such a statement as a premise, ordinary deductive logic would allow us to derive two further propositions:

1. Premise: "We do X"

2. Therefore: "I do X"	Where "I" refers to the person who is asserting "We do X"
3. And: "Others do X"	Where "others" refers to all or some members of the group of which "I" am a member.

Suppose we were to find out that, in fact, the person who told us "We do X" did not himself do X. Worse still, suppose this person actually *confessed* to us that he did not do X. Finally, what if we found out that none of the people whom this person knew in fact did X. Obviously we would have a logical contradiction. Presumably, either this person was lying or his appreciation of logic leaves something to be desired.

This was roughly the situation Jacobs encountered when he investigated the recreational pursuits of the residents of a retirement community.[2] Answers to the question "What sort of things do you do around here?" consisted of litanies of recreational activities that "we" (the residents) engaged in—such as golf, swimming, lawn bowls, shuffleboard. These conversations left Jacobs with the feeling that the speaker, as well as many others, was participating in these activities. However, it had earlier been established through "head counts" during observational periods that very few residents actually engaged in these pursuits, and the question was later asked, "How many of these activities do *you* participate in?" The answer frequently turned out to be "None." What is one to make of this discrepancy? Apparently, the pronoun "we" was used here in the sense that "We won the football game" is used by nonmembers of the team. Individuals felt called upon to talk on behalf of their fellow residents and answer the original question generically. Thus they were talking, not about themselves or their friends, but about "what everybody knows goes on around here."

Such misunderstandings are not easily alleviated by instructing respondents in just what you want from them. They will use their understanding of the situation ("This is an interview") to interpret these instructions. As a result, their definition of the situation can subvert the very instructions given to them to ensure against such subversion. This is what apparently happened when Asch tried to instruct subjects to report only their own perceptions, whether correct or incorrect, in a classic experiment. Witness this explanation, given by subjects who violated his instructions:

These subjects often justified their yielding in a way that seems curious to the outsider. With remarkable frequency they arrived independently at the decision that they should not report their defective estimates, since to do so would "interfere" with the experiment.[3]

There is also the problem that interviews are usually one-shot affairs located some place within the respondent's ongoing personal life. This in itself affects the sort of information obtainable.

First, consider the following problem noted by Sacks: Why is it that friends who talk regularly, on a daily basis, always have some "news" about themselves, whereas friends who have not been in touch for a year or longer may find that they have nothing to tell each other[4]? Items which are seen as "news," noteworthy, or nontrivial if recounted on a daily basis do not have this status if told after longer time intervals. They seem silly or trivial or they are not remembered. The interviewer faces the same problem in this regard as the "long-lost friend."

Second, the way in which someone is likely to respond to interview questions—indeed, whether he is hospitable at all—is contingent upon "which side of the bed he got out of that morning." That is, what's going on in somebody's life at any given time can determine whether and how "what's going on in his life" will be recounted in an interview.

It should be noted that neither the "long-lost friend" nor the "which side of the bed" problem can be solved by interviewing the same person several times.

STRATEGIES FOR OVERCOMING INTERVIEW CONSTRAINTS

Having indicated some problems with interviewing as a way to acquire personal accounts, we will offer some strategies for overcoming them.

It is recommended that the interviewer get to know the interviewee over a period of time before attempting to acquire or assess his or her personal accounts. If successful, this will help to overcome many interviewing problems at once.

Knowing potential respondents means, among other things, knowing something about them. This can be used in two ways. On the basis of what one already knows about them, one can make a better choice of respondents. Not all respondents are good respondents. Which people to talk to might be determined by such things as the researcher's assessment of the degree of rapport he has with another person; his assessment of how insightful and "knowing" this other person is about himself, his life, and its details; and how articulate the other person is (how well he will be able to express what he knows about his own biography). Knowing a little about the respondent's life-world also provides opportunities to sample and select where and when in his life one will talk to him about personal matters. This helps to alleviate the "which side of the bed" and the "long lost friend" problems.

It also means that the interviewer can achieve a certain marginal status. He or she can become something more than a stranger but less than a friend or intimate. As a result, an interview is not exactly an interview anymore. The respondent knows you (the interviewer) a little and knows a little about you, and two persons who know each other don't usually "interview" each other. All this should cut down on the problems of getting information in generic form and having your instructions and suggestions misinterpreted. This marginal status also allows you to talk to another person about personal matters in many noninterview situations.

A second strategy (which is best combined with the first, when possible) to help overcome the constraints of the interview setting is the use of unsolicited written accounts of those being studied—diaries, letters, suicide notes, autobiographies, and so on. These and other written documents which a researcher has reason to believe the account giver did not write with ulterior motives in mind can be used to help evaluate the accounts he received during face-to-face conversation.

One may also use as a check (as in the case of life histories) the recollections of casual or intimate second parties who were a part of the personal accounts presented by the account giver.

OTHER SOURCES OF PERSONAL ACCOUNTS

Often public and private agencies have tapes, transcripts, and written records of personal accounts of the type that has just been discussed. Leaving aside the moral problem of using such resources, these data are often poor for a number of other reasons. They have all the problems inherent in one's own data, plus an additional set of problems. There are now two realities to reconstruct, that of the individual and that of the agency. Both of these realities are needed to make sense of the tapes, transcripts, or documents. Further, the agency was not collecting data for the researcher's particular sociological problem. Thus, what it has, and/or can let him see, is likely to be fragmented, and perhaps irrelevant. Finally, the data in people-processing agencies is notoriously distorted.

A second tack, which is sometimes possible, has intriguing possibilities. Respondents are treated as research assistants. They are told the problem and instructed to keep an ongoing written or taped record of their experiences in connection with the problem. This approach is often invoked in therapy. Smokers are told to note when they feel the urge to smoke, the nature of the impulse, and whether it is translated into action. Nutritionists have people make hourly records of what and when they eat. Psychiatrists instruct depressives to record the times, places, and events that evoke depression. As is obvious from these examples, this strategy is feasible only when there is some way to motivate people to keep up such a regimen, and do it accurately. Care should thus be taken to make the form of note-taking painless and rewarding (by, for instance, having a person talk to a therapist, daily, about his findings) and to arrange for the topic to be intrinsically interesting to those who must make observations about it.

A third possibility is to choose one's own intimates and consociates as the people to receive personal accounts. Kristin Luker used this approach when studying contraceptive risk taking among single males.[5] She got her initial information by asking her male friends about their sexual behavior.

Of course, one does not necessarily have to engage in some semiformal survey of one's friends. Often a person has natural access to a variety of personal accounts of a certain type, just by being embedded in a network of friendships. If you are not personally privy to certain personal accounts, it might be possible to find someone whom you know well who is.

Finally, we have already mentioned certain "natural" written (or sometimes taped) personal accounts that might be available. These have an immense advantage. They are practical documents written for practical or personal purposes that spring from the very fabric of the individual's life. They thus might contain things that no researcher would ever think to ask about and that no "respondent" would ever think to tell someone doing "research," no matter how well he knew the researcher. These might include things that are considered too trivial, too minor, or too silly to be interesting or to explain anything. They might be things that come up in the context of a specific personal relationship or important event and then leave one's attention and memory forever. In summary, what these accounts relate, how they are structured, and the style used to relate them may have everything to do with the person's daily life and virtually nothing to do with research and researchers.

There are many practical strategies and methodological issues associated with written personal accounts. Allport offers one way of organizing these issues, when addressing studies that use written documents as their main source of data:[6]

1. With what sort of first-person material is the study concerned: comprehensive autobiography, topical autobiography, artistic production, diary, letters, verbatim records—or what?
2. What is the history of the documents employed? Were they written for an audience, an order, or without thought of publication or use? And how were the documents acquired by the social scientist?
3. Does the document (or do the documents) stand alone, or is it supplemented by other material? If the latter, is the supplementary material used for confirmation, contrast, as groundwork for generalization, or for what purpose?
4. Are there attempts to establish either the reliability or the validity of the document? If so, what?
5. What statement does the investigator make about his method, about the value of his material?

6. Does the investigator use the document inductively or as illustration for an hypothesis, theory, or dogma; or does he do both? Are his inferences limited specifically to the case in question or generalized to apply to "types" or groups of people?
7. What is the bias or frame of reference of the investigator, and how does it seem to influence the interpretation? Do the interpretations seem compulsory, plausible, or strained? Do the investigator's comments clearly draw their meaning and intelligibility from the personal documents, or does the document take on meaning and intelligibility only in the light of the comments and interpretations?

Case study C (page 156) illustrates one form of analysis that can be applied to a set of written personal accounts—in this case, 112 suicide notes.

Life Histories

Another research strategy used for uncovering the effects of external events upon the internal experience of the individual is the life-history approach. As is true of the other approaches to reality reconstruction we have considered, the life-history approach is not peculiar to sociology. Life histories are a part of, for example, medical histories, psychiatric and psychological profiles, FBI dossiers, social workers' "face sheets," and work histories kept by employment counselors. In fact, in our society there are a great many persons whose professional business it is to concern themselves with other people's business for one reason or another.

What constitutes a "case history"—that is, the questions asked, how they are asked, their relevance, and so on—is contingent upon the "vocabulary of motives" of those asking them. This in turn is related to the work role of the questioner, as well as to his ideological position, "tacit understandings," and "background expectancies,"[7] all of which are related to his "purposes at hand."[8]

For example, psychoanalysts take life histories that often concern themselves extensively with early childhood and "precipitating causes" and very little with what transpired in between. This is consistent with the Freudian notion that one's basic personality is formed in early childhood and that one's way of coping in the world, and success in doing so, will be a reflection of these early childhood dynamics. From this perspective, those who wish to understand an adult's current behavior have only to view it as a reflection of the patient's earlier means of coping, means firmly established in early childhood and now a part of his basic personality.

In short, life histories take different forms and contain different contents for the same person depending upon who took the history and for what purposes. There are of course the added factors of how skillful or competent the history taker is and how motivated to do a good job.

NOMOTHETIC AND IDIOGRAPHIC APPROACHES
TO LIFE HISTORIES

There are two basic orientations to life histories within the social sciences.[9] The *nomothetic* approach (used by "objectivists," "empiricists," "experimentalists," and "hard-data quantifiers") contends that theoretical generalizations should be applicable to *many* individuals and should be derived through systematic experimentation, usually involving the use of statistical validation. Nomothetists usually regard the case study as an excellent pedagogic aid for learning theoretical constructs in the social sciences; they also tend to believe that case studies function to generate new discoveries. Beyond this, however, the uses and contributions of the case study diminish for the nomothetists, since they insist that it is scientifically impossible to generalize from single cases.

The *idiographic* approach (used by "naturalists," "subjectivists," and "soft-data investigators") stresses the legitimacy of investigating and researching the life of a single individual and is concerned only secondarily with the frequency or nature of a variable outside the realm of that individual. This view contends that it is scientifically valid and methodologically correct to study the behavior of one human being and to perceive her not only as a representative of a group, but also as an independent totality from whom generalizations may be drawn.

It further contends that the true goal of the social sciences is *understanding* behavior, not quantifying, classifying, or dissecting behavioral patterns. Idiographists feel that this is best accomplished through the use of the case-study method, since this allows one to study the totality of a single personality on a gestalt level.

These two orientations need not be in conflict. Indeed, they may complement each other. One may in the course of applying the idiographic approach acquire a set of data to which one may then apply a nomothetic approach. That is to say, in the course of acquiring and analyzing the contents of a series of individual life histories, and searching for the patterns *within* each one, the researcher may purposefully or serendipitously uncover patterns *between* them.

SOCIOLOGICAL LIFE HISTORIES

While life-history research is widespread in psychology, it has had very restricted uses in sociology. There are a number of reasons for this.

For example, the whole notion that one's personal circumstances would be useful in explaining individual or group behavior was discredited by Durkheim and mainstream sociology. From the positivist position, life histories smack of "reductionism," "psychologizing," and "philosophizing." Moreover, it was held that information about unique personal histories could not easily be generalized to bear on scientific hypotheses about group behavior. There are, however, some notable exceptions: for example, Ruth Cavan's life-history analysis of suicides,[10]

W. I. Thomas and Florian Znaniecki's study of Polish immigrants,[11] and Harold Garfinkel's study of a transsexual.[12] These and other sociological works deal with constructing and analyzing life histories. Notwithstanding their differences, they have certain features in common.

The data are usually derived from interviews, written documents, or a combination of the two. Interviews may be with the person whose life the researcher seeks to reconstruct or with intimate second parties or others who know of this or that facet of the individual's life and help contribute to the total reconstruction. However, the researcher is sometimes subject to external constraints regarding his choice of strategies. One obvious example is the problem of reconstructing the life history of a suicide. In such a case, the coroner and others who are a part of the "psychological autopsy" must rely upon the accounts of intimate or casual second parties and whatever other documentary evidence is available, such as a suicide note or diary.

In order to serve as useful data, life histories ought to include as many of the following features as possible:

1. The account ought to be autobiographical and, if possible, corroborated by another in order to ensure against distortions in memory, selective perceptions, and the like.
2. The account ought to cover as much of the life of the individual as possible, as opposed to only a brief and discrete segment (or segments) of time.
3. The life history should be as detailed as possible, not only in the number of events included, but also with respect to how the individual felt about these events at the time of their occurrence.
4. Particular attention ought to be paid to the dates of the events in order to be able to reconstruct not only the occurrences and how they were experienced, but their sequential ordering.

As matters now stand, very few life histories of individuals found in the sociological or psychological literature meet these criteria. Indeed, some so-called life histories are scarcely more than "one-liners." One study of suicide attempters gives the following information: "Age 14, slow in school, disliked school and threatened to run away. He had been on probation for petty stealing, was found hanging in the cellar of his home at 11:30 A.M., fully clad."[13]

Life histories can take many forms. As indicated above, the most common is the "case history" presentation. Here, the researcher turns biographer, and by utilizing these sources of data, seeks to write (in the example of the psychological autopsy) a "womb-to-tomb" biography of the victim. Jacobs, in applying this approach to the study of a group of fifty adolescent suicide attempters and a "matched pair" of control adolescents, uncovered a number of interesting findings.[14] Having written a case history for each of the suicide attempters—based upon interviews with the attempters themselves and their parents conducted within seventy-two hours of the attempt, information acquired from psychiatric interviews, the accounts of the attending physician in the emergency room, suicide notes, and intimate and casual second-party accounts—Jacobs rendered these data with an original twist. Using categories of events that emerged naturally from the data themselves (after numerous readings of the case histories)— such as residential moves, onset of serious illness, marriage and divorce of parents, death of a family member or friend—he plotted the life of each adolescent from birth to the time of the attempt, by schematically representing the events in the adolescent's life as a "life tree," with color-coded dots used to represent different categories of events. A notation was also made of how the events were experienced at the time of their occurrence, according to the adolescent's recollections. Each of these life histories was then divided into three time periods: (1) early childhood, (2) childhood to the onset of adolescence, and (3) the onset of adolescence until the time of the suicide attempt. A fourth time period emerged (a subset of the third), the period immediately preceding the attempt. This was loosely defined to be within the year of the suicide attempt, usually the weeks immediately preceding it.

The pattern (or common denominators) to the suicide attempt that emerged from these data is as follows:

1. A long-standing history of problems (from early childhood to the onset of adolescence).
2. The escalation of problems (since the onset of adolescence) above and beyond those usually associated with adolescence.
3. The progressive failure of available adaptive techniques for coping with the old and new increasing problems, which leads to the adolescent's progressive isolation from meaningful social relationships.
4. A chain-reaction dissolution of any remaining meaningful social relationships in the days and weeks preceding the attempt, which leads to the adolescent's feeling that he has reached "the end of hope."
5. An internal process by which he justifies suicide to himself and thus manages to bridge the gap between thought and action.

This pattern proved to be consistent with one that emerged from a later independent study of suicide notes (see case study C). A combination of these two approaches produced findings that were at odds with the main body of literature in psychology and sociology on the causes and dynamics of suicide.[15]

A STRATEGY FOR CONSTRUCTING AND ANALYZING LIFE HISTORIES: BELIEVE WHAT YOU'RE TOLD

We have mentioned, in the section on participant observation, a particular kind of "reality disjuncture"—two different research procedures, each competently applied, that yield different answers to the same question. We now want to talk about another kind of reality disjuncture: a competition between the fact-finding methods of the social scientist (or other professionals) and those of his subjects. More often than not, the person who is the subject of the life history, and his intimate relatives, have a different version of the facts than the one produced by the professionals. Moreover, the fact-finding methods of the professionals and of the subjects may each be internally consistent. Each can be used as the standard with which to evaluate the other.

Under these circumstances, social scientists engage in a diabolical maneuver that simultaneously determines who is right about the truth, gives the scientist the case history he seeks, and establishes the format for analyzing it! We can state this maneuver as a procedure:

1. Treat your own version (that of the professional) of the subject's life, whatever that may be, as his real, objective life.
2. Treat the subject's version of his life as "the member's point of view," as his subjective "beliefs," "interpretations," and "experiences" of the life he actually led.
3. Analyze the subject's life history (item 1 plus item 2) by explaining the social-psychological processes that caused the subject to experience his life other than the way it "actually happened."

It should be noted that the political nature of this maneuver cannot be mitigated by reference to the greater reliability, detail, or rigor of professional fact finding. First of all, this is often not the case. "Professional" fact finding often results in little more than commonsense guessing made by a professional. Indeed, it is the *identity* of the professional that earns his facts the title of "the real," rather than the ways in which they were obtained.

Yet there is a more important point. There is no third party to compare the two sets of methods and facts. Each version of the world establishes the terms under which the other is considered. For example, if chess players examine Monopoly, it is found to be an inferior game since it has no checkered board, pawns, or bishops. On the other hand, according to Monopoly players, the game of chess is found wanting in that it lacks dice and fake money.

When the professional and the subject disagree about the life history, how is the discrepancy resolved? In that the professional is constructing the life history, he is the detective, the defense, the prosecutor, the judge, and one of the involved parties. In conducting and deciding the case, he will unavoidably be guided by his presuppositions concerning who could be right and who wrong.

Thus, whether one presumes for or against what a subject tells you is fraught with political implications. The authors strongly recommend a simple policy in this regard: *Believe what you're told.* Most social scientists find this policy, for understandable reasons, almost impossible to carry out. It requires that one believe statements and stories which one's college training, the professional literature, good common sense, and all else that is held sacred and holy say are dead wrong (if not crazy), and that one treat the problem as lying with the sacred and holy, not the beliefs of the respondent. Yet again and again, we have found that this simple policy of credulousness leads to impressive discoveries. It becomes the creative task of the investigator to find a way to believe.

One reason to do so arises when the goal is to reconstruct another person's life-world. In that case, he is the only possible expert. It makes no sense to describe his life-world from the standpoint of yours. A second, practical reason for this policy is this: The authors and others have found many times that there are unexpected ways in which subjects are correct about things, ways that one would not discover unless *he already suspected they were there* and went about looking for them. For Lemert, it turned out that paranoids were, in fact, being prosecuted;[16] for Jacobs, it turned out that suicide attempters were not mentally ill, but rational, competent decision makers;[17] Narens's hallucinator was not seeing ghosts but was detecting the ghosts' presence by the tactile sensations left by very *real* air currents.[18]

In a study of "subnormality" (case study D, page 168), the policy of "believe what the respondents tell you" led Jacobs to an entirely different evaluation of the case histories of retarded children than that constructed by the doctors.

Notes

1. Jerry Jacobs, *The Search for Help: A Study of the Retarded Child in the Community*, New York: Brunner/Mazel, 1969.
2. Jerry Jacobs, *Fun City: An Ethnographic Study of a Retirement Community*, New York: Holt Rinehart and Winston, 1974.
3. S. E. Asch, *Social Psychology*, Englewood Cliffs, N.J.: Prentice-Hall, 1952, pp. 450–501.
4. Harvey Sacks discusses the problem in mimeoed lecture notes, University of California at Irvine, 1970. Of course we have oversimplified it here. Some find it easy to recount the events of the previous year and hard to describe those of the past day. The main issue here is how the location of a recounting in someone's life determines how and what he can remember and describe.
5. Personal communication concerning a study in progress from Dr. Kristin Luker, University of California at San Diego.
6. Gordon Allport, *The Use of Personal Documents in Psychological Science*, New York, Social Science Research Council Bulletin No. 49, 1942.
7. For a discussion of these concepts, see Harold Garfinkel, *Studies in Ethnomethodology*, Englewood Cliffs, N.J., Prentice-Hall, 1967.
8. Alfred Schutz, *Collected Papers I*, The Hague; Martinus Nijhoff, 1971, pp. 9–10.
9. We are indebted to Daniel Haytin for our discussion of these approaches. For more detail, see Daniel Leigh Haytin, *The Methodological Validity of the Case Study in the Social Sciences*, unpublished Ph.D. dissertation, University of California at Berkeley, 1969.

10. Ruth Cavan, *Suicide*, Chicago: University of Chicago Press, 1928.

11. W. I. Thomas and Florian Znaniecki, *The Polish Peasant in Europe and America*, vols. I and II, New York: Knopf, 1927.

12. Garfinkel, *Studies in Ethnomethodology*, pp. 116–185.

13. Warren A. Stearns, "Cases of Probable Suicide in Young Persons Without Obvious Motivation," *Journal of the Maine Medical Association* 44 (1953): 16–23.

14. Jerry Jacobs, *Adolescent Suicide*, New York: Wiley Interscience, 1971.

15. For a detailed account of these findings and their derivation, see Jacobs, *Adolescent Suicide*.

16. Edwin Lemert, "Paranoia and the Dynamics of Exclusion," *Sociometry* 25, no. 1 (March 1962): 1–20.

17. See Case Study C.

18. Louis Narens, "The Belief Systems of the Insane," in *Topics in Ethnomethodology*, ed. by J. Schenkein et al., Berlin: Suhrkamp Publishers, 1975.

CHAPTER 5

Nonreactive Techniques for Studying Groups or Individuals

Most of the techniques we have discussed thus far—interviewing, participant observation, analyzing personal accounts, and constructing life histories—are what investigators call reactive. They have the investigator going into some arena of social life (and/or diverse social occasions) and "making a mess," so to speak. The investigator becomes a part of the social process he is investigating. His presence and activities constitute events in this process, with their own consequences and effects.

Consequently, there is every chance that the way a social world or an occasion displays itself to him is a by-product of the way in which he becomes a part of that world. Further, his actions in the world may change the very world being examined.

Two classes of techniques, unobtrusive measures and audio-visual strategies, seek to minimize these possibilities. Here the idea is to remove the investigator from the world he observes and, as a result, enable him to look in from the outside, in such a way that "not a hair on the head of the phenomenon is touched" during the looking. The world does not react to his presence by displaying itself in a particular way, nor does the looking process change the world he looks at in any appreciable manner.

Unobtrusive Measures

An unobtrusive measure is any nonreactive measure of group or individual life—any indicator whose investigation does not itself affect the thing studied. In

75

looking for unobtrusive measures in different cultural settings one might ask questions like these: Does a community have roads? Are they paved or littered, and, if littered, with what—beer cans and Coke bottles or the droppings of burros, dogs, or bullocks? Are there public signs, and if so, what do they say, how many are there, and where are they placed?

Other questions might be: Does a community have electricity, radio or television? What is the average consumption of electricity per family per unit time? How many cars go past a given point on the freeway at different hours of the day and different days of the week? How many persons are there per car? What kinds of cars do they drive? How many and what kinds of people use public facilities such as parks or libraries or restrooms? As an indicator of the nature, frequency, and type of social activity in a community, one might look at liquor purchases at neighborhood stores. How much liquor is bought in which areas of the community, on what days?

If these indicators strike the reader as rather gross, there are more intimate indications which are closer to the devices used by detectives. Physical-trace evidence consists of erosion of materials or accretion of deposits which build up over time. The articles strewn around conference rooms and in garbage pails can supply clues to what small numbers of people have been doing, and how often. Wear on floor tiles has been used to indicate the popularity of museum exhibits; dust, particles of food, and fingerprints on chairs, appliances, or doorways has been used as a measure of the articles people have been using, or where they have been walking and sitting.

One can readily imagine other forms of unobtrusive measures that are easily accessible to anyone and supply indicators of group life. Information retrieved in this way has a great advantage over other methods in that it allows for the study of individuals or groups and does not itself influence the thing being studied.

However, while unobtrusive measures provide the investigator with a strategy for transcending the problem of his own reactive influence, they have other serious limitations, at least with regard to the questions those in the reality reconstruction business seek to answer. Unobtrusive measures of the kind given above offer few, if any, clues to what's going on in people's heads. Rather, they are indicative of life styles, behavior patterns, or technological stages, and "world views." Useful as these indicators may be for gaining access to some facets of group life, they offer very little direct evidence of the social meanings of social actions to the participants involved.

NONVERBAL COMMUNICATION

There are, however, other unobtrusive measures that do bear on this matter, among them nonverbal communication. One can observe an interaction between two or more other individuals from a distance, as an outside third party, without influencing the interaction itself. If one is concerned with "what's going on in their heads," he might consider whether the participants to the interaction are frowning, crying, shouting, or whispering. He could also infer a good deal from their "body language."[1] In general, the face is a major source of "emotional comments" in face-to-face conversation. Deliberate manipulation of one's facial "poses" and changes in one's facial expression over time constitute an analogue to series of sentences in that they convey sequences of surprise, amusement, concern, anger, and so on. Researchers have found that other parts of the body (such as the hands and arms) are good indicators of whether someone is deceiving others. Indeed, a trained observer watching two interacting parties can often tell more about the nature and truthfulness of their interaction than the parties themselves.[2] As is evident, depending on the kind of information one wishes to obtain from body language and facial expression, more or less stringent requirements are put on the observer's position with respect to the observed—for example, does he need to see details, notice quick facial changes over time, or merely see locomotion?[3] Such are some of the potentials and pitfalls of nonverbal communication when used as unobtrusive measures.

CONTENT ANALYSIS

Another form of unobtrusive measure (usually quantitative in nature) is content analysis. One of its more influential developers, H. D. Lasswell, has characterized this method as an attempt to ascertain the meanings in a body of discourse in some systematic and quantitative way.[4] Kaplan notes three basic concerns of content analysis in this regard:[5]

1. Content analysis is concerned with the semantic (and sometimes syntactical) features of signs.
2. Content analysis is interested chiefly in political discourse.
3. Content analysis aims at statistical formulations, directed toward empirical problems.

While there is a long tradition for the utilization of this research technique in evaluating the forms and effectiveness of propaganda, it has of late experienced a renaissance with respect to the media's influence on socialization. All manner of people have suddenly become content analysts. Most of their studies are cast in terms of political motives. Thus feminists refer to advertising campaigns as sexist, blacks refer to them as racist, and gays may see them as discriminatory. In this sense, content analysis is used to show how those in power influence socialization patterns in their own behalf, and at the expense of subjugated minorities. In short, content analysis is used in these ways to support the Marxian contention that "ruling ideas are ruling-class ideas," with the rulers defined differently by different segments of the population.

This form of analysis can be applied to novels, newspaper reports, television series, or advertising campaigns. It usually involves counting key words, topics, or themes that appear in such artifacts and noting who "produces" and who "consumes" them. More complicated time-series analysis can, for example, trace evolving conceptions of "workers" or "oppressors," as a newspaper grows and changes in administrative structure.

A central theme of these analyses is to show how this material can be used to socialize the reader, listener, or viewer (on a conscious or subliminal level) to accept negative stereotypes of ethnic minorities or other target groups. The analysis can then be turned to demonstrate the harmful effects of such stereotypes.

Another way to assess harm in the media is to search out the role models that are being presented to large groups of impressionable people. It is this strategy that is behind studies which try to explore the connection between violence on television and crime and violence in society at large.[6]

Here, as in most instances, the methods can be used by either side. The key words are "forewarned is forearmed"; and once they grasp the process, the victims of media attacks may turn these methods against their attackers. In this regard, it is ironic that many militants have advocated "fighting fire with fire" by getting a bigger and better Madison Avenue firm than their adversaries have to act on their behalf, in order to reverse the negative stereotypes imposed on them by power elites.

PERSONAL DOCUMENTS

Another unobtrusive measure (as it relates to individuals and what they are thinking) has been dealt with earlier in our discussion of case histories and personal accounts. Written documents—for example, letters, diaries, autobiographies, and suicide notes—are excellent unobtrusive indicators of individual and group life. But care must be exercised in establishing how such documents were generated, for whom, and why.

THE DOCUMENTARY METHOD OF INTERPRETATION

The thrust of the previous comments was to highlight some ways in which the nature of unobtrusive measures can limit the kinds of information one can obtain by using them. Thus, for example, a researcher can be faced with the choice of finding things out unobtrusively *or* getting a close look at how individuals subjectively evaluate each other or how they think about some common situation.

It would seem that if one is in a position to measure a phenomenon of interest unobtrusively, he has overcome many of the problems of research error. However, there is something endemic to the method of unobtrusive measures that makes them somewhat less than a cause for methodological celebration.

Precisely how does one obtain information using unobtrusive measures? Garfinkel has captured the essence of the procedure with his concept of "the documentary method of interpretation."[7] Some phenomenon that can be observed unobtrusively is singled out and treated as "the document of," as "pointing to," or as "standing on behalf of" some underlying pattern.[8] The underlying pattern and what is known about it are in turn used to interpret the observed phenomenon. Thus, observed phenomenon and underlying pattern are each used to interpret the other. In this sense, each elaborates the nature of the other. A common example of this method is the way we interpret the talk of others in everyday situations. We listen to what they say as an indicator of what they mean. But we also use our knowledge of what they mean in hearing and interpreting what they say.

Take for example this common situation. Suppose you suspect or assume that a person dislikes you. As a method of finding out about this, asking the person point-blank has its problems, both social and empirical. What you need are unobtrusive "indicators." Suppose he happens to tell you in the company of others, "I am certainly glad I met *you.*" Given the assumption of dislike, he has just uttered a sarcastic remark. The sarcastic remark, in turn, is an indicator of, and entirely in keeping with, his dislike. However, if you assume that he really likes you, the reverse is true, and you have just received a "compliment." Insofar as you hear the dislike or the high regard in which you are held in and through the remark, there is no way of determining the true status of the comment independent of your original assumptions about how the person feels about you.

This example illustrates two major aspects of the documentary method. As long as this method is being used, one must make assumptions about the underlying pattern in order to know what to make of the indicators. These assumptions will come from social context and commonsense knowledge. Thus, the same behavior or phenomenon in different contexts will be interpreted as an indicator of different underlying patterns. If one is wrong in the assumptions used to interpret the indicators, there is virtually no practical way to correct them, since there is nothing to refer to outside the assumptions themselves. Second, one must already know a great deal about something before he can find and competently interpret indicators of it. In situations where the investigator knows little about a set of people and their lives, unobtrusive measures not only are of little help but often cannot be competently and correctly employed at all.

Of course, one can simply invoke his expertise as an authority on "heads" to justify his interpretations of indicators. This relieves him of the necessity of first acquiring an intimate firsthand familiarity with his subjects. This is precisely what psychiatrists and psychologists do when they interpret responses to an inkblot test or the Thematic Apperception Test without knowing the respondent in any detail. The obvious criticism of such a procedure is that one may be quite wrong about what the indicators are indicators of. Such an invocation of expertise could be valid only if there currently existed a fairly rigorous science of the mind. In the authors' opinion, such a science does not yet exist. Any social scientist who claims to know the inner significance of others' behavior without first knowing the others themselves is overestimating his expertise. Therefore, unobtrusive measures are best employed in the area of the "head" only after other information-gathering techniques such as participant observation and unstructured interviewing have been used.

What we have outlined in our discussion of unobtrusive measures, and will soon consider in discussing audio-visual methods, are two nonreactive ways to study individuals and groups. But the fact that one can eliminate or minimize his own effects upon the setting and thereby minimize one source of error does not mean that he has finally reached the Godhead. While these methodological procedures help one to study what he has set out to study (natural settings), the fact remains that the investigator, like everyone else in the world, must interpret what he sees. In this sense there is no way to transcend cultural assumptions and be certain of one's reconstruction of reality. We are inclined to support Pirandello's contention that the social world is "absurd" in that there is no way for anyone, lay or professional, to establish "what's really going on out there."

UNOBTRUSIVE MEASURES: AN EXAMPLE

Rather than include an entire case study to illustrate the potential usefulness of unobtrusive measures, we will content ourselves with an example of a "serendipitous finding."

In his study of a retirement community, Jacobs naturally gravitated toward the centers of activity in "Fun City."[9] These turned out to be the Town Hall-Activity Center complex and two large supermarkets. While surveying the supermarkets, observing the nature of interactions, Jacobs made a surprising discovery. Both markets had huge displays of pet supplies—cat and dog food, kitty litter, flea collars, leashes—enough to maintain a large number of domesticated animals. The peculiar thing was that, although he had already spent considerable time observing the streets, homes, and activity centers, Jacobs had rarely seen a domesticated animal in the community. There were only the jackrabbits (natural inhabitants of the area) who happily hopped about at will, devouring (like Thurber's unicorn) what few flowers were to be found in the residents' yards.

At this juncture, the problem presented itself: Either the store management routinely stocked merchandise that no one bought, or there were a lot of cats and dogs in Fun City that were nowhere to be seen. The question, once formulated, resolved itself in time in the following way.

It turned out that one of Jacobs's students was at the time of the study a mailman in Fun City (another serendipitous finding). Through this fortuitous contact, a number of home interviews were arranged with "gatekeepers" (those who had to authorize interviews with themselves and others), who in turn provided interviews with other residents in a "snowball sample." In the course of these informal home interviews, the answer to the question "Where are they keeping all of those animals?" revealed itself. In fact, the animals were kept where the residents were kept—that is, at home, not out in the street in front of their homes or in the yard behind them. "Home" meant within the confines of the tract home proper. Hence, while a great many residents kept pets, few were visible. The discovery of pets within the home itself proved to be a new unobtrusive measure. The question arose: Why are they all kept indoors? In other tract home communities, domesticated animals are frequently left to roam at large.

The answer to this question, which had to await analysis of the home interviews and other informal sources of data, turned upon Fun City's compulsive adherence to the tenet "Cleanliness is next to godliness," coupled with the notion that one ought to respect the privacy of one's neighbors and never give others grounds for offense. These would be difficult goals to meet if one's dog were outside where it might annoy neighbors by barking, digging up a bush, or, worse still, defecating on their gravel "lawns."

Audio-Visual Techniques

Audio-visual techniques as a research strategy are of recent origin. These procedures have a wide variety of applications, including photo essays, filming or videotaping of natural settings for future analysis, films used as therapeutic techniques or teaching devices, audio tapes of natural conversations used by conversational analysts as the sole source of data, and photo analysis of still or motion pictures taken to reveal one's "world view," values, or priorities.

As methods of gaining information, audio-visual methods are the Rolls Royces of data collection. It is popularly thought that they are capable of capturing more social life, in more detail, with more accuracy and less reactive effect, than practically any other method. However, with respect to the question of reality reconstruction, even these techniques have their drawbacks. To see what these drawbacks are and how they might be overcome, it is convenient to catalogue audio-visual methods by their major uses:

1. As direct sources of data.
2. As devices for obtaining "accounts."
3. As special forms of communication.

AS DATA

The major audio-visual media are videotape, film, audio tape, and still photography. More exotic media such as heat sensing cameras and infrared photography (which allow one to photograph in the dark) are at present limited to spies, medical people, military personnel, and others.

Audio and visual "channels" of information are thought to correspond to two main sources of "input" by which ordinary persons become aware of their environment. Our eyes and ears are "distance receptors"—those senses by which we obtain information about things which are physically removed from us. Hall and others have hypothesized that Americans, and other Westerners, rely comparatively more on these distance receptors to put together their world than do people of other cultures. For us the world outside is almost exclusively confined to what we see and hear. In particular, it is primarily audio and visual input which are received through the senses, coded, stored in memory, and processed in the brain, that enable us to recognize "insults," "waiters," and "football teams."

In this model we can detect an implicit solution to what is perhaps the most important problem in qualitative sociology. There are innumerable ways of describing the world, each of which is self-consistent. In studying human subjectivity one must decide which descriptions of the world will be taken as the real world and which will be regarded as interpretations. Positivists and others solve this problem neatly: The real world is the world of physics. "Insults," "waiters," and "football teams" are social interpretations, whereas equally abstract ideas such as "input," "sound," or "stimuli," which were also taught to us by our society, are taken to refer directly to reality.

Given this model, one can see the rationale for considering audio-visual methods as providing the ultimate in data collection. In recording the audio and visual channels of information, one has virtually all the raw material from which Americans build an understanding of "what's going on" in a particular social setting. And cellulose or tape, unlike the original situation, can be reviewed again and again, in as much detail as is desired.

One can also see that this same rationale would require other techniques for individuals or groups that live in a comparatively richer kinesthetic, olfactory, or tactile world. It has been proposed, for example, that the world of children is much more of a kinesthetic world than that of adults.[10] To a child, how something feels or makes her or him feel may be far more memorable than how it looks or sounds.

THE PROBLEM OF SELECTIVE ATTENTION

This points to a major crack in the image of tape machines and the like as accurate recorders of what people perceive. Eyes are not cameras; they cannot zoom, nor can they pan. Ears are not microphones; they fail to hear high- and low-pitched sounds if these sounds are at low volumes (the Fletcher-Munsen effect).

But even if an individual had microphones for ears and cameras for eyes, he is always "situated" within a social environment at some space-time point. Depending on physical barriers, spacing patterns among those present, and his own patterns of locomotion, the same room can look and sound amazingly different to him than it does to others.

This has recently come to the attention of architects. There are now architecture courses designed to re-create for the architect the conditions that the occupants will have to contend with in order to live in the spaces he designs. These situations are simulated by, for instance, asking architects to negotiate apartment spaces in a wheelchair or to try to descend a flight of stairs wearing glasses that simulate astigmatism or glaucoma.

The above points merely relate to the physical aspects of our receptors. But there are also social considerations. The definition of a social situation regulates the perceptions of those within it. For example, how and when one person looks at the face of another is controlled by a complex set of social norms. Perhaps as a result, Ekman notes, most people are poor judges of others' emotions. Many emotions show mainly on the face and vanish very quickly (often in a fraction of a second[11]). One person is simply not able to look at another's face constantly, and in enough detail, to catch these facial clues without violating social norms.

Another important example is the way in which the rules of conversation regulate hearing. While one might be hearing the sound of fellow conversationalists in great detail, the talk of others in the same environment, although of the same volume and clarity, may be heard as mere background noise. Similarly, within the conversation itself, one is required to listen to some things very carefully in order to hold one's own as a conversationalist. Other things can be literally "tuned out," and often are.

In sum, in no possible way can films and tapes directly "recover" the visual-auditory world experienced by different persons within an ongoing social scene. This point cannot be overemphasized, because we have been fed the physics model of reality and have been accustomed to regard a videotape as a direct record of "what happened." Yet if one wishes to know "what happened" from the standpoint of those within the scene, it is necessary to make use of complex contextual information and cultural clues in order to "make sense" of one's film or tape.

Independent of selective attention—of what individuals might become aware of—is the question of meaning. In participant observation or interviewing we can simply ask people about their interpretations of ongoing events. But how do we decide what something like a slow-motion film or a facial movement "means"? It is to this problem that we now turn.

THE MICROSCOPE PROBLEM

In many ways tape and film represent the microscopes of human interaction. They open up a world of detail that is simply not available without their aid. As one consequence, most of the qualitative research that might be called "rigorous" uses audio-visual data as the main resource.

However, this virtue of audio-visual data is also one of its greatest problems. Let us mention a few of the topics that have been studied with the aid of these media:

1. Which people start and stop talking at which places during overlapping speech in multiparty conversation.
2. Pupil dilation and eye and head position as measures of students' attention in the classroom.
3. "Micro-displays" of emotion in the face. These are facial configurations that are so brief, and so confined to particular parts of the face, that they are difficult to see with the naked eye.

As an example of a finding in one of these areas, one-to-one correspondences were discovered between emphasis in one's tone of voice and certain accompanying gestures with the face, arms and body called "illustrators."[12] That is, these illustrators seemed to be synchronized with emphasis in tone of voice. This pattern was found to hold within our culture, within other cultures, and even in the communication of the mentally ill. Finally, efforts to teach people to unsynchronize these two methods of showing emphasis failed.[13] The significance of such findings is that, if they prove to hold universally, they may provide clues to some of the biological bases of human communication.

Yet most of us are not explicitly aware of such small, seemingly inconsequential patterns in our behavior. We do not experience them as such, nor are we likely to tell others about them. In this sense they are not part of our social reality. In fact, according to Weber, synchronizing certain gestures with one's tone of voice is not even a social action; it is merely something people "do." For it to be a social action, we would have to attach a subjective meaning to it.

Yet often we find ourselves responding to the "small" actions of another in some systematic way, although we are not explicitly aware that we are doing so. For instance, it has been shown that variations in a teacher's tone of voice can affect the performance of students.[14] Yet the students would hardly say they were doing better or worse because of variations in the teacher's tone of voice. Do these tonal variations constitute social actions in Weber's sense? Are the students taking them into account or attaching a subjective meaning to them? Or should their responses be regarded as something they are merely "doing"? If the tonal variations have a meaning, how is this meaning to be ascertained? What if a social scientist describes the meaning the teacher's voice has for the students, based on how the students are responding, but the students find the scientist's interpretation strange or wrong. Who is right about the meaning—social scientist or students? Answering such questions, and deciding how to answer them, are critical for sociologists who wish to employ media to reconstruct social realities.

AS DEVICES FOR OBTAINING ACCOUNTS

We have already mentioned the many ways in which photographs, films, and tapes are ethnographies of a culture or situation. They are often used by a researcher explicitly in this way. Instead of interviewing respondents or having them keep written accounts for her, she gives them cameras and tape recorders, trains them in the use of these instruments, and has them go out and compose an audio-visual ethnography of "an argument," "an average day," "a medicine man," "a toaster," or "a blender." Clearly, such people need to select what to film, how much of it to film, when to cut, zoom, and pan, and so on. Insofar as they skip from segment to segment they are engaged in natural "documentary editing." In these and other ways their effort represents a journalistic composition, with their own members' knowledge about "what's going on" used as a guide.

These compositions can be used as depictions of the social settings being recorded, or as indications of the way natives see the world or particular things in it. The latter use is bolstered by various theories such as the famous Whorf-Sapir hypothesis, which asserts that the structure of language affects how its users perceive the world. The former use is helped by the fact that photos, tape, and film are standardized symbol systems in many modern cultures. Thus "poses" act as conventional symbols of cultural events when seen on film or tape. They depict, for example, "Jimmy riding his motorcycle," or "the Jones family with their daughter back from college." There is also the interesting set of conventions associated with professional actors, who behave in certain ways which, if seen on film or stage, are interpreted as faithful portrayals of social events and situations. The same actions if performed by real people in natural situations would be interpreted as unnatural and "dramatic." Similar and complex conventions of this kind apply to newsreels and motion pictures. In short, our culture has already adapted these forms as conventionalized ways to depict itself.

In contrast to verbal descriptions, tape and film essays need to be "composed" at the very times and in the very places they depict. In many ways this is a tremendous advantage, since problems of memory and lack of feedback are mitigated. Second, these media force a certain kind of temporal organization. There can be no insertions, flashbacks, or inserts, as when one relates an account. After one "shoots" the opening of the meeting, there is no way to go back and get more. Third, the interpretive license of the native ethnographer is limited to the freedoms given to her or him by the technical devices in question (volume control, angle of shooting, or stopping and starting the machine).

Obviously, if those being filmed or taped are aware of the filming or taping, we need to worry about their definition of this activity as a certain kind of cultural event. This problem is analogous to how informants define "interviewing" as a social occasion. The difference is that we know much less about how to think about the former problem than about the latter.

A second way to use these data for obtaining accounts is first to make a tape, take photos, or shoot film and then to show these artifacts to members and ask them for their interpretations. This technique, of course, is an old stand-by of clinical psychologists who use projective tests, notably the Thematic Appreciation Test. In effect, this technique uses tape, film, and photos to ask structured and unstructured question in an interview. It has been used to discover cultural and cross-cultural meanings of facial expressions, to study the effect of memory in reconstructing past events, to assess differences in the accuracy with which people can receive nonverbal messages, and in many other ways.

When this method is used as a "projective technique," it runs into a standard problem. Someone is shown an artifact and talks about it. His interpretation must itself be interpreted by the researcher in order to discover what it says about the individual, his personality, or his unconscious. But then, one does not know whose projection has been captured, that of the subject or that of the researcher. Efforts to solve this with reliability measures, multiple sources of validation, and so on meet with the same troubles we discussed in chapter 3—each person's version of the "projection" will undoubtedly be self-consistent.

Another way to use this method, which is becoming more and more popular, is to tape or film one's subjects "in action"—teaching a class, being drunk, participating in therapy—and then show this record to them at some later time (or sometimes simultaneously with the occurrence of the action). As our previous discussion indicated, such a recording will present another symbolization of a social scene than the one available to the participants situated in that scene. When they view and/or hear it in this way, they gain a different perspective, and outsiders gain from their "new insider's" interpretation. The thing that many like about this simple procedure is that it provides a learning service for one's subjects. They get some useful feedback from the research which may help them. In fact, the peculiar mirroring effect of hearing and seeing oneself in action from the perspective of an outside observer is being widely used in behavioral therapy and in teaching interactive skills. For example, it has been found that alcoholics who are filmed while on a binge, and later view the film while sober, are helped a great deal toward rehabilitation by this use of audio-visual technique.

AS A SPECIAL FORM OF COMMUNICATION

Ordinarily scientists communicate with one another using the written symbol system of their culture, amplified by technical nomenclature invented by their profession (tables, jargon, etc.). Tape and film clearly offer a whole other kind of symbol system with which to communicate. The most pervasive way in which this system is currently used is to display data. In professional sports, for example, it is much more convenient for adversaries to study films of another team in order to plan strategies than to get information about the opposing team in oral or written form. This technique is now coming into vogue in sociology in the form of documentary film making and photo essays. Both of these procedures have been subsumed (for good reason) under the title of "visual anthropology."

Used for reality reconstruction, audio and video media can often depict a social world, an individual's daily life, a cultural event, or a certain kind of activity much more effectively than written or verbal reconstructions. By editing a film to display the common elements in the behavior of many professors, a sociologist can literally "film" a social role. Anthropologists can easily capture behavioral rhythms, rituals, or teaching styles.

THE PROBLEM OF IMAGERY

These methods of displaying the world have a unique advantage over other methods. Often qualitative sociologists take it as a goal to create an image of another's world. One of the advantages of words in the natural language, compared to numbers, is their connection to narrative style. Many English courses are dedicated to exploring how words make visual images and sounds unfold in a reader's head. We have learned how to scan the pages of books composed by biographers, journalists, or novelists and experience the sense of being in the world they write about. Qualitative sociologists can take advantage of this ability in a way that quantitative sociologists cannot. A skillfully written verbal account can actually give its readers the feeling they "know what it is like to smoke marijuana," for example.

But there are problems with using natural language in this way. If one read about "turn overlap," "role definitions," or "sequential intentionality," in connection with a discussion of, say, urinating, he would not recognize this subtle, detailed, technical activity as the one he performs when he "takes a leak." The imagery fails, because technical terms and concerns seem to get in the way. One is faced with a familiar problem—going native and describing the world as natives see it, or transcending the natives' world and describing what they do not. Unless he sticks to natives' reconstructions, natives' categories, and natives' ways of looking, collecting, and displaying data, he will not be talking about the world that they recognize themselves to be living in. On the other hand, if he confines himself to acquiring and reporting only natives' accounts of their world, more detailed or subtle aspects of that world will be unavailable.

Film and tape solve the imagery problem in an elegant way. For whatever reason, and however accurate this impression is, films and tapes appear to most people to be accurate re-creations of the worlds they depict. On the other hand, they can be edited, examined frame by frame, slowed down, speeded up, coded and spliced, and otherwise analyzed to reveal aspects of social activities that are seldom naturally seen or talked about. They also easily depict certain phenomena which are awkward or impossible to describe in words with clarity and conciseness.

Depicting reality with the use of media takes the form of documentary film making or photographic essays. (We do not count simple replays of entire conversations and the like. This is because we are concerned with a social scientist's use of media as a symbol system and her consequent editing, selecting, and overall manipulation of these symbols for her own purposes.)

In using media as a symbol system, the researcher must not only concern herself with the meaning systems of those she photographs or tapes; she must also worry about how her audience understands and interprets film and photos. Neglecting the latter problem can result in everything from miscommunication to absolute disaster. Wilson describes such a disaster in connection with a film which was designed to show African natives how to get rid of standing water in their households. [15] After being shown the film, the natives were asked what they saw. They saw no sanitation procedure. Instead, they saw a chicken! How did this happen? They had not focused their eyes in front of the large screen as we do, so as to take in the whole screen at a glance. Instead they scanned the screen like a printed page—segment by segment. And indeed, when the film was inspected frame by frame, a fowl did appear in one corner of the frames for about a second.

SOME GENERAL METHODOLOGICAL ISSUES

SAMPLING

Virtually all uses of audio-visual devices face the problem of sampling. One cannot possibly record everything, not only because this would provide too much information, but because the camera or tape recorder is always situated in some particular place (or places). For different styles of audio-visual research this poses a variety of knotty problems.

One such problem was encountered in a study by Zimmerman and West in which they taped conversations between males and females.[16] They found men monopolizing the floor, usurping the turns of women, while women tended to defer to men. Sexism in conversation?[17] Perhaps—but to see how general this pattern is, one should listen to different kinds of conversations between men and women. But how should this sampling be done? There is no list of "kinds" of conversations similar to a list of the different kinds of occupations available to both sexes. Verifying hypotheses by using media often calls for sampling (and thus enumerating) social activities rather than individual people or groups. It is often difficult or impossible to know how to do this in some practical way.

On the other hand, when a native member takes a film, he uses his own system of selecting shots, poses, and sequences. It then becomes the social scientist's task to fathom how general or representative his or her selections are in putting together a composite sketch of a cultural event.

Finally, in using media as a symbol system, one faces the sampling problem in perhaps its worst form. How will time and duration be shown? Will a wide-angle lens be used, or will the camera move around zooming, panning, gaining detail and perspective alternately? Will activity sequences be followed or particular people? Which shots are revealing or typical, and which give the audience a distorted impression of what is going on?

INFORMATION RETRIEVAL

Rather clearly, film, videotape, or audio tape present some big filing problems. Unlike memos or field notes, they cannot easily be coded, put into folders, and indexed, and they contain an enormous amount of heterogeneous information. To some extent researchers find no way out of this problem. Many simply spend enormous amounts of time looking, listening, relooking, and relistening. They find that the time it takes to translate these data into research papers is much more than for other kinds of studies, because of the retrieval problem. However, there are some devices that can be used.

When the researcher makes a documentary film or videotape, he automatically codes it as he takes it. The various sequences that are followed, and so on (what we have just called "sampling"), automatically re-create for him the way he structured his environment as he viewed it. In this way a researcher, who is familiar with the scene he is studying, can use the ongoing scene to determine how to film it—as it proceeds.

In addition, coding systems have been devised to code tape or film directly. Ekman reports a method of attaching labels (such as "left eyebrow movements") directly to videotape, which can be called back in sequence with the use of a small computer.[18] There are also varieties of labels that can be attached to transcripts, codebooks that can be composed in conjunction with tape "foot meters," and other devices. We strongly recommend that written or taped ethnographic notes be made right after completing each film or tape. This should help greatly with the retrieval problem.

THE QUESTION OF REACTIVE MEASURES

We have put audio-visual techniques in the category of nonreactive measures. By now the reader may be wondering why. There is a three-part answer to this question. Audio-visual techniques may be nonreactive in the following ways: (1) It is possible to record human interaction surreptitiously and get permission to use these data after the recordings have been made. (2) There are cases when taping is a normal part of the phenomenon under study. For example, Hochschild studied television soap operas as a way of locating stereotypes about women and their social roles.[19] Often, in such settings as group therapy or educational classrooms, taping is a normal part of the situation and is used to teach and give normal feedback to the participants. The researcher need not introduce anything new into these settings in order to get audio-visual data. (3) Finally, it has been noted in several studies that the introduction of microphones or cameras, even when they are known to be operating, does not seem to alter social interaction appreciably once they become a normal part of the proceedings.

Yet, as with almost everything else in this book, whether the researcher is getting "poses" and "performances" or taping in on "business as usual" can be decided only by the ethnographic particulars of the study in question.

In the following photo essay Jacobs solves this problem neatly by photographing, not people, but objects which are designed to be seen by people.

PHOTO ESSAY: "NO ANYTHING ANY TIME"

The theme of this essay is signs of prohibition. These can be found in homes, public places, or places of business. If taken seriously, they prohibit when and where one may park; how one may drive; when and where one can eat; when, where, and under what conditions one may transact business; who may take whom to a public playground; who is eligible to enter university facilities; whether one may play games or sell or buy dope; and many other social transactions too numerous to list here.

Why should the nature and number of such signs be of sociological interest? To begin with, we have discussed the methodological virtues of unobtrusive measures. Signs of all kinds constitute unobtrusive measures *par excellence*. The kinds that are found, where they are placed, how prevalent they are, and who is subject to them are all valuable indicators of group life. Furthermore, photographs of these signs confront the reader with an experience similar to the one he would have if he encountered them on the street. In this sense the photos do yeoman service in "reconstructing reality."

But these particular signs are not only methodologically useful; they are theoretically interesting as well. Long ago Emile Durkheim made a case for what he saw as society's linear progression from "mechanical" to "organic solidarity."[20] By this he meant society's evolutionary progression toward a "higher social type" based upon a different form of social solidarity than that found among "primitives," that is, one based not on similarities but on differences. This would result, Durkheim believed, from the expanding division of labor and the reciprocal social needs and bonds it would generate.

In this regard he noted that with the passage of time there were fewer "thou shalt nots" to be found in the law and that the sanctions accompanying these prohibitions, with the coming of contract law, had become less severe. Insofar as he took the laws to be a reflection of the "collective consciousness," he concluded that society was requiring progressively fewer and less severe constraints of this kind in order to maintain social solidarity; i.e., it was becoming more and more moral.

Leaving aside the question of whether the prohibitions of law have truly become less numerous and severe, or if the laws are truly a reflection of collective consciousness, or what the collective consciousness is, there seem to currently be many counterindicators. For example, consider the following perfunctory list of signs of prohibition: no standing, no parking, no loitering, no food allowed, no bike riding, no games, no "dope," no dogs, no smoking, no left turn, no right turn, no U turn, no solicitors or peddlers, no trespassing, no parcels or shopping bags allowed, no adults allowed unless accompanied by children, no children allowed unless accompanied by adults—to mention but a few. Such signs are everywhere. Indeed, it is difficult to avoid these prohibitions and the many constraints on one's activities they reflect.

That there should be so many signs of prohibition in a permissive society currently populated by the "Spock generation" is ironic. This irony is further compounded when we recognize that the following photo essay was taken in what is probably one of the most liberal areas of the country, the Bay Area—San Francisco and Berkeley, California—home of the general strike, the free speech movement, the SLA, and the hippie movement.

In this regard, the authors can only conclude from the study of public and private signs of prohibition that the number of "thou shalt nots" in society is not decreasing but increasing. Not only have the duly constituted authorities formulated and displayed a series of prohibitions upon the populace, but private citizens have joined in this undertaking in earnest. The authors take this to be an indicator of a pervasive lack of trust on the part of the citizenry, which in turn is taken to indicate not a sense of growing morality, but a lessening of it.

If Durkheim was right that a decrease in the number and severity of formal prohibitions was needed to indicate a growing social equity, then let's face it, we're in trouble. This notion is in no way novel. Much of contemporary social science has been led to conclude that, while change is inevitable, "progress" is not, and that the early optimism of Social Darwinists and other neo-evolutionists and neo-positivists may have been, alas, misplaced. With this in mind we invite the reader to peruse on the following pages "the signs of the time."

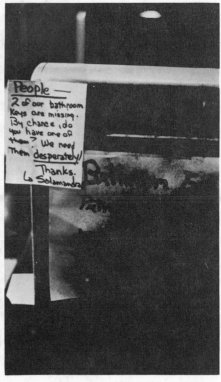

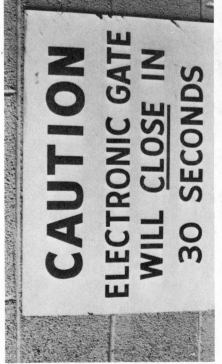

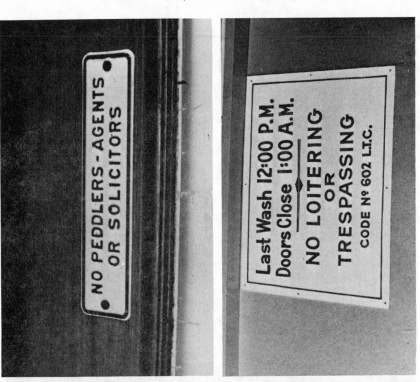

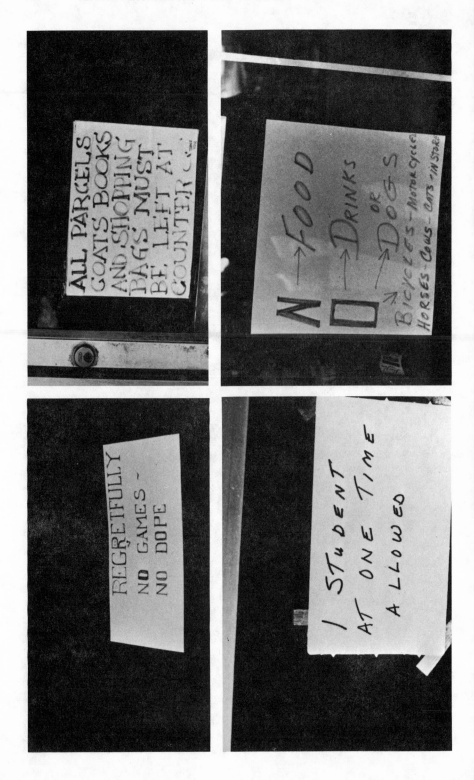

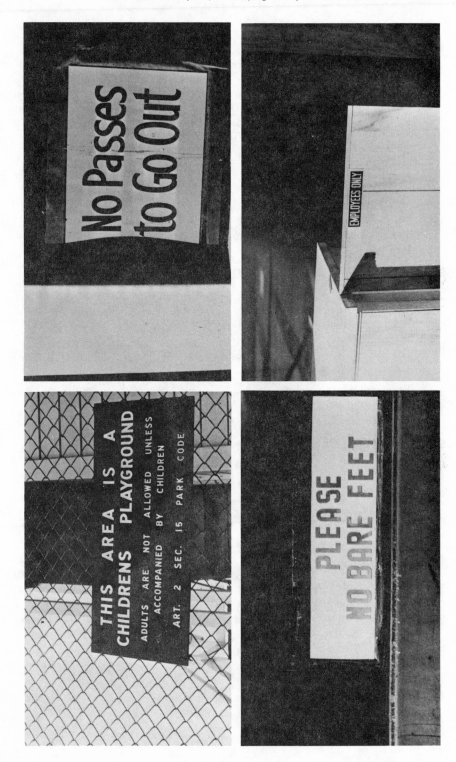

Notes

1. See, for example, Paul Ekman, "Communication Through Nonverbal Behavior: A Source of Information About an Interpersonal Relationship," in S. Tomkins and C. Izard (eds.), *Affect, Cognition, and Personality*, New York: Springer Press, 1965, pp. 390–442.

2. For a description of nonverbal clues to deception, see Paul Ekman, W. Friesen, and W. Scherer, "Body Movement and Voice Pitch in Deceptive Interaction," *Semiotica* 16, no. 1, (1976): 23–27.

3. For a discussion of the characteristics of visual space with respect to varying distances, see Edward T. Hall, *The Hidden Dimension*, Garden City, N.Y.: Doubleday Anchor, 1969.

4. Abraham Kaplan, "Content Analysis and the Theory of Signs," *Philosophy of Science* 10 (1943): 230.

5. Ibid.

6. For research on violence in the media, see: Robert K. Baker and Sandra J. Ball, *Mass Media and Violence*, Washington, D.C.: U.S. Government Printing Office, 1969: Seymour Feshback and Robert D. Singer, *Television and Aggression*, San Francisco, California: Jossey-Bass, 1971; and Joseph P. Murray, Eli A. Rubinstein, and George A. Comstock (eds.), *Television and Social Behavior*, Washington, D.C.: U.S. Government Printing Office, 1969.

7. Harold Garfinkel, *Studies in Ethnomethodology*, Englewood Cliffs, N.J.: Prentice-Hall, 1967, pp. 76–103.

8. Ibid., pp. 116–185.

9. Jacobs, *Fun City*, New York: Holt, Rinehart and Winston, 1974.

10. For a discussion of how children store events in memory kinesthetically, see Ernest Schachtel, *Metamorphosis: On the Development of Affect, Perception, Attention and Memory*, New York: Basic Books, 1959.

11. Paul Ekman, W. Friesen, and P. Ellsworth, *Emotion in the Human Face*, Elmsford, N.Y.: Pergammon, 1972.

12. Ekman, Friesen, and Scherer, "Body Movement and Voice Pitch in Deceptive Interaction."

13. Personal communication from Paul Ekman, 1973. These initial observations did not apply to all gestures which Ekman refers to as "illustrators" but only to a subset of them. However, when Ekman and his associates examined these correspondences more closely their initial observations proved to be incorrect. There were indeed correspondences between voice emphasis and illustrators, but these patterns proved to be far more complex than initially supposed.

14. Robert Rosenthal, "The Pygmalion Effect Lives," *Psychology Today* (September 1973).

15. John Wilson, "Film Literacy in Africa," *Canadian Communications*, 1, no. 4 (1961): 7–14.

16. Don Zimmerman and Candice West, "Sex Roles: Interruption and Silences in Conversation," in B. Thorne and N. Henley (eds.), *Language and Sex: Difference and Dominance*, Rowley, Mass.: Newbury House, 1975.

17. Sentence fragment.

18. Paul Ekman and W. Friesen, "A Tool for the Analysis of Motion Picture Film or Videotape," *American Psychologist* 24, no. 3 (1969): 240–243.

19. Personal communication from Dr. Arlie Hochschild, University of California at Berkeley. To my knowledge Dr. Hochschild has not published the results of her observations on soap operas, although she uses them as classroom exercises.

20. For a detailed discussion of this position, see Emile Durkheim, *The Division of Labor in Society*, Glencoe, Ill.: Free Press, 1947.

Part III

Reality Reconstruction: What's Wrong with It?

The reality reconstruction business as we have described it encompasses three broad goals. It seeks:

1. To make naturalistic observations—that is, to study humans "in their natural habitat," not in situations artificially constructed to facilitate science.
2. To recover the world as it looks from the "inside" (from the point of view of those being studied).
3. To obtain precise, accurate, and scientifically useful information.

Now, it is not at all clear that one can do all three of these things at once. It will be our task in the next chapter to evaluate this program—to see if it can be carried out. In particular, we will try to assess the extent to which one can obtain accurate information while working within the constraints of the first two goals. By "accurate" information we mean information that is undistorted and that can be obtained without using "reactive techniques" which change the thing they are informing about.

In order to accomplish this, the methods of reconstructing reality presented in chapters 3–5 will be summarized by classifying them into several broad categories. Each of these categories will then be evaluated one by one.

CHAPTER 6

The Reality Reconstruction Business Reconsidered

Subjective Phenomena and Reactive Techniques

While sociologists study people, sociologists are themselves (some think unfortunately) people. They therefore find themselves knowing something from the start about why people do the things they do. Within each person there are a host of rather easily observable phenomena—such as emotions, thoughts, or goals—which seem to be the causes of much of what he or she does. In the jargon of psychology, the idea that such things cause and are the reasons for our behavior has "face validity" for each of us.

A common but dramatic example of this phenomenon is the presence of verbal thoughts. As most people read a text they find themselves translating visual images into, quite literally, a voice in their head, which orally narrates the text for them. They can hear this voice just as clearly and distinctly as the physical voice of another person. (The voice in *your* head is probably reading this chapter right now.)

No other person can hear this voice. Observers can know of its presence only in indirect ways. One way is for you to tell them. Or they may assume that people who are reading usually translate visual images into mental auditory sounds. From this assumption they can infer: (1) that your inner voice is talking and (2) what it is saying (it is saying the words of the text). Of course, they could be entirely wrong. The congenitally deaf have never heard oral speech. They probably have no idea of what it is like, just as the congenitally blind would find it impossible to understand what colors are to the sighted. Thus, presumably,

107

when deaf people read a text, think, or reason they don't accomplish this by "hearing" a mental voice saying words.[1] Clearly, to the extent that the voice in your head occurs in a behavioral context with which I am familiar—to that extent I am likely to be able to turn the details of what I observe into inferences about "what is going on inside your head," and the better chance I have of being right. If such thoughts occur in contexts that are unfamiliar to me, such as in the mind of a schizophrenic, chances are that I will find it difficult to predict or understand anything "going on inside."

Indeed, oral thoughts are subjective phenomena of great interest to scientists because they themselves continually need and use them as resources. When they are deducing conclusions, solving problems, or reasoning about data, they are apt to find themselves engaged in an inner verbal dialogue with themselves. Sundry other phenomena, such as emotions, reactions, goals, and even some physical sensations (such as pain), share the characteristic that they are knowable to the one having them in a much more immediate way than to others, under normal circumstances.

Let us, for a moment, regard such phenomena as "real," as concrete things in the world. Thus, the voice in one's head is considered just as "real," as much "there," as a physical voice. The question then arises: Should sociology be concerned with such phenomena? There are three things about them that scientifically oriented people don't like:

1. They don't obey the laws of physics. That is, they do not occupy space and have weight, they do not "have the capacity to do physical work," and so on.
2. They cannot be directly heard, seen, or noticed by anyone but the one having them. (Here we see one reason for the classical meaning of "subjective"—i.e., pertaining to the subject.)
3. The "Heisenberg property": More often than not, the process of observing them, like the process of observing subatomic particles, changes the thing it observes. By "observing" we mean remembering, describing, reflecting back on, thinking about—a subjective phenomenon.[2]

The third property, while hailed by some humanistic theologians, turns life into a methodological nightmare for social scientists.[3] Consider this rendition by Raymond Panikkar:

By experience we may understand any immediate contact with reality. Or, again, experience is that opening of the human being by which the distance between the subject and the object tends asymptotically to zero.

The question about the nature and value of experience arises at the very moment when we begin to think about our experience. But then, we no longer experience: we think, or simply we remember. Or even more generally expressed: the awareness of an experience is not the experience. And even more: an experience cannot be experienced. Experiencing, unlike thinking, does not allow for self-reflection. That is its greatness and its weakness at the same time. This implies that the talk and the reflection about experience have necessarily to be non-experiential.[4]

The reader will note in this quote a distinction between experience and thought. Apparently our "voice in the head" is a thought, which can be remembered, reflected upon, and described, whereas certain other inner phenomena would be destroyed or altered by such a process. In short, *there are subjective phenomena which have the Heisenberg property and others which do not.* Such distinctions are often made by those who are willing to admit subjective phenomena into the world, with all the rights, privileges, and "realness" of their objective counterparts. However, the scientifically minded are reluctant to do this. They disavow an interest in subjective phenomena and deny, in principle, that they exist, or redefine them as something observable or potentially observable to many people. For example, they might insist that motives be treated as complex physiological responses, as social activities, or as a vocabulary used by members of society to explain their own behavior. All these definitions and/or "indicators" of motives are in contrast to understanding them as processes occurring in other people's "heads."[5]

Many of the reasons for scientists' uneasiness about other people's "heads" are well founded. For example, given the definitions and properties of subjective phenomena listed above, how might one go about studying them? There would be two major ways: *a first-person method*, in which each person studies himself and compares notes with others, and a *third-person method*, in which the social scientist studies other people, either by making direct inferences about others' subjective lives from their observed actions and other secondary sources, or by letting others study themselves and tell him the results. Needless to say, actual research does not have to limit itself to one or the other but can use a combination of the two.

Methods of Studying Subjectivity: An Evaluation

THE FIRST-PERSON METHOD

Using this approach, each member of a scientific community would study himself. He would notice, remember, and describe those aspects of his subjective life that were not subject to the Heisenberg property noted above. He would compare notes and communicate with his fellow scientists who were doing the same thing, in order to see if any general laws, patterns, or principles which seemed to apply to his own experience applied to the experiences of others as well.[6] As we all know, this general method (or ones like it) is simply not used in sociology. Not only sociologists, but social scientists in general tend to study "other people"; they do not study themselves. There are many reasons for this, some scientific and some historical. Sociologists in particular have a peculiar problem with the first-person method since it does not fit in well with their avowed subject matter, the study of the characteristics of groups.

We have already considered in chapter 1 why objectivists are not interested in studying what is in their heads or in the heads of others; but why, if subjectivists are so eager to study other peoples' heads, are they so reluctant to study their own? There is a major historical reason, which turns upon the fact that there was a European tradition that did, indeed, employ first-person methods to study human experience. In fact, there were some scientists in American universities who practiced this approach and endorsed its philosophy. However, there followed a struggle between this tradition and behaviorist psychologists.[7] Needless to say, the behaviorists won. This was not merely a scholastic debate, it was political in every sense of the word. Departments were taken over, careers were at stake, and people were put out of work. As a result, the first-person method has become associated with "introspection," a vague, metaphysical, soft, empathetic, unscientific approach to understanding human psychology. Sociologists, for the most part, inherited this attitude. Because of this, very few quantitative or qualitative sociologists have seriously tried to build a rigorous science of human - experience along these lines. Most of them assume that it cannot be done and should not be attempted. Certain phenomenologists are almost alone in developing this approach, which we shall consider in more detail in chapter 12.

The first-person method has the considerable advantage of enabling one to make "direct" observations of subjective phenomena. This follows from our definition of "subjective." However, some phenomena, such as those which Pannikar defined as "experience," are in principle subject to "Heisenberg's horror" if the one who experiences them tries to study them. An example might be the patterns of thought and feeling which therapists refer to as defense mechanisms. If the therapists are right about the dynamics of defense mechanisms, they exist because of their ability to deceive people in a way that makes them feel better. Therefore, if one comes to know about them, their function is thwarted and they automatically change or vanish. On another level there seem to be some aspects of experience that are completely shielded from the intrusions of reflective thought. Experiments have shown that there are events which we explicitly perceive but are unable to recall even a fraction of a second after becoming aware of them.[8] This happens, in part, because the mere physiological act of remembering some perceptions causes us to forget other perceptions.

For such phenomena the possibility of accurate knowledge seems to lie with the third-person method.

THE THIRD-PERSON METHOD: STUDYING SUBJECTIVITY APART FROM STUDYING ONE'S OWN EXPERIENCE

The second way to study subjectivity would be to study "them"—to study other people's subjective lives. The social scientist would need to develop procedures to infer indirectly the presence of emotions, goals, purposes, and so on from another's behavior and the social context of his actions. Of course, as we saw earlier, such inferences are made all the time in everyday life. All of us utilize empathy, analogies between "me" and "you," and commonsense knowledge for this purpose. The question then becomes whether social scientists can devise procedures that are more rigorous but still operate within the messy confines of daily life.

Ah, but now another complication rears its ugly head. When we consider whether the action of knowing some subjective phenomenon originates from the subject or from an observer, the following table emerges:

Heisenberg Property

	The action of knowing changes the thing known	The action of knowing does not change the thing known
The subject tries to find out (first-person method)		
An observer tries to find out (third person method)		

This table offers four categories for the things usually thought of as being subjective. Now, it may be that different subjective phenomena, because of their very nature, dictate how information about them can be accurately retrieved. For certain phenomena such as thoughts, it may be that only the subject can know them without changing them. For other phenomena, it may be that only observers have a chance to discover them without altering them. Obviously, the boxes of the table are not mutually exclusive or exhaustive. In fact, the interconnections involved make for many fascinating empirical problems.

Here we are interested in only one of these interconnections. It might seem that, if a subject could discover some aspect of himself, then we could construct a procedure that would allow an observer to know it also. This would be a two-step process: the observer (1) has the subject find out for him and (2) then finds out from the subject. That is, the lay person discovers and communicates information to the social scientist, using some sort of common symbol system, such as the prevailing natural language. While this two-step procedure is the prevailing method of both quantitative and qualitative research, it is, as we have seen, a particularly crucial strategy for qualitative sociology. Let's consider this procedure, variations on "ask them," in more detail.

VARIATIONS ON "ASK THEM"

Clearly, to invoke this procedure, I must hold two main assumptions: (1) that the person I am talking to knows, remembers, or can find out for me what I want to know and (2) that some common symbol system exists between the two of us that will allow the communication of this information.

The first assumption presents some intriguing problems that psychologists are all too familiar with. Presumably I ask others for information because I cannot easily or morally obtain it myself. Yet the fact that they are able to answer me is not prima facie evidence that they know. There are many things people do not know about themselves; yet, if asked, they can come up with an answer that sounds plausible to both them and others. For example, one popular personality test asks subjects if they have enjoyed sex "almost always," "most of the time," "some of the time," or "very little of the time." It is possible to give the matter a moments thought and circle one of these answers. Yet how many people were keeping count? How many remember that they enjoyed, say, about fifty-eight of the last seventy-five sexual encounters?

Regarding the second assumption, it would seem to exclude various kinds of people from being able to help me out—for example, infants, the very young in general, the insane, anyone speaking a language I do not know, social groups with special argot, the retarded, and others.

If a common symbol system does not exist between me and those I study, there are three basic choices: (1) I learn their communication system, (2) I teach them mine, or (3) I use some kind of translation procedure from one system to the other. All three approaches have been employed. Sometimes all have failed.

When the first is attempted, linguistic techniques such as componential analysis are often used to provide access to the "cultural symbolizations" of such persons as drug addicts, chess players, prostitutes, criminals, or musicians. These are special nomenclatures and ways of talking about things that mark one as "in the know" while permitting competent and coherent discussions to take place on a particular topic.

The second approach is an interesting one in that it attempts to train another person quickly as a research assistant. I teach him concepts, ways of talking, and ways of looking, and essentially send him out to collect data on himself. This might include keeping a daily diary, filling out a self-report form every time he smokes a cigarette, and the like.

Garfinkel and his colleagues employed this procedure when studying how the personnel of a psychiatric outpatient clinic processed their clients. He called upon them to scrutinize their own decision making. Using initial field observations, the researchers came up with a self-report form that seemed to reflect the kinds of things considered in decision making. Personnel were to fill out the form and include it in the clinical records of each client they processed. But it was soon found that the self-report form was being used as a manual on adequate decision making. The staff began to adjust their procedures to conform to the reporting form—which was used as a new definition of their task in preparing clinic folders and processing clients. They were learning not only a new way to describe their job but a new way of doing it![9]

The third approach, the translation procedure, is, unfortunately, widely used by both quantitative and qualitative sociologists—unfortunately because this is the path afflicted with the most potholes in terms of validity. The basic idea of this approach has already been stated: "I know better than you what you are telling me." When we spoke of "translation," some readers may have recalled those famous demonstrations in which a story is told in English to someone who speaks English and German. That person then tells it to someone who speaks German and Greek, and so on. Eventually it gets told to someone who speaks English, by which time the original story has become so transformed that it is virtually unrecognizable. The same sorts of difficulties face sociologists, but the procedure looks a little different.

The sociologist knows ordinary language, and he knows "sociology," a very peculiar way of talking about social life, that he picked up for the most part in college. He has some technical concern, statable in "sociology" but not in plain language. He does not ask people about it directly. He asks them in the nearest ordinary language equivalent—using pictures, hypothetical questions, or other items that he has decided are related to his concern. He may decide this on the basis of impressive statistical calculations, split-half reliability coefficients, Freudian theory, or sundry other technical devices. He then uses some technique, such as factor or discriminate analysis, to translate their answers to commonsense questions into answers to his technical questions. In doing so, he is assuming that he can interpret ordinary talk (or writing) in a way that makes it give information that the subjects did not understand themselves to be giving and that ordinary language is not designed to give. There is a familiar analogue in daily life. It occurs whenever a close friend, boss, junior therapist, or some other person gets "one up" on you by claiming that he knows better than you do what you "really meant" when you said something.

By and large, sociologists do not employ the rather precise criteria developed by linguists to assess the adequacy of translations. Instead, they use statistics, common sense, theoretical and cultural clues, and multiple determinations of the same information to argue for the adequacy of their translations. In fact, in many cases, such as in attitude surveys, the survey researcher does not recognize that he is involved in a translation procedure. Instead, the metaphor of the measuring stick is used, and it is assumed that one is "measuring" attitudes, using ordinary language questions as the "measuring tool."

The reason this problem is so critical for qualitative researchers is that they talk to people in situations that are not contrived. What they ask them, how they ask it, and what they make of the answers are all usually determined in unanticipated ways by the feedback from the ongoing conversation. It is difficult or impossible to avoid translating the subjects' statements into the researcher's own understanding of them as he goes along. It is the latter that gets written down in his field notes as the things that the subjects "said."

Indeed, this frequently takes the form of making spot decisions about whether to take informants seriously. Sometimes a social scientist understands events and circumstances that are related to him as reports on real happenings. At other times he understands them as beliefs, attitudes, and myths. Therapists are often in this position. They seldom, if ever, are in a position, as sociologists are, to check out the facts reported to them by patients. Instead they have to decide about them on the spot, given only "what it sounds like."

Howard Schwartz faced this problem in an unusually nasty form while doing research on mental disorder in a psychotic inpatient ward.[10] He was interested in certain aspects of hallucinations which could be described only by using the technical vocabulary of phenomenology (see pages 356–363). This vocabulary, as Heap has noted, is not a technical language in itself, but makes technical use of ordinary language (in this case English).[11] But ordinary people do not think and talk in the way phenomenologists do, even though both use the same natural language. Schwartz thus faced this dilemma: whether to (1) ask mental patients about their concerns in the ordinary ways of talking that were the closest equivalent to what he wanted to say; (2) ask them in the jargon of phenomenology, explaining what it meant as best he could; or (3) train or find someone who was both psychotic and familiar with phenomenological ways of talking.

He tried ordinary language, but it did not allow him to express certain distinctions that were crucial to the research. He tried the second approach, but it quickly became apparent that the patients did not know what he was talking about. Even worse, such peculiar talking started to make them anxious and suspicious of him (especially the paranoid patients he interviewed)![12] It seemed the third option was really the only feasible one.

As luck would have it, there was at this time on the ward a patient who had gone to a major university and was trained in phenomenology. Further, she was having just the kind of experiences Schwartz wanted to study, chronic hallucinations. There was only one trouble. When Schwartz started interviewing her, *he* became suspicious. In fact, she left one of these sessions abruptly, repeating the phrase "Run—Howie knows" over and over. She had been diagnosed as a "schizophrenic, affective type" because of the hallucinations. Now, with Schwartz's help, it was discovered that she was not a schizophrenic but a "character disorder." She had been lying to therapists for the past fifteen years about hallucinations which she had never in fact had! Anyone who would do such a thing was clearly a "character disorder." Although this discovery helped her therapist, it rendered the data Schwartz had obtained about her hallucinations somewhat less than credible.

As the reader can see, one can only assess an account of someone's inner life if, as Schwartz did, one knows in general "what it should sound like." But it is precisely when a sociologist does not know "what it should sound like" that he is most interested in obtaining such accounts.

Having reviewed the ins and outs of variations on "ask them," let us go on to assess their effectiveness.

CAN VARIATIONS ON "ASK THEM" REALLY WORK?

First, consider the translation procedure. It is true that such a procedure does not present the danger that the researcher will change what he is trying to find out. However, it does contain many possibilities for distortion of information. The issues are extremely delicate here, and only rarely can a translation of this sort be regarded as adequate. Second, consider the strategy of teaching subjects to talk and look at things as the researcher does. In general, this procedure has a large potential for changing the very thing it inquires into.

This occurred in Garfinkel's study for a very typical reason. When people are called upon to scrutinize some ordinary aspect of their lives over a period of time they tend to fuse the question of what they *are* doing and thinking with the issue of what they *should be* doing and thinking. As a result, discovery and creation are united. A more subtle but equally prevalent form of Heisenberg's disease is this: Many of the things we think, feel, and do are done in a rather improvisational way. When others inquire about where, when, and how we think and feel these things, an interesting thing happens: In looking for the structure in what we do, we find a structured way of doing it, often a way preferable to the former way. While that may be good for lay persons pursuing their "purposes at hand," it is bad for the social scientist, since it was the "old" way of doing things that he wanted to learn about.

The last example raises yet another ugly complication. Each part of the two-step procedure might work fine by itself, but when the steps are combined, an "interaction effect" is produced.[13] That is, someone might be able to quickly discover whether she likes or dislikes a stranger. She might be able to communicate this information to another, using the natural language. Yet when a friend asks her to meet his new wife and later give her impressions, both the process of assessing the wife-stranger and communicating these assessments somehow get changed. Finding-out-for-others might be a very different sort of activity than finding-out-for-oneself.

We can summarize our general conclusions as follows:

1. Assume that the subjects know, or can find out, what you want to know about them, without distorting the information in the process of finding it out.
2. Assume that they have a symbol system that can communicate the information, a system that you either know or can learn.
3. Assume that the process of asking for and getting the information does not produce an "interaction effect"—that is, does not result in distorting the information or changing the phenomena.

Only under these conditions can we feel confident of the two-step procedure for finding out about others. It should be mentioned that these conditions apply not only to subjective things like goals and decisions but also to patterned behaviors and actions of those one studies and to the possibility of finding out about them in this manner. Now, these are very stringent conditions and in practice are seldom met in the field. Thus, variations on "ask them" becomes an extremely hazardous strategy for getting accurate information in the field, especially in view of the fact that the qualitative researcher often has no other source of information to rely on.

MAKING INDIRECT INFERENCES

Clearly, if the subject does not know or cannot find out without distortion what we want to know about him, the only alternative is to make indirect inferences on the basis of his behavior and secondary sources. One might think that, at least for certain kinds of subjective phenomena, it is a contradiction to say the subject can be unaware of them, since, without his awareness, the phenomenon does not exist. But this is covered nicely by psychological, sociological, and phenomenological theory. True, by definition, a subject must be aware *in some sense* of such things as motives, emotions, and beliefs. But psychology has described such entities and mechanisms as the subconscious, repression and blocking, while sociology has given us internalization and background expectancies, and phenomenology, the prepredicative, preontological, and prereflective. They all specify ways in which, for one reason or another, someone can be aware of something but unable to describe it or know about it explicitly.

This is not all metaphysics or theory. Consider, for instance, an experiment on "subception," in which subjects were shown a series of nonsense syllables.[14] When some of the syllables flashed on the screen, the subjects received an electric shock. As physiological indicators showed, subjects soon showed signs of expecting and bracing themselves for the shocks as soon as they saw the shock syllables. But they could not say which syllables were the precursors of shock. They *knew* which ones were in terms of behavior, but not in terms of description and explicit awareness. These and other experiments suggest that indirect inference is not just helpful but necessary as an explanatory tool.

There are basically two ways of going about making indirect inferences. One can make them on the spot as he observes and interacts with others, or one can collect relatively enduring records of behavior, such as audio tapes or videotapes, and use them to make inferences at some later time on the basis of some set of reasoned procedures.[15]

The following are some practical considerations for the application of first or second forms of inference. First, the "on-the-spot" form of inference may occur in milliseconds and with no conscious effort on the part of the observer. This happens routinely when one witnesses some event in everyday life and has to surmise what it is that has just happened, almost simultaneous with its occurrence. This situation may apply to circumstances one is a party to, or to events involving second and third parties unknown to the observer. The alternative—to infer what had happened by analyzing a videotape of the same occurrence— might take hours, days, or weeks.

The question arises: Why not always invoke on-the-spot inferences when possible? The answer is that while one can infer more, more easily, and in less time in this way, one may also be very wrong in what he infers depending upon the context in which the inference is made. Furthermore, the application of the second form of inference to the same problem may provide a way of overcoming this error.

In short, second-form inferences offer more possibilities for accurate conclusions than first-form but are severely limited with respect to the kind and amount of information they can provide. This presents our researcher, once again, with a painful choice. He can either put together a relatively complete picture of a subjective reality from pieces of information of questionable accuracy, or he can spend his time filling in small portions of this reality with information obtained by rigorous methods. A vivid illustration of this dilemma will emerge as we give an example of each type of inference.

First-Form Inference: Wrong Again

One morning, Jacobs was sitting in a near-empty coffeehouse, busily devouring a bagel and cream cheese. Looking up, he saw a young man and woman walking down the long corridor leading to the counter and service area. The young man had a beard and long hair and wore blue jeans, hiking boots, and a large knapsack on his back. The young woman also looked as if she had been traveling. They acted as though they were long-time friends. The woman was laughing, joking, and generally playful. They got coffee and sat down at a nearby table. The young woman, before starting her coffee, walked among the customers trying to bum a cigarette (a common occurrence), but was unsuccessful. Finally, she managed to get some pipe tobacco and cigarette paper and returned to the table. She and her companion joked about how hard times were and rolled cigarettes from the fixings.

What would one infer upon witnessing such a scene? The author inferred the following:

1. The young man and woman were good friends and had been traveling together or at least sleeping out for want of funds.
2. They were currently getting along well with each other.
3. The young woman was very happy.
4. They had shared a lot together.

What followed was this: The woman got up without provocation, taking her cup of coffee with her, and walked to the back of the restaurant to a table, where she sat by herself. The man, looking completely indifferent, continued smoking, finished his coffee, and left. A while later, the woman returned from the rear of the restaurant to the coffee bar, asked for credit on a second cup of coffee, and whispered to the owner how depressed she felt (indeed, she now looked depressed). She took her coffee back to her table at the rear of the restaurant and began talking and gesturing as though she were addressing someone else, although no one was there.

At this point the owner asked Jacobs to assist her in repairing a broken table near where the woman was sitting. While the owner left to get a hammer and nails, the woman stopped gesturing and talking out loud to herself and began to talk to Jacobs. In the course of the conversation it was revealed that everything Jacobs had surmised on the basis of his on-the-spot inferences was wrong:

1. The man and woman did not know each other and had met for the first time outside the coffeehouse on the way in.
2. The woman was not happy; she was miserable.
3. The woman had not been camping out, although the man had.
4. The woman was not only depressed but "spaced out."

At the time of the earlier appraisal, only moments before, the scene had seemed totally unambiguous. How could Jacobs have been so wrong?

There is a general principle which explains how one can be so far off the mark in such cases. When inferring (on-the-spot) social meanings from behavior, it is not as if a given behavior has some standard meaning in a social dictionary, analogous to the fixed referent of names, such as who a particular "John Brown" might be in the phone book. Instead, members treat behavior as "indexical."[16] That is, members use an assortment of assumptions, clues, common knowledge, and contextual information to infer meanings from behavior. In this sense, there is no standard meaning associated with a given behavior. The same behavior is given different fringes of meaning if it is embedded in different ongoing social contexts. The story above illustrates this point graphically. New actions and new conversation, by altering the ongoing context of certain actions of the young man and woman, caused Jacobs to reinterpret and change their meaning.

Let's assume that members in general decide on the meanings of observed behavior from the behaviors' social context. But this social context varies fairly independently of the "real" meanings and significances the behaviors have for those doing them. Therefore, by the very method by which on-the-spot inferences are made, we must be chronically suspicious of their accuracy.

The reader might object to this on symbolic-interactionist grounds. After all, if we coordinate our actions with others by assessing their motives, meanings, and morals, and if we were wrong about the latter, would not our actions betray us and lead to correction? In short, would not the truth come out as it did in the above case with Jacobs? The answer provided by a great deal of research seems to be "no." People can think that they know what the others are thinking and feeling and be entirely wrong; they can use their wrong assumptions to decide upon courses of action; and yet rarely, if ever, will it become clear that anything is amiss. In particular, work on conversation indicates that conversation permits a great deal of "misunderstanding." I can be hearing, in many cases, something quite different from what you thought you were saying, and yet we can have a normal conversation which creates the appearance that we understand each other quite well.[17]

If first-form inferences are subject to inherent difficulties, can second-form inferences do better? There is now a considerable literature that indicates they can.[18] The moral is not to abandon on-the-spot inference for more formal or formidable methods. There would be no way to accomplish a general abandonment of this kind and still maintain social life as we know it. Rather, we recommend that, whenever possible, second-form inferences be used as a check upon first-form and that, when one may conveniently choose between them, second-form inferences should be given priority.

Unfortunately, qualitative field methods, given the current state of the art, rely heavily upon on-the-spot inferences. There is at present no way out of this if one wants to reconstruct the reality of individuals or groups in a reasonable amount of time. Reconstructing such realities by the use of rigorous methods involves the analysis of enormous amounts of data. One's great-grandchildren might still be analyzing such data if methods similar to conversation analysis[19]—as illustrated below—were employed. While the fruits of such a harvest may prove to be sweet indeed, one might starve to death ere they ripen.

Second-Form Inference: Who Is "You"?

Consider the following excerpt from a transcribed audio tape of a group therapy session:

DICK: I know I didn't show it, but I really felt close to you—'cause, you know, we have a lot in common, we both think the same.
BETTY: Oh, that day when I went into all that // problem——
DICK: Yeah.
BETTY: Yeah, we're all so much a part of each other, the only person I don't know so much about is *you* [laughs]—I've heard some things——
DICK: Who you talking to? That guy//
BETTY: I'm talking to the doctor.[20]

If we were to hear an exchange of this kind, we would intuitively assume that Betty's remark was ambiguous to Dick—in particular, that Dick did not know to whom "you" referred and therefore asked about it. But how could we *show* that Dick heard "you" as ambiguous? What would a demonstration of this look like?

First, we would need to show that Dick heard the relevant portion of Betty's utterance, in the minimal sense of hearing the actual sound. Second, we would need to show that this sound had a particular meaning for Dick—that he took it to refer to some member of the group but he did not know which. Finally, we would need to demonstrate that Dick heard this ambiguity at the time the word "you" was uttered. None of these three steps can be accomplished by merely examining the next thing Dick says. For one thing, people often say things like "Are you talking to me?" or "Who are you talking to?" because they have not been paying attention. Such a question does not signify that a previous comment was heard as ambiguous, but rather than the asker of the question did not hear the comment to begin with. Or again, Dick might very well *describe* "you" as ambiguous when, in fact, he hears it as quite definite. People often do this sort of thing in order to make jokes. Witness, for instance, the following exchange during group therapy where one patient comments on another who is so drugged he is almost falling off his chair:

MARK: I think this poor fellow should be out there in bed instead of sitting in the chair.
VINCE: Who, the doctor? [Laughter from the whole group]
The question "Who, the doctor?" was similar to Dick's "Who you talking to? That guy //." Yet, needless to say, everyone in the room heard "this poor fellow" as the patient in question.

Does the reader believe that Vince really knew that "this poor fellow" referred to the drugged patient? This may not be true. We have just made a spot inference, presumably the same one made by other members of the therapy group. Vince saw the opportunity for a joke and took advantage of it. But in order to do this, he only needed to know that "this poor fellow" did *not* refer to the doctor. He did not have to know which person it actually did refer to. Our spot inference could have been wrong, since there is no formal way to determine from Vince's response how he actually heard Mark's sentence.

All this can be summarized by saying that if we are after the "truth" and do not wish to be satisfied with fallible common sense, many delicate contingencies have to be taken into account.

One way to demonstrate that "you" in the previous excerpt was indeed ambiguous is based on conversational analysis.[21] When *two* people converse, who speaks next does not depend on what is currently being said. However, in multiparty conversation, this is not the case. A member of such a conversation must monitor the content of each upcoming utterance to see if he should speak next, after it is completed.[22] This seemingly trivial observation has an important consequence. It allows us to claim that *any* nonspeaker in a multiparty conversation listens for certain clues in the talk of *any* current speaker. Thus we need not focus on Dick as a particular person, his relation to Betty, whether he is paying attention to the topic at hand, or what Betty happens to be saying. Minimally, he is listening to see if he is to speak next. What is involved in this kind of listening? There are certain speaker selection rules by which a current utterance selects the next speaker. In particular, Betty's utterance—especially the part "the only person I don't know so much about is you"—employs a "current speaker selects next speaker" technique. This technique has a moral aspect to it. The person selected to speak next by such a procedure has both the right and the *obligation* to speak next. Moreover, no others have this right or obligation. In order to know who this person is, other conversationalists must know to whom "you" refers.

Thus, listening to Betty in order to see who goes next involves: (1) hearing the sound "you," (2) recognizing that Betty has selected someone to talk next, and (3) being concerned with whom "you" refers to, instead of (or in addition to) some other aspect of its meaning.

Although this kind of listening may be what people do, in principle, is there any evidence that Dick is, in fact, listening in this way? Such evidence is provided by part of what he says next. Betty's comment is a "directed" one: It is said *to* a particular conversationalist.[23] In this it is unlike many jokes, stories, or topical utterances which are not directed. In saying "Who you talking to? That guy...," "Dick characterizes Betty's comment as a case of "talking to somebody."[24] He thus shows her (and us) that he understands her remark is a directed one. It is unclear that he could have noticed this without hearing and understanding "you" in the way we claimed.

At this point we have merely established how and why Dick might be concerned with "you" and whom it refers to. We have no basis for claiming we know whom he actually thinks it refers to.

Assume that he knows "you" means the doctor. He could then expect that if he spoke next, (1) he would be talking out of turn and (2) he and the doctor might end up talking at the same time. Talking out of turn and interrupting somebody are, in many cases, sanctionable offenses in conversation—they make other people mad. One might therefore expect Dick to have reservations about committing such offenses, if he knows he might be doing so. Yet he does, indeed, talk next.

Now let's assume that the conversationalists, including Dick, recognize Betty as selecting some unknown person as next speaker. Then what happens next is consistent with this assumption. Somebody will talk next. That person will not know if he is the one Betty is talking to. He thus might be violating a moral rule. One way to deal with this is to show by the very thing he says that his violation is an "innocent mistake." That is, if the content of his utterance consists in asking Betty whom she is talking to, he becomes exempt from the moral rule and will not be heard as talking out of turn or interrupting. This is exactly what Dick does in saying "Who you talking to? That guy...."

Now forget the previous moral problem. Imagine that, at some point, conversationalists cannot figure out who is supposed to talk. In this situation, which one of them, in fact, talks, and what does he say? Conversationalists often employ what Jefferson calls "side sequences" to solve this problem.[25] These are parenthetical exchanges which are exempt from some of the considerations that apply to the main body of talk. This group was talking on a particular topic— their intimate knowledge of one another. Immediately after Betty's remark, this topic is suspended and a new topic is created with a side sequence:

DICK: Who you talking to? That guy //
BETTY: I'm talking to the doctor.

Then they go back to the main topic again.[26] It is like a movie which is stopped, while a technical problem gets solved, and then started up again.

While the notion of side sequence explains *what* can be said when it is ambiguous who should speak next, it does not deal with which person should say it. Why did Dick, instead of somebody else, go next? In research on ambiguity, Schwartz studied situations in which two parties have been exchanging comments (especially questions and answers) and one of them says something to "somebody," but it is not clear who that somebody is![27] Under these circumstances Schwartz found that it is most often the just-prior speaker who speaks next. This is consistent with other findings which indicate a bias in multiparty conversation for the current speaker to select the preceding speaker to go next.[28] Insofar as this tendency is part of common sense knowledge, conversationalists may assume that a current speaker is talking to the just-prior speaker when they cannot tell whom she is talking to. In this exchange Dick is the one who spoke prior to Betty, and Dick is the one who talks next. In sum, the fact that Dick speaks right after Betty, coupled with what he says, gives evidence that he does not know who "you" is. This evidence stems, in several ways, from the formal organization of conversation.

Apart from its aesthetic appeal (?), what does an exposition like the one just given have to offer? It is obvious that, through conversational analysis, it can be demonstrated that a pronoun like "you" is heard as ambiguous. It is just as obvious that the reader probably concluded the same thing without benefit of conversational analysis. Why, then, bother with second forms of inference at all? Why not invoke on-the-spot decisions whenever one can be reasonably sure that they are accurate?

Basically, there are two answers to this question. The first turns upon the fact that the conversational analyst knows what criteria, methods, and theories his inference rests upon, while the reader, in invoking on-the-spot inference, would be hard put to explain why or how he reached his conclusion. It was, like most things one encounters, "obvious on inspection." Why it was obvious or how it was obvious was unnecessary to ask. If, as it is generally held, one is likely to have better grounds for a conclusion if one can demonstrate the basis for it, then the second form of inference, the one that conversational analysis offered in the previous example, should be preferable.

The second answer turns upon the first. It is clear from the example that second-form inferences require one to build theories of social actions that may themselves prove rewarding. Because of these theories, second-form inferences are not simply different ways to discover the same things one might find through on-the-spot inferences. Second-form inferences eventually can ask questions and get answers about phenomena that other forms of observation have no access to at all. They do this by forcing the analyst to attend to details that would otherwise go unnoticed. Here, as elsewhere, how you look has a lot to do with what you will be able to see.

CONCLUSIONS

We have seen that no one method or combination of methods for finding out about subjectivity will consistently give us accurate information. Instead, which person can find out what, using what method, is determined by the *nature of social interaction itself*. Thus, in order to gain consistently accurate information about others' heads, there would have to be a science of subjectivity. We must agree with the positivists that no such science currently exists.

Yet qualitative researchers endorse these methods. If such methods are neither scientifically impressive nor very different from the commonsense methods used by us all, what makes them "social science" methods? More pointedly, what makes them legitimate? It is to this question that we now turn.

The Social Scientific Legitimation of Accounts: Deciding Between Competing Versions of Reality

All forms of sociology, lay and professional, have as their common problem figuring out "what's really going on" in social life. In solving this problem, they face a peculiar logical dilemma. There are many ways of describing social life, all of which may be correct. But these different descriptions convey different inventories of what is present and what is absent; they vary in what they emphasize and what they leave out. In this sense different accounts of social life constitute competing versions of reality. One cannot decide between them by reference to concepts of truth and falsity. For they may all be "true" in a formal sense.

As professionals, social scientists are a group of people whose business it is to describe the lives of other groups of people. Their accounts are therefore, by definition, outsiders' accounts, unless it should happen that they study themselves. How are these accounts to be legitimated? It is in light of this problem that the question of deciding between competing versions of reality assumes importance. Positivists and reality reconstructionists take two divergent routes in solving this dilemma. Positivists wish to see and find the legitimacy of their versions of social reality by reference to science and being scientists. Reality reconstructionists, on the other hand, find little solace in being social scientists. They seek to repair their status as members of some outside group. The accounts of reality reconstructionists (including symbolic interactionists, among others) would be the accounts of "insiders"—those who live the lives or do the things that are being analyzed. The virtue of these accounts would stem primarily from the identity of the people who give them. Such people would not be imposing artificial categories and concepts on some way of life, but would be giving us the "natural" symbolizations, meanings, and significances that a way of life has for those who live it. It is time to look more closely at this solution to the problem of competing accounts.

The conflict just discussed was epitomized in the excerpt quoted at the beginning of this book. Young people became convinced that doctors and scientists didn't know "what marijuana is all about." Yet the descriptions of marijuana intoxication by these experts were both scientific and correct. What was it that they didn't know?

It is not hard for us to unravel this mystery, for there is a kind of folk reasoning behind this conflict. There is a way of evaluating accounts which first asks if another person "knows what he is talking about." One first determines the social identity of a storyteller, then uses it to interpret and evaluate the story. One way to identify the storyteller is by the kind of story he tells. The account itself indicates the identity of the account giver, which in turn can indicate how to interpret the account. Indeed, the drug culture is replete with jargon for talking about drugs. It can be seen merely from the way someone talks about drugs that he is not a "user" and should therefore not be taken seriously. It was in this sense that the scientific description of marijuana was "wrong." It betrayed the describer as an outsider.

"INSIDERS" AND "OUTSIDERS" AS FOLK CATEGORIES

If we make two massive idealizations, we can come up with an interesting issue. For some mode of life or kind of activity, let's divide people into two groups, those who are involved in the activity and those who are not. Assume that within each group there is consensus about who are the authorities on this way of life or activity. Having made these assumptions, a fourfold table emerges:

		The authority on insiders is taken to be an:	
		Insider	Outsider
Which group makes the assumption:	Insiders		
	Outsiders		

The main question becomes: does each group require, as a necessary condition for a competent theorist, that he be one of them? Second, do insiders and outsiders agree or disagree about the necessary identity of an authority on insiders? In this connection, it can be noted that the experts on children are considered to be adults and the experts on the mentally retarded are the mentally normal. On the other hand, blacks insist that no nonblack can be an authority on black life, and feminists similarly say that only women can know what it is like to be a woman. For a case of disagreement, there might be none more graphic than that of Carlos Castaneda and Don Juan.[29] For many of us in the society at large, *our* expert on sorcery is the anthropologist Castaneda. On the other hand, Don Juan and his fellow sorcerers laugh at Castaneda's "anthropology" and use his books about them for toilet paper.

It is clear that we are dealing with an almost political issue. We are dealing with how groups confer "entitlement"—that is, how someone becomes "entitled" to know something from the point of view of others, whether or not he in fact knows it.

THE SOCIOLOGICAL CONCEPT OF INSIDER

Sociologists, like anybody else, are privy to the cultural conventions just discussed. Let's pretend that a sociologist adopted some of these conventions, particularly the view that only insiders are entitled to know about the area of social life that they are "inside." How would such a social scientist go about becoming an expert on some particular phenomenon? He would follow a relatively clear procedure:

1. Choose some phenomenon—for example, motorcycle riding, delinquency, heroin addiction.
2. Locate the collection of people whom the society designates as the insiders with respect to the phenomenon.
3. Either become a member of this group, so that one's reflections and knowledge can be taken as authentic, or solicit accounts and theories about the phenomenon from group members.

This procedure looks very much like that recommended by symbolic interaction as the first step toward understanding social life. In drawing this analogy, we are suggesting that reality reconstructionists have adapted the folk concept of insider. This is their hero, their model of man (or woman) for sociology—the one in the know, the one who "knows what he is talking about."

This perspective puts a new slant on field methods. One of the main things field methods may be about is entitlement. For they are all generally known ways (but not the only ways) of coming to deserve the title "insider." Participant observation is a version of "hanging around" and gaining group acceptance and a group role. All manner of interviewing allows one to claim that one's symbolizations come "from the horse's mouth." The very adaptation by qualitative sociology of the natural language is significant in this regard. In talking among themselves, most social groups use the prevailing natural language, not tables or graphs. By using the natural language, the qualitative researcher is in a much better position to describe a group using the style and jargon which that group sanctions. Thus, in his very way of writing, he can display that his accounts come from someone who "knows what he is talking about."

In using this model, a great deal of common sense culture must be accepted and worked with. One's topics of study correspond to the names members have for aspects of their society—for example, dying, delinquency, voting, tennis. One's target populations correspond to socially recognized groups and networks—teenagers, New Yorkers, prostitutes, sorcerers, witches. One's basic source of data comes to be the theories and stories such groups have about their society and their own lives.

Now, there is nothing intrinsically objectionable about all this. It provides some support for the claim of having the authoritative story on "what's going on out there." But how does it exclude the man on the street from making the same claim? After all, the notion of insider-outsider is dear to his heart as well, and like the reality reconstructionist, he is not misguided by positivist science. Apparently, the only way out of this dilemma is to combine the two previously mentioned sources of legitimacy for accounts. The social scientist must become an insider or speak on behalf of insiders, and, additionally, he must be in a position to be doing science as well. But how can this be?

A SCIENCE OF THE INSIDE?

While most sociologists seem to feel the need to claim science in order to legitimate their activities, deciding exactly what science means has become something of a problem. All of the major figures in sociology have laid claim to science. Clearly, the notion of science that Marx had in mind is very different than that held by Simmel, Schutz, Durkheim, or Weber. Indeed, no two of these held the same notion. Treating the concern for science as primarily a concern with legitimating one's activities explains a number of things—for example, why sociologists feel compelled to see themselves as pursuing science while their actual goals and methods have little or nothing to do with each other. Clearly, if Simmel is doing science, Durkheim and Marx are not. If we understand by "science" positivist science, it is clear that the reality reconstructionists are in trouble. As we have shown in this and previous chapters, there is currently no science of subjectivity. In fact, sociologists of the reality reconstructionist school, in order to retrieve and explain social reality, are invoking common sense notions couched in scientific rhetoric. Whether this means that they know more or less about the social world than the positivists is an open question. As we have previously contended, it may be that sociologists would do well to abandon positivist science as a goal, since it seems that there is no way to apply it fruitfully to answer some of the major problems related to social phenomena. Perhaps they should pursue "understanding" instead of prediction and control. In this regard, sociologists may have abandoned commonsense knowledge prematurely. As things now stand, there is nothing better available to get at an insider's understanding. In this sense, the symbolic interactionists and the man in the street are on to a good thing. It may prove ironic that the former have worked so hard to disassociate themselves from this method.

However, if science is to be everyone's goal, we must decide how the science of social life should and can be done. Is the concept of "insider" an analytically useful scientific category? For it to be so, it would have to reflect certain social realities. There would have to be *in general* similarities in the way those designated as insiders experience the world; there would have to be sharp differences between outsiders and insiders in the way they experience and know social phenomena, and these different patterns of experience would have to be caused by, and cause, individual social actions. Nobody knows whether these general patterns exist, and there is currently no scientific way to find out.

But we do know that common sense endorses these patterns. Indeed, belief in the existence of an inside point of view and the designation of group spokesmen to give voice to it are created and sustained in society without benefit of science. While we do not know how it is created and sustained, it is possible for sociologists to tap into it, because it exists. Yet, it is precisely because it is not a scientific achievement that the sociologist is faced with the choice of knowing the world in this way *or* finding some scientific way to know social life in which the insider and inside would probably disappear as thought constructs.

Notes

1. For a discussion of the sociological aspects of congenital deafness, see Aaron Cicourel and R. Boese, "Sign Language Acquisition and the Teaching of Deaf Children," in *The Functions of Language: An Anthropological Approach and Psychological Approach*, ed. by D. Hymes et al., New York: Teachers College Press, 1972.

2. The Heisenberg principle, as used in physics, is a bit different from what we have called the "Heisenberg property." Let's say that you're interested in getting what statisticians call an "interval estimate" of both the position and the momentum (speed times mass, and the direction of motion) of an atomic particle. That is, you want to know some range of numbers within which one could expect the numbers indicating momentum and position to fall. Let Δx be a horizontal "lane" of a certain width, and let Δm be an interval of numbers within which the particle's momentum is expected to fall. Then, in one form, Heisenberg's principle states:

   $(\Delta x) \times (\Delta m) = p$ where p is a fixed, real number called Planck's constant

   We can roughly interpret this formula thusly:

   1. One cannot know at any given time with the same degree of accuracy both where the particle is and where it is going (a very loose phrase for its momentum).
   2. The more accurately we know where it is, the less accurately we know where it is going, and vice versa.

3. Points 1 and 2 are consequences of the nature of "small" moving particles and the physical laws they obey. No *method* or methods of measuring position and momentum can escape these consequences.

The main difference between the principle explained above and ours is this: The principle says that knowing one thing about an object changes another thing about it. Therefore one cannot know both things about the same object at the *exact same time*. But neither thing is thereby rendered "unknowable" in general. In our formulation, the process of observing something about people changed the very thing it sought to observe.

3. This property is of value to mystics and psychotherapists, among others, because it results in "knowledge which changes the knower." For a description of some of the virtues of this kind of knowledge, see our introduction to part VI.

4. Raymond Pannikar, "The Ultimate Experience: The Ways of the West and the East," unpublished paper, Harvard University, 1971.

5. It should be noted that many aspects of the life-world of the individual, while "objective" from the metaphysical standpoint, still possess one or more of the three properties we have mentioned. For example, it is difficult or impossible for outside observers to observe or learn about one's sexual activities or the daily lies one tells, without altering these activities in the process. Our forthcoming discussion should therefore be understood as applying, at least potentially, to many more phenomena than those which are traditionally called "subjective."

6. This might be called an empirical first-person method. There are other kinds of first-person methods, notably those of the classical phenomenologists. Phenomenologists do not try to determine how general an experience is by having many different people compare notes. Rather, the "generality" of experience (the extent to which it is common to others) is treated as inherent in the structure or "horizontal potentials" of experience itself, and is described as one aspect of experience.

7. For a useful description of this debate, see Sigmund Koch, "Psychology and Emerging Conceptions of Knowledge as Unitary," in *Behaviorism and Phenomenology: Contrasting Bases for Modern Psychology*, ed. by T. W. Wann, Chicago: University of Chicago Press, 1964, pp. 1–41.

8. In one such experiment Sperling flashed single letters on a screen for brief periods of time and immediately asked his subjects to report the letters they saw. Using an ingenious sampling technique, he was able to show that his subjects actually perceived more letters than they were able to report, even a fraction of a second after seeing them. For the details of this experiment, see George Sperling, "The Information Available in Brief Visual Presentations," *Psychological Monographs* 74, no. 498 (1960): 1–2.

9. Harold Garfinkel, "Methodological Adequacy in the Quantitative Study of Selection Criteria and Selection Practices in Psychiatric Outpatient Clinics," in his *Studies in Ethnomethodology*, Englewood Cliffs, N.J.: Prentice-Hall, 1967. The finding described in the text is from the study just cited but is not mentioned in the article cited. Rather it was communicated to one of the authors orally.

10. For a description of some of this research see Howard Schwartz, "General Features," in *Topics in Ethnomethodology*, ed. by J. Schenkein et al., Berlin: Suhrkamp Publishers, 1976.

11. See James Louis Heap, *Figuring Out Grammar: Features and Practices of Explicat-*

ing Normative Order, unpublished Ph.D. dissertation, University of British Columbia, May 1975.

12. In fact, after one patient was treated to a barrage of phenomenological questions most of which he could not understand, he stated: "Well, this interview was good for me. It helped me to see how fucked up I really am." He later voiced extreme suspicions about Schwartz to his therapist.

13. We use the concept of "interaction effect" only as a metaphor here. In quantitative research, an interaction effect is said to be present when, statistically speaking, the whole has a greater effect than its parts—that is, when the effect of some combination of independent variables on a third dependent variable is greater (or different) than the sum of the effects of these independent variables considered singly.

14. Michael Polanyi, *The Tacit Dimension,* Garden City, N.Y.: Doubleday Anchor, 1966, pp. 7–8.

15. We can exclude secondary sources from consideration since they are based upon the efforts of agencies or other people who have already used one of the third-person methods of assessing some target individual (or group). One is then merely taking their word for it. We can exclude, as well, so-called systematic observation for this consists in applying the findings obtained from reasoning procedures to train "superior" on-the-spot observers.

16. See Garfinkel, *Studies in Ethnomethodology,* pp. 4–7.

17. For a discussion of the requirements that must be met for two conversationalists to be aware they have misunderstood each other, see Howard Schwartz, "Understanding Misunderstanding," *Analytic Sociology* 1 (1977).

18. For example, tests to determine the accuracy with which people can determine meanings from facial expressions indicate that those who are trained in systematic observation do better than those who are not.

19. We use the term *conversational analysis* to refer to a method of analyzing natural conversations that was developed by Harvey Sacks and his colleagues. The reader will learn more about this method in chapter 12.

20. The double slashes // indicate points of overlapping speech between the current and next speaker.

21. We are quick to point out that our exposition is not an example of conversational analysis. It is an illustration of one use to which its concepts and findings can be put.

22. For a discussion of "who talks next" and other turn-taking issues in conversation, see Harvey Sacks et al., "A Simplest Systematics for the Organization of Turn Taking for Conversation," *Language* 50 (1974): 696–735.

23. It should be noted that an utterance can be "directed" to a particular person without selecting that person as the next speaker. This occurs, for instance, when one answers the question of another.

24. When a current speaker comments upon or describes a previous utterance, ethnomethodologists speak of this as "formulating" the previous utterances. This is one of the ways in which a next speaker shows if and how he understands a previous speaker.

25. See Gail Jefferson, "Side Sequences," in *Studies in Social Interaction,* ed. by David Sudnow, New York: Free Press, 1972.

26. This fact cannot be seen from the data given but is apparent from the full transcript. Since we intended this exposition as an illustration, we decided to include only part of the data, for brevity.

27. For a discussion of "talking past each other" and what it takes to detect misunderstandings, see Howard Schwartz, "Making Ambiguity Visible: A Study in Sociolinguistics," paper read at the Pacific Sociological Association Meetings, 1975.

28. Sacks et al., A *Simplest Systematics*. While the existence of the bias and its externality to the turn-taking system are mentioned in this paper, they are not analyzed. To our knowledge there is currently no published analysis of this recursive bias, although its dynamics are well known to researchers in conversational analysis.

29. See, for example, Carlos Castaneda, A *Separate Reality*, New York: Simon and Schuster, 1971.

Illustrative Case Studies for Book One

Having presented the ins and outs of various methods of reconstructing reality, we also want to indicate the kind of fruit such methods can bear. We do this with four studies by Jerry Jacobs, each of which employs one of the techniques discussed in chapters 3 and 4 to arrive at its conclusions. Although edited somewhat for this volume, they are presented in substantially the same form in which they appeared in the professional literature. From them the reader can get some idea of what a "finished product"—an article presented to one's professional colleagues—looks like in qualitative sociology. He or she can also see what sorts of findings are obtained when one applies some of the perspectives and techniques discussed in this text to topics like market research, bureaucracy, suicide, and mental retardation.

CASE STUDY A

"Burp-Seltzer? I Never Use It": An In-depth Look at Market Research

Garfinkel (1967) has dealt with the ways in which members do "ad hocing" while pursuing the accomplishment of practical tasks in the here and now, notwithstanding the constraints of more formal sets of instructions or programs. Such tasks range from the routine, everyday activities of lay persons to the expert's active pursuit of "science." The study of the methods used to accomplish these practical tasks in everyday life falls within the general domain of ethnomethodology. While it is not the central concern of this form of analysis, a spin-off of these ethnomethodological studies is the way in which members handle discrepancies between real and ideal practices so that everyone is able to entertain, incorporate, and perpetuate a "nothing unusual is happening" stance (Emerson, 1969; Jacobs, 1967, 1969).

Market Research: A "Success Story"

An interesting illustration of the discrepancy between real and ideal fulfill-ment of routine activities within a scientific framework, and the resolution of this discrepancy to the members' satisfaction, is the way in which market researchers seek to establish a "scientific appraisal" of the opinions, needs, and desires of the

Adapted from paper presented by Jerry Jacobs at the Annual Meetings of the American Sociological Association, San Francisco, Calif., August 1975.

consumer with respect to a wide range of products through market surveys. These surveys are designed to offer the producer rational guidelines for marketing his products—that is, to give him some notion of which segments of society prefer his product over competing brands and why. This, in turn, it is hoped, will permit the rational organization of advertising campaigns that will lead to the successful marketing of the products. Market research need not be invoked exclusively in the name of discerning "needs"; it may also be turned to the task of how to establish "needs." An interesting example of these efforts can be found in the merchandising of over-the-counter drugs.

> There are between 100,000 and 200,000 over-the-counter products available to the bewildered customer.
> And all of them are formulated by some combination of around 200 active ingredients designed to treat about 30 easily recognized symptoms.
> The result is a fierce competition for the huge consumer market. To reach this market, drug companies are spending around $300 million a year on TV advertising alone—with the total promotional cost (including prescription drugs) in the range of $1 billion. . . . Dr. Robert Pitofsky, Director of the Bureau of Consumer Protection of the Federal Trade Commission (FTC), says that drug advertising appears "primarily directed at breaking down consumer resistance, creating consumer acceptance and developing consumer demands." [Christian Science Monitor, November 5, 1971].

A measure of the drug companies' success in this pursuit is indicated in a recent survey of over-the-counter drugs:

> "It is probable that there is an enormous waste of money, not to mention adverse health effects, from misguided consumer experimentation with health products," the study said.
> The agency said its survey of 2,914 persons in 106 communities demonstrated that the United States is an overmedicated society, that a majority of Americans view their own health care unscientifically, and that many people are gullible toward drug advertising. . . .
> Among the study's findings were the following:
> Three-quarters of the American public believe that extra vitamins provide more pep and energy, a finding the study said was "the most common of the misconceptions investigated."
> One-fifth of the public is convinced unjustifiably that cancer, arthritis and other diseases are caused at least in part by vitamin and mineral deficiencies.
> Two-thirds of the public holds the unsubstantiated belief that a daily bowel movement is essential to health.
> Three Americans in eight agreed that ads for health products must be correct or the promoters "wouldn't be allowed to say them" by such agencies as the FDA and the FTC. [New York Times, October 9, 1972]

This marketing success story is truly extraordinary in light of recent studies indicating the ineffectiveness of over-the-counter drugs. For example, a study testing the efficacy of Compoz in "relaxing" or "reducing tension" was summarized as follows by Dr. Paul Rickels, director of Psycho-Pharmacology at the

Philadelphia General Hospital, while testifying at a Senate hearing on drugs: "Neither Compoz... nor aspirin could be differentiated in terms of their clinical efficacy from an inert placebo..." (*Christian Science Monitor*, November 6, 1971). Similar findings were cited for a number of other over-the-counter drugs.

The foregoing might lead one to suppose that market research, through the conscientious application of sophisticated, scientific theoretical and methodological concepts and procedures, has indeed overcome all obstacles and provided for the rational accomplishment of agency goals implicit in the bureaucratic ideal— that is, increased sales and profits. The question presents itself: What practical activities do market researchers routinely engage in to produce these remarkable results?

Excerpts from taped interviews with two market researchers for Burp-Seltzer illustrate standard (as opposed to recommended) worker practices within three major areas: (1) The "orientation" period, (2) "random sampling" and survey neutrality, and (3) coping at the bottom. But the generalizations presented in this study are not based on a "sample of two," for accounts of these two informants are in no way unique. All of the interviewers they work with currently or have previously known have routinely engaged in the practices outlined below. I myself have, through the years, known others who have engaged in marketing research and related research practices that were similar to these. In fact, I have from time to time been asked to stand in as a "bona fide respondent." While the informants in this study are white middle-class homemakers, they refer to fellow workers who are lower-class ethnics. All pursued the same or very similar practices in the course of their "research."

A final indication of the extent and binding effects of "members' knowledge" can be had from one worker who relates how a randomly selected respondent, contacted by phone, spontaneously inquired (following the opening pitch), "Do you need more men or women?" She then went on to ask what the researcher would like her to say so that she could satisfactorily fill in the interview schedule and get paid. In short, the respondent knew what the worker knew, and because of this inside information volunteered to help the phone worker by lying: "You poor thing, I know what you must be going through. I used to do market research myself once." The following accounts, then, are offered as indicative of the general, routine, usual, everyday practices of market researchers, as viewed from the bottom up.

The "Orientation" Period

The "orientation" period for the worker who actually did the data collection and upon whose information future analysis and recommendations would be made was usually very brief and of little or no assistance in instructing the novice about acceptable survey-research procedure.

INFORMANT 1: I was quite surprised at how extremely short the briefing session was. We were supposed to be there at 2:30. The supervisor started fifteen minutes late. One of the housewives brought two of her small children with her, who played on the floor while the briefing was going on. The briefing took maybe five minutes because all she did was go over a short question-naire and read us the same question that we could read for ourselves. . . . After this very brief briefing, the ladies [who were being oriented] went home.

While each study theoretically required (and provided) an orientation period to acquaint the researcher with the format and practice of the particular survey, the successful practicing market researcher rarely attended these sessions. After all, they had little if any effect upon worker practices, and the seasoned profes-sional knew that.

INFORMANT 2: Well, you know, there is a proper way to do this [cheat at market research], and of course you have to use your own judgment. And you have to be, you know, pretty clever about it. . . . I know one woman who's been doing it [market research] for some time. . . . When she picks up a job, she doesn't even bother to go to the orientation sessions.

On a "worse than nothing" level, the orientation period served as a negative model for the new workers. As a reference point for how things "ought to be," it came back to haunt the worker, the supervisor, and the agency.

INFORMANT 2: When they first take you in for the indoctrination session, they lay out the whole job for you and tell you just what they expect and what they want, and then when you bring the job back and they feel that you've spent too much time on it, of course, they'll tell you that too. They'll say, "Gee, what do you mean ten hours for such and such? It should have taken you only five hours. Why did you spend that much time on it?" And then they look over your material and you have a lot of writing and you've put a lot of effort into it and they say, "Achhhhh! You didn't need all that stuff." And they start erasing and cutting corners. Well, then you realize that they're cheating. They're cheating Madison Avenue, or whoever gave them the job.

"Random Sampling" and Survey Neutrality

The "impartial scientific research firm" frequently paid little or no attention to accepted sampling practice in selecting respondents. As a general rule, little effort was made to minimize "skewing" and maximize "internal and external validity." Should the firm make overtures in this direction, they were routinely ignored by those who had to adhere to them if such instructions were to prove effective—that is, field personnel and supporting workers and supervisors. At-tempts to ensure that willing respondents were also appropriate respondents—

that is, that they had used the product, were not friends or relatives, and were not associated with the firm manufacturing it—were also routinely ignored. The following accounts are indicative of these abuses.

INFORMANT 1: Going back some years, I did some sampling and coding for various companies. One company, I think it was the Tarnation Company, seemed to be a little more random than, for example, this survey for Burp-Seltzer. Remember [on the latter job], they just told me to go to page 413 in the phone book and start in. Well, this happened to be names like Rosenberg, and there were like two pages of Rosenbergs—that made for a badly skewed sample. In the one I did for Tarnation some years ago, I had a phone book and I was told to go to page 552 and take every tenth name and address. That seemed to be a little more reasonable, as though it were real sampling, although it has its flaws too. Except even there, I had my own biases. If the tenth person happened to be a lawyer [informant's husband is a lawyer], I would just go down to the eleventh person and use his name. I just didn't think that lawyers needed to be bothered by a lot of dumb questions.

In the broader scheme of things, Informant 1's concern for which of many acceptable sampling procedures were invoked by the agency was, after all, academic. She did not use what she took to be the more legitimate guidelines of the Tarnation Company any more than she abided by the sampling procedures Burp-Seltzer recommended.

INFORMANT 1: I was given a large envelope [in the Burp-Seltzer survey] with my instructions on it. And my instructions said that I was to start on page 413 of the Westside phone directory and that I was to call every number except those that were toll calls. Nothing else was said about skipping or what, so I merely assumed that I had to call every single number in line unless it was a toll call. Therefore, I proceeded to do that, that night. From an interviewer's point of view, this type of thing could be very frustrating even though it is a very short schedule. Some of the problems would be people not being home, that is, no one would answer; people who did not speak English; or maids answering the phone saying that the owners of the home were away. One of the more frustrating things were numbers that were either disconnected, out of service, or had been changed. There was a great number of those—more than I would have anticipated. Out of approximately 247 calls over a period of three days I only spoke to about 90 people, possibly a few more. Of these, I only got two people who met the criteria [set up by the agency] and were willing to accept the free samples and participate in the test. I later found out that even this would not be good because both individuals lived in the same household and we could only use one of them. On the basis of past experience, I knew that interviewers do a great deal of cheating in their work. On the first day I asked one of my friends if he would cooperate in this study. On the second day I called another one of my friends and asked her if she would cooperate even though she frankly didn't use Burp-Seltzer, because her name was also on the page that I was working on.

It was not only the phone worker who ignored acceptable sampling procedures as a means of getting by; supervisors also invoked "ad hocing" procedures in order to cope.

INFORMANT 1: By the fourth day we were told to call [the office] and check in . . . at that point I complained to the supervisor by saying I was having a very difficult time and felt that the pages that I was assigned [in the phone book] were a little skewed, and that I was getting a lot of older Jewish people who could not speak English or understand what I was saying. At that point she just seemed to laugh it off and say, "Oh, well, just go on to some other page. Don't even bother with those, just flip it over." And I said, "Well, I guess I am just having a lot of hard luck." She said, "Well, frankly, if you know somebody who takes Burp-Seltzer you can use them." Since I had had a little training and experience in research I mentioned rather glibly to her that "This isn't really good sampling practice, is it?" And she didn't seem to mind about that, but it was evident to me that she was desperate for people and other people were having just as much trouble as I was, and she said, "No, it's true. It's not good sampling procedure, but we really need the people because we have to get the samples out by next week."

When I heard that, and maybe I'm reading things into it, but it almost seemed to me as though she thought I was naive for trying to stick straight to the rules that were given to me at the beginning. I contacted several friends, and even though I am not quite through with the study yet, I'm sure that by Saturday I will have completed my quota because I will just contact my friends and ask them to cooperate.

INFORMANT 2: I know a woman who has been doing this kind of work for about ten years, and she makes a very good living at it. This is her livelihood, actually, and she has a list of respondents—she takes their names and addresses down, their phone numbers—which you're not supposed to do actually; she has a file, a big file. And these people know her—she knows them. And she gives them several names, so that they go by different names. And she calls them on the phone when she gets a job—she doesn't even bother going out to see them. She tells them, "If you're called back" (a lot of these jobs are checked back on—the office calls back to spot-check to see whether you did the job properly or not), "it's such and such an office—they'll identify themselves—and you're Mrs. Smith for this particular interview," or for another interview they're maybe Mrs. Jones, or whatever, you know—so that they're forewarned in case somebody calls them.

INTERVIEWER: These aren't really all her friends, but just people that she's contacted in the course of doing market research?

INFORMANT 2: Yeh. They're not friends of hers at all. But for her it's like a little business. Her husband [who is not employed by the agency] helps her out with it. And they make a pretty nice living out of it. It's like a little business. And they work it out.

These comments are indicative of the ways in which the phone worker and supervisor were guilty of bending or breaking the rules of acceptable survey research with regard to sampling procedures and ensuring survey neutrality. In a broader sense they are also descriptive of the ways in which top- and bottom-echelon personnel invoke "ad hocing" procedures in order to cope with what both take to be the unreasonable working demands of the agency. However, it is not only (or even) unreasonable agency demands that necessitate their invoking "ad hocing" procedures. It is the research design itself, which the agency gives to the interviewer in the form of acceptable guidelines for achieving legitimate surveys, that top- and bottom-echelon workers must "adapt to." Garfinkel has dealt with this extensively in some of his earlier work (Garfinkel, 1967). Since my informants were survey workers and not supervisors, I cannot deal at length with the question of "coping at the top." However, some indication that this takes place has been noted above.

Coping at the Bottom

As I have indicated, in the name of meeting their quota and making the job "worthwhile," phone workers routinely recorded faulty information. They frequently lied or recruited their friends to lie to the follow-up field workers with respect to a series of questions designed to establish whether or not respondents had used the product in question, when, how often, and their opinion of it on a series of dimensions. The worker, in turn, reciprocated when their friends were "researching." Field workers also falsified information, adopting techniques appropriate to their work context. Such coping mechanisms were invoked by phone and field workers in what may be viewed as a system of "cost analysis," to overcome the constraints imposed upon them by the research firms and subcontractors who frequently made unrealistic appraisals of the time required to complete a survey while still adhering to acceptable research practice. As a result, interviewers and allied personnel were obliged to resort to extensive cheating in order to realize the rate of pay the firm claimed to offer.

INFORMANT 2: On the telephone jobs, that [cheating] is done by saying that you called people and nobody answered. That is legitimate [an account that will seem reasonable to the supervisor] because they know that everybody isn't going to answer when you call. If you do go down a whole page in the telephone book, or two or three pages, and you get maybe only one person who answers, this is legitimate—they expect this, so that's all right. But then again you can get maybe a half-dozen people who will answer and who will hang up. If you've got their name because you got it in the phone book, and if you can hold their attention long enough and say, "Look, I'm doing such and such, will you please cooperate with me," and if you can at least just get them to say O.K., you know, then you can go ahead and do the rest of it yourself.

INTERVIEWER: You mean, make up an interview as if you had talked to them?

INFORMANT 2: Yeh, yeh.

INTERVIEWER: Can you, do you, contact friends to help you, and if so, how does that work?

INFORMANT 2: Well, a lot of the jobs that are given out, or rather, I should say most of the jobs that are given out, you are told not to use your friends or relatives for respondents because they feel that it would be too biased. So most of the researchers, of course, don't pay any attention to this at all. . . . I know of several interviewers who do this. And they have a large list—oh, they belong to organizations, and they go to club meetings and they know everybody in the meeting and they usually come with their pad and their interviews [interview schedules], and they bother everybody there at the meeting and ask them to respond. And they get their interviews done that way. So they sometimes will go to a meeting . . . where there are maybe fifty women, and they will corral maybe fifteen or twenty of them and get their job done in an hour where it might have taken them three days to do it in. And then they can send in a bill for three days' work. So there are all different ways of working at this.

INTERVIEWER: Do you sometimes work with other interviewers on a study?

INFORMANT 2: A lot of the interviewers will work with each other. When they're running into tough situations they will call each other—if they get to know each other—and try to help each other out that way. Also, before they hand a job in, they will check with each other to find out how many hours they put down so that it is always pretty much the same. . . . There was a whole group of women I knew that knew each other, and they would, at the end of the job, call each other up and say, well, how many hours did you put down for this job? And maybe she would say forty hours and the other one would say, "Oh, I put down forty-five." Well, that's all right—you know, about five hours' difference—or another one said she put in thirty-eight. That way they felt they were always within a certain range.

The informants related many other ways in which workers "work" each other, work for each other, and "work" the agency. However, space does not allow for a detailed consideration of all of these variations.

Conclusions

We have seen how supervisors and other training personnel, in the name of staying within monetary constraints or meeting deadlines, implied or openly suggested to the worker that she bend science a bit—that is, ignore instructions but present the data as if she had not. In light of the routine nature of these practices, it does not seem unreasonable to suppose that if the phone interviewer, follow-up field worker, and supervisor were all guilty of "ad hocing" in the name of such pragmatic pursuits as "meeting goals," "padding bills," and "making deadlines," others in the organizational hierarchy (for example, those who code and analyze the data, write it up for presentation, or design programs and strategies based upon the findings) may also have been guilty of transgressions. Indeed, Garfinkel suggests that "ad hocing" is a general phenomenon. Support for this contention is noted below:

INTERVIEWER: What percentage of all of the offices that you worked for do you think were doing market research more or less legitimately?

INFORMANT 2: Well, I didn't work for too many, but I would say that out of, oh, maybe half a dozen, only one was legitimate. The majority of them are not.

If we mean by "legitimate" that the survey research firm provides an orientation period for new and tried workers; that workers attend these sessions; that the orientation period is successful in orienting the worker to acceptable survey research practice; that lower- and higher-echelon personnel do not falsify their data or suggest to others that they falsify it; that the research design is sound in terms of established survey research practice; and finally that the research design is such that it allows, in principle and in fact, the workers to pursue and accomplish its goals without intentionally or inadvertently invoking "ad hocing" procedures—then I would suggest that 0 out of 6 would be a more accurate estimate than 1 out of 6, for marketing research firms able to fulfill these goals.

We have noted some of marketing research's successes. What about the failures? Marketing research firms and their customers feel much the same as hospitals, courts, universities, and other people-processing agencies; that is, they are much freer to acknowledge their successes than their failures. This is not surprising. Goffman (1967) has astutely observed the heroic efforts that interacting individuals are prepared to undertake in order to avoid embarrassment. Lemert (1962) also gives an excellent description of how organizations seek to avoid embarrassment in his portrayal of how they simultaneously go about manufacturing and managing in-house paranoids.

That such organizational embarrassments sometimes occur for marketing research firms and their customers is noted in an article (*Wall Street Journal,* 1975) describing a lawsuit filed by Time, Inc., against its marketing-research firm, charging that "a study prepared by W. R. Simmons and Associates Research, Inc., contained 'biased and unreliable statistics.'" As a result, Time asked the court to hold that it should not have to pay the $188,346 it was billed for Simmons's service. More important than the outcome of the suit itself is the wider implication. According to one advertising agency executive (who preferred to remain anonymous), the suit has "opened up a Pandora's box on the question of such surveys' validity."

Given the worker practices outlined above, it should come as no great surprise that marketing research sometimes fails. What is surprising is that it ever succeeds. The question arises: How do we explain the apparent successes if they are not a result of rational guidelines laid down by market research and workers' strict adherence to them?

Perhaps spending a billion dollars a year on the advertising of prescription and over-the-counter drugs, an expense the consumer absorbs, is enough to ensure some measure of success, however ineptly the money is spent. Perhaps top-echelon decision makers, while they pay for these surveys, routinely ignore their recommendations and base their marketing decisions on other criteria. Here, as in most cases, it is easy to speculate. In order to answer this question we must "await further research." Let us hope that we have not long to wait.

References

Christian Science Monitor, November 5, 1971, p. 3.
Christian Science Monitor, November 6, 1971, p. 5.
Emerson, Joan, "Nothing Unusual Is Happening," paper read at the September 1969 Annual Meeting of the American Sociological Association.
Garfinkel, Harold, *Studies in Ethnomethodology*, Englewood Cliffs, N.J.: Prentice-Hall, 1967, pp. 186–207.
Goffman, Erving, *Interaction Ritual*, Garden City, N.Y.: Doubleday Anchor, 1967, p. 99.
Jacobs, Jerry, "Symbolic Bureaucracy: A Case Study of a Social Welfare Agency," *Social Forces* 47, no. 4 (June 1969): 413–422.
Jacobs, Jerry, "A Phenomenological Study of Suicide Notes," *Social Problems* 15, no. 1 (Summer 1967): 60–72.
Lemert, Edwin, "Paranoia and the Dynamics of Exclusion," *Sociometry* 25, no. 1 (March 1962): 1–20.
New York Times, October 9, 1972, pp. 1, 13.
Wall Street Journal, January 16, 1975, p. 8.

CASE STUDY B

Symbolic Bureaucracy: A Case Study of a Social Welfare Agency

Bureaucratization offers above all the optimum possibility for carrying through the principle of specializing administrative functions according to purely objective considerations. Individual performance is allocated to functionaries who have specialized training and who by constant practice learn more and more. The "objective" *discharge of business* primarily means a discharge of business, according to Calculable Rules and "without regard for persons."[1]

Weber's classic analysis of bureaucracy is largely responsible for sociology's general orientation toward the subject.[2] His presentation rests primarily upon the construction of an "ideal type" where it is assumed that the organization best approximating the central conditions of an ideal bureaucracy will function with the greatest efficiency and that any increase in deviation from the ideal type will be accompanied by a decrease in efficiency. The basic conditions of Weber's model as given by Blau are as follows:

1. "The regular activities required for the purpose of the organization are distributed in a fixed way as official duties." The clear-cut division of labor makes it possible to employ only specialized experts in each particular position.
2. "The organization of offices follows the principle of hierarchy; that is, each lower office is under the control and supervision of a higher one."

Adapted from Jerry Jacobs, "Symbolic Bureaucracy: A Case Study of a Social Welfare Agency," *Social Forces* 47 (June 1969): pp. 413–422.

3. Operations are governed "by a consistent system of abstract rules . . . [and] consist of the application of these rules to particular cases." This system of standards is designed to ensure uniformity in performance of every task, regardless of the number of persons engaged in it.
4. "The ideal official conducts his office . . . [in] a spirit of formalistic impersonality, 'Sine ira et studio,' without hatred or passion, and hence without affection or enthusiasm."
5. Employment in a bureaucracy is based on technical qualifications and is protected from arbitrary dismissal. "It constitutes a career. There is a system of promotions according to seniority or achievement, or both."[3]

Blau sees this model as faced with several dilemmas—for example, maintaining a hierarchy of command without submitting subordinates to feelings of inequality and anxiety, coping with anomie while retaining standardization, maintaining hierarchy and close supervision without causing resentment in a democratic culture, and providing for social cohesion while maintaining impersonality.[4] His findings in *Bureaucracy in Modern Society*, and the findings of others, led Blau to take issue with Weber on the point that unofficial change is inherently detrimental.[5]

Blau contends that unofficial change may increase or decrease administrative efficiency.[6] He refers to unofficial change which expedites administrative functions, reduces the dilemma inherent in the "ideal type," and does not prove detrimental to the attainment of the organization's objectives as "adjustive development." This process is one of gratification through self-imposed rules, unofficially created and mutually subscribed to by the subordinate group. So long as this fully internalized system provides a rigorous standard of workmanship, increases efficiency, and does not violate the organization's intent, its effects will be beneficial. What must be guarded against is the acceptance of a policy that is detrimental to efficiency or the achievement of organizational ends, since this too may develop through unofficial change. Blau recognizes this danger and in several instances enjoins the administrator to be ever-watchful. However, conspicuously absent is a description of what to watch for or how to watch for it. Blau deals with the problem in these terms:

> To establish such a pattern of self-adjustment in a bureaucracy, conditions must prevail that encourage its members to cope with emergent problems and to find the best method for producing specified results on their own initiative, and that obviate the need for unofficial practices which thwart the objectives of the organization, such as restriction of output. What are these conditions? We do not have sufficient empirical evidence to give a conclusive answer to this question. But some tentative hypotheses can be advanced, although these must be qualified by the recognition that the same conditions may not be required for adjustive development in other cultures or in other historical periods.[7]

As I see it, the problem is not so much what conditions are necessary for the achievement of adjustive development as how to recognize them if they exist. I find this question especially troublesome since my own observations and experiences with "bureaucracy" have convinced me that it is possible for an organization to conform barely or not at all to the conditions of bureaucracy while maintaining an image of complete adherence to bureaucratic ideals. Such situations will hereafter be referred to as "symbolic bureaucracy." Under these conditions, the relative success of the organization in realizing its ends efficiently would not easily be subject to accurate assessment, either by the agency's administrative personnel or by the outside observer. It was just such a situation that I witnessed as a participant-observer in a year-long study of a unit of a public welfare department.

The following discussion is, in one sense at least, not intended as a critique. I would agree with Blau that a strict adherence to Weber's ideal type would render "bureaucracy" inoperative and that unofficial change is a necessary addition, at least to save Weber. Whether or not bureaucracy is saved as well by this addition remains to be seen. It is this aspect of Blau's thesis that I feel warrants attention. It is my contention that implicit in Blau's hopeful position toward the utilization of unofficial change in the furtherance of administrative efficiency is the possibility of destroying the necessary conditions of bureaucracy (if ever they existed) while retaining an image of complete adherence to bureaucratic ideals. If such a state is achieved, the basic elements of a functioning bureaucracy cease to exist, while at the same time the organization is unaware of any apparent deviation from the bureaucratic principles which seem to govern operating procedures. There would exist no objective criteria to discern the positive or negative effects of unofficial change since no significant change would be apparent. Since the organizational arrangement was defined at the start as a bureaucracy, everyone concerned would remain convinced that it was continuing as one. The possibility of such an organization's fulfilling its goals would actually be more random than "rational." The department I studied closely approximates an instance of "symbolic bureaucracy." The following discussion will concern itself with whether or not this department functioned within what Blau considered to be the four most essential conditions for bureaucracy: specialization, hierarchy of authority, system of rules, and impersonality.[8]

Specialization

Did specialization exist within the department? The only prerequisite for taking the civil service examination for the position of "social caseworker" was a college degree, and even this had not always been the case. Professionality was not a prerequisite. It is true that anyone passing the exam and "placed" was by definition a caseworker. However, this did not presuppose any professional schooling, training, or experience in the methods of casework. Very few persons holding a master of social welfare degree were employed by the agency. Most "caseworkers" at the agency were historians, artists, sociologists, etc. Commendable as this liberal hiring policy may have been, it did not constitute specialization.

One can achieve a better grasp of this lack of specialization at the agency and/or the need for it by briefly describing the duties of the caseworker. These involved essentially two tasks: determining eligibility, and dispensing services to eligible clients according to agency policy. The determination of eligibility rested primarily upon a consideration of residency and the availability of other resources. If an applicant had not lived in the state for at least a year, he could not establish residency and was by definition ineligible for aid, notwithstanding his needs or his inability to meet them in other ways.[9] Then, too, if he had income available from other resources—relatives, outside income, real property— sufficient to maintain himself according to the minimum set forth by the county, he was again ineligible for service. If he could prove residency *and* show that he was temporarily unable to support himself through no fault of his own, he was eligible for aid. The point to keep in mind here is that since it was primarily the client's problem to prove to the worker's satisfaction his eligibility according to these criteria, it required little skill or insight on the part of the worker to decide whether or not the client met the criteria. It was not surprising to find that many other persons in the agency holding offices lower in the hierarchy than "caseworker" could easily have fulfilled this function, given its demands.

The second duty of the caseworker—dispensing to the eligible client the various services prescribed by the agency—was not a task requiring any special skill or insight either. Assistance took one of several forms, and which of the available options was offered to the client and for how long were often left to the discretion of the worker. (This was a matter not of agency policy but of worker policy.) Clients were eligible for assistance in the form of bus tokens for transportation, rent payments on an apartment ($30 to $45 per month), plus a food allowance of $30 per month, or $1 per day payment in scrip for "hotel accommodations" and $1 a day in scrip for food, or, in place of any of the above, "camp." "Camps" were located in outlying districts and constituted a kind of ghetto. One found at "camp" food, lodging, medical assistance, and the company of persons in similar circumstances—that is, indigent single males. Little else was to be found there that is generally associated with a "normal" outside environment. "Camp" was, then, a "total institution," subject to all the ramifications of that form of society.[10] It was considered by the client the least desirable option in a series of services offered by the agency. Very few clients intended or desired to go to "camp."

Fulfilling the duties of a caseworker in the department required little expertise that could not have been mustered by many, if not most, of the agency's noncaseworkers. For example, going down the scale from caseworker, there was the position of mailboy. Many of the mailboys could have administered the duties of a caseworker, while any of the caseworkers could have doubled as mailboys. Clerk-typists had no special training beyond being semiproficient typists. Many caseworkers in my office were better typists than the "clerk-typists," and I have small doubt that some of the latter could have performed as caseworkers. In fact, one such woman, who received her B.A. degree from a local college a few months after my arrival (having attended night school for several years), did receive a position as caseworker in the agency. The transition was noteworthy. On Friday she was a "clerk-typist." The following Monday she returned to work as a "social caseworker."

Going up the scale from caseworker, there was the supervisor, who also had no professional schooling and came up "through the ranks." She knew more of company policy than her subordinates, but functionally this was inconsequential since it was not on company policy that the organization ran, unless it was particularly expedient for the worker. When the supervisor left on vacation, a subordinate assumed the position of supervisor for two or three weeks at a time, and no change in the unit or in the organization in general was evident beyond a marked increase in morale. So long as persons occupying positions upscale and down in the hierarchy were, to a large extent, functionally interchangeable, there was little real evidence of specialization or expertise. There was only a division of labor, conveniently mistaken for specialization in the name of expediency.

Hierarchy of Authority

Consider now a hierarchy of authority, the second condition of bureaucracy. Was this condition operative at the welfare department? Obvious at the outset is a chain of command ranging from subordinate or superordinate. However, what did these rankings actually mean? For example, our immediate superior, the supervisor, held a unit meeting every week or so, as the fancy took her, where a long list of new policies, directives, and form changes were aired. This was followed by a question-and-answer period, in which all seemed to participate earnestly. An outside observer might suppose the existence of a keen interest on the part of the workers and that a great effort was being made by them to remember these changes and institute them as company policy. However, no change in working procedures (from the workers' perspective) occurred as a result of these meetings and discussions during my year on the job.

There were, of course, the indispensable duties of the higher-echelon members, who could be seen at any time of the day staring out the window of an outer office or conversing in the cafeteria over tea. The inactivity of higher-ranking agency personnel was not necessarily a function of lack of interest or industry but was rather a by-product of the lack of essential duties. Parkinson's Law applied fully here. The most single important function of members of this group, in terms of the daily routine operations of the organization, was to affix their signatures to the many quadruplicate copies of official paper that passed through their offices. Once this operation was set in motion, the process was automatic. The paper work continued through an increasing chain of command, members at each level presumably giving their consideration and approval, when, in reality, they contributed little more than their signatures. It was true that the supervisor's signature was required on all cases to ensure proper adherence to company policy. The supervisor actually did review the cases and, as a matter of fact, was very conscientious in pursuing her duties. However, as I have already noted, the supervisor's considered opinion seems to have had little influence upon whether or not worker practices conformed to the agency policies.

Since the heads of command contributed little to any actual change in the organization's working procedures, their position as policy makers held little import for the worker or client. As persons responsible for checking on and improving the decisions of the lower echelons, they were to a large extent operationally superfluous. In sum, the organization gave every appearance of maintaining a vital and necessary formalized hierarchy, but in reality it is difficult to imagine how this hierarchy of command could have justified its existence in the name of increased organizational efficiency.

Rules

Did the agency have a set of standardized rules to which its members referred in making decisions, a code that would ensure standardization of administration and provide for impartial and unbiased service? A cursory search revealed the "welfare and institutions code," which, having presumably anticipated every contingency, had set down in an orderly and precise manner the way in which the worker was to expedite company business as it arose: which forms, for which case, how many copies, and with or without notary. What function did these tomes play? Were they taken as gospel, or was each worker seeking his own salvation? A few examples that could be extended many times in this agency setting will give some indication.

It is possible for the worker to handle only a certain number of cases at a given time. When this "caseload" was exceeded, as it often was, it became the sole objective of the caseworker to dispose of the excess, in any way possible. The organization actually encouraged this activity, for the "best" worker was the one who "expedited" the greatest number of cases per unit time. Since the supervisor had to read and approve all cases to ensure adherence to company policy, the solution to the problem of disposing of excess cases had to come within the limits of action provided by the rules. This would seem to ensure impartiality to the client and the standardization of agency procedures. The fact is that it did not. For example, in interviewing the client, the worker was asked to list on a form provided for the purpose all persons who might be of some assistance to the client. Such persons were then contacted by letter or phone. The case remained open until answers to such inquiries had been obtained. If none was forthcoming, a second letter was sent. This process might have been expected to continue for weeks, during which time the worker was to aid the client and as a consequence was unable to "expedite" the case. As a result of this situation, an interview might take the following form:

WORKER: Are there any persons who might contribute to your support, Mr. Jones?

CLIENT: Yes, twelve: four cousins, my mother, father, and six brothers, all out of town. But I doubt that they will help me.

WORKER: (Records answer: None. Mother and father deceased. No friends or relatives to contribute to support.)

When reviewed by the supervisor, this case would give no indication of a breach of the rules. The supervisor had never met the client, the questions were asked, the answers given, and the spaces on the form appropriately filled. Everything would seem to be in order. With this obstacle out of the way, the worker was now in a position to "expedite" the case as best he could, within the limits of the "rules." He was no longer subject to that particular constraint.

As another example of the way in which workers succeeded in "expediting" cases, persons with hospital appointments were to be aided until such appointments had been completed. This presented the worker with another type of case that was impossible to "turn over." On interviewing a new client, the worker would ask: "Are you in good health and have you any hospital appointments, Mr. Jones?" The answer might be: "I have an ear infection and my first appointment is in two weeks." The worker experiences a temporary setback, but there are still the impartial and equitable rules to refer to which require the client to show an appointment slip as proof of the appointment.

WORKER: Have you your appointment slip, Mr. Jones?

CLIENT: No, it was stolen with my wallet last night.

WORKER: (Records answer: Mr. Jones has no hospital appointments and is apparently in fair health.)

This is yet another instance of overcoming the constraints of the rules and maneuvering a case into position for a quick turnover. The appearance is of meeting the rules and the reality is of beating them. Space permitting, I could extend this list to include violations of a great many other routine "casework" procedures at the agency. The fact is that the rules were essentially meaningless with respect to their ability to standardize operating procedures and ensure adherence to company policy.

The illustrations given above were of the consistent-lie variety. They were one means of "working" the rules and were part of the process by which the fiction "symbolic bureaucracy" was created and perpetuated. Another method was to use acceptable exceptions to the rules. For example, the rules stated that caseworkers were to come to work professionally attired. This meant, for males, wearing a tie but not a festive sport shirt, an open collar, or sandals. As a result, a typical exchange might have taken the following form:

SUPERVISOR: Mr. B., why are you wearing sandals? Are you going to the beach?

(As a matter of fact, this is precisely what Mr. B. and a co-worker had in mind for the afternoon, but it would never do to explain the sandals.)

WORKER: (Chuckles) No, Mrs. L., I have a toe infection and my podiatrist requires me to wear this ridiculous footwear lest I lose my toe.

SUPERVISOR: Oh, I'm sorry to hear of your illness, Mr. B. It isn't contagious, is it?

To indulge in such a system of lies and acceptable exceptions was to provide for individual subjectivity regarding personal action toward co-workers and especially clients, while indulging all outsiders in the illusion of abiding by the impartiality ensured by the rules. If one persisted in the process over time, he became convinced that this state of affairs (whatever it was), not bureaucracy, was the "given," and proceeded accordingly. Since the new worker soon reevaluated the nature of his task from that of learning and doing bureaucracy to that of learning to do in bureaucracy, and since he succeeded in doing this in such a way that those who had defined their task as establishing and perpetuating bureaucracy would not recognize the difference, everyone was happy. Both sets of persons were convinced that they were achieving their desired goals. The result is that whether we take Weber's conception of bureaucracy or Blau's, it may well be the case that neither exists, when either and/or both seem to.

Impersonality

The last condition, that of impersonality between ranks, was perhaps the one phase of bureaucracy best adhered to. This did not exclude favoritism. But such cases were not overt and, because of the potential embarrassment in having them pointed out, were few in number. However, this generalization did not hold so well in the relationship between worker and client. Since it was actually within the worker's discretion to aid the client or not, independently of rules, those clients exhibiting belligerent attitudes were soon "straightened out," while those who created the impression of the "nice guy" stood a better chance.

One method of "straightening out" the client was to offer him "camp." This was, after all, one of the agency's legitimate services, and it was left to the option of the worker to offer "camp" sooner instead of later in the event it became expedient. "Camp," because of its unpopularity among the clients, was a very popular option for the overburdened worker looking for ways to "expedite cases." If the client, having been given "outside" help for a week or so, was unsuccessful in finding employment (as most were), he could be offered "camp" as a way of either "straightening him out," in the case of a particularly troublesome client, or, in a more neutral vein, simply disposing of the case. If the client refused this service, he was free to seek service elsewhere and the case was closed. This was one way for the worker to "work" the client.

On the other hand, this procedure caused something of a dilemma for the worker. Because of the popularity of this form of assistance among the workers and the limited number of spaces at "camp" facilities, there was often a long waiting list. The worker was obliged to assist the client "outside," if he accepted "camp" as a form of aid, until a "camp" opening became available. The clients came to know this. Indeed, many of them knew agency policy better than the "caseworkers" did. This, of course, provided the client with a way of "working" the worker. The client had only to accept "camp," be assisted outside until his turn on the "camp" list appeared, and then not show up for placement. The case was then closed with one of the two epitaphs "whereabouts unknown" or "refusal to accept assistance." The client was temporarily without assistance, but he might show up at the agency in a week or two and, having been assigned to a new worker, report that he "fell ill" on the day of the "camp" appointment. It was now for the new worker to turn over the case as best his experience or lack of it allowed, within the guidelines provided by the agency.

There were many such transactions between worker and client that were characterized by the reciprocal act of "conning," followed by a period of "cooling out the mark."[11] In fact, so subtle had these unofficial transactions become, and so skillful the participants, that it was often very difficult to establish who had been the "mark." For example, in the instance described above, it was, after all, the client who sought out the worker, and the subordinate standing of the client in this relationship placed him at a distinct disadvantage in trying to "work" the worker. In the situation of offering "camp," another member of the agency, referred to as the "camp man," was interposed between worker and client. The "camp man," who was in charge of administering "camp" placements, was very popular among the workers, since it was left to his discretion (again, not according to agency policy but according to worker policy) to assign "camp" dates to clients. In the case of a particularly difficult client, the worker had only to enlist the aid of the "camp man," who could be relied upon to "unexpectedly" uncover an available placement for the client by moving his name forward on the list.

In short, the worker had greater resources available to him within the agency than were available to the client. This handicap did not prevent the client from trying to manage his affairs as best he could under the circumstances. Indeed, it is more than an idle proverb that "necessity is the mother of invention." The very disadvantage of his position with respect to the worker, and the necessity of overcoming it, provided a strong and constant source of motivation toward invention. For example, bus tokens were another source of assistance to enable the client to get to and from the agency and to investigate possible employment opportunities. The client's task became one of talking the worker out of as many tokens as possible. There were many approaches to this problem. Perhaps the most common was to draw up a long list of appointments with prospective employers and, in one way or another, try to convince the worker of their legitimacy. Having secured as many tokens as possible, the client had only to walk to the nearest bus stop and sell them at a cut rate to persons waiting for a bus. He could thereby unofficially enlist the agency's help in raising his subsidy.

The worker in time became aware of this procedure and, depending upon his predilections toward the client that day, would dispense or withhold bus tokens accordingly.

Another unofficial transaction took place between the client and his local merchant. The task here was to negotiate the exchange of scrip for wine, a commodity that the scrip was specifically designed to exclude the client from purchasing. The transaction generally required little effort on the part of the client. It simply meant that the merchant, in exchange for this service, would charge the client more than the usual retail price for wine. In short, the client found that food scrip and tokens were negotiable, but only at a disadvantaged rate of exchange. While the merchant and the public at large had managed to negotiate a "good deal" at the expense of the client, the client was at least partially consoled by the knowledge that he had once again "worked" the worker. The public's resourcefulness in negotiating favorable rates of exchange in "tokens" has recently taken on the aspect of big business. An article in the *Wall Street Journal* notes:

> If you can stand a guilt-edged investment, go long on subway tokens.
> Subway riders—and many non-riders—are doing that here, hoarding the 20-cent tokens as a hedge against a fare increase. Speculation has become so rampant than many of the 840 token-short booths are limiting sales to one or two at a time. . . .
> Its shortage is so acute that 5 million new tokens have been ordered. A transit man estimates that 29 million tokens are in circulation—but that 7 million are held by hoarders. Normally the agency has a stockpile of 6 million tokens; now it has practically none.
> One Wall Street broker, for example, began buying tokens two years ago when they cost 15 cents: he made a handsome profit when the fare was increased by a nickel. . . . The farsighted broker who says he's no longer hoarding concedes that he never was in it for the money. "Token hoarding is peanuts," he says, "but it's a matter of principle to try to stay ahead of the game."[12]

I need hardly point out that such dealings were unlikely to instill basic trust into the worker-client relationship. In fact, there were in these agency transactions what can generally be described as mutual suspension of trust. This is not to say that all clients and workers spent all their efforts at conning each other. Some clients, after all, did use their bus tokens to reach prospective employers in search of work. Some clients may have even been teetotalers. Caseworkers, within the constraints of the "caseload," sometimes assisted the clients according to the intent of agency policy. However, because of the characteristics of the general population of persons seeking assistance from this particular department of the agency, these practices on the part of the client and worker were common. Most of the clients seen at the agency were unskilled, unemployed single men, generally in poor health, nonteetotalers, isolated residents of "skid row," and generally unemployable. In my year on the job I can recall only three clients who were sent for "rehabilitation" by the workers of my unit. Some clients did find work. Others spent time in and out of "camp," while many moved to other locales. However, there was a hard core of clients whose case records went back many years. These were on what could be described as a "revolving account." No one at the agency, least of all the clients, believed that agency services would suffice to extricate them from this situation. For these clients, the practices and procedures described above had become a way of life.

Workers were not always unsympathetic toward clients. An example of caseworker sympathy for the lot of the client, even when the latter had officially placed himself outside the pale, is as follows: Clients at "camp" were allowed to accept farm employment outside of "camp." They were not required to do so and might refuse such work when it was offered. Many took this course. This was not surprising when one realized that the client, once he had accepted a farm job, had to pay for his own transportation to and from "camp," his meals on the job, and any other operating expenses for the day. Because of this, the low wages paid, and the fact that clients were not steadily employed at farm work and were not in the best physical condition, such employment often amounted to working a long hard day for a net gain of a dollar or two. One might better stay at "camp" and recuperate. Not everyone thought this way, however, and some welcomed the opportunity to get away from "camp" and make some "spending money." If an individual elected to accept farm work, he had to show up on the job at the appointed time and work the day. If he did not, it was considered a case of "refusal to accept assistance" or "whereabouts unknown," and he became temporarily ineligible for all aid, "camp" included. In one instance, a group of men at "camp" contracted to work at a farm picking vegetables. When the trucks transporting the clients arrived, they found they were asked to pick a vegetable other than that for which they had contracted. Picking is a specialized task. Picking one kind of fruit or vegetable can be very different from picking another variety. As a result, those familiar with one kind of work cannot even cover expenses if required to do another. Because of this, the men refused to work. The agency took the position that the men had refused services and were ineligible for aid in or out of "camp." A list of these clients was circulated to the agencies in the surrounding districts so as to alert the caseworkers who might otherwise have unwittingly assisted them. The workers upon hearing of this expressed general indignation at what they felt constituted an arbitrary and unjust act on the part of the agency. Some threatened to take it up with the union, while others threatened to write an exposé. To the best of my knowledge, nothing was ever done. However, it was an example of the caseworkers as a group expressing sympathy for the clients as a group, even when the latter had acted contrary to agency policy.

Conclusions

The foregoing are only a few examples of the many discrepancies between the real and the apparent workings of one "bureaucratic" organization. If a list of actual worker practices at the agency were compared to a list of supposed worker practices and the discrepancies were evaluated for how they affected the workings of bureaucracy, I believe that little more than an image of bureaucracy would remain. Since the actual operation of the agency seems not to have been according to bureaucratic principles, it would be an area of interest for future research to determine in what manner it *is* operating. I say "is" because I doubt that worker practices have changed very much, despite changes in agency policy that may have occurred with time. It was the opinion of some of the long-established workers at the time (there were not many because of the considerable turnover in agency personnel at the "caseworker" level) that things have not changed for many years in the sense that workers' policy was designed to meet workers' needs as opposed to clients' or agency needs.

I would agree with Blau that deviation from the "ideal type" is necessary to contend with the dilemmas outlined at the beginning, such as having a hierarchy of command and not generating feelings of inequity and anxiety, and, more specifically, to meet the obvious objection that in this agency the conditions described by the "ideal type" are nowhere to be found. However, in introducing "adjustive development," it becomes crucial to discern which unofficial changes are beneficial and which are detrimental, if we are to be able to save Blau's dynamic bureaucracy. This presents us with a dilemma that seems to have thus far received little attention. I would suggest that unofficial positive change cannot easily be distinguished from unofficial negative change and that in providing for the one, we must contend with the other. The real problem lies in the fact that it is possible to institute unofficial change while maintaining the appearance of no change at all. If the change is not discernible, it is impossible to subject it to criteria which will allow for the recognition and retention of beneficial change while guarding against the unknowing acceptance of detrimental change. It seems unlikely that bureaucracy will be saved by introducing the notion of "unofficial change" as long as persons within the organization (or outsiders looking in) find it difficult, as they must, to assess whether they are operating in a bureaucracy (or ever were) or whether they have lapsed into a state of "symbolic bureaucracy."

Notes

1. From Max Weber, *Essays in Sociology*, trans. by H. H. Gerth and C. Wright Mills, New York: Oxford University Press, 1946, p. 215.
2. Ibid., pp. 196–244.
3. Peter M. Blau, *Bureaucracy in Modern Society*, New York: Random House, 1956, pp. 28–30.
4. Ibid., pp. 59–60.
5. Ibid., p. 36.
6. Ibid., p. 57.

7. Ibid., p. 61.

8. Ibid., p. 19.

9. *Montgomery* vs. *Burns* declared state residency requirements unconstitutional in the state of California (April 19, 1968). This case is now on appeal from the U.S. Ninth District Court, Northern California, to the U.S. Supreme Court.

10. Erving Goffman, *Asylums*, Garden City, N.Y.: Doubleday Anchor, 1961, pp. 1–124.

11. Erving Goffman, "On Cooling the Mark Out: Some Aspects of Adaptation to Failure," *Psychiatry* 15 (1952): 451–463.

12. *Wall Street Journal*, January 16, 1968, p. 1.

CASE STUDY C

A Phenomenological Study of Suicide Notes

Suicide notes offer an invaluable source of insight by providing us with an unsolicited account of the victim's thoughts and emotions regarding his intended act and, often, what he felt was responsible for it.[1] A study of suicide in Philadelphia by Tuckman, Kleiner, and Lavell reveals that of the 742 suicides which occurred between 1951 and 1955, notes were left in 24 percent of the cases.[2] Shneidman and Farberow note that in each year of a ten-year period (1945 to 1954), from 12 to 15 percent of those committing suicide in Los Angeles County left suicide notes.[3]

There seems to be no significant difference in social, mental, or physical condition between persons who leave notes and those who do not.[4] With few exceptions, suicide notes are coherent.[5]

Tuckman et al. further acknowledge: "the writers were impressed with the possibility that in a number of cases, the suicide could have resulted from a conscious 'rational' decision . . . although, to a lesser extent, unconscious factors may have been operating."[6] Having analyzed 112 notes of persons successful in suicide in the Los Angeles area, I also was taken with their rational and coherent character. These conscious, rational factors were after all obvious in the notes themselves, whereas the unconscious factors to a lesser extent "may have been operating."

Most theories of suicide make some provision for both psychic and environ-

---

Adapted from Jerry Jacobs, "A Phenomenological Study of Suicide Notes," *Social Problems* 15, no. 1 (Summer 1967): 60–72. Copyright © 1967 by the Society for the Study of Social Problems; reprinted by permission of the Society.

mental factors. But whereas environmental factors are often cited and categorized by those who analyze suicide notes, no one has offered an explanation of psychic factors which can be verified by the notes themselves. The psychic formulations of psychiatrists and psychologists are always of an inferred nature.

I believe that an explanation of suicide can be empirically derived from the notes themselves without the necessity of referring to a synthetic outside system. There is no need to proceed in the traditional fashion, either imputing meaning to the notes or, since there are an infinite number of categorical distinctions to be made, categorizing them on whatever common sense ground strike the analyst as potentially "fruitful" or expedient (for example, demographic, environmental, physical, or psychological categories). A description of suicidal motivation and the experiences and thought processes involved in acquiring it is not likely to be arrived at without some broader theoretical perspective which in turn is given some empirical validation by the notes themselves. I intend to offer such a formulation after first briefly considering some sociological theories of suicide.

Sociological Theories of Suicide

A full-scale critique of previous sociological theories of suicide is beyond the scope of this discussion. However, by way of giving some general indication of how my formulation differs from others, it may be noted that the theories of Durkheim, Gibbs and Martin, Henry and Short, and Powell[7] have in common the fact that they are based on an analysis of official suicide rates which they attempt to explain by imputing meaning to the correlations found to exist between the rates and certain social conditions. They are not based on actual cases of suicidal persons, their beliefs, or their writings.

Some of these theories incorporate psychological and psychoanalytical notions as well. Durkheim, for example, was aware that if social norms were to act as a constraint, they must ultimately be internalized. Having acknowledged this, however, he did not involve himself in how this was to be accomplished. The formulation presented here not only recognizes that norms must be internalized if they are to constrain the individual (or inversely, that the constraints of internalized norms must be overcome if one is to act contrary to them) but sets forth the process whereby this is accomplished. It also views suicide as a social fact, with antecedents in previous social facts. It differs from Durkheim's formulation in that it undertakes to establish these previous social facts through the analysis of suicide notes.

Basis of the Formulation

This formulation is based on two main sources: the notes left by 112 adults and adolescents who succeeded in suicide in the Los Angeles area, and insights gained through participation in a two-and-a-half-year study of adolescent suicide attempters.[8]

A sampling of the suicide notes, from various categories identified by the author, will be analyzed and discussed within a theoretical framework designed to account for the conscious deliberations that take place before the individual is able to execute the act of suicide and for the broader context of what the individual must experience in order to become capable of these deliberations. The notes provide the basis for the formulation and, at the same time, offer a means of verifying it. It is my belief that such verification is not contingent upon these particular notes but that any set of notes collected from the same cultural environment would do as well.

The key to this formulation is the concept of trust violation and how the individual accomplishes it while remaining convinced that he is a trusted person. This is taken from Donald Cressey's classic work on embezzlement, *Other People's Money*.[9] In its final form, the hypothesis reads:

> Trusted persons become trust violators when they conceive of themselves as having a financial problem which is non-sharable, are aware that this problem can be secretly resolved by violation of the position of financial trust, and are able to apply to their own conduct in that situation verbalizations which enable them to adjust their conceptions of themselves as users of the entrusted funds or property.[10]

This concept of trust violation is here extended to the act of suicide—the individual's violation of the sacred trust of life—and to the verbalizations he must entertain in order to reconcile the image of himself as a trusted person with this act of trust violation. An excellent source of data for this undertaking is the transcribed accounts of these verbalizations found in suicide notes. Here the similarity with Cressey's work ends, since the method I used in studying suicides is not one of analytic induction.

Both suicides and suicide attempters are considered. The events and processes leading to these acts are held to be equatable within the following definitions of these terms: an act is considered to be a suicide attempt only if death was intended but did not result. This excludes persons "attempting suicide" with the intent of using the "attempt" as an attention-getting device, a manipulative technique, and so on. Such attempts may miscarry and result in death, just as persons genuinely attempting suicide may, through some fortuitous circumstance, continue to live. This in no way alters their intent or the experiences that led them to entertain the verbalizations necessary for establishing this intent. It is in this sense that suicide and suicide attempts are considered by the author to be synonymous.

The three categories of suicides, suicide attempters, and attention seekers were distinguished from one another in the following way. The authors of the 112 notes to be discussed in this case study were all considered to be suicides on the basis of a designation assigned to them by the Los Angeles County Coroner's Office upon investigating the circumstances of their death. The distinction between suicide attempters and "attention getters" was based upon the adolescents' accounts of their intentions at the time of the act. All adolescent suicide attempters in the study were seen within forty-eight hours of the attempt. Their intentions were related to three separate persons during their voluntary commitment at the hospital—the attending physician who treated them in the emergency room, the psychiatrist during a psychiatric interview, and the author or his assistant in an interview which lasted about two hours. The designation (by the author) of suicide attempter was based on a comparison and assessment of these three accounts.

Introduction to the Formulation

Nearly all the suicide notes studied were found to fall within one of six general categories: "first-form notes," "sorry illness notes," "not-sorry illness notes," "direct accusation notes," "will and testament notes," and "notes of instruction." What I have called "the formulation" is a systematic explanation, for all but ten of the 112 notes studied. The exceptions are noted later. The ten-point process to be discussed is characteristic of "first-form notes." Thirty-five of the 112 notes took this form. In addition, "sorry illness notes" also contained all or most of the characteristics found in first-form notes, depending upon their length. The reader is cautioned not to view the other four forms of notes as exceptions which tend to negate the process associated with first-form and sorry illness notes. These four forms and the explanations accompanying them are not exceptions but qualified additions that supplement the scope of the original ten points.

By way of analogy, consider the statement "Light travels in a straight line," except when it encounters an opaque object, except in the case of refraction, except in the case of diffraction, and so forth. One does not say of these "exceptions" that they tend to negate the principle of the rectilinear propagation of light. They simply work to narrow its scope and set its limits. (The recognition and discussion of the four categories of notes cited above serve the same purpose.) To the extent that one is able to explain the "exceptions" in such a way that the explanations are consistent with the evidence, the sum total of these explanations constitutes a more detailed and inclusive understanding of light, or, in the case of my formulation, of suicide. I also believe that the formulation will provide an explanation of suicide, within this culture, that is both empirically derived and more consistent with the evidence than any I have thus far encountered.

The Formulation

Trusted persons appear to become trust violators when they conceive of themselves as having a certain kind of problem: a view of the past plagued by troubles, a troubled present, and the expectation of future troubles erupting unpredictably in the course of their lives. Paradoxically, these unpredictable troubles occur with absolute predictability in that it is held that they are sure to come. The problem is thus seen to be as absolute as life and must be resolved by something no less absolute than death. Since it is impossible to dispose of the problem of change, where change is viewed as unanticipated, inevitable, and inevitably for the worse, and since one sees it as necessary to resolve this problem in order to live—that is, to fulfill one's trust—and since the absolute nature of the problem makes it amenable only to absolute solutions, and since there is only one absolute solution, one finds it necessary to resolve the problem of living by dying. To put it another way, one appears to betray one's most sacred public trust by the private act of suicide.

Implicit or explicit in most of the suicide notes is the notion that the suicides "didn't want it this way, but . . ." From this perspective, they are in a position to view themselves as blameless—that is, as trusted persons—while at the same time knowing that they will be regarded as trust violators because the outsider has not experienced what they have and therefore cannot see the moral and reasonable nature of the act. With this in mind, they beg indulgence and ask forgiveness. In short, they know what they're doing, but they also know that the recipient of the note cannot know.

Life's problems, which one is morally obligated to resolve in order not to violate the sacred trust to live, can be resolved only by death. This is a not-too-pretty paradox, but from the perspective of the potential suicide, it is a necessary and consequently reasonable and moral view. The absence of choice gives rise to the greatest freedom—the recognition of necessity. Thus the suicidal person sees the act of suicide as the potential freedom he has long sought in life. This can be seen from the notes themselves. The writers are rarely "depressed" or "hostile." The notes are by and large very even, as though at the time of writing the suffering no longer existed and a resolution to the problem had been reached. Tuckman and his associates state that 51 percent of the notes they studied expressed "positive affect without hostility" and another 25 percent expressed "neutral affect."[11] Similarly, Farberow, Shneidman, and Litman found that the period of highest risk was not during the depression or "illness" but just after it, when the patient seemed much improved.[12]

FIRST-FORM NOTES

The outline that follows describes the formal aspects of a process that the individual must experience before he can seriously entertain the thought of suicide and then actually attempt it. The extent to which this process is operative will be illustrated through an analysis of first-form notes. The extent to which the other five forms of notes deviate from the characteristics found in first-form notes will be discussed in the explanations of the five remaining forms.

Durkheim went to great lengths to show that private acts contrary to the public trust are irrational and/or immoral and are constrained from occurring by public sanctions. In order to overcome these constraints and appear to others as a trust violator, the private individual must (1) be faced with an unexpected, intolerable, and unsolvable problem; (2) view this problem not as an isolated unpleasant incident but within the context of a long history of troubled situations and the expectation of future ones; (3) believe that death is the only absolute answer to this apparently absolute dilemma of life; (4) come to this point of view (a) by way of increasing social isolation, whereby he is unable to share his problem with the person or persons who must share it if it is to be resolved, or (b) by being subject to some form of incurable illness which in turn isolates him from health and the community, thereby doubly ensuring the insolubility of the problem; (5) overcome the previously internalized social norms which view suicide as irrational and/or immoral; (6) succeed in this because he feels himself a less integral part of the society than others and therefore is held less firmly by its bonds; (7) apply to his intended suicide a verbalization which enables him to adjust his conception of himself as a trusted person with his conception of himself as a trust violator; (8) succeed in doing this by defining the situation so that the problem is (a) not of his own making, (b) unresolved, but not from any lack of personal effort, and (c) not capable of any resolution known to him except death (he doesn't want it this way, but it's "the only way out"); (9) define death as necessary by this process and thus remove all choice and with it sin and immorality; and finally, (10) make some provision to ensure against recurrence of these problems in the afterlife.

Thirty-five out of 112 notes were first-form notes, characterized by begging forgiveness or indulgence. These notes expressed all or most of the aspects listed above, depending on their length. For example:

It is hard to say why you don't want to live. I have only one real reason. The three people I have in the world which I love don't want me.

Tom, I love you so dearly but you have told me you don't want me and don't love me. I never thought you would let me go this far, but I am now at the end which is the best thing for you. You have so many problems and I am sorry I added to them.

Daddy, I hurt you so much and I guess I really hurt myself. You only wanted the very best for me and you must believe this is it.

Mommy, you tried so hard to make me happy and to make things right for all of us. I love you too so very much. You did not fail, I did.

I had no place to go so I am back where I always seem to find peace. I have failed in everything I have done and I hope I do not fail in this.

I love you all dearly and am sorry this is the way I have to say goodbye.
Please forgive me and be happy.
Your wife and your daughter.

First, the problem is not of the suicide's own making. At first glance the suicide seems to be saying just the opposite: "You did not fail, I did," "I have failed in everything." However, having acknowledged this, she states: "Tom, I love you so dearly but you have told me you don't want me and don't love me. *I never thought you would let me go this far.*" Then, of course, she loves them. It is they who do not love her, and this is "the problem."

Second, a long-standing history of problems: "Mommy, you tried so hard to make me happy and to make things right for all of us. I love you too so very much. You did not fail, I did" and "Tom . . . you have so many problems and I am sorry I added to them." It seems from this that she has created a long-standing history of problems. She was, nevertheless, subject to them as well. "Daddy, I hurt you so much and I guess I *really hurt myself.*"

Third, the recent escalation of problems beyond human endurance: "It is hard to say why you don't want to live. I have only one real reason. The three people I have in the world which I love don't want me" and "Tom, I love you so dearly but you have told me you don't want me and don't love me."

These particular problems are clearly of recent origin and of greater magnitude than any she had previously experienced. By her own account, had she experienced problems of this order before, she would have taken her life before, since they caused her to lose what had previously constituted sufficient reason for her to go on living.

Fourth, death is seen as necessary. "It is hard to say why you don't want to live. I have only one real reason. The three people I have in the world which I love don't want me" and ". . . but now I'm at the end . . .," and finally "I love you all dearly and am sorry this is the way I *have* to say goodbye."

Fifth, she begs indulgence: "I love you all dearly and am *sorry* this is the way I have to say goodbye."

Sixth, she knows what she's doing, but they cannot know: "Daddy . . . You only wanted the very best for me and *you must believe this is it.*"

The suicide's message in point 3 is the same as that given by nearly all those who attempt suicide, insofar as this is a particular case of the general condition of "progressive social isolation from meaningful relationships." Ellen West, whose case history is perhaps one of the most famous, wrote in her diary less than a year before taking her life:

> . . . by this fearful illness I am withdrawing more and more from people. I feel myself excluded from all real life. I am quite isolated. I sit in a glass ball. I see people through a glass wall, their voices come to me muffled. I have an unutterable longing to get to them, I scream, but they do not hear me. I stretch out my arms toward them; but my hands merely beat against the walls of my glass ball.[13]

ILLNESS NOTES

Requests for forgiveness or indulgence may be omitted when the writer feels that the public may have made an exception to its general indignation at suicide—for example, in the case of persons suffering from incurable disease or suffering great pain. In such cases, the suicide may feel that no apologies are necessary, and requests for forgiveness may be included or excluded, because of the ambiguity surrounding the degree of public acceptance of the above view.

Thirty-four notes were included in the "illness" category. Twenty-two of these omitted requests for forgiveness; twelve included them. This category has most of the same general characteristics as those of the first form. How many conditions of the first-form notes are met by those of the illness category depends primarily on their length. The two formal distinguishing features of these two sets of notes are that the illness notes may or may not beg forgiveness, for the reasons stated above and, compared with first-form notes, the source of the problem is generally better defined and is restricted to the area of illness, pain, and the like, and its social and personal implications for the individual. Some examples follow.

Sorry Illness Notes

Dearly Beloved Children: For the last three weeks I have lost my blood circulation in my feet and in my hands. I can hardly hold a spoon in my hand. Before I get a stroke on top of my other troubles of my legs I decided that this would be the easier for me. I have always loved you all dearly. Think of me kindly sometimes. Please forgive me. I cannot endure any more pains. Lovingly, mother.

Not-Sorry Illness Notes

If you receive this letter you will know that I have emptied my bottle of sleeping pills.

A second note by the same author addressed to the same person included the line: *"Surely there must be a justifiable mercy death."*
Another reads:

Dear Jane: You are ruining your health and your life just for me, and I cannot let you do it. The pains in my face seem worse every day and there is a limit to what a man can take. I love you dear.

Bill

NOTES OF DIRECT ACCUSATION

None of the notes in this class begs forgiveness or offers apology. The suicide not only feels that the problem is not of his making but knows who is responsible. As a result, he feels righteously indignant and omits requests for indulgence, especially when the note is directed to the guilty party. Direct accusation notes are generally very brief, rarely more than a few lines long. Ten of the 112 notes studied were of this type. For example:

You Bob and Jane caused this—this all.

Goodbye Jane. I couldn't take no more from you. Bob Mary, I hope you're satisfied. Bill.

If you had read page 150 of Red Ribbons this wouldn't have happened.

LAST WILL AND TESTAMENTS AND NOTES OF INSTRUCTIONS

None of these notes contained requests for forgiveness or indulgence. They usually concern themselves exclusively with the manner in which the suicide's property is to be apportioned and make no mention of the circumstances of the suicide. As a result, there is no need for the note writer to admit guilt or request forgiveness.

LAST WILL AND TESTAMENTS

I hereby bequeath all my worldly goods and holdings to Bill Smith. $1 to Chris Baker, $1 to Ann Barnes. Signed in sober consideration.

Mary Smith

NOTES OF INSTRUCTION

Notes of instruction are almost always very brief. The reason why relates to the comments made about last will and testaments and apply here as well.

Call Jane. S Street, Apt. 2. Thank Officer No. 10.

I have gone down to the ocean. Pick out the cheapest coffin Jones Bros. has. I don't remember the cost. I'll put my purse in the trunk of the car.

Precautions Taken to Exclude This World's Problems from the Next World

To guard against the eventuality that a similar set of troubles will erupt in the afterlife, the very thing one is dying to overcome, one of six possible courses of action is formulated and internalized. These forms first came to my attention while studying suicidal adolescents; the suicide notes tend to bear them out.

1. The potential suicide who was in the past a diligent churchgoer rather abruptly stops attending church and starts considering himself a nonreligious person. He thereby disposes of heaven and hell, makes death absolute, and secures for himself all the benefits of the nonbeliever with respect to the act of suicide.

2. The person who attended church irregularly but had enough religious training to make him ambivalent about an afterlife suddenly begins to make

inquiries of very religious persons, asking whether "God forgives suicides" or "Will God forgive anything?" Those to whom the question is put, pleased that it was asked, eager to make a convert, or perhaps in all sincerity, say "Yes, of course, if you really believe, God will forgive anything." At this point the suicidal person suddenly "gets religion" and tries very hard to "believe," thus securing a place in heaven free from future troubles.

The following note is illustrative. Both its author, a sixteen-year-old female suicide attempter, and her mother reported that the girl's preoccupation with religion had begun unexpectedly within the last few months.

> Please forgive me, God. . . . In my heart I know there is a Christ everywhere in the world that is being with everyone. Every second of every day and he represents God in every way. I know that in my brain I think evil things about different situations and sometimes I think that Christ never existed. But my heart always is strong and that when I think that Christ never lived I know that in my heart He did. . . . *Mother thinks that there is no hell and no heaven (I guess) and I know there is a hell and heaven. I don't want to go to the devil, God, so please forgive me to what I have just done. John L. said that if I believe in and accept Jesus that I would go to heaven. Some people say that if you ask forgiveness to God for things you do to yourself or others, that he would forgive you (if you believe in Jesus and love him). . . . Heaven is so peaceful and the earth is very troublesome and terrifying.*

3. The religious person, believing that suicide is an absolute, irreversible, and damnable sin, will make an attempt to resolve this by asking his or her mother or some other authority "Will God forgive anything?" knowing full well that suicide is the exception. He or she will be answered, "If you believe." The pope's pronouncement to the contrary notwithstanding, the suicidal person will accept this and act as though it were true.

4. The religious person, believing that he is unable to secure a place in heaven or ensure an absolute death or any other resolution to his present problem, will fly in the face of God: for example, "Even if I go to hell, at least I won't have those headaches and worry about the baby and that will be one thing anyway." At least you don't have to violate a trust in hell, for no one on earth has ever told you how to act in hell, and you are left to your own resources without the problem of becoming a trust violator. The very ambiguity of the hereafter allows for a happy ending, or beginning.

Parts of a lengthy note written by a man to his wife and family serve to illustrate the uncertainty of the hereafter.

> My Dearest Ones:
> When you get this it will all be over for me on earth *but just the beginning of my punishment for what I have done to you all.* . . . I have given what I am about to do lots of thought and each time I have thought about it there seems no other way . . . *I don't know what's on the other side perhaps it will be worse than here.*

It is interesting to see that the author of the note begins by stating that his punishment in the hereafter is just beginning. It is a very positive statement; the punishment seems a certainty. However, the letter ends on this note: "I don't know what's on the other side *perhaps* it will be worse than here." The tentative nature of this statement allows for the possibility that "perhaps" it will be better. In the hope of tipping the scales in the right direction, the suicide concludes his note:

> I love you all *May God help me and forgive for what I am about to do.* Again good-bye.
>
> Jack and Daddy

5. Another group concerned with the prospect of hell will request in a suicide note that others "pray for my soul" or that "God forgive me" and—having taken this precaution—hope for the best.

6. Reincarnation is the last form of possible salvation: "Maybe it will be better the next time around; it couldn't be worse." This resolution to life's problems and the hope of preventing future ones was discovered through interviews with adolescent suicide attempters. One fifteen-year-old Jewish boy, who until a year earlier, when the family moved from New York, had been attending synagogue regularly, suddenly stopped attending services and became preoccupied with the prospect of reincarnation. A fourteen-year-old black Baptist girl, who had been a steady churchgoer, also stopped attending church and became interested in reincarnation. It is perhaps unnecessary to point out how peculiar it is for a Jew and a Baptist to undergo conversion to a belief in reincarnation, especially without any external indoctrinating influence. Both adolescents also recognized the peculiarity of reincarnation to the outsider, and although they mentioned its existence, refused to discuss it in detail.

In brief, religious convictions do not appear to be ultimately binding upon the individual as constraints against suicide, since one tends to interpret religious dogma as one has a need to interpret it.

It is true that Durkheim dealt at length with this notion by establishing the degree of social integration within various religions as the constraining factor against suicide rather than the religious dogma *per se*. However, he did not discuss the way in which religious dogma specifically intended to prevent suicide can serve to encourage it, with the proper "rationalization."

I acknowledge that there were some exceptions to these six categories. But among the 112 suicide notes studied, the paucity of cases falling into a "residual category" is heartening. There were only ten of these in all, four of which contained the only elements of humor found in all of the notes. For example:

> Please do not disturb. Someone sleeping.
> (Hung on the dashboard of his car.)

Conclusions

If it is true, as Hume believed, that "such is our natural horror of death, that small motives will never be able to reconcile us to it,"[14] it is also true that the horror of life is no small motive. I believe that most people prefer the uncertainties of life to the uncertainties of death because in life they have defined for themselves the possibility that certain sets of events will occur, and live in the expectation that "anything can happen." If one's view of life excludes uncertainty—that is, if life is not full of ups and down but only downs, and anything *can't* happen, things can only get worse—then one might better try the uncertainties of death. Accepting death provides a possibility of resolving life's problems, while at the same time ensuring against future problems (or at least providing the possibility of resolving future problems when they arise).

I believe it is necessary to take what the suicide writes seriously in attempting to understand why he is committing suicide. I am further convinced that a fuller understanding of suicide will emerge only if one's procedures for "transcending the data" do not end in ignoring it, and if the "data" transcended have some direct relation to the real-life phenomenon under study.

Notes

1. Jacob Tuckman, Robert J. Kleiner, and Martin Lavell, "Emotional Content of Suicide Notes," *American Journal of Psychiatry* (July 1959), p. 59.
2. Ibid.
3. Edwin S. Shneidman and Norman L. Farberow, "Appendix: Genuine and Simulated Suicide Notes," in *Clues to Suicide*, New York: McGraw-Hill, 1957, p. 198.
4. Tuckman et al., p. 59; Shneidman and Farberow, p. 48.
5. Tuckman et al., p. 60.
6. Ibid., p. 62.
7. Emile Durkheim, *Suicide*, New York: Free Press, 1951; Jack P. Gibbs and Walter T. Martin, *Status Integration and Suicide*, Eugene, Ore.: University of Oregon Press, 1964. Andrew F. Henry and James F. Short, *Suicide and Homicide*, Glencoe, Ill.: Free Press, 1954; Elwin H. Powell, "Occupational Status and Suicide: Toward a Redefinition of Anomie," *American Sociological Review* 23 (April 1950): 131–139.
8. Adolescent Attempted Suicide Study, supported by the National Institute of Mental Health and conducted at the Los Angeles County General Hospital under the direction of Joseph D. Teicher, M.D., Professor of Psychiatry, University of Southern California School of Medicine, and Jerry Jacobs, Ph.D., Research Associate, University of Southern California School of Medicine.
9. Donald R. Cressey, *Other People's Money*, Glencoe, Ill.: Free Press, 1951.
10. Ibid., p. 30.
11. Tuckman et al., p. 61.
12. Norman L. Farberow, Edwin S. Shneidman, and Robert E. Litman, "The Suicidal Patient and the Physician," *Mind* 1 (March 1963): 69.
13. Ludwig Brinswanger, "The Case of Ellen West," in *Existence*, ed. by Rollo May et al., New York: Basic Books, 1958, p. 256.
14. David Hume, "Of Suicide," in *Hume's Ethical Writings*, ed. by Alasdair MacIntyre, New York: Collier Books, 1965, p. 305.

The Clinical Organization of "Sub-Normality": A Case of Mistaken Identity

In an essay on "Tacit Knowledge of Everyday Activities," Aaron Cicourel states that sociologists "seldom concern themselves with the properties of everyday social life" but take them for granted. Furthermore, both the "natural" and "laboratory" events studied "are not established by asking first what a 'natural order' is like, and then what it would take to generate activities members... would label 'unnatural' or 'natural.' Instead, the problems taken as points of departure are assumed to be 'obvious' instances of *the* 'real world.'" Any sociologist insisting that such a study should begin with an examination of the properties of routine practical activities in everyday life "is not likely to meet with the approval of colleagues who have already decided what the 'real world' is all about, and they have already been studying 'it' for a long time."[1]

This description of certain key assumptions routinely made by sociologists applies equally well to psychiatrists. Psychiatrists also take as a point of departure the "obvious" instances of the "real world" without being overly concerned about what it would take to generate activities that members of society would label "unnatural." I am here concerned with psychiatrists who evaluate the possibility of mental retardation in children and with the ways in which these evaluations generate and preserve certain categories of mental retardation. I will also consider

Adapted from Jerry Jacobs, "The Clinical Organization of 'Sub-Normality': A Case of Mistaken Identity," *Deviance: Field Studies and Self Disclosures*, by permission of Mayfield Publishing Company (formerly National Press Books). Copyright © 1974 by Jerry Jacobs.

the reasons why these categories do not seem "unnatural" to those who accept and perpetuate them. I will begin by considering one class of "severely retarded" children—nonverbal, nontestable children with no discernible organic pathology—and the general belief among physicians that all children so diagnosed relatively late in childhood have no prospect of ever achieving a normal or above-normal level of intellectual performance. When such children have miraculous recoveries later in life, it is invariably held, in retrospect, that they were wrongly diagnosed to begin with; that is, it is usually assumed that the retardation must have been a case of childhood schizophrenia all along. On the other hand, when children who had been diagnosed as childhood schizophrenics miraculously recover, it is *not* assumed that they might have recovered from severe retardation, or from a combination of schizophrenia and retardation. The evidence seems not to warrant such assumptions, especially when it is so difficult to establish the existence or influence of either schizophrenia or retardation at the time of the diagnosis,[2] let alone several years later. The issue is further complicated by the fact that so many of these cases seem to carry a mixed diagnosis of severe retardation and childhood schizophrenia, with an emphasis on one or the other.[3]

The question then arises: Why, in cases of the recovery of children initially diagnosed as severely retarded, and later found to possess a normal or above-normal level of intelligence, is it invariably assumed in retrospect that the inconsistency between the physician's initial prognosis and the child's later performance is best explained by presuming against the original diagnosis? A more convincing hypothesis in many of these cases seems to be that severe mental retardation (at least in the class of children noted above) is sometimes reversible. The reason this position is never entertained, let alone accepted, must be sought in the fact that it is a psychiatrist who is called upon to rationalize any apparent contradiction between the anticipated "before" and the resulting "after." This he does by entertaining the possibility that the original diagnosis was faulty and then accepting this possibility as "given." The reason for this is to a large extent based upon the psychiatrist's prior "background expectancies,"[4] which in turn rest upon certain assumptions in the medical model of mental retardation, assimilated by physicians in the course of their professional training. These have been succinctly presented by an influential spokesman as follows: "In the light of present knowledge, mental retardation is essentially irreversible. This does not deny the possibility of prevention or amelioration; but though many therapies and other maneuvers have been hailed, few have survived the test of time. Preventive measures ... have had some limited success; but *adequately diagnosed mental retardation probably never is reversed to normal.*"[5] (Emphasis added.)

Psychiatrists' attempts to rationalize "contradictory" findings depend upon their acceptance of some generally held position on mental retardation, which in turn is determined to a large extent by the assumptions and practices of the particular institution or agency they work for. Garfinkel has formulated the general case of this influence as follows: *"recognizable* sense, or fact, or methodic character, or impersonality, or objectivity of accounts are not independent of the socially organized occasions of their use. Their rational features *consist* of what members do with, what they 'make of' the accounts in the socially organized actual occasions of their use. Members' accounts are reflexively and essentially tied for their rational features to the socially organized occasions of their use, for they are *features* of the socially organized occasions of their use."[6]

For example, a psychiatrist—a consultant at several children's services—recently told me that he had had occasion to see the same child in five different clinical settings, and in each instance the child received a different diagnosis. In a psychiatrically oriented evaluation center, "nonverbal" "nontestable" children without discernible organic pathologies are likely to be diagnosed as cases of "childhood schizophrenia"; in an "organically" oriented center they are likely to be diagnosed as "brain-damaged." One authority has referred to "the diagnostic schizophrenia that exists in many states . . . where certified psychiatrists in one institution claim a patient is primarily retarded, whereas in another they say, with the same conviction, that the person is primarily psychotic or mentally ill, making an individual patient a virtual football between two teams of experts. The commissioner in the state house usually referees these games."[7]

This practice is so routinely accepted that an authority on mental retardation lecturing to an audience of doctors got a big laugh by opening with this gambit: "Let's see, I must get oriented. Am I lecturing at X clinic or Y clinic? Oh, yes, this is X clinic; they're all schizophrenic here, aren't they?"

Apart from the inconsistencies in orientation and practice, the confusion of terminology within any one camp can be overwhelming. The use of the terms *functional mental retardation* and *mental deficiency* is a case in point. Functional retardation means that the child is functioning at a subnormal level of intelligence; in addition, it implies that the child may possess the potential to operate at a much higher level of intelligence than his current performance would indicate. Autistic children are often given this diagnosis. Whereas those who are "functionally retarded" may improve even to the point of achieving a normal level of intellectual performance, those who are "mentally deficient" are given no hope of recovery. Mental deficiency usually assumes organic pathology for which no known remedy exists. Where it is impossible to isolate the particular organic pathology that a diagnosis of "mental deficiency" implies, such pathologies are not infrequently inferred on the basis of "clinical insight." Then, too, there is considerable disagreement among practitioners regarding the concept of childhood schizophrenia. For example, some consider the terms *autism* and *childhood schizophrenia* to be synonymous, while others believe they are distinct entities.[8]

Quite apart from whether or not they are the same, there arises the prior question of what they are: "In planning such corrective remediation, the therapist inevitably assumes a theory of etiology though it is most often more implicit than explicit. . . . Indeed, one must not lose sight of the additional fact

that the descriptive entity childhood schizophrenia is grossly defined and differences among the children within any schizophrenic sample are as striking as
are the similarities. Certainly the notion of a disease in the sense of a single
definable pathologic agent remote in time, an inevitable course of development,
and a predetermined course of treatment is still a mythical one."[9]

Arbitrary distinctions such as those we have noted need not cause undue
confusion here if we keep in mind that among the class of children being
discussed, the position of the medical community is that those whose intellectual
performance reaches or exceeds the normal level at some later date are by
definition not "really" retarded (for example, in the case of childhood schizophrenia), whereas those whose I.Q.'s do not reach a normal level at some later
time are considered retarded or retarded and schizophrenic.

The popularity of this medical position notwithstanding, an alternative
hypothesis can be drawn: severe mental retardation, at least in some instances
and for whatever reasons, is reversible. Furthermore, since it is extremely difficult to determine whether a child is autistic or retarded or both (or what these
terms mean), one cannot help wondering if some cases of miraculous recovery by
"autistic" or "schizophrenic" children were not instances of recovery by retarded
children.

Edgerton has noted over one hundred "causes" of retardation in the literature.[10] Another authoritative source gives twice this number.[11] As things currently stand, it is the exceptional case that allows for a causal relationship to be
shown. "With present knowledge regarding the causal factors in mental retardation, it is possible to identify precise causes in approximately 15 to 25 percent of
cases. In such cases, organic pathology as a result of disease or injuries is often
demonstrable, most readily in instances where the degree of retardation is severe
and there has been gross brain damage."[12]

The problem of isolating the causal factor or factors in retardation for the
group of children being considered here is graphically illustrated by the following
excerpts from case history accounts. They are taken from a large metropolitan
clinic offering treatment and evaluation services for the mentally ill and mentally
retarded. All names, dates, and places have been changed to ensure the anonym-
ity of the patients.

Case No. 1

Paul Jones is a seven-and-a-half-year-old Caucasian boy. Both parents are
professionals, are well educated, and occupy a high socioeconomic status. Paul is
nonverbal, nontestable, and not toilet trained. He seemed to develop normally
until about the age of nine months. It first came to the mother's attention at that
point that Paul was "slow," and the parents began to be concerned about his rate
of development. In 1961, at the request of their pediatrician, Paul's parents took

him for a psychological examination. In March of that year, his I.Q. on the Kuhmann and Cottel scales was 74 and 61 respectively. By August, his I.Q. on the same scales was 55 and 46. In August of 1962 he was tested a third time by the same doctor (one of some eminence in the field of retardation), and his performance had regressed to I.Q. 31 and 28. The diagnosis and prognosis were stated as follows: "There can be no question of this child's retardation, and the failure to make any progress on the tests during a year, all of which were given by me, indicates lack of ability to develop beyond the infantile stage." Paul's parents went to great lengths to establish the reasons for his retardation. He has undergone psychological testing, observations, chromosome analysis, pneumoencephalogram, EEG, neurological exams, skull films, and more. All findings were either negative or ambiguous. The case records note: "Paul's current status is an enigma. No medical person has been able to give a diagnosis of his condition. The Joneses have been to a series of professionals, all apparently quite eminent people."

The professionals' inability to offer a reason for Paul's retardation presented the parents with a series of dilemmas. For example, should they have another child? The case record notes that when Paul's parents put this question to the geneticist, "he could not predict what the chances were of their having another retarded child and made no recommendation as to whether they should have other children." On the other hand, their pediatrician recommended that the Joneses have more children and have Paul put in an institution. Another question was, What could they realistically expect of Paul? Whereas the doctor who tested Paul felt he would not progress beyond the infantile level, others were more cautious in their prognosis, since the cause of his retardation could not be established.

The contrary inferences drawn by different professionals regarding the same pieces of information have led to much frustration and anxiety for Paul's parents. This account is not intended to reflect upon the competence of practitioners (although this is sometimes an important factor); it is intended only to give some indication of how difficult it can be to establish the cause or causes of retardation, even among the "severely retarded," where it is supposed to be most easily established.

Problems of diagnosis, as previously noted, result from more than the imperfect state of the medical sciences. They are also a function of the orientation of the particular agency for which the clinician works. In this regard, we find that Paul has recently undergone another medical and psychological evaluation at still another agency. There he was diagnosed as both "severely retarded" and "psychotic." The prognosis for his future development is poor. An optimistic prediction at this point would be that he is "trainable." The current evaluation, like the past ones, has left the question of the cause or causes of Paul's retardation unanswered. Furthermore, it has added for the first time to the long-standing diagnosis of "severe retardation" the diagnosis of "psychosis."

Case No. 2

The next case presents an example of a diagnosis of childhood schizophrenia being made where the question of mental retardation cannot easily be ruled out. Retardation in this case was deemphasized in much the same manner that childhood schizophrenia was in the preceding case.

Joanne is a thirteen-year-old Caucasian girl who lives with her mother. The father and mother are divorced. When first seen in 1959 Joanne was five years old and characterized as isolated, "bordering on mutism," and nontestable. All physical, neurological, and laboratory findings were within normal limits. Her diagnosis at the time was "schizophrenic reaction, childhood type." By 1961 the psychologist stated: "In summary, Joanne's functioning is on such a higher, more integrated level than at the previous evaluation that an I.Q. test can be administered to her." Upon testing she was found to be "in the upper range of borderline defective level."

In 1964 the psychologist's report stated: "Joanne readily understands highly abstract concepts . . . her test responses as well as her behavior indicate many changes during the last one and a half years. Her performance on the Information and Similarities Subtests and Sequin Form Board were adequate, and her spontaneous use of language suggest above average verbal ability."

Currently, Joanne has just completed the sixth grade of normal classes in public school. The case record notes: "She is very verbal and demonstrates an above average intellectual endowment. The reader will, no doubt, be struck by the marked difference in the case summary of 1959 of an autistic child 'bordering on mutism.'"

Case No. 3

The first two cases were both instances of mixed diagnosis, the first with an emphasis on retardation, the second with an emphasis on childhood schizophrenia.

The case to be presented next was also one of a mixed diagnosis, in which the diagnosis of retardation in childhood was replaced ex post facto with a diagnosis of childhood schizophrenia; currently neither the retardation nor the schizophrenia is in evidence. In none of these three cases were the clinicians involved able to offer a conclusive statement regarding the etiology of either the retardation or the childhood schizophrenia.

Johnny is a fifteen-year-old Caucasian boy who lives with his mother and two siblings. The father died in 1956. The case record notes: "John's development was slow from the beginning. He sat at nine months and did not start to walk until age two. He had no speech until age six. He could not yet distinguish colors at the age of six. At age five, mother attempted to enroll him in kindergarten. He sat in the middle of the classroom screaming, soiled and smeared himself and all he could reach. Mother was asked not to bring him back. He was seen by a psychiatrist at that time and diagnosed as 'mentally retarded'... and needing special education, to be started at age eight."

For the next three years, Johnny did not attend school and was kept at home. Most of his early years were spent in England. There were a number of moves during this time, and when he was ten his mother enrolled him in a special school in Germany. "He was there evaluated by a German psychiatrist in a residential setting. The conclusion was that John was not retarded, but severely neurotic. John did very well in the special school. In six weeks he learned German and caught up with the class."

Johnny remained in the special school until he was fourteen. By then he had learned to read and write. At the age of fourteen he was no longer eligible to remain at the school because of an age limitation. His mother emigrated to the United States and Johnny, because of his past history of "retardation," was initially enrolled in an "educable" class for the mentally retarded within the public school system. It was soon apparent that he was capable of normal work, and he was placed in regular classes. He is now enrolled in junior high school in regular classes and getting A's and B's.

An explanation of Johnny's recovery with respect to the diagnosis of mental retardation is noted in the case records as follows: "In childhood, John was severely retarded and was apparently suffering from a psychosis which is not apparent at all at present."

"Severely retarded" as used here referred to severe "functional retardation," a distinction previously noted. I believe that there is good reason to question this diagnosis imposed by hindsight. Johnny's slow development indicated retardation, his past social and intellectual performance indicated retardation, and he was diagnosed professionally by a psychiatrist at age five as being retarded. To suddenly state in retrospect, in the light of his recovery, that the retardation was in fact a case of childhood schizophrenia (he was diagnosed as "severely neurotic" at age ten) is a position that is not easily tenable. It seems to me more reasonable to suppose that he was in fact severely retarded and for some reason recovered. Such a position was not even entertained by a group of psychiatrists who heard this case. Indeed, they all spontaneously enjoyed a good laugh at the "obvious error" of the original diagnosis. Nor was this case unique. Several others of this kind have been brought to my attention within a single clinical setting. A final one is offered for the reader's consideration.

Case No. 4

Joan is a four-year-old Caucasian girl who resides with her foster mother. She was first seen at the age of two and a half, when she was functioning at the six-month level. The case record states: "Diagnostic impression was mental deficiency, severe idiopathic, with severe stress being extreme emotional deprivation and lack of care by parents." Joan was unable to walk or talk and was totally unresponsive to her environment. Her behavior was characterized as "essentially placid and unresponsive." Prior to this, she had received an inpatient medical evaluation elsewhere and was found to be "physically and mentally retarded without specific detectable cause."

A few months after she was first seen, she was taken from the care of her natural mother and placed in the care of a foster mother. Within about a year, Joan had shown striking progress. "She now feeds herself well, is completely toilet-trained, well-groomed, verbal, affectionate and responsive to adults, and engaging in play with obvious pleasure with other children."

It is true that Joan still shows some residual symptoms in terms of her prior emotional disturbance. However, the case record states: "It was clear, a striking change in this girl had occurred in response to a change in her mothering relationship. In a few months' time, a girl who had originally been considered to be severely mentally defective at the late age of two and a half years demonstrated capacity for rapid growth and development, physical, mental, and emotional. . . . The diagnosis of severe mental deficiency is of course not appropriate at this point and further evaluation is indicated to clarify the nature and extent of her emotional disturbance as well as more definite evaluation of the degree of any remaining functional retardation as indicated perhaps in her play and speech."

There is no way to know for certain whether Joan will eventually reach a normal level of intellectual performance. However, based upon her miraculous rate of development in the past year or so, there are at the very least promising indications. It seems almost certain that she will reach at least a level of "mild retardation" and may well go on to become a normally intelligent child.

How many other cases of this kind can be brought to light is a question that warrants our attention. An attempt at a systematic collection of recorded cases of miraculous recovery among "severely retarded" or "autistic" children and a reevaluation of these and new cases in the light of the above analysis might prove very rewarding, given the serious implications for diagnosis and treatment of accepting per se the widely held set of assumptions described above.

The key question is really whether or not in the case of miraculous recovery of nonverbal, nontestable children (when no organic pathological cause can be established) from a state of severe retardation to one of normal or above-normal intellectual functioning, it needs to be assumed that the potential to realize this new intellectual level had always existed in the individual and that it remained only to liberate it. Case-history accounts indicate that the potential to perform at a normal or above-normal level of intelligence may be lost at one point and recovered at some later period. Should this prove to be true, the prognosis for the class of severely retarded children discussed in this paper may not be so hopeless as is now supposed. The author believes that in light of the evidence, this possibility has been too quickly and easily disposed of—or, perhaps more accurately, has not yet been entertained.

Notes

1. Aaron V. Cicourel, *The Social Organization of Juvenile Justice*, New York: Wiley, 1968, pp. 3–4.
2. S. A. Szurek and I. Philips, "Mental Retardation and Psychotherapy," in *Prevention and Treatment of Mental Retardation*, ed. by I. Philips, New York: Basic Books, 1966, p. 221.
3. Lauretta Bender, "Childhood Schizophrenia: A Review," *Journal of the Hillside Hospital* 16, no. 1 (January 1967): 10–20.
4. Harold Garfinkel, *Studies in Ethnomethodology*, Englewood Cliffs, N.J.: Prentice-Hall, 1967, pp. 35–65.
5. E. A. Doll, "Recognition of Mental Retardation in the School-Age Child," in *Prevention and Treatment of Mental Retardation*, ed. by I. Philips, New York: Basic Books, 1966, p. 62.
6. Garfinkel, *Studies in Ethnomethodology*, pp. 3–4.
7. A statement made by Dr. Peter Bowman, Superintendent, Pineland Hospital and Training Center, Maine, in the *PCMR Message*, no. 11 (April 1968), p. 1.
8. B. Pasamanick, "Etiologic Factors in Early Infantile Autism and Childhood Schizophrenia," *Journal of the Hillside Hospital* 16, no. 1 (January 1967): 42–52.
9. William Goldfarb, "Corrective Socialization: A Rationale for the Treatment of Schizophrenic Children," *Journal of the Hillside Hospital* 16, no. 1 (January 1967): 58–71.
10. Robert B. Edgerton, *The Cloak of Competence*, Berkeley: University of California Press, 1967, p. 2.
11. "Mental Retardation," reprinted from the *Journal of the American Medical Association* 191, no. 3 (January 18, 1965): p. 1.
12. President's Panel on Mental Retardation, "A Proposed Program for National Action to Combat Mental Retardation," Washington, D.C.: U.S. Government Printing Office, 1962, pp. 6–7. Also see "Mental Retardation," p. 1.

BOOK TWO

Formal Sociology

Part IV

Formal Sociology: What Is It and Why Do It?

"The bathroom has also another attraction which the outreach worker recognizes: This is the only downtown public john. A lot of kids come to the center for no other reason than to go to the bathroom."[1]

This quote comes from a research project which focused on paid outreach workers; their job was to find youthful drug users and attract them to a treatment facility. Both the researchers and the outreach workers were interested in what attracted drug users to the center. If they were to follow the recommendations of scientific sociology, they would look to social facts. If they were to follow the recommendations of symbolic interaction, as outlined in chapter 2, they would look to morals, meanings, and motives. Yet none of these did much to explain why users came to the center. In fact, it turned out to be the public bathroom that was behind the youthful "rush" to the center.[2] How embarrassing for us all, sociologists and outreach workers alike!

In chapters 7 and 8 we shall be considering, among other things, the serious study of trivia. While age, sex, marital status, and occupation are all well-recognized independent variables in sociology, the presence or absence of toilets has yet to achieve this status. Along with many similar factors, this "variable" is ordinarily considered too mundane, silly, and "unsociological" to receive much attention by social scientists. Yet such mean details of practical existence may turn out to have more significance than the factors which currently strike us as so much more serious, important, and scientific.

All of the authors considered in chapter 7 and 8 are concerned in one way or another with the study of interaction in everyday life. The reader might wonder how this differs from the focus of the reality reconstructionists. The distinction between symbolic interaction and formal sociology turns upon two key considerations. The first is what each school means by everyday life; the second is how each goes about studying it—that is, the language each uses to describe it and the conceptual and methodological focus.

By "everyday life," symbolic interactionists mean a collection of "places" located in social time and space. That is, they study collections of people in conjunction with settings, activities, and problems which they all face and which make them a group. They ask what the world looks like to members of this group, and use this information to explain the actions and interactions of these members. In this sense "everyday life" might mean the everyday life of prostitutes, drug addicts, or secretaries.

On the other hand, formal sociologists mean by "everyday life" the situation in which each of us finds himself between the time he regains consciousness in the morning and the time he goes to sleep. Everyday life is a set of sociological *circumstances*, a set of circumstances faced by almost everyone in day-to-day existence. Such circumstances include, but are not limited to, communicating with others using some common symbol system, making a sequence of practical decisions about "what to do next," and using whatever knowledge one has at hand to "get through the day."

The way these circumstances are studied is, first, to find out what they are.

Formal sociology is interested in what people know in a different sense than what the world looks like to them. It is interested in what people know how *to do*. What does it take to be a socialized adult? What does one have to know, and be able to do, in order to lead a day-to-day life in society, of whatever sort? It is almost as if daily life were regarded as a work site and each adult as a worker whose job it is, during his waking hours, to say the ordinary things, think the ordinary thoughts, eat the ordinary lunch, take the ordinary route home from the market, and watch the ordinary television shows. What are the technical skills needed to do this? In what ways do geniuses, mentally ill persons, or cultural strangers "fail" at the job of being ordinary?

The minute one consider these topics seriously, he is led directly to the study and importance of what most people regard as trivia, a preoccupation with the minutiae of daily life and with a series of topics, concerns, and explanations of social phenomena that appear strange to the rest of sociology.

These topics, concerns, and explanations don't just pop out of everyday life. They are the outcome of the work of certain social scientists. By outlining some of this work, we will suggest some of the theoretical underpinnings of formal sociology.

The term "formal sociology," however, hides a dangerous oversimplification. Many practitioners will be unhappy with our division of qualitative sociology into reality reconstruction on the one hand and formal sociology on the other. They would argue that this distinction is about as real and as informative as the one that characterizes people as either "mentally healthy" or "mentally ill." We agree wholeheartedly. Our two categories, supposedly corresponding to two types of qualitative sociology, are employed primarily as an organizing device for the sections of the book. In particular we use Georg Simmel's term "formal sociology" to encompass the work of such diverse authors as Goffman, Garfinkel, and Schutz. We believe there is a common nexus of concerns among these authors and have included those aspects of their work that are germaine to the topics and problems we have collected under the term, formal sociology. Yet the diversity of their work is undeniable and, indeed, has been mirrored somewhat in the diversity of our presentations. With these cautions in mind we invite the reader to proceed.

Notes

1. This quote and the accompanying example come from "Outreach," a program evaluation study prepared by the SMDP Evaluation Research Team, Institute for Social Science Research, University of Montana, 1974.
2. Obviously the bathroom was not the sole attraction of the center, but it was a major one.

CHAPTER 7

The Sociology of Everyday Life: Nothing Unusual (or Otherwise) Is Happening

In this chapter we examine some of the results of giving serious sociological attention to seemingly mundane events and activities. We look at the work of Georg Simmel, Erving Goffman, and Alfred Schutz, all of whom were instrumental in opening up these phenomena as major study-topics for formal sociology.

Formal sociology's study of the trivia and minutiae of everyday life will prove to be no easy task. By the very act of making trivia a topic of study and recognizing its prevalence and importance in everyday life, formal sociologists change the very thing they seek to study. That is, trivia is no longer trivial; it now becomes important. To the extent this is true, the sociologists' rendering of trivia in everyday life cannot by definition correspond to the actors' experience of trivia. Nor can the way members encounter and contend with trivia, "the how to" of trivia, be dealt with accurately, given this inadvertent transformation.

This is true of Goffman's work. While his analyses of forms of interaction in everyday life are engaging and insightful, they are not, in the sense described above, "true to the phenomena." In his work, these forms become key features of everyday life, while in the lives of those he describes, they are taken for granted and go unnoticed.

Another problem with describing or analyzing trivia turns upon the sociology-of-knowledge dilemma that one cannot transcend the thought system of a group to which he belongs. How, then, will middle-class college professors of sociology manage to see and study trivia when it is invisible to other members of their class? The claim is, of course, that they can transcend common sense reasoning; as a result, things taken for granted by others can become a topic of investigation for them. They manage to do this, as previously noted, by embracing "science." However, we have also noted that social science, upon closer scrutiny, frequently ends up being nothing more than social rhetoric.

Another question presents itself. Why have sociologists of every persuasion tended to avoid the study of trivia? Positivists are interested in general social laws, whereas many early symbolic interactionists were concerned either with social disorganization or with interesting, unusual, or just plain kinky topics of study. Classic field studies were concerned with "street-corner society," "hustlers, beats, and others," the activities of homosexuals in public men's rooms, skid row drunks, or doomsday cults. Few studies were concerned with "the man in the street." Descriptions of people in more mundane occupations, such as schoolteachers, librarians, or public accountants, are scarce. The question arises: Why? The reason revolves, we think, about the topic of trivia itself. In this connection, many sociologists from various schools comment: "Goffman is fine, but how many Goffmans are there?" Many say the same of Simmel. What do they mean by this? They mean that while the formal analysis of everyday life is a legitimate, indeed important area of study, it seems that very few are capable of describing it, especially in terms of its formal features. Again, why? The answer seems to turn on the fact that few lay persons or social scientists can look at trivia and see it. If you can't see it, you can't describe it. If you can't describe it, you can't analyze it. If you can't analyze it, you can't uncover its formal features. The problem seems to be that it takes a Goffman or a Simmel to succeed in this. Why should they be able to succeed where other college professors have failed? By "failed," we mean failed to see the importance of trivia or failed to find a way to study it adequately. Actually, the question is rhetorical; we have no conclusive answer. One possibility, however, may be found in Stonequist's notion of "marginal man" or Mannheim's "free-floating intellectual." That is, Goffman and Simmel are marginal men, even by the standards of their peers, which are taken to be more liberal than those of the man in the street. This means that they can more easily transcend accepted models, because they are less a part of the social group than others and are therefore less constrained by the norms or thought processes of others.

Another reason why the study of trivia has been neglected turns upon the notion of using a pile driver as a nutcracker. Why turn so prodigious a method as "science" to the study of trivia? After all, common sense reasoning (which science is invoked to transcend) is good enough for that. And what of the scientist looking for "revolutionary breakthroughs"? Would he be likely to find them studying trivia? Laymen seem to think not. Members of the U.S. Congress were recently incensed to find that grant money had been allocated for the social scientific study of cocktail parties. Why were they troubled by this? After all, cocktail parties are a part of social life and even have a classical heritage in the literature on "forms of sociation."

While some formal sociologists have dealt with the question of trivia in a serious way, others have avoided it as studiously. There have been studies of witches, shamans, transsexuals, the mentally retarded, kung fu, microscopy, magicians, and cartography. While the findings of such studies may prove, in a formal sense, to have general implications for how the man in the street gets through an average day, they are not seen by the man in the street as constituting the trivia of *his* everyday life.

Finally, there are political and economic reasons for social scientists' neglect of trivia and their conscientious pursuit of novel, interesting, or deviant cases. A textbook or monograph on shopkeepers, librarians, or accountants, if it gets published at all, is unlikely to make the best-seller list. Given the fact that sociologists are not usually considered to be overpaid professionals and are further under the constraint of "publish or perish," a key concern of theirs becomes how to publish and sell books based upon their research efforts. In this regard, it is generally held that witches are likely to outsell accountants.

The irony of all of this can be painted in broader strokes. Isn't it peculiar that anyone, lay person or social scientist, should criticize Goffman or Simmel for studying "trivia"? After all, 99 percent of all one encounters in everyday life is trivia. However, its importance stems not from the fact that one is confronted with a lot of it, but rather that its effect is important. In fact, the unimportant details of life act rather like Durkheim's social facts, in that they are ubiquitous, ambiguous, and constraining upon the individual in the most powerful way. No matter how hard one tries to transcend the trivia of everyday life—by becoming a yogi, having an affair, experiencing a primal scream, having an encounter, or getting a massage—upon returning home one is always confronted by the dirty dishes and yesterday's garbage. Trivia indeed! It is the attempt to transcend trivia that is trivial. If man is but a pimple on the nose of God, the extraordinary is but a speck in the universe of mundaneity.

Georg Simmel and Formal Sociology

By now the reader may think that we have laid social facts to rest, those objective conditions that are external to the individual but nevertheless exert a force upon his life. They are about to be resurrected. Perhaps one of the baldest of these facts is the sheer number of individuals in a group. What bearing does the number of interacting individuals have upon their forms of social life?[1] One way to start finding out is simply to go down the list of numbers starting with one and see what might, and does, happen.

Two would seem the minimal number of people required for a genuine "social" life. The simplest social relationships—such as "friends" or "enemies," "husband and wife," "leader and follower"—are binary. The simplest social activities are two-person activities—conversation, tennis, a quarrel. But in a sense, social structure is not possible within a two-person group. When we speak of social structure, we usually have in mind a relationship of individual to "society" or "group" in which the latter is more powerful and autonomous relative to the former. But in dyads, the individual does not find himself confronted with some totality that can exist and act independent of himself. In the dyad the whole has a unique relation to its parts. Its greatness is that it balances the individual and the group and puts them on parity in many ways. For the group depends upon each of its members for its very life, independent of their identity, role, or placement within the group. With larger totalities, such as a class, only certain individuals achieve this power and independence. Without a teacher there is no class, whereas the class can easily survive without any particular student. In this sense, the students are dependent on the class, but not vice versa. Yet there is another kind of dependence in the dyad. The continuation of the marriage, the friendship, or the tennis match awaits the pleasure of the individual; it cannot survive without him or her. Anything that might make either individual withdraw is a "threat to society."

Another reason social structure is absent in dyads is that in dyads the agents of society cannot be separated from those they must control. If there is a fight, it must be settled by the fighters. If there is a game, its rules must be policed and enforced by the very ones who are supposed to obey them. There can be no disinterested judges, referees, or policemen.

Finally, agreement also takes a peculiar form in the dyad. In a group of one hundred people, there are potentially one hundred different meanings that may be given to any word—say, "cat." Supposedly, because of this, the larger the group, the tighter and more complex the mechanisms of socialization and social control must be in order to ensure cooperation and communication. Yet when these mechanisms result in a common meaning for "cat" for ninety-nine people, the remaining individual and his interpretations can have little effect in changing that meaning. He is rendered powerless in matters of social change, unless he combines with others. In dyads all of this is different. Initial agreement can easily occur without social controls or rules of decisions making. By chance alone two persons will agree half of the time on yes-no decisions, such as whether to see a particular movie. For a group of three persons the probability that they will agree on such decisions by chance alone drops to one-quarter.[2] Yet, having come to an agreement, let one individual in a dyad change his or her mind and the agreement crumples or dissolves.

When we consider a three-person group, tremendous changes take place in the situation. Social structure becomes possible. For now the individual is, indeed, confronted with a totality which is external to and independent of himself. It becomes possible to be a nonconformist or deviant. The majority and minority appear for the first time as possibilities. Impartial agents of society, arbitrators, intermediaries, and scorekeepers enter the stage. More complex social relationships also emerge. One can now be *indirectly* related to another person—for example, by being "a friend of his wife." There can be binary relationships between groups and individuals—one can be "their daughter." The structure of power and conflict is greatly affected. For instance, by dominating one member, another member can control the whole group (in democratic decision making). Finally, new problems and social forms of interaction present themselves. It becomes possible to talk behind another person's back, to backbite, to engage in "gossip." In connection with gossip, one can now give and receive "secrets." For the first time in conversation a "speaker-selection problem" arises; we need mechanisms to decide who talks next.

We have been talking about social life in a style and form that is quite similar to Simmel's. Three elements can be identified in our discussion:

1. Objective conditions—in this case, the number of people in a group.
2. Forms of activity and kinds of relationships, such as majority-minority or leader-follower, which are possible within the objective conditions.
3. Individual interests, motives, and passions, which find expression through particular relationships and activities with others.

For Simmel, pure or "formal" sociology consisted of the study of forms of "sociation"—the processes by which members of a group affect and are affected by one another's actions. When one asks how these actions are organized, he finds certain patterns or "forms" which humans use to deal with one another, forms somewhat independent of the content of the dealings. If one concentrates on decision making, for example, he finds "majority rule," "might makes right," or "the leader and the followers." Such decision making is found in politics, religion, or settling who should wash the dishes. Additionally, one is just as likely to find "majority rule" or "might makes right" used between nations or private companies as between individuals.

This brings up an important point. Simmel noted that dyads or triads could exist in families, street gangs, or football teams, as well as among individuals. For not only do human beings relate to one another so as to form totalities; these totalities in their turn become related as elements of more complex social totalities.

Thus we arrive at Simmel's offering of a subject matter unique to sociology—the study of *social forms*. Whatever human passions, needs, or propensities are, they somehow translate themselves into repeated forms of mutual dealings. Sociologists can isolate those forms, as one isolates a virus. That is, forms of interaction can be identified and described taxonomically. Complex forms can be expressed as combinations of certain basic (and in this sense "simple") forms. In this regard, Simmel often used a geometric metaphor. If human beings are the line segments and points of social space, then what varieties of figures can be made from them and are, in fact, made from them? An obvious way to find out was to observe concrete human interactions, such as family fights or queuing up at a movie, and then seek to locate the patterns of mutual action and abstract them from their particular content. One would then examine the causes and consequences of the patterns, the way they combine (or failed to combine) with other patterns, and the content that could be "contained" within such formats or social molds.

This geometric metaphor makes Simmel out to be a crass formalist. But an examination of our discussion of triads corrects this impression. For him, the individual and the social structure rise and fall together. Neither has a separate existence; each achieves its identity in relation to the other. For many symbolic interactionists, the individual and his actions and interpretations are the primary reality ("society" is an abstraction), while for structuralists, society exists as the real and external "thing," and individuals and their lives are treated as its parts and by-products. Simmel, in his approach to sociology, skillfully managed to interweave part and whole so as to slight neither and fuse their contribution to social life. A well-known example is his conception of the relation of individual and society. In society a person is less than a complete individual, since social forms limit which aspects of his personality can come into play in the course of interacting with others. On the other hand, that personality is, in large part, made available to him by society, and part of his identity consists of his position in, and relation to, social forms and social structures. The-individual-in-society is thus both more than a single person and less than a total personality. More to the point, he and his fellows are the creators of social forms which allow expression of his interests and passions. Yet it is these same forms, when they gain their own autonomy and momentum, that begin to "create" him and his identity.

But how are these conceptions related to everyday life and to individuals? Logically one might just as well study forms of sociation in international relations as consider roommate selection in a dormitory. This is true in part—except that by sociation Simmel implied interaction among *individuals*. His image of society was of millions of individuals simultaneously interacting with, for, and against one another, on a day-to-day basis. When they did this, they made little patterns between themselves which combined into larger patterns, ultimately forming "society."

Since everyday life was seen as a field of sociological snowflakes among which repeated patterns could be found, it was not conceived of as a collection of subgroups each with its particular life-world. For example, in isolating the features of what Simmel called "sociability" with respect to a particular form—such as "play"—one might study cocktail conversation on Monday, children's games on Tuesday, and sexual coquetry on Wednesday. The essence of sociability for Simmel was a detachment of a form from the original serious interests and purposes that spawned it.[3] Thus in many conversations talk goes on for hours for its own sake, with no particular need to give or receive serious information. This example illuminates an often encountered puzzle. Formal sociologists often fly like butterflies from substantive topic to substantive topic, in a way that outsiders find puzzling. The connecting threads between these topics are provided by the formal sociologist's own developing theoretical scheme—in the above example, the essence, causes, and consequences of play.

In this approach to studying forms such as "play" is the kernel of another style of (formal) sociological research. Sociologists are accustomed to relying on a certain familiarity with their host culture as they carry out their studies. They discover and explain patterns in a society which is known to contain such things as "drug abusers," "cocktail parties," and "grade-point averages." Now, Simmel suggests taking a giant step backward and exploring one's own culture as an anthropologist might. Instead of a collection of familiar groups, places, and culturally defined activities, society will be observed and *redescribed* as an arena of social forms. Using this perspective, distinctions and similarities, ways of looking, names, and vocabularies will be found that allow one to see his culture in detail through the eyes of a sociologist.

Although Simmel pointed the way to such a program and suggested methodologies with which to carry it out, his work was primarily theoretical. What remained was to put many of his ideas into empirical practice. This was done with unexcelled brilliance by Erving Goffman. Instead of remaining "only theories," Simmel's ideas were grounded and expanded in the colorful world of unexpected activity that Goffman was able to uncover in everyday life.

Erving Goffman and "Finding Everyday Life"[4]

The first sociologists sought a social physics. They looked for it where Newton or Kepler might have looked, in the "heavens," in a domain filled with objects of cosmic proportions moving about over vast distances, but coordinating their journeys with respect to each other in accordance with certain elegant laws. The planets of sociologists were composed of vast numbers of people, bound together by geography, national affiliation, race, or social class. It was hoped that through statistics and census bureaus we would learn that the average income of the middle class was ever and always the square root of that of the upper class, or that for every Catholic who committed suicide there were 2.14 Protestants who took their lives. But alas, bundles of people were not planets, and they did not govern their lives with elegant mathematical formulae.

But perhaps these sociologists were looking in the wrong place. Perhaps the physics they were looking for was right around the corner instead of in the heavens. Perhaps Newton's laws of motion were being played out, not among the nation-states around the globe, but among people in the laundromat. Let us take the reader to such a place. Let him gaze with us through our telescope down through the ceiling of a cubical structure, peppered with metal machines grinding away close to the floor. Imagine a collection of people-molecules arrayed around the room in some geometric configuration, all but motionless but vibrating about their fixed positions like the molecules of a crystalline solid. We notice that their "vibrations" are hardly random—a leg crossed by one instantly produces a turned head in another. Yet these people-objects are not in a state of static equilibrium. At regular intervals one of them is propelled toward the machines, and what follows is a hurricane of chaotic Brownian movements between man or woman, machine, pieces of cloth, and sundry plastic baskets. Although such episodes occur at regular intervals, it is not immediately obvious how to tell which person will be propelled next or where (that is, to what machine) these sporadic invisible forces will pull her or him. Although the patterns of motion are far from clear, one can observe that people-objects are coordinated to one another. No two people, whether moving or static, ever get closer to each other than a certain limiting distance.[5] As one approaches this distance, with respect to another, he is propelled away, as if by some magnetic force. Heads and eyes seem to act like compass needles turning toward and away from each other in complex, integrated patterns. The laws of motion are here, all right. It just remains to uncover them.

In traditional parlance, a laundromat is a "public place," a more or less bounded area of physical space where any and all members of the community are entitled to cohabit together, independent of their relationships to each other or their connection to the establishment itself.[6] It is one of the paradoxes of public places that perhaps nowhere else does our suspending a front of social graces and simply "being ourselves" have fewer or milder consequences; yet nowhere is our behavior with respect to others more stringently controlled and constrained. And we do it ourselves, voluntarily. Here is an environment full of people we do not know and may never see again in our entire lives. There are no bosses, or policemen. We can say anything, dress however we like, whistle, chew gum, and who knows what else. The worst that may happen is a momentary dirty look or a passing expression of displeasure. But we don't do these things; we never even think of being "free" in such environments. Instead, as Goffman points out, men scrupulously inspect their trousers to see that they are zipped and that an erection bulge is not showing. A positive finding initiates camouflaging action such as crossed legs or a newspaper or book used as a protective cover. Newspapers and books also find service as "involvement shields" hiding the face and its telltale expressions from onlookers, preventing the possibility of eye contact, and giving the person a legitimate preoccupation which excuses him from paying the amounts and kinds of attention to the rest of the environment that "any normal person would."[7]

For as Goffman points out, the physics of public places is not only one of behavior but one of consciousness and attention as well.[8] In such environments, merely by doing what he does and looking the way he looks, a person "emits" or "exudes" information about himself and his current activities to strangers, information that he does not have much control over giving to or withholding from them. And as he is a source of information to them, they are a source of information to him. Each gives and receives a continual stream of information about the other, and *knows this*. Perhaps as a result, there is a very basic social order in public places, a set of norms which govern an individual's handling of himself during and by virtue of his immediate physical presence among others.[9] Such norms strictly control the amount and kind of attention one can pay to others and how that attention is to be displayed. Upon entering a situation such as this and becoming part of a bona fide public "gathering," an individual is expected and obliged to "come into play" and display a certain "interactional tonus." A vast and disciplined management of clothes, surface decorations, movement, and other personal appearances produces a visible "personal front" which displays that he is an ordinary, competent, knowledgeable person who is situationally "present" to others. [10]

Of particular interest in this regard is the incredible control required of a person over the composition of his face. It must not be blank; it must not be turned toward the wall; if its muscles display surprise, joy, or humor, this must be for certain time intervals and in connection with certain appropriate events. The whole symphonic accompaniment of wrinkled forehead, puffed-up cheeks, open mouth, and eye movements is delicately sequenced and coordinated to the newspaper being read, the person who just walked in, or the "wash that I'm now going to put in the dryer." Failures in maintaining personal fronts of this type are frequently treated as the first signs of mental illness by lay persons and professionals alike. [11] "Disturbed" people often find that they can't "put on their face"; they start "neglecting personal appearance and hygiene," or their reactions and displayed attention become ill-timed, too slow, or nonexistent.

In general, "normal" people handle themselves in such situations so as to have publicly visible "good reasons" for doing or seeing anything—whom they look at and why they look, where they go and why they are going somewhere, and so on. Even the most fleeting meeting of two pairs of eyes might constitute a delicate social ritual, heavily controlled by social norms and delicately managed:

> In performing this courtesy the eyes of the looker may pass over the eyes of the other, but no "recognition" is typically allowed. Where the courtesy is performed between two persons passing on the street, civil inattention may take the special form of eyeing the other up to approximately eight feet, during which time sides of the street are apportioned by gesture, and then casting the eyes down as the other passes—a kind of dimming of lights. [12]

We learn from Goffman that such a ritual is done to display "civil inattention"—to show that one appreciates that the other is present (and to openly admit having seen him), but that he does not constitute a target of special curiosity or design. In attending to such minutiae as this, a tremendous amount of information can pass between two consciousnesses in a fraction of a second:

> By according civil inattention, the individual implies that he has no reason to suspect the intentions of the others present and no reason to fear the others, be hostile to them, or wish to avoid them. (At the same time, in extending this courtesy he automatically opens himself up to a like treatment from others present.) This demonstrates that he had nothing to fear or avoid in being seen and being seen seeing, and that he is not ashamed of himself or of the place and company in which he finds himself. [13]

In *Behavior in Public Places*, Goffman goes on to discuss further layers of structure in these situations. In focused interactions such as conversations, some sustained, concentrated focus of attention or behavior is required of a group of people over time. He discusses who can and who must enter into various kinds of focused interaction and how entries into them and exits from them are accomplished. He considers the relations of those bound together in dominant involvements to the spectators and onlookers who comprise the remainder of the "gathering."

We need not follow him up these roads. It has already become clear that a social physics of sorts is indeed to be found around the corner. The questions before us now are "Which corner?" and "What sort of social physics?"

At one time ethnomethodologists made the claim that they had discovered everyday life as a topic of study. Goffman never made such a claim himself, but he might well have done so:

> My ultimate interest is to develop the study of face-to-face interaction as a naturally bounded, analytically coherent field—a sub-area of sociology.[14]

> We need to identify the countless patterns and natural sequences of behavior occurring whenever persons come into one another's immediate presence.[15]

As can be seen from these quotations, Goffman is mainly concerned with one "slice" of everyday life, that part of it which pertains to face-to-face interaction. Consequently, one of Goffman's main jobs is the same as Simmel's—to find and identify patterns.[16] This may look like a librarian's task, but it is different. For it is not as if everyone already knows "what's going on in everyday life" and needs only to have someone classify and catalogue it. As Goffman points out, sociology before him had not concerned itself much with face-to-face interactions, with especially those aspects of it which are trivial and ordinary:

> Sociology does not provide a ready framework that can order these data, let alone show comparisons and continuities with behavior in private gathering places such as offices, factory floors, living rooms, and kitchens. To be sure, one part of "collective behavior"—riots, crowds, panics—has been established as something to study. But the remaining part of the area, the study of ordinary human traffic and the patterning of ordinary social contacts, has been little considered.[17]

THE ONTOLOGICAL SCIENCES

The dictionary defines ontological science as the science of being, the investigation of those things that "are."[18] Let us take this to be a main part of Goffman's task. He must isolate the elements of say, walking on the street (as a biologist isolates a virus), must distinguish them from similar and surrounding phenomena, and then describe them in some systematic way. Such a task requires that one combine the activities of looking and naming. But how should they be combined? What methods are appropriate to such a task? Ordinary social scientific methods are of little help in answering such a question since they are predominantly concerned with how to tell if, when, where, or why something is happening. Ontological inquiry asks the prior question "What is happening?" "Finding" everyday life (or face-to-face interaction) in this sense consists in learning to see and know it in a way that makes it available as a world to study in the first place. This is a bit like setting out to make a map of some domain without knowing in advance whether that domain is the rapid transit system of San Francisco, the interior of a computer-science building, or the circulatory system of the human body. If one knows so little about the sort of "world" he is charting, he does not know in advance what tools and methods are best suited to finding out about it. For the latter depends on the structure of the world itself.

How can we possibly characterize everyday life and the interaction within it—this very place where we (and Goffman) live most of our lives—as such a strange and mysterious land? The answer, in part, is that Goffman wants to "find" everyday life in a level of detail beyond that used by, or required of, the ordinary "practitioner" of everyday life. Second, he looks at things that most of us know how to deal with when they come up, but which we take to be unimportant (in the sense that there is no reason to discuss them with our friends, put them down in our diaries, or otherwise be explicitly concerned with them for any amount of time). Third, he seeks to make a kind of general "map" applicable to many diverse individuals making decisions, choices, and assessments in the course of negotiating the rapids of daily existence.

Putting these three concerns together, we can justify the characterization of Goffman's topic as a new "world"—that is, a huge area of practical life that is there but that has not been subjected to scrutiny or concern by most of us, lay or professional.

For example, Goffman has mapped out the following among other areas of everyday life:

1. The presentation of self[19]—the techniques by which individuals and groups project images of themselves (and their actions) to others.
2. A sociology of "occasions"[20]—the rules, definitions, and contingencies that govern people's mutual conduct when they are copresent or "face to face" in a common physical environment.
3. Strategic interaction[21]—those aspects and types of interaction that are "gamelike" and involve "players," "winning," "strategy," and so on.
4. Face work[22]—a concerted "line" of verbal and nonverbal actions through which an individual expresses his evaluation of a situation, those within it, and especially himself (who he is and what worth he possesses).
5. Stigma[23]—the management of labels and characteristics which spoil individual identity.

In work such as the foregoing Goffman made a major contribution to sociology by providing a plethora of new sociological phenomena along with conceptual frameworks for ordering them. But his contribution proved a mixed blessing for his colleagues. It was clear that the work was both good and more than "mere description." But how was it to be formally evaluated? Here the mapmaking analogy breaks down, since forms of social interaction are not fixed terrains which can be measured off in inches and feet. What, then, would be the data that validated Goffman's conclusions? He was not reconstructing the reality of particular individuals and groups. Instead he wanted to study "the syntactical relations among the acts of different persons mutually present to one another."[24] But he did not study these relations by making counts of what black Americans or female college students do in laundromats "on the average," "in the long run," "with all other variables statistically controlled."

To evaluate Goffman's worth effectively, sociologists would need new theories and research methods compatible with these new theories. For example, sociologists were accustomed to using common sense categories like "female college students" or "black Americans" to define the populations to which their generalizations refer. But to trace who accords, say, civil inattention to whom, and under what conditions, people and kinds of people would have to be defined differently. We would count, not single people, but pairs of people in relationship. For instance, Goffman distinguishes between "unacquainted" persons, who need an excuse to interact with each other, and "acquainted" persons, who need an excuse *not* to interact when they meet. We might thus find (as Goffman did) that while two unacquainted individuals give each other civil inattention, two acquainted ones, under similar circumstances, engage in a different kind of nonverbal exchange. One "recognizes" or "acknowledges" the other using a variety of devices—a passing smile, a nod of the head, or a peculiar hand gesture that looks somewhat like three-fourths of a wave.

Armed with appropriate categories to define populations and variables, there is still another problem. Full-blooded people will not always act as our hypotheses dictate. Two acquainted people may "acknowledge" each other one time, exchange verbal greetings a second time, and use civil inattention to "snub" each other a third. Actual behavior will vary around some standard. But to assess how it varies or conforms to such a standard—and why—we would have to know, or at least specify, what the standard is. We would have to specify typical motives, competencies, and kinds of situations that lead to (typical) civil inattention.

In short, new vocabularies and theoretical models which incorporate these vocabularies have to be constructed.

Goffman did not concern himself explicitly with constructing these models or with the philosophy of science that served as their foundation. But another man was working on just this kind of a problem. Alfred Schutz was attempting to specify methods of social science that would be appropriate for studying everyday life. In particular he wanted to clarify the relationship between commonsense interpretations of everyday life, and scientific models of the same domain. Before discussing Schutz, it is best to examine the nature of "common sense" in more detail.

Alfred Schutz: The Problem of Common Sense

We may then say conclusively: the term "suicide" is applied to all cases of death resulting directly or indirectly from a positive or negative act of the victim himself, which he knows will produce this result. An attempt is an act thus defined but falling short of actual death. [25]

This is Emile Durkheim's "scientific definition" of suicide as it appears in his pioneering study of suicide rates. Strangely enough, it is not very different from the common sense, unscientific definition of suicide. True, rigorous application of Durkheim's definition might evoke some disagreement from the man in the street. But it is clear that both are talking roughly about the same sets of people, in connection with similar kinds of action. What makes this similarity strange is that Durkheim hated common sense thinking. He all but defined his job as replacing it with scientific thinking.

> The sociologist ought, whether at the moment of the determination of his research objectives or in the course of his demonstrations, to repudiate resolutely the use of concepts originating outside of science for totally unscientific needs. He must emancipate himself from the fallacious ideas that dominate the mind of the layman; he must throw off, once and for all, the yoke of these empirical categories, which from long continued habit have become tyrannical. [26]

It can be seen why Durkheim had some trouble in banishing common sense reasoning to the conceptual outlands. What if he found the everyday conception of suicide to be scientifically inadequate? Then the "suicide" that he defined in order to achieve greater scientific rigor would not be the same phenomenon we know. The farther away he gets from "our" suicide, the farther he gets from our world. On the other hand, the more his conception is derived from and is commensurate with ours, the more scientifically useless it might be (at least from Durkheim's point of view).

In seeking something that would be both a science and a sociology, we have repeatedly found a kind of schizophrenia. It would have to be objective, verifiable, logical, inductive, rigorous, and so on. At the same time, to be sociological, it would have to be about the world of social life. Yet there is no way to locate the world of social life except through the complexes of interpretations, concepts, and theories which those within it invest with reality and therefore base their actions upon. Thus, sociology needs common sense however much it might hate it. Without common sense, where would Durkheim come up with the concept of suicide, how would he know that it goes on in the world, and how would he find his way to the agencies that might have records of it?

But how far can one stray from folk reasoning, once it takes him to the general social vicinity of his phenomenon? To what extent can this "ladder" be dispensed with once one is "up in the tree"? This constitutes the empirical and moral issue involved in answering "What should be done about common sense?"

Weber, and later Schutz, opted for maximizing their connection to the world that people actually live in. They did this by placing common sense over sociology as a judge. Not only must sociological models be scientifically adequate, they must also be commensurate with commonsense. As Schutz wrote:

> Each term in a scientific model of human action must be constructed in such a way that a human act performed within the life-world by an individual actor in the way

indicated by the typical construct would be understandable for the actor himself as well as for his fellow-men in terms of common sense interpretation of everyday life.[27]

But how can this trick be performed? How can one construct a model of the man or woman in society that is both scientifically adequate and acceptable to common sense? For sociology is competitive with common sense. They very point of sociology is supposed to be how to know society and its workings *better* than the man on the street. In fact, the thing that upsets almost everybody about common sense is that it is very often wrong. It shows itself to be subjective, illogical, vague, inconsistent—the very antithesis of scientific thought. If this is so, how can one manage to be both commonsensical and scientific at the same time?

Positivists did not even try. They opted for science over common sense. Symbolic interactionists, however, did attempt a solution. Common sense interpretation enters their model as "the actor's point of view." One need not believe in all the gods and witches people once populated their world with. But one would have to know about them and discover the connections between these interpretations and the burning of middle-aged women at the stake or the periodic killing of "two he-lambs without blemish mingled with oil" and leaving them to rot on an altar while people were starving.

Yet the strange thing about this solution is that, upon closer examination, it turns out to be the same one that Durkheim had. Symbolic interactionists try to identify emotions, purposes, and motives that people *really have* and which *really determine* what they do, and how they do it. For example, insofar as one verifies that love, as it is commonly understood, "really" exists as such and "really" affects people's lives in the way it is popularly thought to do, one's models of men and women can be acceptable to common sense thought. But if love does not motivate and affect people in the way they think it does, one must stray from common sense thought in order to find objective knowledge. Blumer, like Durkheim, could reconcile science and common sense only to the extent that the latter was *already* compatible with the former. But in this case, one has merely validated what the man on the street has known all along, and certainly this is nothing to write home about.

To summarize the problem, common sense thought, if used as a resource, is somewhat like home cooking. It is inefficient, time consuming, and prone to error, and it varies from person to person. But inevitably, to the extent that one abandons it in favor of "modern methods," one just doesn't come up with the same conceptual meal. Like grandma's chicken soup and McDonald's hamburgers, common sense thought and scientific sociology seem inevitably irreconcilable.

COMMON SENSE: WHAT IS IT?

So far we have dealt with five uses for common sense thought under two major headings. First, *as a topic of study*:

1. Commonsense concepts and interpretations may be used to explain the actions of those who hold them.
2. Ordinary practical reasoning in everyday life is a topic of study in its own right.

And second, *as a resource*:

3. Commonsense interpretation finds the social world for us. Without using it as a take-off point, at the very least, we cannot locate topics, problems, and possible explanations.
4. Commonsense fact finding appears to be the best and most practical method of discovering how others interpret everyday situations, how this is related to what they do, and why they do it.
5. It has been proposed that our theories of social life must pass a "test of commonsense"—they must agree with commonsense conceptions of what might plausibly happen in the world as we know it.

The fifth item was incorporated by Schutz in his "postulate of adequacy": Scientific models of social action *must* be understandable to the social actor and his fellows in terms of common sense interpretations of everyday life. Schutz proposed to satisfy this postulate thus: A scientific model of action would be a mock-up—a make-believe actor endowed with certain purposes, knowledge, and competencies which the social scientist imagines he needs, to perform some typified course of action. The model would employ concepts that were consistent with both science and common sense. They would be consistent with science because they would satisfy the requirements of clarity, distinctness, and internal consistency that are compatible with formal logic. They would be consistent with common sense because the scientist's concepts would be "second-order constructs" derived from, and commensurate with, commonsense concepts. But, more important, they would refer to a bundle of purposes, knowledge, and abilities that we know can exist in an individual, because of what is known about common sense thought. That is, a real person, if endowed with all, and only, the attributes of our theoretical puppet, should be capable of performing the typified course of action under study.

If we reflect on the sociological knowledge that would be needed to construct these imaginary people, we notice a peculiar lack. It is not clear what we mean by "common sense." Hence it is unclear how to satisfy Schutz's postulates. This is true, in part, because we have so far given very little attention to the second stipulation in the previous list. We have been so busy trying to satisfy or transcend common sense that we have neglected to study it. We do not even know if there is such a thing. Is there a form of thinking common to a population of people (or perhaps even to our species) called common sense thinking, or is one person's "common sense" qualitatively different from another's? Is "everyday reasoning" merely a label for any mode of thinking that varies from those taught in college? The lack of answers to these questions is quite understandable if one looks at items 1, 3, 4, and 5 of the previous list. Sociologists can use common-sense thinking as a tool without knowing how it works.

Happily, while we the collective readership might only have ideas about what common sense is not, Schutz has endeavored to tell us in some detail what it is.

The common sense reasoning Schutz was talking about *produces* the world of everyday life in and through its use. For the moment, think of a "world" in the subjective sense, as a *method* (or methods) of making sense of anything what-soever. In this sense, seeing everything as "a man," "a woman," or "neither," where "everything" includes thoughts, dialectical materialism, and orgasms, would create or "constitute" a "world." Thus, in studying the world of everyday life, we would try to locate and identify a method of thinking and interpreting through which environments are rendered "everyday" or "ordinary." We would call this way of thinking (of making sense of things) "common sense reasoning." Yet there is an obvious difficulty with this approach—it is too simple to handle the problem. Under "everyday reasoning," we would want to include at least these heterogeneous topics:

1. *Reasoning:* e.g., practical fact-finding, making judgments and evalua-tions, deciding on actions.
2. *Meaning ascription:* interpreting things in the here and now on all levels—that is, putting things in categories, synthesizing separate events into comprehensive wholes, or translating marks on a piece of paper into "poems."
3. *Social knowledge:* acquiring and using a certain stock of information about all aspects of the world one lives in.
4. *Constitutive accents:* a "flavor" or "tone" that all aspects of an environ-ment have because it is a feature of the way one is looking at the environ-ment, for example, "boring" environments, as seen by a bored person, "dangerous" events and circumstances, as seen by a frightened individual, and so on.

Schutz has devoted conceptual time to all of these topics; here we will deal with only one of them, the "natural attitude."

THE NATURAL ATTITUDE AND ITS ASSUMPTIONS

In considering topic 4 a natural question presents itself: Does an environment become "ordinary" for a person in the same way it becomes "boring" or "danger-ous"? Is there a set of characteristics that all environments commonly thought of as "ordinary" possess *because* they are attributes of the methods of seeing every-thing in such environments? Schutz thought so. For him, the world of everyday life was characterized by a certain "cognitive style" which he called "the natural attitude."[28] It is possible, although misleading, to describe this cognitive style as a set of working assumptions. If they functioned as assumptions, they would be analogous to the basic axioms of a mathematical system; they would have to be:

1. "Taken for granted"—simply assumed to be valid without proof or evidence.
2. "Tacitly" understood, in that they contain the basic undefined symbols of the system. These symbols are grasped intuitively and not explicitly.
3. "Constituting"—that is, through their use, all of the other theorems and new symbols are defined and proved to be valid.
4. "Background" assumptions: They form the backdrop against which all of the particular theorems, definitions, and mathematical structures of the system acquire meaning. To eliminate or change one of them is to alter the whole system in a major way.

This analogy between the natural attitude and axioms of a mathematical system is not without merit. The working assumptions of the natural attitude have also been characterized as "background," "tacit," "taken for granted," and "constituting," to emphasize certain aspects of their working in everyday life.

In particular, what do I assume about an environment when I expect it to be an "ordinary, everyday" one? My assumptions revolve around two topics: the way in which everyday settings are experienced as "intersubjective" and the "sense of reality" they possess.

INTERSUBJECTIVITY

While presumedly I know intellectually that people can and do "live in different worlds," only seldom do I *experience* the world in this way. In his essay "The Stranger," Schutz gives a vivid picture of what it is like to be in a strange culture—to literally feel, and be, cut off from other people, despite their physical presence.[29] But this is not so in everyday environments. They are places where I am not an isolated human being with my own private interpretations of what's going on. Rather, everyday life is an area where, by and large, others know and see the same world as I do. But how do I manage this? Why do everyday settings seem to be this way, regardless of whether or not they actually are? The sense of being in a world known in common with others is brought about by several tacit assumptions:

1. Assuming the Existence of a Common Scheme of Communication

When I walk into a restaurant or go to teach my class, I assume that I am in the presence of English-speaking people, and act accordingly. Of course, I may be wrong. Perhaps there is someone in the class who speaks only German. If he speaks to me in German, I will notice it, be a bit surprised, and assume that he did not understand my lecture. However, what I will not do is start worrying about what language everyone else in the class speaks. Insofar as the classroom is an "everyday environment" for me, my lecture will continue in English and I will assume that the audience understands, unless there is reason to think otherwise.

However, as Schutz points out, assuming a common scheme of communication is far more than assuming the presence of a common language. It involves using categories, names, and interpretive schemes to make innumerable "typifications"—i.e., seeing environments as composed of "typical" people pursuing "typical" projects in predictable ways. Thus, for example, I confidently walk through a door merely marked "Men" and expect to know what will be found there. Or again, I may fail to leave money near my dirty dishes after finishing a meal at a restaurant. As I pay the check and leave the restaurant, I can picture how the waiter who spilled my drink will receive a "message" as he discovers what is *not* on the table.

Such typifications result in the feeling that "what I say is what they hear"—a feeling that allows millions of misunderstandings to occur silently without being noticed. And what happens when they are noticed? What happens when tests or questioning later reveals that the students have not understood my lecture? I am likely to interpret this as reflecting the students' lack of attention, effort, or intelligence, instead of realizing that a common scheme of communication, in fact, does not exist between us. For when I take the latter possibility seriously, I am no longer confronted with an "everyday" environment.

2. The Assumption of the Reciprocity of Perspectives

In the world of dreams, I can be a character in a drama while simultaneously witnessing the whole thing from the standpoint of an outside observer. However, this is not true of the wide-awake "real" world. In the latter, I am always situated in some social and physical place, some "here." The other person is always "there." Certain objects are "out of my reach": I can't see or hear them, but the other person can. The reverse is also true. Further, I bring to an environment certain knowledge that came from outside of it, and so does the other person. I alone may know that such and such a person is an FBI agent, or that the building will close in five minutes. Because we are different beings with different biographies, our current purposes, schemes of relevances, capacities for knowing things, and "knowledge at hand" can be wildly different.

Common sense takes these contingencies into account. But how, then, can we possibly get the feeling (in general) that everyday environments are known in common? Schutz describes two working assumptions that overcome this embarrassing knowledge about private experience:

a. The interchangeability of standpoints: I assume of my fellow man, and assume that he assumes of me, that were we to change places so that his "there" becomes my "here" and vice versa, he would see and know things in essentially the same way I do.[30] Thus, while our actual worlds might not correspond, I assume that my actual world—my actual sights, sounds, knowledge—is his potential world, and vice versa. The picture that I see in back of him thus acquires, as one of its features, that it is the same picture he would see if he were to turn around.

Interestingly enough, some of the mentally ill suspend this assumption. They adopt the very reasonable belief that there are certain experiences and bits of knowledge in a given environment that only they can see and know—in other words, that there is private knowledge and public knowledge. This produces for them a four- instead of a two-valued logic. Statements are not only true or false, they are privately true or false or publicly true or false.[31] Communication between a person who holds a four-valued logic like this and one who thinks in a two-valued logic produces disagreements and confusion. Indeed, the very assumption that, in an ordinary environment, standpoints are not interchangeable may be seen by others as a symptom of mental illness.

b. The congruence of relevances: What about all our different purposes and relevances "at hand," in given situations? They are clearly major determinants of what is seen, heard, or taken into account. Schutz describes an idealization that simply says, "Forget that." It asserts that the differences in our perspectives are simply irrelevant for the "purposes at hand." While you may be seeing, knowing, and feeling things differently, I assume we select and interpret things similarly enough for "all practical purposes"—for instance, for sitting on the same park bench or buying and selling a newspaper.

These two assumptions together describe how and why the everyday world comes off to us as a more or less "public place," containing people, events, and happenings that are actually or potentially available to everyone. A common way to understand the behavior of the mentally ill is to assume that they inhabit a world distinctively "their own." One might therefore speculate that they suspend the assumptions that produce a feeling of being in a world in common with others. Interestingly enough, as the following case illustrates, this is often not the case. It is the attempt *to hold onto these assumptions* in the face of abnormal events that causes them to act in ways that we interpret as symptomatic of mental illness.

WHO'S LYING?[32]

In an initial intake interview, a seemingly paranoid patient wished to introduce the therapist to an invisible (to the therapist) friend who, he claimed, had accompanied him and was present in the interviewing room. The therapist refused either to shake hands with this friend or to introduce himself and exchange greetings. Instead, he asked the patient why he had diverted attention to some other person just when they were to discuss the patient's problems. At this point the patient became very suspicious and uncooperative. Communication was not restored for the duration of the interview.

Let us assume that, somehow, the patient knew and saw this "friend." Assume as well that the patient, from his point of view, was in an everyday environment. Therefore he was in a public environment. The friend whom he saw was, of course, the same person the therapist saw, or would have seen if he had looked. Why would somebody refuse to greet a friend of yours *whom he saw*, not talk to him at all, and treat your wanting to introduce him as an "evasion"? If this happened to you, would you not be suspicious and hostile to such a person?

3. The "Reality" of Everyday Life

As Schutz pointed out, from the subjective point of view "to call a thing real means that this thing stands in a certain relation to ourselves."[33] By holding the natural attitude we place a certain kind of "accent of reality" on the objects and events we encounter. The following understandings describe in part how this kind of reality is created.

THE SUSPENSION OF DOUBT

In scientific research, we are accustomed to a certain cynicism that derives from the so-called scientific attitude: nothing is to be taken as what it appears to be without evidence. In certain kinds of philosophy there is an even more radical *epoché*, or suspension of belief. Descartes recommended that we suspend belief in all the knowledge that we have thus far accumulated in order to start afresh to build a personal knowledge. Husserl suggested that, to this end, we should suspend belief in the existence of the world, its objects, and even ourselves, as one of its objects. Yet the scientist or philosopher (unlike many paranoid patients) confines this cynicism to classroom discussion. He does not continue to think this way as he takes the bus home and greets his pet ("Pet?"—how do I know it's my pet? True, it looks like my pet and it *is* in my house. "House?"—Or is this my house?—etc.).[34]

In daily existence our epoché, the epoché of the natural attitude, is not the suspension of belief but the suspension of doubt. We assume that things are in fact what they appear to be unless we have reasons to do otherwise.

In a way we are forced to do this by the sheer volume of interpretations, predictions, and presumptions that must be made in an average day. Because of time constraints we are forced to take most of them for granted without "checking them out." Yet even when checking one interpretation out, in order not to take it for granted, we must do so by taking other interpretations for granted. For instance, if I think I may have misinterpreted what you said a minute ago, I might ask you if my interpretation was correct. But in order for this strategy to work, I must trust my interpretation of what you say to me now.

PRACTICALITY

Schutz regarded the idea of work to be at the core of what everyday life was all about, in several ways. In work there is some project, some goal, known to the doer, into which his actions fit as steps, means, or as mini-ends in themselves. This can be true for fixing a car, composing music, or selecting and getting to a movie. As a scheme of interpretation, "the job and its accomplishment" provides a way to structure the meaning of all acts occurring in connection with it. Most of our fact finding and reasoning within daily life have a practical, not theoretical, motive. The motive is the mastery and manipulation of the world so as to realize our various aims. All this can be summarized thus: We chronically assume about the people, events and happenings of daily life that we can be affected by them and can affect them, in imminently practical ways.[35] Because of this, we are anything but disinterested observers of this world. Its events and happenings are addressed with an eye to what they will do to us and what we can do to them.

THE TIME PERSPECTIVE OF EVERYDAY LIFE

As compared with other environments in other "worlds," daily scenes are addressed with a distinctive time sense. We can get a feeling for this time perspective if we compare it with that experienced in dreams, in reading a novel, or when viewing a play. In the last instance we permit a man to be born, grow up, and marry in a manner of minutes, while a single argument with his wife takes a half-hour.

Moreover, within his life, in the world of the stage, the next chronological event after his fight with his wife can be a similar fight with his mother when he was three. Not only does the scheme of time in plays differ from that used in ordinary life, but the time in a particular play need not coordinate to time in the "real" world within which it is placed. Thus Edna St. Vincent Millay's "Conversation at Midnight" can be performed at nine in the morning.

Interestingly enough, a coordination of the time in *two* "worlds" is required within everyday life. In the outer world is a socially approved scheme of temporal relationships, put into practice with paraphernalia like clocks, calendars, and names like "spring semester," "middle age," or "sundown." There is also our personal time sense, or *durée*, which is intimately related to the contents of our ongoing social life. Being in a queue, for instance, seems to automatically make us concerned with time in the form of "getting through the queue as quickly as possible." This concern occurs somewhat independently of whether there is any practical reason that we need to get done quickly. Yet here, "quickly" is defined by the queue, not the clock. Imagine that someone chooses a supermarket line that is shorter than another in order to get home faster. Then imagine that the longer line starts moving faster than the short one. In such a situation, this person might feel that it took a "long time" to buy the groceries, independent of the number of minutes that elapsed on a clock and whether or not he had any pressing need to leave the supermarket.[36]

Everyday life is characterized by the more or less constant coordination of our personal inner time experience with the standardized time and temporal reckonings of the society at large. This is done in the interest of scheduling interactions and projects with others. How "inner" and "outer" time are coordinated makes fascinating study material. If they are not coordinated, we become, on many occasions, functional incompetents in daily life.

This kind of incompetence is the daily nightmare of many centers for the treatment of heroin addicts. Addicts often do not wear or use watches, since their world and its time sense revolve around when they want or need drugs. Time is not measured in this world with the prevailing scheme of temporal reckonings. As a result, despite everyone's best efforts, they seem incapable of showing up for appointments anywhere near the time when they are due.[37] For almost any bureaucracy, that sort of failing in clients is fatal.

To characterize the time sense of everyday life in detail is extremely complex and will not be attempted here.[38] However, we have tried to give some indication of the kinds of things one would need to characterize in order to succeed in such an undertaking.

MULTIPLE REALITIES

Schutz regarded the world of everyday life as the "paramount reality." Other realities were worlds within the everyday world, produced by changing or modifying some of the assumptions of the natural attitude. One can readily see some of the reasons for this. Even while we are watching a play, dreaming, or working on a scientific problem, the everyday world is always "waiting in the wings," so to speak. In powerful and numerous ways, it may intrude upon and interpenetrate other worlds (corresponding to other cognitive styles) at any time. To the "you" in daily life, a dream comes off as an event within that life. Yet to the "you" in a dream, your waking life in society does not come off as an event in the dream world. Similarly, the waking world provides a standard piece of furniture, a special room, and a particular (horizontal) posture by which one enters the dream world, but there is no similar furniture, room, or procedure by which one enters the waking world from the dream world. Of course, you say, for the waking world is the "real" one. It is precisely because of assumptions like this that Schutz came to consider it the paramount reality.

A SCIENCE OF THE EVERYDAY WORLD?

There is now another way to put the problem of common sense. If everyday life were a "new place," we could study it and learn to understand it. But it is not a new place. We already live here, and only here, and understand it as natives. Our problem is to *replace* one form of knowledge with another. And doing this involves a lot of operations of the type "Do not think of the number three." That is, we must forget or pretend to forget what we already believe, know, and see.

Schutz finds our ability to do this in the world of everyday life itself. One reason we can succeed in this is that this world is structured so that one of the worlds within it (one of the "cognitive styles" that one can find, learn, and use) *is* the scientific attitude. Because this attitude is "around" in the world, there is the practical possibility of abandoning our naive participation in common sense thinking. Instead of believing and taking for granted most of the constructs of common sense thinking, we can pick up a practical and workable way to call these into question. In this undertaking we are assisted by society, insofar as "science" is a profession, "scientist" a job that brings pay, and "sociology" an activity which is both tolerated and accepted in social life. For example, instead of suspending belief, there are situations in which one is allowed critical doubt—such as in classrooms or scientific journals. In such situations, one is permitted the luxury of "not knowing what people mean without a linguistic analysis." In contrast, one is not permitted this attitude with his wife, or at the supermarket.

But there is a paradox here. If a world is a way of making sense of things, how can someone who adopts the *scientific* attitude study everyday life, which is literally produced in and through the use of the *natural* attitude? Imagine having a conversation with a friend within a dream. You would hardly approach the same friend after waking up and continue this conversation. Is there not an analogous situation when one compares the world of everyday life with the world of scientific theorizing? To what extent can the God whom you as a Christian, say, literally believe in be the same God that you as a scientist regard as the social invention of a group of people? Schutz defined the very stuff of reality, its very core, to consist in the cognitive stance one takes toward something. In that sense, is not the "reality" of a world created by *your* current cognitive attitude? Thus, could there be an everyday world to look at for someone who does not adopt the natural attitude and its component assumptions?

Here we have an old dilemma in yet another form. Either you stay in the world people live in, and thus naively participate in their myths, or you alter your cognitive style and leave this world for another one in which scientific knowledge is possible. Schutz believed that there was a way out of this dilemma, whether it arises scientifically or, as in this section, phenomenologically. However, Schutz's path to salvation is narrow, long, and rocky. We will not attempt to traverse it here, especially since we are convinced it leads not to heaven but to hell.[39]

While the effectiveness of Schutz's methods is a matter of reasonable debate, there is little debate about the importance of the topics that these methods were designed to deal with. It is common sense thinking, the ability to communicate with others about a world known in common, and the assumptions of the natural attitude that get sociologists and those they study through an average day. It is these assumptions, skills, and resources that enable sociologists to carry on the activities of their profession and somehow create, each day, the spectacle of institutions, social structures, and social facts which they believe in and undertake to study.

Notes

1. For Georg Simmel's treatment of number as it relates to social forms, see "The Number of Members as Determining the Sociological Form of the Group," *American Journal of Sociology* 8 (July 1902): 1–46 and (September 1902): 158–196.

2. Since a three-person group can agree in two ways (by all saying yes or all saying no) and disagree in six ways, the probability of their agreeing by chance alone is $2/(6 + 2) = 2/8 = 1/4$.

3. For Simmel's treatment of sociability, see "The Sociology of Sociability," *American Journal of Sociology* 55 (November 1949): 254–261.

4. Goffman has done several very different types of sociological work in the past and is currently developing additional modes of analysis. In this section we introduce the reader to only one variety of his work.

5. We are alluding to the concept of personal space here. However, social science does not treat this idea in the mechanistic way we have chosen for purposes of our metaphor. For a good introduction to the issues involved, see Robert Sommer, *Personal Space: The Behavioral Basis of Design*, Englewood Cliffs, N.J.: Prentice-Hall, 1969.

6. For Goffman's theoretical treatment of public places and the concepts relevant to their analysis, see his *Behavior in Public Places*, New York: Free Press, 1963, pp. 3–32.

7. For a discussion of involvement shields, see Goffman, *Behavior in Public Places*, pp. 38–42.

8. The reader should be made aware that the metaphor of "social physics" is ours, not Goffman's. Nowhere in Goffman's writings does he construe his work as mapping out a new social physics. We employ the figure for imagery only.

9. Goffman speaks of such norms in terms of "situational properties." For a discussion of situational properties and the significance of their violation, see Goffman, *Behavior in Public Places*, pp. 216–241.

10. The terms *gathering, coming into play, interactional tonus, personal front*, and being *present* to others are all used in various technical senses in Goffman's works.

11. In fact, Goffman contends that we recognize others as mentally ill, in part, by recognizing that they are violating the situational norms of face-to-face arrangements.

12. Goffman, *Behavior in Public Places*, p. 84.

13. Ibid.

14. Erving Goffman, *Strategic Interaction*, New York: Ballantine Books, 1975, p. ix.

15. Erving Goffman, *Interaction Ritual*, Garden City, N.Y.: Doubleday Anchor, 1967, p. 2.

16. When in note 4 we promised to elucidate only one aspect of Goffman's work, it was this one we had in mind—sociological "mapmaking."

17. Goffman, *Behavior in Public Places*, p. 4.

18. Actually we employ the concept of ontology somewhat loosely here, although it has been so used (or misused) by others. Often ontological inquiry is taken to be inquiry directed to the nature of "being" and "existence" (and types of existence) itself, not to

developing assertions about the sorts of things that "are" in some domain and the nature of their existence within that domain. However, even in a latter, stricter sense of ontology it serves as a philosophical grounding and methodological guide for sociological mapmaking.

19. See Erving Goffman, *The Presentation of Self in Everyday Life*, Garden City, N.Y.: Doubleday Anchor, 1959.

20. Goffman, *Behavior in Public Places*.

21. Goffman, *Strategic Interaction*.

22. Goffman, *Interaction Ritual*.

23. Erving Goffman, *Stigma: Notes on and Management of Spoiled Identity*, Englewood Cliffs, N.J.: Prentice-Hall, 1963.

24. Goffman, *Interaction Ritual*, p. 2.

25. Emile Durkheim, *Suicide*, N.Y.: Free Press, 1951, p. 44.

26. Emile Durkheim, *The Rules of Sociological Method*, Glencoe, Ill.: Free Press, 1962, p. 32.

27. Alfred Schutz, *Collected Papers I*, The Hague: Martinus Nijhoff, 1971, p. 44.

28. For Schutz's treatment of the natural attitude, "Common Sense and Scientific Interpretation of Human Action" and "On Multiple Realities," see parts I and III of Alfred Schutz, *Collected Papers I*.

29. Alfred Schutz, "The Stranger," *American Journal of Sociology* 49, no. 6 (May 1944): 499–507.

30. This is our paraphrase of Schutz's formulation. For his exact words, see Schutz, *Collected Papers I*, pp. 11–12.

31. Dr. Louis Narens of the University of California at Irvine made this observation in the course of his research with the mentally ill at the Los Angeles Neuropsychiatric Institute and pointed it out to us.

32. This case was taken from a videtaped interview with a paranoid patient made at the Los Angeles Neuropsychiatric Institute.

33. Schutz, *Collected Papers I*, p. 207.

34. Paranoid schizophrenics often address ordinary settings with what clinicians call the "hypothetical attitude." If one asks such a patient if he sees his mother in the waiting room, he might reply, "Maybe." From his point of view, what appears to be his mother may or may not actually turn out to be his mother.

35. Again, this is our paraphrase of Schutz's observation. For his treatment of our practical interest in the world, see various parts of his essay "On Multiple Realities" in Schutz, *Collected Papers I*, pp. 207–245.

36. This is not a hypothetical example. In research on queues Schwartz gathered much data to support the contention that people use the structure of a line to count and experience elapsed time.

37. Personal communication from Andrew Walter, Harvard University, who made a study of the time sense of heroin addicts in New Haven, 1973.

38. For a characterization of the time sense of everyday life, see Schutz, *Collected Papers I*, pp. 214–218.

39. In learning about the natural attitude, Schutz considered it critical for the scientist to

adopt a particular cognitive style which would make the features of this attitude available for scrutiny. The so-called scientific attitude could accomplish this in part. However, for certain problems, such as exploring how communication is possible, Schutz recommended more radical phenomenological methods which yielded more radical cognitive stances. Detailing these methods is beyond the scope of this book. However, the interested reader can consult the following works: *Collected Papers I: The Problem of Social Reality*, The Hague: Martinus Nijhoff, 1971; *Collected Papers II: Studies in Social Theory*, The Hague: Martinus Nijhoff, 1964; *Collected Papers III: Studies in Phenomenological Philosophy*, The Hague: Martinus Nijhoff, 1966; *The Phenomenology of the Social World*, Evanston, Ill.: Northwestern University Press, 1967; *On Phenomenology and Social Relations*, Chicago: University of Chicago Press, 1970; and *Reflections on the Problem of Relevance*, New Haven: Yale University Press, 1970.

CHAPTER 8

The World of Everyday Life: Reconstructing Sociological Knowledge

Once formal sociologists started to study everyday life, they found that they were not merely exploring a particular topic. They began to find affinities between their own professional concerns and those of the people they studied. If sociology is an inquiry into the nature, causes, and consequences of social action, then this activity is not limited to professionals. Sociological theory can be heard on any radio talk show, sociological data are gathered whenever an employer tries to figure out whom to hire, and sociological analysis is employed by members of a jury as they decide who is guilty and why. In fact, since sociologists are typically members of the very society they study, information about everyday living is information about professional sociology, considered as a collection of daily actions.

For all these reasons formal sociologists were all but forced to consider their own interpretations and activities, and those of their colleagues, as merely another set of instances of the phenomena they studied. This was a feature of their work—not a problem to solve or an obstacle to overcome. As a consequence they found themselves reconstructing sociological knowledge. They evolved new conceptions of sociology's topics, its methods, and the nature of sociology itself, construed as an everyday activity engaged in by lay persons and professionals alike.

In this chapter we shall be concerned with two of the major architects of these reconstructions and how their work led them to new understandings of what sociology is, or could be.

Harold Garfinkel and Ethnomethodology

Some time prior to the birth of ethnomethodology, Garfinkel was invited to participate in a study in which researchers had taped conversations in a jury room in order to examine how jurors go about their deliberations.[1] The situation of jurors had immediate interest. Here was a group of ordinary people who, in principle, could be anybody and everybody. They were being called upon to make extremely important decisions about other people's lives and other people's money. Yet their resources for making these decisions were scant at best. They might have to sift through facts and come to conclusions about things that completely transcended their personal experience—such as mental illness, murder, drugs, or elaborate financial manipulations. How could they do this? After all, jurors were usually people who were untrained in data analysis, cultural anthropology, clinical observation, or criminal law. In no clear way were they technical experts in analyzing other people's affairs. They were not even practiced at being jurors. There is no extensive folklore about juries obtainable from mothers everywhere or an apprenticeship program for prospective jurors. Under these circumstances, what makes them jurors? How do they know what they should do and if they are successfully doing it?

Whether or not they knew what to do, Garfinkel found in examining the tapes that they were actively doing it. "Doing it" meant, among other things, engaging in complex sociological reasoning:

> Those common sense models are models jurors use to depict, for example, what culturally known types of persons drive in what culturally known types of ways at what typical speeds at what types of intersections for what typical motives.[2]

In deciding such issues jurors did not feel at liberty to invent procedures. Far from it. They wanted to be fair; they wanted to be legal. They were concerned with such things as adequate accounts, adequate descriptions, and adequate evidence. In fact, if these people had been social scientists, we would say that they were using and discussing "methodology." But where did their "technical methods" come from and what sort of methods could they be? These were questions that Garfinkel asked as well:

> Here I am faced with jurors who are doing methodology, but they are doing their methodology in the "now you see it, now you don't" fashion. It is not a methodology that any of my colleagues would honor if they were attempting to staff the sociology department. They are not likely to go looking for jurors. Nevertheless, the jurors' concerns for such issues seemed to be undeniable.[3]

Garfinkel coined the term "ethnomethodology" to serve as a label for the methodology jurors invoked in reaching decisions. Used in this way, "ethnomethodology" acquired a perfectly reasonable, if undramatic, significance, a significance similar to terms like "ethnomedicine" or "ethnobotany" (meaning folk medicine, folk botany). Ethnomethodology would refer not so much to a discipline as to a subject matter: The subject matter would be the "methodology" used by ordinary people in everyday life when they reason about their society and its workings.

But who would these people be? Would they be lay persons or "folk" as opposed to scientists and professional sociologists? Would ethnomethodology be the study of folk reasoning as opposed to scientific and logical reasoning? We can begin to answer this question by considering how Garfinkel set about studying practical reasoning.

PRACTICAL REASONING AS PRACTICAL ACTION

It might have struck the reader that the jurors were a bit casual about their situation. They offered no protestations to the judge or to each other about their lack of preparation or the vagueness of their instructions. They simply and unabashedly proceeded to reach serious decisions about other people's lives.

Yet accepting the practical situation and working within it are not peculiar to jurors and lay persons, as compared with professionals. Garfinkel found it in every kind of social reasoning he investigated. For example, in studying how social scientists determine the cause of death at a "psychological autopsy," Garfinkel found them willing and able to use whatever evidence was available to make a determination:

> And *whatever* is there is good enough in the sense that *whatever* not only *will do*, but *does*. One makes whatever is there *do*. I do not mean by "making do" what a Suicide Prevention Center investigator is too easily content or that he does not look for more when he should. Instead I mean: the *whatever* it is that he had to deal with, *that* is what will have been used to have found out, to have made decidable, the way in which the society operated to have produced *that* picture, to have come to *that* scene, as its end result.[4]

Observations such as these pointed to the fact that people are not only willing to work within any given situation but able to do so. Members know how to take rules of counting, deductive logic, or the code of juror conduct into any situation where they have to use them, and *use* them. That is, members are able to adapt and articulate ideal procedures to concrete situations. Because of this, a whole orientation for studying practical reasoning presented itself. Garfinkel now had to ask, "What are the practical ways of counting?" "What are the practical ways of being moral?" or "What are the practical ways of using logic?"[5]

With such questions in mind he found a rich lore of social "savvy," not mentioned in any textbook or manual, whenever he studied any of the sciences. For instance, while deductive logic defined the procedures of adequate proof, these procedures were almost never used by logicians when actually proving something. Instead, abbreviations, references to "what we all know," skipping steps which are "trivial," and sundry other informal practices were the stuff of the classroom, the journal article, or the office discussion. Questions such as how formal to get, how much detail should be given at what points in the argument, or how important it is at this point not to make a mistake were decided by reference to the social situation, not the rules of logic.

Garfinkel's genius was in developing positive amnesia for his formal academic background, so as to sift out the actual things people worried about and the actual abilities they employed in getting a concrete job done in the real world. He took any and all of these contingencies deadly seriously no matter how "important" or how "unimportant," how "sociological" or how "silly." While one's politics or social class may very well have a lot to do with how he votes on a jury, so, it turned out, did an urge to go to the toilet, the wish not to look like an idiot, or how bored one was at the time.[6]

To Garfinkel, any credible theory of social action would now have to answer the following question to be taken seriously: How do members get concrete jobs done in the real world, using whatever resources are at hand? In answering this question, Garfinkel began to discover some of the methods of thinking and acting that he first encountered in the jury study. The reader can find descriptions of these abilities in Garfinkel's writings[7] under such titles as:

1. ad hoc practices
2. dealing with vagueness
3. etc. rules
4. making do
5. wait and see
6. enough is enough
7. glossing
8. let it pass

THE CONCEPT OF MEMBER

In looking at sociological reasoning as an activity done in practical situations, the distinction between lay and professional reasoning has no place. Any and all methods people employ to learn about their society are "folk" methods in the sense that they are sensitive to the requirements and benefits of everyday situations within that society. With this in mind, we would want to study competencies that are endemic to different social circumstances. If ordinary English is to be used, it would be necessary to endow some set of arbitrary "people" with these competencies for the purpose of discussion. To talk about competencies that are tied to practical situations, Garfinkel employed the dummy variable "member." Just as infinity is not a number like other numbers in mathematics but is to be read as one anyway, so "member" is not a person (or "members" a group of persons) but serves the syntactic and semantic functions of one for the purpose of talking about competencies.[8]

At the risk of oversimplifying several complex issues, the reader might understand a "member" as someone who possesses and displays sets of competencies in natural settings when faced with practical problems in daily life.[9]

PRACTICAL ACTION AND SOCIAL ORDER

Having cultivated an interest in practical reasoning, the next question becomes "How does one study it in a way that would shed light on major sociological issues?" When looking for a major sociological issue, one can hardly go wrong in selecting "How is society possible?" The notion of practical action in daily life makes it possible to rephrase this question as "How is everyday life possible?" For there they are, millions of people, lying motionless in the wee hours of the morning on ornamented contraptions situated within sheltered enclosures. At some point in the morning they sequentially come to life. Each composes a daily sonata of decisions, actions, and encounters. Put together these individual melodies, and society is re-created every day, complete with economic structure, interlocking directorates, municipal bus systems, motherhood, and McDonald's hamburgers. There is only one problem with this. Garfinkel found that society and its structure could not possibly be the product of everyday activities in the sense presented above. To see why, and to see what the relationships between society and everyday life might be, we must take up the topic of "rational accountability."

RATIONAL ACCOUNTABILITY

Imagine a perfectly reasonable possibility. Imagine sociologically "ignorant savages" whose ignorance consists in this: Their real world is made up of only those objects, events, and happenings which they directly encounter in the course of their daily lives. It is these things that are real to them. It is these things that they take into consideration in their practical plans and projects, take seriously, think about, explain, and analyze. That which transcends their daily lives—things they never actually come in contact with—are not real to them. Such phenomena are regarded as fictions, myths, mere intellectual abstractions—in fact, anything but the hard facts of life. In a way, this "ignorance" under another name is simply the critical attitude sometimes recommended in philosophy as the only sure road to valid knowledge. If people were critical in this way, they either would have no conception of such things as the national economy or the world supply of crude oil, or would not take them seriously.

But there are probably no people on the face of the globe that match this description of "ignorant savages." Individuals in society have always been dramatically aware of social facts and happenings that transcend their particular everyday lives. They have always portrayed and even celebrated such events through symbol systems, rituals, art, and folk science. And they have always linked such "cosmic" events to their concrete personal lives. The defeat or victory of the invading army was determined before deciding whether to plant crops; the temperament and disposition of the king was ascertained before consecrating a marriage; and knowledge of ghetto life obtained from TV was applied in deciding whether to convict a black man of robbery.

From this perspective, professional sociologists' concern with and belief in social facts per se is merely one, somewhat recent example of an activity and a preoccupation that has characterized societies for centuries. Such social facts, no matter what their nature, how they are known and discovered, or which group of people know and use them, are what Garfunkel has called "rationally accountable" features of everyday life:

> Not only does common sense knowledg portray a real society for members, but in the manner of a self-fulfilling prophecy the features of the real society are produced by persons' motivated compliance with these background expectancies.[10]

The above observation suggested a notion of social facts that contrasts with that ordinarily used by many sociologists. For most sociologists, social facts are real characteristics of society (as established and verified by professional social scientists) which individuals are subjected to. Societal members may or may not be aware of these facts, may or may not have accurate information about them, and may or may not actually take them into account in daily activity.

In contrast to this view, Garfinkel would take as social facts the rationally accountable features of social structure. That is, social facts would be:

1. Features of the society that members knew, discovered, used, and (above all) *talked about* in the context of daily activity.
2. Features of the society which were "accomplished" by practical reasoning in everyday life.

Thus knowledge of social facts in the above sense would be used in making common sense choices, in putting together excuses for violating traffic laws, in planning projects of action—in literally seeing, knowing, and displaying to others that one is acting rationally, that one is a reasonable person, "capable of managing his or her everyday affairs without interference." It is this sort of knowledge that Garfinkel referred to as "common sense knowledge of social structure."

But in what sense would the social structures of which members have common sense knowledge be "facts" or "factual"? In particular, in what sense were these facts "accomplished" by practical reasoning in everyday life? Would they be mere beliefs and theories about society which individuals "accomplished" a belief in? Would these beliefs be "real in their consequences" in the sense of W. I. Thomas?[11] Clearly we are asking one of the main questions ethnomethodology would have to answer: What is the relationship between social structure and practical reasoning in everyday life? It is to a preliminary exploration of this question that we now turn.

1. PRODUCTION ACCOUNTS

Consider the following edited transcript from a call-in radio talk show in New York:

CALLER: I have a gripe.

ANNOUNCER: What's the gripe, dear?

CALLER: Well, eh, the trains. You know, the people—— Uh, why do not they respect the so-called white cane? In other words, if they see me with the cane traveling the city et cetera, why do they not give me the so-called right of way?

ANNOUNCER: Well they probably do, once they see it. Hu, the trouble is——

CALLER: No, they don't, Brad.

ANNOUNCER: How d'you know?

CALLER: Because I've been on the trains before and they don't care whether I live or die.

ANNOUNCER: Well——

CALLER: (interrupting) Uh——

ANNOUNCER: Dear, *wait*, wait, wait, *wait*!

CALLER: Go ahead.

ANNOUNCER: Now, N——

CALLER: (interrupting) Okay——

ANNOUNCER: Don't ask a question and then answer it.

CALLER: Go ahead.

ANNOUNCER: Uh, you see, what happens, 'specially with New Yorkers, is that they get all preoccupied with their own problems...

CALLER: Yes.

ANNOUNCER: ... with the fallout and the pollution and the landlord...

CALLER: Yeah, mm hm.

ANNOUNCER: ... and they don't——

CALLER: (tries to interrupt)

ANNOUNCER: Now, wait a minute, let me finish.

CALLER: Go ahead.

ANNOUNCER: And they don't *notice*.

Here the radio announcer is confronted with a sociological problem which, in all likelihood he has never thought about before. Given this lady is blind, people should be considerate of her. So why aren't they? Yet the announcer does not behave like a social scientist. He gathers no evidence, does no interviewing, and makes no systematic observations. Instead he produces a theory that explains the behavior *in a fraction of a second*. He converts the place where the incidents occurred (New York subways) into who the people in the incidents were (New Yorkers). He identifies typical worries possessed by people in this category. Now these worries make them blind to her blindness—they are "preoccupied," they "don't notice," et cetera. What an elegant explanation! She above all people should appreciate the difficulties of being blind!

Clearly nobody knows what percentage of the people she actually encountered were New Yorkers, whether they did or did not notice her white cane, whether they were worrying about "fallout" or "pollution," or how representative they were of the general population. But his explanation does not have to be true in some ideal, scientific sense. It only has to be as good as her problem. In fact, it is built to have certain relationships to her problem, as she verbally presents it. Note the following symmetries:

1. She speaks in generalities.	He replies in generalities.
2. Her problem is a complaint.	His explanation is an excuse.
3. She has problems.	They have problems.
4. She is blind.	They are blind.

In Garfinkel's terms the announcer's story is an example of a "production account."[13] It is a sociological explanation, built on the spot, during the course of an interaction, exactly when it is needed, using whatever time, evidence, or knowledge is on hand. We ironically pointed out that the announcer's explanation might not be true. But this is a serious mistake. In constructing production accounts, members are not necessarily concerned with "truth" (although they might be). It might be far more important that the account be funny or plausible. In general, the adequacy of a production account is to be sought in its relationships to the interaction at hand. It is for this interaction that the account is consciously being built.

From production accounts we see that common sense knowledge of social structure is not learned and used in the way one learns and uses a list of items, stored somewhere in that mnemonic warehouse called the brain. Instead, it consists of *collections of procedures* which allow members to build endlessly new and different stories about society, to meet the needs of situations within that society.

To get a better idea of what might constitute a "situation in society," and how it might evoke accounts, let's look at perhaps the most pervasive situation of this kind: natural conversation.

2. FORMULATIONS

In studying how natural conversations are socially organized, Garfinkel and Sacks encountered the following phenomenon:

> A member may treat some part of the conversation as an occasion to describe that conversation, to explain it, or characterize it, or explicate, or translate, or summarize, or furnish the gist of it, or take note of its accordance with rules, or remark on its departure from rules. That is to say, a member may use some part of the conversation as an occasion to *formulate* the conversation.[14]

Formulations are descriptions of a conversation (or its parts) which are themselves utterances within the same conversation. They can be viewed as one way in which conversations describe themselves. From this point of view, what can be said about a conversation, when it might be said, who will say it, and how such a comment will be understood are all largely determined by the ongoing progress of the conversation itself (and the rules of conversing in general):

A: Isn't it nice that there's such a crowd of you in the office?

B: You're asking us to leave, not telling us to leave, right?[15]

If the ongoing conversation affects the sorts of things that get said about the conversation, then, as can be seen from the above, the things said about the conversation return the compliment. Not only do formulations define and describe previous talk, but they guide the course of future talk by calling forth replies, introducing new topics, and starting new kinds of sequences. As a consequence, perhaps nowhere are a socially structured activity and descriptions of that activity so organically welded, in so many ways, and in such detail as in ordinary conversation. As a result, the study of talk has given ethnomethodologists a whole cornucopia of metaphors for understanding the interweavings of the fabric of social order and practical reasoning. For example, consider the "etc." clause.

3. THE ETC. CLAUSE

A celebrated way to get society (through its members) to talk about its own structure is to break its rules. In the previous section we spoke of the "rules of conversing" putting a constraint on what could be said in any particular conversation. But what is the nature of a set of social rules, how do they constrain conduct, and how are they invoked and talked about in order to deal with trouble? In preliminary trials with games, Garfinkel, rather immediately, found interesting examples of trouble. He could find no game whose rules sufficed to cover all the problematical possibilities of action. Taking advantage of this, he engaged others in play and then acted in ways that were unusual but not prohibited by the rules of the game. His opponents insisted his actions were deviant and illegitimate. They made him promise he would not "do anything" in the next round of play. More interestingly, they wanted to assert that his actions were illegal, and suspected that they were illegal, but in terms of rules which they did not know and could not state.

Following up this lead, Garfinkel tried a similar procedure in connection with social rules and agreements. He would engage someone in conversation while he had a wire recorder hidden under his coat. At some point he opened his jacket to reveal the recorder, saying, "See what I have?" Seeing all kinds of new possibilities, subjects wanted to know what he was going to do with the recording. They claimed the breach of an agreement that the conversation was "between us," an agreement that had never been mentioned and, indeed, did not previously exist.

Apparently, any list of social rules, conventions, or agreements contains an "etc." clause at the end of it. This clause refers to an open-ended list of additional rules and agreements which members treat as binding and as "there all along."

Yet these rules remain unknown and unstated until some problematic action brings them to the fore.

If an etc. clause can add rules to a social arrangement, then apparently it can be used to subtract them as well. For when Garfinkel studied the rules of scientific inquiry, he found a situation that contrasted with the one encountered with the rules of games. In every case that he studied, practitioners permitted one another to relax these rules in various ways and still count the results of their actions as adequate scientific procedure. Witness this report of an informant, from case study A, on some of the practices of scientific sampling in practice, as opposed to sampling in theory:

> In the one I did for Tarnation some years ago, I had a phone book and I was told to go to page 552 and take every tenth name and address. That seemed to be a little more reasonable, as though it were real sampling, although it has its flaws too. Except even there, I had my own biases. If the tenth person happened to be a lawyer (informant's husband is a lawyer), I would just go down to the eleventh person and use his name. I just didn't think that lawyers needed to be bothered by a lot of dumb questions.

We do not want to be ironic here; Garfinkel did not want to be ironic, or to complain. He wanted to notice that *this is the way (or one way) that social rules are understood, talked about, and carried out.* In fact, he showed in various experiments that there is no way to eliminate or repair the etc. provision of social rules without making it impossible to carry out the rules themselves. Through practices like "etc.," socially organized conduct and talk about socially organized conduct are able to interact so as to make each other plausible, practicable, and even possible.

THE REFLEXIVITIES OF ACCOUNTS

The three previous study topics (and many others) can be summarized in the following way: We offer as an empirical observation that society produces depictions of itself, as part of its workings. We do not pass judgment on the relative accuracy of these depictions. We merely note that, somehow, society constantly provides its members with opportunities, motives, and methods for thinking about and analyzing it.

Garfinkel subsumed this observation and others under the heading of "the reflexivities of accounts." In mathematics, to be reflexive is to be related to oneself. The reflexivities of accounts, in Garfinkel's sense, consist in the many ways in which accounts about society and its workings are constituent parts of the very thing they describe. Let us be clear about what he is saying here. It is not that there are two things—(1) social order and (2) our methods of seeing, knowing, and talking about social order, which are nevertheless "connected." It is not that one causes the other or that one is a symbolic representation of the other. Rather the "two" are so inextricably interwoven into one cloth, in so many interesting ways, that another question becomes more interesting: Why do we separate them? What is it about sociology as an activity that makes us separate our social creations from ourselves and our activities, on so many levels, in so many ways?

INDEXICAL EXPRESSIONS

Now, this question could easily turn into a cliché. It is often said in social philosophy that human beings have a tendency to disconnect, or alienate, themselves from their own creations. But we do not know that yet, or even what it might mean for the case of social facts. To explore such a claim in a nontrivial way, two steps would be required:

1. Study if, and how, people who engage in sociological reasoning encounter Garfinkel's reflexivities—that is, the ways in which their descriptions of social order are embedded within, and are part of, that same social order.
2. See what they do about these reflexivities once they encounter them.

In pursuing this program, we immediately run into a problem. To "do something" about the reflexivities, members would have to be aware of them. But members hardly see themselves as engaged in "formulations," "production accounts," or "etc. practices." Is there some natural and consistent way in which members themselves become aware of these aspects of their reasoning? Garfinkel's answer was yes. He said that "reflexivity is encountered by sociologists in the actual occasions of their inquiries as indexical properties of natural language."[16] Before deciphering this statement, it is necessary to give a simple version of what is meant by "indexical expression."

In traditional philosophy various linguistic terms were encountered whose meanings depended on the context of their use, that is, on the person saying them, that person's biography, where and when they were said, and so forth. Such expressions included "I," "you," "here," "now," "this." When these "indexical expressions" appeared in an assertion, this assertion had no fixed truth value, since it had no fixed meaning. Sentences like "I am hungry now" could be true or false depending on when they were said and who said them. To avoid these wobbling meanings, philosophers repaired indexical expressions by replacing them with objective ones which possessed fixed meanings. Starting with "I am hungry now," for example, one might replace "I" with a proper name and "now" with a clock time and date.

Expanding on this simple idea, Garfinkel noted that everyday communication had indexical properties as well. The meanings and significances of talk depended on the contexts in which it occurred, but for rather different reasons from those envisioned by philosophers. When one speaks of an expression like "I" as being an indexical expression, one treats it as a linguistic symbol with a standardized meaning of the type found in the dictionary. It just happens that, in terms of its dictionary meaning, "I" refers to different persons, depending on context. But this is not why people habitually take context into account in practical situations. In particular situations people are not interested in idealized, standardized, or typical meanings per se. They are interested in *particulars*. They want to know what *that* particular woman meant or did not mean by *that* particular thing which she said at *this* time, in *this* place. It matters not what the dictionary says she means. For the dictionary may or may not be relevant to the situation at hand. The problem with members is that when they try to be practical, they really *are* practical. In this case, that means being ready, willing, and able to consider any bit of information which might bear on what is happening "here," "now," with "this one." And this contextual information is not only consulted to interpret things which are atypical and unusual. It is also used *to recognize the typical as typical*. It is just that, as social scientists, we have difficulty in seeing these artful abilities at work in situations where the dictionary would have sufficed to understand the meaning of a conversation or a newspaper article. This in part explains the rationale behind some of Garfinkel's attempts to introduce disruptive or senseless behavior into otherwise normal social settings (see chapter 10). Only by watching how members make sense of unusual, deviant, or bizarre behavior does it seem possible for us to notice some of the powerful interpretive abilities they employ in recognizing that which is unnoteworthy, ordinary, and mundane.

It might be thought that, if the desire to be practical is what is behind members' delicate attention to context, then children should be somewhat less interested in context than adults. After all, "being practical" is reputed to be something that happens to you only after you grow up. Actually, Garfinkel and his students found the opposite to be true. Children were willing, even happy, to let "Howard Schwartz" be a person, a stuffed animal, a repeatable noise, or whatever else it seemed like a good idea for this phrase to mean "this time." They had perhaps less loyalty to the dictionary than we, and they had yet to attend the sociology classes which explained how they were constrained by social norms and social structure. Perhaps as a result, children turned out to be unexcelled masters in the use of indexical expressions.

INDEXICAL PARTICULARS

For all of these reasons and more, Garfinkel abandoned the philosopher's concept of indexical expressions in favor of something he called "indexical particulars." A particular could be any concrete aspect of a situation which someone attends to—a word, a story, an action, or an event. What was the significance of that word, the implications of that story, the motive for that action, the consequences of that event? In studying how members answered such questions, it became necessary to wean many of the concepts that surrounded the notion of "indexical expression" from their philosophical mother. Instead of multiple and changing meanings being a property of idealized linguistic expressions, they were now a property of the way *people* happened to interpret actions, talk, and events. Instead of looking at the meanings of verbal and written communication only, attention was payed to actions, events, circumstances, future possibilities, and all manner of other "particulars" which may be relevant in a setting. Meaning no longer refers only to things like the person referred to by "I" or the clock time implied in "now," but encompasses various motives, implications, nuances, prospects, and whatever else members see in a particular. Finally, in philosophy and linguistics one can distinguish the expression itself from its different meanings. But alas, in sociology, where social objects "are" whatever people take them to be, one is not permitted this luxury. In a crowded theater, "Howard Schwartz" may not be a proper noun at all, but a noise—a noisy noise that is interfering with the movie (and to which the proper response may be "Shhh"). In short, in Garfinkel's hands the concepts of "meaning," "object that means something," and "context" have all turned into research topics. In pursuing these topics, the constant query was "How are they doing it?" What are the methods by which members create and define "meanings," "contexts," and "particulars," on an ongoing basis?[17]

To see what the answers to such questions might look like in a particular case, let's go back to an old friend. In discussing the jury study we permitted ourselves the liberty of speaking of jurors making "decisions." Ordinarily a decision is thought of as a certain type of social-psychological act. In taking such an action, one makes a "decision." Yet the jurors did not find it that simple to identify their decisions. Understandably, they were concerned with justifying their conduct in their own eyes and those of others. To that end, they would look back on what they had said and done and analyze it as one analyzes a set of data. The purpose of this analysis was to assign past events their "legitimate history," that is, to find ways in which what had been done was reasonable, fair, and legal. It was in the course of this analysis that past actions were collected together and described as "a decision about such and such, made for the following reasons." In other words, many decisions came into existence not so much by the jurors' taking certain actions as by their interpreting past actions *in a certain way*. And this "way" of analyzing and interpreting past actions was not learned in high school. It was learned and perfected, in large part, by engaging in the jury deliberations themselves. Apparently the relationships between an action, its meaning, and its context would prove to be complex indeed.

CONSTRUCTIVE ANALYSIS

The nice thing about indexical expressions (and indexical particulars) is that they are no surprise to members, nor are they our discovery. Most of us are vividly aware of how (and that) we use a wide assortment of assumptions, clues, and contextual information to dope out what other people are talking about. In ordinary informal communications we would have it no other way. Garfinkel showed, through numerous demonstrations, that such things as indexical expressions and vagueness are not merely allowed in everyday interaction, they are demanded. Fail to use and respect them, and you soon start losing friends (and you are lucky if it stops there).

But there is another side to this coin. What happens when sociologists encounter indexical expressions in their data—in the talk of a respondent during an interview or in the transcripts of courtroom proceedings? What happens when they discover them in their own professional communications—in their field notes or their articles and research reports? Graphs, tables, and numbers, for example, often become indexical expressions when sociologists try to use them as indicators of social processes. As an illustration of how this happens, consider a study of fertility and family planning in Argentina.[18] A common "indicator" of the family stability in a particular group is its divorce rate. Survey data from the study indicated that, indeed, few divorces, separations, or second marriages occurred among urban dwellers. Does this indicate family stability? It might, except for the awkward fact that there is no legal means of obtaining a divorce in Argentina. So it might equally well indicate that few people had the time or money to get a divorce from other countries. In fact, it turned out that some members of the middle and upper classes did obtain their divorces by mail or by traveling to other countries. But the survey not only revealed few divorces, it revealed few separations. However, the meaning of "separation" here is problematic. It was common in the lower classes, when marriages were in trouble, for both partners to take up other relationships, while retaining the "fact" of their marriage. Further, common-law marriages were widespread. In such arrangements husbands frequently would come and go over the course of a few years, although such movements were not official "separations." Thus the statistics on divorce and separation were indexical in the sense that, to know what they meant or "indicated," one had to know or assume things about the very phenomenon which the statistics were supposed to tell about. In the trade we call such problems "problems of validity" (does your statistic measure what it is supposed to measure, and how do you know?).

Although our example was confined to professional social science, Garfinkel found a similar pattern when the man on the street attempted to find out about some aspect of social life. To sociologists of all kinds, indexical expressions acted like harbingers of disease. Whenever they appeared, sociologists encountered various concrete problems in their research.

Why should indexical expressions be such convenient friends in everyday communication, and such nuisances for those trying to learn about society? A general answer may be sketched as follows: By and large, there is no way merely to observe the elements of society. The existence of a status sytem or the nature of family relations only becomes known through complex communications among society's members. To interpret these communications, one must know the contexts in which they occur. But finding and understanding "contexts"— answering such questions as Who? What? Where? and Why?—requires one to possess (or think he possesses) and use massive amounts of knowledge about the very social order he is trying to learn about. It is for this reason that indexical expressions confront members with various connections between their own practical reasoning and the social world they are reasoning about.

Previous studies had convinced Garfinkel that there was no remedy for this reflexivity. What fascinated him was that people who were engaged in sociological reasoning almost instinctively sought a remedy. When they encountered indexical expressions, they saw troubles, they had names for these troubles, and they devised all sorts of techniques for eliminating or mitigating them:

> If whenever housewives were let into a room, each one on her own went to some same spot and started to clean it, one might conclude that the spot surely needed cleaning. On the other hand, one might conclude that there is something about the spot and about the housewives that makes the encounter of one by the other an occasion for cleaning, in which case the fact of the cleaning, instead of being evidence of dirt, would be itself a phenomenon.[19]

What fascinated Garfinkel even more was that sociological "housewives" actually succeeded in cleaning up this indexical "dirt" to their satisfaction. By studying how members repaired, replaced, or otherwise dealt with indexical expressions and particulars, he had a way to locate and study the concrete, bread-and-butter procedures people used to transcend their membership in society. These were (often ingenious) techniques by which one psychologically, conceptually, or methodologically disconnected himself and his research activities from the social order he was trying to learn about. Of course, as always, this was done "for all practical purposes." Any form of analysis which, by its nature, used, and must use, these techniques was given the title "constructive analysis."

With the study of constructive analysis, ethnomethodologists faced a major fork in the road. They were committed to studying practical reasoning. All the reflexive relationships between social order and practical reasoning which others were trying to escape from, they wanted to study as phenomena. But what kind of reasoning would Garfinkel himself adopt in order to study practical reasoning? Would he, for example, engage in constructive analysis? He could not do that. For in constructive analysis many critical aspects of reflexivity (such as the indexical properties of language) had to be repaired, eliminated, or ignored before one could find out *anything*. To use it to study practical reasoning would be rather like examining the dirt in a room by employing a vacuum cleaner to clean things up a bit so you could see better.

It would seem that Garfinkel needed a way of working that welcomed reflexivity as a friend rather than treating it as an enemy. He needed, for example, to allow indexical expressions to show up anywhere and everywhere—whether in the talk of a respondent or in one's own theories—and yet present no "natural" difficulties. The ethnomethodologist would be a "member" of the society he studied. He and his research activities would exhibit the same properties as the activities he studied. Yet, somehow, this would not constitute a methodological problem on any level.

Such a way or ways of working (if they could be found) would constitute ethnomethodology's claim to being a radical discipline. We will not attempt to describe such methods here, or the thorny conceptual issues that surround them. We had a hard enough time just describing the work that led up to them.

THE STATUS OF ETHNOMETHODOLOGICAL "THEORY"

As the inventor of the term *ethnomethodology*, Garfinkel has been elected as the father of a radical discipline by a constituency that was not of his own choosing. A discipline, of course, needs theories; it needs methods; and it needs findings. Consequently Garfinkel's work was turned into Garfinkel's "perspective," Garfinkel's "approach," and Garfinkel's "concepts." Yet it was never clear that he wanted to create, or be part of, a "discipline." Quite the reverse. He came to believe that the methods used to study a particular social phenomenon should be *unique* to that phenomenon. Nothing could be more disastrous to such a program than the use of such ideas as "reflexivity" or "indexicality" as standardized, theoretical concepts. Consequently, all that we have said about ethnomethodology is best read as tenative, tenuous, and praxiological. It does not constitute a theory of social structure in the ordinary sense. If it is useful in making phenomena visible, use it. If not, don't. With Garfinkel we recommend that, if you are serious about finding out what ethnomethodology is, or could be—go do some.

It is to Garfinkel's credit that many who have followed this recommendation found themselves doing work which was not "ethnomethodological." A striking example of this is provided by Aaron Cicourel, a contemporary and collaborator of Garfinkel's during the formative years of ethnomethodology. In his early research Cicourel used some of the ideas of Schutz and Garfinkel to uncover hidden resources and assumptions used by his colleagues when they arrived at professional sociological "facts." This naturally led to an interest in how "facts," of whatever sort, are assembled, displayed, and authenticated within a society, institution, or social group. In pursuing this topic, Cicourel found himself adapting concepts and techniques from such a variety of disciplines that his work defied a unifying label. So he invented his own: "Cognitive sociology" would be the study of how language and meaning are acquired by individuals and used to create and make knowable a "real world."

Aaron Cicourel and Cognitive Sociology

A Zen master once asked his disciple to draw a perfect circle, freehand. Understandably, the disciple's attempt produced a wobbly figure that looked rather like a lopsided egg. Yet the master praised the disciple and even went so far as to call his effort "perfect." When asked how this wobbly figure could possibly be considered a perfect circle, the master replied: "It is not a perfect circle; however, it is a perfect whatever."

The wisdom of this story seems to have found its way into the sociology of everyday life. Instead of average people who clumsily muddle their way through each day, one gets the feeling that authors like Goffman and Garfinkel are writing about magicians. Just saying "Hi" to somebody seems to require pulling rabbits out of hats. For in doing so, one attends to "background expectancies," "conditional relevance," "situational improprieties," "membership categorization devices," and sundry other contingencies, most of which none of us has ever heard of. Yet these authors have found it necessary to coin terms such as these for the endless, complex things most of us seem to do in the course of performing an ordinary action.

It is of course possible to consider human beings as competent experts in any and every ongoing situation. One merely treats whatever they do, not as a failed attempt at something else, but as a successful example of whatever it is. Every action and every recognition becomes "a perfect whatever."

Even small children can be regarded as talented artists or social engineers if we conceive of "kids' talk" or "game playing" as technical achievements, accomplished with the use of specific knowledge, skills, and artful improvisation. In fact, this has been a traditional ethnomethodological stance toward children.[20] They are not imperfect adults but full-fledged members of "kids' culture," a distinct world of daily activities with its own demands and its own possibilities. In contrast, adults, both lay persons and professionals, frequently construe children as practicing to be grown-ups and interpret their actions as faulted versions of corresponding adult actions.

Cicourel was privy to an intellectual tradition that emphasized and beautifully elaborated all of this. To all of this he put a single question: "How did they get that way?" Where did all these skills and capacities come from? He noted that one can describe the rich and artful things that people do; one can explain how they are doing it. But in carrying out this program, one presupposes full-blown competence. The disciple of such a Zen master as we have described is incapable of making a mistake. Everything he does is a perfect "whatever," skillfully accomplished by however he accomplished it.

Thus we put our finger on a serious limitation of the ethnomethodological orientation. It postpones or obscures developmental issues. If Cicourel were to understand how social activities, skills, and collections of knowledge came about, he would have to find some perspective more conducive to answering "How did they get that way?"

THE PROBLEM OF LANGUAGE ACQUISITION

As an example of the need for such a perspective, consider language acquisition. We all know how to talk. Speech is perhaps the most common skill and the most pervasive activity of the human species. Whether young or old, black or white, American or South African, we all know how to talk. That says a lot. It says that we possess a skill of a complexity and subtlety that are far beyond the capacities of even our most sophisticated computers.[21] It says most of us (not just some of us) take to talking as fish take to water. It is widely held that the kind of communication we call language is unique to our species. We somehow "learn" how to produce and understand an infinite number of sentences, most of which we have never heard or uttered before and which bear no simple correspondence to anything we have ever encountered others saying in the past. No theory of learning currently known can account for how such a skill is acquired.[22]

Of course, the fact that learning theory cannot explain how we acquire language competence does not mean that we do not, in fact, learn it. It may simply indicate deficiencies in learning theory. But the trouble is that in fact we don't learn language in the usual sense of learning. For the most part, parents do not know how to teach it.[23] Even if they did, their efforts appear to be super-fluous. Put even retarded children in front of a television set, rob them of the physical presence of competent language users, deprive them of any teaching and learning (whether good or bad), of any schedule of rewards and punishments, and some of them will acquire a surprising amount of language competence anyway. In fact, it appears that good language development is not contingent on specific training measures. A wide variety of rather haphazard factors seems to be sufficient.[24]

Thus, looking at language, we are confronted with a dilemma. To the question "How did they get that way?" psychologists usually answer, "They learned it." But learning theory is incapable of dealing with language acquisition.[25] To the same question, sociology's answer is "They got socialized." But this is little more than saying, "Those who got it somehow gives it to those who ain't." Advances in ethnomethodology and formal sociology did no more than deepen the mystery, for they revealed that natural communication was even richer and more complex than linguists had imagined. New skills, new accomplishments, new "whatevers" were unveiled for explanation.

For Cicourel the question remains: Where do I go from here? Interestingly enough, linguists had some ideas which suggested a direction. They claimed that the languages of every culture have certain "universal" characteristics and postu-lated that these universals were present in all speaking cultures because of certain biological features of the human species. The ability to acquire and use language was an innate, biological characteristic of human beings.[26]

Yet Cicourel could not be satisfied with vague references to human biology or language universals. Here was one of the most basic human activities, an activity that many have suggested is at the bottom of the mystery of common culture—of social life itself—and nobody knew why human beings were capable of it in the first place. The problem was especially acute because of the many and deep connections between language competence and sociology itself. It is to these connections that we now turn.

LANGUAGE AND SOCIOLOGY

Did you ever wonder what our lives with one another would be like if we couldn't talk? That is, let's assume that the linguists are right, that the ability to acquire and use language is biologically programmed. Without these innate abilities, what would social life look like, what would society be?

The "taking other people into account" that the symbolic interactionists speak of would be absent or drastically altered. For some kind of communicative scheme resembling language is universally found at the center of all human interaction, human organization, or organized conflict. In fact, one finds it in any and all actions where one person must be in complex intersubjective "touch" with another. If, indeed, language abilities make complex coordinated action possible, and if such actions combine to produce families, bowling leagues, and nation-states, then the simple and universal fact that we all know how to talk may be what makes society itself possible. There are many who strongly believe this.

Second, once language is somehow mastered, it is constantly used in order to learn almost everything else—including new languages, driving a car, and technical nomenclatures such as are found in calculus, physics, and sociology.[27] It is unclear how many of these abilities would survive, and in what form, without the mastery of language.

Third, a distinct world of actions and objects would be unavailable to us. There would be no poets, jokes, soap operas, or gossips. Indeed, there might not be any sociologists insofar as most sociology consists of talking and writing.

Finally, our knowledge of the world and of one another would be unimaginably altered. For natural language (and its derivatives) is the idiom through which we assemble and display knowledge to one another and to ourselves and the idiom within which we think. What would a sociology look like whose practitioners could not think and talk in English, French, or any other natural language?

In summary, talking in many ways is the primordial social activity, an activity which is fundamentally done "together" (even when it is done alone) and one that, more than any other, makes it possible for us to be "together" in the first place.[28] With all of this in mind, one might think that sociologists would be tremendously interested in this topic. In fact, they are not. Most sociologists know little about language and care less. Sociolinguistics remains a relatively underdeveloped specialty with little impact on the rest of the field.[29] In fact, Cicourel is one of the very few researchers who treats the mystery of language competence as one of the basic problems of sociology.

COGNITIVE SOCIOLOGY

The last sentence gives a clue to how Cicourel answered "Where do I go from here?" and to why problems in communication have not become central issues in sociology. Ordinarily, speaking and hearing are thought of as activities done with the vocal chords and the ears. More pointedly, the cognition of speech is a matter of perceiving sounds and translating them into meanings by means of a "code" called language. Thus, under this conception, the sending and receiving of sounds and the code called language can be studied apart from the other skills and competences associated with social life.

Is language the ability to send and receive sounds with the use of a linguistic "code"? Should the lines be drawn in this way? To answer this (actually he had already tentatively answered no), Cicourel went looking for universals of a different sort. Instead of studying different languages, he studied different kinds of languages—for example, improvised and highly developed sign language as used among the congenitally deaf, communication among the retarded, and talk among small children. Instead of studying different cultures, he and his students studied different social situations—interaction in encounter groups, interchanges between teachers and grade-school children, even scientific communication in the context of sociological research.[30] Through all this the prevailing question was "What sorts of things do people do when they communicate with each other?" Universals of sorts were found, but not linguistic universals. The common elements in these different communicative situations, listed below, provided a very different vision of what language is.

1. Multiple sources of information, sights, sounds, body cues, and biographical knowledge are selectively attended to as the need arises and are integrated together in order for one to understand and be understood.
2. Meanings are not obtained from sounds by means of a "code." What is meant is always more than what is said, in that background knowledge and social contexts are continually used to fill in the gaps in messages, to pass back and forth from what is being said to what is meant.
3. To talk and to listen are to improvise in most of the popular senses of that word—to guess, to invent new meanings and conventions on the spot, to let things pass, to wait and see later what was meant now, to select from multiple courses of linguistic action any of which are "correct," to fudge, to gloss, to make do.

These observations suggested a tentative, if surprising, conclusion. Ordinarily in sociology, a sense of social structure—that is, the ability to tell "who's who," "what's going on," "what's expected of me," and so on—is considered to be a secondary set of skills, acquired after language is acquired and taught through the use of language. The feeling Cicourel now had was that these two achievements had to be put on at least an equal basis. In all the diverse communicative situations he had studied, the ability to produce and decode sounds could not be separated from the ability to know and use a sense of social structure. At the very least this suggested a redefinition of language.

But there are eerier implications here. One might have little difficulty in combining a few social and linguistic concepts into a new definition of language.

But what if the social skills are independent of and *prior to* the language skills? What if the innate capacities used to acquire language were social *from the outset*, not linguistic? That is, there might be a set of cognitive abilities through which human infants acquire a sense of social structure, and it is through these abilities that particular languages, among other things, are acquired. From the conventional way to think about this issue, this would be inconceivable and outrageous. However, Cicourel was willing to conceive of it, and he had been outrageous before.

The first hints of the possibility came from studying esoteric languages. The congenitally deaf, after all, display complex social "savvy" far before being taught to speak by the oral method in school. Yet, however they engage in thinking, however they engage in reading, it cannot be through a voice talking to them in their head. For they have never heard, nor will many of them ever hear, a human voice.[31] Similar hints were available from the blind. One of Cicourel's students reported a blind woman's description of how she followed complex directions in walking through the city.[32] She said she translated the verbal directions into a tactile map and that she imagined this must be something like what sighted people call a visual map. Indeed there were similarities. However, she described puzzlements such as this: She could not understand how, starting on one street, one could walk down a cross street, turn right and walk down a street parallel to the first, turn right again walking up another cross street, and finally end up on the same street she had started from. Clearly when such a person "imagined things," it was not through a series of pictures in her head. In short, pictorial imagery and verbal dialogue appear to be the main thinking idioms of most adults. Yet there are people who use their minds in completely different ways and yet are able to figure out the culture. Perhaps a sense of social structure is available by multiple means, means other than what we ordinarily treat as language competence. Or again, maybe we had better widen our concept of language competence far more than we previously dreamed of doing.

The next step was clear: Begin at the beginning and look at children. So Cicourel and his students entered the field of psycholinguistics and performed such experiments as the following:

> We employed a procedure in which sentences having direct and indirect object constructions (in active and passive voice) were acted out and imitated by pairs of pre-school and kindergarten children (aged three to six years). There was a table of toys beside the children which they identified before the test began. The sentences typically required one child to give an object to, or receive an object from, the other child.[33]

He and his students looked at more complex situations such as teacher-child interaction in the classroom.[34] These episodes were meticulously scrutinized using videotapes and supplementary interviewing strategies.

It appeared that long before they mastered what adults would consider a rudimentary grammar and vocabulary, children constructed a world that was undeniably social, a world that included such things as "monsters," "bad guys," and "orange worms." Yet their social world was not our social world. Adults find it all but impossible to give satisfactory accounts to very young children of such things as "property," "privacy," "why it is dangerous to cross the street," or "why something is poisonous although it looks like candy."[35] Yet these same children daily engaged in complex socially structured activities among themselves and with adults. Cicourel found that even in acting out the simple instructions, they were attending to an impressive array of visual, kinesthetic, biographical, and contextual information. How could these children's social world and socially organized conduct be explained? Surely not by reference to the common culture known to adults. They did not know the culture yet; they had not learned a natural language worthy of the name. Not only did they not have any "values" or follow any "norms," many of them did not know what a social norm or value could possibly be (or if it was permissible to eat one).

Given these observations about children, the deaf, and the blind, we have to credit the possibility that social orders and social worlds can exist without many of the things dear to the hearts of sociologists, such as languages, roles, and values. With this in mind, Cicourel embarked on a search for what he called "interpretive procedures."

INTERPRETIVE PROCEDURES

Cicourel's peculiar research problem seemed to be this: Locate a set of skills that are perhaps innate, perhaps learned, but not linguistic. Locate a set of inherently social skills through which one can acquire language competence and a sense of social structure *as part of a single process*. These skills would have to be "generative" in the sense that "they constitute a few (but not exhaustive) procedures interacting together so as to produce instructions for the speaker-hearer for assigning infinitely possible meanings to unfolding social scenes."[36] They would also have to be "universal" in that they could be known and used without knowing a particular language or a particular culture.

In his search for these skills, Cicourel supplemented his work on children with studies of animal social behavior, findings in information theory and artificial intelligence, and some original work on the development of entire language systems in other cultures. Through this work he tried to identify a set of "interpretive procedures" which would be used to acquire language and culture. He even speculated that "What seems plausible despite little or no empirical evidence is that children acquire interpretive procedures *prior* to their use of language" (emphasis added).[37]

Here we cannot describe these procedures or how Cicourel uses them to analyze the activities of children and adults. We can do little more than give the reader some idea of the questions this kind of analysis is designed to answer.

One such question is the following. Social scientists commonly conceive of speaking in a language, or performing any other social action, as a process of using general rules to decide on particular actions. The term "general rule" here has the widest possible meaning and includes values, norms, roles, strategies, rules of grammar, and so on.

Cicourel's central concern is this: Assuming that a person is in possession of a motley collection of diverse social "rules," we have yet to explain how and why he treats one or some of them as relevant or necessary guides to particular actions and interpretations. For obviously, whether they are traffic laws or rules of grammar, rules are not uniformly applied to all and only those situations where they are appropriate. Instead rule invocation is "spotty." This is all but necessitated by the fact that many different rules and combinations of rules are applicable to the same particular cases, yielding incompatible lines of action. So how is it that members determine when to articulate which sets of rules to use as a guide in connection with which sets of practical actions?

For an answer to this and similar questions which utilize "interpretive procedures," we refer the reader to Cicourel's book *Cognitive Sociology*.

The "Fact" Construction Business

In carrying out his research program, Cicourel encountered huge (sometimes preposterous) methodological difficulties. For example, how does one identify and describe nonverbal and perhaps preverbal abilities—in words?

> As I review the tape over and over again, I find it difficult to describe what I think I "see" and "hear." I think I "understand" many kinesic, visual, and auditory nonverbal activities that are "happening," but find it difficult to represent them verbally for the reader. As I notice the children communicating to one another with glances, one word statements, pointing gestures, non-verbal auditory outbursts, touching each other, and the like, I assume that various kinds of information are being exchanged but I cannot be explicit about the presumed content.[38]

In exploring the question "How did they get that way?" Cicourel encountered a second question: How am I reconstructing how they got that way? He had already documented how statistical methods produced representations of human beings, what they did, and how they did it that were artifacts of the statistical methods themselves. As Cicourel put it, "They package people in mathematical containers and then they discover the features of their own packages as the features of the people in them."[39] Yet now he had to perform the same task for his own work. In studying children and their talk, he found himself imposing adult conceptions of language on their verbal and nonverbal actions as means with which to understand what he was seeing and hearing. He found this to be prevalent in psycholinguistic and educational research as well. He was not a child, he did not remember what it was like to be a child, and he had only the most fanciful images of what the world of children was like. Yet he was constituting himself as an expert on child development and explaining children's lives as seen through his socialized, rational eyes and accompanying instruments, measurements, and theories. In studying sign language among the deaf, Cicourel found himself to be someone who had always lived in a world of sound, who was all too familiar with the conceptions of language invented by hearing people who had always used oral communication as their main resource; he found himself to be someone whose very profession consisted in thinking and communicating in an idiom which was fundamentally foreign to the congenitally deaf. Indeed, how could his version of language acquisition apply to someone who had learned to produce English sounds with her vocal chords, and yet had never heard a sound in her entire life? The reader might find these to be unusual problems. But Cicourel was convinced that they were not unusual in terms of how sociologists produce data. They always employ cultural abilities and tacit information, acquired prior to witnessing a social scene, in order to recognize the scene for "what it is"—for example, a "teacher asserting authority" or "a sergeant playing his role." They describe such a scene using criteria that are foreign to the scene itself. Diverse idealizations and concepts are taken from their own discipline and pressed into service to represent the scene as a set of abstract, objectified people and events. This is the process that eventually produces the tables, sets of numbers, or transcripts of conversations which find their way into texts under the section marked "Data." Along with their own special ways of being read and understood, these products—these data—would be what was reaped from the harvest of empirical research. In their terms, theories and hypotheses about people would be validated.

About all of this, Cicourel asked a question of himself and his colleagues: Exactly how do you obtain and produce your facts? What are the activities, the processes, the involved parties, and the notional conventions responsible? Only by finding this out could Cicourel decipher the significance of particular studies, including his own, or sociologists' relationship to the people and situations they study and learn about. To this end he devised what has become for him almost a standard research procedure. He would do a study on some topic, be it fertility or toilet training. Simultaneously he would arrange for a study of the study, concerned with the means by which the primary study produced and validated its findings. This is different from the customary practice of describing the ongoing progress of one's research in a methodological appendix. In the formal study of the study, he arranges for structured observations and experiments to occur in connection with his own efforts. In effect, the researcher and the research become a subject for research and a social phenomenon. One can get some sense of the flavor of this strategy from the following passage. In it Cicourel describes how he produces "basic data" from repeated viewings of a videotape of a classroom:

> An initial problem we face is deciding the kind of stimulus field the children attend and understand and how the teacher orients herself to the children's responses. In examining the video tape I presume much more than is available from the tape itself because I know something about the classroom independently of the tape. My memory provides background information which is imposed on the film and integrated with my viewing of the tape as I make observational claims which seem to be clear and

obvious. Depending on what I think I see or hear and imagine the teacher and children to be doing in the setting captured by the perspectival view of the video camera, I selectively attend information and create judgments in a context that I hope represents what is happening on the video tape in some logical fashion. My description trades on terms I presume will be intelligible and convincing to the readers of the paper.[40]

It should be noted that this strategy is *not* designed to ensure the validity of the primary study. For it could be asked: Why stop with a study of a study? Why not continue with a study of a study of a study? If the validity of a research project is threatened by the fact that one was not aware of his own tacit assumptions and activities, could this not be said of the study of the study as well? Clearly, if one is worried about validity, and looking at one's own activities with the primary motive of checking the research for logical problems and fallacious inferences, an endless infinite regress presents itself.[41] But if one is merely gathering information on how people assemble and display facts, the situation is quite different. This is especially true if one suspects that all fact gathering has certain things in common. For in that case, a study of a study will reveal the same properties of "fact-finding activities" as will a study of a study of a study. In short, to learn about fact finding as an activity, one need not start an infinite regress that will be eventually handed over to one's grandchildren.

INDEFINITE TRIANGULATION

Nevertheless, Cicourel produced practical versions of the infinite regress so that he could study it. In asking how people (including himself) assembled versions of "what really happened," he devised procedures which produced an indefinite number of different accounts about "what really happened" in some social setting. He also generated accounts of these accounts, accounts of the accounts of the accounts, and so on. An example of one of these "indefinite triangulation" procedures is provided by Marshal Shumsky's study of an encounter group:

> Shumsky placed one of the older members on the "hot seat" of intensive group focus soon after the session began. As soon as attention was diverted from him, he was removed from the session and asked to provide an account of what had occurred in the group to that point. After this account was audio-taped, he was shown portions of the video tape which depicted his "hot seat" experience and he was again asked to address particulars identified by the interviewer.
>
> The group member with limited experience arrived an hour and a half after the group started. She was allowed to participate for about ten minutes, then she was removed from the group and was interrogated in the way described above. Of particular interest here was the way she described the part of the session she did not experience directly but saw on video tape.
>
> Finally the participant with the least experience in the group was interviewed. One month later the same group members were interviewed independently of each other. . . .[42]

Using procedures like these, Cicourel found ways to realize yet another of his aims. He did not wish to leave social science behind in a search for some sort of esoteric knowledge about obscure topics. His research should be commensurate with that of other practitioners in similar fields and should be understandable to them. One way this could be done was to treat the results of other research as take-off points from which to start his own inquiries, inquiries that might ground and deepen the original studies. There was really no choice but to do this anyway. His experiences with the deaf, with the blind, and with children alerted him to the many modalities that human beings attend to while they communicate and interact with one another. Simultaneous attention to sights, sounds, smells, kinesthetic cues from one's own body, and social knowledge was the rule, not the exception.[43] All of these things were taken into account in planning coherent lines of action and interpretation with one's fellows. No one academic discipline could possibly encompass all the theories and methods needed to study such processes. For these processes knew nothing of the division of knowledge into special departments at major universities. They simply were what they were. In dealing with this fact, Cicourel has thus far found it necessary to delve into the following specialties, among others:

1. Transformational linguistics, psycholinguistics, and sociolinguistics.
2. Computer programming and mathematical modeling.
3. Memory and attention theory (psychology).
4. Artificial intelligence and information-processing theory.
5. Social biology (social behavior among animals).
6. Ethnomethodology and phenomenology.

All these orientations and many others not mentioned here were integrated into an area of investigation which Cicourel has called "cognitive sociology." Cognitive sociology would address the sociological issues inherent in what is ordinarily treated as human cognition, the activity of grasping "what's going on" and acting accordingly. In Cicourel's own words:

> My current research seeks to [examine] the general problem of how persons in different social and cultural groups have sought to develop, represent, and evaluate their communicational strategies. . . .
>
> Stated another way, this means how social or cultural groups create something we have called "language," the way this representational form captures and truncates our experiences and the way we use language to make claims about knowledge.[44]

Latter-Day Followers

Garfinkel and Cicourel represent two of the most well-known social scientists who have attempted to reconstruct sociological knowledge by coming to grips with everyday activities. Yet there is an increasing number of their colleagues who are attempting similar reconstructions, but along slightly different lines. The result has been a proliferation of schools of thought, orientations, and disciplines in recent years, all of which, in one way or another, focus on everyday life as a method of doing sociology.

It has been claimed that many of the disciplines which claim Schutz, Garfinkel, Cicourel, Goffman, or Simmel as their "fathers" are not disciplines at all but "clubs." That is, they are collections of people, many of whom are in informal contact and collaboration with one another, who use labels like "phenomenological sociology" or "ethnomethodology" as umbrellas for very different kinds of work. There is no question but that this "critique" is true, if it be a critique. We shall list many of the current practitioners who have been inspired and informed in one way or another by the sociologists discussed above. Yet work in formal sociology at this time does not permit its division into a number of neat piles. The reader should therefore be advised that the assignment of "mentors" to these researchers is a loose approximation, undertaken for convenience.

1. Simmel-Goffman: Forms of Sociation
   Marvin Scott   Stanford Lyman
2. Husserl-Schutz: Phenomenology
   Phillip Roth   Edward Tiryakian
   James Heap   Peter Berger
   George Psathas   Thomas Luckmann
   John O'Neill   Burkart Holzner
   Jack Douglas
3. Garfinkel-Cicourel: Ethnomethodology–Cognitive Sociology
   Don Zimmerman   Lindsey Churchill
   Larry Wieder   Thomas Wilson
   Albert Adato   Melvin Pollner
   Alan Blum   David Sudnow
   Peter McHugh   Egon Bittner
4. Harvey Sacks: Conversational Analysis
   Emmanuel Schegloff   Roy Turner
   Anita Pomerantz   Matthew Speier
   Alan Ryave   Gail Jefferson
   Jim Schenkein

Notes

1. For a discussion of this jury study, see Harold Garfinkel, *Studies in Ethnomethodology*, Englewood Cliffs, N.J.: Prentice-Hall, 1967, pp. 104–115.
2. Ibid., p. 106.
3. Roy Turner (ed.), *Ethnomethodology*, Baltimore: Penguin Books, 1974, p. 16.

4. Garfinkel, *Studies in Ethnomethodology*, p. 18.

5. Some of these questions represent actual studies undertaken by Garfinkel. For example, he studied counting in the context of enumerating bed patients at an inpatient mental hospital. In Garfinkel's words, the procedures for doing this turned out "not to satisfy the requirements of 'Piano's postulates.'" Similar studies were undertaken to determine the practical procedures used by logicians in doing mathematical logic.

6. These examples are not used by Garfinkel but are employed by us to illustrate the problem in common sense terms.

7. Discussions of these subjects can be found not only in *Studies in Ethnomethodology* but also in the following works: Harold Garfinkel and Harvey Sacks, "The Formal Properties of Practical Actions," in *Theoretical Sociology*, ed. by John C. McKinney and Edward A. Tiryakian, New York: Appleton-Century-Crofts, 1970; Harold Garfinkel, "A Conception of and Experiments with 'Trust' as a Condition of Concerted Stable Actions," in *Motivation and Social Interaction*, ed. by O. J. Harvey, New York: Ronald Press Company, 1963.

8. The analogy between Garfinkel's use of the term *member* as a noun and mathematicians' use of the symbol ∞ (infinity) as if it referred to a number like 3 is not without merit. Both shorthands are designed to avoid complex expositions in favor of convenient metaphors. For example, in mathematics one might say, "As the number n goes to $+\infty$, the fraction $6/n$ goes to the number 0." If written out literally, this assertion looks something like this: "For any small number x, there exists a large number y, such that, if n is greater than or equal to y, then the fraction $6/n$ is less than x." Clearly the second exposition is not only longer than the first, but qualitatively unlike it, in terms of the image it conveys.

9. Actually there are more subtle considerations involved in understanding the notion of member. Our rendition of "member" is not Garfinkel's, although we hope it can be used to "find one's way into" Garfinkel's usage.

10. Garfinkel, *Studies in Ethnomethodology*, p. 53.

11. For those unfamiliar with this phrase, W. I. Thomas pointed out that if people take something to be real, it is real in its (social) consequences.

12. These data—from a recording of the Brad Crandel Show in New York City—and the outline of their analysis come from Harvey Sacks. His own analysis is available in his unpublished lecture notes, University of California at Irvine, 1970.

13. Actually Garfinkel uses the term *production accounts* in a much broader sense then we do here. Strictly speaking, our example would be only one *kind* of production account.

14. Garfinkel and Sacks, "The Formal Properties of Practical Actions," p. 350.

15. Ibid.

16. Ibid., p. 338. See this article as well for Garfinkel's treatment of indexical expressions, indexical particulars, and constructive analysis. A review of indexical expressions, as treated in philosophy, can be found in Yehoshua Bar-Hillel, "Indexical Expressions," *Mind* 63 (1954): 359–379.

17. Actually, things are far more complex than we have presented them here. Garfinkel found that "meanings," "objects," and "contexts" shifted, expanded and contracted, and collapsed into each other after the manner of what he called a "swarm" (as in swarm of bees).

18. Aaron Cicourel, *Theory and Method in a Study of Argentine Fertility*, New York: Wiley, 1973.

19. McKinney and Tiryakian (eds.), *Theoretical Sociology*, p. 306.

20. For a discussion of this view of children's culture, see Mathew Speier, *How to Observe Face to Face Communication*, Pacific Palisades, Calif.: Goodyear, 1973, pp. 138–159.

21. For a discussion of some of the problems in computer simulations of language competence, see Aaron Cicourel, *Cognitive Sociology: Language and Meaning in Social Interaction*, New York: Free Press, 1974, pp. 99–140.

22. For a well-known discussion of these issues, see Noam Chomsky, *Cartesian Linguistics: A Chapter in the History of Rationalist Thought*, New York: Harper and Row, 1966.

23. This is not to say that parents do not instruct their children in language use or that these efforts do not somehow bear on the acquisition of language. However, there are certain critical elements of language that cannot be taught in the ordinary sense. For a discussion of the intricate issues involved, see Cicourel, *Cognitive Sociology*, pp. 42–73.

24. See E. H. Lenneberg, "On Explaining Language," *Science* 164 (1969): 635–643. By this we mean that one method of teaching children language does not seem superior to another, that children can be exposed to adults with varying language capabilities who speak to them in varying amounts and in different ways. Yet such children appear to acquire language at about the same rate with about the same degree of fluency. Many other "variables" of this kind do not seem to appreciably alter language acquisition.

25. More precisely, behaviorists can explain *why* children acquire language—they are rewarded for language behavior by parents and others. But they cannot explain *how* it is done—how children figure out the amazingly complex behavior that adults seem to like and reward.

26. Lenneberg, "On Explaining Language."

27. For a fascinating account of how the congenitally deaf employ natural sign language as a take-off point for learning both formal sign systems and normal oral language, see Aaron Cicourel and R. Boese, "Sign Language Acquisition and the Teaching of Deaf Children," in *The Functions of Language: An Anthropological Approach and Psychological Approach*, ed. by D. Hymes et al., New York: Teachers College Press, 1972.

28. When we say that talking is done "together" even when done alone, we have George Herbert Mead in mind. In "talking to oneself" one listens to one's own talk from the standpoint of a "generalized other" member of society, and uses what this "other" hears to decide on what to say next. As we mentioned in our discussion of Mead, inner dialogue is more like a conversation between two social role types, such as "sinner-moralist," than it is like self-reflection.

29. This statement is more our opinion than established fact. However, it is a widely held opinion.

30. For accounts of this work, see the various articles in Cicourel, *Cognitive Sociology*.

31. For an account of the various problems of the congenitally deaf in a hearing world, see Cicourel and Boese, "Sign Language Acquisition."

32. Personal communication from Dr. Kenji Ima of San Diego State University, who has studied the blind extensively.
33. Cicourel, *Cognitive Sociology*, pp. 124–125.
34. Ibid., pp. 142–149.
35. Ibid., p. 50.
36. Ibid., p. 88.
37. Ibid., p. 58.
38. Ibid., pp. 143–144.
39. Personal communication from Cicourel. This colorful metaphor was given concrete reality in such works by Cicourel as: *Method and Measurement in Sociology*, New York: Free Press, 1964; *The Social Organization of Juvenile Justice*, New York: John Wiley, 1968; *Theory and Method in a Study of Argentine Fertility*, New York: John Wiley, 1973; and Aaron Cicourel and John Kirsuse, *The Educational Decision Makers*, Indianapolis: Bobbs-Merrill, 1963.
40. Cicourel, *Cognitive Sociology*, p. 142.
41. For a discussion of the problem of infinite regress, see Thomas Wilson, "The Regress Problem and the Problem of Evidence in Ethnomethodology," paper presented at the American Sociological Association Annual Meetings, Denver, 1971.
42. Cicourel, *Cognitive Sociology*, pp. 126–127.
43. For a discussion of "cross modal communication" and its implications, see Cicourel, *Cognitive Sociology*, pp. 141–171.
44. Ibid., p. 9.

Part V

Making Everyday Life Visible: How to Do It

Introduction: The Problem of Visibility

Everyday life is the place where society touches the individual. Sociology would hardly have much meaning if it did not find its way into the bars, the buses, and the sinks full of dishes that make up someone's average day. Yet everyday life needed to be "discovered" in sociology. The task was primarily one of going places and looking at things. The reader might rightfully wonder why such a field of study needed to be discovered. The reason is then to be found in the kind of person most sociologists are in this society. We are natives, we are members, and we are also sociologists. Each of these identities plays its part in robbing us of the sight of everyday life.

First, as natives of our culture, discovering everyday life—looking at it and describing it—amounts to functioning as anthropologists in our own society. The reader can already see the contradiction in that. It is always the natives who know their own culture and the anthropologist who finds out from them. But when the natives become anthropologists what is there to find out? How can we rediscover what we already know? There is no set of raw data or raw experience that is yet to be structured and ordered. Instead the explanations—the where it came from, who is who, what is going on—are already naturally available. The laundromat, the post office, and the freeway are for us preanalyzed domains that already make too much sense.

Let us be clear about the nature of this problem. Following Schutz, an environment becomes part of one's everyday world when he makes sense of it by using a cognitive style called the "natural attitude."[1] If cognitive styles make worlds, then the very aspects of the natural attitude to which Schutz called attention prevent the holder of such an attitude from "seeing" an environment addressed under its auspices.

Such an environment cannot be an "interesting" place (at least in a theoretical sense). It presents no consistent array of intellectual puzzles and intriguing observations. There are only practical puzzles. To the extent that one "does questioning," the questions that arise are of the order "How can I pay as little income tax as possible?" or "Why are they late for the movie?" Intellectual curiosity is not available as the recurrent motive for discovering and learning things about taxes and movies. Second, there is the global suspensions of doubt—the millions of things that are taken for granted. Everyday life is filled, for its inhabitants, with the hum of washing machines that have been running for so long that nobody hears them anymore.

Schutz mentions other aspects of the natural attitude that render daily events invisible—the general feeling of being in a world known in common with others, or the assumption that one is communicating and can communicate with people at the bus terminal.

In previous chapters we all but defined everyday life as that open field of situations, decisions, and events which almost everybody in the society faces in his daily existence. Thus this field is just as ordinary and natural for sociologists as for anyone else in society. Indeed, it is *our* everyday life as much as it is anybody else's.

Now the scientific attitude[2] was supposed to remedy all these problems. It was through our economic position in society (our jobs as sociologists) that we obtained access to the scientific attitude and it first occurred to us to use it in the places where our "natural attitude" usually prevails. But there is something awkward about the scientific attitude; it is a luxury. Society permits it only in certain places and at certain times. Indeed, *we* will permit it to hold sway on only relatively rare occasions. One's spouse and friends have a limited tolerance for this attitude when it is brought home (as many of us have painfully discovered). When a fight breaks out about who should do the shopping, it will be hard to invite others to settle the issue by using deductive logic or empirical data. Indeed, as Garfinkel has noted, while clarity and "reason" are valued in scholarly communication, vagueness is not just normal but demanded in everyday discourse:

ESTHER: My husband remarked that he was tired. I asked, "How are you tired? Physically, mentally, or just bored?"
SAM: I don't know, I guess physically mainly.
ESTHER: You mean that your muscles ache or your bones?
SAM: I guess so. Don't bo so technical. . . .
SAM: (after watching TV a little) All these old movies have the same kind of old iron bedstead in them.
ESTHER: What do you mean? Do you mean all old movies, or some of them, or just the ones you have seen?
SAM: What's the matter with you? You know what I mean.
ESTHER: I wish you would be more specific.
SAM: You know what I mean! Drop dead![3]

Efforts to export scientists' ways of explaining things into everyday life have been no more successful than attempts to export scientists' modes of communication. As one example, when an ardent feminist challenged one of the authors for his continued use of the word "chick," he tried to explain that this was the result of prior "linguistic conditioning." His "explanation" literally spelled the end of their relationship, for she took it as evidence of his unwillingness to talk to her seriously. Instead he was feeding her "that intellectual bullshit."

As long as you are in a class, at a sociology convention, or safe in the home of a professor, you can think and talk about everyday life in a scientific manner. But you yourself will not be able to sustain scientific interest in "behavior in lines" for very long while standing in line at the motor vehicle bureau. You can try it, you can know how to talk and what to look for (that is, the relevant "sociological issues"). You can be willing, even eager, to do it, but it will get boring. After a short while, you won't know for the life of you what to look at next.

It is perhaps because of these phenomenological facts of life that, as sociologists, we find ourselves in the peculiar position of becoming the stage performers for ordinary situations.[4] Ironically, it is only within the university classroom, with its peculiar structure of attention and relevances, that the welfare agency, with the aid of appropriate talk, taped transcripts, and embellishments from the professor, can become a marvelously interesting, exciting place. Make the mistake of going there, and this whole image evaporates. Even in the very citadels of sociological theorizing, the halls of universities, it is disquieting how easily and how often we slip from the stance of the curious spectator of life who takes little for granted back to finding the right zip code or "bad-mouthing" somebody else's research study.

Although this discussion has been fanciful, we are talking about an extremely serious psychological reality for those who would learn about everyday settings. It is difficult, if not impossible, to sustain the scientific attitude in the very situations where, as a sociologist, you need it most—everyday situations. This difficulty comes not from personal inadequacies but from the very properties of everyday life itself.

THE SOCIOLOGIST AS A KIND OF PERSON

If being a native and possessing a natural attitude makes it difficult for us to understand everyday life, our profession itself causes us more trouble. It might be wondered why, as users of common sense knowledge, we are so interested in transcending it, especially in view of its many benefits. It is not merely because we wish to be scientific. As Schutz so rightly pointed out, in any given situation we all find ourselves with certain biographical "purposes at hand." As professional sociologists we inherit a pervasive purpose at hand: *finding out things other people do not know.* In this sense, it is because of our particular profession that, as natives, we become interested in transcending common sense thought about social life. But this means that common sense knowledge, whether true or false, becomes something that is not very interesting in its own right. It becomes interesting to find out that it was wrong, to explain how it got that way, or to use it as a take-off point for finding things everybody did not know.

In the realm of systematic observation, this purpose at hand makes it interesting to discover patterns that are not visible to the man on the street but affect him anyway. Traditionally there have been two major kinds of data used to make such discoveries. Macroscopic data capture patterns that are too "big" to be seen and known by the man on the street, patterns and objects that transcend the situations of everyday life. Not the boss but authority structures are scrutinized. There is little interest in how specific people get into a car, walk into a booth, pick up a pencil, and vote, but the national voting patterns produced by innumerable such excursions become the data.

The other time-honored method for uncovering things that are "hidden from the vulgar" is to look at the very small instead of the very large—that is, to employ microscopic data. This tradition has given us such memorable studies as "eye contact among bus riders," "leg movements as indicators of lying," or "the movement and placement of arms while waiting in lines."

There are of course innumerable practical strategies for discovering things other people do not know. Unfortunately, much of the study of everyday life appears to consist in *rediscovering what we already know*; that is, both the data and the findings are "news from nowhere." Indeed, this is the feeling many readers get when reading, for example, the works of Erving Goffman. They are being told what they knew all along. The profession of sociology has considered the previous statement as a charge against it and has been defending itself against this charge for years. As a result, sociology has no theoretical conception of this form of knowledge, nor does it know how to value it explicitly. Thus much of everyday life lies fallow in the field as a topic of study.

Uncovering hidden knowledge is only one goal in what Schutz would call the whole "system of relevances" which determines how sociologists select topics and problems.[5] In this connection it is true that sociologists have traditionally shared with society at large some common priorities about what is important to study. For example, the causes and consequences of such social problems as delinquency, mental illness, and riots have long been considered worthy of great investments of sociological time, effort, and money. In addition there are various subjects, issues, and problems that acquire importance only through technical considerations internal to the discipline itself. For instance, innumerable papers and studies have been devoted to assessing whether "friends of friends are really friends,"[6] and the like. Unfortunately, everyday life turns out to be a veritable storehouse of the inconsequential, in terms of almost everybody's system of relevances. Lay persons, state senators, and sociologists alike find it difficult or impossible to devote any time or energy to the inconsequential. For there is no payoff, no importance, or no point in doing so.

To take just one illustration, consider the petty work of our lives—the dishes, the garbage, the making of six copies of our latest paper, the finding of the right zip code. Wulbert has made the interesting observation that in neither commercial nor sociological films are people often shown *working* (at least for any length of time).[7] What to us are places where we spend countless hours devoted to practical work are to Warner Brothers or the soap operas but staging grounds for extramarital affairs, existential crises, or bank robberies. Never for any length of time do we see a secretary tediously and endlessly typing letter after letter. For every video millisecond that she is at the typewriter, she spends a half-hour flirting with the boss. Similarly, as Garfinkel has noted, sociological studies of the professions contain information about roles, status systems, labeling—everything but work. The last things Howard Becker, himself a jazz musician, tells us about jazz musicians are the details of their playing music.[8] In his study of the medical profession, Eliot Freidson takes us up to the very door of the doctor's office but fails to tell us about the practical ins and outs of a day's work behind that door (in particular, about treating patients).[9] Even Karl Marx, the very champion of the "worker," rarely concerned himself with real work but instead concentrated on the political-economic aspects of the worker's life. Indeed, the whole field of political sociology is almost devoid of experts on practical politics (running campaigns and so on).

Again, one can understand these omissions phenomenologically. In daily life the question "What is it important to know about?" is a situationally determined, practical question. It is important to know the things that fit into one's practical projects. The Israeli-Arab war may be of no consequence, while how to change the ribbon on a typewriter may become a priceless gem of knowledge. There appear to be many things that can become important to someone only in this situated, practical way. They do not acquire generic relevance as parts of a sociological subject matter, as pressing social problems, or as indicators of fundamental human abilities and dilemmas. It is true that some theory or intellectual problem one picks up in college may, on occasion, make some of these things relevant. But it will not lift that general curtain of "of course" and "so what?" that hangs over most of our routine life, making it fundamentally uninteresting outside of a particular practical context. For that reason it becomes difficult and recognizably absurd to start a sociology of typewriter ribbon changing.

Finally, even if one could find ways to make many aspects of everyday life into sociological "news," and relevant or interesting news at that, there remains the problem of methodology. When sociologists study some topic or problem, they need to report their findings publicly, in print. As a consequence they are unusually interested in avoiding being wrong about these findings, even provisionally. In this connection, everyday life turns out to be an awkward experimental laboratory. It contains too much "noise." It is hard to isolate one phenomenon from everything else that surrounds it, to compare and sample behaviors, or to control irrelevant and extraneous variables. As a result it is hard to study natural situations in a way that guards against being wrong. On the other hand, if sociologists take the phenomenon out of everyday life, they study it under conditions that are so different from those in which it originated that generalizing from the one to the other is often out of the question. As a result, one is often confronted with a choice between studying everyday life *or* using currently available research methods. For the former is difficult (sometimes impossible) to learn about by using the latter.

So far we have indicated the following demons which tend to cloak much of daily life in a veil of invisibility, irrelevance, or impracticality:

1. *Our own identity as natives of our culture and members in good standing of everyday life.*
    a. Daily life is a preanalyzed domain for us.
    b. Our natural attitude: it renders things invisible because they are taken for granted.

2. *Our identity as sociologists.*
   a. Our concern to see and know things other people don't see and know.
   b. Our sense of the theoretically relevant and important.
   c. Our preoccupation with avoiding false conclusions.
   d. The flimsiness of the scientific attitude as a personal orientation in everyday life.

Formidable enemies all—yet the methods presented in the following chapters need to be primarily directed against them. The major function of these methods is to make a familiar world look strange—to discover topics, problems, and sociological phenomena in a world that formerly seemed to contain little or none.

Notes

1. For a description of this attitude and how it is used to interpret events and happenings, see our discussion of Schutz, pages 194–205 above.
2. Schutz defined the scientific attitude as a cognitive style contrasting to the natural attitude in its underlying assumptions. For example, whereas in the natural attitude one suspends doubt, in the scientific attitude one suspends belief and takes nothing for granted without evidence. For a discussion of the scientific attitude, see the section on Schutz, pages 194–205 above.
3. Harold Garfinkel, *Studies in Ethnomethodology*, Englewood Cliffs, N.J.: Prentice-Hall, 1967, p. 43.
4. We use the term *phenomenological* here to indicate that it is the structure of conscious attention one gives to a line or a park bench that makes it difficult to perceive intellectually interesting events occurring there.
5. We thank Dr. Roland Wulbert for bringing this goal of "uncovering the hidden" to our attention.
6. In particular, this equation was part of the research generated by "balance theory," in the study of social networks. Insofar as the equation held, groups should eventually decompose into two "cliques," each made up of people who liked one another but disliked everyone in the other clique.
7. Personal communication from Dr. Roland Wulbert.
8. Howard S. Becker, "The Professional Dance Musician and His Audience," *American Journal of Sociology* 57 (September 1951): 136–144.
9. Eliot Freidson, *The Profession of Medicine: A Study of the Sociology of Applied Knowledge*: New York, Dodd, Mead, 1970.

CHAPTER 9

Participant Observation in Formal Sociology

If we want to find something, one way to do it is to look for it out in the world in different places. Another way is to change our method of looking at the world in order to discover it. Traditional participant observation is primarily concerned with the first procedure. It seeks to achieve an intimate relationship between the researcher and a particular set of people and places.

Formal sociology introduces an additional premise and an additional concern.[1] The premise is taken from Schutz and more generally phenomenology: Changing someone's cognitive style (the way he makes sense of things) *literally* changes the world for him. Translated into a strategy, this means being concerned directly with changing the inner cognitive attitudes of the researcher and only indirectly with people and places. We thus ask how we might place ourselves in social situations which would fundamentally alter our system of practical relevances, commonsense assumptions, or habitual methods of interpreting events in everyday life.

In this chapter we introduce the reader to a few devices that have been found unusually versatile in accomplishing this goal. We begin by considering first-person strategies which seek to directly alter the cognitive attitudes of the researcher(s).

Social Identities and the Problem of Visibility

If the natural attitude makes for familiarity, then suspending it should be a powerful device for making the familiar strange. As we have seen, the adoption of the scientific attitude is only partially successful in this regard. As a psychological identity, "scientist" more often than not offers rhetoric, but not things to notice when in an actual setting. It is an attitude that not only is difficult to sustain but doesn't indicate what to do next. What we need is far stronger medicine. We need identities that provide workable, practical ways of suspending the natural attitude on a continual basis. The identities of the stranger and the novice accomplish this, to a greater or lesser extent, by depriving the researcher of his social and technical competence.

THE STRANGER

In a memorable essay, Schutz described the situation of the stranger in an unknown culture and the bewildering position in which he finds himself.[2] Such a role necessitates an attitude which in many ways is almost the opposite of the natural attitude. While there can be numbness of attention for those with member's knowledge, the stranger must be on the edge of his cognitive seat. There is no problem in being constantly suspicious of his own view of what's going on since he literally does not know what's going on and is continually rediscovering this awkward fact. It is a sobering position to be in, and tends to prevent conceptual complacency.

What makes the identity of stranger so strong psychologically as compared to that of scientist is practical involvement. It is of the utmost importance that the researcher be both a stranger to a scene *and* enmeshed in it in practical ways. He must continually be in the position of having to *do* things. Thus he avoids the liberty of "hit and run" ethnography—of being able to zip in and out of a situation for purposes of analyzing and theorizing. Instead, he is subjected to the same practical conditions and situations as other members but is without the equipment to handle them competently.

"LINE? WHAT LINE?"

This was the position—and the plight—of Howard Schwartz during a visit to India. He had arrived at Bombay airport and in several hours was to take a plane from there to the city of Poona. However, he did not speak Hindi or Marathi, he had not yet bought the plane ticket for this flight, he was unfamiliar with the Indian monetary system, and he did not know the precise time his plane was to leave or from what gate. Unless he learned a lot of culture fast, Schwartz feared he would be spending many a sleepless night in the Bombay airport. Many of the practical contingencies involved in getting on his plane involved standing in lines—ticket-buying lines, luggage-checking lines, customs-clearance lines, boarding lines, and so on. This was fortunate since the author was an "expert" on lines. He had given lectures and written papers on lines in his home country. There was only one trouble: Bombay lines were not at all like San Francisco lines. It seemed that all the author's sociological expertise was not going to get him onto the proper plane at the proper time.

Disturbing things like the following started happening: At a certain point almost all passengers placed their luggage around various unmarked pillars in the room. Schwartz had no idea who would retrieve this luggage or when, nor did he know which pillar was associated with which plane, although apparently everybody else did. Or, again, at certain points groups of people would line up in front of one or two clearing posts where they would be checked for weapons and then allowed to board planes. However, the same two clearing posts were used for all planes, and one's ticket had no indication of which clearing post went with which plane. Yet, clearly, certain clearing posts were used for certain planes and not others. Needless to say, there was no scientific leisure possible for figuring all this out. Unless the right cultural conventions were deciphered, and quickly, a plane would soon be taking off leaving behind a somewhat deflated sociologist and expert on lines. To allay the reader's fears, Schwartz somehow did manage to get himself and his luggage on the right flight, but it was a close call.

The big payoff in situations like this is finding oneself confronted with endless puzzles, problems, and issues where others in the same place hardly see anything worth mentioning (nor do they even know how to mention it). It is an especially elegant situation for making visible the "silly" little details of social life that are almost always left out of sociology. Indeed, we called attention to such a detail in the quote that opened chapter 7—the presence or absence of toilets. Indian toilets themselves provided a technical education in alternative means of attending to one's bodily necessities (instead of sitting upon many of these toilets one squatted on them). The reason the stranger cannot ignore these things while the sociologist can is, of course, that the former has to get things done, whereas the latter only has to talk about how they got done. This is why devices like "the stranger" were heavily employed by Garfinkel initially in developing notions of "practical" actions.

In this regard, the cultural stranger is a particularly nice device for exploring competencies in a culture that everybody learns without ever having been explicitly taught. For instance, who taught most of us how to participate in the many different kinds of queues in our society, or how to instantly obtain impressions of strangers and use these as the basis of action and interaction? Undoubtedly much indirect teaching and learning takes place in connection with such things. However, they are not part of any curriculum, nor are parents everywhere charged with imparting them to their children along with toilet training and proper grooming.

The social and cognitive situation of the stranger is also of intrinsic interest. It provides a contrasting attitude which helps to uncover the features of the ordinary natural attitude. It provides, as well, a first-person approach to studying improvised actions.

Finally, the particular environment or setting can be chosen so as to have a special relationship to a particular topic in everyday life. To utilize Simmel's metaphor, one can hold some social "form" constant but vary the "content" in selecting an environment. This strategy in part explains the zoo of studies one finds in ethnomethodology—studies of kung fu, microscopy, African religious cults, mapmaking, professional magicians. It was not kung fu that was being addressed so much as learning and using instructions. It was not the microscope that was of interest so much as competent "seeing" as a daily practical task. It was not magicians and their world that were being investigated so much as the practical necessity of creating appearances for others. If one studied one's *own* seeing, one might not be able to "see" it; if one studied one's own impression making, one might not be impressed.

STRATEGIES FOR USING THE STRANGER

In matching an investigator and a set of environments, several of the things which will contribute to making the stranger "strange" are within our province of manipulation.[3] In considering all of these parameters, one thing should be borne in mind. "The stranger" as a research device attempts to create ignorance in the *investigator*, so as to force him to take note of things that might otherwise be trivial, irrelevant, or invisible. A number of issues arise in this regard.

1. Exactly What Will It Be That He Does or Does Not Know?

If we are studying common symbol systems, we might deprive our researcher of the natural language. If the topic is the use of context in determining social meanings, we might divest him of a definition of the situation—we might send a Tibetan lama into a bowling alley to play a few games, or a rural sociologist into a gay bar. Clearly, ignorance is hardly a two-valued "yes-no" variable; the kind and amount of ignorance will greatly affect the ways in which a given person is strange to a given environment. The California surfer who has never been to a nude beach will have a different set of practical problems than an Eskimo who has also "never been" to a nude beach (or for that matter, any beach at all). Importantly, will our ignorant investigator *know* what he does not know, or will many of his deficiencies appear to him in the form of nasty surprises?

2. What Practical Tasks Will We Assign to the Researcher?

The particular kind of ignorance we are looking for must be chosen with an eye to what the stranger will have to do in the environment. Will it be using a pay telephone, keeping up a conversation, or finding his way to an address in a strange city? Whatever it is, the investigator must be placed in situations where real practical success and failures are all but unavoidable.

3. Selecting an Environment

In our example of "an American in India," we presented the somewhat tired image of the stranger in a strange land, the proverbial "Martian." Opportunities of this type do not abound for sociologists. Yet mild equivalents of the "foreign country" within our own society are not totally inaccessible. Many public places can be frequented by any member of the community; yet distinctive social worlds are created by their regular clientele (the "members" of these worlds). Bars (and various types of bars) are excellent examples of such places and such "worlds." In looking for "foreign lands" we are not usually directly interested in the people and the place. We select them primarily because of their ability to make us uncomfortable—that is, to force the abandonment of the natural attitude.

4. Selecting an Identity

We have some control over the stranger's identity with respect to others—that is, what kind of stranger the stranger will be. A crucial question in this regard is whether the stranger will try to "pass" or will present himself to others as some variety of incompetent (such as a visitor, trainee, or researcher). Each strategy has special potentials and disadvantages. The presence of a known incompetent often turns an environment into a technical place for its members. That is, members start attending to what he needs to know, giving him unsolicited instructions, and so on. On the other hand, such an identity takes the cognitive pressure off the researcher in many ways.

5. Optimizing and Recording Practical Problems

In using the stranger device, the main idea is to put a dent in the researcher's attitude by manipulating his state of knowledge with respect to the practical tasks he has to do. To maximize the effectiveness of such a device, the following conditions should be optimized:

1. There will be a consistent stream of things the researcher *has to do* which can only be accomplished through members' knowledge.
2. These things have to be done quickly, "right now." Real practical misfortunes and mistakes are possible if not probable.
3. He can't talk his way out of failure; explaining "I am a sociologist" simply will not get him on the plane. This means that the practical tasks are so designed that verbal accounts cannot excuse or mitigate the practical and emotional consequences of failure or misinterpretation.

The last point is particularly important, for anthropologists routinely are cultural strangers to other societies. Yet allowances are made for them, and to the extent that they acquire "times out" and are given many chances, they can retain their natural attitude while leisurely acquiring the knowledge of another culture.

There is another important difference between the functions of the stranger and the situation of the anthropologist. The attitude created by being a stranger—the sense of being on the edge of one's cognitive seat—can decay extremely rapidly. A newcomer can impose massive amounts of social structure on a situation in a very short period of time. Very quickly one finds himself with sufficient "savvy" to negotiate through a world without constant detection or disaster. As a case in point, one researcher reports that newcomers to a city get sufficient spatial "bearings" within a few days to feel confident in finding people and places by car without getting hopelessly lost.[4] To study the process by which strangers imposed geometric structures on the city, the researcher had to get to them very soon after they first arrived. The same might be said for becoming initially familiar with a new work site, or with new people and their tastes and attitudes. For this reason the researcher in this role usually can be immersed in the target situation for only a few days, or even a few hours, before he becomes, psychologically, a native who no longer worries much about what will happen or what's going on.

Having done all we can to make certain that our newcomer encounters unavoidable practical problems and that he does not become accustomed to his new environment, there remains the problem of how to retrieve the observations which emerge from the process. Here we face a problem analogous to the description of drug-induced experiences. Our great hope is that our researcher, as stranger, will encounter sociological problems in a completely different way than we encounter the same problems when we study them as sociologists. But if this happens, there is every reason to believe he may not be able to remember or describe much of what he notices. If these things are not somehow dramatic, if he does not have names or theories for them, if he is not already looking for them or for their absence, how will they find their way into his memory and notebook? Chances are many of them will not, especially if they come up in quick succession in the context of practical problems. Therefore special precautions have to be taken.

Optimally, observations should be recorded as the ongoing process proceeds. Yet this is often difficult or impossible. The setting simply does not grant the kinds of "time out" necessary for the researcher to "jot a few things down" in his notebook. Sometimes it is possible for the stranger to talk into a tape recorder. For example, in following a map to another's house located in an unfamiliar area of town, he can describe the ins and outs of getting there to his portable Sony, as they come up. Another strategy is to work in pairs, one member being a native and the other a stranger. Garfinkel and Cicourel had planned such a trip to Mexico, since Cicourel speaks Spanish and knows the culture, while Garfinkel does not. As the stranger negotiates his way through the day and its succession of situations, a continuing dialogue can be kept up with the native, providing interesting feedback for both parties. The native, unburdened with the stranger's practical problems, can act as a human tape recorder of sorts. In a post mortem discussion, the stranger's dilemmas may be easily recalled by the native, who could automatically conduct himself appropriately while reserving his cognitive and mnemonic apparatus for noticing the travails of his friend.

If one does not bring along one's own native, it is often possible to retrospectively interview other "natural" natives concerning their impression of the stranger-researcher and his status and/or business among them. Their point of view can suggest many additional, hidden aspects of culture to which the stranger was an unknowing party. For example, Schwartz, when he had his troubles at the Indian airport, at least had the advantage of a proper outfit—or so he thought. He wore clothes in Bombay which he had bought in the Indian countryside, clothes all but indistinguishable from much of the attire seen around him. Much to his embarassment and surprise, he was later tactfully informed by a native that his outfit had the same significance in a public place in Bombay that shorts and a T-shirt might have at a wedding.

6. Selecting a Stranger

Up until now it has been assumed that the pool of employees who are available for hire as strangers is limited to sociologists and academics. But given all that has been said about the delicacies involved in matching particular people to particular environments and social requirements, this employee pool would seem to be too limited. Why not include members as well? Why not enlist the aid of medical doctors, union carpenters, or ghetto homemakers in studying race tracks, sociology conventions, or yacht racing? This would greatly increase the possibilities of obtaining novel and distinctive observations about a particular environment.

The most common use of this strategy has been to "put one man in another man's shoes." Several studies of psychiatric treatment have been conducted by having psychotherapists openly or secretly admitted to mental hospitals as patients.[5] Such an arrangement offers unique possibilities. The doctors now see their own practices from the other end and can compare what they as doctors imagine patients to be thinking and feeling with the actual thoughts and feelings experienced in the patient role. The uniform result of these studies has been that the doctor-researchers find dehumanization, oppression, and incompetence in their own profession when its practices are viewed from the point of view of their recipients.

THE NOVICE

Many things about daily life that are second nature to most of us are the object of pedagogical interest for certain groups. Confidence men have an abiding interest in the "natural" occurrence of "spontaneous" conversations and friendships. Magicians have well-developed theories of body language and eye contact. Psychotherapists have a special interest in reading emotional affect in faces, as other people read passages in books. There are also all manner of teachers, schools, and programs designed to teach the skills practiced by such groups and to initiate strangers into their cultural life.

These provide golden opportunities for selected ignorant sociologists to become novices or bona fide students in a common culture. In apprenticing oneself to such groups, one taps into a semi-automatic program for penetrating the fog of the natural attitude in favor of a calculating, explicit awareness of some aspect of ordinary life. In this pursuit, one does well to become a novice rather than a visiting scholar, for the people in these groups more readily impart their knowledge by teaching it than by describing it.

The utility of "the novice" is by no means confined to the study of groups such as confidence men whose talents somehow bear on everyday interaction. It can be used, among other ways, to (1) become a group member, (2) re-create ignorance, and (3) construct "grounded theory."

BECOMING A GROUP MEMBER

In groups of people whose identity as a collectivity depends upon a distinctive set of competencies, a strong criterion for membership arises. If one wishes to be a dancer, musician, lawyer, or medical doctor, membership depends on what one can *do*. There are those who advocate this criterion for the sociologist-participant-observer as well. We saw earlier that it is possible to become an insider merely by mixing with the natives—i.e., by acquiring a legitimate identity among them and participating in their common culture. But in the present case a much stronger demand is made. To count oneself a member, an insider, one must be able to do what they do—not only learn to do it, but do it. In this view one cannot possibly be a medical sociologist without learning to be a doctor, nor can one do research in the sociology of law without going to law school. It is argued that the most important sociological phenomenon to understand and explain for a group defined by competencies *is* its competencies. We must first know exactly what is involved in treating a patient or how plea bargaining is done before explaining or theorizing about doctors or lawyers. And the best way to know this is not to ask or observe people. Doctors and lawyers are not, after all, sociologists; they are doctors and lawyers. They have idealized versions of what they do; they can construct pictures of their reality. But they cannot isolate and describe the complex sociological contingencies involved in learning and doing a complex skill. Secondly, mere observation of these practitioners will not help either. It has been shown that even in a simple conversation the participants do not convert their spoken sounds into meanings in the same ways as those listening in on their conversation.[6] It is for this reason that, in general, one cannot "overhear" the same meanings that conversationalists hear.

To translate this into a general principle, the practitioner attends to a complex set of details, contexts, and systems of relevances in accomplishing his art, a set determined primarily by his practical tasks. An observer simply will not and cannot attend to the same things, especially when it comes to details. He does not have to do anything, and so he will not (and cannot) structure and analyze ongoing activity in the same way as the practitioner. Neither will the practitioner be able to communicate his systems of relevances to the observer, since they come and go automatically as his work proceeds. His skill lies in the doing, not in the telling of the doing.

RE-CREATING IGNORANCE

If one does not like the previous perspective, for philosophical reasons or from sheer laziness, the novice role might still offer some interesting possibilities. Through its use one can arrange to be reborn to an old skill. If one is interested in studying improvisation, one can become a jazz musician. If the topic is following rules, one can learn the Japanese tea ceremony. By starting with something one knows how to do in one area of life and relearning it in another, one is reestablished as a neophyte.

Here again the important thing is that the researcher submit himself to the constraint of actually having to deliver. A sociologist interviewing or "observing" other piano players is permitted all sorts of cognitive and verbal liberties. But as a beginner, no matter how smart he is and how much he knows about music, it won't help at the keyboard. As David Sudnow points out, he can talk for a week and not a single tune will come out of the piano.[7] The only way to "know what he's talking about" in the piano-playing situation is to find ways to make his fingers negotiate a keyboard as easily as they ordinarily type up sociological theories. Thus the researcher is forced to attend explicitly to sundry details and practicalities that are usually ignored so long as he is merely watching. In this way, what is ordinarily sociologically trivial becomes painfully important.

Why would a sociologist, as such, want to learn jazz piano? One reason is to use this learning to learn about something else. Sudnow, for example, has studied language (in part) by learning and practicing jazz piano. While some readers might see this strategy as fanciful, we believe it is a brilliant way to proceed. The simple act of talking exhibits one of the most important features of action in everyday life. It is improvised, in the sense that one ordinarily does not have the foggiest idea what he is going to say until he is saying it. Still, most adults can spend hours talking to each other without ever being at a loss for words. When the time comes, there is almost always something "on the tip of one's tongue," and once one has said *that*, there is the next thing to say, and the next, and so on. And all this comes easily, without effort, without rehearsal or calculation, and without any deliberate searches of the mind. We invite the reader to perform an experiment. Just start talking. Say anything and keep going. Can you describe how you are finding the words coming out of your mouth and stringing them together into coherent and meaningful patterns? Most adults have no idea how they produce speech sequentially and would not even begin to know how to talk about the issues involved. If one is such an adult, what does one do?

One way to proceed is to find a "similar" activity, start from scratch, and keep close tabs on the technical problems that come up as one learns to do the activity fluently. Inasmuch as in talking one produces sequences of sound improvisationally, jazz might have something to say about improvisational talking. And indeed it does. When Sudnow inspected talk for the issues of production to which he had become sensitized in playing jazz, he found he was beginning to know how to "talk about talking" and perhaps about improvisation.[8]

CONSTRUCTING GROUNDED THEORY

When a formal sociologist, as a novice, sets about learning some complex skill with the help of others, he gains access to an unlimited field of trial and error, instruction and instructors, achievement and failure. The whole vocabulary and orientation that surround him revolve around one of his pet issues, technical competence. He has a first-person way to experience the whole process by which something that was once unfamiliar to him and undoable by him turns into something that is second nature. On the other hand, the researcher has the advantage of engaging in the whole process with another motive than just learning a skill. And that motive might well be to search for a "grounded theory" of competence. (See pages 26–33 on Glaser and Strauss.) That is, many investigators have found that the experience of being a novice has provided invaluable ideas and concepts for theorizing about competent improvised action of any kind. From the perspective of formal sociology, this can only be viewed as a good thing in that sociology has yet to develop a detailed conception of practical social action.

We have discussed above, in a general way, how the researcher as novice can gain a level of competence held by members. We have also seen how he is in the enviable position of not only being able to learn how to do something but being able to describe the process of doing it. One way in which this is accomplished is through getting and giving instructions.

INSTRUCTIONS

Reality reconstructors conceive of their subjects as "insiders" with an authoritative "picture" of a certain reality. For gaining access to this reality, the abiding tool is "the description." As naturally occurring activities and artifacts, descriptions provide the researcher with the picture others have of their world.

If the predominant image of the human being in formal sociology is that of a worker, then the tool corresponding to description is "instructions"—those items that describe the "how" of members' skillful actions. Unlike reality reconstruction, the prevailing issue is not what they *see* but what they can *do*.

But here formal sociologists run into an enormous problem. Almost all of our methodological wisdom concerning observation and data is built upon description. Our prevailing notions of validity, reliability, misplaced concreteness, sampling, and so on proceed by starting with the correspondence theory of truth: There is the real world of people, events, and circumstances, on the one hand, and one's own observations and descriptions of this world, on the other hand. Competent observation and description depend principally on achieving certain formal relationships between the former and the latter—that is, by producing good "pictures" of reality.

The problem this poses for formal sociologists is that instructions are not, and were never intended to be, pictures of something else. The criteria for an excellent photo essay on pottery making are completely different from the criteria for an excellent manual on how to use a potter's wheel (although the latter may contain selected photos as well). The two are written differently and, most important, are to be *read* differently.[9]

As a result, when the researcher interacts with a group of others in the capacity of novice, he receives feedback in a unique way. Instead of describing their activity to him, they are trying to show him how to do it. What they select to describe in detail, what they gloss over, what descriptive categories they employ, and how materials are displayed are all determined by this task. The researcher, in his turn, no longer assesses information using interview schedules but takes what has just been said and tries to imitate it, compares the enactments of a teacher with his own and with fellow students', and so on. In short, he receives a distinctive kind of information in a distinctive way.

Frankly, many students of interaction have not found themselves at home in the idiom just described. They did not know how to take full advantage of this information or how to assess whether their efforts were adequate. For this reason instructed action has become a topic of increasing interest to formal sociologists, as a sociological topic of study, as an ethnographic resource for getting information, and as a way to communicate findings among themselves.[10]

Let us now consider, for the sake of brevity, only the third of these foci of interest and the way in which it leads to a radically different concept of data.

INSTRUCTIONS AS RESOURCES: DISPLAYING THE PHENOMENON

It is clear that teaching someone how to do something is a distinctive way to impart knowledge. If, as sociologists, we wish to incorporate teaching into our methodology, we can do so in several ways. We already do it implicitly in teaching our own art to students and colleagues instead of only describing it to them. Some researchers are doing it by apprenticing themselves to their subjects and becoming students during participant observation. But when we communicate among ourselves about what we have learned about others, we do so by means of description. In field studies we give our colleagues a picture of other people's picture of reality. The question arises: Why not skip the translation? Why not create that reality directly, instead of merely describing it through symbolic data? Surely this is one of the strongest possible ways to communicate information about another reality.

But is this form of communication really necessary? While it may be very empathetic, colorful, and dramatic, as the old argument goes, "I don't have to be able to lay an egg to tell a good one from a bad one." For what research purposes must we actually "taste of the fruits of knowledge"? The outlines of these purposes start to emerge when we consider research experiences like the following: In a study of the creative movement, Margaret Theeman endeavored to answer the question "Who are the creative movers in dance?"[11] What tendencies, motives, and characteristics lead one into this movement? In this case it was not age, social class, or any other such factor that explained individuals' attraction to dance. They simply liked the way it *felt*. In exploring "how it felt," Theeman found a whole world of kinesthetic communication among people within creative-movement circles. But what about data? How could she retrieve kinesthetic sensations—with a tape recorder, by interviewing, by observing others? How could she report on such data—in words, statistical tables, photographs?

There seemed no alternative but to devise techniques through which the nature of this kinesthetic world and the way it was organized could be displayed directly. (Indeed, as part of Theeman's Ph.D. examination on this topic at Harvard University, she had her examiners participate in a movement workshop.)

But there is yet another step to take. In speaking of the reality of dancers or musicians, groups of people are given titles to a particular reality as families obtain title to a tract home. Why not forget about who "owns" a given reality and simply display the nature of that reality itself? This has been the radical proposal of some formal sociologists.[12] In studying everyday life (or certain aspects of it) they advocate abandoning the use of data to depict phenomena symbolically in favor of procedures by which colleagues can be placed directly "in the presence" of these phenomena. Such a program requires the development of instructions which, if followed, will actually *produce* the phenomena being studied. We shall give two short examples of such techniques, to give the reader some idea of what they might look like. Paradoxically, in the following two demonstrations Mehan and Wood provide instructions for encountering the properties of instructions. In the first, one discovers how and why vagueness, incompleteness, and the like are essential properties of instructions. One cannot, from the standpoint of instructed action, literally describe how to do something:

> Researchers are instructed to learn a new activity from a set of written rules. Hoyle's book of games, cookbooks, and sewing manuals provide a large set of possible activities. Researchers are directed to do only what the instructions say. They are neither to improvise nor to make allowances. They are to approach the document as "strict constructionists."
>
> Researchers discover that the activities cannot be done. In following a recipe, for example, instructions are given for preparing the food and for preheating the oven. There are seldom explicit instructions to put the food in the oven. Sometimes the instructions indicate that eggs still in their shells are to be placed in mixing bowls, or beaten with a stick, or whipped with a belt. Cookies sometimes must be dropped on the floor, not on cookie sheets. Researchers search in vain for behavioral representations of "cook until tender," "sauté," "blanch," "fold."
>
> Card games and sewing rarely even begin. Interested researchers must discover the reason for this themselves.[13]

Having seen the disadvantages of literalness, Mehan and Wood then go on to demonstrate the advantages of vagueness. One encounters in detail the practices of "ad hocing," filling in, making do, and so on that are employed when one person tries to show another how to do something. In progressively getting better at their mutual task, both parties create a structured form of communication tailored to a common purpose:

> One researcher devises a simple geometric shape: A second researcher stands at a blackboard. The first researcher talks to the second, telling him or her what to draw. Neither researcher looks at the other. Some self-correcting mechanisms of ordinary conversation are thus suspended.
>
> The first researcher usually gives instructions like, "Draw a vertical line. Then draw a horizontal line off one end." When the instruction giver is satisfied that a full description has been given, the drawings are compared.
>
> The discrepancies are always enormous. Researchers experience the complexity of descriptions. If they continue to practice with new figures, they learn to produce similar drawings. They learn to do new descriptive practices within a new language game. These new games compare with the descriptive practices they first employed, much as scientific description does with everyday description.[14]

MULTIPLE OBSERVERS

The previous strategies, while adequate for some purposes, suffer from a serious defect. The formal sociologist is supposedly interested in "situations, not people." As a novice or stranger, one studies and observes situations from the standpoint of a *single individual.* Yet social situations (at least many of them) permit, indeed demand, participation by all sorts of people. In studying dying as a set of coordinated activities, Sudnow had to deal with doctors, nurses, patients, families, clergy, and all manner of other "social types" who typically entered into the process. In examining public places, Goffman had to take into consideration an open-ended list of kinds of "characters" who might or did enter the scene of a restaurant or a bus at some point, each with his own personal business, point of view, knowledge at hand, and the rest. In such environments, social interaction occurs among heterogeneous people living in partially different worlds, dealing with each other as best they can.

In order to see how all these people and activities coalesce into social realities, "teams of phonies" are sometimes sent out into the field.[15] Many different observers can be selected, each with a particular cognitive style, kind of knowledge, or practical task, thereby producing interesting interactions between them and some environment or set of activities. In particular, some environments, such as hospitals or banks, are used by a definite collection of categories of people. In such cases it is possible to assign one investigator to each category in the manner already discussed under participant observation.

The "team of phonies" strategy is enormously flexible and is not limited to the use of researchers. Various combinations of researchers and natural participants can be employed as observers to see how diverse actions and interpretations fit together to produce an orderly arrangement of activities.

As we have already described, Cicourel took advantage of this flexibility in his "indefinite triangulation" procedures. The problem was to explore how the conditions under which accounts were produced resulted in different accounts of the "same" social events. To this end, various people were pulled in and out of settings at different times. In the course of these procedures, some gave repeated accounts, others had to reconcile their own accounts with those of another or with that given by a tape recorder, and so forth.

CULTURAL MISFITS

The previous strategies (the stranger, the novice, and multiple observers) suffer from the handicap that the researcher must go to an environment or situation with which he is unfamiliar in order to learn how to observe the familiar. But his own daily existence remains shrouded in "of course." If one cannot explicitly estrange oneself from everyday situations, another strategy is to go looking for those who can. In particular, one can search for people who, for one reason or another, find activities which everyone else does as a matter of course to be difficult or impossible to achieve.

The two names for these individuals in the literature roughly correspond to the types of relationships they have to society—cultural misfits and cultural troublemakers.

A cultural misfit is one who is trying, more or less successfully, to pass. In one way or another, she is trying to fool the normal, natural people of this world into thinking that she is one of them. Garfinkel's analysis of Agnes is perhaps the best-known study of a cultural misfit.[16] To most people of our society, "male" or "female" is something you are, always were, and always will be. Along with this identity go certain definitive physical "insignia," among them the possession of a penis for males and a vagina for females. In conjunction with this identity go a set of appearances, surface decorations, tendencies, and behaviors (some of which are optional but expected and others necessary and required). With their aid, one typically recognizes that another is either male or female, immediately, initially, and without the possibility of later changing his mind on the basis of new information. Normals treat "male" and "female" not as social roles but as natural biological categories. For this reason they find it strange and difficult to give credence to the notion that both male and female characteristics are randomly distributed among persons; to a procedure for deciding sexuality by adding up lists of male and female characteristics and taking the excess of one as the criterion for establishing an individual's gender; to the idea that the first three years of child rearing should be used to determine sexuality; or to the presence in society of males who have vaginas and females who have penises.

If the foregoing constitutes some of the assumptions which define sexuality for adult members of our society, then Agnes did not satisfy these assumptions. She was a woman who possessed both well-developed breasts and a functioning penis. She was also a woman who was not practiced at being a woman, having been raised as a male. This put her in a position somewhat similar to "the stranger." For she had to "accomplish" various social tasks without having the ordinary resources for doing so. In particular, she became adept at "accomplishing" being a woman.

The major benefits conferred upon us by people like Agnes might best be described with a simple physical analogy. To the ordinary eye, a tree or a star is an object which exists, while to the physicist they are events which are happening. The tree, as matter, is energy vibrating at a certain rate. The star is a source of atomic fusion which has moved to another region of the heavens, perhaps hundreds of years before its light reaches earth. This light portrays it as an object at a certain point in the sky—a point it might have occupied centuries ago.

Although less dramatic, social activities and events have a way of crystallizing into "things" which just exist, when looked at by ordinary members of society. The more automatic, easy, and second nature certain activities become, the more they are reciprocated and supported by our fellows—the more they lose their processlike identity and solidify into social facts. A woman, a family, and a classroom become things which an individual, a group, and a place merely "are."

What the misfit does for us is to reverse this process and show us how to see social facts as complexes of social activity (including accounts and interpretations). In this sense, Agnes's practical problems and strategies for passing do not just inform on the knowledge and skills required to "do" being a woman; she shows us some of the things involved in creating and sustaining *any* social identity.

In general, Garfinkel gave us a program for studying social facts as accomplishments: (1) take anything that is ordinarily regarded as a social fact—a fact of life, things people "are," events that just "happen," etc.; (2) search for the ways in which this fact is seen, displayed, and talked about as a fact, for and by members of society. Cultural misfits must carry out the second part of this program in detail in order to successfully pass. We have only to ask them, judiciously, for their "findings."

The Recruitment Problem

This might seem like an extremely flimsy research strategy. After all, how many Agneses are there? How many individuals are, in some continual way, pretending to be what they are not? Further, how might they be found? Often, the very purpose of the passing behavior is to avoid being identified and perhaps punished or incarcerated. In this sense, the most interesting misfits may be ones we do not know about. The better they are at what they do (passing), the less likely it is that we can ever find them.

Secondly, even if one came upon such a person, how would his confidence be gained? It is seldom that one has an item like a sex-change operation to trade off for cooperation in the "cause of science," as in Garfinkel's study. Such people are not concealing things and creating appearances for fun. Exposure is frequently emotionally painful, embarrassing, or otherwise undesirable. The consequences may be compounded for those in institutions. They may be trying to convince their captors that they are not the sort of people who should stay in that institution. In these cases, cooperation with the sociologist constitutes a serious practical risk. Further, even if one finds such a person and gains his confidence, his skill at deceiving the researcher may be no less effective than it was in deceiving others. Indeed, Agnes's sweeping deception of Garfinkel and his colleagues is a well-known case in point.[17]

Finally, after passing all of these hurdles, there remains the problem of retrieving the right information. To this end, overkill seems advisable. The researcher, if possible, should take a case history, gain access to spontaneous personal accounts, perhaps induce his informant to keep a diary, and so on. The basic goal here is to obtain and accurately interpret the details of the actual interactions in which the misfit attempts to pass, details that he may not easily remember or be able to describe.

There is a device which lessens the recruitment problem a bit and thereby expand the usefulness of misfits for studying action. Many people do not consistently pretend to be something they are not but do so only occasionally. The deaf sometimes want to appear to others as if they hear; the retarded often wish to be regarded as people who can tell time when in fact they cannot, the marijuana user wishes the police officer to see him as an unhigh, unstoned, average guy, and so on.[18] Since passing occurs in a more restricted context in these people's lives, it is somewhat easier to find them and interview them without being immoral or ineffectual. They can more easily talk to a social scientist in a truthful way without putting themselves in jeopardy.

CULTURAL TROUBLEMAKERS

On a slightly different plane from cultural misfits are "cultural troublemakers." These are people who have been identified as defective in some area of social life and who, for one reason or another, are considered incapable of performing some of the tasks falling to the normal, natural adult member of the society. We might include in this category children, the mentally ill, the retarded, and certain types of criminals. These people are interesting in two ways—the way they deal with society, and the way society deals with them.

Such people are called troublemakers precisely because others regard them as a source of what is, for the sociologists, interesting social troubles. The various incompetents of our society share the possibility of creative deviance. Competent members, by their very status as competent members, may be limited to highly structured deviant actions such as cheating or revolting. In the way known social structures define the world of normal people and in the way it is *this* world that they live in, all sorts of actions and perceptions would "have no point," "be boring," "be silly," or simply never come up. This is so because the deviance of normals, in one way or another, is oriented to the *known existence and nature of the structure it deviates from*. Thus, for the competent normal adult, the discovery of novel deviance takes on the character of a project. It takes work, sustained motivation, and time and effort to do it. The last place that one finds such deviance is in one's own spontaneous behavior and perception in varieties of settings. In this sense cultural troublemakers are a continual source of naturally occurring disruption, for they break rules that are seldom broken, they say things that are never said, and they have technical problems that others do not. Such people provide us with the provocative contrasts to the normal and the ordinary that we so ardently sought in taking the roles of stranger and novice.

Cultural troublemakers also allow us to see how society responds to people and events that it does not see often and is not well equipped to deal with. One such response is to create, discover, and describe social structures for these people to fit in. That is, the very presence of such people in a normal environment and/or their unusual acts (including the failure to perform expected acts) transform an environment into a place where its participants engage in sociological analysis. Only in their presence do we explicitly recognize that we were speaking the English language, that our dinner is to be kept off the floor, or that we are to wear clothes in this particular place. In fact, our general response to cultural troublemakers is evident in the names we give to them and the institutions we provide for them. These institutions have it as their task to make a normal, natural life possible, to a greater or lesser extent, for the retarded, the blind, the emotionally disturbed, the mentally ill, and others. In performing this task, cultural troublemakers make society give accounts of itself and its normal workings in general, and amid the small incidents of daily life.

Finally, students of everyday life have found it immensely helpful to study cultural troublemakers from the perspective of the Zen master mentioned in our discussion of Cicourel. That is, the actions of these people are treated, not as an imperfect version of what *we* do, but as a perfect example of what *they* do. In short, we abandon the practice of measuring cultural troublemakers against a standard of the normal and the usual and try to understand their actions in their own terms.

When their actions seem incomprehensible or defective, this is the sociologist's fault, not theirs. Cultural troublemakers become, in effect, denizens of an unknown culture with its own activities and possibilities, which it is our job to decipher or figure out. This perspective results in identifying abilities in, for example, the retarded or in children which we never knew they had, with immense practical significance for their treatment and education.[19]

Previously, we have stressed the strategy of estranging oneself from others in order to understand everyday life. The reason for this was not hard to find. We were trying to understand a domain of action which was already quite familiar in terms of empathy. We were not looking to decipher the life of urban guerillas or terminal cancer patients. But in dealing with cultural troublemakers, the opposite strategy seems to be implicated. It is of the utmost importance that the researcher learn from them, using all his powers and devices of empathetic understanding. Here the goal is to mesh one's perspectives with those of children or the victims of dyslexia, so that one sees what they see, knows what they know, feels as they feel. One thus enlists all the strategies of reality reconstruction in the service of formal sociology. To this end, Goode and other researchers have found it invaluable to spend large amounts of time in the company of "troublemakers." One must not be under institutional or other obligations to train them, teach them, or otherwise treat them as people in need of social servicing. Instead, the researcher and his subjects must be free to do whatever it is that they wish or are able to do, if they are not interfered with. Ordinarily it is difficult, immoral, or both to be the constant companion of another person throughout her daily existence. However, in the case of institutionalized cultural troublemakers, this becomes not only possible but often helpful in many ways to those one studies.

When this program is successful, there is a fringe benefit in addition to having met another human being on her own terms. The researcher will have another cognitive attitude available with which to view everyday life.[20] She will have given him that. He need not invent additional attitudes to supplement the stranger and the novice in his attempts to make the familiar strange. There are all kinds of people out there, already in possession of "unnatural natural attitudes" which they use to find their way through social existence. He has only to find them, exercise a little humility, and let nature take its course.

In case study E (page 381–395) Goode incorporates most of the strategies discussed in this chapter. In attempting to inhabit the world of a very different human being, he encountered that peculiar interplay of empathy and estrangement that seems to be required for such a task.

Notes

1. The contrast we make here is not a black-and-white one but one of relative emphasis between field methods and formal sociology.
2. Alfred Schutz, "The Stranger," in Collected Paper II: Studies in Social Theory, The Hague: Martinus Nijhoff, 1964, pp. 91–105.
3. The discussion here implies two social scientists—one who is interested in a particular research problem, and a second who is chosen by the first and sent into some environment to which he or she is a stranger. Only when a researcher is interested in studying an environment in which he is already a cultural stranger will it be possible for the device of "stranger" to be employed by a single researcher.
4. Personal communication from Dr. Kenji Ima, San Diego State University, 1975.
5. A well-known example of such a study is D. L. Rosenhan, "On Being Sane in Insane Places," Science 179, no. 4070 (January 1973): 250–258.

6. For a review of the information-processing issues involved in listening to speech, see Donald A. Norman, *Memory and Attention: An Introduction to Human Information Processing*, New York: Wiley, 1969.

7. See David Sudnow, *The Ways of Hands*, Cambridge, Mass.: Harvard University Press, 1978.

8. Sudnow treats conversing as an *embodied activity* involving integrated attention to pace, rhythm, muscle movement, and so on. He found that such traditional concepts as "hearing with one's ears" were dangerously misleading when it came to understanding the facilities used in the actual production of speech.

9. Some social scientists call the practice of reading a description with the intention of trying to do what it describes "giving the material a *praxiological* reading." This involves, among other things, scanning the page differently from the way one scans when giving the same passage a "narrative reading."

10. For a treatment of instructed action as a topic and as an ethnographic resource, see George Girton, "Kung Fu: Toward a Praxiological Hermeneutic of the Martial Arts," unpublished manuscript, Department of Sociology, University of California at Los Angeles, 1975; and Bennetta Jules-Rosette, "Reflexive Ethnography, Part I: Instructions as Data: The Apostolic Case," unpublished manuscript, Department of Sociology, University of California at San Diego, 1974.

11. Margaret Theeman, *Social Configurations of the Movement, "Movement": A Study in Alienation and Ecstasy*, Ph.D. dissertation, Department of Sociology, Harvard University, 1973.

12. See Hugh Mehan and Houston Wood, *The Reality of Ethnomethodology*, New York: Wiley Interscience, 1975, pp. 225–38.

13. Ibid., pp. 234–235.

14. Ibid., pp. 233–234.

15. Our thanks to Dr. Andrew Walker and Dr. Charles Lidz for calling this strategy and its attendant problems to our attention.

16. Harold Garfinkel, *Studies in Ethnomethodology*, Englewood Cliffs, N.J.: Prentice-Hall, 1967, pp. 116–185.

17. Ibid., pp. 285–288.

18. Both the deaf and the retarded sometimes employ "props" in this passing activity consisting of hearing aids and watches, respectively.

19. For a vivid illustration of this, see case study E, "The World of the Congenitally Deaf-Blind: Toward the Grounds for Achieving Human Understanding" by David Goode, pages 381–395.

20. It is interesting in this connection that persons on mind-altering drugs often report "learning" how to feel high. That is, they find that they can later reproduce their drug-induced feelings without the drugs themselves.

CHAPTER 10

Reification and Reactive Measures as Research Strategies

Only occasionally is everyday life experienced as introductory sociology textbooks make it out to be. Only occasionally does one literally notice and come in contact with "rules," "social networks," or "role conflict" as such. The rest of the time one is just bowling, talking to Bill, or having a cigarette. But there are ways to turn everyday settings into sociological places. If the mountain is not the sort of thing Mohammed says it is, one can bring in strip-mining shovels and see to it that the holy Koran is not contradicted by a mere mountain. In sociology, such a repair operation can be carried out in two ways—either by physically changing events and activities, or by altering our customary interpretations of these events and activities. When we do the former we have employed reactive techniques, whereas when we use the latter procedure we have "reified" an environment. To reify an environment, in Karl Marx's sense, is to replace its concrete material reality with one's own abstract representations of that reality.

Both reactive techniques and reification are usually considered to be mistakes. In this chapter we treat them as research strategies. We seek to turn an environment into a place which it actually is not, to turn it into a sociological place, and to do so deliberately. The concrete ways of accomplishing this are what now await discussion.

Producing Multiple Realities

One way to reify a social situation is to arrange for members to interpret it as something it actually and obviously is not and govern their actions accordingly.

266

This is most commonly done by arranging to "fool" one's subjects through some experimental procedure

In one such experiment subjects were told they would receive a new form of counseling consisting of "yes" or "no" answers to their questions about personal problems. In fact, the answers of the "counselor" consisted of a fixed series of yeses and nos determined by the use of a table of random numbers. A similar device consists in using a computer program which engages in conversation as though it were a client-centered therapist. Depending on the input, the computer says such things as "Say some more," "That's very interesting," and "You seem to be very upset." Subjects are fooled into thinking they are talking to a real person.

After such experiments researchers can inspect data so as to find subjects engaging in practices of "cognitive consistency," "imputing meanings," or "socially constructing reality." But notice that the procedures are reversible. Suppose that it is the researcher who was deceived. Imagine that the yeses and nos in the counseling experiment were really answers to the subject's questions and that the researcher was falsely told that they were random. The subjects could then examine the researcher's journal article and discover the practices by which *he* constructs social reality!

What are we to make of this symmetry, and, in particular, what happens to the validity of the journal article in the face of it? What these procedures really do is produce operative multiple realities. Both researcher and subject are provided with interpretive schemes *which they really believe in* and which they use to interpret the other's actions. Each scheme reveals the other person's interpretations as a systematic distortion of the real "facts" of the situation. Why would we want to do a thing like this?

Phenomenologically, the irksome problem in making the construction of reality visible is this: On the one hand it is easily possible, at least intellectually, to construe one's interpretations as imposing meanings on a world that possesses none of its own. But whenever we interpret things, it appears that we are giving an object the name or interpretation that it deserves, i.e., we are calling the boys "boy," and the insults "insult."

One way to overcome this difficulty is to provide ourselves with a means of seeing another person as imposing meanings on things that do not "really" possess them. We do this here by providing ourselves with a version of reality different from the one being entertained by the member. It matters little which version is the correct one. It matters only that we truly believe in our version. In this sense we are setting up the experiment, with all its accompanying hardware, only to do what we have to do to believe ourselves and our version of what is happening. This will produce recognitions and observations that would otherwise be impossible. Just as a placebo will not work unless the patient really believes it will, so we cannot merely decide to adopt a version of reality for intellectual reasons. Paradoxically, if we were Azande sociologists instead of American, we might have to employ potions and spells instead of computers and statistics in order to believe ourselves. [1]

More esoteric techniques based on this same data attempt to produce simultaneous multiple realities within the same individual. Castaneda reports that it was the apparent strategy of his mentor, Don Juan, to provide him with two such realities, that of the sorcerer and that of the Western college student.[2] The result presumably would be to make visible how *any* reality is an ongoing construction of the individual and that any reality consists of such a construction.

Schwartz located a similar phenomenon in connection with the mental disorder of paranoia. It was discovered that certain paranoids engaged in what he called nondiscursive reasoning, consisting in perceptually "seeing" conclusions about others and their actions. At the same time, ordinary discursive thinking and common sense knowledge remained intact. It was thus possible for a paranoid patient to "hear" a lie when another person spoke to him, but to "know" in terms of common sense that it was, in fact, not a lie. This situation appeared to allow the paranoid to observe how he constructed suspicious meanings while he listened to other people speak.[3]

In considering strategies which produce multiple realities, we have probably left the more scientific readers far behind. They may refuse to credit such devices as bona fide research techniques. For the study of reality construction inescapably involves some of the most ancient paradoxes in epistemology and philosophy.

Any social scientist who presumes to study the construction of reality is a perennial reality constructor himself. Like everyone else, he believes in his particular version of the world and in the hardware that produces it, be these computers or magic spells. He therefore ends up by describing how "they" construct their reality, as seen from within his reality, except that his reality is real while theirs is constructed. Is there another way to do business here? Can one study this topic without fragmenting it by addressing the world as seen by others as a phenomenon and using one's own world as a privileged resource? Should this be done? Such questions have been bandied about for centuries. There appears to be no escape from them if one wishes to study "reality" seriously as an empirical topic. An important illustration of this is provided by the next research strategy to be considered. Merely presuming (as most sociologists *must*) that people do activities in some structured "way" can result in major changes in those activities themselves.

Making Methods

In a very real sense, competent practitioners do not know what they are doing. Their "doings" are just done innocently, without explicit awareness. Indeed, the naming, describing, and laying out of the steps in the process are the crutches (the Wittgensteinian "ladders") used by the neophyte and his teacher while he learns. Increasing competence is synonomous with the progressive discarding of these crutches. Indeed, efficiency, fluency, and speed demand it.

It is often the task of the formal sociologist to reverse this process. He must turn a doing into something that is done, and thus make a member's competent actions an object of his own scrutiny. One way to accomplish this is to propose to people that they use certain "procedures" to accomplish their actions. When using this tactic one often must make methods rather as one makes a cake—a recipe is needed. For often enough, competent practitioners find inquiries about their "methods"—the "how" of what they are doing—strange and unanswerable. Frequently they may have nothing to say, unless the researcher has some workable strategy for enabling them to "find" their methods.

In one study, the discovery of these methods was crucial not only for the researcher but for the members as well. A drug-abuse prevention and treatment program was funded for rural Montana, and some forty people were hired to implement it. After the center had operated for about a year, nobody—politicians, evaluators, even the workers themselves—could "find" the program. Although the workers went to work each day and did something or other, it was not clear to them or anyone else just what they were doing, or if they were doing it. In an effort to produce a visible drug program from these activities, researchers put a plausible proposition to the workers:

> The staff members were encouraged to take into account the indexical nature of their work or more specifically understand that all activity occurs somewhere, and that if place or "somewhere" could not be articulated, the very occurrence of any activity was doubtful and indeed then only subject to gloss.[4]

In short, in suggesting that they must be doing their work "somewhere," researchers were inviting the staff to consider their activities as possessing a spatial organization. They were asked to locate on maps the areas of the town where they ordinarily conducted their work, to photograph these places, give an account of their nature, and explain the relationship between the place they photographed and the work that occurred there. Confronted with these plausible questions, staff were able to successfully discover "work sites." The front of the treatment center became the "greeting area," where secretaries paired clients with workers. The bathroom became the "sanctuary" where one escaped temporarily from the phone and the people. Divisions of labor emerged, insofar as one outreach worker covered the bars while the other went to the schools.

In short, staff discovered ways of seeing what were once aimless, confused activities as definite jobs carried out in particular "ways," with definable results and plausible rationales. They discovered as well new ways of doing those jobs. This seems altogether typical, since coming to see the structure underlying what one is doing simultaneously provides one with a structured way of doing it.

Another reason why this procedure is pregnant with reactive possibilities is the potentially moral nature of most action. Explicit reflection on what one is doing seems to lead easily and simultaneously to reflection on what one *should* be doing. There are of course settings which are especially sensitive in this regard. In his study of group therapy, Schwartz found that almost any aspect of the therapy process was addressed by psychiatrists with moral eyes. "Is it good for the group?" "Should it be stopped or let alone?" "Should it be mentioned to everybody?" "Why are you telling me about this, Schwartz?" "Do you think i: is wrong?"

As is clear from the example, different "method making" recipes will produce different versions of activities and different activities. In the drug study, it could just as easily have been suggested that whatever the staff does, it does at certain times. Why don't they see how much time they spend on paper work, how much on travel, and how much talking to clients? How are activities spaced throughout the day? When are the breaks, the "off hours," and how long do they last? In short, what is the temporal organization of outreach work, and what should it, and will it, become?

PRACTICAL CONSIDERATIONS

In selecting a method-making recipe, many practical contingencies present themselves. One has to consider the preexisting interpretive skills of the members in question. Will they be capable of seeing and describing what they are asked to see and describe? Will they be willing? One has to consider the settings and activities themselves and whether the fact-finding procedures being proposed can be performed within the practical constraints of these settings and activities. If members cannot discover what they are doing while doing it, there is frequently a way out. The researcher can provide reconstructions of the activities, which members later review. He can keep a log of the police officer's day and review it with him when he gets off duty. He can videotape a classroom and show the tape to the teacher after the class is dismissed. In this way members are allowed to inspect their activities in a manner that is unavailable to them when they are engaged in doing them. There is now some "time out"; there is the possibility of seeing it again; and so on. Yet in using such devices, one had best tread lightly. For the manner in which members are asked to put together their stories will have as much to do with the final tale as the selection of the story they are asked to tell.

Finally there are moral problems. One can expect changes in people's lives to emerge from this kind of process, as it did in the case of the drug program. That puts an enormous responsibility on the social scientist, and what he decides to do or not to do.

USES FOR METHOD-MAKING RECIPES

Obviously method-making recipes do not give information about activities in their natural, innocent state (prior to research intervention). However, if a setting in its innocent state is not of the type that some researcher wants to look at, he can simply and brazenly transform it into one that is. If he is willing to take this step, the results can be used in several ways. For example, method-making recipes offer an unusually nice way to study "reflexivity," as discussed by Garfinkel. Let's say someone takes the position that there is no way to separate the structure of action and interaction from the ways in which members see, know, and talk about these structures. The method-making recipes offer the researcher a sequence of events, one that he himself instigated, in which the structuring of action, and the finding of structure within action, occur together in one process.

In studying such a process, he would do well to have many sources of information about what is going on. This is one reason Cicourel's indefinite triangulation procedures are often so useful (see pages 233–234). They require someone to see and describe the structure in his or her behavior, while simultaneously allowing the experimenter to manipulate that behavior and the manner in which it is described.

Manipulating Social Situations

A second set of ways to turn everyday life into a sociological arena is to actively construct, destroy, and otherwise alter social situations so as to make them bear on some predecided problem. This might seem sacrilegious to researchers who pride themselves on being sociological "naturalists" whose only interest is in the direct study of human action within "natural settings." In fact, many formal sociologists feel just this way about manipulation and regard it as both unethical and counterproductive. However, there are good rationales for manipulating settings if one's goals are clearly spelled out.

Disrupting Social Settings

Disruption is a classical technique by which to reveal the otherwise hidden aspects of everyday life. One way to do this is to find ways to conduct oneself "badly" within a social setting. First some set of concepts from sociology is used to describe the setting as it normally operates. Let's call this the "script" for the setting. Then one finds himself a part to play within the scipt, using it as a reference point to see how to behave in ways that are unusual from the point of view of others. It is convenient to consider three types of scripts:[5]

1. Scripts which are absurd to both the sociologist and the member.
2. Scripts which describe the setting and/or its activities to the sociologist, but not to the member.
3. Scripts which describe the setting in terms of the understandings of both the sociologist *and* the member.

SCRIPTS WHICH ARE ABSURD TO BOTH THE SOCIOLOGIST AND THE MEMBER

Disruption experiments are often spoken of as "breaching people's ordinary reality" or "violating their common sense assumptions." There is a certain unwarranted egotism in these phrases, since their implication is that the sociologist knows what other people take to be real and ordinary. But sociology does not give us this information; in fact, this is precisely what we are trying to find out through disruption procedures. Our dilemma thus becomes: How does one do otherwise than usual when the usual is not known in any detail? One way is intuitively to pick some way to act that is outrageous and hope for the best. That is, in whatever ways one's conduct turns out to be senseless or strange, it will suggest what the usual and the familiar might be, and how it is sustained.

A well-known example of this strategy is Garfinkel's experiment in which students were instructed to use the role set operative in a boardinghouse to guide their behavior in their own homes.[6] Garfinkel reported situations in which students took the boarder role and treated other family members in polite and formal ways. The metaphor was not applied in further detail, by, for example, asking the students to treat the father as the house's "owner" and the rest of the family as fellow "boarders." Garfinkel utilized this procedure in two forms. In the first form, students looked at their homes from the standpoint of boarders and wrote accounts of their observations. In the second form, they actually acted as boarders.

TECHNICAL PROBLEMS

At least one goal for such procedures is to find a heuristic device for continually behaving in senseless, strange, or deviant ways. To that end the scheme selected has to meet several practical requirements:

1. Your privately known scheme of interpretation has to repeatedly suggest things for you to do.
2. You must be able to sustain your interpretive scheme for some time in the face of what is going to happen when you start, without lapsing into independent reactions to others' behavior, explanations, repair jobs, etc.
3. Your resulting behaviors must consistently come off to others as deviant in some way.

In practice, these conditions are extremely hard to fulfill. With respect to the first condition, you must select roles that you know about (in fantasy or fact) in some detail and that mesh with the situation to the extent that you can at least imagine "someone of your sort" being in the situation and doing the thing being proposed in the first place. Garfinkel's students reported being confronted with situations in which they were not sure what a boarder would do. Another experiment appeared to fail from a technical standpoint because the students were not practiced in the use of their roles. Students were instructed to adopt the stance of a paranoid in listening to others—to hear hidden motives, misinformation, and so on.[7] They reported an acute awareness of "being in an artificial game," being "unable to live the part," or being "at a loss as to what to do next." In the course of listening to other people, students would lose sight of the experiment. Often they put so much effort into maintaining their novel attitude that they were unable to follow the conversation.

Another contingency is interpersonal. Others will be ignorant of your imaginary role. They will therefore not adopt complementary roles for themselves (they will not act as boarders). Consequently their initial responses to your behavior can produce situations for which the person you are pretending to be has no ordinary response. Further, you "know" who you are on several levels. As a result, Garfinkel's students reported lapsing back into "familiar" emotional responses based on their real identities and those of others.

One way out of some of these difficulties is to engage in "hit and run" disruption. One thinks up some well-defined unusual behavior that can be performed in a small amount of time within various settings by various people, for example:

> I walked into a small luncheonette carrying my own plate, knife, fork, spoon, and napkin under my arm and quite conspicuously set my own place setting at the counter. I was met with several glances and expressions of bewilderment but no verbal responses.[8]

In this instance, it is not difficult to figure out what to do on an ongoing basis. The short duration of the whole episode makes it easy to sustain. Furthermore, since it is done in the presence of strangers, matters are not complicated by the personal histories of those involved.

NOTES ON VALIDITY

What possible use could such a strategy have, besides providing a source of sadistic amusement to oneself and embarrassment to others? Acting like a boarder in one's home is reification, all right. There is no question that an abstract scheme of interpretation is being applied to a reality that is incompatible with it. There is also no question that the scene has been physically transformed, as well as symbolically misrepresented. But so what?

What could the interactions that result from such a procedure have to say about either normal households or boarders? One no longer has a normal household and its accompanying behavior. That has been distorted. One also does not have a boardinghouse. For the family sees no boarder, only a continued stream of offensive formal behavior whose motive and warrant are obscure.

This is all quite true and would invalidate such a procedure from a conventional point of view. But Garfinkel was not interested in either households or boardinghouses per se. He was interested in normality itself. He asked, as Schutz had asked, "What is responsible for the normal, natural appearance of *any* social environment?" With this in mind, the purpose of such a demonstration is not to demonstrate anything; *it is to supply ideas.* The many small events, emotional reactions, and accounts produced by such disruptions will, it is hoped, suggest something about what ordinary actions and ordinary interpretations of action might be, and how they are sustained. In Garfinkel's words, these suggestive events function as an "aid to a sluggish imagination."[9]

In this connection, one of the most important outcomes of these experiments has been negative. An ever-popular metaphor for conceiving of the "ordinary" is the game with rules. Obey the rules, and you are recognized as an ordinary social player, acting in a normal fashion. Disobey the rules, and you disrupt the game and its attendant reality. Yet this metaphor has been all but destroyed by disruption procedures.

Again and again, clear violations of a social "game," instead of being treated as senseless or nonordinary, merely started a new "game." The ordinary nature of the gathering itself was retained intact. Consider, for instance, this exchange where an experimenter constantly asked her husband to clarify his common sense remarks:

> "As far as I am concerned, dropping off your shirts—whichever shirts you mean— could mean giving them to the Goodwill, leaving them at the cleaner's, at the laundromat, or throwing them out. I never know what you mean by those vague statements."

The husband responded thus:

> He reflected on what I said, then changed the entire perspective by acting as though we were playing a game, that it was all a joke. He seemed to enjoy the joke. He ruined my approach by assuming the role I thought was mine. He then said, "Well, let's take this step by step with 'yes' or 'no' answers: Did you see the dirty shirts I left on the kitchenette, yes or no?" . . . In the same fashion, he asked if I picked up the shirts, if I put them in the car; if I left them at the laundry and if I did all these things that day, Friday.[10]

On the other hand, when Garfinkel actually studied games, he found actions which did not directly violate the rules and yet were treated as disruptive, unusual, and—more interestingly—*illegitimate* behavior. Such an action was exchanging the position of, say, his two knights in chess, leaving the overall board position unchanged:

> On the several occasions in which I did this, my opponents were disconcerted, tried to stop me, demanded an explanation of what I was up to, were uncertain about the legality (but wanted to assert its illegality nevertheless), made it clear to me that I was spoiling the game for them, and at the next round of play made me promise that I would not do anything this time.[11]

SCRIPTS WHICH DESCRIBE THE SETTING AND/OR
ITS ACTIVITIES TO THE SOCIOLOGIST, BUT NOT
TO THE MEMBER

As we have pointed out, in no clear way is everyday life a sociological place for its inhabitants. In no explicit sense are members attending to roles, interpretive procedures, and so on. This puts the sociologist in a bind similar to the psychiatrist's. What the latter sees as crazy and bizarre behaviors are only fleeting moments in the life of most mental patients. Most of their lives are perfectly ordinary and unremarkable. Similarly, the aspects of life that preoccupy sociologists are ordinarily mere incidents in the everyday existence of those they study. Most of the day seems to consist of far more plebian events such as putting on one's shirt or doing the dishes.

Most sociologists contend with this by theorizing their concepts into the member's underworld—by speaking of "internalized norms," "tacit understandings," or "implicit assumptions." In other words, they imply that members really are living the lives sociologists say they are; they just don't know it.

Imagine that as a social theorist I wish to show that individuals have background understandings that they do not know they have. How do I do it? Disruption procedures provide one tool. First I must make a theoretical commitment: I must describe some set of assumptions or expectations that people implicitly hold. I know what they are and can explicitly describe them, but the people do not and cannot. Nevertheless, they are definitely "there." These implicit assumptions are then used as a scheme of reference in two ways:

1. By consulting them, I devise behavior that violates them.
2. I interpret the reactions of others to this behavior in terms of the assumptions.
   a. If they get angry, complain, show confusion or anxiety, this indicates that they tacitly hold the assumptions.
   b. If they respond quickly, fluently, and as if nothing unusual is happening, they may not possess these tacit assumptions after all.

Such procedures have been used to show, for instance, that members expect one another to speak vaguely and accept the vagueness in one another's remarks,[12] or that around each of us is an invisible bubble of "personal space" which others are expected not to violate.[13]

Of course, things need not be, and seldom are, as simple as that. In using disruption in the second way, I get slightly closer to "legitimate" procedures of inference, but only slightly. At least I state my assumptions about other people in advance, before undertaking my experiment. But there is still no good way to validate my version of what will happen in this experiment, as opposed to alternative explanations and interpretations of the same data.

This otherwise commonplace methodological malady is aggravated by the nature of tacit assumptions themselves. When one talks of tacit assumptions, one buys into a whole universe of sociological theory. There are "definitions of the situation," "background expectancies," "residual rules," "situational properties," and on and on. More often than not, the planned disruption is not a violation of some single expectation but of a whole set of different kinds of expectations which collectively render events real, ordinary, and meaningful. Given these complexities, there are bound to be many plausible, but competing, ways to interpret people's reactions to some supposedly disruptive action or actions. Which one of these should we choose and why? To illustrate the logic involved in such a choice, let's continue to explore "ordinary-ness."

UNMAKING SENSE: PRODUCING SENSELESS ACTION

Symbolic interaction explains that we get our cues about how to act by observing and interpreting the actions of others. This presupposes that the others' actions are interpretable to begin with—that we can make sense of them. And indeed it would seem a minimal condition for socially organized conduct that individuals be able to make sense of one anothers' actions in some consistent, coordinated way. It would thus seem to follow that persistent amounts of sense-less behavior would start to make for social disorganization (either at the indi-vidual or group level). Thus the logical question becomes: What kind of behavior would be senseless in a particular social occasion? The question is a very tricky one because it is difficult to fail at the task of giving actions some meaning. Even if the meaning is "He's weird" or "That's uninterpretable," it is adequate to provoke structured responses.

But let us assume that wit and ingenuity triumph and we produce an event that is initially uninterpretable. Castaneda indicates the difficulties in making this event remain senseless:

> Imagine going into a restaurant and having the waitress ask you how many are in your party. You respond by joyously taking her in your arms and showering her with hugs and kisses. For a moment, you have her; she stops making sense of the world. But she recovers *immediately* and thinks or says, "Ah, he's crazy."[14]

Because of this incredible adaptability, it is all but impossible to prevent an event from eventually acquiring a meaning.

Then, too, the researcher has his own problems. Producing a string of unin-terpretable behavior is a bit like trying to consistently produce sentences whose words are in random order. As an on-the-spot task, it is almost impossible for a native speaker. So it is with senseless action for a socialized adult. Therefore one cannot employ a shotgun strategy, such as acting like a boarder. The experiment must be set up very carefully, or it will not work.

After all of this, the reader may be discouraged. Don't be, for there are orkable procedures for generating no-sense.

Readers will recall Schutz's discussion of the natural attitude, that set of assumptions, interests, and attitudes which gives environments their normal, ordinary feeling. In addition, there is a large store of expert information we draw on to know a situation as a bridge game, a traffic jam, or a union meeting and to interpret events accordingly. Put all these resources together and presumably one gets reality at a given time and place. Presumably if one could produce an action or event that resisted these resources, he would have an uninterpretable phenomenon, a "something" without a name, a reason for happening, or a coherent connection to everything else that is going on. But an additional condition must be met: The "victim" must be trapped into using the interpretive resources commensurate with "where he is" and "what's going on" to make sense of this problematic event, without being able to redefine the situation somehow so as to bring new assumptions into play. Such a redefinition could be accomplished in two ways. He could modify his "natural attitude," which is equivalent to deciding that this is not an ordinary situation. Schutz describes such modifications and how they turn an initially everyday environment into a "game," a "playful exchange," a "conspiracy," and so on.[15] Another way is to redefine the occasion as something other than what it was at first taken to be. What seemed to be a German class turns out to be a faculty meeting; what he thought would be a talk about his raise turns out to be the day he was fired. While such a process can and does occur, there is evidence that it (1) takes time to do, (2) is best done in conjunction with others, and (3) is hard to sustain unless one's redefinition is consensually supported by the others present.

Thus, if we require of a person that he must manage the redefinition by himself, in insufficient time, and without being able to assume that he will be supported by others, it should be difficult or impossible for him to do it. Finally, he must be prevented from "leaving the field" by physically withdrawing, daydreaming, reading, or by engaging in other kinds of situational withdrawal, such as conversing in the corner with a confederate.

With all these conditions met, we should have a genuine senseless event for an individual. In order to make things even tougher on him, he should be obliged to respond to the event in front of witnesses—to talk about it, comply with it, and so on. We thereby make someone not only initially confused or surprised but acutely confused and anxious about what to do.

This was roughly the battle plan when Garfinkel set up interviews between premedical students and a bogus "representative of an eastern medical school." Students were told they would hear a recording of an interview between a med-school applicant and an admissions examiner:

> The recording was a faked one between a "medical school interviewer" and an "applicant." The applicant was a boor, his language was ungrammatical and filled with colloquialisms, he was evasive, he contradicted the interviewer, he bragged, he ran down other schools and professions, he insisted on knowing how he had done in the interview.[16]

After the premedical students were asked to evaluate this "applicant" and his potential, they were told how this same applicant had been evaluated by (1) Dr. Gardner, the medical school interviewer, (2) six members of the admissions committee who had also heard the tape, and (3) other students. They were also given general information from the applicant's "official record":

> The information was deliberately contrived to contradict the principal points in the student's assessment. For example, if the student said that the applicant must have come from a lower class family, he was told that the applicant's father was vice president of a firm that manufactured pneumatic doors for trains and buses. Was the applicant ignorant? Then he had excelled in courses like The Poetry of Milton and Dramas of Shakespeare. . . .
> That the applicant was stupid and would not do well in a scientific field was met by citing A's in organic and physical chemistry and graduate level performance in an undergraduate research course.[17]

While the student was recovering from these "facts," he was also told that this applicant had been admitted to medical school and was living up to the promise that his interviewer, the admissions committee, and other students had seen in him on the basis of his fine performance in the interview.

After this, the premedical student was invited to listen to the recording a second time and to assess the applicant again.

Notice the way in which this experiment produces a senseless event. The event is not uninterpretable but too interpretable. A "reality disjuncture"[18] is produced: Common sense says the applicant is an idiot, and, simultaneously, equally trustworthy sources (an interviewer, the medical school, etc.) say he is wonderful.

In such situations, Garfinkel suggests that a person's confusion should be directly proportional to his moral commitment to the "natural facts of life." But how are we to measure "confusion"? Fortunately, there is a nice way to do this in the case of reality disjunctures. As Pollner points out, good common sense reasoners "know a problem when they see one," and when they see one they endeavor to solve it in a convenient (for us) way: They check out the sets of assumptions that led to the dilemma to see which might be at fault. How fortunate, since when they do this in the course of an experiment, we are there to see which assumptions they check, in what order, and why.[19] Does our experiment justify such a conclusion? Unfortunately, the answer is no, and we shall now show why.

Endowing People with Assumptions: A Methodological Problem

Let us distinguish two ways in which a member comes to know of the existence of assumptions and expectations. There are occasions when these words correspond to psychological events which someone can remember and describe. The young woman anxiously "expects" the doorbell to ring at about six o'clock and to find at the door her date for the evening; the sociologist "assumes" something about social roles while working out a theory.

At other times there may be no subjective event to remember and describe. Nevertheless, it makes sense to say that people engage in actions "as if" they held certain assumptions about themselves, others, and the world. When I begin to give my lecture in English, one might say that I have "assumed" that the students (or most of them) speak English. Yet one might just as well construe my lecture as a "verbal" performance and conclude that I must have "expected" that my audience was not deaf. Depending on how one categorizes the behavior in question, it will make sense to explain it by reference to different assumptions and different kinds of assumptions. In each case it is possible to devise disruption experiments which violate these assumptions and thus show that they were there all along. In fact, the number of assumptions someone can be endowed with in this manner seems to be limited only by the number of ways we can devise to surprise him.[20]

How does one decide which of these "assumptions" were really there and which are merely reasonable ways to talk? There is no way of settling such an issue by reference to the views of the subjects. By definition, we are looking for their tacit assumptions—assumptions that they do not know they have. Consequently there will be no psychological event for them to remember and describe. However, some "assumptions" will make sense to them for explaining their reactions. But so what? In some cultures it makes sense to explain behavior by reference to the presence of demons in the mind. In short, it would seem that the decision of how to explain behavior is left to the researcher. Yet his common sense is no more trustworthy than theirs. Something is obviously very wrong here.

In experiments such as Garfinkel's, one relies on common sense reasoning in an extremely dangerous way. By analogy, it is like arranging for the car of an auto mechanic to fail to start. One then watches him successively check out the points, the condenser, the spark plugs, and so on, and treats each of these actions as evidence that he "assumes" each of these parts is working whenever he starts the car. It would seem better to say that his mind goes to these parts *only* when he turns the key and finds that nothing happens. Consequently, one cannot find out what people are expecting "all along" by doing something unexpected. One can discover only what resources they muster to deal with the unusual action.

But what makes the event unusual in the first place, if it is not prior assumptions? Actually it is the researcher as much as the subject who makes sure that his disruption is a disruption. He does this by using his own understandings to interpret any and all reactions to it. Consider some of the ways in which the premedical students handled their situation:

1. Some decided that the medical school had accepted a good man and that their original assessments were off base.

2. Some trusted their own assessments and decided that the medical school had accepted a boor.
3. Three subjects were convinced that there was a deception and acted on this conviction throughout the interview.
4. Three others regarded the interview as an experimental one in which they were required to solve some unknown problem. They thought they should not abandon their honest views since to do so would interfere with the study.
5. One student, who alone among the subjects was confident of getting into medical school, showed no appreciable disturbance or attention to a "problem" throughout the interview.
6. Another subject regarded the information as semantically ambiguous, so that common opinions about this information were difficult or impossible.

It is difficult to claim that these diverse reactions and interpretations were all attempts to cope with the "same" senseless events. Instead, the same words and deeds constituted different events to different students, in terms of their meaning. In fact, for some students the supposed "puzzle" was no puzzle to them and consequently required no "solution." They readily understood "what was going on" and therefore what to do about it. It should be pointed out that Garfinkel was aware of these difficulties.

An Alternate Conception of Anticipation

So far, expectations have been treated as primordial assumptions which people bring to social situations and try to hold onto at any cost. But "to expect" and "to anticipate" are verbs. Why not treat them as referring to activities rather than to the holding of "assumptions"? Coming to expect something, altering one's anticipations, throwing out previous assumptions, and so on can be thought of as flexible activities done differently by different individuals, who remain sensitive to many different horizons of possibilities. There is a place for disruption procedures in all of this, but disruption used far more delicately than in the examples presented thus far.

SCRIPTS WHICH DESCRIBE THE SETTING IN TERMS OF THE UNDERSTANDINGS OF BOTH THE SOCIOLOGIST AND THE MEMBER

Of course, there are some expectations, assumptions, and understandings that are no secret to the member. Everyone might know and agree that here we have a department store or there a game of tic-tac-toe. In such cases, sociologists are mercifully spared some of the problems of strategies 1 and 2, but not all of them. One might wonder what disruption procedures have to offer in well-defined situations, when one need not look for underground expectations or hidden realities.

Producing Unusual Social Events

Here disruption's greatest value is in producing events in the society that may be genuinely new, that is, events that may not naturally occur with any frequency, may never have occurred before, and may never occur again. Of what interest are such events to the sociologist? Often we wish to know how a social system will respond to certain contingencies. For example, Durkheim pointed out that the constraining nature of social rules is not visible so long as one behaves in conformance with them. It is only when one attempts to do otherwise that one becomes aware of the existence of constraints. But *will* people do otherwise so that we can observe what happens to them when they do?

The reasons many rules are seldom violated can be easily catelogued:

1. For adults of our society, violating such rules may never come to mind. Only children, the retarded, foreigners, and other cultural troublemakers would even think of doing this.
2. If this does come to mind, there is no motive for doing it, such violations are not "somethings" in our society, they confer no rewards, fit into no practical projects, etc.
3. Social sanctions and beliefs about rules act in such a way that nobody ever puts himself in a position to test what would happen if they were violated. In this sense the consequences of disobeying social rules constitute social myths.

Here again sociologists become special kinds of people in the society with respect to all three reasons. Our intellectual topics and problems are played out on the field of everyday life. These topics and troubles will suggest things to do in everyday life that very few others might ever consider. Such actions, and what happens when they are done, might have crucial implications for sociological theory, but might happen, like the passage of Halley's Comet, only once in seventy-five years.

Further, by the use of disruptions we have the advantage of producing these events right in the midst of our field of interest (in everyday situations). Our motives for creating these things are provided by our abiding concern with "background expectancies," "functional theory," "interpretive procedures," and so on. As one sociologist put it:

> The seen but unnoticed backgrounds of everyday activities are made visible and are described from a perspective in which persons live out the lives they do, have the children they do, feel the feelings, think the thoughts, enter the relationships they do, all in order to permit the sociologist to solve his theoretical problems.[21]

Finally, our inner conviction that we are indeed professional researchers sustains and protects us from those inhibitions and emotional reactions that might otherwise make the performance of unusual actions impossible. It is interesting in this connection that motivational and emotional factors tend to limit the population of "normal" people who deliberately engage in "pointless" behavior to sociologists and people like them. Garfinkel found, for instance, that students, unexcited by the problem of "indexical expressions," could not complete certain demonstrations because they got bored too soon.

An important kind of unusual action is one that tends to produce social disorganization. In a now famous article, Garfinkel told his readers: "Procedurally it is my preference to start with familiar scenes and ask what can be done to make trouble."[22] Now, why should Garfinkel be so interested in making trouble for people? The fact is that he was interested in making trouble not for other people but for the social order. As we have seen, in Garfinkel's conception, social structure is relatively hardy and flexible. But how hardy? What sorts of events and actions within a social occasion constitute difficulties for social order? What sort of difficulty is a "difficulty," and how is it perceived and responded to by individuals? Such questions must be answered in connection with a whole plethora of sociological topics. We will consider only one, the social organization of emotions.

An old sociological problem, perhaps best articulated by C. Wright Mills and Max Weber, is the following: There are many rules of social conduct that may be vital to the preservation of social order. Yet within the occasions when they will have to be enforced, there can be no police, game wardens, or other agents of society. Further, in no clear way is it to anyone's personal interest to see to it that these rules are enforced. The problem then becomes: How do you marshal people's emotions in the interest of society? Exactly how are personal reactions like fear, anger, and embarrassment organized so as to preserve social order—or do they act in this way? With such issues in mind, Garfinkel assigned students the task of bargaining for one-price merchandise.

> When the bargaining episode was analyzed as consisting of a series of steps—
> 1. anticipation of the trial
> 2. approaching the salesperson
> 3. actually making the offer
> 4. the ensuing interaction
> 5. terminating the episode
> 6. and afterwards
> it was found that fears occurred with the greatest frequency in anticipating the assignment and approaching the salesperson *for the first time.*[23]

The amount of discomfort declined with each successive step in the sequence, and after two or three trials most students reported that they were enjoying the assignment. Conversely, in terms of the salespeople, it turned out one could indeed bargain (on occasion) for one-price items with some realistic chance of success, if it occurred to one to try it. In summary, it appeared that this particular rule achieved its status as a known rule principally because few people ever put themselves in the position of seeing what would happen if it was violated. However, if one thought of doing this and overcame the initial anxiety, the constraining nature of the rule might quickly evaporate.

While Garfinkel's students had to overcome fear and anxiety in order to complete their assignment, many other persons are either not constrained in this way or overcome this fear at some time prior to being observed. Jacobs noted one example in his study of retired persons who shared an on-campus dining hall with students. They had the privilege of eating there at the same rates per meal as the students paid—a fixed rate. While students were never observed bargaining for a meal at a reduced rate, many retired persons were: "I'm old, I don't eat so much"; "I don't like what's on the menu so I won't each much"; "I don't feel so good today, I only want a little to eat, how about eighty-five cents?"

RECORDING DISASTERS

Since a main benefit of procedures like the foregoing is to provide ideas, it is of the utmost importance to obtain material that evokes one's memories, feelings, and thoughts about what happened during the demonstrations. This is not always easy, since the things one wants to have "recorded" are often not easily captured by the tape recorder or camera. Such things include ongoing emotional responses, one's image of others' images of him, and perceived emotions in others. It is therefore a good idea to conduct post mortem sessions soon after the incident occurs. One format for doing this is to work in pairs. One member of the team engages in the problematic behavior in a context where the other can view the proceedings. Then the other "interviews" the experimenter about the events in question, and this interview is placed on tape for review. Notebooks do yeoman service here, in that all manner of brilliant insights and little "noticings" can be jotted down before they disappear, never to be remembered again. Often, when one restores the situation with one's victim, he can be asked about his reactions, thus obtaining the three major perspectives on a social action: that of the actor, that of the recipient of the action, and that of an outside observer.

MORAL QUESTIONS

Ethnomethodologists and other sociologists have raised a hue and cry about disruption procedures, almost from the time of their inception. The complaint is that these procedures cause people varying amounts of emotional distress— everything from mild surprise to torturous anxiety. Paradoxically, such demonstrations continue to be popular classroom exercises for sociology students. We feel that no general yes or no answer can be given as to the morality of these procedures. In some cases, one can be reasonably sure that the inconvenience or discomfort they cause will be minor or nonexistent. In other cases, either this is not true or one simply does not know. This is so, in part, because the investigator's problems do not end with the experiment. From the standpoint of moral worries, the experiment includes its aftermath. Experiments frequently "turn serious" and, in the manner of a psychodrama, the distinction between those parts of the scene that were simulated and those that were real becomes blurred. Experimenters report finding themselves "really angry" or "really suspicious" after getting into an episode that started out as a mock-up. Conversely, victims are sometimes left with "revealing glimpses" of new aspects of the experimenter's character or of their own.

In addition to this, there is the problem of restoring the situation. In cases of mildly eccentric behavior, the purposes of a disruption might well remain a trade secret. Yet if the disrupting behavior "disrupts" to any extent, moral considerations would seem to dictate that the victims be debriefed. It is here that the "no time out" feature of daily life presents nasty problems. It is often not possible to subject a stranger to a peculiar, annoying, or antagonizing interaction and then simply wipe the incident out by explaining that you are a researcher doing science. Instead of allaying fears and restoring strained relationships, these explanations may prove more disruptive than the disruption itself. Instead of showing how past actions were understandable and legitimate, they may redefine them as even worse than they first appeared. After all, the victim was initially confronted merely with an eccentric individual engaging in bizarre conduct. But now he is in the presence of a "professional" who deliberately deceived, annoyed, or even frightened him without his consent merely to complete an assignment for a sociology class or write a paper on something called "the problem of social order." The more personal your relationship with the "victim," the worse this situation can be.

The victim well may assume that your consideration for him, his feelings, and his life should take precedence over your other claims and goals. In using him as a guinea pig, you show that this may not be so and provide grounds for his reassessment of your relationship (or you, for that matter):

> Subjects were only partially accepting of the experimenter's explanations that it had been done "as an experiment for a course in Sociology." They often complained, "All right, it was an experiment but why did you have to choose me?" Characteristically, subject and experimenter wanted some further resolution than the explanation furnished but were uncertain about what it could or should consist of.[24]

It might be imagined that a way out of this problem is to perform experiments with strangers who revere science. This helps (in principle) in producing an incident that does not have to be integrated into an ongoing history of mutual dealings with another person. Furthermore, your first identity after "stranger" would be "scientist" or "student acting on behalf of scientist." If you were lucky enough to pick a stranger who revered science (a vanishing breed, these days), all might be well. Yet all of the nasty potholes of social science have yet to be unveiled. Having begun a relationship with a stranger by showing your willingness to deceive or manipulate him, why in the world would he believe all this stuff about science?

> Seven subjects had to be convinced that there had been a deception. When the deception was revealed they asked what they were to believe: Was the experimenter telling that there had been a deception in order to make them feel better?[25]

THE DILEMMA

The nasty thing about disruption experiments is that the very thing that makes them so interesting (unpredictable responses) also makes them morally unmanageable. That is, we generally have some measure of control over the following in setting up demonstrations:

1. Who will act as the experimenters.
2. Who will be the victim.
3. Within what situations the thing will be done and at what point in the ongoing action the disruption will occur.
4. The amount and kind of the disruption itself.

If we could standardize all these things, and perhaps engage in some "pretests" to see how the experiment works, we might well proceed with our efforts in the confident hope that humanitarian concerns would not be totally overlooked. But in order to do this, we must be able to anticipate responses. Unfortunately, the more accurately we can anticipate responses, the less interesting the disruption experiments are. For, as we have noted, they are undertaken mostly to discover how the social world will react to novel or rare events in its midst.

In fact, the disruption procedures themselves show us how ineffectual we are at anticipating the responses of our fellow human beings and (embarrassingly) how, as social scientists, we tend to regard them as "cultural dopes." All sorts of actions that we might think would land a person in an institution, get him arrested, or cause panic in the streets are treated as if they happened every day. People know exactly what to make of them and what to do about them, without fuss. Apparently "normality," however it is recognized and produced, could encompass a Martian landing with ease:

> Our next interaction was staged in a barber shop and acted out by Andy who has a great abundance of hair growing in just about any direction it pleases. As we entered, the barber was seated in a chair and after a quick look at Andy quipped, "The beauty parlor's down the street." Not to be deterred, Andy calmly walked over and confided to the barber that he had a serious problem at home. He explained, "My mother has refused to let me inside the house until I get some hair cut and I told her I won't have anyone touch a hair on my head. So do you think you could shave my arm pits?" Before the barber could say anything Andy had taken off his shirt and undershirt and was standing, bare-chested, before him. But the barber refused to get upset or take the request seriously and still sitting in his chair answered back, "If you want to do it, do it

yourself. The machine is right over there." He showed no embarrassment, anxiety, or frustration and remained completely detached from the dilemma placed before him.[26]

Certain members of the research community have proposed a sardonic solution to this problem of unpredictability: Perform one's disruption experiments on one's sociological colleagues. They above all others should appreciate the value of sacrificing their own emotional comfort for the sake of a possible advance in science.

This policy was put into effect in one of Garfinkel's classes, where students were instructed to knock on doors in various disruptive ways. Among the assignments, one was supposed to knock on the door of somebody he did not like. Soon after giving out the assignment, Garfinkel received a knock on his office door from one of his students.

FIRST-PERSON STRATEGIES FOR DOING DISRUPTION EXPERIMENTS

If we retreat from our sardonic attitude a bit, the suggestion that social scientists use themselves as guinea pigs has a certain amount of moral merit. They have unlimited access to their own daily lives and may be willing to conduct themselves in ways that others would find less than exciting. But they wouldn't play tricks on each other; they would employ first-person strategies designed to "mess up" their own lives. One way to do this is to perform ordinary daily activities while robbing oneself of the usual resources for getting them done.

In pursuing this strategy, students of everyday life have participated in their daily rounds blindfolded; they have worn glasses which reverse the visual field for long periods of time. Some have made daily decisions by using the I Ching (the ancient Chinese book of divination) or by throwing dice instead of using good old common sense. The idea here is quite similar to that employed in the "third-person" disruption strategies already discussed: Find a way to make the familiar strange.

But the reader might get the wrong idea from the phrase "make the familiar strange." In using dice to make decisions, students of everyday life are not trying to conduct themselves in a different way than they ordinarily do. Instead they assume that, in carrying out the "advice" of the dice, they use many of the same interpretive abilities which are employed in ordinary decision making. The advantage of the dice is that they provide a more recent, novel, and unusual way to make decisions and thus make the details of decision making more noticeable. Of particular interest in this regard is the way new, factual features of the real world start to appear around one's new method of dealing with, and grasping, the world. The dice thrower soon finds a certain "logic and rationality" in the decisions of the dice. The blindfolded experimenter soon discovers certain laws of form which enable him to predict where the door might be and so on. With diaries and tapes of such processes, another way of studying how people discover and create the facts and features of their daily lives is available.

Case study F (pages 397–404) enables us to see in greater detail how disruption works and some of the things it can tell us about social life. It deals with a disruption of the third type, in which the rules of pool are violated. The game is played between a supposedly "normal" social scientist and a mentally retarded adult, who is accustomed to regarding his actions and perceptions as defective. How will this person react when someone considered to be "normal" apparently starts doing things wrong? For the answer to this question, and for whether it could be answered in this way at all, we refer the reader to the study itself.

Notes

1. The idea that these experiments are designed to capitalize on the beliefs of researchers is our interpretation. The originators of such experiments (needless to say) do not necessarily view their efforts in this way.
2. Carlos Castaneda, *A Journey to Ixtlan*, New York: Simon and Schuster, 1972.
3. For a more detailed discussion of how this happens, see Howard Schwartz, "Mental Disorder and the Study of Subjective Experience," Ph.D. dissertation, University of California at Los Angeles, 1971, pp. 249–277.
4. John H. Newman, "From Space to Place: Locating a Rural Drug Program," paper read at the Annual Meetings of the Pacific Sociological Association, San Jose, Calif., 1974, p. 2.
5. This classification of disruption is our own, supplied so as to relate disruption to research goals. However, the experiments we cite under these headings may or may not be understood by the original researcher in the way we describe them.
6. Harold Garfinkel, *Studies in Ethnomethodology*, Englewood Cliffs, N.J.: Prentice-Hall, 1967, pp. 47–49.
7. Ibid., p. 51.
8. John L. Pates, "Violation of Social Expectations," unpublished paper, Harvard University, 1972, p. 3.
9. Garfinkel, *Studies in Ethnomethodology*, p. 38.
10. Quoted in Harold Garfinkel, "A Conception of and Experiments with 'Trust' as a Condition of Concerted Stable Actions," in *Motivation and Social Interaction*, ed. by O. J. Harvey, New York: Ronald Press, 1963, pp. 222–223.
11. Ibid., p. 199.
12. Garfinkel, *Studies in Ethnomethodology*, pp. 42–44.
13. One such experiment is reported not in written form but in a documentary film, *Invisible Walls*, available from Pyramid Films, Santa Monica, Calif.
14. This is our dramatized paraphrase of the remarks of Carlos Castaneda during a lecture at the Massachusetts Institute of Technology, 1972.

15. Alfred Schutz, *Collected Papers I*, The Hague: Martinus Nijhoff, 1971, pp. 207–259.

16. Garfinkel, *Studies in Ethnomethodology*, pp. 58–59.

17. Ibid., p. 59.

18. Dr. Melvin Pollner of the University of California at Los Angeles coined the term *reality disjuncture* for the situation in which two trustworthy methods of determining some factual state of affairs are each competently applied but yield inconsistent results.

19. The medical school experiment is not well suited to exploiting this aspect of common sense reasoning. For a better experimental setup in this regard, see S. E. Asch, *Social Psychology*, Englewood Cliffs, N.J.: Prentice-Hall, 1952, pp. 450–501.

20. Thanks to Dr. Melvin Pollner for calling this to our attention.

21. Garfinkel, *Studies in Ethnomethodology*, p. 37.

22. Ibid.

23. Ibid., pp. 68–70.

24. Ibid., pp. 72–73.

25. Ibid., p. 64.

26. Pates, "Violation of Social Expectations."

CHAPTER 11

Hunt-and-Peck Ethnography: Studying Topics, Not People

Traditionally, ethnography has been understood as a process by which an anthropologist discovers and describes "a people and their culture." But the concerns of formal sociologists pull against anthropological ways of selecting target populations and corresponding topics. Formal sociologists do, indeed, engage in ethnographic field work, in the sense that they employ all of the methods of obtaining information that were detailed in chapters 3, 4, and 5. However, they do a very strange kind of ethnography. They jump around in the world in ways that seem haphazard to the onlooker. Today the sociologist might be attending modern dance classes, tomorrow interviewing welfare workers, and the next day we find the same person apprenticed to a gourmet cook.

If we know that the integrating thread in these exploits is the study of instructions in daily situations, the whole thing might make a little more sense. In that case, we are in the business of studying sociological topics, not people. That is, if there is to be ethnography, it will be the ethnography of such things as gazing and staring, practical decision making, or giving and getting impressions. Since hunt-and-peck ethnography is concerned with studying topics, and in view of what has already been said about the problems of making everyday life visible, hunt-and-peck ethnographers tend to conduct themselves in a shameless fashion. They pay little attention to the logic of causal inference, to verifying and validating hypotheses, or to systematic and "unbiased" observation. Instead, their logic is the logic of the mapmaker. Their job is to make a set of integrated observations on a given topic and place them in an analytic framework (the symbolic analogue to the cartographer's map).

Although the analogy is misleading in some ways, we invite the reader to consider the hunt-and-peck ethnographer as a social mapmaker. Forget the scientist and his concern with cause and effect, problem and explanation, hypothesis and data. Instead consider "Making Friends" or "Using and Following Rules" to be the title of a yet-to-be-produced travel brochure which describes an entire social "resort area," complete with indigenous population, points of interest, things to "do," alternate routes, and so on. Imagine yourself the technical writer in charge of preparing the brochure. You yourself have vacationed in the area, but now you must describe it to prospective visitors. It will not suffice to know how to live in the area. You must display it to newcomers, quickly and in some useful way, as a place of this and that sort. How can this be done? In what follows we discuss some of the methods, rationales, and controversies that surround this task.

Getting Started: Single-Case Analysis

One way to get one's bearings in a new terrain is to find a central reference point and reckon from there. In this framework, the detailed analysis of single cases acquires a new dignity. What is often done is to use some preselected topic to locate a single case, which is from the outset treated as a single case of "something"—storytelling, misunderstanding, rule violation, or some other topic. Then one produces a theory for why this event or action came about as it did. Such a theory consists of many informed speculations, based on whatever intuition, member's knowledge, and sociological findings are at hand. Often the purpose of the theory is to explain or describe one's own cultural intuition about the data. For example, it becomes "obvious" from a transcript that two people misunderstood each other. Now, why is it obvious, exactly how does one define a misunderstanding, and what enables a reader, a speaker, or a hearer to detect that such a thing happened in the world?

More often than not, such theories can be put in pseudo-deductive form. This has the advantage of decomposing one's initial conjectures into several more specific assumptions which together imply the initial conjecture. In this way, one's first case and reflections on it can act as a foothold, showing one not only what to look at next but what needs further thought.

Thus a group of problems, issues, and things to say starts to emerge, along with the data that evoked them and that they evoked.

At this point the selected case takes on more of the characteristics of a reference point. If one started with different cases, one might well come to produce different maps for different purposes. It would therefore seem advisable to select initial cases with caution. It would be nice to have a "central," "interesting," or "important" case. The trouble is that it is often only after the ethnography is completed that it becomes clear what is interesting, central, or important.

However, it is frequently possible to choose initial cases that have special advantages. Schwartz started his research into the process that leads to paranoia by examining a single case of drug-induced paranoia. The advantage of drug-induced incidents is that the whole process, from start to finish, occurs in a matter of hours, not years. One can often obtain direct recordings of its onset, development, and end (as in fact Schwartz was able to do). Some patients may even be, on occasion, college educated and fluent in the vocabulary of social science.

FOLLOWING UP LEADS

There is a widespread belief, often called "the myth of induction," that empirical data suggest hypotheses about patterns which in turn can be tested to yield news about the world. Yet facts, in and of themselves, do not imply or suggest anything. Facts, in this sense have nothing to "say." It is the judicious combination of facts with the restless mind of an analyst, suitably fertilized, that yields patterns and problems This is why one does well to follow up leads for manipulating one's own subjectivities in conjunction with the panorama of facts being considered. In doing this, one meets with problems quite different from those encountered in ordinary sampling. There is no question of trying to select items which are representative. Instead a whole circus of personal strategies for arriving at initial conjectures is employed. Some researchers compose an analysis from one piece of data and successfully expand and alter it as they look at new material. Others superficially consider a large number of examples that bear on their topic to find some common problems of patterns, then use this information to select a single case to look at in more detail. Although there may be a single best path to follow in order to arrive at winning guesses quickly and efficiently, there is no way to know what that path is until it is too late. For this reason we will not bore the reader with a recitation of discovery procedures for hunt-and-peck ethnography.

Suffice it to say that a collection of examples, cases, theories, and issues start to develop around one's topic. The examples and cases will eventually become one's data. The theories and issues will, hopefully, be integrated into an analytic framework (or frameworks) which order the data.

The Method of Examples

In everyday life certain behaviors obtain for their observers a unique form of generality. They are understood as "for-instance" objects. For-instance objects are addressed as representative of some totality of which they are a part. In observing the characteristics of the for-instance object, one sees the characteristics of the totality as well. Strategies for making a good impression are based explicitly on this idea. In certain contexts, such as job interviews, first dates, or other first contacts between strangers, common sense knowledge informs all parties that behavior will be addressed as for-instance objects. That is, specific displays of kindness, intelligence, or rudeness, say, will permit the inference that the doer is a kind, intelligent, or rude *person*. Armed with such knowledge, an individual can take his seat at the piano, play the one piece he knows, and leave the situation as an accomplished pianist in the eyes of others.

From the point of view of many sociologists, what we have just described is the logic behind the most prevalent form of data in qualitative field studies. Data in such studies are most commonly reported in the form of examples, illustrations, or instances. Some generality about the world of the aged or of suicide attempters is offered together with a case (or cases) in point. Within such a format, example and general point mutually prop each other up. The example helps one to interpret the general point. The general point, in its turn, shows one how to understand the specific case as an example of the point. Like the piano player, the field researcher wishes us to treat his "case in point" as representative of some general pattern in social life.

THE EMPIRICAL STATUS OF EXAMPLES

The method of examples has been the butt of wry and knowing satire under the title of the "I know a lady" procedure or the method of "buttonhole" sampling. The procedure is simplicity itself. One starts out with a point to make—for example, that blacks are less intelligent than whites, or that criminals have small heads. One then "samples" evidence by selecting cases that conform to the main contention and eliminating those that contradict it. This form of "data" is what is called in common parlance "examples."

Of course, examples may be as easily invoked to refute a claim or assertion as to support it. Just reverse the procedure and find a black person who is a genius or a murderer with a large head. The truth which counts on examples for its life can just as easily die by the same kind of evidence.

This is all very true in connection with the use of instances, as verifying data. The fact is, examples don't verify anything. But having established what they do not do, can we discover what they do do?

PEDAGOGICAL USES

Although the use of illustrations tends to be looked down upon in research monographs, it is joyously accepted in textbooks and classroom lectures. In fact, in almost all pedagogical situations, the use of illustrations is a major teaching tool, whether the activity be wrestling, jazz piano, meditation, or sociology. In learning complex activities which are impractical or impossible to describe literally, illustrations teach us something very important. But what do they teach us, and how do they do it?

What better way to answer these questions than by introducing an example! Consider a game such as chess. How might one introduce a beginner to the game so that he will be able to interpret the complex situations that come up in actual play? Most manuals do this by displaying and commenting upon a few representative situations and problems. Somehow, once one knows these "basics," he can use them as take-off points with which to "see his way into" much more complex situations of play. The "basics" are not representative in the sense that they occur many times in actual play. Counting is not involved here. The basics are "basic" in terms of the *structure of the game.*

We suggest that sociological mapmakers have a similar problem. How does one introduce a reader to a complex system of interactions, of which only some aspects can be discussed in a monograph? One way to do this might be to select "key" aspects of this interactive system for discussion. These aspects would be "key" in the same sense that certain situations in chess are "basic"—that is, they would be take-off points from which a person could "find his way into" the complexities of the full interactive drama. And indeed, "finding one's way into the phenomenon" does seem to be made possible by this procedure. The authors think that researchers have been implicitly using illustrations as pedagogic tools for quite some time. Yet the logic of illustrations in this new sense has scarcely been explored. In particular, what is a "key" or "central" illustration in a pedagogical sense? At this point the reader's answer is as good as our own, for the subject has never come under serious study.

EXAMPLES AS PROMISSORY NOTES

Ordinarily, to test a generalization, a social scientist samples some representative items from the total collection of items to which the generalization refers. But to do this he must be able to describe the total set. He must be able to list them or, at least, know some of their general characteristics. For without knowing anything about the total set, how can he select a sample from it and how can he know that this sample is representative? When studying people, this problem is seldom encountered. One can specify one's interest as confined to black Americans, to college students, or to female children below the age of seven. But formal sociology studies activities and situations. How does one define the total set of different situations?

In the light of this problem, we can appreciate another service that examples provide hunt-and-peck-ethnographers. Often we find in their research reports, some statement about a situation or activity: Telling jokes is governed by such and such a rule, or staring has such and such a significance in public places. The author may cite one or more cases in which his assertion holds and then give it a pseudogenerality with phrases like "typically," "regularly," or "often." One reason this is done is that the author does not yet know how to define, or even locate, the set of different public places or kinds of jokes. At this stage of the research there is thus no meaningful way to test the generalization. Yet he may have good reasons to believe he has noticed a pattern that is both general and important. At this juncture examples serve as promissory notes for research that is forthcoming.

The research that eventually "redeems" these notes may not be what many quantitative sociologists would suspect. These sociologists, when encountering the claim that something happens "sometimes," "frequently," or "often," usually assume that the next step in the research process is to discover just who does it, under what circumstances, and what percentage of the time. Indeed, this might be the case. But more often, examples and cases are treated differently. The mere fact that human beings are observed to engage in a certain activity *at all* may have crucial implications for a developing analysis. This is especially true for formal sociologists who focus on human competencies. If they notice a given occurrence, and have informal ways of finding it happening again and again, this suffices to establish that members "do" it. If they do it, they must be capable of doing it, and the next step in the research process may be to analyze the social competencies that account for this capability.

This was the situation in case study H (pages 418–428) when Ryave presented examples of an innocent but interesting observation: When people talk to each other about the real world, they "regularly" report incidents that are remarkably similar. They may have similar characters, courses of action, moral points, and so on. When he inquired into how these similarities were produced, he found something unexpected. In the data he analyzed, similar stories were not the product of like-minded individuals sharing and exhibiting a common point of view. It turned out that a second person could knowingly undercut and challenge the perspective of a first in such a way that it appeared to observers (and perhaps to the first person as well) that they were in perfect agreement. In exploring the dynamics of the procedures that accomplished this, Ryave uncovered some unexpected ways in which "points of view" emerge and are created in the course of ordinary conversation.

In Ryave's study, and in many others, the importance of examples lies, not in their ability to lead us to simple generalizations, but in their ability to point us toward new aspects of social action.

HOW TO "MAKE" AN EXAMPLE

In finding and dressing up some happening to serve as an example, there are some general guidelines that can be followed:

1. Examples can come from anywhere—from diaries, other studies, personal experience, rigorously collected data, or, indeed, from any area of social life.

Since formal sociologists are not in the verification business when using examples, nor are they looking for general explanations, evidence and cases from a large variety of heterogeneous sources can be collected within the framework of a particular study. Indeed, this is sometimes considered a virtue in that it maps out a social terrain, in the sense that it integrates a variety of otherwise unrelated phenomena into one analytic framework.

Given that a candidate example can in principle be anything and can come from anywhere, what conditions does it have to meet (if any) to gain entrance to our ethnography? A deceptively simple and basic criterion would seem to be this:

2. The example has to have "actually happened" or be "actually there."

That is, one criterion for any sort of valid map would be that it marks off trees, mountains, or blades of grass that actually exist. But the idea of something being "actually there" takes a peculiar form in sociology. For unlike the proverbial tree that exists independently of whether there is anybody to perceive it, jobs, mothers-in-law, and greetings are literally created by the perceptions and interpretations of human beings. Therefore, what an action is an example of depends on how it is interpreted by individuals in everyday life. But which individuals are we talking about? Are we talking about the producer of a greeting, the one she greets, or observers of this verbal transaction? Does a greeting, once perceived as such, remain a greeting, or does it turn into a sarcastic remark after the greeter hands you a court summons? Here lies a very tender area in the practice of hunt-and-peck ethnography.

In order to demonstrate what an action is a "case of" for the different people within a social setting, a number of extremely delicate arguments are required.[1] However, if one ignores this issue, one can treat an action as an example of any number of things by describing it in different common sense ways, within his text. In this regard, Erving Goffman has been accused of sometimes interpreting behavior from the point of view of an outside observer, sometimes as the doer of the behavior might interpret it, and sometimes as the recipient might. Thus a single action can become a source of an unlimited number of examples of different points, depending on the argument one wishes to make.

The Use of Models, Paradigms, and Frameworks

We have seen how formal sociologists look for patterns, structures, or forms of interaction in natural settings as opposed to the content of any particular interaction and its resulting "definition of the situation." In this regard Goffman notes:

> I assume that the proper study of interaction is not the individual and his psychology but, rather, the syntactical relations among the acts of different persons mutually present to one another.[2]

The question becomes, not what is this or that person thinking and how does this perception of reality influence behavior, but:

> What minimal model of the actor is needed if we are to wind him up, stick him in amongst his fellows, and have an orderly traffic of behavior emerge? A psychology is necessarily involved, but one stripped and cramped to suit the sociological study of conversation, track meets, banquets, jury trials, and street loitering.[3]

Hunt-and-peck ethnographers have been concerned not so much with answering this question as with dealing with the question posed in the first quotation—that is, describing "the syntactical relations among the acts of different persons." They do this by using an assortment of models and frameworks which describe and unite heterogeneous bits of experience and activity. Having formulated a framework that would allow for how these micro-social phenomena (track meets, jury trials, street loitering) can exist and perpetuate themselves in an orderly fashion, the search is on for examples that such frameworks implicitly encompass. These, once found, serve to justify the framework, while the framework serves to locate the examples, as examples of part of that framework.

In one such construct, Goffman's dramaturgical model, the world of interaction is conceived of in terms of front stage, back stage, stage management, stage presence, competent actors, audiences, and so forth. Having recognized the utility of this metaphor, Goffman then seeks convincing illustrations of situations to which one can apply these concepts. Insofar as these are taken to be formal features of interaction, examples of stagings, audiences, and actors can be found in a variety of social settings. In fact, Goffman has devoted whole books to this sort of analysis. For example, one of his works, *Strategic Interaction* (1969), deals with, among other things, forms of interaction between spies and counterspies, and how the notion of information control can be applied to the mundane circumstances of everyday life.

Unfortunately, while such frameworks are useful analytical devices for locating and describing forms of interaction, they are not, from a phenomenological perspective, true to the phenomena. That is, societal members do not see themselves either as actors who perform for the benefit of audiences or as spies and counterspies. Only professional actors, theater critics, or spies might naturally describe social settings in this way, without the benefit of having heard of Goffman.

One way in which such a framework might be validated is by reference to the psychology of the actor—by the specification of an ideal "competent member" who, by virtue of the motives, consciousness, and abilities we attribute to him, is capable of performing all the interactional acrobatics which we describe as characteristic of everyday life. Unfortunately, neither Goffman nor anyone else has yet formulated and tested such a model. Consequently, the diverse behaviors he describes cannot be integrated in one actor, a group of actors, or even an ideal theoretical actor.

In light of the foregoing, formal frameworks such as these are currently validated through the examples of social life which they serve to locate and integrate. The search for examples of social life to illustrate the validity of one's model is nothing new. Symbolic interactionists and positivsts also seek to find illustrative cases to demonstrate the validity of models generated from within their perspectives. In this search one never has far to look, in that anything can serve as an example, if properly interpreted.

The reason that so few frameworks fall and so many appear to stand is that most social science is dedicated to the search for supporting data, not for contradictory data, at least from *within* schools of thought. This is true since most sociologists claim science, and science, as we know, seeks order, not chaos. Fortunately, there is a fierce competition for converts *between* sociological schools, so that competing frameworks are generated, if for no other reason than to discredit existing frameworks in other camps. Formal sociology is not exempt from the complaint that it, too, seeks to perpetuate its models of social reality, notwithstanding certain internal contradictions. In fact, it does so in the same way that positivists and symbolic interactionists do—by accentuating the positive and eliminating the negative.

The "What's New?" Problem

In choosing which episodes of daily life to place in one's monograph and what frameworks to employ in ordering and talking about them, ethnographers face an unusual problem. As we have already stated, sociology's concept of knowledge is status oriented. The value of what one knows is, in part, proportional to the extent that other people do not know it. If one studies everyday life, this kind of knowledge can be hard to come by. For much of one's data from daily life will refer to things that all of us, lay persons and social scientists alike, have seen, heard of, or done ourselves. Secondly, one's analysis of the causes, consequences, and implications of these activities may sound like news from nowhere for an interesting reason. Qualitative sociologists, by and large, have chosen to use the natural language of their host society (rather than statistics, equations, and the like) to report their findings. This makes the researcher's own analysis directly comparable to the common sense explanations constructed by the "natives" (in this case, most of us). In making such a comparison, either his analysis will or will not make good common sense. If it does, it may come off as something (1) that everybody already knows, (2) that anyone could have found out, given a moment's reflection or a look around the corner, or (3) that is dull, obvious, or trite. In a way this is not fair, since there are many stories one might tell about an event, all of which are plausible in terms of common sense. It takes research and observation to discover which of these are correct in terms of what people actually do. Yet when written down, "the true story" will not come off as a finding.

On the other hand, if the researcher indicates that an implausible explanation (in terms of common sense) is the one that truly represents what's going on, people may not believe such claims. They may cite the inadequate and inconclusive nature of hunt-and-peck ethnography and may insist that such outlandish claims can be justified only by rigorous experiments or mathematical data. Ironically it may be that only the legitimating devices of science will validate an explanation of daily life that violates the common sense beliefs of those who live it.

The existence of common sense reasoning gives us a third problem. There are some theoretical questions to which the solutions, when presented to others, appear to be bright, new, intelligent, or shrewd. Other questions are problems only when one is on the "wrong" end of the solution. That is, it is difficult to find the solution given only the problem; but once found, the solution does not seem to be hard to come by.

One way out of this is to have your audience be in the same position you occupied before making a discovery. Following their failure to find what you did, your success becomes available as something more than trivial. This device is available to sociologists who, for example, study social problems like crime prevention or drug addiction. Yet this avenue for showing that time and money were well spent is generally closed to formal sociologists. The community at large and other sociologists have not been working on understanding behavior in elevators or where people choose to sit on buses.

The usual way out of these dilemmas is to report to one set of people the exploits and activities of others about whom they know nothing. But formal sociologists cannot do this, since they are committed to studying circumstances common to us all.

Maybe all these difficulties seem like social, not scientific, problems. But they arise in large part because (1) the subject matter of formal sociology happens to be everyday life; (2) therefore, common sense reasoning and the use of natural language are both topics of study in formal sociology; and (3) formal sociologists must use common sense reasoning and the natural language as resources for discovering, reporting, and interpreting their own findings. In light of this, perhaps formal sociologists should not seek ways out of the "What's new?" dilemma. Perhaps they should develop new forms of knowledge which allow us to "find out what we already know."[4]

But this has not been the reaction of ethnographers. Escaping the "What's New?" problem has become a primary criterion for selecting data and the frameworks that order them. Given the hard realities of the sociological community, we trust this will probably be true for the reader as well. In that event we owe it to him or her to describe some of the solutions to this problem that others have evolved.

In choosing frameworks and vocabularies, ethnographers have sought ways of talking about common events that are or sound new, inventive, interesting, or unexpected. Paradoxically, scientist becomes showman, and claims to knowledge become equivalent to the dramatic effect of a text. The problem becomes not the discovery and communication of new information, but finding ways to give old information a new significance. To this end the ethnographer may speak of problems and their solutions, perspectives and their implications, previous errors and how his interpretations set things right, and other demonstrations that he is a smart person engaged in worthwhile pursuits.

Another approach to this problem is to search for knowledge that is "locally hidden" to members. That is, only in certain social contexts do we possess certain types of social knowledge. In other contexts we "don't know we know it." For instance, if a man calls a woman and inquires, "What are you doing Wednesday night?" the woman may know perfectly well that this is not merely a question but a prelude to an invitation. She may display such knowledge by providing unsolicited additional information in her reply: "I have a night class Wednesday, but I'm not doing anything on Friday." Yet she has no name for these kinds of questions, seldom discusses them at parties, and, in general, does not know or remember they exist except at the times and places when she has to respond to them. Someone like Sacks can identify such questions as "pre-invitations" and proceed to examine their properties.[5] They then become interactional objects that "exist in the world." We can notice, remember, and describe them independently of the contexts in which they occur when formerly we did not know of them in this way.

A third strategy is to seek the noncommonsensical by looking at ordinary happenings in much greater detail than the man on the street is capable of or interested in. This strategy has incensed many sociologists and intelligent lay persons, who have criticized formal sociologists for being overconcerned with detail—for fruitlessly counting the number of leaves on the social trees. In their view the topics, the explanations, and the things that are explained were all absurdly "small." Schwartz studied the operation of queues and lines, Sacks and colleagues spent years examining how conversationalists take turns at talking, and Goffman became preoccupied with distinguishing "gatherings" from "situations" and "social occasions." Who cares? Meanwhile, political extremists mount wars against the police, the divorce rate soars, and the elderly are denied proper medical care.

The feeling that in such projects time and money are being wasted stems not only from the urgency of more practical problems but also from a vision of society. Durkheim's dictum that social facts can be explained only by prior social facts has often been understood as "Big effects have big causes." Yet in everyday life there is much reason to think otherwise. Many small events and happenings can generate chains of events which result in gross alterations of individuals or groups. This has long been a problem in psychology. An individual's personality is the product of millions of daily happenings and reactions, most of them insignificant in themselves, and most of them not remembered and impossible to retrieve.[6] In tracing these aspects of personality, one looks in vain for monsters of the id or for catastrophic events after birth. Instead of major causal events, one finds that the individual notices some acne pimples, feels some embarrassment, which causes him to withdraw from social occasions, making it hard to develop social skills, which results in awkward behavior in the presence of others, thus giving them a bad impression of him, which makes him feel even more socially unacceptable, et cetera. In the end, we are confronted with someone with something called a "negative self-image."

In everyday life there is even more reason to acknowledge the momentous effects of detail. Modern urban life turns the events of even one person's average day into a veritable zoo of heterogeneous happenings. The weather, the daily traffic, what is on television in the evening, who decides to call you and when, what mood your roommate is in—all of these items, and how they happen to combine or conflict with one another, can make up the general pattern of your day, your week, or your life.

It is here that the frameworks developed in the process of hunt-and-peck ethnography can give priceless service. They permit one to isolate and observe a complex process of details—by disengaging and disentangling it from its surrounding environments.

Natural versus Contrived Settings

As we have seen, from the standpoint of orthodox methodology, hunt-and-peck ethnography is unrigorous, unclean, and uncouth. Its proponents justify its use in an interesting way. They claim that only through such methods is it possible to gain an understanding of ongoing interactions of everyday life. It is often said that the study of everyday life necessitates looking at "naturally" occurring phenomena, presumably as opposed to unnatural or artificial phenomena. In studying these natural phenomena, many if not most kinds of conventional sociological data are regarded as useless. Such data include:

1. The results of experiments.
2. The product of interviews set up for the purpose of studying people.
3. Case folders and other "people data" collected by social institutions in the course of their operation.
4. The codified and tabulated results of questionnaires and surveys.
5. Information about social totalities larger than individuals, such as families, countries, or interlocking directorates.
6. Historical reconstructions of the past by anthropologists, historians, and archeologists.
7. Coded summaries of naturally occurring phenomena.
8. Macroscopic data of all kinds (crime rates, cost-of-living indices, and so on).

The reader might already suspect that this back-to-nature movement in the study of everyday life is pernicious. It seems rather analogous to the distinction between natural and unnatural living made by many critics of modern society. The world is divided into two parts: the natural and the unnatural. The former is good, the latter is bad. Who decides which is which? Naturally (pun intended), the critic himself. Plants, animals, and inanimate objects, together with all they make and do, are "natural." Human creations, on the other hand, are unnatural. The beehive and the beaver's dam are natural; the city and the hydroelectric plant are unnatural. The sweetener made by bees from pollen is organic; the sweetener made by humans from sugar cane is "processed" and unnatural.

In summary, the human being and whatever he does in the world are treated as intrinsically foreign to, not a part of, that world itself. He doesn't really belong there.

If we replace "the human being" by "the sociologist," we seem to arrive at the very core of the distinction between natural and contrived situations. Again, it is the critic who divides the world up into two piles, the one unequivocally good and the other bad. All the usual procedures by which his opponents ("unnatural" sociologists) gather information are singled out as artificial and foreign to everyday life. The experiment or the interview is not a natural situation in everyday life, while the phone conversation or the party is. "If God had meant men to be experimented upon, he would have called them subjects."

At this point we must seriously ask what's so natural about natural situations and what makes them so different from, or superior to, the situations created by social scientists? There are two major answers to this. We will consider them in order.

THE PROBLEM OF COMPARABILITY

Simply put, the first argument states that sociologists study behavior in situations that are not comparable to those found in everyday life. Here, "situations of everyday life" are defined as all those except the ones set up by the social scientist to study behavior. Although this sounds circular, it need not be.

To take one example, people's impressions of other people's personalities have been studied experimentally by showing subjects photographs, movies, or actual people in order to elicit their impressions. Yet in everyday life, in contrast to the laboratory, we find impression formation occurring under conditions like these:

1. Each person is not a mere observer of the other but assumes that the other can affect and be affected by him in practical ways.
2. Each forms an impression of the other, not because he was instructed to

do so, but because of the natural structure of the situations and/or his own relevances and concerns.

3. One person has practical reasons to present himself to the other as a certain kind of person, with certain traits.

4. Each person, while getting impressions of the other, is simultaneously a source of impressions himself, and knows this.

5. Impressions are formed not through observation but during the course of an interaction between two persons, such as a conversation.

6. Impressions occur within a particular social setting, such as a party or a job interview, with its own distinctive "definition of the situation"; this, in its turn, affects the "definition of the people within it."

Needless to say, many of these conditions are extremely difficult to duplicate experimentally. In the vernacular of experimental methodology, these factors cannot easily be "controlled" or systematically varied. Apparently then, situations in everyday life have certain characteristics in common, all or many of which affect impression formation. These common conditions are ordinarily, and specifically, absent from the experimental situation and they are difficult or impossible to include within such a situation. Therefore, the impression formation of everyday life is not the impression formation of the experiment.

While the forgoing is the traditional argument for advocating the "natural" over the contrived, it has certain inherent weaknesses. The argument, for instance, cannot be applied to the very topics that qualitative sociology specializes in. If a phenomenon as it occurs in daily life is poorly understood, then the factors which affect it are *unknown*, in whole or in part. That is the reason for studying the phenomenon in the first place. It is therefore impossible to know at the outset that these factors are present in everyday situations and absent in experiments. But for the sake of argument let's grant that, say, impression formation in the psychology laboratory does not proceed as it does in job interviews. Yet this process, as seen in job interviews, might be equally dissimilar to impression formation as it occurs in bars. To justify the dichotomy between natural situations and experiments, one would have to show that all or most natural situations *shared* certain characteristics which affect a phenomenon of interest, while experiments lacked them. Otherwise experiments represent merely one more, equally good or equally bad, situation in everyday life. But to do this one would have to know what these characteristics were. And if one knew that, one could probably build them into the experimental situation!

Yet it might be argued that the burden of proof is being wrongly placed. Experiments and the like certainly *might* differ in significant ways from natural environments. Quantitative sociologists are thus in chronic danger of being wrong in their generalizations. But are they really in worse danger of being wrong than hunt-and-peck ethnographers, who, by their own admission, have abandoned traditional logical and scientific safeguards in order to study natural situations?

In short, construing the situations constructed by sociologists as artificial and somehow out of everyday life does indeed seem to constitute a prejudice, similar to the distinction between natural and unnatural foods.

THE PROBLEM OF NATURAL OBSERVATION

Yet there is an answer to this criticism. First, as in the case of impression formation, it is sometimes possible, using qualitative research, to demonstrate that contrived situations are special, in the sense of justifying this dichotomy between them and "natural" setups. But in general, the consistent preference for uncontrived environments is justified by reference to other considerations. It is precisely because the factors that comprise and affect impression formation are often unknown that we should not construct a social context on our own within which to look at the process. Why? Because the major question may not be "What are the causes and consequences of impression formation?" but instead may be the naturalist's question, "What are the varieties of impression formation that occur in our society? As we have repeatedly pointed out, the question "What's going on?" is logically prior to the question "Why (or how) is it going on?" Thus we can fancy ourselves as sociological "botanists," asking what sorts of social vegetation grow in the situational soil of our society. We can take as our major premise that *all or most interaction activities occur differently in different social situations.*

The botanist would hardly search out the indigenous growth of a new land by growing his own plants in his own greenhouse and observing the results. The analogy to this, for the sociologist, is to start out with a common sense concept such as impression formation and then construct an experimental mock-up of the process, examine this mock-up, and treat the results as an indication of the way people actually do business in social life. Such a procedure will never do. The sociologist must first have a taxonomy; he must start with that concept and use it to *search everyday life* for the kinds of processes to which it might refer. Armed with this information, he might then know enough to set up experiments which were comparable to "natural situations." For now he would have some idea what these natural situations were.

Here we have the crux of the problem and of the argument. It is not so much that some situations are natural and some are contrived. Rather, it is that we do not yet know what the range and variety of "situations" in everyday life are in the first place.

The more strongly one believes that interactional phenomena are sensitive to social situations, the more cogent becomes this argument for looking at uncontrived situations first. The argument is especially important when one is dealing with meanings. We have already indicated the "indexical" nature of social understandings—how ongoing social contexts, common sense knowledge, and biographically determined purposes are the resources employed in daily life to see, discover, and know meanings. If the researcher changes these contexts or takes talk or social action out of its usual contexts, there is every chance that his subjects' interpretations of their meaning will be different (in unknown ways) from those made in practical situations.

The reader will be able to see this graphically in case study G (pages 405–417). In his study of psychotherapy, Schwartz found that doctors had a way of interpreting the beliefs of patients that was neither "scientific" nor "commonsensical." Using a unique mode of reasoning, they assessed whether these beliefs were true or false, in a psychological sense. Had he not studied psychotherapy in detail, he would never have discovered such a way of thinking. Yet once he had discovered it, Schwartz found that this mode of thought was not peculiar to psychotherapy but was a common way to evaluate beliefs in many other situations.

Notes

1. For a hint or two regarding these complexities, see our discussion of a child's story ("The baby cried. The mommy picked it up.") in chapter 6, pages 317–322.
2. Erving Goffman, *Interaction Ritual*, Garden City, N.Y.: Doubleday Anchor, 1967, p. 2.
3. Ibid., p. 3.
4. A major problem for formal sociologists is the structure of their host natural language. For instance, in English *male* and *female* are nouns. It is thus easy to describe "femaleness" as something you "are," rather than something you do (that is, as an activity). On the other hand, English has no convenient terminology for other aspects of daily life, thus forcing sociologists to describe them in awkward and long passages of words. It is therefore difficult to ignore the presentational effect of descriptions of everyday life couched in natural language.
5. Harvey Sacks, unpublished lecture notes, University of California at Los Angeles, 1966.
6. In this connection, see Howard Schwartz, "General Features," in *Topics in Ethnomethodology*, ed. by J. Schenkein et al., Berlin: Suhrkamp Publishers, 1976, which demonstrates how sequential properties of conversation, combined with certain accidents, can literally turn a normal individual into a paranoid.

Part VI

Analyzing Everyday Life: How to Do It

Introduction: Sight versus Thought in Formal Sociology

Throughout intellectual history there have been two overwhelmingly accepted bases for human knowledge: sight and thought.[1] Intuitively these were two different modes—I can observe or experience something without thinking about it, and I can think about it without observing it. Yet neither mode of knowing will suffice by itself, nor does one have precedence over the other, and the relations between them are not particularly clear. It has been one of the basic problems of epistemology to grasp the complex web of relations between these two. In particular, does experience constrain abstract thought and vice versa, and if so, how?

Different disciplines have tended to emphasize one or the other of these two sources of knowing. In particular, sociology has tended to emphasize thought over sight. What do we mean by this? In part we refer to the sheer quantity of each activity done in the course of a week's work. In sociology, as opposed to anthropology, it is still possible to get a Ph.D. and have an illustrious career without ever watching social life directly for any length of time in any detail. Indeed, in quantitative sociology it is the "slaves" who actually commandeer the agency records, conduct the interviews, and code the questionnaires. The professional sociologist's job starts only at the point when there is an abstract data set to inspect, a data set whose relation to the world he grasps through an additional set of abstract assumptions and representations.[2]

Another thing we might mean when we say that sociology emphasizes knowledge through thought is this: What does sociology take to be its technical problems? What are the how-to-do-it books and methodology courses primarily concerned with? They are mostly concerned with making accurate abstractions through proper thinking. They give advice on how to tell if, when, where, and why something is happening rather than *what* is happening. Textbooks and instructors tell how to represent and summarize data, how to put them into abstract categories, how to assign numbers to them, and how to inspect them for statistical regularities. But in general one is not shown how to observe them in the first place.[3] In short, observation per se—how to see—is not taken to be a major technical problem in sociology.

There are some obvious reasons for this and some not so obvious reasons. To tease out the latter, let's look at a contrasting discipline, clinical psychology, and its pragmatic concerns. Because of their purposes and goals, psychotherapists often seek out reactive measures in thankfulness. That is, they look for ways in which the process of finding out about oneself will change the very thing that is found out. While logically the classic statement "All Cretans are liars" as made by a Cretan is to be avoided because of its paradoxical properties, it might be the very thing some Cretan needs to say from the point of view of personal growth.[4] Admitting the chronic dishonesty of himself and his fellows may be the first honest thing he ever said. In fact, coming to this realization may be the best, perhaps the only, route to a truthful life with others. In a similar vein, if someone can admit to others that he is afraid of them, this very admission can be his first act of bravery. With this in mind, if we ask what therapeutic knowledge has to *do*, the answer is not "It has to be true or false" but rather "It has to change people." It has to change their behavior, their attitudes, or their self-conceptions. Gnosis (knowledge that changes the knower) becomes its goal. What kind of knowledge will achieve this goal? Sometimes it is paradoxical knowledge.

But sometimes it is knowledge by "sight" instead of by thought. That is, it won't do to discover a personal characteristic by "testing a hypothesis" about one's own behavior. That would only be intellectual; that won't change one's personality or behavior. But there is another way to know the same thing. One can "see" this thing about oneself, one can "realize it," one can attain a genuine insight. Only knowing this thing about oneself *in this way* will generate the emotional and psychic energy to change the behavior patterns connected with it so that one "frees" himself of it. This distinction between intellectual knowledge and insights is made by many psychotherapies and psychotherapists.[5] In their reports and those of their patients, the use of terms associated with vision is repeatedly found in connection with talk about particular insights and insight in general.

Now, if we ask about the pragmatic situation of sociologists—that is, what their knowledge must *do*—we get a very different answer. Sociologists have no clients in the sense that therapists do. In general, they are not investing other people's money or building anything, nor is there any direct sense in which "the car does or does not run" as a result of their knowledgeable efforts. What sociologists mostly do is talk and write. This is what they use knowledge for—to make lectures, books, and articles. This is what their knowledge has to "do." As a result, to sociologists, understanding something is *being able to talk (or write) about it in a certain way*. This is one of the most important reasons why knowing something, in the sense of knowing how to talk and write about it, is emphasized in their discipline. This is their job, this is what they primarily get paid to do. Other skills are to some extent optional. But it is not possible to be a sociologist without knowing how to construct verbal representations of society and its parts, quite independent of how good or bad they are. This is also why observational skills, in and of themselves, are not central to the discipline. Although it is necessary that *somebody* have these skills and use them, it is not necessary that *everybody* have them and use them. The observing can be done by the Bureau of the Census, graduate students, or other sociologists while you do the analyzing. In contrast, other disciplines, such as microbiology, radiology, archeology, and psychotherapy, require almost every practitioner to learn how to observe and recognize things in detail.

There are other reasons, unrelated to sociologists' working conditions, why observation is deemphasized. There is, after all, their subject matter. As natives, sociologists already know how to "observe" riots or television sets. Consequently, the main observational problems are not how to recognize these things in the first place but how to get different observers to scrutinize them in the same way, or a single observer to notice them consistently over time.

Secondly, many sociological phenomena can, by definition, be grasped only in and through abstract thinking. There is no coherent sense in which one can observe a suicide rate or a kinship system. Indeed, such things as a kinship system consist of and are literally created by systems of thinking. If a group of people abandon such thinking and reasoning, the kinship system simply, and literally, vanishes.

Finally, by their very nature, many sociological studies are not easy to replicate. For example, it is not particularly simple for any interested party to "get another look at" how people rank occupations in the United States. In fact, the NORC study described in chapter 1 has been replicated only once in the past twenty-eight years![6] One can readily understand why. Collecting such data requires a lot of personnel, time, and money. Government agencies, foundations, or university institutes have to be persuaded to supply researchers with these resources! These agencies are hardly impressed with a rationale such as "We just want to see if the people at NORC were right." But it is not only large-scale phenomena that are subject to this limitation. Much of qualitative field research is directed toward studying activities and people that are in no sense available to all interested parties, people such as black militants, flying-saucer cultists, or Polish peasants.

For all these reasons, certain methodological conventions have emerged in sociology which we all live with and have come to consider quite reasonable and practical:

1. Do it once and do it right.
    a. A high premium is put on avoiding error in observation and inference, not only in the long run, but *within the confines of a single study.*
    b. The reward for "mere replication" of studies and experiments is low.
2. "Knowledge through thought" rather than "knowledge through sight."
    a. Only one of us will study the Polish peasants. The rest of us will know about them indirectly, through data sets, journal articles, and so on.
    b. A *methodological "division of labor"* prevails: *the sociologist who* analyzes and explains something need not be the same person who actually observed and described it.

Although these conventions are hardly general canons of scientific procedure, many of us now take them for granted, and many schools of sociology use them to evaluate formal sociology and its methods of studying everyday life. But the study of everyday life generally proceeds under working conditions very different from those noted above.

First of all, many of the phenomena in everyday life are directly "observable" in a reasonable sense of this word. In this they are unlike the gross national product or the average income of female engineers. Second, these phenomena do not come into view only after expensive and time-consuming national surveys or prolonged negotiations with the Black Panther Party. Insults, eye contacts, and people standing in lines are readily available to single observers on low budgets. Observations are easily made again and again, and many replication studies are feasible under comparable conditions. Third, at the present time there are respectable numbers of people who are all independently working on the same problems and topics. And finally, observation is at least as crucial a technical problem in studying everyday life as are analysis and inference.

SOME PRIORITIES OF FORMAL SOCIOLOGY

As a result, in formal sociology there are some ways of working and of evaluating work that are exactly opposite to those noted previously:

1. Know what you're talking about.
   a. There is an emphasis on firsthand observation and a tendency to avoid using secondary sources of data.
   b. The moral convention "The one doing the talking (the analysis) should be the same one doing the looking (making the observations)."
   c. The convention that proper interpretation of an analysis requires firsthand observation of the phenomenon in question. This leads to many different investigators making many comparable observations.
2. "I might be wrong, but I've found something to be wrong about."
   a. Freedom from error is sought, not so much within the confines of a single study, but over the course of many cumulative studies, conducted by different investigators.
3. Alternatives to "the study" as a work unit.
   a. Many papers about everyday life consist of diverse observations and experiments collected together under a central theme. They are not put together' as an integrated text revolving around a single, central research problem.

The knowledgeable reader might wonder where all these conventions were hiding when he read Garfinkel, Cicourel, or Goffman. For we have, indeed, presented a coherent research orientation. But we have given only a laundry list when it comes to describing the actual work practices of a group of people. Some formal sociologists use some of these orientations, others use other parts of them, and still others do neither. This just happens to be the way things are at this time.

Luckily, however, our job is not to be historians. This text, like any other, distills proverbs and recipes from the world and tabulates them in what we hope are convenient forms. The relationship between these recipes and how people past and present actually go about becoming gourmet cooks remains obscure.

In the next pages we shall try to describe in more detail how some of these conventions are implemented. In particular we shall talk about the distinctive ways in which formal sociology goes about "knowing through thinking."

Notes

1. We thank Dr. Steven Riskin for introducing us to this topic. For his discussion of it, see Steven Riskin, "The Philosophical Grounds for Some Sociological Certainties," paper read at the Annual Meetings of the Pacific Sociological Association, Portland, 1972.

2. Of course, things don't go like this every single time. Yet there is a disturbing statistical relationship between a sociologist's fame and status and his never actually collecting the data he analyzes.

3. In interpreting our statements, we ask the reader to be kind to us, for the word "observation" is fraught with ambiguities. In particular, "making observations" in sociology sometimes means getting ideas.

4. The statement "All Cretans are liars" is an example of what logicians call the "liars' paradox": Assume that the statement is true. If a Cretan makes the statement, it is false because by definition he is a liar. Alternately, assume the statement is false. Then there must be at least one Cretan who is not a liar. If this Cretan makes the statement, it must be true.

5. For a discussion of this distinction, see case study G, "On Recognizing Mistakes" by Howard Schwartz, page 405.

6. Here we speak of a strict replication. Studies like the one by North and Hatt have been done in other countries, and small duplications, using small regional samples, have been done in this country.

CHAPTER 12

Making Patterns I: General Orientations

We have just indicted ourselves for specifying a set of orientations that does not correspond in some definite way to the things that practitioners are actually doing. But there are certain general policies and procedures (some used formally, some informally) that have proved unusually helpful in coming to terms with everyday life. They have been used by various investigators, utilizing different forms of analysis. It is to the description of these orientations that we now turn.

Type I versus Type II Errors

Imagine a quantitative sociologist who suspects that older people tend to be more politically conservative than the young. A typical test of this idea would go something like this: A dummy "null hypothesis" is set up which asserts that there is no relationship between age and political affiliation in the general population. Taking this as a premise, it is possible to calculate the probability that this relationship might be observed in a small group of people by chance alone. Next, one samples a small group and looks to see if the relationship is present. Only if the relationship observed in this group is extremely unlikely (it could happen only five times in a hundred), given that the null hypothesis is true, will the researcher reject the null hypothesis. Of course, even though what he observes is extremely unlikely, it could still happen. If it does, his decision to reject the null hypothesis will be a mistaken one. He will have made a type I error and will think there is a pattern when in fact there is none. Statisticians call the reverse situation, failing to detect a pattern when in fact there is one, a type II error.[1]

311

While the foregoing is a slight vulgarization of certain statistical ideas, it is accurate enough for our purposes. Here it suffices to notice that quantitative sociologists are much more afraid of type I than type II errors. One of the major goals and guiding principles of quantitative methodology is to avoid being wrong. This is done by designing ways to rule out every possible alternative explanation for an observed relationship before finally accepting it.

Yet there is a momentous choice to be made here. All other things being equal, the more one designs his methodology so as to avoid type I errors, the greater are his chances of making type II errors. That is, if the chances are minimal that one will think he sees a pattern that is not really there, then the chances become greater that one will overlook a pattern that really is there.

Furthermore, there is another and perhaps more important consequence of trying at all costs to avoid mistakes. To be confident that a relationship or pattern is really there, one must bring it into a laboratory in order to disentangle it from the other events and happenings within which it usually occurs. One must measure and count its occurrence in carefully controlled ways. Phenomena which evade such procedures cannot be safely studied.

Many quantitative sociologists take it for granted that avoiding being wrong, *within a single study*, is a major and important goal of any research. It is not just that one must eventually not be wrong about the world. One must, if possible, avoid being wrong at each step of the way. Consequently, these sociologists take it as a serious, if not devastating, fault of qualitative methodology that it easily allows for all kinds of false conclusions, because of its lack of controls.

As a general rule, this is true about the methods employed in formal sociology. But a proneness to error is not a fault of these methods. For immunity from type I errors is intentionally traded off in order to acquire a greater immunity from type II errors. Why is this done? There is the "easy" answer already given: Researchers can risk being wrong in the short run because they will be corrected by others in the long run. They can organize their efforts to permit many different verifications of the same findings.

But there is a more important reason. Practitioners find everyday life to be a shockingly new sociological place. What is meant by this can be gleaned by considering the following story recited by a small child: "The baby cried. The mommy picked it up."[2] Sacks taught an entire semester course on the sociological problems inherent in this story. Yet to many sociologists, it probably takes on a deadly, opaque appearance. Someone who has spent four long years in graduate school being trained in the theory and practice of sociology may find himself at a complete loss in trying to deal with it. In no coherent way does the story have causes and consequences. Even if it did, what would they be— socioeconomic status, or peer-group pressure? It makes absolutely no sense to consider this child's "relations to the means of production." Nor does it help much to inquire into whom she is "taking into account" or what her "point of view" is. It is completely unclear what to measure or how to measure it, or even what is sociologically relevant.

This is one of the most prevalent problems that formal sociologists currently face. They are repeatedly confronted with ordinary happenings which they do not begin to know how to talk about in a sociological way.

Under these circumstances, how does one "cut into the phenomenon"? It's a familiar problem, but it takes on some special twists when the topic is everyday life:

1. Cutting into the phenomenon is a major methodological problem. It deserves as much technical concern and formal credit as do verification and accuracy.
2. Because of this, individual investigators are always discovering concepts, issues, and methods that everyone else does not know about firsthand. That is, everyday life, because of its nature, will encompass the study of diverse, noncomparable topics.

To put our dilemma in traditional terms, there is reason to reverse the priorities concerning discovery and verification. Currently, discovery is left to the individual and is done informally. Research aimed at discovery is considered preliminary to research aimed at verification.[3] Instead, we want discovery to be done systematically and *cumulatively* among a group of research colleagues. We want these discoveries to be formally reported and credited as the nonpreliminary products of a single study, equally as valuable as a tested hypothesis or a verified theory. The question then becomes: What are some social conventions that would organize a group of researchers so that they discovered concepts, issues, and modes of analysis *together*?[4]

We shall now offer a few such conventions. They are presented as semiformal proposals, of the type that one finds in a text. Yet we have not worked out the optimal solution to the discovery-versus-verification controversy. Rather, we state as methodological canons what is informally going on among investigators anyway.

The "What If" Mentality and Its Alternative

As we mentioned, sociologists take great pains to avoid being wrong in their empirical conclusions. They do this not only because they hold a particular philosophy of science. They do it for self-preservation in a sociological community full of trained conceptual vipers. One of the hallmarks of graduate training is the fostering in all of us of the so-called critical attitude. The critical attitude consists in learning to scrutinize the theories and research of others to detect the presence of mistakes, oversights, incompleteness, inadequacies, holes in the argument, fallacies, contradictions, vagueness, inadequate data—you name it.

As a result, it is currently possible to invalidate a piece of research completely by the "what if" method. The "what if" method does not require additional research or data; it requires only that one find some way in which the researcher might theoretically have been wrong. The phenomenon might have been caused by another variable than the one cited; things might have gone differently if not for the particular setting in which the research was conducted; the informant could have meant something quite different from what the researcher claimed he did, et cetera.

Now, imagine that some inadequacy is found in a given person's research. Imagine that, because of this, the researcher might be wrong, and there is no way to demonstrate that he is not. In such a case, it could be said that the conclusions are not adequately supported by the data. As things currently stand, this can completely invalidate the research.[5] Given the difficulty of replicating other people's work and the lack of value placed on "mere replication," it makes good sense to allow studies to be refuted by mere verbal argument. Some consider it a virtue that this is so.

Now consider another point of view. What if, by the "what if" method, it can be shown that somebody might be wrong? This does not mean that he is wrong. He might also be right. Moreover, he has done some research and looked firsthand at the things that he is talking about. So why presume against him on the basis of some theoretical possibility? Why not instead require the same thing of the criticizer as of the researcher? What if someone who does the original research is considered tentatively right until another future research *shows* him wrong? Such a policy makes a lot of sense in the study of everyday life. First, comparable data are readily available. Second, it is in the interest of a community of scholars in this area to adopt conventions that maximize the possibilities of one person looking at data comparable to those considered by another. Finally, if we require that refutations be done only empirically and not by theoretical "what ifs," we change the process of criticism and refutation into one that automatically get us more data and more empirical findings. For these reasons and others, Sacks has recommended the following policy: A researcher studying everyday life is considered innocent until proven guilty by additional research.[6] According to this policy, it is insufficient to find ways in which an analysis might be wrong. The criticizer must now engage in research similar to that of the person criticized in order to perform his critique. This may be done in various ways:

1. By collecting empirical counterexamples—*not* by making up counterexamples.
2. By giving an alternate analysis of the same or comparable data.
3. By demonstrating through research that a certain kind of error might indeed occur. For instance, it would not suffice to claim that an informant might have been lying to the researcher. One would have to study lying and show that, in a situation comparable to the original, people are prone to lie.

In summary, formal sociologists (at least some of them) are rather "kind" to one another when it comes to their analyses. This is done to promote discovery.

But there is another side to this coin. Strangely enough, in the interest of this very same goal, they are rather hard on one another when it comes to permitting free choice of the topics and problems to be analyzed. The next few pages will suggest why this is so.

Discovered Topics

One of the things that has to be decided is what part of our work as sociologists is to be constrained by the world and what part is to be left to our own discretion. In this connection, sociological problems and topics are usually left to the researcher's discretion. These may be chosen according to his particular scientific purposes, inclinations, or interests. When we argue about what is in need of explanation (what to study), we argue about our own subjectivities— about the relevant literature, useful and neglected topics, what is trivial and nontrivial, and so on. On the other hand, when we evaluate and justify the explanations themselves, we do it by reference to the world. Here we invoke data, findings, videotapes, "facts," and so on.

In light of this, many of the articles currently available in formal sociology have a peculiar format: It is sociological problems that they explicate and work out in great detail. Often evidence is cited and collected to show that a certain issue really exists, or that something is in need of explanation. On the other hand, the explanations and solutions to these questions often seem preliminary, fragmented, and inadequate.

The reason for this is that many formal sociologists regard discovered topics and problems as empirical findings. Indeed, entire studies are undertaken with this in mind. Investigators insist that one needs evidence for the claim that something is a sociological problem. One needs to prove it with data, just as one needs data to validate hypotheses.

As a result, one cannot at one's own prerogative or by sociological convention ask whether a child's age or sex affects how she tells stories. One must now prove (that is, give evidence) that these are appropriate questions to ask about storytelling. As the reader knows, the situation is usually the other way around. Investigators usually must prove that conventional variables, such as sex and age, are *not* relevant, insofar as they wish to neglect them and still have their research regarded as legitimate.

This might seem rather strange to the reader. First of all, why should we be required to prove that young children tell stories differently from adults, or that girls tell them differently from boys? Second, in what sense can a topic or problem be an empirical finding? How do you prove that something is a topic?

Let's deal with the first question first. Imagine entering into a sociological discipline that considered it very important to look at blood-sugar level. Whatever one's topic of study, be it storytelling or deviant behavior, it will be important to consider whether blood-sugar level explains the phenomenon, in whole or in part. If one is interested in things other than blood-sugar level, then one must either hold blood-sugar level constant or randomize it. For undoubtedly it will have some effect on the thing being studied.[7] Without question, people with low levels of blood sugar could be expected to tell stories differently than those with high levels.

Is this a ridiculous analogy? Has it been demonstrated beyond question that such factors as sex, age, and social status provide ways of classifying people that are relevant to most social phenomena? Does it make sense to speak of male versus female behavior in lines, or staring among high-status persons compared with staring among the lower classes? You might believe it does. Many formal sociologists do not. Here again, you either believe it or you don't. If you don't—if you think that traditional sociological concerns may not be relevant to the study of everyday life—then it becomes a waste of time to be chronically concerned with them. For it is clear that one can find patterns in connection with any conceptual scheme once one has decided that the scheme is relevant.

One could discover that for the same amount of clock time spent waiting in line, men take it to be psychologically longer than women, or that older people take it to be longer than the young. One could then go on to construct a theory to explain such findings, perhaps contending that the work orientation of men versus the adaptive training of women leads them to experience the passage of time differently. But how might one notice that people are using the structure of the particular line and not the clock to tell time?[8] There is no ready methodological answer. There might be an answer, however, if we had systematic, instead of informal, methods of determining which conceptual scheme to employ when studying a particular phenomenon.[9] Formal sociology provides a few of these procedures. In such undertakings, it is suggested that we eliminate two ways of validating a given topic or variable:

1. Common sense doesn't count. It is not sufficient that a given issue makes good intuitive sense.
2. Sociological conventions don't count. The conventional variables and issues in sociology have emerged from the study of topics that are qualitatively different from those found in everyday life.

Now let us consider the second question: In formal sociology, how does one "prove" that a topic of study is "correct," using data, in much the same way as other schools of sociology prove that a hypothesis is correct?[10] This question cannot be answered in general. Rather, the procedures used to solve a particular problem are specific to the phenomenon being studied. Obviously, for example, one demonstrates that turn taking is a topic of study in queues in a different way from showing that turn taking is an issue in natural conversation. Having to prove topics of study are correct has the following consequences:

1. There are no general topics and no general variables. That is, topics and problems become tied to particular phenomena. Thus we avoid fitting the

rest of everyday life into conceptual shoes that were designed only for the study of turn taking in queues.[11]

2. Once something has been validated as a sociological topic, it must be dealt with. In this way, research tends to multiply the richness of everyday life. As opposed to ways of working that seek to find simplicity in apparent chaotic diversity, this way of studying everyday life uncovers complexity and richness in apparently simple and uncomplicated events.

Since the use of data to validate a topic of study is different for each phenomenon, there is no alternative but to demonstrate these uses through a concrete example.

AN EXAMPLE OF A DISCOVERED TOPIC: IS A BABY BY ANY OTHER NAME STILL A BABY?[12]

Consider the small child's eight-word, two-sentence story cited earlier in this chapter: "The baby cried. The mommy picked it up."[13] The story identifies two people, "the mommy" and "the baby." As our candidate for a discovered topic, we will consider the following issue:[14] Why did the child choose to identify these imaginary people in this way? How might one show that the selection of identifications is a proper topic of study with respect to storytelling?

Let's start by showing that the conventional orientation toward this issue is wrong. Traditionally, anthropologists have treated the issue of identification as a problem of finding rules which match people to linguistic titles.[15] This has been seen as a problem of proper reference. So conceived, the issue is linguistic (and cognitive), not sociological. In particular, people call someone a "mommy" because she *is* a mommy. Sociologists have been concerned with identifications primarily in connection with stigmatizing labels such as "criminal" or "crazy." Here identifications are treated as tags which, once assigned to people, have various social consequences. But again, the main focus is on the process by which tags get pinned on individuals.

In understanding this process, there has been a kind of schizophrenia. On the one hand, Becker defines a deviant as anyone whom others successfully label deviant:

> Social groups create deviance by making the rules whose infraction constitutes deviance, and by applying those rules to particular people and labeling them outsiders. From this point of view, deviance is not a quality of the act the person commits, but rather a consequence of the application by others of rules and sanctions to an "offender." The deviant is one to whom that label has successfully been applied; deviant behavior is behavior that people so label.[16]

On the other hand, Becker wants to understand such things as bias in law enforcement, "crackdowns" on prostitution, or undetected crime. Yet by his earlier definition there can be no undetected crime since, sociologically, a crime *consists* of an act that others have successfully labeled as a crime. To get around this problem he suggests that there is a "correct" way to use the term *deviant*. The term should be used to refer to chronic rule breakers. Given this definition, we can distinguish "real" deviants from persons who are recognized as such. We do this by using the following scheme:[17]

	Obedient Behavior	Rule-breaking Behavior
Perceived as deviant by others	falsely accused	pure deviant
Not perceived as deviant by others	conforming	secret deviant

Thus we see that Becker's procedure is similar to that of the anthropologists.[18] First one finds which people are correctly identified with a certain label in the society. If this label is correctly applied, there is no sociological problem, for in this case, someone was called an X because he is correctly recognized as being an X. If the label is incorrectly used—for example, if insane people are called sane, or innocent people are convicted as criminals—there is a potential sociological issue. In such cases, one must analyze the social conditions that explain the incorrect use of the label, conditions like race prejudice, selective law enforcement, or political interests.

In contrast to this, consider an instance in which someone names or identifies himself or others in the course of some daily interaction. Will Becker's orientation work here?[19] In particular, is proper reference (whether one identifies people correctly) a relevant issue? Observations such as the following suggest that it is not: It is easy to show that there are *many* categories, names, and descriptive phrases which identify a given person correctly. We would have to explain why one of these and not another was selected for use. But this still assumes that the referent of a term is relevant to its selection for use in daily interaction. This may not be the case. Voluminous data show that linguistically incorrect identifications are often socially appropriate in a given situation, while correct identifications can be regarded as socially outrageous. Consider the following transcribed conversation between two male teenagers during a group-therapy session:[20]

ROGER (TO KEN): Fact is you're a poor little rich kid.
KEN (TO ROGER): Yes, *Mommy*, thank you. [Empahsis added.]
ROGER: Face the music.

Or consider a statement by the mother of a retarded child:

> The doctor was blunt. He didn't seem to want to talk. All he said was, "It is my personal observation that the child is *mongoloid.*" My head swam. I fell backwards, gasping.[21] [Emphasis added.]

In summary, it is not necessarily the case that one calls another person a mommy because that person is a mommy. The term might be applied because in the context it's funny or insulting. This does not constitute a mistake on the speaker's part. It is our business to find which factors he is concerned with when he chooses to identify himself or others in a certain way. "Correctness," far from being a generally useful consideration, is but one of these factors. Thus we have established a sense in which the selection of identifications is a sociological, not a linguistic, issue.

Our next order of business is to clarify the nature of this issue in the case of storytelling. We want to do this empirically if possible, not by arbitrary definitions. Consider "mommy" and "baby" as they are used in the story. Since they are names for imaginary, not real, people, the child could not possibly have chosen them because they are "correct" in terms of reference. But might not the child's emerging ability to match the labels "mommy" and "baby" correctly to real people have something to do with her ability to use the terms in stories? There are reasons to think that these two abilities might be independent of each other. In order to see why this is so, let's consider an important sociological ability people use when they tell, and listen to, stories.

The reader will notice that the events depicted in the story do not seem like metaphor or fantasy but strike him as something that could possibly happen. That's an interesting observation since it means that people construct and recognize what Max Weber called ideal types. They can describe and talk about theoretically possible events in their society even though those events may not actually have happened or, if they did happen, were never witnessed. In fact, on any radio talk show one can hear numerous cases of someone discussing with utter seriousness events and situations with which he has no familiarity and which he has never experienced. We already discussed one such talk show, in which a blind woman called in and complained of having received inconsiderate treatment on the subways. The announcer immediately explained the subway riders' behavior on the basis of their mental preoccupations and worries. He came up with these "real-sounding" worries and preoccupations by using a social logic, in connection with the blind woman's initial remarks. In all probability he had no knowledge of the people involved, how they characteristically treat blind people on subways, or what was actually on their minds.

Thus we have some basis for claiming that whether the child can correctly describe real events may be independent of whether she can correctly describe events that sound real. If this is so, then her ability to use the categories "mommy" and "baby" correctly in connection with real people may be somewhat independent of her ability to use the categories "correctly" within a story.[22] In fact, this conclusion fits in nicely with many observations about verbal behavior in children. They can, indeed, use "mommy" in a story correctly prior to the time they start using "mommy" to refer to women with children.

Allowing that we can recognize a story as representing events that could possibly happen in our society, then this might be a possible goal in constructing a story. If this is so, then imaginary people might be named in such a way as to facilitate this goal. For we might not accept as literal "The basketball player cried. The baby picked him up." This of course would be one way to conceptualize the sort of issue we have here. If we could show that the child had certain "goals" in putting together her story, if we could show that using the categories "mommy" and "baby" helped to achieve these verbal goals, and if we could finally show that she deliberately chose these categories as *means* to these ends, then we could have both our issue and its potential answer. This is the road we will take. In order to travel it further, we must first specify one more goal the child may have in telling her story: exhibiting social relationships.

Although no possessive was used (that is, the storyteller did not say, "The baby cried. *Its* mommy picked it up"), we don't take it on hearing this story that some mommy picked up some baby. Rather, we sense that these persons are related in the customary way—that is, the baby has been picked up by *its* mommy. How is it that we surmise the existence of a relationship that we are not directly told about, between two real or imagined persons of whom we have no knowledge? The problem is far more general than accounting for a particular tacit assumption in a particular story. Sacks notices that there are some extremely important connections between the way we actually perceive people we don't know and the way we understand descriptions about such people. For the events depicted in the story could happen on the street: Seeing a woman pick up a crying child, we would probably recognize the existence of a familial relationship that is in no direct sense there to see. Indeed, it is the imputation of such relationship that allows potential kidnappings and rapes to be seen by onlookers as "family fights that are none of my business."

We now have two "goals" ready to be achieved. Next we will give some procedures for selecting names for the characters in a story and show that these procedures, if followed, will achieve these goals.

It's likely that most of us would have little trouble passing the following test in common sense knowledge:

Which of the following categories "go together"?

teacher
pitcher
woman
student
shortstop
man

Obviously, most of us know how to group various social categories into collections of categories, in various ways. So what? In terms of the problems we are discussing, this ability has significance. For it is just as obvious that we often select names and phrases to identify people with, not one at a time, but with respect to one another.

Our child's story might be a case in point. The names "mommy" and "baby" have a clear relationship. These are among the terms used to describe family members. Let us therefore assume, for the moment, that the categories "mommy" and "baby" were selected not separately but with respect to each other. Let's assume that in some general way all the characters in the story are doomed to be labeled with names for family members. Why would someone choose a whole naming scheme for her main characters all at once?

Sacks gives us a possible reason. Names for family members form a collection in a different way than names for race or sex. These names identify the players on a social "team," the family. Sacks proposes a rule in connection with the categories of such a collection, which he calls "duplicatively organized" categories:

1. Assume that some collection of people is categorized by using a set of categories which are duplicatively organized.
2. Then, if it is possible for these people to be understood as members of the same "team," they will be understood in this way by hearers or readers.[23]

Thus, merely describing the characters in one's story with names for family members will semi-automatically imply they are in the *same* family and will display various familial relationships among the people so named. These relationships, in their turn, will become part of the story. So we see, at least potentially, how and why the mommy is heard as the mommy of the baby.

But there's a problem with all this. In the case of real people we can pick a category for a person on the basis of adequate reference (call the sister "sister"). But in the case of imagined people there must be some other way of deciding which of the family-member categories applies to the character about to do the crying or the picking up. Otherwise, the previous rule does not bar any of the following stories:

1. The daddy cried. The mommy picked it up.
2. The mommy cried. The baby picked it up.
3. The mommy cried. The daddy picked it up.

As luck would have it, we are in the business of making our story "sound real." When naming imaginary people, there is a criterion which is analogous to adequate reference. There are certain cultural stereotypes which link activities to categories of people who are known to "do" them. When cultural knowledge links an activity to a category of people in this way, Sacks speaks of the category as being "bound" to the activity. These stereotypes are not empirical propositions. They are used primarily in constructing and interpreting meanings. For example, knowing that babies cry, one can readily understand what another means when he says, "You're acting like a baby," if you are an adult and you are crying.[24] Yet it would not make sense to say, "You're acting like a baby," because the person drinks milk, although in terms of empirical knowledge, babies drink milk.

Because these stereotypes are learned and are used differently than empirical knowledge about the world, it is possible for a child to know that babies cry with or without witnessing some number of babies crying, knowing anything about statistics, or even knowing precisely what babies and crying are in the first place.

Sacks proposes that if a category of people is bound to an activity in this sense, then the statement that a member of this category did the activity—that a baby cried—becomes recognizable as something that could possibly happen. Thus, selecting "baby" as the family member who will be doing the crying is in part a means of constructing a real-sounding story.

SUMMARY: PROVING THAT IDENTIFICATION SELECTION IS A TOPIC

At the beginning of this analysis we posed a problem:[25] How does one prove that people *select* the way they identify story characters, and that they do this, not in a linguistic, but in a sociological manner? Employing a means-end scheme, we treated the display of social relationships and making something sound as though it could really happen as story-goals. We then showed how one might select identifications for the characters of a story so as to achieve these goals. The next step (a difficult one) would be to show that people consciously and deliberately make selections like these in order to achieve story-goals. We shall not attempt this analysis here.[26]

Hopefully, our discussion of this story has illustrated some of the ways formal sociologists go about setting up a problem. We shall now go on to discuss one way in which they arrive at solutions. In particular, we shall consider distinctive ways in which they verify and elaborate hypotheses.

The Traditional View of Hypotheses

There is a particular philosophy of science that is important in sociology because it is used to guide the writing of publications and articles. According to this philosophy, if sociology is to be a science, it needs both armchair speculation and naturalistic observation. We must have theories, explanations, and hypotheses which are inherently conceptual (in that they are not direct descriptions of the world), and we must also have precise generalizations which answer directly to data sets.[27]

But how are the former to be linked to the latter? The prevailing recommendation is that this link ideally consists in the following: Theories about the social world are formulated in deductive, axiomatic fashion, so that a few basic concepts and assumptions logically imply a series of empirical generalizations.[28] It is the latter that are tested by observation and experiment.

We need not concern ourselves with the correctness of this philosophy of science. Our concern is with one of its major spin-offs. It makes a sharp distinction between two kinds of hypotheses, the theoretical and the empirical, and recommends that these two be used and evaluated in strikingly different ways.

Theoretical hypotheses are in no sense directly connected to the world, nor need they be descriptive of concrete events and happenings. Thus they are not, in any direct sense, true or false. Rather, they are subject to conceptual laws. Such hypotheses are required to be consistent, not with the world, but with each other in terms of the rules of theory, logic, and deduction. These assertions can come from most anywhere—the literature, one's own head, or so-called hypothesis-generating studies. Their function is not so much truth as usefulness—usefulness in deriving empirical hypotheses, in providing sets of ideas that help one to look at the world, and in summarizing heterogeneous facts and findings into general statements.

Empirical hypotheses are the heroes of scientific sociology. As purported descriptions of the world, empirical generalizations are the things which are true or false, probable or improbable. It is these which data subject to substantiating tests, and which counterexamples or contrary evidence can refute directly. It is here that type I and type II errors are considered in setting up the criteria by which empirical generalizations are to be rejected or not.[29] When we consider these criteria, a general methodological issue presents itself. How hardy does one want his hypothesis to be? If it gets revised or rejected upon encountering any single case where it does not seem to hold, one has a house of cards easily knocked down by even a small wind. Unless one just happens to hit on the right sequence of cases to look at, in connection with just the right hypothesis, chaos may reign, and it would be all but impossible to discover order in the world. On the other hand, if one makes his assertion too hardy, so that it is impossible to knock down, there is a sense in which it can no longer teach him anything about the world.[30] One way to grapple with this dilemma and obtain an assertion that is hardy, but not too hardy, is to meld both theoretical and empirical hypotheses into the same assertion. One such union produces a hybrid called "conceptual laws."[31]

Conceptual Laws

Consider this conversation between myself and my son just turned three. We are traveling through the country-side and he remarks that sheep eat grass. I concur and ask if other animals eat grass. "Oh yes, cows, and goats, and horses, and cats, and . . ." My seven year old son interrupts: "Cats don't eat grass." "Yes they do," retorts the three year old, "I saw a cat eating grass!" The seven year old replies that O.K. perhaps *that* cat was eating grass but cats don't eat grass. The three year old comes back with yes they do, lots of cats do, and besides he asked that cat if cats eat grass and the cat said that they did. This stops the seven-year-old briefly until he decides that the cat must have been mistaken. The three year old, sensing the direction in which victory must lie, states that lots of cats say that cats eat grass. The seven year old concedes the argument but ends by muttering that they can say what they want but cats don't eat grass.[32]

In this account, Riskin dramatically captures the somewhat annoying characteristics of what have sometimes been called "conceptual laws." Their features may be summarized as follows:

1. Conceptual laws are not tautologies. They are not true by definition. ("Cats don't eat grass" is not automatically true by virtue of a definition of the word *cat* as a carnivorous animal.)
2. Unlike theoretical assertions, conceptual laws refer directly to things in the world. One must be able to pick out cases in which these laws seem to either hold or not hold.
3. Conceptual laws are what Gasking calls "incorrigible proportions." They cannot be refuted by counterexamples:[33] "For it is clear (and I think it was clear to the three year old) that mere numbers wouldn't win the argument. That is, if seven, or thirty or *all* the cats were eating grass, still the assertion that cats don't eat grass might yet be true. There can be many sorts of temporary reasons why some or all the cats of a region may take up vegetarianism."[34]

Why would we want to work with a proposition in this way? Why would we commit ourselves to interpreting the world in such a way that our "law" always turned out to be correct? Before answering this, let us first note a somewhat perplexing property of conceptual laws. They are neither empirical nor theoretical hypotheses but something queerly in between. They give us new information about the world, but not by virtue of being true or false. Instead they function as tokens of obligation, showing us what events and happenings are in need of explanation and in what direction an explanation might lie:

The strong and interesting shift in the argument comes when the younger adduces the cat himself as an expert witness. For cats really ought to know what cats do or don't. Afterwards I asked the older child if he really thinks the cat was mistaken about whether or not cats eat grass, and he replied it had to be. I pressed him and asked what if all cats averred that cats eat grass, and he retorted that then cats would be liars.[35]

To find events in need of explanation, we use our law to search the world for mysteries. In the case of Riskin's older son, such a mystery is provided should he encounter a cat contentedly chewing grass. His sworn duty then becomes one of protecting his cherished belief against the onslaughts of an unsympathetic world. To accomplish this, the following courses of action are among those open to him (and to us):[36]

1. Monster barring: rejecting the case as an instance. (It is eating grass, all right, but it's not a cat.)
2. Monster taming: accepting the case as an instance, but finding some way in which it does not contradict the law. (It's a cat, and it's eating, all right, but what it's eating is not grass.)
3. Filling in the "etc." clause: postulating a hitherto unexplicated condition of the law's application. (Cats don't eat grass unless they are hungry and there is nothing else to eat.)
4. Monster accommodation: redefining definitions and concepts so as to accommodate the new case. Notice that this is not the same as items 1 and 2. The latter saves our law by examining the world, while the former proceeds by examining, explicitly, our own ideas and concepts. (Well, I guess what I really meant by "cat" was . . .)
5. Starting an escape clause: Cats don't eat grass, except toms, tigers, Persians, etc.
6. Naming the monster: collecting exceptions to the law into a new class (or classes) of objects and giving it a name. (Call those crazy cats "grass-eating cats.")

These procedures are familiar enough to any researcher. Practically every study of fact finding, whether in physics, market research, or sociology, has come up with these as things people actually do.[37] But the reader will look in vain for such procedures in methodology textbooks. In terms of the morals of methodology, what we have given is a catalogue of cheating practices. For this reason, conceptual laws and the reasoning practices that sustain them are seldom, if ever, recommended as the products of a sociological study—as the thing one ends up with and reports to his colleagues. Yet this is precisely what we are about to recommend:[38]

1. That conceptual laws be reported to others as findings of a particular study.
2. That they be used by many investigators, over the course of many individual studies.
3. That they be treated in the manner described above—that is, those working with them decide that such a law "is going to be true if it kills us" and proceed to inspect the world accordingly.

These three items are not merely recommendations. They are descriptions of what actually happens in the course of formal sociological research.[39] Why this is so and whether or not it is a good thing are matters that must now be taken up. In particular, conceptual laws are unusually helpful in solving three research

problems: finding out what you already know; conceptual mapmaking; and studying distinctive topics.

FINDING OUT WHAT YOU ALREADY KNOW

There are certain times when a researcher arrives at a finding about which
the following can be said: "There's no doubt that you're right about something.
The question now is, what are you right about?" Such was the situation when
Sacks, at an early stage in his work, proposed the following "rule" for natural
conversation: *At least and at most one party talks at a time.*[40] Again, clearly
there is something true about it, but it is not at all clear what "it" is. In order to
test such a rule one would have to know how to count instances of its violation.
In order to do this, one would have to answer questions like these:[41]

1. What counts as a "natural conversation?"
   a. How do we decide who is "in" it and who is "out" of it? Must the
      number of talkers remain fixed? If an onlooker "chimes in" with a
      comment while others are talking, is he violating the rule?
   b. How does one tell when a conversation begins and when it has ended?
2. The phrase "at a time" implies that speakers take *turns* at talking. But
   what counts as a "turn"?
   a. If a speaker stops talking in the middle of his utterance, waits, and then
      continues, has he taken one or two turns? If another person says
      something during this pause, is that a violation of the rule?
   b. How much overlapping speech counts as a violation of the rule? How
      much silence in between speech counts as a violation of the rule?
3. What kind of a "rule" is the above rule?
   a. Is it a behavioral rule? Is the rule supposed to describe how people
      actually talk in conversation?
   b. Is it a moral rule? If somebody violates it, is he sanctioned by others?

These questions can be answered in two ways. One could rush to arbitrary
operational definitions, in a search for immediate rigor, or he could wait. As we
have seen, if he does not wait, he may have to pay a price: type II error. That is,
he might throw out the rule prematurely as invalid because it did not fit the data
in terms of his arbitrary definitions.

One is reluctant to take such a step when there is the conviction that something is right about the rule. But where does this conviction come from? What
convinces the researcher that he has a hypothesis "dripping with truth" if only he
could find where it lay?

Often enough this conviction comes from a native's intuition. One recognizes something in a piece of data because of common sense: "This one interrupted that one" or "So and so has paused but is not finished talking." The

research program then attempts to explicate one's own common sense knowledge. How was it possible for me to have recognized such things? How would one explain to a "Martian" how to notice an "interruption" and how to tell who interrupted whom? Exactly what did I mean by "pause"—do silences in conversation belong to people? By reference to such questions as these, one may be led to the rule "At least and at most one party talks at a time" and to its possible significance.

Yet the conviction mentioned previously need not come solely from the cultural intuitions of a native. Often it comes because a rule has worked surprisingly well on some initial set of data. In Sacks's case, his rule fit an enormous number of initial conversations perfectly, in the sense that it described exactly what people did. The problem was to work with apparent counterexamples in such a way that the nature and scope of the rule was discovered empirically.

We can see here the first rationale for the use of conceptual laws in research. The rationale is based on an assumption which has often been vindicated in the history of science: *There are patterns in the world which cannot be found unless one already knows (or believes) that they are there.*[42] The person who thinks he knows of such a pattern is in an unusual position. Ordinarily one has a hypothesis, knows pretty well what it means, and wants to know if it is true. Here one has a hypothesis, is pretty sure it is true, and wants to know what it means (wants to know *what* is true). In order to answer this question, he treats his hypothesis as a conceptual law and puts a bit of knowledge beyond question for a while in order to "see where it will lead."

But how long is "a while"? What will it take to make Sacks give up his rule as wrong or fruitless, once it has been converted into a conceptual law? To answer this question we must discuss another use of conceptual laws in social scientific research: conceptual mapmaking.

CONCEPTUAL MAPMAKING

In the previous discussion we decided not to test our rule immediately because we did not know how to count. Except in an intuitive, common sense way, we did not really know what a conversation was. We did not know how to tell who was in one and who was not, or when it started or ended. Paradoxically, the rule itself helps us to develop those ways of looking, listening, and thinking about conversation which will permit the rule to be evaluated in a meaningful way. In considering turn taking, we start to divide "conversation" into subtypes. For examples, there are two-party and multiparty conversations. Only in the latter does who goes next become a problem which, if not solved, results in a violation of our rule (in overlapping speech or nobody talking). "Conversation" itself becomes distinguished from other types of talking and listening to which other sets of rules might apply:

It does not hold for members of a household in their living room, employees who share an office, passengers together in an automobile, etc., that is, persons who could be said to be in a "continuing state of incipient talk. . . .

Persons in such a continuing state of incipient talk need not begin new segments of conversation with exchanges of greetings, need not close segments with closing sections and terminal exchanges. [43]

In short, a lot of definitions and ways of looking and listening start to revolve around the rule in question. When this happens, one gets, in Riskin's words, "locked into a level of discourse." One can no longer "merely" change "At least and at most one party speaks at a time" without also changing one's notion of "turn," "pause," "conversation," "speaker," "hearer," and so on. It thus becomes far easier to accommodate novel cases within an already existing system than to throw out a whole set of concepts and research procedures just to deal with one measly new counterexample. This is not to say that the researcher has been backed into a conceptual corner and refuses to see the truth. Far from it. Our law has merely become embedded in an entire paradigm, which can be refuted only by another full-blown paradigm that handles the same data—only better.

The reader might object to this situation on the ground that we have betrayed our ideal. Did not Sacks commence by shunning arbitrary definitions that might prematurely topple an otherwise valuable rule? Now what has happened? Perhaps some of the definitions and procedures for looking at conversation mentioned above have sprung from meaningful observations about how people talk. But others must have been constructed by the researcher to support his rule. And now, it seems, "empirical realities," once constructed by the researcher and embedded in paradigms which support them, tend to perpetuate themselves. It becomes more and more difficult to muster evidence which will knock them down. All quite true. All this has been thoroughly discussed in the sociology of science. [44] Some find the situation reprehensible; others see it as actually helpful.

Whatever the reader thinks of this, it is going to happen to him anyway. He will at some point find himself using hypotheses as conceptual laws because they are centrally located within his conceptual household. We are merely giving the situation a name and suggesting how to proceed.

Yet there is an additional aspect to this situation that might give solace to an otherwise disgruntled reader. When first testing an empirical hypothesis, the question the investigator asks the world is: Is it true or not? But after the hypothesis has been around for a while, after it has achieved the kind of centrality we have described above, the social scientist becomes less interested in this question. He begins to ask another question about the same hypothesis: Where does it hold and why? With this shift in emphasis an empirical hypothesis is transformed into a conceptual law. The same procedures which constitute cheating if one wants to know "Is it true?" are perfectly legitimate methods of determining where a given law holds and why. The reader can check this for himself.

When used in this fashion, a conceptual law functions more as a scheme of interpretation than as an empirical law. It is not that it must hold everywhere. But in those places where it does not hold we are under an obligation to explain why. Often both the phenomena which satisfy the law and those which do not receive "pet names." Hitherto unrelated happenings thereby become appreciated as "similar sorts of things" and "different sorts of things."

In short, what starts out as a hypothesis may well end up as an entire theory, mapping out different forms of social interaction and identifying their constituent elements. This metamorphosis allows us to achieve what has long been heralded as an essential feature of life in society—a way to make order out of chaos.

In case the reader thinks this process is peculiar to the social sciences and their "soft" procedures, let us take him back to high school physics where he was told that "light travels in straight lines"—except for "refraction," where light bends; except for "reflection," where light behaves like a billiard ball; except for "dichronic crystals," where light neither travels straight nor reflects nor bends but instead becomes "polarized"; except for "black bodies," where light does not travel straight, bend, reflect, or polarize, but is partially or completely "absorbed."

DISTINCTIVE TOPICS

Knowledgeable readers might have balked at our presentation so far, since it presupposes a "social physics" in which one formulates "laws" of social action. However, sadly or joyously, the study of human interaction seldom focuses on laws of behavior similar to "Cats don't eat grass." Instead the mainstay of our theoretical meals is made of more intangible stuff, such as motives, intentions, and meanings. Such intangibles, interestingly enough, are not viewed as intangible but as real, as "there," and as affecting and being affected by the actions of individuals. It is in the process of analyzing the connections between these "intangibles" and concrete actions that conceptual laws become an important resource.

Such an analysis typically proceeds as follows: By various techniques already discussed, one discovers that various "rules," "intentions," or "goals" are present on the social stage. By reference to these, one infers the things people *might* do. These statements about possible actions are then used as conceptual laws to analyze and understand what people actually do. There are several distinctive sociological topics that seem to require this kind of analysis, and it is to an explication of these topics and their accompanying modes of analysis that we now turn.

THE ANALYSIS OF INTENTIONS

Imagine seeing a man aimlessly walking about a room uttering gibberish: "One, two, Charlie Brown—hello, hello, ah—hey—." To almost anyone, such behavior might present a natural puzzle in need of explanation. Suppose we were told that this behavior was, far from being psychotic, quite rational. It was a means to an end. The man was an audio engineer who, together with co-workers, had set up a public address system. He was testing the sensitivity of microphones by walking around the hall emitting sounds of various frequencies and volumes while his co-worker watched the dials of VU meters for signs of distortion or bad signal-to-noise ratios.

Apparently we have "explained" the behavior. It has become rational, and understandable. But what kind of explanation is it? It is not of the traditional sort found in the philosophy of science. We have not described the causes of the behavior in the sense of a cause and an effect. It is not as if the engineer's project literally *causes* him to make those particular noises. Nor have we subsumed his behavior under some set of general laws—for example, by characterizing him as engaged in the "three o'clock noise-making ritual." In general, we have not given a scientific explanation at all. If this is so, what kind have we given?

In situations like these, where reference is made to human goals, motives, projects, or reasons, there is a core thrust to the explanation. Basically we have explained that these actions were done "on purpose" and have explained what the purposes were. He engaged in these behaviors because he "intended" to engage in them. But unlike the relationship between causes and their effects, the relations between intended actions and actual actions have the following well-known but extremely annoying characteristics:

1. One can intend to do something and not do it.
2. One can not intend to do something and yet do it.

The courts are all too familiar with these characteristics. How do you prove somebody intended or conspired to do something when he didn't do it? Or, conversely, as in the Patty Hearst case, how does one demonstrate that someone did not intend to do something which she obviously, and methodically, did? Actually, court records are a good place to look for a sophisticated methodology for determining intentions from actions and vice versa.

The problem presented above is an important one. In understanding so-called rational actions, in considering human goals and practical projects, in analyzing all manner of motives and motivations, actual actions are explained by reference to human intentions. Yet how can one test a hypothesis that asserts a connection between intentions and actual actions? Clearly there is no direct route from the former to the latter. Not only is this connection not one of cause and effect, but there is no necessary statistical connection either. That is, it is not the case that 67 percent of the people who intend to do X will in fact do X, if other extraneous variables are controlled for. Why is this so? For one thing, one needs to consider the enormous implications of the fact that human actions can be mistaken; electrons, unlike people, never mistakenly move in the wrong direction.[45]

Imagine, for instance, a shopper intending to buy some laundry detergent who places a box, packaged and colored like the detergent, in his shopping cart.

A market researcher, observing this action, writes on his tally sheet "Buys one box of non-fat, powdered milk." These two people have made very different kinds of mistakes. In correctly interpreting the connections between purposes and action then, one obviously must consider the current stock of knowledge of the actor and how this knowledge indicates to him how his current actions fit into his general projects. One must discover what he thinks he's doing when he's doing something on purpose and use this information to analyze the relations between his goals and his actions. This was precisely the kind of analysis needed in the following excerpt from a case in traffic court.

JUDGE: M. Dale, you're charged with violating 21654—driving slower than normal traffic. I take it that you heard and understood my statement concerning your legal rights?

DEFENDANT: I understand my rights, yes sir.

JUDGE: And having that in mind are you ready for your plea?

DEFENDANT: Ah, guilty in part, sir. With extenuating circumstances. I entered the freeway at Lopez, and I remember having the thought at that time that since there are several right-hand on-ramps that I would stick to the center lane. And I was proceeding down the center lane, at about the speed. And this is what the officer could not have known. I was going at fifty-five miles an hour and if I had gone sixty-five I would have been following too close. Or driving the guy in front of me off the road. Because the speed of fifty-five miles an hour was being set by the person in front of me. The officer didn't take this in consideration. And as he pulled me over, he blamed me for obstructing traffic in the central lane and I feel that, well, I'm guilty of that I was going fifty-five—I mentioned this to him but he——-

JUDGE: What did he say?

DEFENDANT: He said that he considered that it was my car, which is a camper bus, that was obstructing traffic, so I feel I was guilty of going at a safe speed.

JUDGE: Well of course the difficulty with having a camper bus is that people can't see around you very well, can they?

DEFENDANT: Yes, and people tend to look at this huge thing and say, "This is really obstructing traffic. Everybody else must be held up by him."

JUDGE: [They] can't see anything in front of you, huh?[46]

From the police officer's point of view, what the driver *was doing* was "driving too slow," yet from the driver's point of view he was *not doing* something—he was not tailgating the car in front of him. Since the same action and its implications can be described in many different ways, all of which are correct, it can be "doing" many different things depending on how it is construed by the actor or the observer. In fact, many experiments have shown that observers tend to attribute the actions of others to their stable personal dispositions, while the actor tends to attribute them to his immediate situation and its accompanying circumstances.[47] In such situations, the judge as a third party functions as a social scientist in deciding such things as:

1. What was he "doing"—going too slow or keeping a safe distance away from the car in front of him?
2. If he was going too slow, was it done on purpose or was it a mistake?
3. If it was a mistake, what kind of mistake was it—an innocent mistake or incompetence?

THE ANALYSIS OF FUNCTIONS

Structural functionalism has had a long and honored history in sociology but is now on the wane as a theoretical approach. Durkheim early admonished his fellow sociologists that an adequate explanation of a social fact required specification of its causes and its functions.[48] Here a simple meaning of the term *function* is implied. The causes of a social fact are prior social facts which produce it. The functions are other social facts caused by the original social fact. An expanded view of "functional analysis" is easily generalized from this concept of function, which still operates within the framework of cause and effect. In this view, functional analysis consists in considering an entire system of social parts and analyzing the relationships of the various parts to the whole and to each other.

All this may suggest a machine and the kind of analysis that enables one to understand the workings of a machine. But there's the rub, one that gets functionalism in a lot of trouble in sociology. Machines have purposes, and purposes cannot be discerned or analyzed within the framework of cause and effect. For example, the main "purpose" of a car is to travel along a road. However, this purpose is not discoverable merely from an examination of the vehicle. That is, from the standpoint of what causes what, the fact that the wheels turn, moving the car forward, is no more significant than the fact that the pistons move up and down. There is no way to know if the purpose of the machine is to move the pistons up and down or make the wheels turn any more than there is a way to establish if the end of the acorn is the oak. Engineering is not physics. Although the principles of engineering must operate within the principles of physics, the one discipline cannot be reduced to the other.[49]

Within the human sciences there are certain situations in which functional analysis is both necessary and appropriate. It is easy for an efficiency expert or evaluation researcher to locate functions, since either he or his clients specify desirable goals in advance. It is then possible to analyze a drug abuse program or a plant operation in terms of "maintenance," "efficiency," "repair," "malfunction," "shortcut," "superfluous procedures," and so on, all by reference to the relationship between what the behavior system is doing and what it is supposed to be doing.

But what if we apply this kind of analysis to face-to-face interaction? Who says what the functions are then? Here sociologists must infer the functions of forms of interaction, such as civil inattention or taking turns at talk, by observing the interactions themselves. The universal complaint against this procedure is that social phenomena have no intrinsic functions. Imputing purposes to them must, in the final analysis, be an arbitrary decision of the analyst. Thus in the previous section we have considered the difficulties in establishing that some human being has a purpose or intention. How, then, do forms of social interaction have purposes or functions, and on what basis do students of interaction swear to their existence? There is a unique warrant for this claim that is not always found in other areas of sociology. People themselves bring functions into existence by treating various objects, words, and actions as having standard uses. In case study E (page 381), for instance, one way that others "accomplished" seeing a child as mentally incompetent was by noticing that she did not use a cultural object in accordance with its "function." She did not shake a rattle; instead she sucked it, probed with it, and so on. Since members engage in functional analyses of this type, we must do so as well if we are to understand their interpretations.

THE ANALYSIS OF RULES

It is perhaps one of the most cryptic and uniquely sociological explanations of human behavior to claim that someone is doing something because she is following a rule. Rules of various sorts—mores, laws, agreements, norms—are mainstays of sociological theory.[50] Yet they are even more peculiar than intentions or functions. When a person follows a rule, she is not acting in accordance with some behavioral law. It is not that kind of a rule. It is not a description of the actor's point of view concerning her behavior. It is not a goal, purpose, or intention. She can follow a rule without explicitly taking it into account.

> We can know a rule even without being able to articulate it, if we can act in accordance with it. Or we can "know a rule" if we can state it. Whereas the competent interactant need know a rule only in the first sense, the sociologist must know a rule in *both* senses.[51]

With this in mind, what kind of a rule is a rule, anyway? Where in the vast reaches of outer and inner space do we place "rules"—in the subconscious, in the collective unconscious? Often enough we place them in neither. We speak of forms of interaction themselves as having their rules—rules of classrooms, games, or conversation. Then, enter the cast of people onto the social stage we have set for them, and they proceed to perform. Some of them may know our rules, some may not. Some may care about our rules, some may not. It is our job to analyze the interaction between these diverse characters and the stage we have set for them, so as to explain how normal, organized interaction emerges from the alchemic combination of different people and social rules.

The Place of Rigorous Theory in Formal Sociology

Quite frankly, the reader is going to find many of the formal remarks of this chapter all but useless in his actual research. We say this from our own experience and the experience of others. The reason for this turns upon Garfinkel's observation that sociology, as a science, is a daily job, done in the very world it studies. On the one hand, there is the desire to develop and display rigor, precision, and logic in our work, so that the world can see that we are professional specialists doing an excellent job. On the other hand, there is our desire to learn about social life. Strangely enough, or perhaps not so strangely, the two conflict with each other. The reaction of some to this conflict was to develop what John Horton called "more and more sophisticated ways to find out less and less."[52]

For whatever reason, the following of rules or procedure, the careful use of concepts and their operational definitions in research, and the testing of generalizations to find in detail their scope and their exact truth, all seem to involve a lot of boring work and boring reading that simply do not have much of a payoff in understanding everyday life. We are not defending this statement—we are not saying that is the way it should be.[53] We are simply reporting our own experience for better or for worse. Nor are we saying that in some specific research, these procedures might not pay off admirably—for they sometimes do. However, in general it appears that, at this time, if one prizes learning about daily life above other goals of formal sociology, one does best to approach one's task as an art form rather than as a science (as positivists understand science). In this connection, our previous advice will not be wasted, for many of the questions, problems, and answers which we discussed do, in fact, regularly come into play in the "art form" of formal sociology. It is just that they come up in times, places, and ways that are strikingly different from the formal contexts we have described. Insofar as the reader finds this to be true, his reading will not have been done in vain.

Notes

1. Properly speaking, one never "accepts" a pattern as real on the basis of confirming data. Data never confirm hypotheses but are merely consistent with them. Officially one either rejects or fails to reject the null hypothesis that the pattern, in fact, is not there. For a detailed treatment of this subject, see William L. Hays, *Statistics for Psychologists*, New York: Holt, Rinehart and Winston, 1963, chapt. 9.

2. From E. G. Pitcher and E. Prelinger, *Children Tell Stories: An Analysis of Fantasy*, New York: International Universities Press, 1963.

3. Again we play historians here, without a survey to back us up. However, let the reader survey methodology texts in sociology and we think he or she will find our view confirmed.

4. We thank Harvey Sacks for sensitizing us to many of the issues to come, and for the general idea of attending to the social organization of *ourselves* for the purpose of optimizing the chances of learning things.

5. Schwartz even gives a "recipe" for invalidating research in this manner. See Howard Schwartz, "Towards a Phenomenology of Projection Errors," paper presented at the Pacific Sociological Association Annual Meetings, Portland, 1972.

6. Although Sack's admonition has not to our knowledge, found its way into print, it has found its way into the ears of many of his students.

7. In conventional terms, we mean the following: Blood-sugar level directly or indirectly "affects" some other variable, like one's emotional mood, if there are statistical associations between these two variables. Therefore, if one wishes to study the effect of time of day on mood, one must eliminate the effect of blood-sugar level on the process in order to study time of day and mood in isolation. One can do this either by selecting people all of whom have the same blood-sugar level and watching their mood changes at different times of day or by randomizing people's blood-sugar levels (somehow) so that they have no systematic statistical effect on mood. The whole subject is treated in a far less fanciful fashion in almost any text on experimental methods.

8. See the section on Schutz for a discussion of the sense of time in queues, pages 203–204.

9. Considering the question of how to measure or classify phenomena, we find perhaps the largest methodological inadequacy in sociology. For a discussion of some of the problems involved, see Aaron Cicourel, *Method and Measurement in Sociology*, New York: Free Press, 1964.

10. Note that, in asking this question, we have used the terms *topic, issue, problem*, and *variable* more or less interchangeably. This was done on purpose. In posing a question to ask about a particular phenomenon, the formal sociologist usually marshals evidence for the claims (1) that the question is appropriate and (2) that he is conceptualizing the question in an appropriate way. For instance, sex may be related to storytelling in the sense that women deliberately tell men different kinds of stories than they tell other women. Or the question may be whether most members of our society, men or women, tend to portray certain kinds of characters in a story as male or female.

In quantitative sociology many of these complexities are avoided since almost every question is conceptualized by asking whether some "variable" statistically affects another. To show that the sex of a child is related to how she tells stories, one turns storytelling into a variable by, for example, measuring how long stories are or how many female characters they contain. One then shows that sex, as a variable, statistically affects the storytelling variable.

11. For the rationale (and some methods) for making descriptive terminologies unique to particular phenomena, see Howard Schwartz, "Data: Who Needs It?" *Sociology* (Journal of the British Sociological Association), forthcoming.

12. It should be emphasized that the ensuing discussion is semitheoretical, designed to illustrate how one might discover a topic (or topics) of study and go about formulating it properly as a sociological problem. This example should not be thought of as a valid empirical analysis of storytelling. This is true in part because of the following: (1) It is based on inadequate data, that is, an isolated story taken from a book written by another, with little or no additional information about the context in which it took place. (2) Later work by Sacks and his colleagues indicated that, to be valid, an

analysis of the type we present requires a different type of data. It requires, for instance, a tape of *an entire conversation* within which one or more stories are told.

13. The ensuing discussion assumes that our punctuation of this story corresponds to the way it was told and/or heard. (Alternate reading: "The baby," cried the mommy, "picked it up.") The reader might consider how one might gather evidence in favor of a given punctuation.

14. Our analysis is an adaptation of Sacks's, from which it differs in several ways. For his treatment, see Harvey Sacks, "On the Analyzability of Stories by Children," in *Ethnomethodology*, ed. by Roy Turner, Baltimore: Penguin Books, 1974, pp. 216–232.

15. For a discussion of this issue as it relates to anthropology, see Michael Moerman, "Who are the Lue?" *American Anthropologist* 67 (1965): 1215–1230.

16. Howard Becker, *Outsiders*, New York: Free Press, 1963, p. 9.

17. Table is from Becker, *Outsiders*, p. 20.

18. For a discussion of this orientation and some of its consequences, see Melvin Pollner, "Sociological and Common-Sense Models of the Labelling Process" in *Ethnomethodology*, ed. by Turner, pp. 27–40.

19. Notice that we are not indicting Becker's approach. Insofar as those who label others as "deviant" are, in one way or another, consistently concerned with whether they are or are not labeling people "correctly," his approach is perfectly appropriate.

20. The conversation and the observation about it are from Harvey Sacks, after he had had attended a seminar.

21. Jerry Jacobs, *The Search for Help: A Study of the Retarded Child in the Community*, New York: Brunner/Mazel, 1969, p. 29.

22. Actually the issue is much more subtle than this. Children may be *able* to use categories as adults do before they *choose* to do so. For example, in children's culture, what adults would consider instances of "misidentifying" things are perfectly accepta- ble, often enjoyable things to do, such as misidentifying a body part with a "dirty word" such as "butt."

23. Notice the qualification "if it is possible," indicating that actual cases require a complicated analysis.

24. Sacks uses data like these as evidence that a particular category is bound to a particu- lar activity.

25. As is now clear, we have offered not so much a "proof" that our topic is relevant to storytelling as a series of reasoned speculations supported by data.

26. The interested reader can find this topic dealt with in Alan L. Ryave, *Aspects of Story Telling Among a Group of "Mentally Retarded,"* Ph.D. dissertation, Department of Sociology, University of California at Los Angeles, 1973.

27. For a case of this distinction offered in terms of theoretical versus operational defi- nitions, see Hubert Blalock, *Social Statistics*, New York: McGraw-Hill, 1960, pp. 8–11.

28. Although Hans Zetterberg and others have extolled the virtues of axiomatic theory in sociology, we know of no real axiomatic theory that has been constructed in sociology to account for a substantive phenomenon (except as a trivial demonstration). This is true in part because most sociologists are unfamiliar with mathematical logic.

29. Methodologists in quantitative research usually make a finer distinction than the one made here. It is not really the empirical generalization they test but a statistical hypothesis which is derived from it. For example, one might propose that the income of whites is higher than that of blacks, for some set of jobs. Depending on what one wants this assertion to mean, one might translate it into statistical terms in any of the following ways:
    1. The mean income of whites is higher than that of blacks.
    2. The median income of whites is higher than that of blacks.
    3. The mode of the income of whites is higher than that of blacks.
    If we choose alternative 1, then what is statistically tested is not alternative 1 but the hypothesis that the means of the two groups are the same. Given a sample of whites and blacks and their respective incomes, one can obtain sufficient contradictory evidence to reject this latter hypothesis. Thus we see that, literally speaking, there is a trail of additional procedures and assumptions that connects even the empirical generalizations to the "world."

30. One might think that sociology already has a flexible way to handle this problem, since it (at least the quantitative variety) deals in probabilities, not truth or falsehood. But this is not strictly true. Statistical hypotheses are assertions about definite characteristics of groups (population parameters), which are either true or false, not probable or improbable. Probability comes in only when one estimates the relationship between the characteristics of a sample and those of the population. While it is possible to use a probability logic instead of a two-valued (true-false) one, in sociological *theory* sociology does not currently have such a logic.

31. In the following treatment of conceptual laws, we borrow heavily from Steven Riskin, "Reasonable Accounts in Sociology: The Problem and the Logic of Explanation," Ph.D. dissertation, Department of Sociology, University of California at Los Angeles, 1970.

32. Steven Riskin, "The Philosophical Grounds for Some Sociological Certainties," paper read at the Pacific Sociological Association Annual Meetings, Portland, 1972, p. 3.

33. These statements are more widely known as "incorrigible propositions" than as "conceptual laws." See Douglas Gasking, "Mathematics and the World," in *Logic and Language*, ed. by Anthonly Flew, Garden City, N.Y.: Doubleday Anchor, 1955.

34. Ruskin, "Philosophical Grounds," p. 3.

35. Ibid. It has long been recognized that beliefs of all types perform this service for their adherents. Those events and happenings which conform to the belief become "normal," "natural" events and produce no surprise or confusion. It is by reference to the belief that it is possible to spot the bizarre, the peculiar, or the puzzling things of this world.

36. Our terminology, in part, is taken from I. Lakatos, "Proofs and Refutations," *British Journal for the Philosophy of Science* 14, no. 53 (May 1963). We recommend this article highly as a manual on the strategies of discovery (particularly on how to work with counterexamples).

37. A favorite social scientific research topic is how various groups (religious, political, etc.) sustain their beliefs in the face of inconsistencies and contradictory evidence. Our "cheating practices" are frequently among the research findings of such studies.

38. Actually we are more than a little embarrassed by our talk of single "hypotheses" or "conceptual laws." Quantitative or qualitative sociologists seldom work with single assertions in isolation which they "test," "revise," and so on. Instead, research (and its attendant monograph) involves simultaneously working with many interconnected assertions, integrated into a unified analysis. However, our discussion is not pointless, since the *practices* underlying conceptual laws are used in the latter kind of analysis.

39. This is difficult to document precisely because these things are done informally. In part, in making this claim, we report our own personal experience and that of our close colleagues.

40. Although the story we are about to tell about Sacks's research does not correspond to a series of day-to-day events in real time, it is surprisingly accurate. The source of its accuracy (or lack of accuracy) comes from Schwartz's close association with Sacks during the time this "rule" started to be explored.

41. For the eventual answers to questions like these given by Sacks and colleagues, see Harvey Sacks et al., "A Simplest Systematics for the Analysis of Turn Taking in Conversation," *Language* 50 (1974): 696–735.

42. This often happens because a relationship is so hidden in the world that only an irrational, unreasonable search can find it.

43. Emanuel Schegloff and Harvey Sacks, "Opening Up Closings," in *Ethnomethodology*, ed. by Turner, p. 262.

44. A well-known discussion of "normal science" and its attendant paradigms is found in Thomas Kuhn, *The Structure of Scientific Revolutions*, Chicago: University of Chicago Press, 1970.

45. One argument for why intentions and actions are not related statistically is this: The world can intervene between a person's intentions and his actions in an indefinite number of ways, each qualitatively different than the other. For example, it can provide someone with faulty knowledge about how to carry out his intentions; it can put an obstacle in his way; or it can introduce a more important, but incompatible, goal. These contingencies would result in different kinds of action, all somehow related to and stemming from the same initial intention(s). Such contingencies could not be easily treated as variables, since they continually cause changes in the original independent variable, that is what a person, from his viewpoint, "intends" to be doing, and vice versa.

46. Melvin Pollner, "Mundane Reasoning," *Philosophy of the Social Sciences* 4, no. 1: 50.

47. For a summary of some of these experiments, see Edward E. Jones and Richard E. Nisbett, "The Actor and the Observer: Divergent Perceptions of the Causes of Behavior," Morristown, N.J.: General Learning Press, 1971.

48. Emile Durkheim, *The Rules of Sociological Method*, Chicago: University of Chicago Press, 1938.

49. For an elucidation of this point and a theory for human knowledge surrounding it, see Michael Polanyi, "The Logic of Tacit Inference," *Philosophy* 41, no. 155 (January 1966): 1–18.

50. For a well-known article that explores the implications of this fact, see Thomas Wilson, "The Normative and Interpretive Paradigms in Sociology," in *Understanding Everyday Life*, ed. by Jack D. Douglas, Chicago: Aldine, 1970, pp. 57–79.

51. From an unpublished classroom handout by Dr. Harvey Segal, Department of Sociology, California State University at Sonoma.

52. Personal communication from John Horton.

53. Many students of everyday life believe that micro-sociology within natural settings has yet to find its technology but that whatever the technology will eventually be, one thing it will *not* be is a way to discover and test rigorous hypotheses.

CHAPTER 13

Making Patterns II: Two Exemplary Procedures

Up until now we have been talking only about general orientations, problems, and procedures. It is time now to consider how (or if) these generalities become crystalized in specific forms of analysis. To this end two important methods of analyzing everyday life, conversational and phenomenological analysis, will be described in more detail than has been possible thus far. It should be noted, however, that these are merely examples of a wide variety of analytic traditions from which the enterprising sociological shopper can choose.

Conversational Analysis[1]

If we choose to be anthropologically naive about conversation, we might propose that it is a social activity in which participants take turns at making noises. As such, it seems to be almost a compulsion among humans. Of all the social activities they engage in, this one seems to be their favorite. They do it everywhere, under all sorts of conditions, at great length, and, more often than not, without immediate practical purpose or results. The groups that do it show almost infinite variation in size and composition. Furthermore, as an activity, conversation seems to display the paradox of triviality. Its occurrence within daily life strikes us as remarkably unmomentous. Yet these millions of small verbal episodes may be the main vehicle for shaping what each of us become, know, and experience throughout our social life. Like the incessant sculpting of rocks by the sea, natural conversations may have more to do with shaping the nature of individuals and societies than wars, child-rearing practices, and political elections. Conventional wisdom already credits natural language with such properties as these:[2]

1. It structures the thought process of those who think in it.
2. It determines one's perception of the world and its meanings.
3. It is the main vehicle by which the man in the street receives, accumulates, and transmits beliefs and information.
4. It is one of the fundamental social skills which determines one's personal, economic, and social life chances.

Any activity that does all these things to people's "heads" and people's lives, day in and day out, in practically every known society, should be studied in detail. Conversational analysis is one way to do this. Let us now outline how.

THE SUBJECT MATTER

The primary subject matter for conversational analysis is the activity of conversing. This may sound like an obvious conclusion, but there are some hidden elements to it. First, it represents a fundamentally different orientation from that which is found in linguistics or sociolinguistics. The former regards language as an entity, a "thing," with a particular structure. This means that actual linguistic activity, as such, is not the subject matter of linguistics. Rather, the act of talking or listening is conceived of as a "performance" which utilizes "language" as an idiom.[3] The task of linguists is to discover from speech acts the structure and component parts of language(s), not the "performances" which utilize language. If this is what linguists do, sociolinguists take the component parts of language (as defined by linguists) and examine their social correlates. That is, they ask how children acquire language, what accounts for the differing vocabularies used in the marketplace as compared with the home, or how one explains the fact that people of different social status speak with different intonation patterns.

Conversational analysts, in contrast, are not interested, in any direct way, in the structure of "language." They come at the problem from a completely different angle. If they are interested in structure, it is the structure of conversing, complaining, telling jokes, or storytelling. They do not treat language as a "thing" but as a series of social activities, like tennis or grocery shopping. They then ask: What are those activities, and how are they accomplished?

It is now safe to say that one of the verbal activities that occurs in daily life can be called "natural conversation." That seems like a banal enough statement, but actually it needs justification. By "natural conversation" we refer to a form of verbal interaction with a very specific structural organization—an organization that is quite different from the exchanges that occur between teacher and student, in debates, or when hailing a cab. For the moment, think of "natural conversation" as a kind of mutual talking that can and does go on under any and all circumstances in our society. It is a "game" whose "rules" specify no special time and place, no special set of circumstances for it to be "played." It can legitimately go on between anyone and everyone, over the phone or in the street, for a few seconds or for many hours. Any topic or no topic can be discussed through its occurrence. In short, the structure of natural conversation is so defined as to allow it to occur in every nook and cranny of social life. This is one of the reasons its effects are so far-reaching. In exploring what this structure is, conversational analysts have pointed (for openers) to the following layers of organization:

1. A *turn-taking system* determining who talks next and when to talk next.
2. A *"recursive" organization* by which previous utterances determine how to listen to and how to produce a current utterance.
3. An *overall structural organization* through which conversations are divided into bounded "sections," such as beginnings, endings, first topics, second topics, and so on. Each section, in turn, has its own internal structure, its own particular placement within the entire conversation ("beginnings," "endings," etc.), and a definite structural relationship to the other sections.
4. An *intra-utterance structure*: Single utterances, such as complaints or requests, have their own series of "parts" which are constructed and ordered by particular principles of organization.
5. An *interconversational structure*: In the course of conversing, members relate entire conversations to other entire conversations.

Of course, the previous discussion was not so much a description of an activity as a list of possible study topics. It should suffice here to point out that we are talking about a distinctive, if pervasive, form of "making noises." It took considerable research effort on the part of conversational analysts to establish the fact that there was something called a "natural conversation" (in the sense defined above) and that it had a structure that was somewhat independent of the diverse situations in which it occurred.[4]

This, then, is conversational analysts' answer to linguistics. Instead of an *entity* with a structure (language), they take as their major topic an *activity* with a structure. It serves a function for the conversational analyst similar to the one "language" serves for the linguist. It is his main take-off point, so that other forms of mutual talking, such as psychotherapy, can be analyzed as modifications of, or variations upon, "natural conversation." This is not merely a theoretical device, since members treat other ways of talking and listening in this way as well. For instance, a discussion between intimates is recognized as an "intimate conversation," in part because each party suspends some of the rules that operate in ordinary conversation and can see that the other has done so as well.[5]

DATA COLLECTION

So far this form of analysis has been concerned primarily with naturally occurring conversation in the English language. These are first tape-recorded or videotaped and then transcribed in as detailed a manner as possible. There has been a general preference in this kind of work for surreptitious recording (when it can be morally done), for excluding any and all conversational analysts from participation in conversations that serve as data, and for refraining from influencing the course of the conversation in any way.

It has also been found valuable for the researcher to be conservative about conversational context. That is, even when an analysis revolves around just one sentence, that sentence should be reported together with as much of its surrounding talk as possible—preferably the entire conversation. The reason for this is that future and past remarks (verbal context) can dramatically affect what is said and heard "now." Since we don't know the intricacies of these connections, it is wise to prevent the elimination of potentially relevant contextual data.

There have been three basic approaches (not necessarily mutually exclusive) to collecting data in connection with a particular problem. First, one can choose a problem in advance for which relevant data can be found in almost any conversation, or at least it is clear where to find the conversations that contain the needed data. Here one might focus on beginnings, turn taking, and so on. However, certain kinds of data occur fitfully and unpredictably in naturally occurring talk, so that there are no particular social times and places where they can be expected to be found. Someone studying jokes, verbal put-downs, or descriptions of people's moods might run into this problem. To handle this, some investigators have amassed a "library" of diverse transcripts made by themselves and others which they can tediously plow through in search of data that bear on a particular issue. Instead of having to hunt for one's data in this manner, a third alternative is to first collect a set of data and then choose or discover a problem that fits the data already at hand. Many dissertations using conversational analysis have invoked this third strategy.

DEVELOPING A TECHNICAL "EAR"

Whatever the strategy employed for a given transcript, it has been found to be all but essential, as part of one's general apprenticeship, to actually listen to and transcribe a variety of tapes in great detail. There are several reasons for this. First, it has been found again and again that people do not actually converse as we think they do (that is, as our common sense and memory tell us they do). Second, the kind of attention that is required in transcribing an "impersonal" recording is so different from that which is present when one is himself a conversationalist or is thinking about how people talk that it forces many new recognitions, even upon the seasoned analyst.

Such an undertaking functions to develop, first, the analyst's conversational intuition and, second, his knowledge of what to make of transcripts: It helps him interpret marks on a page in terms of sounds and overlapping sounds, to know when a transcript might be sufficient and when the tape must be listened to, or when both are required. It also allows him to spot where mistakes might have been made and where refinements are needed. In short, it helps turn a naive speaker-hearer into a technical expert on conversation.

SOME EXCLUSIONS

There has been a tendency for researchers to steer away from transcripts produced by agencies and investigators who are not normally engaged in this kind of work. The reason is that such agencies produce artifacts, whether they be transcripts or crime statistics, consistent with their own daily operation and practical requirements. In this regard, conversational analysts have found that transcripts made by others contain many errors, omit much acoustic detail, and incorporate a great deal of editing. In addition, they are frequently recorded under unknown conditions, which renders them unfit for this type of analysis. Also excluded are data from experiments on language or other verbal interactions. The "conversation-in-an-experiment," while one form of interaction, is of limited interest in itself. For experimental talk is structured with respect to special roles, tasks, and definitions of the situation which are intimately related to specific research goals. The way people talk in such situations is, in all probability, quite specialized. Studying such talking will not help us to discover the structure of natural conversations, since these occasions do not comprise natural occasions. Finally, in exploring the rules, conventions, and conditions under which mutual talking occurs in a society, it seems self-defeating to start by deliberately molding these conditions and conventions so as to create hybrid activities with unknown relations to naturally occurring activities.

Using the same logic, the conversational analyst will obviously have little use for categorized, coded, content-analyzed, or classified data, for they are already too far removed from the events that produced them. That is, if I am interested in the structure of "complaining"—who complains, where complaints occur in conversation and why, how one "builds" a complaint with words and how others see it as such—what am I to do with the information that 32 percent of the comments of women in group therapy sessions were complaints directed to men? The researcher has already used his intuition to make the counts. God knows what varieties of comments were counted as complaints, or what words were in them, or to whom and when they were said in any particular session. In short, these kinds of data will not bear upon the questions that are ordinarily asked in conversational analysis.

Finally, made-up data are excluded as well. The reader might say "of course" to this, but this exclusion is not at all a general rule in linguistic analysis. Linguists assume that the basic resources used by most speaker-hearers to produce and understand grammatical sentences are similar or identical.[6] Consequently, the researcher who is a native speaker is every bit as good an informant as anybody else. With this in mind, linguists often invent candidate sentences to prove points or argue for or against possibilities. Through the use of such data, important arguments have been carried out about, for example, the nature of English grammar.

However, this procedure cannot be allowed in conversational analysis for several reasons. First, in making up sequences of conversation, we do not use the same resources that natural speakers use. A made-up utterance or sequence of talk is produced and interpreted so as to make some theoretical point. In contrast, in naturally occurring talk, people use the ongoing social context, in particular what has been said thus far, as their main resource in producing and interpreting a "next thing to say." Since we don't know exactly how these resources work, we can hardly claim that they are the same for us as for them. Thus we can hardly claim that our made-up data could have been said or heard that way in conversation. Second, it has been a simple, gross finding that tape recorders capture things which most of us don't know we do. No matter what point we were trying to make, we couldn't invent such things because they are not rememberable or even imaginable in the ordinary sense of the word.

THE ANALYSIS

Having taken care of most of the "window trimmings," we are now faced with outlining the kind of analysis involved in conversational analysis. Alas, we cannot do it. Such an undertaking is too complex for a text of this kind. What we will do is give a few of the topics, assumptions, and strategies found in this analysis and let the reader take it from there.

There are three broad strategies to be found in the literature, each particularly suited to certain study topics and not others.

THE EXCAVATION OR ANNOTATED TRANSCRIPT

Consider the following street exchange reported by a black doctor:[7]

Policeman: What's your name, boy?
Doctor: Dr. Poussaint. I'm a physician...
Policeman: What's your first name, boy?
Doctor: Alvin.

The "excavation" is an extensive, detailed analysis of a single piece of data in order to open up some particular study topic of interest. An excavation typically starts with a sociologist's staring blankly at an opaque piece of data. Using as much native intuition and conversational expertise as it takes, he begins by finding a topic and a few observations in the data. In the exchange reported above, it does not take a conversational analyst to detect the presence of racism.

In particular, the maneuvering for status seems to revolve around the identification categories "boy," "Dr.," "physician," and "Alvin." However, this initial intuitive observation contains a multitude of presuppositions about the people and the exchange. In order to unearth these presuppositions and use them to dig in further, we create a sort of main analysis. This consists of many reasoned possibilities, buttressed by facts already known about conversation and subsidiary analyses and supporting data that come up as we proceed. This is called an "excavation" because, proceeding in this fashion, one tends to come up with millions of detailed, complex issues contained within a seemingly simple exchange:

> How does mis-identifying a man as a "boy" degrade somebody? Does it do this only for blacks? In what sense are "Dr." and "physician" competing categories to "boy"? Can we use the fact that the doctor slips in unasked-for information as evidence that he interpreted "boy" as degrading? Would he have told the policeman his job if he was a waiter? Might a waiter have lied and claimed to be a physician? From this can we see what verbal needs might create lying in our society?

In coming to terms with such issues one creates a mini-theory or analysis. This analysis is challenged by proposing alternate analyses for the same data or by giving different analyses for comparable data. The original excavation also helps here in that it provides hints on where to find additional exchanges of "this sort." In the present case, one might look for cases of racism and status display achieved through the use of identification categories. Thus it becomes progressively clear what additional kinds of data are needed to settle the original issues in a more definitive way.

This kind of analysis is especially helpful for exploring how the innocent properties of talk are marshaled for rather important social and personal goals. Conversational analysts, for instance, may weep at the doctor's strategic error in not replying with "Dr. Alvin Poussaint, I'm a physician." For it is a property of question-answer sequences that the asker of the first question, upon receiving an answer, has the right to ask another question.[8] By leaving out "Alvin" in the reply, the doctor hands the policeman his next question on a platter: "what's your *first* name, boy?" Further, the question is potentially degrading in that it allows the policeman to force the black man to tell him a piece of personal information (his first name). Schwartz has found that people often see threats like this coming and head them off at the pass. They offer the information first, so that the other is robbed of the chance of displaying his verbal power.[9]

Hunt-and-Peck Conversational Analysis

Some topics present a grab bag of ongoing issues, requiring many different kinds of data. When examining the general structure of verbal activities, one tends to encounter issues like this: How does one end a conversation? What are the component parts of a conversational beginning? In such cases one proceeds much in the fashion already discussed in chapter 11, "Hunt-and-Peck Ethnography." The runners go out in search of many different pieces of data all of which bear in one way or another on some general problem. Many mini-analyses are initiated to deal with specialized observations in connection with such data. Finally these diverse data, observations, and theories are patched together (a more dignified word is "integrated") into a unified theory that applies to the general problem. An example of this kind of analysis is Schegloff's treatment of the ways in which people describe places and locations to each other.[10] In *The Image of the City* Kevin Linch treats members' descriptions of places as indicators of their general geometric perception of a city. Schegloff's analysis casts doubt on this perspective, in a typical interactionist way. After looking at many kinds of data, he found that members will talk of places "out there" quite differently, depending on three situational contingencies which they take into account: (1) the current physical location of both speaker and hearer, (2) the identities of speaker and hearer (American, New Yorker, German, etc.) or the relationship that exists between them, and (3) the topic or verbal activities currently being engaged in (giving directions, telling a friend about one's vacation).

CONVERSATIONAL-ANALYTIC INDUCTION

Finally, either an excavation or hunt-and-peck conversational analysis may lead to a theory or set of generalizations which can be applied to a large set of comparable pieces of data. Such was the case when Schegloff asked the general question "What does it take to begin a conversation?" He focused upon sequences of talking and listening, which he called "summons-answer" sequences, and showed that these sequences had certain general properties. Because of these properties, summons-answer sequences could perform the *interactional work* required to get a conversation started and keep it going. These ideas could readily be tested on telephone conversations, for all of these start with a ring (a summons). In validating this theory on a large number of phone conversations, Schegloff wrote an entire dissertation, appropriately entitled "The First Five Seconds: The Order of Conversational Openings."[11]

SOME UNDERLYING CONCEPTS OF CONVERSATIONAL ANALYSIS

Many of the general ideas discussed in previous chapters have paid off superbly when applied to conversational materials. Below we exemplify how this application was done and what its results might be in selected cases.

INTERACTIONAL WORK

One can "do" various activities, such as complaining, joking, or displaying one's status, through the use of talk. In fact, there are verbal activities which several people can cooperatively "do" together through talk. Analysts have taken it as one of their tasks to identify the sorts of things that get done in and through talk, and to explore exactly how they are done.

STRATEGIC INTERACTION

Thus one can speak of people intending to do certain things, using various verbal tactics to get them done, and running into difficulties and opposition in the process. In short, one can study conversational "tactics" together with the sense in which people "win," "lose," use "ploys" or "delaying strategies," and so on.

"CONVERSATIONAL OBJECTS" AND THEIR FUNCTIONS

In and of themselves, talk and sequences of talk such as greeting pairs ("Hi," "Hi") or "pre-invitations" ("Are you doing anything tonight?") "do" certain interactional work. That is, they have standard functions. Speakers and listeners know of these functions and orient to them when using and responding to them. Because of this it is possible to speak of talk and sequences of talk as "objects" and to examine their properties much as chess commentary examines the properties of moves, independently of the motives or thoughts of players during actual games.

CONSCIOUS "ORIENTATIONS"

One of the most important developments in conversational analysis has been the discovery of methods to retrieve what people are aware of by examining what they say and do not say. Here we need not interview them later to discover their "point of view," but have ways of discovering what they notice, think about, and attend to in the very midst of their daily activity.

One of the key resources for doing this has been the fortunate fact that people are not merely cognizant of "what's going on" but *deliberately display* this awareness to others through behavior. For example, listeners are often obliged to display that they understand a speaker by using a variety of conversational devices such as eye contact, gesture, listening noises, or replying.

An interesting illustration of these concepts is provided by a demonstration devised by Ryave. When someone tells a story, you can display that you are listening by inserting standardized "listening noises" such as "hm," "oh," or "uh-huh" at certain points in the unfolding story. In fact, the storyteller often provides spaces for you to do this and may not continue until you fill those spaces with listening noises. In order to demonstrate the improvisational nature of social organization, Ryave instructed his students to display their listening "badly" by making a listening noise every few seconds at regular intervals. At first this interfered with the storyteller's pacing and caused him or her some trouble.[12] But soon the storytellers began pacing themselves in their recounting so as to fit the rhythm of the story to the rhythm of the listening noises!

SOME USES OF CONVERSATIONAL ANALYSIS AS A TECHNIQUE

Many readers may find our presentation and the techniques of conversational analysis itself over technical and of little sociological importance. Instead of trying to argue against this reaction, we shall suggest a few of the benefits other practitioners have found through acquaintance with this method. We shall then show how it can be used to arrive at concrete sociological payoffs.

1. If, indeed, verbal activities have a structure, then this structure will affect whatever people do with each other using talk as an idiom—from getting married to negotiating a nuclear arms agreement. It therefore pays to know what these structures are and what can and cannot occur within them.

2. Another approach to conversational materials is to treat natural talk as a medium through which the culture operates. Thus, in analyzing how status, race, or storytelling operates in conversation, one learns much about the nature of status, race, or the myths of a culture *in general.*

3. Independently of interest in conversation per se, this kind of analysis has produced, and is producing, a fund of detailed concepts and methods for analyzing any kind of social interaction. Thus conversational materials are an excellent proving ground for developing sociological hardware to analyze social action in everyday life.

4. Finally, many practitioners of phenomenological sociology and ordinary language philosophy are looking at natural conversation as an example of how people "make the world up as they go along." Without being committed to the theories of conversational analysis, they employ it as a preliminary road map of the sorts of events and happenings to be found when people talk with one another. An example of this constitutive tradition has been provided by Ryave's demonstration of how speaker-hearers produce on-the-spot social structures.

We have presented thus far an outline of what conversational analysis is, its potential importance to sociology, and some of its underlying assumptions. Of course, an outline is only an outline. The reader still does not know, in a concrete way, how conversational analysis gets done and what it can do. The best way to solve the "how it gets done" problem is for the reader to do some analysis himself. For this purpose, there is already one good manual on the subject, and, doubtless, others will be forthcoming.[13]

AN ILLUSTRATIVE APPLICATION

For our part, we can do something about the "What can it do?" problem by considering the following excerpt from a natural conversation:

Bob
Really?I haven't seen the Valley on a clear day f'r about four years.   It's jus'so smo:ggy all the time.
       Yeah   It really surprised me becuz y'know   I don't go to L.A. that often so I
John

The talk of Bob and John above overlaps in several places. In fact, it looks more like the base and treble parts of a musical composition than several separate "turns" at talking. Each "tune" is complete and coherent in itself. If we collapse them into two single utterances, they make perfect sense as two things said, one a response to the other. On the other hand, the "notes" of each part (what is being said) are timed to blend, harmonically, with those of the other. Both the timing and content of what Bob says seem to be responsive to the timing and content of what John says, and vice versa.

We will give substance to this musical metaphor in only one way—by looking at why these two speakers stop and start talking. We ask the reader's indulgence as we present some rather technical concepts and observations. We promise a sociological payoff from these if the reader perseveres:

POSSIBLE COMPLETION POINTS

In timing his music to that of others, the classical musician has an advantage that conversationalists do not; he knows what other people are going to play before they play it. Listeners make up for this "handicap" by estimating the exact point at which a speaker may be through. When such "possible completion points" arrive, a listener may start talking immediately without, for instance, waiting to make sure his estimate is correct. This strategy explains why John comes in (that is, starts to talk) at four points in Bob's talk with virtually no acoustic silence in between:

BOB: 1. Really?
BOB: 2. Really? I haven't seen the valley on a clear day f'r about four years.
BOB: 3. Really? I haven't seen the valley on a clear day f'r about four years. It's jus' so smo:ggy.
BOB: 4. Really? I haven't seen the valley on a clear day f'r about four years. It's jus' so smo:ggy all the time.

"NEXTEDNESS"

Of course, in estimating when another is finished you can be wrong, as John was. What do you do then? The situation has an analogy in daily life. Imagine being in the middle of doing something when another demand is made on you that takes precedence. For instance, you are talking to somebody or ironing clothes and the phone rings. How much more of the first activity do you do before abandoning it in favor of this "next" activity? In conversation, when someone is in the middle of saying something and discovers he needs to stop talking, he does not necessarily stop that instant. Depending on context he may complete some "unit" such as a word, phrase, or sentence before lapsing into silence.

In the case of John's first "false start," the following procedure seems to be employed:

1. Assume that you are in the middle of saying something and discovers you are "talking out of turn."
2. If you can complete your turn "quickly" relative to what the other person is probably going to say, talk till the end of your "short" turn and stop.

Notice that John starts talking after Bob says, "Really?" It becomes clear that Bob was not done at the point he continues with "Really? I———." At that point John has already uttered "Y———," but he does not go silent. He completes "Yeah," which is a one-word answer to John's question, "Really?" and thus a complete turn at talk. Then he stops.

As bad luck would have it, John makes a similar wrong estimate after Bob says, "It's jus' so smog:gy." He starts talking again and gets to "Y'k———" when Bob can be heard to continue. In this case John proceeds to the end of one of his favorite phrases, "Y'know," and stops. The analysis of this stopping point is more complex. Let it suffice to point out that "Y'know" can often act as a "lead-in", similar to the standardized musical introductions to popular songs. Lead-ins like "Y'know" are good things to be saying when someone else is simultaneously talking. They are relatively content-free and are not part of what you mainly want to say. If your partner doesn't hear them, he hasn't missed much. In light of these considerations, let's describe John's pause and restart as a procedure:

1. When you start an utterance with a lead-in and discover your partner is not through talking, complete the lead-in and wait for the partner to finish.
2. After that, you can restart, as John did, with the actual "tune" (with your main sentence).

PROJECTIBLE UTTERANCES

One way to show another person you "know his mind," and thus display intimacy, is to listen to him until what he is saying becomes "projectible"—until you think you know what he is going to say. At that point, you reply to what he would have said, had you let him finish. Insofar as not just anyone could have anticipated him like that, you show him, in a small way, how well you know his mind.

Of course, this strategy is hardly limited to intimates; it is done by strangers all the time. If the reader heard John say, "It really sur———," and knew the context, he might be able to project it to "It really surprised me," which would be a complete utterance. In fact, Bob starts talking right after John completes "It really sur———."

Not only do members project future talk and use their forecasting to decide when to start talking; they also use it to decide when to stop talking. If you find yourself talking at the same time as another, often you can "see the end" of his remark coming. At that point you pause in your own remark to "make room" for him to finish his remark—and then proceed again. Notice that John starts to say, "It really surprised me becuz——," stops talking right in the middle of his sentence, pauses, and then continues. Why? Notice he stops at the point Bob has said, "It's jus' so smog:——." This is projectible to "It's jus' so smo:ggy," which is a complete sentence, and it is at the end of the word "smoggy" that John ends his silence and continues talking.

CONVERSATIONAL STRUCTURE AND PERSONALITY

At this point the reader might be asking the question that has plagued sociology since its inception: So what? While the foregoing observations shed light on the subtleties of turn taking in conversation, they seem terribly technical and picky. Yet their import may not be. The data presented here were part of a study by Candice West, in which male-male conversations were compared with male-female conversations for patterns of dominance and deference.[14] This conversation happens to be between two males. Notice that, unlike Bob, *every single time* (in this case four times) John starts talking, he does so only when he has good reasons to think his partner is done. Also notice that each time John discovers that he is talking at the same time as Bob (in this case three times), he proceeds to an appropriate stopping point and stops—instead of finishing what he was saying. Thus we have seven potential cases of deference within a flurry of talk that lasted perhaps two or three seconds. It may be tiny patterns like these that we intuitively notice when we notice that someone is timid or that, in some funny way, one person seems to dominate another. Conversational analysis has shown that people are capable of such sensitive reactions to each other—if not more sensitive.

In analyzing turn taking in ways like these, we carry out Simmel's program of locating the social forms within which personalities and types of relationships express themselves in numberless ways. In fact, it may be such forms that make personalities or relationships visible within a society to begin with.

For a more dramatic example of what conversational analysis is capable of doing, we urge the reader to consult case study H by Alan Ryave, "The Art of Talking About the World" (page 418). He analyzes some of the not so obvious reasons people discuss the world with each other while conversing, and draw the morals and messages they do from these discussions. He also shows how concern with seemingly technical details can yield surprising sociological and practical payoffs.

Yet despite our efforts to "sell" readers on the importance of earthly detail, there are undoubtedly still those who prefer the sky. To them the phenomenological approach to social science which follows may strike a more sympathetic chord. For it sprang from a philosopher's concern with the nature of personal, human knowledge.

Classical Phenomenology

There is a growing distrust in America of secondhand knowledge, knowledge that comes from television, newspapers, college professors, religious authorities—anywhere but from you and your personal experience. Presidents and government agencies are being revealed as liars; scientists are becoming "prostitutes" enlisted in the service of private companies and government agencies who hire them to prove some preestablished point. Textbooks used in public schools for years are now all but laughable. In them are found distorted versions of history and human events which accentuate certain persons, groups, and values while omitting or recasting the contributions of minorities and women, the defeats and atrocities of our country, and the alternative values and life styles that have characterized our national growth.

In such an atmosphere, a recommendation of Edmund Husserl, the founder of phenomenology, might fall on sympathetic ears: Return to personal knowledge.[15] At some point in your life, attempt to rebuild your conception of the world by rejecting, totally, all forms of authority. Reject the authority of the book, the teacher, the scientist and his science, the group and its spokesmen. Most particularly, reject the authority of the past and your knowledge of the world that comes from the past. In the past you accepted countless beliefs about the world from countless sources, for countless reasons, most of which you no longer know. It is now time to start anew, to build up a conception of the world that is consciously put together to be satisfying to *you.*

Anyone confronted with such a proposal might immediately object: "But I cannot possibly do this. I am a creature of my culture, bound by social habits of thought and feeling. I have a past, full of experiences that left their imprints on my mind, which in turn inexorably control my current perceptions and beliefs. In short, I am not a transcendental being but someone located in relative time and space. One cannot transcend one's own relative existence."

To all that Husserl would calmly reply, "Of course—throw out all of those assumptions as well. For they were handed to you in college, partially validated by your own experience in ways you do not know, and are now accepted as dogma." All this occurred "before," before the conscious rebuilding of personal knowledge that is now before us. Husserl wants a fresh start, a start that would allow a person to discover whether, indeed, he is bound in all the ways which psychology and sociology insists that he is.

But what about this new journey? Having proposed that it be undertaken, and being unimpressed with the claim that it cannot be accomplished, Husserl must see it as a real possibility. But even the claim that we *could* attempt such undertaking Husserl regarded as a prejudice that must be abandoned before we can proceed. As he puts it:

> At the beginning, . . . to presuppose even the possibility of that goal would be prejudice. We are satisfied to discover the goal and nature of science by submerging ourselves in scientific activity.[16]

In short, he wants us simply to start the journey, not to evaluate its potential for success or estimate what it could or could not come to. The nature and goal of the journey are to be determined by one method only, by undertaking it. What the rebuilding of one's own knowledge can or will come to will be revealed in and through the rebuilding itself. All prior assessments, pro and con, are rather like the philosopher's knowledge of a food he has never tasted.

For this reason, Husserl should not be read as describing facts about a world common to us all. He is not a scientist reporting findings which can be verified by anyone. He is reporting on his journey and the view of the world produced in and through it. The reader will not find this world unless he embarks on a similar journey. If one refuses to undertake such a journey, then his world will continue to be the one he has been putting together by making a patchwork quilt out of diverse knowledge that comes his way through leading a life in society. He will accept the world and its knowledge naively as reality and its structure. To him Husserl will have little that is comprehensible or credible to say. Instead, Husserl will appear to be merely another man among men, engaging in some kind of personal introspection.

Secondly, even for those who attempt to reconstruct their store of knowledge, Husserl's journey may not be their journey. What he comes to accept as self-evident may not be what they decide upon as such. For is not the key to the enterprise the pursuit of personal knowledge? As he writes: "We thus everyone for himself and in himself, with the decision to disregard all our knowledge."[17] For this reason, what follows is what we previously said not follow: We are about to depict someone else's epistemological journey we who have never taken one. We must look in from the outside and try to life and reality as it appeared to Husserl through his reconstruction of knowledge.

it is all very well to embark on the task of rejecting previous knowledge, technique is needed. Specifically, how do you do it? Husserl does it variety of epochés (as a verb: to stop, check, or hold).[18] He suspends concerning any and all assumptions and beliefs that came into existence this new journey. He does not deny them; he does not affirm them. puts them "out of play" or "in brackets." This reduces these assumptions to "stuff." They are no longer true or false to him but just "there," as a here.

cessfully employed this epoché, we reenter a state of deliberate which:

... We now have neither knowledge that is valid for us nor a world that exists for us. We can no longer say that the world is real—a belief that is natural enough in our ordinary experience—; instead, it merely makes a claim to reality. This skepticism also applies to other selves, so that we rightly should not speak communicatively, that is, in the plural. Other people and animals are, of course, given to me only through sensory experience. Since I have questioned the validity of the latter I cannot avail myself of it here. With the loss of other minds I lose, of course, all forms of sociability and culture. In short, the entire concrete world ceases to have reality for me and becomes, instead, mere appearance.[19]

But the goal is to build up new knowledge. So some source of evidence that we indubitably trust must be found. What science calls data are merely codified collections of beliefs and conclusions. Can we find a source of data upon which to base judgments that is not itself merely one or several of our judgments?

Such a source of evidence reveals itself after we have successfully carried out the epoché in a radical fashion—carried it out so thoroughly that no nook or cranny of our prior knowledge system escapes it. What the epoché does is to allow us to experience our entire life somewhat as we experience an innocent walk down the street.[20] We are making no assumptions, nor are we "affirming" or "denying" anything. For walking down the street does not demand all that much theorizing. If assumptions, emotions, and other aspects of subjective life are thought of as *activities* which occur in and through consciousness, the reader can begin to get some idea of what presents itself to a person who successfully performs the epoché. The chair is just "there." The conviction that it is a chair, insofar as a conviction arises in consciousness, is just "there" also. It becomes [the chair is there] just happened. The existence of the chair becomes ⁘[the existence of the chair].[21] In effect you become a mere observer of your own convictions, beliefs, and interpretations, which come and go in consciousness like a passing parade. They become mere phenomena. In this radical sense you no longer believe in your beliefs—none of them, not a single one. Again, it must be emphasized that this is something that *happens* to you when you perform the epoché. It is not a description of what beliefs "really are" (that is, mere "subjective interpretations").

What is left after all this? What is left is everything!—the real world, yourself as a particular individual, your convictions, other people's convictions, dirty garbage cans—everything. But it is all transformed. It is all phenomena which you, the radical philosopher, have successfully disengaged yourself from and can merely observe, in ideal scientific fashion. Reality is no longer real, it is a phenomenon. The horse that is seen while daydreaming becomes "the dreamlike horse." The horse seen in the meadow becomes "the horse that comes off as real." Every conceivable aspect of life and creation remains available, not as something known, but as something observed to happen in consciousness. One can say that you have entered a new world, or one can be tenaciously mundane and say that you have transformed the way the world presents itself to you. In either case, here is the domain of evidence we sought, the domain prior to any and all beliefs. Phenomenologists speak of the epoché as the phenomenological "reduction" and speak of the world as naively lived in, as having been "reduced" to a new domain—a new world. It is this new domain that is the subject matter of phenomenology—the domain that will be talked about, scrutinized, and described. We have reached this domain in classic fashion, by finding a way to "look at it":

> I reach the ultimate experiential and cognitive perspective thinkable. In it I become the disinterested spectator of my natural and worldly ego and its life.[22]

PHENOMENOLOGICAL ANALYSIS

Now the genesis of the term *phenomenology* can be seen. Phenomenology would be the study of the "phenomena" that are made available to a person by using the epoché. Now comes the rebuilding. With this domain taken as given and furnishing a source of evidence, new judgments can proceed.[23]

What is the situation here? In particular, what is the structure of this domain? The answer is, like all of Gaul, divided into three parts. First there is an "I," a subject. But this is not the "I" as I used to conceive of myself—that is, as one human being and one consciousness that are merely part of a larger world. Rather, the "I" conceived as a particular person, the real world itself, and the world of fantasy are now *mere parts* of the gigantic display we have called phenomena. These show up as complex interconnected acts of belief, conviction, and recognition within consciousness. The newly intuited "I" (which Husserl calls the transcendental ego), the subject of *all* experience, can never be an object of experience in the ordinary sense.

Second, there are acts of conscious life; there is remembering, discovering, knowing, fearing, imagining, liking. Third, there are objects of consciousness—appointments that are remembered, people who are feared, foods that are like. In short, the phenomenological domain has a tripartite structure consisting of "ego," "cogitations," and "cogitatum." The fact that consciousness is always consciousness of something was called by Husserl the *intentional* structure of consciousness.

Having just arrived in this new domain without a travel brochure, what can we do here? Well, we can "look" at things. In particular, one of us can look at one of those "somethings" that are the objects of consciousness. On the desk in front of me stands a red cube, one inch square. In the natural attitude I perceive this object as unquestionably real. I perform the phenomenological reduction(s). The cube retains all of its qualities. *The cube as-it-presents-itself-to-me* is still "real," "red," and "one inch square." But now these qualities are addressed as phenomena. Suppose I am interested in finding out about the common qualities of all cubes. "Imaginary cubes" are "phenomena" as well with all the rights and privileges possessed by real cubes. So I imagine such a cube and ones like it. I transform this imagined object in my fancy by successively varying its features—

its color, its size, the material of which it is made, its perspective, its surroundings and background, and so on. During this "free-fantasy variation," it might be noticed that all cubes have certain characteristics in common, such as being corporeal and having six square sides. Without them, "whatever it is" in my consciousness is simply not a "cube" for me. These essential characteristics Husserl calls the "essence" or "eidos" of the cube.

The search for such essences and the methods of finding and analyzing them constitute the "eidetic approach" in phenomenology. Through these methods Husserl found unique ways to deal with what is ordinarily called "the problem of meaning."

Strangely enough, in the eidetic approach we seem to have an analogy to geometry. Geometry is an eidetical science in the sense that it deals with the relationships between *possible* shapes and figures. Insofar as any possible figure obeys the laws of geometry, any real figure must satisfy these laws (to an approximate extent) as well. Thus geometry discovers things about real objects only indirectly, by considering their ideal equivalents. Similarly, by examining the common features of anything I can imagine as a cube, I discover the features common to all possible cubes. Of course, these need not be the same as those spoken of in geometry. For now I am dealing with conscious experience. Independently of the laws of geometry something might very well come off to me as a cube. And if it does, it is a cube, at least within the realm of consciousness. The more important question becomes: In finding the common features of the cubes of my imagination, have I not found features that would be present in any cube-as-it-appears-to-me on the street or on my desk? In short, in examining the ideal and the possible, have I not found features of the "real" as well?

Let us not be too hasty in answering yes. I have been playing fast and loose with words by using terms like "the object cube" as if they corresponded to *phenomena*, as described previously.[24] So let me go back to my desk for the moment and gaze upon this object. As I do this, moving from side to side, around to the back, blinking my eyes and looking again, I do indeed seem to be confronted with a unitary object. But why? More pointedly, how? How are these varieties of appearances, succeeding one another in internal time, often interrupted, often interspersed with other appearances, constituted in my consciousness as "the cube from the front," "the cube from the back," "the cube again, after I blinked," and so on? In short, how is conscious experience *synthesized* into unitary objects? Here we have another vital and important question of phenomenology, to be asked in connection with any kind of "object" whatsoever, be that object a cube or a person called Howard Schwartz.

At this point we must leave Husserl, for space does not permit delving into the intricacies of his journey and his science. In fact, the previous presentation itself would be considered extremely loose and theatrical by bona fide phenomenologists. Our intention was to give the reader some idea of what Husserlian phenomenology was all about. And now we must confess that there are other phenomenologies—phenomenologies equally intricate and, alas, equally different from one another as they are from Husserl's original concept.

Among the best known are the approaches developed by Maurice Merleau-Ponty, Martin Heidegger, and, in the social sciences, Alfred Schutz.[25]

PHENOMENOLOGICAL "DATA" VERSUS SCIENTIFIC DATA

It should be noted that in this search for personal, yet certain, knowledge, the sciences have been killed off, in particular the social sciences, for a rather important reason. While the ideal of the sciences is to accept nothing without evidence, science as it is now practiced proceeds on an enormous amount of intersubjective trust. Most of what I learn through science is based on written symbolizations of what other people have supposedly seen and heard. I read about them in written texts, I hear other people tell me about them. I translate their words into what I take to be the "facts" on the basis of a culturally learned symbol system that is common to us all "for all practical purposes." When I do research myself, my whole approach to the subject, including what I take for granted and what I feel I must find out for myself, is based in countless ways on prior scientific information which I have accepted and trusted.

In contrast, the phenomenological method has led me to "transcendental subjectivity." I have been led there, paradoxically, by my search for certainty, by my unwillingness to trust anything that was not given to me immediately in experience. I find that I *must* describe and examine my "own" consciousness, because this is the only domain that is available to me without trusting others or accepting prior beliefs. There is simply no other place to go. In this sense it is too bad I have to speak of "subjectivity," since hidden within that term are all kinds of presuppositions about "minds" and "personal experience," all of which have been abandoned. In ordinary science, complex abstractions (often mathematical) are built up over time by many different people and interpreted in accordance with social conventions and cultural sign systems. These are regarded as the hard facts upon which to base judgments. The immediate "stuff" of my own experience, on the other hand, is regarded as subjective, undependable, and "soft." Strangely enough, the evidence that is most immediately available to me is taken to be undependable. Yet evidence that requires a great amount of trust on my part and is quite far removed from my experience is socially sanctioned as the definitive criterion for valid knowledge.

THE RELATIONSHIP BETWEEN CLASSICAL PHENOMENOLOGY AND PHENOMENOLOGICAL SOCIOLOGY

The reader may be familiar with a social scientific discipline called "phenomenological sociology." This is a peculiar discipline in exactly the way

Husserl's phenomenology is peculiar. For many years, everyone granted that such a discipline was being practiced. Yet nobody—neither practitioners nor spectators—could figure out exactly what this discipline was, how it was being practiced, or what its results were or could be. In effect, everybody knew that "it" existed, but nobody was sure what "it" was.

The previous pages constituted an admirable exhibit of this. No such radical introspective program is evident in the work of current phenomenological sociologists.

There is good reason for this. As Heap and Roth point out, the phenomenological reduction(s) produce or reveal a domain of inquiry in which social life as we ordinarily think of it does not exist.[26] Husserlian phenomenology does and must study a completely different "subject matter" than is found in sociology, a subject matter from which roles, occupations, motives, and meanings are conspicuously absent. Either such phenomena do not exist at all in the domain of phenomenology, or they are so completely transformed by the reductions as to be unrecognizable, in the sense that there are no simple correspondences between the "roles" found by Husserl and those spoken of by either professional sociologists or the man on the street.

Here we once again have the obstinate problem encountered first with Durkheim and the positivists and later with qualitative sociology. How does one abandon one's naive trust in the world and society without simultaneously (cognitively) taking leave of that entire world and society as well?

It is from this standpoint that we can understand what phenomenological sociology is, what its relations to Husserlian phenomenology is, and why these relations came about. Most phenomenological sociologists attempt in one way or another to straddle the fence by doing only a "little sociology" so as to be able to practice a recognizable social science. In particular, they abandon some of their trust in the world and its objects and knowledge, but not so much as to make it impossible for them to see and recognize what sociologists call "meanings," "roles," or "interpretive procedures." There are several ways in which this can be done.

PHENOMENOLOGY AS A BAG OF THEORETICAL TRICKS

One use for phenomenology in sociology is found simply by borrowing concepts, ideas, and methods of phenomenologists and employing them, in altered form, in sociological research. With this goal in mind one indeed finds a rich fund of ideas in the phenomenological literature with which to talk and think about people and the study of them. Among the most popular of these ideas which have been borrowed and altered in various ways are:

1. The idea of eidetic science or a science of the possible.
2. Intentionality and intentional analysis.
3. Cognitive attitudes, their manipulation and significance.

4. Personal knowledge and the structure of intersubjective trust.
5. Distinguishing the act of awareness from the subject of awareness; from the object of awareness.

PHENOMENOLOGY AS A NEW SYMBOLIC INTERACTIONISM

Many sociologists have employed the dictum "Back to the things themselves" or "Start from ongoing conscious experience," not as a call to radical reflection, but as a new justification for what we called "subjectivism" in chapter 1. They take the position that the world of sociology is not a real world but a world of abstractions. Jobs, friendships, or money would not exist as such without the thinking and interpretations of people who sustain and create them. Consequently, it is illegitimate for sociologists to take, as their basic data, abstractions based on these original abstractions—i.e., their own definitions of jobs, friendships, or money. The primary data of sociology should be the subjective experience of other individuals or of oneself. By subjective experience, this perspective means the things which are ordinarily taken to be subjective experience, things like "interpretations," "opinions," "attitudes," "selective perception," and "points of view." In contrast to symbolic interaction, no assumption need be made regarding the relationship between subjective experience and objective social actions. It is merely asserted that subjective experience, as understood above, is more basic and real than the codifications of it which sociologists call data.

REFLEXIVE SOCIOLOGY

Phenomenology has been used to sensitize us to the importance of the subject (as analyst) as the source of all knowledge. Reflexive sociology pays close heed to the practices by which researchers create, display, and defend the existence of facts about the social world. Complete research here involves showing how the researcher's activities generated the world and the facts he finds and vice versa.

PHENOMENOLOGIES OF THE SOCIAL WORLD

Some practitioners, notably Schutz and his followers, have attempted to give a philosophical analysis of the social world along the lines of Husserl's program. They do, indeed, perform reductions, engage in intentional analysis, and so on. The purpose of these programs is to clarify such underlying problems as:

1. How is communication possible?
2. In what sense is the social world an intersubjective one, shared by others like ourselves?

In answering these questions they hope to ground sociology, in the sense of explicating its foundations.

A "SCIENCE" OF YOURSELF?

As can be seen from Husserl's presentation, phenomenologists would be most unhappy with a description of their method as a way to "observe oneself." For such a description employs assumptions about people, the real world, and the relation of the former to the latter that phenomenology had to abandon to even get started. However, for the reader's conceptual convenience, let us examine the efficacy of the formula "study oneself" independently of its actual or possible relation to what "true" phenomenology is.

Perhaps the largest problem we have encountered in this entire book was that of gaining access to the life-world of individuals. It was this project that we claimed at the outset was somewhat better realized by qualitative than by quantitative methods. But even at the outset we asked a very serious question: can one human being inhabit the life-world of another to any reasonable degree? Jacobs proposed that if the answer was no, sociology might be out of business. This gloomy projection was based on the assumption that to understand social life, one must do so in terms of the life-world of the individuals within it.

Throughout the book an inventory of the problems inherent in this task has been growing. There was the extreme difficulty of knowing the thoughts, strategies, feelings, and other subjective aspects of another person's ongoing conscious life. There was the pseudo-physical problem of "being around" to observe the detailed structure of another's average days, without dipping in at the wrong times and places or altering his daily life in the process. There were the enormous problems inherent in getting others to report on the details of natural situations, details which they usually do not remember, describe, or talk about. In short, it seemed that society was so constructed that it did not allow time out for social scientists. Social scientists simply could not hop around within society collecting information and making observations while the rest of us went about our daily business, as if the social scientist and his motley collection of computers, questionnaires, and ways of living were not even there. Everyday life might be the area of society that is most pernicious in this regard. For, in its innocence, in its "nothing unusual is happening" flavor, it is protected against the intrusion of scientists. Everyday life, like much experience and myth, has a way of presenting a photogenic face to any epistemological intruder who has the temerity to try to capture its nature and essence. It transforms itself into an arena of noteworthy, elegant, technical, sociological activities for its photographers, so that they go away happy. But this picture of life is not the life of those in the picture. Only in getting up and having a cup of coffee, going down to the office to look over the data, picking up the sleeping bag at the dry cleaners—only in leading an everyday life—can the sociologist truly know its structure and essence. His image of the everyday life of others will ever be a crudely distorted painting whose twisted lines can be justified only in light of the practical requirements of something he calls "science."

In light of all this, a first-person method of sociology would seem to offer enormous practical benefits. After all, you are the constant companion of yourself throughout every minute of the day. It would be like having a trained ethnographer riding on the back of your subjects—an unheard-of situation. Were the events of your life to be scrutinized, remembered, and described, there would be no legal permission to obtain and no interview time and place to schedule. You would be continuously available to yourself for any variety of interrogation that might arise. In short, each person has unprecedented and literally awesome access to his own life-world, both its "inner" and "outer" events, in a way that could never be approached by another.

But it is widely held that there is a dear price to be paid for data obtained in this way. Social scientists generally believe that the data obtained from observing oneself is in principle inferior to those obtained from observing others. This inferiority comes in two parts:

1. Self-observation is intrinsically subject to bias, distortion, deception, value judgments, and the like.
2. There is no way to generalize knowledge about oneself to knowledge about other people or groups of people in society.

Here we can spot a kind of unreasonable paranoia in the scientifically minded as regards first-person methods of any kind. On the one hand, as scientists we are admonished to look upon others with objectivity—to avoid bias, distortion, interpretation, and the rest. On the other hand, it is said to be difficult or impossible to maintain this same attitude when observing ourselves. Is there really vastly less potential for distortion when a conservative Republican social scientist examines the writings of Fidel Castro than when he examines his own political attitudes? If we ask what specifically makes it possible for an individual to adopt an objective posture, and what subverts this posture, we find many empirical studies devoted to just this question. While these studies identify numerous and varied factors, there is no evidence that these factors divide neatly into two categories so that those favoring objectivity tend to operate when observing others and those inhibiting it tend to come into play when observing oneself. From this point of view, associating self-observation with bias in some general way must be looked upon as a prejudice. If the objective attitude is possible *at all*, it must be possible with respect to oneself.

But what about the second point? How can one generalize from oneself to society at large? The differences among personalities, subcultures, and societies are celebrated attributes of social life for qualitative sociology. In light of these differences, how can one possibly know about others by knowing about oneself? But here again one finds a paranoid reaction. Positivists and other "hardheads" are interested not in individual differences but in general patterns. It is for this reason that they concern themselves with aggregates of people, with averages and trends, and with contrasts and comparisons. On the other hand, the search for general patterns is based on the assumption that people everywhere are very much alike—that their so-called individual thoughts are but a kaleidoscopic combination of the concepts of society, that their particular speech is but an application of the rules of syntax common to the whole culture, and so forth. It would seem that the more universal, lawlike, and "scientific" a general pattern is, the less it matters which particular individual one looks at in order to find it. To use a biological analogy, "if you know how to look, when you've seen one eye, you've seen them all."

It is awesome to conceive of the entire history of civilization as having been crystallized in one's own being—in the way one thinks about the world, in one's desires, emotions, activities. This leads us to take our own life experiences, and those of others close to us, extremely seriously in trying to understand ordinary conversation, social stratification, or, for that matter, the nature of human beings. There are many in our profession who have been doing this for a long time, informally, and dressing up their hunches with experiments, data, and other rituals of the times. Phenomenology has given us perhaps its greatest gift by providing a warrant for doing this formally and without apology.

Notes

1. If Harold Garfinkel is the father of ethnomethodology, the late Harvey Sacks was the father of conversational analysis. Unfortunately few of his works were published in his lifetime. However, through the efforts of his students and colleagues, more and more are being made available in published form.
2. We are quick to point out that those who engage in conversational analysis have a different conception of language than do others and thus do not necessarily agree with this list.
3. More specifically, modern transformational linguistics regards knowledge of such things as the rules of grammar as part of the "competence" of an ideal speaker-hearer. This ideal person is a fantasy of the linguist, who endows him or her with the capabilities needed to speak in or understand the language, as the linguist conceives of it. Any actual talkers and listeners may depart from the competence of the ideal speaker-hearer in various ways. They may also depart from using the language as the linguist conceives of it in various ways. This is what is meant by the distinction between "competence" and "performance."
4. Sacks and his colleagues have given this idea a general formulation in their concept of "context-free-context-sensitive" rules. Context-free rules of conversation are those that members regard as relevant to any particular conversation, somewhat independently of the particular circumstances involved. However, by reference to these rules, conversationalists find ways to tailor their talk to their particular situation via suitable adaptations, alterations, and adjustments of the context-free rules.
5. For example, one party may have rights to interrupt the other at the point where he sees what the other is "talking about." Thus the interruption itself and its accompanying utterance show how well one understands the other.
6. As a theoretical assumption, this is held by many but by no means all linguists. However, as a way of working, many more linguists do research "as if" they held this assumption.

7. Matthew Speier, *How to Observe Face-to-Face Communication: A Sociological Introduction*, Pacific Palisades, Calif.: Goodyear, 1973, p. 188.

8. For a discussion of question-answer chains and chaining, see Speier, *Face-to-Face Communication*, pp. 97–100.

9. For a detailed example of the excavation form of analysis, see our previous treatment in chapter 12 of the story "The baby cried. The mommy picked it up."

10. See Emmanuel Schegloff, "Notes on a Conversational Practice: Formulating Place," in *Studies in Interaction*, ed. by David Sudnow, New York: Free Press, 1972.

11. For a summary of some of this work, see Emmanuel Schegloff, "Sequencing in Conversational Openings," *American Anthropologist* 70, no. 6 (1968): 1075–1095.

12. Of special interest under this heading is the recent work of David Sudnow, who is treating the production of speech as (among other things) a problem of producing sequences of sound. He considers such issues as timing, pace, and rhythm as vital to this production.

13. See Speier, *Face-to-Face Communication*.

14. Candice West, "Communicating Gender: A Study of Dominance and Control in Conversation," Ph.D. dissertation, University of California at Santa Barbara, forthcoming.

15. The presentation given here is a theatrical adaptation of the first essay of Husserl's *Cartesian Meditations* and of a similar essay published under the title *The Paris Lectures*. Our purpose in departing from a strict presentation was to present some of Husserl's ideas in what might be an initially more understandable form. For a literal version of these essays, see Edmund Husserl, *Cartesian Meditations*, The Hague: Martinus Nijhoff, 1970, and *The Paris Lectures*, The Hague: Martinus Nijhoff, 1970.

16. Husserl, *The Paris Lectures*, pp. 5–6.

17. Ibid.

18. There is much controversy among scholars concerning how many "epochés" there are, what they are, and how they are interrelated. One well-known scheme divides them into three types:

    1. The phenomenological epoché by which one suspends judgment about the existence of the world and/or the objects within it.
    2. The transcendental epoché by which one suspends the belief in one's own existence as a particular human being.
    3. The eidetic reduction through which one progresses from the world of the actual to the world of the possible.

    For the purpose of our exposition, we ignore these details and deliberately leave the term *epoché* (or "reduction") ambiguous, often speaking as if there were but one epoché.

    After performing these reductions or epochés, one's assumptions, strictly speaking, continue to be true or false to him. He believes some of them and doubts others. The difference is that one no longer "believes in the belief," so to speak. One merely *notices* that he believes an assumption as one notices, say, that the telephone is black.

19. Husserl, *The Paris Lectures*, p. 7.

20. This analogy is a dangerous one. Assume that at various points in one's daily life he is

not explicitly noticing, categorizing, or thinking about his surroundings. How could he recall them? What are we asking our readers to remember? If one is unaware of things, can he simultaneously be aware of his unawareness? Can he remember both *that* he was unaware and *how* he was unaware?

21. When a phenomenologist suspends belief in the existence of something this is often indicated by putting it within brackets to depict the fact that it becomes, for the phenomenologist, a phenomenon—something that happens in consciousness. In our example the chair, its location, and *its existence* become a panorama of interrelated events within consciousness.

22. Husserl, *The Paris Lectures*, p. 15.

23. The manner in which phenomenological knowledge is built up cannot really be described as the making of "judgments." However, this technical subject is beyond the scope of this text.

24. In a recent critique of phenomenology, Heap focuses upon just this point. He shows how phenomenologists employ the nomenclatures and structures of a particular natural language (which they know) as searchlights for examining the nature and structure of conscious experience. What they end up with, therefore, may have more to do with the structure of language than with the structure of consciousness. For a full exposition of this idea, see James L. Heap, "Eidos, Sociology, and Language: A Criticism of Free-Phantasy Variation," paper read at the Annual Meetings of the Eastern Sociological Association, Boston, 1975.

25. For those whose appetites have been whetted, we suggest the following sources in which the concrete outlines of these approaches are brought out more explicitly. Edmund Husserl: *Ideas: General Introduction to Pure Phenomenology*, New York: Collier Books, 1962; *The Crises of European Sciences and Transcendental Phenomenology*, Evanston, Ill.: Northwestern University Press, 1970; *Cartesian Meditations*, The Hague: Martinus Nijhoff, 1970. Maurice Merleau-Ponty, *The Phenomenology of Perception*, London: Routledge and Kegan Paul, 1962; *The Primacy of Perception*, Evanston, Ill.: Northwestern University Press, 1964; *Signs*, Evanston, Ill.: Northwestern University Press, 1964; *The Visible and the Invisible*, Evanston, Ill.: Northwestern University Press, 1969. Martin Heidegger, *Being and Time*, New York: Harper and Row, 1962; *An Introduction to Metaphysics*, Garden City, N.Y.: Doubleday Anchor, 1961.

26. James L. Heap and Philip A. Roth, "On Phenomenological Sociology," *American Sociological Review* 38 (June 1973): 354–367.

Part VII

Formal Sociology and Reality Reconstruction: What's Wrong with Them?

We have devoted this book to the theoretical and methodological concerns of qualitative sociology. Early in the work we formulated the problem of "retrieving the world." The question was asked: Do we recover or create the social world we live in, or is it the product of some combination of the two?" Is there an external, objective, knowable, social world that can be retrieved through the diligent application of the scientific method, or is reality, as Pirandello suggests, a matter of "Right you are, if you think you are"? Can a study of the external objective world of "social facts" produce any real sociological understanding, or must its products be only a monumental gloss or, worse still, a fraud? Do we need to establish the reality of a social scene in order to acquire sociological understanding, and if so, is there any way to do this?

Then there is the question "How is society possible?" The answer would seem to rest upon the discovery of patterns of human behaviour and experience which somehow cause our species to create such things as nation states, world religions, and hamburger stands.

In the next chapter we attempt to examine these questions from a much broader perspective than has thusfar been possible. Can qualitative sociology help us to understand, in some significant way, how and why we both create social worlds and become subjugated to them?

CHAPTER 14

Patterns? What Patterns?

In previous chapters we mentioned the sociologist's concern with the question "How is society possible?" We have also noted throughout the book a number of sociologies and their various assumptions, understandings, and methodological procedures as they relate to ways in which researchers have sought to answer this question. Clearly, all of these sociologies are very different from one another, and one might rightfully ask, "What is it that they hold sufficiently in common that makes us call them all sociology, and their practitioners sociologists?"

Actually, many not only have very little in common but hold mutually exclusive sets of assumptions. As a matter of fact, when the smoke clears, there seems to be little more left than the proverbial "opposable thumb." If "human nature" has been reduced to one common denominator, sociology has two: (1) the claim to being scientific and (2) the claim that social life is patterned life.

We have already dealt to some extent with the claim to science. Let us now consider the question of patterns. The notion that social life is patterned life has taken many forms. For example, patterns have been dealt with in terms of norms and values, class, SES (socioeconomic status), roles, tacit understandings, and background expectancies. That society ultimately rests upon patterns is a given. Structuralists demonstrate their existence with respect to what happens when the patterns shift or change abruptly—namely, social disorganization, disequilibrium, and alienation result. Symbolic interactionists assume patterns with the notion of the "generalized other," that is, learning to see yourself in the light of the expectations of others and adjusting your behavior accordingly. Many formal sociologists also deal in patterns of behavior. Simmel was concerned with the forms of sociations. Goffman treats social occasions as replete with rules for appropriate conduct, where their violations constitute "situational improprieties." Ethnomethodologists concern themselves with patterns as well. However, they don't assume that situational patterns are the result of preexisting sets of rules and norms. Instead, they are concerned with how people display to one another that rules and norms exist in a given situation. Here it is held that people create for one another a sense of social structure using certain "methods." For them, patterns emerge because these "methods" have certain invariant characteristics. For example, they are always "reflexive," they are always "indexical," and so on.

In short, there is a long and honored commitment in sociology to the notion that, however it turns out that society is possible, it would be impossible without patterns. This basic tenet rests not only upon the conceptual models that sociologists use to explain the existence and perpetuation of society but also upon their almost universal commitment to science. Science, even in the loose sense of the word, is (whatever else it might be) a search for regularities and generalizations. Without this, scientists could not realize their goal of a systematic and parsimonious explanation of the social world.

Notwithstanding all of the above, there are some sociologists whose main concern is not with "How is society possible?" but with "How are patterns possible?" Their disconcerting query is "Patterns? What patterns?" Upon what reasonable basis could such a question rely? Actually, there are as many well-established traditions for contending that there are no universal social patterns as there are for accepting patterns as givens. In order to understand these conflicting traditions it is necessary to go back to the problem of social order and its traditional solutions in sociological theory. For it was here that these controversies and traditions were spawned.

The Problem of Social Order

In all societies humans incessantly organize themselves in complicated ways so as to produce institutions, cooperative activities, and social structures, which take on a life and stability of their own. One seems to be able to talk about the goals, motives, functions, and characteristics of societies, institutions, and other social totalities as if they existed objectively and independently of the persons who make them up. Individuals seem to arrange themselves in such cooperative arrangements in the manner of organs of the body, parts of a machine, or other symbiotic metaphors. This they do despite the enormous difficulty of establishing such arrangements. Typically, there are no systems analysts to plan the way persons are to be organized. In many cases there is little conscious planning involved at all. Individuals making up these groups are, or can be, heterogeneous in all sorts of ways. They can speak different languages, come from different cultures, have different values and goals, possess different and incompatible skills and abilities, and vary over a wide range of intelligence. More often than not, it is not in the personal interest of the individual to perform the tasks required of him by the group. These and many other classically cited circumstances could be catalogued. But still humans keep doing it again and again: arranging themselves in intricate symbiotic relations to form living entities larger than themselves. The question presents itself: How and why do they continuously manage to do so?

This has become a classical question, with generations of literature devoted to answers. In sociology this question gave us Emile Durkheim, and the so-called order theories of society, of which the theories of Talcott Parsons are often cited as a prototype. While these theories attack the problem of social organization in a wide variety of ways, they all have in common the fact that on the social psychological level they require certain uniformities in persons' "heads": People participate in a "collective conscience"; they all have common norms, natural language, goals, values, reciprocal role frames, and so forth. The particular uniformities depend on the theory. The basic functions of the uniformities in these theories are to explain the presence of intersubjectivity—of a world of social realities known in common.

A simple definition of intersubjectivity might be formulated as follows: First there are behaviors, events, and other factlike phenomena on the ground floor. Then there are individual "persons" that inhabit the world; and finally, there is, for each person, a stream of accompanying interpretations, beliefs, and perceptions of the fact-world that parallel them on the second floor. Intersubjectivity (or a world known in common) results when the potentially distinct meaning structures in a group of individual persons turn out to be the same, become the same over time, or mesh in certain ways.

The similarities and convergence of meaning structures make good intuitive sense. The only question is: How can this happen? First, there is the old chestnut "Everyone is different" or "We are all individuals." If we take this folk wisdom literally, how does it happen that in so many ways we are presumed to be the same—that is, we fit this or that category of persons who in turn make sense of the world in this or that typical way? There have been many attempts to resolve this apparent dilemma. The general idea is to shift the problem of explaining patterned behavior to the problem of explaining patterned meanings. We behave in patterned ways, in part because we hold common meanings. The nasty question then presents itself: Where do common meanings come from? How is it possible that these various uniformities in persons' heads exist and persist?

Socialization and the Problem of Social Order

The most accepted and revered answer to this employs the concept of socialization. When used in conjunction with order theories, the concept is formulated by first dichotomizing the individual and the society (or social group). The individual, as a new initiate or recruit, is then confronted with society. Henceforth, these two beings commence to interact. As noted in various ways and senses by Durkheim and others, the society and its structure are always "already there" for the individual who will be, or is, within it. New recruits to a social totality, be it a whole society, a business firm, or a street gang, are confronted with an already established, organized, functioning social order—or so the theories say. Whether the recruit are babies, immigrants, or new employees, their situations are similar in one respect. There is an enormous asymmetry of power between the recruit and the social order. The overwhelming probabilities are that when individual and social group interact, the social group can and will affect the structure of the individual far more than he can or will affect its structure.

The classical objection to this perspective is that it overestimates the extent of consensus and homogeneity within social totalities. In particular, if there is to be significant changes within such a totality while its order still remains "orderly," the explanation for this must be found in the dynamics and structure of the totality itself or its relationship with the outside—with other groups, necessary resources, recruitment pools, and so forth. For if a preexisting social order is stable in its organization, and if relations with the "outside" are stable, there is no reason for any significant changes in the structure to occur, except over long periods of time. But this flies in the face of many historical and contemporary observations of significant, sweeping, and quickly occurring changes in societies and groups, under seemingly stable conditions.

This leads us to a consideration of conflict theory. Unfortunately, conflict theorists are subject to many of the same criticisms as the proponents of order theory. For example, they also see socialization as the coercive molding of individuals' attitudes, values, and the rest, by agents of the established order. However, instead of finding this to be one of society's services, they consider it as a complaint. Further analysis locates this conspiratorial process with the inevitable attempts of elites or other social classes to sustain the subjugation of others.

Indeed, it is hard to find a conception and use of socialization which are divorced from the assumptions of conflict or order models of society. For these notions have deep and strong roots within our common sense. If we reflect upon what our parents were about, what school was like, or what it felt like to be a "new man" at an employment site, it is easy to find the assumptions about socialization made by these theories to be intuitively reasonable. These assumptions may be given as follows:

1. The dichotomizing of the individual on the one hand, and the agents and resources of the society on the other.
2. The assumption of the existence of a stable, factlike social structure that "recruits" are socialized to fit into.
3. The asymmetric allocation of power in the interaction between recruit and social order, which allows treating the former's influence upon the latter as negligible.

The substitution in conflict theory of "Ruling ideas are ruling-class ideas," for the "collective conscience" as a means of resolving the problem of intersubjectivity does little to lift the fog. The one is certainly as big a "gloss" as the other. Furthermore, whether conflict is the natural state of affairs, and the life of man is indeed "solitary, nasty, brutish, and short," or order is the natural state of society, the question remains (apart from one's political philosophy): How is society possible? or Where did all those patterns come from?

Contemporary examples of the enigma surrounding patterns, with respect to the convergence of meanings and ideas, often border on the bizarre. For example, both conflict and order theorists would be hard-pressed to explain why the founding fathers and mothers of the Symbionese Liberation Army (SLA) were the sons and daughters of doctors, ministers, or, in the case of Patty Hearst, one of the wealthiest and most influential men in the country. Furthermore, why were they trying to destroy the very social order, class, and lifestyle that they and their parents were so much a part of? It would seem that such persons should have been busy maintaining the social equilibrium. The idea of ruling ideas being ruling class ideas takes a peculiar turn here as well. Patty Hearst and William Randolph Hearst seem to be at odds on about every conceivable issue. The ideas held by SLA members who were the children of doctors and ministers also showed a very poor fit to those held by their parents or others of their social class.

The reader should realize that these critiques of theories of socialization, while they seem extremely reasonable to us, are in no way binding upon the adherents and proponents of these models. The reader might wonder why. The reason is straightforward. Conflict and order models are usually formulated as closed systems. As such they can be used to explain anything, including the sort of contradictory situations noted above. However, while such theories are capable of explaining everything, they explain nothing at all, at least not in such a way that the explanation itself can be subject to science's "empirical disproof." As Kuhn notes, any general collection of ideas, assumptions, and observation procedures cannot be disproved, because it is not a specific hypothesis but a device which generates numerous hypotheses.[1] Second, any concrete hypotheses which are derived from the theory can be disproved without disproving the theory. We will not go into the many reasons for this here.

What does it all come to? We've hit on it before in our discussion of the general problem of transcending models. If you believe, you believe; if you don't, you don't. The authors don't. However, we feel that in the final analysis, this is not "only" a matter of opinion. There is, as indicated above, plenty of reason for skepticism if one is an optimist, and outright pessimism if one is not.

Qualitative Sociologists: Do They Make Better Patterns?

If the reader, along with us, is not a believer when it comes to the previous story about organized behaviors, common meanings, and socialization, has he found any solace in this book? Has he found any theoretical stories that depart from the classical perspective sufficiently to give hope for patterns? In other words, has qualitative sociology anything new and convincing to offer in the search for how society is possible?

It would seem that symbolic interaction, and reality reconstruction in general, explain social organization not by common or converging meanings, but by patterns in people's heads. In social situations individuals negotiate meaning structures between them, they take one another into account, and they create and display images of themselves and others. All this results in organized behavior on the microscopic level which somehow concatenates into social organization on the macroscopic level. For this view of society to become the basis for a science, the structure of the ongoing interpretive processes of individuals and its relation to behaviors would have to be discovered and described. We have seen some of the difficulties of this program. We currently have neither an adequate vocabulary with which to describe ongoing conscious life nor a scientific methodology for tapping into it. Further, it is not clear that concepts like "motives," "meanings," and "morals" literally describe the interpretive process itself so much as they represent the prevalent idiom by which members (lay and professional) talk about and account for coherence and sensibility in our actions and those of others.

If one is not taken with the reality reconstructionists' explanation for the origin of patterns, he can find in formal sociology a new suggestion: that we abandon the distinction between objectivity and subjectivity. That is, we should not separate the "real" order that exists in social dealings among humans from the interpretations and accounts of that order produced by society's members (including sociologists). It is not that the perception of order on the part of individuals is the *cause* of the emergence and existence of actual order in social behavior. Rather, the two are so inextricably intertwined that they should be collapsed into one problem. Garfinkel went so far as to equate the two kinds of "order":

> In exactly the ways in which a setting is organized, it *consists* of methods whereby its members are provided with accounts of the setting as countable, storyable, proverbial, comparable, picturable, representable—i.e., accountable events.[2]

If our goal was to make a "science" based on this proposal, we would be faced with the following task: We would have to discover and verify the patterns in the ways members went about seeing, describing, discovering, and displaying order and "reality" in any and all situations and behaviors, which, as theorists, we wanted to dub with the label "social." Having found these regularities in the sense-making activity of humans, we would have accounted, at least in part, for the externalities, rationalities, organization, and objectivity that humans everywhere incessantly find themselves confronted with in the course of their daily lives.

Yet, in order to do this, we would have to know what knowledge and competence was, from a sociological point of view. For Garfinkel's orientation, like others in formal sociology, envisions members as skilled experts practicing their arts and crafts. If symbolic interaction was concerned with retrieving members' points of view, it is probably fair to say that formal sociologists have been mainly concerned with retrieving members' knowledge. But what is knowledge in the first place? The metaphor involved in ideas like "point of view" or "perspective" is curiously geometric. However, the metaphor thus far used in talking of knowledge is outrageously capitalistic. We spoke of background assumptions which members "hold" when they interact with others. We spoke of "stocks" of knowledge which members "possessed," almost as if knowledge were a collection of merchandise that either was or was not in stock in a person's warehouse of skills and memories.

But this is not how these things are given in our experience. *As one engages in action*, in no clear way is he assuming things or using knowledge as one uses a screwdriver. Further, just as members explain and talk about their actions in terms of "motives," "meanings," and "morals," so do they speak in terms of their "assumptions," "beliefs," and "knowledge." In short, the concepts used by formal sociologists to talk about social action are just as much the product of common sense thinking as are the concepts of symbolic interactionists. In both cases, the literal meaning of this talk in terms of ongoing action remains mysterious.

Further, we have already seen the complexities involved in retrieving ongoing subjective experiences and meanings by observation and/or interviewing. But this task is child's play compared to the job of retrieving members' knowledge, using the same resources.

At least members were well acquainted with what we were talking about when we inquired about their "opinions," "attitudes," or "feelings." But they ordinarily do not talk "well" about their "background assumptions," "tacit expectancies," or "interpretive procedures." Their activities and modes of thought must often be changed appreciably before it becomes possible for them to even speak of such things.

On the other hand, endowing others with knowledge and skills on the basis of what they do is fraught with arbitrary prerogatives left to the investigator. By exercising such prerogatives one can start from the same action or actions and infer that its doer possesses a potentially infinite number of different assumptions, expectations, or skills. The methodology behind these inferences, and therefore what distinguishes a good one from a bad one, has yet to be clarified.

In summary, it is currently unclear what knowledge or competence is from a sociological point of view, and therefore how to retrieve it, whether scientifically or otherwise.

All of these problems are compounded even further by the more daring formal sociologists who reject the idea that studying everyday life consists of studying "other people" as they interact within a real world. These sociologists see themselves and their own activities as irreparably part of what they are studying. Science, as ordinarily construed, is abandoned in favor of a transcendental way of learning about social life that collapses "us" and "them," "the real" and "the apparent," or "the subjective" and "the objective." This is all well and good. Yet, as far as we the authors are concerned, no one has come up with a workable way to do this and still answer "How is society possible?" in any meaningful way.

Phenomenology seemed to offer a promising way to do this. Yet there have been many (often famous) phenomenological attempts to account for intersubjectivity.[3] So far, all have failed. Worse yet, there is a growing body of evidence that phenomenological methods themselves use one's mastery of a particular natural language as a resource, and that this colors phenomenological findings in a very untranscendental way.[4]

Ethnomethodology has claimed that any and all methods of seeing and knowing social order have certain "invariant properties" and that these properties can be used to account for social order. Yet others have scanned the world and found no such properties. They claim that these properties are artifacts of ethnomethodology's methods, and that they are neither invariant nor general. There is no ready reply to such criticisms until ethnomethodologists can clarify how it is possible for something to be "there," "general," and "invariant," but not in the sense that it is a real property of a real, social world.[5]

Thus, for both formal sociology and reality reconstruction, their "patterns" are currently in doubt, their programs have up until now not been carried out, and counterexamples and anomalies abound in connection with each.

Given all of this, the reader has basically three choices:

1. He can attempt to do scientific qualitative sociology.
2. He can seek his science of society elsewhere, in yet uncharted theories and methods of studying human beings, their consciousness, and conduct.
3. He can abandon the call to science and embrace the more modest goal of "understanding" or "interpretation."

The reader is doubtless wondering by now, with the recapitulation of these dilemmas: What does it (qualitative sociology, or sociology in general) all come to? This depends upon how you define it, that is, its assumptions, methods, and goals. If the goals are seen to lie in the positivist's dream of recovering some fixed, external, knowable social world of "social facts," in order to be able to explain, predict, and control the world of individuals or groups, then, as things currently stand, sociology doesn't come to much. It is indeed, as Mazur has noted, "the littlest science." In fact, it has yet to generate a single "law" of human behavior, in the sense that the word "law" is applied in the physical sciences. All of this is dealt with by sociology's more optimistic practitioners, by invoking the following save: Of course sociology (one might throw in psychology and anthropology) is the littlest science, it's the newest one. All we need to do is to persevere and our science's cumulative and self-corrective features will ensure our ultimate success in retrieving reality. After all, "all's well that ends well."

As we say, these are the optimists, and not everyone is so optimistic. The pessimists, as we have shown throughout the book, have good grounds, if not for pessimism, then at least for skepticism. It is not clear that a positivist science can succeed in saving sociology. If this is so, the question may rightfully be raised: Should sociology pursue science, either as a goal or as a method, in an effort to (1) establish a social science or (2) acquire sociological understanding? Our answer is implied in the title of the book, *Qualitative Sociology*, and what the reader has by now come to understand this to mean. We see no optimistic signs that qualitative sociology has unearthed the tools that will eventually make a science of society possible, be that science of the phenomenological, ethnomethodological, or symbolic interactionist variety. However, this would not exclude the possibility of achieving sociological understanding. To achieve that, qualitative sociology holds some promise, at least in principle. Nevertheless, it has yet to overcome many of the methodological and theoretical problems discussed throughout the book and especially in the "how to do it" sections.

A Word to Anyone Rarely Suffices

In the final analysis, what we have offered was a discussion of the theoretical and methodological problems of doing qualitative (and by implication quantitative) sociology. This was couched in terms of "What is it?" "How to do it," "Who has done it?" "What have they done?" "What's wrong with it?" and "What has it to offer?" We have made certain observations and recommendations regarding sociological methods, especially qualitative methods. Here, as in most cases, these recommendations will be heeded by some and ignored by others. It is a good bet that guiding this decision will be the reader's prior commitments to, and understandings of, the discipline. This will turn upon his assessment of what sociologists ought to observe and describe, and how and why they can succeed in such an undertaking. As a result, it is unlikely that this book (or any other) will make many converts. It may, however, win some of those who are new initiates to the sociological order, or now occupy the proverbial "uncommitted middle." If so, we shall be content. As for the other souls lost (if we may be allowed to mix a few metaphors and spin a few adages in their graves), it might be said: What shall it profit a man to preach? A word to anyone rarely suffices.

Notes

1. Thomas Kuhn, *The Structure of Scientific Revolutions*, Chicago: University of Chicago Press, 1970.
2. Harold Garfinkel, *Studies in Ethnomethodology*, Englewood Cliffs, N.J.: Prentice-Hall, 1967, p. 34.

3. Of these attempts, the best known (to social scientists) are those of Husserl and Schutz. There is wide opinion that the attempt of Husserl failed, while that of Schutz was not completed, because of his death.

4. For one version of this argument, see James L. Heap, "Eidos, Sociology and Language: A Criticism of Free-Phantasy Variation," paper read at the Annual Meetings of the Eastern Sociological Association, Boston, 1975.

5. For one discussion of this ethnomethodological problem, see Hugh Mehan and Houston Wood, *The Reality of Ethnomethodology*, New York: Wiley Interscience, 1975, pp. 162–176.

Illustrative Case Studies for Book Two

Our general purpose in presenting these case studies is the same as for the previous studies by Jacobs. Although we discussed the process of doing formal sociological research, we did not deal in any detail with its products—with packaging data, information, and conclusions in the form of an article. As illustrative "packages," the following articles are more or less self-contained. They have their own arguments, their own methodological overviews, and their own styles of thought. They should therefore not be read as passages designed to illustrate some point in the text. However, they do illustrate how the general themes of formal sociology get translated into concrete problems and findings. For instance, all of these studies focus on members' skills and competencies rather than their perspectives and points of view; all of them study a major topic of formal sociology in concrete form. By now these topics should not be new to our readers: intersubjectivity, "passing" behavior, practical reasoning, and giving common sense "accounts" of reality. Yet we hope their application to concrete problems, such as treating the mentally retarded or conducting psychotherapy, will render the forthcoming studies both informative and helpful.

CASE STUDY E

The World of the Congenitally Deaf-Blind: Toward the Grounds for Achieving Human Understanding

DAVID GOODE

For a year and a half I conducted an ethnography of a state hospital ward for congenitally deaf-blind, retarded (rubella syndrome) children. I entered this research enterprise as a social scientist but with no particular theoretical or methodological issues in mind. Rather, I let these concerns emerge during the course of the research. I did not know what my involvement with ward personnel or residents would come to in the long run but was motivated by a genuine interest in the interaction of the congenitally deaf-blind with normally seeing-hearing persons. This paper represents one extremely important part of this ethnography.[1]

Ordinarily we take it for granted that we live in an intersubjective world, a world whose physical, social, and psychological aspects are communicated and shared with reasonable accuracy. Yet on this ward there were in a sense two "worlds," one shared by myself and the staff (normal perceivers) and another inhabited by the residents. Indeed, by the very differences in our sense organs,

This research was supported by PSH Grant No. HD04612 NICHD, The Mental Retardation Research Center, UCLA, and No. HD-05540-02, Patterns of Care and the Development of the Retarded. My special thanks for their assistance in guiding my enterprise to Robert B. Edgerton, Harold Garfinkel, Melvin Pollner, and Michael Gaddy. My thanks to Harold Levine for his editorial assistance.

the residents were living and acting in a different perceptual place than I—one in which the reception of audio-visual stimuli had been degraded as a result of a prenatal viral infection. It was decided that only intimate and persistent interactional contact with the residents would be likely to enable me to enter into their world. A major obstacle to such a task stemmed from the variation in perceptual abilities displayed by particular residents; it was not the case that they inhabited a deaf-blind world at large; rather, each exhibited a specific configuration of perceptual/cognitive skills and deficiencies. Consequently, I decided to concentrate on a nine-year-old female resident, Christina (Chris), and spend a number of daily cycles (24-hour periods or longer) with her, sharing "average days" in her "ordinary life." In addition to naturalistic observation of her behavior, I employed videotaping and viewing of normal ward routines and other interactional procedures ("mimicking" and "passive obedience").

My relatively long-term involvement with Chris gave me access to observational data unavailable to medical practitioners, who would see her during relatively short, structured, and "nonordinary" medical examinations. From our interactions and my observations over a period of a few months, I gathered the following information about her perceptual, motor, behavior, and language abilities (see also Goode, 1974a, 1974b, 1975b).

Medical and Behavioral Profile

Medical examination records, developmental assessments, and interviews with the child's mother were used to construct a medical/behavioral profile.

During Chris's prenatal existence, she (the fetus) was subject to an "attack" of a virulent and destructive cyclical virus (rubella). During the second or third week of pregnancy, the rubella virus entered her mother's bloodstream and attacked the sensitive, rapidly multiplying cells of the embryo (rubella embryopathy), causing damage in the forms of hemorrhage, brain lesions, lysis damage to the cochlea, cataract, and so on. As a result, Chris was born with a severe syndrome of multihandicaps (the rubella syndrome) whose sequelae included bilateral çataracts, congenital heart disease (patent ductus and stenosis), functional deafness (the "intactness" of Chris's hearing mechanism has never been established), clinical microcephaly, central nervous system damage (a low-grade diffuse encephalopathy), abnormal behavior patterns, and severe developmental retardation. The degree and nature of Chris's multihandicaps have been difficult to assess since medical procedures for making such determinations are usually designed for normally perceiving and communicating persons (see Goode, 1974a). At the age of five Chris was diagnosed as legally blind, legally deaf, and mentally retarded and was placed in a state hospital for the retarded.[2]

VISION

Chris was able to orient visually to large objects in her path and would normally "fend" against these by using her right arm. She was also able to inspect objects at a very close range and was observed to eat by bringing the spoon to her right ("good") eye to a distance of perhaps one to two inches, for the apparent purpose of inspecting the food's color and consistency. Chris's visual acuity varied considerably depending on such factors as setting, emotional state, motivation, and quality of visual stimulus. In close face-to-face presentation, she sometimes seemed to be studying my physiognomy.

HEARING

Chris's auditory acuity also seemed to vary considerably. When motivated, she seemed to be able to orient to the sound of my guitar being played at a considerable distance from her, and in a number of "natural experiments" she was observed to "home in" on this sound from distances of more than twenty feet. She loved sound stimulation of all types—especially music, with its regular rhythms and variety of frequencies. She attended to my singing to her or speaking to her in her ear (she used her right ear more than her left and would maneuver herself so that she could turn this ear toward the sound stimulus). It was difficult to assess the amount or quality of sound she was receiving, but several clinicians concurred with my belief that she *received* a variety of sounds but had problems in "processing" the sound as normal hearers do.

TOUCH

Chris was extremely touch oriented. She used her tongue as her primary organ for perception whenever possible and would lick anything within her reach. I learned to conceive of this activity as Chris's way of asking, "What is it?" although repetitive licking of smooth surfaces (apparently for purposes of sensory gratification) was also observed. Chris was a "ticklish" person and usually responded to being touched all over her body by laughter (sometimes, as her teacher noted, this laughter may have been defensive—that is, an effort to curtail interaction rather than to fully participate in it). While she could easily distinguish between textures by touching objects with her hands, her sense of heat and cold seemed depressed relative to mine.

AUTOSTIMULATORY BEHAVIORS

Light and sound for Chris were often a matter of self-gratification and self-stimulation, that is, compared with normal youngsters of her age. She exhibited many autostimulatory behaviors, including "finger-flicking" (autophotic behavior), repetitive licking of smooth surfaces (autotactual behavior), rocking, and head swinging (autokinesthetic behaviors). We developed a number of games (described below) based upon her pursuit of perceptual gratification. It is important to note that Chris's use of her senses was not purely autostimulatory. She also used them in goal-directed activities (for example, finding a toy, building up some objects so that she could climb on them and get her ear closer to the radio in the day room, looking for the ward door, fending against objects, finding the guitar sound). The autostimulatoy use of her senses was, however, a characteristic and conspicuous feature of her behavior.

GROSS MOTOR BEHAVIOR

Chris enjoyed gross body activities of all kinds and was in this regard a fairly active deaf-blind child. She loved to interact with me by having me pull her up while she simultaneously grasped my neck with her arms and my waist with her legs. From this rather common position between parent and child, she would engage in a variety of head-swinging and head-rocking movements. Often I would bounce her and throw her into the air, and she seemed to enjoy her helplessness—abandoning herself to the sensations these activities provided for her. Common to most of these activities was genital contact and rubbing. Chris also characteristically rocked her body to music and in autophotic reactions to strong light sources (such as an overhead fluorescent light). In a life described as one of "scattered achievements," Chris's most significant ones were in the areas of gross body interaction and in her use of the sensation of touch.

SELF-HELP SKILLS

At the time of my study Chris was almost totally untrained in all areas of self-maintenance other than eating. Urination and defecation "accidents" often occurred during the course of data collection (and in a gesture of good faith vis-à-vis the staff, I took care of these). Chris was unable to dress, wash, bathe, or walk without assistance. Teaching such skills to the congenitally deaf-blind-retarded is a very time-consuming and difficult enterprise, and given the paucity of staff in general and trained staff in particular, Chris had never mastered these skills. Of course, she could engage in elaborate behavior schemes in order to gratify herself (she could get up without any cue, go to the music room, and let herself in), but she could not master the skills and rationale behind toileting and dressing. By hospital regulations these matters were usually taken care of as a matter of routine. Chris was cleaned and dressed whether she participated voluntarily or resisted violently.

COMMUNICATION SKILLS

Chris did not seem to share any awareness of what a linguistic symbol was. However, this is not to say that she did not regularly communicate with me and with staff. To communicate her wishes, she used gross physical actions which relied heavily on "background expectancies" (Garfinkel, 1967)—for example, walking into the dining area and sitting at her table ("I'm hungry") or going to the ward door and waiting ("I want to go out"). She also used gross body movements to indicate that I should continue or cease some of our activities (for example, grabbing my arm and simulating a strumming movement apparently to indicate her desire that I continue playing, or pushing me away to indicate her wish to terminate interaction). At one point her language teacher claimed to have gotten her to say the word "more," and I have seen her use the gestural symbol (Signing Exact English symbol) for "more" when I rigorously structured the activity and coaxed her by reward/punishment conditioning. It is doubtful that Chris had any grasp of the symbolic character of these actions. At the time of this writing Chris can receive a modified version of the "food" sign but has not been seen to use the sign expressively.

GENERAL BEHAVIOR SUMMARY

When I was present in the research setting and interacting with her, Chris appeared to possess an inquisitive and active intelligence, housed in an extremely flawed body. She was oriented toward getting physical and perceptual satisfaction in any way she could. She displayed her dissatisfaction and liked to have things "her own way." She actively pursued contact with adults and was socially sophisticated relative to other areas. At an educational conference at the hospital, one administrator commented on her ability to "wrap me around her little finger" and, in some sense, this observation was true. Granting all the difficulties in making a determination of this kind, I felt that Chris's primary difficulties stemmed from her lack of intact audio-visual perceptual fields, upon which we build our systems of symbolic communication and organize our practical interactional activities. She had never had an intact behavior model and did not understand our "recipes," "motivational relevancies" (Schutz, 1970), and courses of rational activity. This is not to say that Chris was an acultural being, only that in many areas of her life the skills we find manifested by normal cultural members were not evident.

Meeting Chris on Her "Own Grounds"

The staff's institutional rationale and its concomitant "purposes at hand" (maintenance and teaching) were directly related to the particular features they formulated about the residents. I came to understand that I could take advantage of my institutional position (my not being charged with maintenance and teaching) to pursue a particularly interesting line of research. I could examine the staff's construction of certain of the residents' behaviors as retarded (that is, as faulted) to discover the logical underpinnings behind their system of practical reasoning—a system which produced behavior-displays-as-faulted. By doing this I hoped that I might also be able to unmask some of the skills the children exhibited—skills which the remedial stance of the staff was "hiding." This enterprise would entail establishing intersubjectivity with the residents on a somewhat different basis from that of the staff. I wanted to avoid—as Jean Itard failed to do with the "Wild Boy," Victoire of Aveyron[3]—seeing the children as tabulae rasae, as deficient cultural beings who needed cultural repair work done on them. While they were culturally deficient, to make them seeable and describable in only those terms was to ignore a whole storehouse of skills which they had developed but which were not specifically cultural achievements. Mannoni (1972) rightly noted that if Itard had accompanied Victoire to live in the Caune Woods (where Victoire had survived for eight or nine years as a youngster), Itard's storehouse of cultural knowledge would have been quite beside the point. Stripped naked, battling the elements, *he would have had to learn from Victoire in order to survive* (the woods creatures' "purpose at hand"). In that setting an understanding of Victoire's world, using only the stock of knowledge at hand in eighteenth-century French culture, would have been maladaptive. Metaphorically speaking, I decided to "go to the woods." To make this journey I had to locate where I was.

I saw my task as an attempt to establish intersubjectivity with Chris in more or less her "own terms." The problem was how to recognize what her "own terms" were. First I attempted to approximate her perceptual environment by the simultaneous use of ear stops and blindfolds. I discovered that I was quick to make the necessary adaptations to the features of the visual/auditory world I already took for granted. This is not to say that the blindfolds and ear plugs did not cause me a lot of trouble, that they did not render me essentially helpless without the aid of a sighted and/or hearing person. Rather, the cognitive categories I already possessed allowed me to be deaf and blind in a fashion which bore little resemblance to the *congenital* deaf-blindness of the residents. There was no simple technology by which I could accomplish my purpose—any procedures would have to be accompanied by a "willing suspension of belief." It seemed impossible to bridge this gap between our worlds and the consciousness interior to each. My "world" was thrust into relief by Chris's, and I started to perceive it as perceptual biological mechanisms accompanied by rules for their use—that is, a relatively coherent gestalt of seeing-hearing beliefs and practices which allowed me to produce a stock of practical knowledge about my life-world. This body of knowledge had taken on a *sui generis* character, since the activities I had been taught to realize were the same activities by which the knowledge was "validated." The knowledge was Castaneda's "description," it was a perceptual "bubble" (von Uexkull, 1934) in which I was trapped. On the level of discourse, I had been experiencing a natural language version of my phenomenology, reified but kept alive by the activities which comprised *doing* my phenomenology. It was a bubble I had to burst in order to discover Chris's "own terms."

Obviously Chris did not share the staff's evaluation of her behaviors. The construal of these behaviors as deficient was clearly an interpretation of our seeing-hearing world view. I thought I could begin my task of willing suspension of belief by attempting to separate the evaluative from the descriptive components in my accounts of Chris's actions. This pursuit was manifested in the following field notes:

> Watching Chris walk it was clear that her arm movements were spastic, her gait wide, and her movements and balance awkward. She also did not seem to walk purposively—that is, she would walk a few steps, stop, bend over or stare into the sun, run, twist around, laugh, sit down, get up, walk, etc. *She seemed to enjoy the physical sensations involved in her admittedly "abnormal" techniques for ambulation.* While it is clear that she does not walk correctly, it is equally clear that it is only incorrect with respect to the dominant seer-hearer culture's version of walking—a version, by virtue of her impaired sensors, almost inaccessible to her. Most importantly, while watching her we were occasioned to ask ourselves, "Who is getting more from the activity of walking, Chris or us?" It is no great cognitive accomplishment, no mystery, no great analytic task to watch Chris walk (eat, play, excrete, and so on) and to find her actions "faulted," "wrong," "abnormal," and so forth. Any competent cultural member (Garfinkel and Sacks, 1970)—that is, anyone who understands the rational and socially sanctioned set of activities for which walking (eating, playing, excreting) is an appropriate name could and would find Chris walking abnormally. The question is, how *should* we evaluate what we see? Is it "wrong" to act abnormally, and does one's detection of "abnormal" or "faulted" behavior require that remedial work be done upon the child to correct the observed flaws? These questions seem particularly important when asked with regard to persons who, in very obvious ways, do not share the perceptual cognitive world that occasions "normal" walking.

Evaluations ("fault finding"—see note 5) seemed inextricably involved in my simple descriptions, my direct experience of Chris's behavior. To find a "way out" of these evaluations-embedded-in-experience, I had to turn not to a cognitive reshuffling of categories, but to a change in my practical activities with the resident. In other words, a suspension of belief could emerge only if I reorganized the material, concrete interaction which Chris and I produced.

I felt I could use certain interactional procedures (changes in my purposes at hand) in order to provide myself with an experiential basis for the kind of understanding I sought. Achieving this understanding was to be my new purpose at hand. I stopped trying to remedy the obvious faults I perceived in Chris and tried instead to intuit, while interacting with her, what purposiveness or rationality her activities might have from her perspective. My first major change in interactional strategy was to allow Chris to organize activities for both of us by *"remaining obediently passive."* On the first occasion I did this, she organized the following activity for us:

> Activity No. 1, or *"MMmmm . . . mmm . . . K . . . h"*
>
> Chris maneuvered me in such a way that she was lying on my lap face up and had me place my hand over her face. By holding my hand she eventually maneuvered it in such a way that my palm was on her mouth and my index finger was on her right ("good") eye. She then indicated to me that she wanted me to tap on her eyelid, by picking my finger up and letting it fall on her eye repeatedly, smiling and laughing when I voluntarily took over this work as my own. (She has also "shown me," by moving my body, that she wanted me to speak in her ear and flick my fingers across her good eye.) While I tapped Chris's eye, she licked and sniffed my palm occasionally and softly hummed seemingly melodic sounds. We *did this* for about ten or fifteen minutes.

I named this activity by the sound Chris produced while doing it, in order to remind myself, even in the reading of my own material, that my purpose was to burst the "bubble." To do this consistently I could not *properly* code my sensory experience of the activity into a natural language (as Chris apparently cannot do) because the "bubble" and the "language" were so intimately related that to sort one from the other would have been a practical impossibility. Thus, in my first encounter with Chris's desired form of interactional activity, I became aware that in my writing about the activity I necessarily transformed what it was she could possibly intend in organizing it as she did. The description I sought to suspend belief in was itself imbedded in the very language I used to formulate my attempt. I realized that *my enterprise was a standing contradiction*, but I was willing to let this be, since to do otherwise would have meant to abandon all attempts to communicate to others what I was discovering. I was in much the same position as the anthropologist trying to code the native's language into his (the anthropologist's) own tongue. I was like Castaneda trying to speak of the world of the sorcerer by employing the language of the layman—admittedly the "old" language left much to be desired in terms of its descriptive power in the "new" world, but it was for him, as it was for me, the only language available.

An interesting example of the use of natural language categories in "making sense" of the residents was the staff's use of the category "play." Resident-initiated activities were considered by staff "play" activities and not particularly relevant to their purposes at hand. Usually these activities merited a smile from the staff or an utterance such as "Cute." There was an interesting parallel between the staff's approach to these and Itard's approach to his walks in the woods with Victoire (seen by Itard as play periods and not relevant to his teaching of the boy except insofar as the walks provided Victoire with relief from the stress of the pedagogical situation). It was not as if Chris hadn't played with ward staff before I arrived on the ward. It was a question of how they, normal seer-hearers, interpreted and categorized her actions and what consequences these interpretations had in formulating the resident as social objects.

Chris quickly expanded our repertoire of activities to include many varieties of bodily exchange and perceptual play. Patterns of the activities were constantly being refined and varied, sometimes in very subtle ways. These activities consisted of *gross body interaction*—swinging, jumping, rocking, running—and generally long-term and repetitive *perceptual playing*. They also included volitional participation in the activities of perception in order to achieve gratification—for example, including such things as having me play with her light reception (as above), singing and jumping from a baritone to falsetto range (which delighted her), or putting my fingers in her ears to rhythmically "stop" sound. When I began to cooperate with her in such pursuits, these activities often culminated in Chris's reaching peak periods of excitement. Sometimes these peaks would result in her urinating and defecating.

I introduced Chris to a small toy electric organ and observed the following:

> Chris would place her left hand on the keys of the organ which produced the lower frequency sounds. She would then engage in two related sets of body movements. One was to move her head and body in a rhythmic rocking motion which brought her right (good) ear closer and farther from the organ sound source. The other set of movements involved her leaning her head back so as to face the overhead light, and swiveling it back and forth, from side to side, accompanying these actions with vibrating her lips (something like the way little children imitate motorcycle sounds but without the vocal component). In both sets of body movements there was an obvious rhythmic quality—such as to suggest the kind of thing seer-hearers do when they are engrossed in the activity of keeping beat to music. In Chris's case, however, there was no clearly available beat to the droning sounds she was producing by holding the organ keys down.

As with Chris's brand of walking, my initial encounter with these behaviors was characterized by my engaging in the "vulgarly available."[4] I "naturally" saw that these behaviors were obstacles which I would have to overcome in my pedagogical enterprise (my initial purpose at hand)—a pedagogy designed to make Chris attend to sound in the "right" way. Once I gave up this remedial stance toward Chris, her alternative treatment of light, sound, and tactile stimulation took on a rational and even intelligent quality.

> I decided to *mimic her actions* in order to gain more direct access to what such activities were providing her. I utilized wax ear stops (placed more securely in the left ear—i.e., Chris has "better" right ear than left ear) and gauzed my left eye with a single layer of lightweight gauze to simulate the scar tissue which covers Chris's left eye. I proceeded to imitate Chris's behaviors at the organ. While the procedure had its obvious inadequacies, with respect to my gaining access to Chris's experience of these activities, I did learn a number of interesting things in this way.
>
> In both sets of body movements *the motion of the head itself gave the experienced sound a beatlike quality, and this was uniquely present by virtue of performing those movements.* In adapting to deficient eyes and ears and their resultant degraded perceptual fields, Chris had developed a way of "doing" hearing, so as to make any long-term and reliable sound source available as a source of music. For example, when Chris was wearing her hearing aid, I would sometimes find her engaging in similar kinds of body movements even though there was no hearable sound source in the

room. This became a clue for me that Chris was probably getting "white sound" (feedback) from her hearing aid. I knew that Chris was able, when presented with appropriately amplified music, to keep "accurate" beat to that music in the fashion described above. I had also found Chris keeping completely inappropriate beat to music while listening to a small transistor radio with low amplification and a small speaker, which was unable to emit bass notes. Put simply, when beat was not a "hearable" feature of the mechanically given sound stimulus, Chris had learned to endow her experience of that sound with that quality.

Rolling the head on the shoulders (the other set of body movements Chris engaged in) was a difficult practice for me to mimic in that Chris's neck muscles were supple and loose in comparison with my own. Her muscles allowed for apparently painless and easy rolling movements, while my own head rolling was somewhat less comfortable. Nevertheless, I discovered that Chris's head rolling provided not only for a beat to the music (which in its performance it does), but also for what one observer called a "light show." By "light show" I mean that the head rolling, which Chris performed with her head leaned back and her eyes facing the overhead fluorescent light, provided an overall effect something like the following: Alternative musical beats, occurring when the head was accelerating from one extreme position to the other, were culminated, when the head came to rest, in either light stimulation (when the head rested on the left shoulder, thus directing her good eye toward the light) or a lack of light stimulation (*when the head rested on the right shoulder, thus interposing her nose between the light source and her good right eye*). Chris was providing her otherwise impoverished perceptual field with a richness her eyes and ears could not give her. She accomplished this by the use of her available and intact bodily resources—her good eye, her nose, her muslces, and her skeletal frame, which provided for the possibility of making such movements. I was, and still am, struck by a certain inventiveness in this activity.

Another excerpt from my field notes is relevant to the present discussion. This was written after a particularly interesting teaching session with Chris (Goode, 1974a). I was trying to demonstrate the use of various music-making toys vis-à-vis the "familiarizing" procedures described by Robbins (1963).

Chris demonstrated skill in *"alternative object readings."* By this I mean that Chris's inability to grasp the intentional meaning and activities for which "triangle" or "rattle" are appropriate glosses—that is, "rattle" or "triangle," as members' glosses for the practices entailed in recognizing, picking up, and shaking a rattle to make rattle sounds or banging a metal triangle with a metal bar so as to produce triangle sounds, allowed her to constitute a rattle as an object which could provide for her a number of alternative experiences. Initially, our play sessions consisted in precisely my attempting to provide for her the "proper" cultural formula—that object X is a rattle and is to be used (in satisfaction of the criteria of a rational course of action) in such and such ways. I would hand her the rattle after demonstrating its use to her by placing the rattle in her hand and placing her hand within my own, then engaging in the appropriate shaking motion. While such demonstrations were successful in that Chris would hold and shake the rattle appropriately and unassisted (for ten seconds or so), she invariably brought the rattle to her right (good) eye or mouthed it. She would bring it within two inches of her eye with the apparent purpose of determining what it could visually supply for her (parts of the rattle were metal and reflected the fluorescent light in the room). This visual examination would be of short duration (less than fifteen seconds). Of the longest duration, often lasting till I would interrupt her somewhat intense involvement, was her use of the rattle as an object with which she could obtain various forms of stimulation in and about the mouth. Parts of the rattle were employed as tongue thumper or lip thumper, licked inside and outside the mouth, rubbed against the front teeth, banged against the front teeth, pushed against the cheek, and so on. Characteristically, when Chris was through with or had exhausted the immediately present and interesting possibilities of the rattle, she would drop it with no concern as to where it fell, its breakability, or its future uses. While such actions were easily accessible as "problems" with regard to teaching Chris to use objects appropriately (similar behavior was observed with regard to many objects), I was occasioned to ask myself: Who is getting maximum mileage out of the rattle? Is it we, who use it singularly and for specific purposes, or Chris, who uses it in a variety of ways? Let's put it another way. What Chris's not knowing how to use a rattle might mean is problematic. Her not knowing disqualifies her from membership in the category of persons who know how to use a rattle. However, it also *qualifies* her as a member of a category of persons who, by virtue of their not knowing how to use a rattle, do things with it which are inaccessible to persons who "know" its proper use. *The superordinate ranking of our use of the rattle, on the basis that we realize its intended purpose by our actions, constitutes the "ground" for the pejorative figure "Chris does not use the rattle appropriately."*

It is quite reasonable, given Chris's deficient eyes and ears, that she should place rattles or triangles or paper or fingers in her mouth. The tactility of the relatively sensitive tissue of the lips and tongue, as well as the ability of the teeth to conduct vibration, make her mouth the organ around which she can successfully organize reliable perceptual activities. Her adaptations to her perceptual handicaps have allowed her to become an "expert" in the use of the mouth as an organ of primary perception (something like the use of the mouth by young infants). From this perspective, her behavior is available to normal seer-hearers as an alternative set of mouth perceptual practices against which our mouth perceptions are deficient versions of her more active pursuits. Yet most of her mouthings are inaccessible to the competent cultural member. Chris will put almost anything into her mouth which does not frighten her. For example, she will not mouth a lit match, does not like toothpaste or a toothbrush, but would undoubtedly try to lick a broken piece of glass or the porcelain parts of toilets if given an opportunity to do so. The researcher was not able to adopt this stance toward objects—I was unable to overcome the culturally engrained notion that "something bad" would happen to me were I to lick a window, the floor, and so on.

My initial reading of these observations provided me with two general categories of findings. One concerned the reasoning embedded in my (and the staff's) "fault finding procedures"[5] with the residents, and one concerned the rationality or purposiveness (from Chris's point of view) behind these same behaviors. It was not as if Chris's behaviors, or the meaning ascribed to them, existed apart from the procedures and circumstances by and in which she was apprehended. Her behaviors were "rational" *to me,* "faulted" *to the staff,* and this multifacetedness of Chris was an important finding. As a material object, Chris's "horizons" were open. Like her rattle, she could be seen as multifaceted, or she could be discovered to be singularly "dumb."

With regard to Chris's purposiveness, she was basically self-seeking, hedonistic, and amoral in her interactions. She would often rub her genitals against me or pantomime her (our?) recognized "behavior display" to denote a rocking or swinging activity. She did not seem to care whether I was getting pleasure from the activity. Instead she focused on structuring the interaction so that she could get as much of what she inwardly recognized as "good feelings," though I really don't "know" what these words index in terms of her experience. This seemed quite understandable to me since, in terms of her life on the ward, Chris did not live a life particularly filled with gratification—especially when she was interacting with others. However, left to herself, she was quick to provide herself, through varieties of autostimulatory behaviors, with experiences which she apparently enjoyed. Generally she occupied a powerless and frustrating position in many of her interactions and did not have the cognitive equipment (concepts, language, logic) through which she could rationalize (understand). She could only accept or reject, and on rare occasions "puzzle." She did not have the physical capability to aggress or, for that matter, to even defend herself against "attack." Compliance with sometimes not understood pulls and pushes from staff was characteristic. When staff could not force compliance (for example, when her language teacher could not get her to make the sound "Mmm"), she seemed to sit in a sort of dull passivity. Other times she seemed to be puzzling—that is, trying to "code" what it was I was trying to do into some understanding or feeling she could deal with—what a program administrator called her interior "language" system. Generally when she initiated interaction it was to seek as much pleasure as she could, however she could. We often index such a behavior pattern by the term "infantile," but Chris was no infant. She was nine years old and had lived long enough to have gained some sophistication in achieving her pleasure-seeking activities.

Within the limits of hospital routine, I cooperated with her in achieving her goals. I became a sort of "superplaymate"—perhaps (with the possible exception of her father) the only one in her life she had ever had. While there were a number of sympathetic and loving custodians and teachers in her life, the institutional definition of their relationships to Chris prevented them from simply cooperating with her. From time to time I did observe activities in which the staff's role was precisely to be Chris's playmate (for example when it was hot out and they would sprinkle the residents with a hose, or when they took the residents to the pool to "swim"), and on these occasions the staff and residents seemed to enjoy themselves immensely. By the end of my stay on the ward I had become a little sad about the way in which the institutional and medical "contexting" of the children seemed to victimize the staff as well as the children.[6] An even sadder thought was the impossibility of ever changing this situation under the present approach in the fields of human servicing.

By employing the kind of procedures I have described above, I felt as if I had discovered in Chris the "internal contradictions" by which she was propelled into relation with others and by which she could be particularly distinguished from other social beings (Mao, 1971). This was evident in my concluding remarks on Chris's rattle activities.

> Perhaps the most interesting feature of Chris's mouth perceptual practices is the way in which they can be seen as illustrating how *she is both wise and deficient in how she constitutes objects and experiences the world.* I described her alternative object reading of the rattle and I noted how Chris used the rattle for three general purposes: what she could make seeable with it; what she could make hearable with it; and what she could provide tactually with it. I claimed that her not grasping the intentional meaning of the object allowed her to get, in some sense, more out of the rattle than *members* who attend to the rattle singularly and employ it in satisfaction of a set of rational guides for use. The "kicker" here is that, seemingly, the very thing which allows her to get more mileage out of the rattle (her visually and auditorally deficient body and her development of perceptual practices appropriate to such a body) is that very same thing which delimits her experience of the world as it is composed for us and by us—as a world of intentional meanings. For Chris, *objects can only be sources of perceptual stimulation of the sorts outlined above.* When I watched her "do her thing," it was with both joy and sorrow that I appreciated what I was seeing. *Her blindness and her deafness constituted her strongest asset as well as her greatest deficiency.* They sometimes provided her with incredibly intense enjoyment of the simplest things. At other times they were a source of "troubles" as equally intense.

My abilities to see and hear allowed me to engage in the practices by which the culturally defined objects and activities of my world were realized. These abilities allowed me to experience certain pleasures as well as pains. Obviously, Chris did not comply with culturally prescribed courses of rational activity. Yet in a most generic sense, she seemed to conduct herself quite rationally. Perhaps she could not give her hedonistic pursuits names like "self-realization," "the pursuit of personal power," or "transcendence," but that she was a pleasure-seeking creature made her quite understandable to me. In this most basic enterprise, we were in basic agreement. We just used different technologies to accomplish our goal.

Concluding Remarks

All creatures, that is, all subjectivities, seek, in their own terms, to fulfill needs and to gratify themselves. They do not do this in any haphazard fashion. Certain needs must be met before others (this is Maslow's insight), and in Chris's case survival-related needs were almost exclusively taken care of for her by others. Next in her "motivational" hierarchy were emotional and perceptual gratification, and in this regard she was not dissimilar to other humans. She differed primarily in the forms in which these needs would be met. Many of the rational activities of our culture are built upon these very motivational projects. But the specification of these enterprises into culturally acceptable forms is not what defines our humanity to ourselves or to others. If we learn to believe this, then we have stopped one of our basic self-deceptions and have moved away from a view of man which raises us above other creatures—which affirms our presence here as an "emergent" phenomenon. We are not "better" than other creatures. We are "different." I was not "better" than Chris. I was, in many ways, "different."

Given this view, what is to be made of my personal attempt to share a world with a very different human being? What can we learn from this attempt, and what is its future use? In this regard there are several positions to take. One can "believe in" the phenomenon of intersubjectivity; one can take it as possible that human beings "really" or "in fact" can, and do, share their worlds. Starting from there, my experiences can be seen as providing technical resources and interactional methods for accomplishing this goal—for "starting with two worlds and (to a greater or less extent) making them into one." Insofar as the methods and their results are taken to be valid, the further question can be asked: How is it possible for two worlds to become one in the course of intimate human interaction? That is, are there species-specific characteristics, activities, or aspects of our common "habitats" which make this accomplishment possible? If so, what are they?

Another kind of lesson that might be drawn from my experiences with Chris proceed from a different perspective. In this approach to the text, either one does not accept the "real" possibility of intersubjectivity or one is not interested in discovering whether what we take to be a common world *is* a common world in actual fact. Instead the question is "How do people start out with the feeling of being cut off from each other and together achieve the mutual feeling of being in touch with each other in the same world?" For example, Schutz, among others, has described some of the working assumptions that constitute people's sense of being in touch with each other. The previous ethnographic field notes can be read as my attempts (and those of Chris) to find ways of being, such that our interaction could be characterized in part, by the kinds of working assumptions about which Schutz has written. That is, we progressively developed common schemes of communication, congruent practical relevancies, mutually defined things to do in the world, and so forth. But even if it is the *sense* of a shared world we achieved, the question can still be asked: How is it possible for human beings to accomplish this?

These perspectives are not necessarily mutually exclusive, but from either of them intersubjectivity becomes a *practical and empirical issue*—an issue for which, it is hoped, this paper has provided some initial technical resources. By utilizing procedures appropriate to the particular setting in which ethnography is conducted, field researchers can collect data from which the procedures for constituting intersubjectivity can be made objects for analysis.

Notes

1. In the spirit of this text, designed to deal with issues of field method and procedure, this article focuses almost exclusively upon the interactional strategies used in collecting ethnographic *data*. Conspicuously absent are analyses of these procedures—that is, conclusions about how my involvement with the deaf-blind allowed me to produce findings about the nature of human intersubjectivity. At least two modes of analysis are suggested in my concluding remarks. I plan to publish analyses of the data along these lines as well as with regard to more ethological concerns.

2. If the reader finds that this writing is "very scientific," he should bear in mind that the work was motivated by very human concerns. Foremost among these was my desire to improve the life situation of both deaf-blind resident and normally perceiving staff. The staff regarded their charges as prospective cultural converts. Much like the religious missionaries of the eighteenth and nineteenth centuries, they attempted conversion without any true appreciation of the "natives' culture," and this had the consequence of creating confusion and frustration for both residents and staff. While there was no easy solution to this problem, clearly attempts had to be made to understand the deaf-blind "in their own terms." This present writing tells of such an attempt with a particular resident. In some sense I have tried to discover Chris as a creature whose existence is comparable to my own. This was a strong motive for the work. But it must be made clear that very human interests often lead to problems which must be dealt with technically and rigorously. This can be true whether the objects of analysis are atoms or persons. Readers concerned with the application of my approach in actual programming for the deaf-blind are referred to Goode and Gaddy (1976).

3. The work of Jean Itard (an eighteenth-century teacher of deaf-mutes) with Victoire of Aveyron (a "wolf boy," or child raised in the woods) was, in various ways, quite instructive during the course of my research, even though Chris was a product of a humanly ordered world (home, schools, and hospital), while Victoire was not.

4. Harold Garfinkel, personal communication, 1974.

5. "Fault-finding procedures" is a phrase suggested by Dr. Harold Garfinkel (personal communication, 1974). I have adopted the phrase (not Dr. Garfinkel's sense of it) to refer to a structure of practical reasoning in which the deaf-blind retarded are found to be faulted with respect to some setting occasioned normative criterion of action. While the specific flaws located will vary from setting to setting (for example, a child can be found to be an incompetent eater at lunch, or an incompetent test subject for normal audiometric examination procedures, or an incompetent ambulator in walking from the ward to the classroom, and so on), the *form* of the reasoning—that is, the judging of the child as deficient with respect to a normative criterion of behavior or action—is invariant from setting to setting. The ethnography of the ward indicated that staff (and other normals) also engaged in "asset-finding procedures" which, in similar fashion to the faulting practices, find the child as competent with respect to some "normal" behavioral capacity. Both asset and fault finding are suggested as possibly basic structures of practical reasoning in that all settings are seen to produce "their cast of local heroes and villains" (Dr. Melvin Pollner, personal communication, 1975). For a more detailed discussion of these matters, see Goode, 1975*b*.

6. Toward the end of my stay on the ward the staff began to resent my presence and complained that my playing with Chris was interfering with her programming. I feel

that at least part of this resentment stemmed from my relatively enviable position—that is, I could play with Chris and not be responsible for her training and maintenance. I began to notice that when staff were allowed to simply play with the residents (for examples, when they took them to the pool or to the trampoline), both staff and residents seemed to enjoy themselves a great deal. "Play" was that time in hospital routine when the normative rules and goals for interacting with the children could be suspended and the staff were afforded the opportunity to experience the residents in nonideologically defined activity. Play, activity, for the sake of itself, transcended the institutional goals of remedialization and provided for the staff a time when they could "meet the residents on their own grounds."

References

Garfinkel, H.
  1967 Studies in Ethnomethodology. Englewood, N.J.: Prentice-Hall.
Garfinkel, H., and H. Sacks
  1970 "On the Formal Structures of Practical Actions." In J. C. McKinney and E. A. Tiryakian (eds.), Theoretical Sociology: Perspectives and Development, Appleton-Century-Crofts.
Goode, D.
  1974a "Some Aspects of Interaction Among Congenitally Deaf-Blind and Normal Persons." Working Paper No. 1. Unpublished paper. Mental Retardation Research Center, UCLA Medical Center.
  1974b "What Shall We Do with the Rubella Children?" Unpublished paper. Mental Retardation Research Center, UCLA Medical Center.
  1975a "Some Aspects of Embodied Activity on a Deaf-Blind Ward in a State Hospital." Unpublished paper. Mental Retardation Research Center, UCLA Medical Center.
  1975b "Towards the Grounds for Achieving Intersubjectivity: An Initial Report from a Ward for the Congenitally Deaf-Blind, Retarded." Department of Sociology and Mental Retardation Research Center, UCLA.
Goode, D., and M. P. Gaddy
  1976 "Ascertaining Choice with Alingual, Deaf-Blind and Retarded Clients." Mental Retardation 14, no. 6.
Mannoni, O.
  1972 "Itard and His Savage." New Left Review 74 (July/August).
Mao Tse-tung
  1971 "On Contradiction" (originally written 1937). In Selected Readings from the Works of Mao Tse tung. Peking: Foreign Language Press.
Robbins, N.
  1963 "Auditory Training in the Perkins Deaf-Blind Department." Perkins School Publication no. 23.
Schutz, A.
  1970 On Phenomenology and Social Relations. Chicago: University of Chicago Press.
von Uexkull, J.
  1934 "A Stroll Through the Worlds of Animal and Men." In C. Schiller and K. Lashley (eds.), Instinctive Behavior. New York: International Universities Press.

CASE STUDY F

Imitation and Competence: A Study of Retarded Adults

ARNE T. BJAANES

In the course of making observations of the mentally retarded, one area of behavior, that of imitation, came to interest me considerably. The function of imitation in the coping behavior of the retarded has not been dealt with in the literature. The question posed here is this: Is imitation part of the general process of getting by in the world of the mentally normal, or is it undertaken in order to get along with a particular person? If a "normal" person does some activity differently than a retarded person, does the retarded person imitate the normal person in order to get along with him and reduce conflict? If this is so, he could do this while retaining his own understandings of the activity and how it is properly done. Alternately, does he imitate the normal person as a strategy for correcting his own "faulty" understandings about how to do things in the world? If this were so, the retarded person might adopt the new way of doing the activity with others in the future. Further, he might change his own understandings of how the activity is properly done.

To gain insight into this problem, an experiment was designed, in much the same manner as some of the experiments of Garfinkel and his students.[1] The objective was to take a situation in which a retarded individual was known to have an understanding which is shared and known by others, and to deliberately violate that common knowledge or understanding.

A second goal of this experiment was to see how far the retarded person would go in doing imitating behavior. The basic question being approached here was: To what extent will the retardate use another's set of rules and understandings to

Unpublished paper, reprinted with the permission of Arne T. Bjaanes.

determine his own behavior? To examine this, the experiment was divided into two sections. In the first part of the experiment I would violate a common practice whose violation does not per se destroy or contradict the situation. In the second part I would violate a rule which is essential to the very doing of the situation. That is, if the rule is violated, the situation can no longer go on without strong contradictions and will in effect become meaningless.

The situation chosen for the experiment was a pool game. Conveniently, there was a pool table in the game room of a residential facility for retarded adults. Several of the residents were proficient at playing pool. From Mrs. Brown, the caretaker, I learned that John was very good at pool. He frequently played with Mike, the caretaker's son, and at times with Sam, the caretaker's husband. He played well enough to win quite frequently. In addition, John and I had developed a friendly relationship in the course of the observations. It can be assumed that I had come to be, at least to some extent, a significant other to John, in that there frequently was behavior designed to show affection and friendship.

I initiated a conversation with John with the objective of getting him to ask me to play pool with him.

ARNE: Hi, John. I hear you like to play pool.

JOHN: Yeah. I sure like it. I win. I win. I win over Sam some time.

ARNE: How long have you been playing pool?

JOHN: I play pool a lot. A lot.

ARNE: How long?

JOHN: Oh, I don't know. Don't know that. No, I don't know that. Maybe six month.

According to Mrs. Brown, John had been in the home over four years and had played pool ever since they got the pool table, shortly after John came.

ARNE: I would like to see you play pool some time.

JOHN: Yeah, I play pretty good. Pretty good. I play Sam Brown. I win over him. He don't like that. He sure don't like that. He sure don't. He pretty good too. You wanna see me play pool? I play pool. I play you. Yeah, I play you. You wanna play me?

With that we went into the pool room.

The following points can be made at this time.

1. John knows how to play pool.
2. He has a working knowledge of the rules of the game.
3. He has established a friendly relationship with me, the observer.

The strategy for the experiment was as follows. During the first part of the game I would follow the rules, but I would shoot with the blunt end of the stick. This is a violation of a common practice, but it does not destroy the game. In the middle of the game, while continuing to shoot with the blunt end, I would immediately replace all balls shot into the pockets back onto the table. If I missed, I would push the ball I missed by hand into the pocket. Furthermore, I would do the same to the balls hit and missed by John. This is not only a violation of common practice, but it also destroys the game as such. The first violation is labeled A and the second, B.

We went to the game room; all the while John was talking about his prowess in pool. John got the balls out, arranged them properly on the table, and positioned the white ball. He then went to the rack and selected a cue stick.

JOHN: This mine. Sam Brown gave it to me.

I also selected a cue stick. John chalked his tip, and I proceeded to do the same. He then asked me if I wanted to break. I suggested that he should do that. After breaking and shooting two balls into the pockets, he missed and it became my turn. I chalked my stick again and proceeded to prepare to shoot with the blunt end. John noticed this immediately. He stood for a moment with a very perplexed look on his face, rubbing the cue stick against his chin.

JOHN: Hey . . . you holding the stick the wrong way. That's wrong. That's wrong. You suppos'ta shoot this way. [He demonstrates the correct way.] That's wrong.

When I missed, John smiled and got ready to shoot. He chalked his stick and shot in the conventional way. He missed and it became my turn. Again I chalked the tip and shot with the blunt end. This time I succeeded in getting a couple of balls in the pockets. Again John stood with a very perplexed and worried look on his face but did not say anything. When his turn came up, he chalked his stick, shot in the conventional way, and missed. Again I shot with the blunt end. A couple of pockets were made. This time it appeared that John was really worried. He was scratching his head, his brow knitted up, and his mouth hung open. Clearly something was amiss. When his turn came, he chalked the tip of his stick and proceeded to shoot *using the blunt end.* He missed and then stood up shaking his head and looking at me.

JOHN: That's not right. You like to play pool?

I did not give an answer and proceeded to shoot using the blunt end. After getting one ball down, I missed. John chalked his stick and proceeded to shoot with the *blunt end.* Again he missed.

JOHN: Shiieet!

At this point I decided to include violation B in the experiment. I shot, using the blunt end, made a pocket, and immediately put the ball back on the table. On the next shot I missed and proceeded to roll the ball into the pocket by hand. John appeared to be very surprised. He did not say anything, but his mouth was wide open. I then told him it was his turn. He chalked his stick and shot with the blunt end. He missed and I proceeded to push the ball into the pocket. Again nothing was said, so I proceeded to shoot, again with the blunt end. One ball went into a pocket, and I immediately replaced it on the table. The next shot missed, and I pushed the ball into the pocket. This apparently was too much.

JOHN: You like to play pool?

ARNE: Yes, I sure do.

JOHN: That's the wrong way. You not suppos'ta push the ball. You like to play football?

ARNE: Yes I like to play football.

Note that John made no mention of the way in which I had been playing, but he was obviously irritated.

JOHN: Let's play football.

ARNE: Why don't we play pool?

JOHN: No, let's play football. It's too hot in here.

> The reference to heat was obviously a ruse to get out of playing pool; the game room was air conditioned.

I left the home shortly after this. I returned three days later. Mrs. Brown told me that John had been talking about the pool game.

MRS. BROWN: Do you really know how to play pool?

ARNE: Yes, I do.

MRS. BROWN: Well, I guess John really got confused then, because he didn't think you knew how to play. You know how confused they get about simple things sometimes.

In the hope that further feedback might be forthcoming, I decided not to tell her about the experiment at this point. After a while, John came in, and after the usual greetings he started talking about his bowling ball.

JOHN: You want to see my bowling ball? I got a new bowling ball.

ARNE: How would you like to play some pool?

JOHN: You want to go fishin' with us next week? Sam is taking me fishin'. Yeah, Sam is goin' ta take us fishin'. Good. Good. [He rubs his hands together as he talks.]

ARNE: You want to shoot some pool?

JOHN: Did ya see the patio, Brown? Is it clean enough?

MRS. BROWN: Yes, you did a real fine job today, John. It looks real good.

JOHN: O.K., Mrs. Brown.

It appeared that the idea of playing pool with me was not a very comfortable one, and it was quite clear that John was trying to avoid it. The behavior going on was typical of what I have labeled "keeping safe."

ARNE: Come on and let's go shoot some pool.

JOHN: O.K., we play pool.

He seemed quite unhappy about this. He motioned to me to come along, and we went to his room. He started to take out his "family pictures" but then changed his mind. He kept searching for something in his duffel bag. Finally he gave up.

JOHN: O.K., we shoot pool.

With that we went out to the game room. John set up the balls and selected his cue stick.

JOHN: This my stick. Sam Brown give to me. Sam and I go fishin' soon.

He spent some time chalking his stick and then looked over the table for about two minutes. It appeared that he was trying to postpone the game. Finally he started the game shooting with the conventional end of the stick. As he aimed, he looked at me and then shot. He pocketed four balls before he missed. He stood up with a big, proud smile on his face. He was obviously very pleased with the results.

JOHN: Hey, I was lucky. Yup. Good shots.

As I started chalking my stick, he watched me very intently. When I looked at him, he quickly looked away. I got ready to shoot, using the conventional end of the stick. I shot and made a couple of balls. While this was going on, John started smiling.

JOHN: You shoot pretty good now. That's much better, much better.

After I missed, I did not immediately move away from the table. John stood watching my hands. When I moved from the table without pushing any balls into the pockets, he was visibly relieved.

JOHN: That's good. You play pretty good.

At this point Mrs. Brown came into the room with a couple of glasses of lemonade.

JOHN: It's O.K., Mrs. Brown. He know how to play pool pretty good. Pretty good.

MRS. BROWN: Well, that's what I told you, John.

In the middle of the game, I decided to see if suggesting another game would have any effect.

ARNE: You want to go out and play football?

JOHN: No, it's too hot. Pool is more fun. You like to play pool?

It is interesting to note that John used the same excuse for not playing football as he had previously used for not playing pool. At the beginning of the game, John was quite tense, but as the game proceeded, he became more relaxed. This gives some indication of the tensions that had built up during the experiment.

Discussion of the Experiment

It is clear that one experiment cannot be the basis for any clear-cut conclusions, but it does indicate some tendencies. It was hypothesized that imitation which would become a permanent part of the behavior vocabulary of the subject would be an indicator of the use of imitation to structure behavior. Conversely, if the behavior imitated was used for a short period, then imitation can be seen as a means of coping with an unknown and un-understood set of rules, and thus as a means of getting along in that particular set of behaviors. If this is the case, then it is clear that John was in part trying to cope with my ignorance of his understood and known set of rules. Once we had established a friendly relationship, getting along with me was a desired objective for him. A further confirmation of this notion is that when the game was played subsequent to the experiment, John chose to use the conventional way of shooting, that is, to abide by the rules of the game as he understood them. Two other types of behavior were also involved at this point. The first was an attempt at "keeping safe" by avoiding playing the game at all. The second type was "acceptance testing." When he shot in the conventional manner, he was keeping a close eye on me to gauge my reactions to his violation of my rules.

The second notion that was central to the experiment was the extent to which a retardate was willing to violate rules with which he was comfortable in the process of imitation, or, as we have tentatively interpreted it, coping with a difficult situation. Imitation ensued after a minor rule had been violated a number of times. However, when a major rule—a rule central to the game—was violated, there was no imitation at all. Instead there was considerable tension and irritation. Rather than go along with a major violation, he sought to abort the whole activity and suggest an alternative. The process of aborting the activity and suggesting an alternative can be seen in terms of "playing safe." That is, the current activity had become un-understandable, not in terms of John's knowledge of the game, but in terms of my behavior relative to the commonly understood and taken-for-granted rules of the game. A switch of roles had thus, in effect, taken place. John was in the position of being competent, and he was confident in his competence to the point of telling Mrs. Brown that I did not know how to play pool, while I was in the position of being incompetent. One can thus speculate as to the motive for imitating. Could it be that John, seeing my obvious incompetence, was merely humoring me lest perhaps I become violent? Doing humoring would certainly have had precedents in the Brown home, and thus could have conceivably been a part of John's behavioral vocabulary.

Of interest here also is the fact that the relationship between John and myself was strained during the experiment but reverted to being a friendly relationship once I started complying with the rules of the game as John understood and knew them.

The last idea brings into focus the set of relationships between the residents and Mrs. Brown. In the case of John and myself, it is clear that the relationship was friendlier when there was a convergence between the rules and behavior as experienced by both. It could be posited that a similar process operates between Mrs. Brown and her residents. Mrs. Brown's notions of what mental retardation is centers on her perception of the retarded as children or childlike. As a consequence, she tends to play the mother role. If friendly relations are to occur, a compatible set of behaviors must be done by the residents. This clearly is the case when there is face-to-face contact. The residents frequently adopt childlike gestures and mannerisms. Mrs. Brown reacts to this like a mother, and a friendly relationship goes on. On the other hand, while some of this carries over—for example, references to Mrs. Brown as "Mamma Brown"—there are clear differences. There tend to be small and brief revolts, at times demonstrated to visitors. An example of this is John's use of "damn" and "shieet" after Mrs. Brown has made clear that she gets angry when such language is used.

Conclusions

This study has been largely exploratory, and the findings are at best sketchy. Very little has been written about how the mentally retarded act, since the majority of the studies relevant to mental retardation have been medically and biologically oriented. Others have dealt with I.Q.'s and adaptive behavior. A notable exception to these studies is Edgerton's *The Cloak of Competence*. [2]

The notion of "passing behavior" has been defined as that type of behavior which the retardate engages in so as to appear normal and thus hide evidence of mental retardation. That this type of behavior is frequent has been demonstrated by Edgerton and was observed in the course of this study. The fact that passing behavior does take place has some implications which stand contrary to popular notions of how the mentally retarded see themselves. In order for passing types of behavior to take place, the individuals engaged in such behavior must have some notion of their subnormality. It could be argued that they do, in that the retarded have been told that they are retarded, and in all likelihood they have also, at one time or another, been institutionalized.

What is significant here is that not all behavior is passing behavior. That is, some acts are chosen to be used as passing acts, while others are not. If the. labeling process is to be assumed to be the major factor in determining passing behavior, then the specific areas of incompetence must have been labeled, thus providing the retardate with a guide as to which areas he needs to do passing in. There is little information as to whether such act-specific labeling takes place. On the other hand, if the labeling process is not assumed to be act-specific, then it must be considered possible that the retarded, in some areas at least, have reasonably well-developed competencies. Cases of the "idiot savant" provide some reason to believe that this is the case. Certainly the data in this study show limited areas of well-developed competence that is resistant to manipulation.

This line of reasoning suggests a somewhat different conceptualization of what mental retardation is. Laws and Ryave have suggested that mental retardation be viewed in terms of competence rather than incompetence, claiming that the latter point of reference tends to blind one to areas of competence. [3] In line with these notions, mental retardation can be regarded as a segmented set of competencies, in which some sets are relatively well developed and others are relatively poorly developed. That is to say, competence is not uniform for a given person, and one may be equipped with areas of competence, as well as with areas of incompetence.

If mental retardation is viewed in this fashion, then the fact that the retarded show remarkable competence in some areas, while at the same time showing little or no competence in others, is not surprising. The observations in this study tend to support this view of retardation.

Notes

1. Harold Garfinkel, *Studies in Ethnomethodology*, Englewood Cliffs, N.J.: Prentice-Hall, 1967.

2. Robert Edgerton, *The Cloak of Competence*, Berkeley: University of California Press, 1967.

3. Donald F. Laws and A. Lincoln Ryave, "Toward a Sociology of Experience: The Abandonment of Concepts of Defectiveness," unpublished paper, California State College, Dominguez Hills.

CASE STUDY G

On Recognizing Mistakes: A Case of Practical Reasoning in Psychotherapy

HOWARD SCHWARTZ

Introduction

As is rather obvious, the concept of subjectivity has long had deep connections with the concept of mistake. For this reason I became interested in studying practical mistakes made by people in everyday life. Because I was concentrating on mistakes in order to learn about subjectivity, I decided to look for occasions when people discovered that they were "wrong about the world" or mistaken in a previous conclusion or assertion. To make such a discovery, one would need certain epistemological hardware. One would need some version of evidence, truth and falsehood, and so on. So I went looking for a method of evaluating conclusions that would permit people, in daily life, to discover that they had been "wrong about the world."

I found such a method in psychotherapy, a method designed, in a sense, to help patients recognize mistakes in their thinking. What follows is an exposition of that method which stems, in large part, from my research in 1969 as a professional intern at Langley Porter neuropsychiatric institute. Unless otherwise noted, data and examples come from my transcriptions of tape recordings made during group therapy sessions.

Let us begin the discussion of this method by describing the pragmatic context within which it must function.

Abridged from *Philosophy of the Social Sciences* 6, no. 1 (March 1976): 55–73.

Psychological Self-determination for Patients

If the first reform movement in psychology (starting with Dorothea Dix and others) concerned itself with gross physical abuse of the mentally ill, then a second reform movement, still under way, might be said to be concerned with psychological abuse. The therapist has been characterized as a new kind of policeman.[1] Persons having experiences or engaging in behaviors that are, for one reason or another, unacceptable to the community at large are conceived of as "sick" and are handed over to psychologists instead of to the police or the priests. Such persons are incarcerated, stigmatized, degraded, and manipulated in the name of treating their various "illnesses."

The response of humanistic psychology to this has presented an interesting dilemma. There was a reluctance to conceptualize patients as sick people. But, on the other hand, they were going to be given treatment. How can there be treatment without sick people? Secondly, treatment was construed as a process by which an individual freely makes certain decisions, arrives at certain insights, and changes his or her outlook and behavior. A psychologist does not and cannot cure the person. He should not control another's behavior, tell him what to do or think, or otherwise infringe upon his autonomy as a human being. He merely facilitates, acting as a catalyst, creating conditions conducive to a healthy self-exploration.

However, this ideology must come to terms with the fact that therapy is something done at a certain time and place with a certain kind of paid professional. The results of therapy, whether good or bad, just do not happen without the professional. Indeed, it is often precisely because self-help or trusted friends have failed that people arrive at the therapist's office, as a last resort.

Thus, to be cynical, a psychologist who embraces the previous ideology has this problem: How does one manipulate another person's thoughts, feelings, and behavior while making it appear both to him and to oneself that he is perfectly free? Second, how does one assess the psychological weaknesses, strengths, and progress of somebody while creating the feeling for all concerned that therapy is a place where acceptance and lack of value judgments are the rule?

The Concrete Problem

Overwhelmingly, one of the things insane people do that strikes others as "insane" is to talk wrong. One of the ways they talk wrong is to say things that are not so. Such statements can be of at least two types. On the one hand, there are what we might call patients' theories of social structure—collections of hypotheses and beliefs about the structure of the world, the nature of people, or the course of one's life. Equally important, but less studied, are reports of definite, particular occurrences which sound distorted, incorrect, or slanted. Here is an example:

> THERAPIST: This is another example of the defense of undoing. Thinking about killing had to be undone by the counterbalancing behavior of thinking of doing good. Associated material indicated that Robert's concern about his uncle served to cover his feelings about his father's death. In this exchange he was attempting to atone for murder, *feeling that he had killed his uncle and had committed patricide when he was two.*[2] [emphasis added.]

Here a patient makes reference to a certain past event, a murder. The doctor just does not believe it happened that way, but presumably the patient does. Such a patient will make many such claims and relate many such incidents during a given session. Many of these claims will obviously be relevant to his psychological problems. After such a claim is made, the doctor will have to do something immediately. It will be his turn to talk. Some next thing to say will have to be chosen. Moreover, it may be "now or never" for dealing with the claim. These interactions have their own distinctive continuities, emotional momentum, and issues of timing and pace. Something that is a crucial matter now is often emotionally dead later, or next time. We can summarize these considerations thus: There is going to be a steady stream of patient's statements that need to be evaluated immediately, by making spot assessments. There will be no practical way out of it. Moreover, many of these spot assessments will be negative.

This poses one part of a two-part moral dilemma. How do you treat another human being in an open, accepting way when you do not believe much of what he tells you about himself and the world (or, at the very least, don't take it at face value)?

Putting off the answer to this question for the moment, let us inquire further into the pragmatic situation. What resources are available for these spot assessments? In "I killed my uncle," we have a specific past event that is gone in the sense of experience. We have a therapist faced with a patient on a ward containing no persons, records, or artifacts that could possibly bear on whether or not this patient killed his uncle. A therapist is usually without the resources to bring empirical evidence to bear upon such a story, and his interest in such evidence borders on apathy. Patients are massively denied the role of reporter since, sociologically, the relevant roles are patient-therapist, not defendant-judge or victim-policeman. The relevant activity is treatment, not fact finding. This is of course one of the ways that patients are robbed of the opportunity of being taken seriously, as discussed by R. D. Laing and others.

In any case, our much maligned therapist merely has an intuitive conviction that the patient's report is both false and psychologically motivated, a conviction grounded in a native's common sense and his own prior knowledge and training. How can he make the patient see what he sees? How can an insight be achieved? A traditional method of doing this is the Socratic dialogue: Let someone know that you doubt his convictions and try to convince him, by judicious questioning, that these doubts are well founded.

Of course, this method will not work. The psychologist often lacks the resources needed to change a person's mind in a logical or empirical manner. General beliefs frequently have the character of so-called closed systems. An example from the same case history illustrates this beautifully:

> On another occasion he told me he was afraid that if he touched my desk I would die. I told him I didn't believe it and suggested that we carry out an experiment—that he touch the desk and we observe the results. He replied that he was too frightened to do this.[3]

The problem inherent in this is obvious. This patient had feelings of guilt about being an evil person, one who caused others harm. Assume that he really believed the doctor would be killed if he touched the desk. It certainly would not be worth another person's life just to test his ideas about causality. Indeed, only an evil person would even consider making such an experiment.

Of course, even if logical and empirical evidence could be brought to bear upon such statements, there are additional problems. It has long been noted in clinical work that people no longer take kindly to Socratic dialogue. In these sensitive situations they are likely to construe such dialogues as personal attacks on themselves and their credibility and to become offended rather than convinced. Obviously a direct challenge to another's beliefs, even if successful, would hardly create the feeling in him that he is being treated with acceptance and trust.

Finally, the changes of mind and heart which are called insights are not considered to be intellectual. The psychiatrist's aim is knowledge that changes the knower in some deep way. Mere intellectual conviction will not suffice.

For these reasons, dialogues, evidence, debates, and arguments of the usual sort are of little value. Yet, in changing his mind about a false idea, a patient gives an important sign that he is getting better. This can indicate a cessation of hallucinations, delusions, or defense mechanisms.

Here we have the second half of the moral dilemma. How do you change another person's conception of himself and/or the world while simultaneously respecting his right to self-determination? In particular, you must change another's mind without telling him that you are doing so, or want to do so, and still see yourself as not engaging in psychological manipulation.

This two-part dilemma will be solved by the method of reasoning about to be discussed.[4]

The Skills

To use this method of reasoning, patients need to learn several cognitive skills. First there is a way of listening which amounts to changing language levels during a conversation. Using philosophical terminology, we can speak of the symbols of the natural language being "used" to "mention" something else. Then our present concern is with listening to what is *used* rather than what is *mentioned*. To put this in another way, a person notices such things as how something is said, or that it is said, rather than what is said. Call this skill "listening metalinguistically."

One way to listen metalinguistically is to hear a speaker "doing things with words." More and more comments are heard, not as somethings which are said, but as verbal activities which do something:[5]

A: I keep getting these funny twitches.

B: Jesus, A, every time something real comes up you try to change the subject. Consider the difference, in listening to someone say, "I keep getting these funny twitches," between hearing a description of a current physical problem, and literally *hearing*, instead, "the topic-being-changed." I am not implying, however, that these two possibilities need to be mutually exclusive.[6]

Here, rather complex interpretations are involved. Years of technical training allow a psychologist to recognize the elaborate and intricate psychological things a verbal comment might be "doing." These things are infinitely more sophisticated than doing bragging or doing complaining. Patients as well need to learn many of these intricacies:

> DOCTOR: He then said that he had just received a mental telepathy message from a former doctor, in which the doctor said he would kill him with a shock treatment. This imagined punishment followed his evil thought. What, at this point, with his archaic superego he called evil was actually beginning feelings of competence or competitive strivings. He therefore gave himself an imagined shock treatment which relieved his anxiety and expiated his guilt, just as his previous imagined shocks had punished him for harming his friend's hospitalized mother.[7]

The Logic of Personal Motives

At this point we do not have the necessary tools to assess the truth of a belief. At best, hearing a statement as "doing" some verbal job could render the truth of the statement irrelevant. But it cannot make the statement false. For that, more is needed. More is provided when we add the use of personal motives to our equation.

The following statement may be difficult to understand for a reader who has not had experience with therapy. In many psychiatric settings the notion of correct motivation replaces the notion of truth as the criterion used to determine the validity of descriptions. If it is determined that the patient's motive for saying he killed his uncle is pathological, then he did not kill his uncle. The doctor, and later the patient, do not believe the statement or, better, do not believe *in* the statement. We can say that the statement is rendered invalid, but it is closer to the actual experiences involved to say it is false, in a sense of false that transcends the usual epistemological hardware used to determine truth. Just substitute evaluation procedures that employ personal motives for those that employ what scientists think of as evidence, then retain the subjective way one feels about something when he thinks of it as true or false—and that is how a belief is invalidated in many of these settings. I hope this claim will become more cogent when the logic of motives is described in more detail.

To use this logic one must learn, first, a "vocabulary of motives" peculiar to a given psychiatric environment.[8] Second, one needs to see which of his personal motives are involved in the way he describes events and situations. One of the important ways this happens is by therapists and other patients telling a patient what they see as his recurrent personal motives.[9] Equipped with this information, he is encouraged to learn to see these motives operating in the things he says and does. As his relationships with staff and other patients become stabilized, his distinctive personal motives can become relatively public knowledge. Finally, there is a complex system of assessing the validity, or authenticity, of motives in terms of their psychological origins and consequences. While such motives as buying indulgences or avoiding self-responsibility might be invalid, wanting to be part of the group or desiring to "come out" may be assessed as laudable.[10]

When we combine these factors—the ability to listen metalinguistically, the ability to detect interpersonal actions which are "done" by verbal comments, the ability to see personal motives for descriptions, and the use of a logic of personal motives to assess truth—we have the basic ingredients of a rather general method for changing people's minds. The same method can be applied to a diverse collection of descriptions. When successful, it will replace what was once thought of as a fact with a personally motivated interpretation.

The Problem of Apprenticeship

If talk was the medium through which a patient earned the label "mentally ill," then help will come, overwhelmingly, in the form of talk as well. Yet it is clear that the kind of verbal interaction that characterizes psychotherapy must be different from the kind that characterizes most everyday encounters. Otherwise, why go to a therapist? It would seem that new skills are involved.

If these skills were like other skills, one would presumedly have to learn and practice them first and actively use them later. This would mean that teaching patients the verbal abilities needed to participate in therapy would occur apart from the therapy itself. But therapeutic interaction appears to be so designed that rehearsal and performance need not be separated but can occur together. In socializing new patients, teaching and learning occur, but without any visible students and teachers. That is, new patients come to see and know certain things without receiving explicit instructions about them from others. We will mention only one vehicle for this learning, a vehicle which ethnomethodologists call formulations.[11] Imagine a patient makes some comment. His psychiatrist may reply by describing or "formulating" the comment and what it is "doing,"—for example, it is an "evasion," a "brag," or an "attempt to change the topic." In this sense, he is commenting on the comment. Let us illustrate the process:

PATIENT: If you do a pleasure without a reason, that makes you a pleasure seeker. That's just sexual pleasure, not intellectual happiness. That's why people who do the twist go to the mental hospital.

DOCTOR: Do you need to defend yourself against pleasure?[12]

In making this remark, the doctor invokes a deceptively simple procedure for inferring personal motives from speech acts. First, he finds some psychological thing the patient's comment is "doing." In particular, his reply formulates the patient's comment as a case of "defending oneself against pleasure." Having found what his comment is "doing," both doctor and patient may infer that he made the comment *in order to do* that thing. He can thus be sensitized to a personal motive and to a method of inferring personal motives from speech acts. Of course, there is a problem with this method. There are all sorts of things which a verbal comment can be described as "doing." How does one know which one of these the patient intended in making the remark? Luckily, our job is not to evaluate the validity of this reasoning, but just to point it out.

In employing reasoning like this, therapists use formulations differently from the way they are used in other kinds of conversations. They do this in two ways: (1) by *which* of the patient's remarks they formulate and (2) by *how* they formulate (or describe) these remarks. By controlling the content and placement of his formulations, a therapist can display a pattern. New patients can then pick up this pattern. But picking up this pattern amounts, in effect, to learning new ways to talk and listen.

Yet there are many ways that this sort of program can run into snags. Clearly, specialized kinds of verbal fluency are involved together with particular ways of conceiving of oneself and the world. One would imagine that such skills would vary considerably with sociological categories. Indeed, it is rather easy to discover that various types of people in these psychiatric settings have what are clearly, for me, technical problems in this regard. They don't know how to talk, think, and listen in these ways. The technical learning problems involved tend to be over-looked in such settings where the model is illness, treatment, and recovery rather than that of a school with students. Thus a patient's failure to recognize personal motives is more likely to be regarded as a psychic problem than a learning problem. A change in this ability is more likely to be seen as a change in personal attitude or the growing of personal insight rather than a verbal skill having been acquired. A hilarious case of a patient just not knowing what to attend to in-volved the admission on a ward of a white, upper-class, Protestant mother. These categories, in particular, the Christian, religion furnished the customary idiom she employed to describe events in daily life. It seemed impossible for her to think of herself as doing something for a personal motive, or at least to talk that way. This was because, in her view, she was always a case of "somebody," not a particular person. When discussing an action of hers, she immediately attended to morals instead of motives or feelings—should "someone" do that, was that a justified action, and so on. If one proposed she did something out of fear, she would launch into how "individuals" should learn to conquer their own fears. The problem here was providing the woman with a conception of personal identity so that she could take personal possession of her actions, in a conceptual sense. She irritated the staff to no end with this business. In the face of what they saw as blatant rigidity and repression, they spoke of her prospective treatment in terms of "killing a Christian."

LEARNING THE SKILLS: A SUMMARY

In illustrating how certain cognitive skills are learned, we have been emphasizing formulations. But this is only the tip of the iceberg. Many other forces are operating to bring about similar results. Most of these results happen, not by design, but by one human being adapting himself to others while the others simply hear what they hear and say what they say. In this sense psychotherapy both is and is not a technical activity.[13] For it provides ways for beginners to immediately engage in it, understand what is happening (more or less), and simultaneously pick up the competencies that will make them skilled practitioners.[14] It does all of this by just being what it is.

The Procedure

Let us collapse our previous observations into an idealization. Let us describe a kind of logic, a step-by-step "procedure" by which the falsehood of certain assertions may be ascertained:

1. Let X be some assertion about the world.
2. Skip to a metalinguistic level and consider X as a conversational object.
3. Find some verbal activity which is "done" by the statement X.
4. Find a personal motive, a reason why someone would do this activity. (Sometimes, as already discussed, the activity done by X, and the motive for that activity, will be one and the same.)
5. Evaluate the personal motive as healthy or unhealthy, normal or pathological, etc.
6. If the motive is found to be invalid or inauthentic, the statement X is false. Don't believe in the statement.

Of course, our idealization is an idealization. It leaves many issues unanswered. Foremost among them is the empirical status of the procedure. For there is no procedure, in the sense of an explicit logic used by a group of people. Yet our idealization does capture a form of common sense thought which really exists. The question is, can we be more concrete in describing this form of thought as it occurs in everyday life?

Mistakes as Sequences of Interaction

The author is not entirely a neophyte in connection with this form of thought. In fact, my versatility in this regard revealed itself dramatically during an interaction with a friend who is a family therapist. I related certain personal problems to my friend. He, in turn, suggested several solutions. I, in my turn, recited a series of practical facts which indicated that his solutions would not work. He then interpreted my "facts" thus: We had a pattern of talking together. I would recite problems, he would make some proposals, and then I would automatically find fault with his proposals. Consequently, if we were to get anywhere, we would have to get out of this pattern. Here was a classical double bind.[15] What was I to say? If I denied the existence of this pattern, I would be acting in accordance with the pattern (I would be rejecting what he proposed), thus proving his point. Similarly, assenting to the presence of the pattern would also validate his claim. In either case, my "facts" would be revealed as personally motivated, and thus suspect. I was a "fault finder," and my facts were brought out and displayed in order to find fault.

Which course of verbal action did I take? I capitulated, turning the definition of the situation over to my friend. This course was all but necessitated by elegance of the double bind. After assenting to such a pattern, any subsequent disagreements between me and my friend would automatically be decided in his favor. Yet it was only after the interaction had taken place that I realized all these strategic contingencies.

It was not by accident that the previous interaction took the form of a first-person account. There are two ways we might study the form of reasoning involved here. We could use empirical science. For example, we could videotape such interactions and analyze them in detail However, behavioral science proceeds by studying "other people." The knower is philosophically and methodologically disengaged from the known. While there is much to be gained in this way there are certain endemic problems in studying other people's mistakes. As a structure of conscious attention, "my mistakes" have the following obvious, but important, characteristics:

1. They are committed by *me*, not anybody else.
2. I always become aware of them only when it is too late, that is, after they have been committed.
   a. In this sense one could hardly set out to make a real mistake in the same way one sets out to make dinner.

In contrast, the set of experiences I undergo while witnessing someone else's mistakes has an altogether different structure. Here he is in error, not I. While the error may be consequential or crucial to him, it has no such practical connection with my current projects of action. While he was fooled initially, I was never fooled. As someone looking in from the outside, I knew what was going on all along. Yet for him there is no outside, nor any experiences connected with it.[16]

Given the above, how might one best describe the structure of ongoing thought and attention that occurs when one consciously makes a mistake? For this, phenomenological, not empirical, methods are needed.

What I have been calling a method of reasoning would show up as sequences of events like the foregoing. A phenomenological analysis of such sequences, it is hoped, could replace the term *method* with descriptions more "true to the phenomenon."[17]

Some Functions of the Method

At this point, author and reader alike can appreciate how elegantly this method of discovering mistakes is suited to the circumstances within which it takes places.

In one small way, acquiring and using this method solve many of the moral dilemmas we have previously outlined for therapy. Patient and therapist come to draw on common resources in arriving at a common conclusion. Patients can learn these resources, and therapists can teach them, without seeing themselves as doing so. The method works immediately, using only conversational sequencing, common sense reasoning, and the plausibility of certain interpretations. Nothing additional is required, no additional information, added time, lengthy dialogue—nothing. The procedure does not employ the correspondence theory of truth. Therefore it is not important "what really happened" (that is, the relation of the description to what it described). For this reason, this method of evaluation can, potentially, be applied to diverse, concrete, factual claims of all sorts.

Further, the method is "sneaky." In interpreting your facts in terms of personal motives, a therapist need not directly accuse you of lying or being wrong. He can challenge your facts without "challenging your facts," so to speak. Also, recognizing mistakes in this way is valuable for therapy. It reveals personal motives, and it is capable of producing genuine personal insights. The reasons for the latter are external to this paper and cannot be detailed here.[18]

Finally, in coming to such insights you change your mind yourself; the psychologist does not change it for you. In terms of the needs and requirements that exist between doctor and patient, who could ask for more?

CASE STUDY H

On the Art of Talking About the World

A rather commonplace conversational activity is telling and hearing stories about the world.[1] Frequently such stories appear in a conversation in clusters of two or more.

In the data to be focused upon here, in each case presented, there occurs a cluster of two stories and related story commentary, told at separate times by two conversationalists. In the second instance presented below, Peter tells a story about a dangerously close call he experiences at a fairgrounds, and then Gordon follows with a story dealing with the possible prevention of trouble in amusement park rides in Long Beach. In the first instance, Blanch presents a story dealing with the fact that an accident was witnessed which evidently was not subsequently reported on by the media, whereupon Beth tells a story of a witnessed event that received the same fate. These instances are presented immediately below, and the reader is encouraged to examine them carefully before proceeding to the ensuing analysis.[2] In my analysis, particular attention will be given to instance 2.

Instance 1

BLANCH: Say did you see anything in the paper last night or hear anything on the local radio, Ruth Henderson and I drove down to Ventura yesterday.
BETH: Mh hm.

Abridged and revised by Howard Schwartz. Reprinted with the permission of Alan L. Ryave.
418

phenomenological analysis, see the excellent summary in Alfred Schutz, *Collected Papers I*, pp. 99–197.

18. Recognizing mistakes in this way allows a person to engage in what I have treated elsewhere as "nondiscursive reasoning." The latter kind of reasoning is one way to achieve an insight in contrast to a mere intellectual realization. For a discussion of these matters, see Howard Schwartz, "Mental Disorder and the Study of Subjective Experience: Some Uses of Each to Elucidate the Other," Ph.D. dissertation, University of California at Los Angeles, 1971, pp. 249–276.

19. See note 17.

Notes

1. See, for example, Thomas Szasz, *The Myth of Mental Illness*, New York: Hoeber-Harper, 1961.
2. K. H. Blacker, "Obsessive-Compulsive Phenomena and Catatonic States—A Continuum," *Psychiatry* 29, no. 2 (May 1966): 189.
3. Ibid., p. 188.
4. There are inherent simplifications in words like "method." The body of this article, it is hoped, indicates that the author appreciates the subtleties involved. The words themselves ("method" and "procedure") are used only for expository convenience.
5. I do not refer to sheer quantity here. I refer to a change in the pattern of one's metalinguistic listening, as one adapts to new styles of interaction found in therapy.
6. The extent to which these possibilities are separate and the nature of their interrelations are best left to experimental psychology.
7. Blacker, "Obsessive-Compulsive Phenomena," p. 188.
8. See C. Wright Mills, "Situated Actions and Vocabularies of Motives," *American Sociological Review* 5 (December 1940).
9. Others discover these motives from your behavior and talk, and then feed this information back to you.
10. These are not made-up motives but were obtained from taped conversations.
11. Strictly speaking, formulations are descriptions of a conversation or its parts which are themselves utterances within the same conversation. Formulations are briefly discussed in Harold Garfinkel and Harvey Sacks, "On Formal Structures of Practical Actions," in *Theoretical Sociology: Perspectives and Developments*, ed. by John McKinney and Edward Tiryakian, New York: Appleton-Century-Crofts, 1970.
12. These conversational excerpts coupled with commentary do not, of course, constitute analyses. They do, however, indicate topics for analysis.
13. I am aware of the tremendous number of philosophies and mutual activities that go under the title "psychotherapy." However, I am impressed, and others are as well, with their many commonalities, in spite of these differences. Why this is so is unclear. That it is so gives some hope for a sociology of mental illness.
14. Competencies which are characteristic of socialized adults need to be at one's command in order for one to participate in the thinking, talking, and learning that I have been talking about. Therefore the considerations of this article become all but inapplicable to certain kinds of severe mental illness.
15. For a discussion of double binds, see Gregory Bateson et al., "Toward a Theory of Schizophrenia," *Behavioral Science* 1, no. 4 (1956).
16. In this brief account I am referring to only one variety of the phenomenon, "his mistake."
17. A little-known but extremely interesting suggestion by Maurice Merleau-Ponty is this: The collection of many different cases of a phenomenon such as "mistakes" can accomplish phenomenological functions similar to Husserl's methods of fantasy free variation. Thus ordinary empirical research, if differently construed and differently handled, can be made to serve phenomenology. For an explanation of

Conclusions

As many have noted, human beings seem to be "reality-detecting" organisms. Pretty much anything from various gods to the effect of the stars on personality to the gross national product can be invested with external, independent existence. The ways of doing this are as diverse as the number of human groups and human situations. But we are equally capable of seeing and knowing subjectivity, of seeing almost anything as mistakes, experiences, perceptions, interpretations, or opinions. When a sufficient number of the activities through which human beings create reality and unreality have been located and described, it will become possible to ask an interesting, if classic, question. What do they all have in common?[19]

Methodological Notes

The previous account undoubtedly seemed ideological and polemic. It painted a black-and-white picture without qualifications and without a specification of where, when, and to whom this kind of picture really applied. Substantiation came exclusively in the form of examples, not data. Finally, circumstances, requirements, and procedures were fitted together like a watch. How many of these things go together so perfectly in the world and how many only in the author's own mind?

All of these criticisms are thoroughly justified. Yet certain clarifications are necessary. Qualitative sociology has recurrently bit off more than it could chew in its selection of problems. Phenomena have been chosen which were not easily validated by some symbolically representable collection of data, but which were interesting anyway. The phenomena under consideration here exhibit this problem as well.

In addition, if these observations are to be used to clarify subjectivity and lead to an eventual phenomenology of mistakes, then the question "Who are you talking about, and where?" is out of place. Notwithstanding all of this, qualitative observations have been fitted together into an analytic framework, a framework that can be used again.

Finally, I was not attempting an "argument from design" or suggesting some kind of functional hypothesis. It is not claimed that malevolent psychologists produced the ways of talking and thinking discussed, in order to satisfy their professional needs. It is also not claimed that a homeostatic mechanism was operating to adapt human behavior to a set of environments and circumstances. Yet there do seem to be some ecological arrangements here. Why this is so I simply do not know.

is no procedure, in the sense of an explicit logic used by a group of people. Yet our idealization does capture a form of common sense thought which really exists. The question is, can we be more concrete in describing this form of thought as it occurs in everyday life?

Mistakes as Sequences of Interaction

The author is not entirely a neophyte in connection with this form of thought. In fact, my versatility in this regard revealed itself dramatically during an interaction with a friend who is a family therapist. I related certain personal problems to my friend. He, in turn, suggested several solutions. I, in my turn, recited a series of practical facts which indicated that his solutions would not work. He then interpreted my "facts" thus: We had a pattern of talking together. I would recite problems, he would make some proposals, and then I would automatically find fault with his proposals. Consequently, if we were to get anywhere, we would have to get out of this pattern. Here was a classical double bind.[15] What was I to say? If I denied the existence of this pattern, I would be acting in accordance with the pattern (I would be rejecting what he proposed), thus proving his point. Similarly, assenting to the presence of the pattern would also validate his claim. In either case, my "facts" would be revealed as personally motivated, and thus suspect. I was a "fault finder," and my facts were brought out and displayed in order to find fault.

Which course of verbal action did I take? I capitulated, turning the definition of the situation over to my friend. This course was all but necessitated by elegance of the double bind. After assenting to such a pattern, any subsequent disagreements between me and my friend would automatically be decided in his favor. Yet it was only after the interaction had taken place that I realized all these strategic contingencies.

It was not by accident that the previous interaction took the form of a first-person account. There are two ways we might study the form of reasoning involved here. We could use empirical science. For example, we could videotape such interactions and analyze them in detail However, behavioral science proceeds by studying "other people." The knower is philosophically and methodologically disengaged from the known. While there is much to be gained in this way there are certain endemic problems in studying other people's mistakes. As a structure of conscious attention, "my mistakes" have the following obvious, but important, characteristics:

1. They are committed by *me*, not anybody else.
2. I always become aware of them only when it is too late, that is, after they have been committed.
   a. In this sense one could hardly set out to make a real mistake in the same way one sets out to make dinner.

In contrast, the set of experiences I undergo while witnessing someone else's mistakes has an altogether different structure. Here he is in error, not I. While the error may be consequential or crucial to him, it has no such practical connection with my current projects of action. While he was fooled initially, I was never fooled. As someone looking in from the outside, I knew what was going on all along. Yet for him there is no outside, nor any experiences connected with it.[16]

Given the above, how might one best describe the structure of ongoing thought and attention that occurs when one consciously makes a mistake? For this, phenomenological, not empirical, methods are needed.

What I have been calling a method of reasoning would show up as sequences of events like the foregoing. A phenomenological analysis of such sequences, it is hoped, could replace the term *method* with descriptions more "true to the phenomenon."[17]

Some Functions of the Method

At this point, author and reader alike can appreciate how elegantly this method of discovering mistakes is suited to the circumstances within which it takes places.

In one small way, acquiring and using this method solve many of the moral dilemmas we have previously outlined for therapy. Patient and therapist come to draw on common resources in arriving at a common conclusion. Patients can learn these resources, and therapists can teach them, without seeing themselves as doing so. The method works immediately, using only conversational sequencing, common sense reasoning, and the plausibility of certain interpretations. Nothing additional is required, no additional information, added time, lengthy dialogue—nothing. The procedure does not employ the correspondence theory of truth. Therefore it is not important "what really happened" (that is, the relation of the description to what it described). For this reason, this method of evaluation can, potentially, be applied to diverse, concrete, factual claims of all sorts.

Further, the method is "sneaky." In interpreting your facts in terms of personal motives, a therapist need not directly accuse you of lying or being wrong. He can challenge your facts without "challenging your facts," so to speak. Also, recognizing mistakes in this way is valuable for therapy. It reveals personal motives, and it is capable of producing genuine personal insights. The reasons for the latter are external to this paper and cannot be detailed here.[18]

Finally, in coming to such insights you change your mind yourself; the psychologist does not change it for you. In terms of the needs and requirements that exist between doctor and patient, who could ask for more?

BLANCH: And on the way home we saw the:: most gosh-awful wreck.

BETH: Oh::::

BLANCH: —we have ev— I've ever seen. I've never seen a car smashed into sm—— such a small space.

BETH: Oh::::

BLANCH: It was smashed from the front and the back both it must've been in— caught in between two cars.

BETH: Mh hm uh huh.

BLANCH: Must've run into a car and then another car smashed into it and there were people laid out and covered over on the pavement.

BETH: Mh.

BLANCH: We were s— parked there for quite a while but I was going to listen to the r— news and haven't done it.

BETH: No, I haven't had my radio on, either.

BLANCH: Well I had my television on, but I was listening to uh the blast-off, you know.

BETH: Mh hm.

BLANCH: The uh ah— // astronauts.

BETH: Yeah.

BETH: Yeah.

BLANCH: And I–I didn't ever get any *local* news.

BETH: Uh huh.

BLANCH: And I wondered.

BETH: Uh huh.

BETH: No, I haven't had it on, and I don't uh get the paper, and uhm

BLANCH: It wasn't in the paper last night, I looked.

BETH: Uh huh.

BETH: Probably didn't make it.

BLANCH: No, no you see this was about three o'clock in the afternoon.

BETH: Uh huh.

BLANCH: Paper was already off the press.

BETH: Uh huh.

BLANCH: Boy, it was a bad one, though.

BETH: Well that's too bad.

BLANCH: Kinda // (freak)—

BETH: You know, I looked and looked in the paper—I think I told you f–for that uh f–fall over at the Bowl that night. And I never saw a thing about it, and I // looked in the next couple of evenings.

BLANCH: Mh hm.

    (1.0)

BETH: Never saw a th— a mention of it.

BLANCH: I didn't see that, either.

BETH: Uh huh.

BETH: Maybe they kept it out.

BLANCH: Mh hm, I expect.
BETH: Uh huh, deli//berately.
BLANCH: Well I'll see you at— at—
BETH: Tomorrow // night.
BLANCH: —at six at— hehhehh.

Instance 2

HAL: They're-uh-they::'re uhm, they're easy.
PETER: Boy, don't go at the fairgrounds through.
    ((whistles "wow"))
STAN: Oh(hh)o Go(hh)d'   00'.
HAL: Why?
PETER: C'z uh, —(2.0)— have one a' them things, they break loose up there.
GORDON: Oh wuhnyuh buildin that yeah I know about that. —They're prob-
    'bly— there's cables wasn' uh strong enough tuh, —pull'm *back*.
PETER: Uh-no those big cable cars. Y'nuh the ones up on the, track.
GORDON: Mm.
STAN: Wih A one Boat YUH::: UHLON DOHLENKO, — ETCHEruh
    WOOOOOPS.
    (1.7)
HAL: I wouldn' ride on them (cars.)
STAN: Gah' No *me*.
    (1.7)
GORDON: Aw me I'd ride onna *bumper* car.
PETER: An ah know who almos' got hit bah one a' them things.
STAN: YOU?
HAL: (((You?   )
    (   )
(STAN): Go::d.
GORDON: Mm hm.
GORDON: Not me.
PETER: ((with mouth full)) If I didn' stop bout; —
GORDON: ((with mouth full)) Eh w'z this— ((chewing))
(GORDON): (   )
PETER: (The cable car jus' went past me'n:: dropped. —dat, close to me.
HAL: Jeez.
GORDON: (   ).
PETER: That's how far ah was 'way fm that cable car.
STAN: ((whispered))   Go::d.
HAL: *Wow*.
STAN: (*Yeah.*)

how this significance can be appreciated in and through the way these events are recounted. The "and/or" was not an incidental usage, but was meant to indicate that these two concerns of storytellers are intimately interrelated and, together, dictate just how to present the tale in question.

In general, recounting events is done by reciting a number of separate utterances which are tied together by some developing course of action. Showing the significance of these events takes the form of an abstract assertion, accomplishable within a single utterance.[4] In Peter's case, for example, both of these aspects of story organization are exemplified. There is a recounting of a particular event that once occurred at a fairground, which is prefaced by a general statement admonishing and warning the other participants about visiting such places. The admonition seems to show the relevance of recounting the dangerous event which occurred at the fairground. The recounting, in and through its presentation, serves as a source of evidence and support for producing the admonition in the first place.

What happens next is critical. I want to propose that Gordon produces an utterance whose function is the same as Peter's original admonition. That is, Gordon's "They should check those things out— When they rent'm" is designed to describe the significance of Peter's story. Support for this contention can be obtained by a few observations. First, Gordon makes this comment after Peter completes his entire story. Second, it is a response to the story as a whole. In this it contrasts to the utterances produced by Gordon, Hal, and Stan that appear within the confines of Peter's unfolding story and which are directed to concrete elements of what is being recounted. Third, it is "reflexively" fitted to what Peter has said. That is, what Peter recounted stands as a source of testimony for what Gordon said and, at the same time, what Gordon said suggests one conclusion that can be drawn from what Peter has recounted. Fourth, notice that one can actually remove Peter's opening significance statement (his admonition) and substitute Gordon's statement "They should check those things out—," and Peter's entire story and all intervening commentary still make perfect sense.

Of course, it is no news that a given story can have two different significances. What might be news is that, within conversation, a listener can give a story a second significance which is different from the one announced for it by the teller of the story, and that this second significance need not be derived from, or commensurate with, the first. Apparently this is morally permitted in conversation, and there are ways to do it. In particular, notice that Gordon places his "second significance statement" in a certain "slot"—he says it right after Peter completes his story. These observations will give us a "road home" in terms of solving the problem which started this article. They will suggest one reason why conversationalists deliberately design their "talk about the world" so that it takes the form of a series of stories—a consecutive set of tales which are visibly tied to one another like the links of a chain. We will also see why the views of the world expressed in a conversation may be as much the result of the unfolding talk in the conversation itself as it is the product of the beliefs of those who express them.

actually done; I am pointing to something that the conversationalists can *see* he has done. That is, I am raising the possibility that Gordon constructs his story so as to deliberately show that it was motivated by his own preceding utterance. Before attending to the implications of this observation, I would like to provide substantiating evidence for it.

It is not unusual to find instances in conversation where a story is being told so that it can be seen as occasioned by, or derived from, some preceding or succeeding utterance. For example, one might state a maxim, proverb, rule, or assertion and design a story so it can be seen as an illustration, proof, explication, or demonstration of such an assertion. In such cases the very design of the story displays the motive for telling it, that is, to substantiate some asserted state of affairs. For a story to be heard in this way by others, it cannot be produced in just any manner, but has to be worked up with an attention to this state of affairs.

Gordon's story illustrates one way of doing this. It is organized so that its *developing conclusion* ends up being an utterance—"Boy he check dem out 'e finally tol'm you guys better check the equipment out. hh(an' *now*"—that markedly resembles the preceding utterance that motivated the story in the first place: "They should check those things out— When they rent'm (they should check'm out.") What I am pointing to here is not some concluding remark which is tacked onto the story as an afterthought. Instead we have a series of events, related to us in succession so as to properly and reasonably culminate with the presentation of Gordon's preceding utterance as the story's conclusion.

The import of these observations is that they challenge our earlier definition of a "series of stories." Recall that we wanted to discover the process that spewed out a particular product—two or more adjacent stories which possessed many common elements. We assumed that such a product was produced by each next person designing his tale so it was similar to the one told by the person before him. Now, it is proposed that Gordon's "next" story was not designed to be similar to Peter's but was instead designed to be an instance of Gordon's own maxim, "They should check those things out." How then do we get what clearly looks like a series of stories when Gordon was not designing his story to be one in a series?

The Significance and Recounting Aspects of Storytelling

Two major concepts can be introduced here in order to solve this problem. There are two separate, but deeply related concerns which people frequently have in telling stories. I refer to these concerns as the *significance aspect* and the *recounting aspect* of storytelling. Conversationalists not only involve themselves in the relating or recounting of some event(s) but are also concerned with expressing the import, relevance, or significance of those events and/or indicating just that either leads up to or out of the faulty operation of amusement park rides. Finally, each storyteller constructs his story in such a manner as to make a moral point or illustrate a maxim. The storytellers do not leave this matter to be understood from the specifics of the events they relate. Peter and Gordon both describe the moral point independently of the actual relating of the story. And both moral points are so constructed as to relate to the issue of faulty amusement park rides. The reader is encouraged to make the previous observations for himself so that he will be better acquainted with the data and the phenomenon to be addressed in this paper.

Although these observations by no means exhaust the number of relationships that exist between the two tales told in instance 2, they do suggest the following possibility: The relations between these stories are not capricious and happenstance, but are instead the product of the careful attention and management of the conversationalists. They may have reasons for producing and exhibiting these relationships within a conversation; indeed, they may be obligated to do so. In this sense "talking about the world" is a markedly different activity within conversation than it is on a news show or in a classroom. For who says what about the world, and when, will all be highly contingent on the unfolding sequences of talk within the conversation itself.

When two adjacent stories are *designed* by their tellers to be related in these (or other) ways, I wish to speak of them as a "series of stories" rather than a mere "cluster." How could this be done? One procedure would be for each "next" storyteller to construct his own tale so that it had definite observable relationships to the previous one. This would require him to listen to the story before his own, in very special ways. Thus the occurrence of a "series of stories" would not be a preordained, pregiven matter, but would reside in each succeeding storyteller's *decision and achievement*. But if this is so, the question arises: Why would conversationalists want to do such a thing?

Having stated this preliminary but primary problem, we can turn our attention to a more detailed consideration of the particular data under investigation.

Refining the Problem

Implied in the above problem is a way to search for a solution. Since the resources for Gordon's succeeding story are presumably in Peter's preceding one, the researcher should begin by carefully comparing the contents of the two sequentially adjacent stories. However, closer inspection of instance 2 calls this approach into question. The origin of Gordon's succeeding story seems to be more directly traceable to one of *his own prior utterances*—"They should check those things out— When they rent'm (they should check'm out")— than to Peter's story itself. Further, when I speak of Gordon's story being *derived* from his previous utterance, I am not only pointing to something Gordon might have

PETER: I woulda been pinned under it.
    (4.0)
GORDON: They should check those things out— When they rent'm (they should check'm out.
    (
STAN: Yea::h.
    (3.0)
HAL: W'sometimez they don't—
    (1.7)
GORDON: Th–they should— they (should
HAL: —check'm.
    (5.0)
GORDON: If they're gonna rent'm (through the day), the:n, they should sheck'm out. —(2.0)— or the boss should— sorra, "Got this thing checked up?" "No," "What's duh mar:: wih you." — "Y' be'r check it out." —(4.0)—Cuz down here in Long Beach idjuh— anh-an bumped inna the bass'n I say "Hey. (one a'yuh rides goin out over here"— "Well which izzit.") — "Yerruh:: merry g'round ennuh::: dee— deh d'bump'm cars." —"What? I'll go to um *now*." Boy did he *go*. ('E really *told*'m though.)
    (3.0)
PETER: One time I w'z pinned, in the bump'r car one time.
GORDON: Boy he check dem out 'e finally tol'm you guys better check the equipment out. hh(an' *now*.
STAN: En hyou know(a' jing go ups go down eh duh — de(awduh
GORDON: (check'm out.)   (
    Better check'm out.
GORDON: ((He) did:d too.
    (2.0)

The Series-of-Stories Problem

By using the term *cluster*, I mean to point out that the stories being referred to occur in close proximity to one another. However, it is clear that the relationships that exist between them extend well beyond the fact that the second is told immediately after the first.[3] For example, in instance 2 each story is devoted to a similar topic, amusement park rides, also suggesting that each event being related occurs in a similar setting. More refined, each story focuses, in some manner, on the faulty operation of these amusement park rides and not, for example, on how much fun they are or which ones are too expensive. Second, in each story the storyteller is somehow implicated as a principal character in the story he is reporting. In fact, all character portrayal is built in and around the issue of the operations of the amusement park rides. And each story has a course of action

BLANCH: Mh hm, I expect.
BETH: Uh huh, deli//berately.
BLANCH: Well I'll see you at— at—
BETH: Tomorrow // night.
BLANCH: —at six at— hehhehh.

Instance 2

HAL: They're-uh-they::'re uhm, they're easy.
PETER: Boy, don't go at the fairgrounds through.
     ((whistles "wow"))
STAN: Oh(hh)o Go(hh)d'   00'.
HAL: Why?
PETER: C'z uh, —(2.0)— have one a' them things, they break loose up there.
GORDON: Oh wuhnyuh buildin that yeah I know about that. —They're prob-
     'bly— there's cables wasn' uh strong enough tuh, —pull'm *back*.
PETER: Uh-no those big cable cars. Y'nuh the ones up on the, track.
GORDON: Mm.
STAN: Wih A one Boat YUH::: UHLON DOHLENKO, — ETCHEruh
     WOOOOOPS.
     (1.7)
HAL: I wouldn' ride on them (cars.)
STAN: Gah' No *me*.
     (1.7)
GORDON: Aw me I'd ride onna *bumper* car.
PETER: An ah know who almos' got hit bah one a' them things.
STAN: YOU?
HAL: (((You?   )
     (   )
(STAN): Go::d.
GORDON: Mm hm.
GORDON: Not me.
PETER: ((with mouth full)) If I didn' stop bout; —
GORDON: ((with mouth full)) Eh w'z this— ((chewing))
(GORDON): (   )
PETER: (The cable car jus' went past me'n:: dropped. —dat, close to me.
HAL: Jeez.
GORDON: (   ).
PETER: That's how far ah was 'way fm that cable car.
STAN: ((whispered))   Go::d.
HAL: *Wow*.
STAN: (*Yeah*.)

BLANCH: And on the way home we saw the:: most gosh-awful wreck.
BETH: Oh::::
BLANCH: —we have ev— I've ever seen. I've never seen a car smashed into sm—— such a small space.
BETH: Oh::::
BLANCH: It was smashed from the front and the back both it must've been in— caught in between two cars.
BETH: Mh hm uh huh.
BLANCH: Must've run into a car and then another car smashed into it and there were people laid out and covered over on the pavement.
BETH: Mh.
BLANCH: We were s— parked there for quite a while but I was going to listen to the r— news and haven't done it.
BETH: No, I haven't had my radio on, either.
BLANCH: Well I had my television on, but I was listening to uh the blast-off, you know.
BETH: Mh hm.
BLANCH: The uh ah— // astronauts.
BETH: Yeah.
BETH: Yeah.
BLANCH: And I–I didn't ever get any *local* news.
BETH: Uh huh.
BLANCH: And I wondered.
BETH: Uh huh.
BETH: No, I haven't had it on, and I don't uh get the paper, and uhm
BLANCH: It wasn't in the paper last night, I looked.
BETH: Uh huh.
BETH: Probably didn't make it.
BLANCH: No, no you see this was about three o'clock in the afternoon.
BETH: Uh huh.
BLANCH: Paper was already off the press.
BETH: Uh huh.
BLANCH: Boy, it was a bad one, though.
BETH: Well that's too bad.
BLANCH: Kinda // (freak)—
BETH: You know, I looked and looked in the paper—I think I told you f–for that uh f–fall over at the Bowl that night. And I never saw a thing about it, and I // looked in the next couple of evenings.
BLANCH: Mh hm.
    (1.0)
BETH: Never saw a th— a mention of it.
BLANCH: I didn't see that, either.
BETH: Uh huh.
BETH: Maybe they kept it out.

The Same-Significance Procedure: Type 1

We can now state a general procedure for constructing a succeeding story which others can see to be related to the first—i.e., to be "one in a series." One can use the significance statement for the first story as a "blueprint" for remembering, inventing, and organizing a tale which has the same significance. One way to do this has already been described. One can use a "developing conclusion methodology" in organizing one's own tale. That is, one can "recount" a succession of events, which naturally culminate in the preceding storyteller's significance statement as their conclusion. Alternately (as additional data demonstrate), one can restate (or paraphrase) the preceding significance statement, and use it as a "story preface" to one's own tale.[5]

However, one need not be as blatant as this. Merely recounting events in a manner that *can be heard* as having the same significance as the first recounting, will allow others to hear it that way.[6] In fact, this third procedure is apparently employed in instance 1. First the issue of the media failing to report a newsworthy event is introduced by Blanch, and an instance of this given. Beth achieves a clear connection and series of stories relationship by recounting her events in strict conformance with this significance. Support for the contention that this procedure is often used (and that it works) can be obtained by noting the following: It is common to find the first story in some series containing both a significance statement and an appropriately organized recounting, while succeeding stories may lack any explicit indication of their significance. Yet they are heard by all parties as a "series of stories."

Additionally, it should be noted that all the similarities between adjacent stories which we discussed initially may be an *indirect* consequence of the same-significance procedure. That is, in recounting events in such a way as to exhibit that they have a particular significance, one may have (or be able) to include in them similar characters, similar settings in which they occur, and so on. Yet, importantly, events with a visibly similar significance need not be similar in other ways.[7]

Finally, one of the benefits of using the same-significance procedure is that it allows one, in the very way he tells his story, to show that and how he understands, supports, sympathizes, or agrees with the preceding story.

Same-Significance Procedure: Type 2

As already indicated, Gordon does not use the procedure we have just discussed. He uses another kind of same-significance procedure by making his intervening utterance function as a significance statement for both the story he later tells and for Peter's last story. Why does he do this? Why does he not employ the significance statement introduced by Peter? Relatedly, if the type 1 procedure allows one to show support, sympathy, or agreement with a preceding story, what does the type 2 procedure do?

Recalling our earlier discussion, we can see that being the "first" person to tell what will be a series of stories gives one strong control over the subsequent conversation. It is the first storyteller who not only provides a maiden recounting (with all its implications of topic, setting, characters, and so on) but also gets first crack at indicating the significance of that recounting. Any succeeding storyteller must pay close attention to what the first one did, or risk the possibility that his own tale will not be heard as one in a series, that is, it may seem irrelevant, off the topic, and so forth.

One way to deal with this is to provide new material (as Gordon did) for connecting two stories in a manner that might not be in any way apparent. This supplies the listener with a new sense of what the preceding story was actually about. Further, if the new significance statement is quite different from the first, it will be the second that becomes the only one that can meaningfully interrelate the two independent recountings. Recalling that "telling a story" includes both recounting events and displaying significance, we can now see that the second significance statement is, potentially, "competitive" with the first, for it can challenge, question, or correct what the first recounting is taken to mean.[8] Finally, the type 2 procedure provides a way to recount something that might otherwise be heard as quite out of line with what was said before and yet have it heard as commensurate with, and similar to, the first tale that was told. One might thus give a series of events a particular significance, merely to exhibit their connection to what was previously related. But such a significance statement will, in turn, affect how the events themselves must be described.

We see, then, that when one talks about the world within conversation, one does not merely report information; one undercuts or agrees with the view of another, talks on, or tries to change the topic, and so on. Because of these contingencies, talk about the world, in conversation, frequently takes the form of a series of deliberately interrelated stories. Both the events related and the significance attributed to them are as much the result of conversational dynamics as they are of the personalities and attitudes of the conversationalists. In fact, we can venture further. If a person's general "point of view" is, in part, the product of the proverbs and stories he relates to others in daily life, then he may end up with a particular viewpoint on, say, sex or politics because of the conversational sequences he happened to get into!

The Import of the Analysis

At this point there may still be some readers who are waiting for a "punch line." After all, while the preceding may be interesting and plausible, what does it have to do with sociology? We have uncovered some methods by which competent, socialized adults "talk about the world." It is now time to point out that the data we analyzed from instance 2 were not produced by adults who were "competent" and "socialized"—at least from the standpoint of our society. It represented a conversation between two males who resided in an institution for the mentally retarded. Insofar as what they do and understand when they talk is structurally similar to what the rest of us do and understand when we talk (as evidenced by instance 1), perhaps we had better reexamine our conception of the retarded. Perhaps the initial intuitive feeling that their communication is somehow "defective" is superficial. Before deciding what about their behavior is defective and what is normal, we had better learn explicitly what the "normal" consists of and how what they are doing might be different. This article represents a partial effort in that direction.

Notes

1. The study of storytelling in conversation, as a topic of research, was established by Harvey Sacks. For a number of uniformities and regularities uncovered in his researches, see Harvey Sacks, unpublished lecture notes, University of California at Irvine, spring, 1970. The basic thrust of this report is deeply indebted to features of this work, although I accept full responsibility for uses made of these materials.

   A couple of additional clarifying remarks follow. First, by the notion of "story," I mean, for now, the telling of some event in more than one utterance. Second, when I speak of the "telling of a story in conversation," I have in mind not only the utterances of the storyteller but also the comments made in the course of a story presentation by those who are the recipients of the story. The fact that recipients make these comments can affect the in-progress unfolding of some relating of an event, and consequently the very meaning that a series of utterances might obtain. This is a distinguishing characteristic of stories told in conversation as opposed to, for example, stories told in performance situations. This characteristic not only differentiates our concerns and interests in storytelling from those of, say, students of folklore, who show an abiding interest in this phenomenon, but it also affirms the sense in which storytelling in conversation is an interactionally collaborative achievement.

2. Instance 2 is part of a larger corpus of tape-recorded conversations made at a Los Angeles County Board and Care Home for the mentally retarded. Instance 1 was supplied by Harvey Sacks and consists of a telephone conversation between two adult females. Any interested reader can obtain additional instances of the conversational phenomenon discussed in this article by writing to Alan Ryave, Department of Sociology, California State University at Dominguez Hills, California.

3. The present line of discussion should not be construed as undercutting the fundamental importance of proximity to the general phenomenon of telling "another" story. For example, on occasion, a prospective storyteller is unable, for whatever reason, to adequately present a succeeding story in the sequential place they deem relevant. When this occurs, there are special conversational devices for indicating the slot in

428   ILLUSTRATIVE CASE STUDIES FOR BOOK TWO

which the story should have appeared. Thus, in the conversation from which instance 2 was taken Peter attempted to start up a story, following Gordon's, with the utterance "One time I w'z pinned in the bump'r car one time." He was interrupted. When the opportunity came to start up again, he began his story again, but in a slightly different manner: "'N' like I w'z goan say about bumping cars . . ." With a preface like "'N like I w'z goan say . . .," Peter is able to link the present unfolding story with his prior effort and thereby indicate where his story should have been told.

4. By "utterance" I mean a complete turn at talk in conversation.

5. As articulated by Sacks, "story prefaces," often framed in the form of a question, serve to "clear floor room" for a prospective storyteller. That is, they announce his intention to tell a story, give listeners some idea of what is coming, and allow them to give him the floor for a certain amount of conversational time, in order to accomplish his task.

6. One import of this hearer's maxim is that a previous story does not have to be an immediately preceding one in order for the series-of-stories phenomenon to be obtained. That this is the case can be appreciated by the way in which this maxim is invoked by lawyers in locating and determining a precedent for some story they are presently involved in constructing. For further articulation of this point, see Michael Moerman, "The Use of Precedent in Natural Conversation," *Semiotica* 7 (1973). There are numerous other analytical disciplines that require practitioners to know and work with intricacies of this procedure, e.g., historians, psychological counselors and therapists, analytical interpretation of open-ended interviews, doctors, etc.

7. When the same-significance device is employed, it is not uncommon to obtain two related stories whose story elements (such as characters, setting, time, and topic) do not display any sense of strict commonality. Therefore, searching for common story elements as a means of substantiating their status as a series of stories will not necessarily yield valid results.

8. There is a sense in which Peter's and Gordon's significance statements stand as alternatives to Peter's recounting. It can be observed that Peter's significance statement, which prefaces his impending recounting, takes the form of a "warning." It uses a conventional frame for doing "warnings"—"Don't do X" (that is, don't go to the fairgrounds). Where his succeeding recounting stands as an evidential instance of a dangerous thing that can happen to you if you choose to do X. In contrast, Gordon's appended significance statement locates specific blame and explanation for the fairground's catastrophe, thereby providing potential resolution to the troubles, and dangers described in Peter's story. That is, the danger as developed by Peter in and through his story is presented as embedded in the setting, whereas Gordon, by assessing specific blame, shifts the attention from the setting to certain individuals; the danger is not irremedial. If "they" would check those things out, then presumably the sort of danger incurred by Peter could be avoided—and, along with it, the propriety of Peter's warning.

Bibliography

Allport, Gordon
   1942   *The Use of Personal Documents in Psychological Science.* New York: Social
          Science Research Council Bulletin no. 49.
Anthony, Dick, et al.
   1974   "Reply to Bellah." *Journal for the Scientific Study of Religion* 13 (December):
          491–95.
Asch, S. E.
   1952   *Social Psychology.* Englewood Cliffs, N.J.: Prentice-Hall.
Austin, J. L.
   1961   *Philosophical Papers.* London: Oxford University Press.
Bar-Hillel, Yehoshua
   1954   "Indexical Expressions." *Mind* 63: 359–379.
Becker, Howard S.
   1951   "The Professional Dance Musician and His Audience." *American Journal of
          Sociology* 57 (September): 136–144.
   1963   *Outsiders: Studies in the Sociology of Deviance.* New York: Free Press.
   1958   "Problems of Inference and Proof in Participant Observation." *American Socio-
          logical Review* 23: 652–660.
——————, ed.
   1964   *The Other Side: Perspectives on Deviance.* New York: Free Press.
Bellah, Robert
   1970   "Christianity and Symbolic Realism." *Journal for the Scientific Study of Reli-
          gion* 9:89–96.
Berger, Peter, and Thomas Luckmann
   1966   *The Social Construction of Reality.* Garden City, N.Y.: Doubleday.
Bittner, Egon
   1965   "The Concept of Organization." *Social Research* 32: 239–258.
   1967   "The Police on Skid Row." *American Sociological Review* 32: 699–715.Blalock,

Blalock, Hubert
  1960 *Social Statistics.* New York: McGraw-Hill.
Blum, Alan, and Peter McHugh
  1971 "The Social Ascription of Motives." *American Sociological Review* 36, no. 1: 98–109.
Blumer, Herbert
  1954 "What Is Wrong with Social Theory?" *American Sociological Review* 19: 3–10.
  1956 "Sociological Analysis and the "Variable." *American Sociological Review* 21: 683–690.
  1966 "Sociological Implications of the Thought of George Herbert Mead." *American Journal of Sociology* 71 (March): 535–544.
  1969 *Symbolic Interactionism.* Englewood Cliffs, N.J.: Prentice-Hall.
Castaneda, Carlos
  1968 *The Teachings of Don Juan: A Yaqui Way of Knowledge.* Berkeley: University of California Press.
  1971 *A Separate Reality.* New York: Simon and Schuster.
  1972 *A Journey to Ixtlan.* New York: Simon and Schuster.
Cavan, Ruth
  1928 *Suicide.* Chicago: University of Chicago Press.
Chomsky, Noam
  1965 *Aspects of the Theory of Syntax.* Cambridge: M.I.T. Press.
  1966 *Cartesian Linguistics: A Chapter in the History of Rationalist Thought.* New York: Harper and Row.
  1968 *Language and Mind.* New York: Harcourt, Brace and World.
Churchill, Lindsay
  1971 "Ethnomethodology and Measurement." *Social Forces* 50: 182–191.
Cicourel, Aaron V.
  1964 *Method and Measurement in Sociology.* New York: Free Press.
  1968 *The Social Organization of Juvenile Justice.* New York: John Wiley and Sons.
  1974 *Cognitive Sociology: Language and Meaning in Social Interaction.* New York: Free Press.
  1973 *Theory and Method in a Study of Argentine Fertility.* New York: John Wiley and Sons.
  ———, and R. Boese
  1972 "Sign Language Acquisition and the Teaching of Deaf Children." In D. Hymes et al. (eds.), *The Functions of Language: An Anthropological Approach and Psychological Approach.* New York: Teachers College Press.
  ———, and John I. Kitsuse
  1963 *The Educational Decision Makers.* Indianapolis: Bobbs-Merrill.
  ———, et al.
  1974 *Language Use and School Performance.* New York: Academic Press.
Coleman, James S.
  1968 "Review: Studies in Ethnomethodology." *American Sociological Review* 33: 122–130.
Comte, Auguste
  1853 *The Positive Philosophy of Auguste Comte.* Translated and condensed by H. Martineau. London: J. Chapman.
Denzin, Norman K.
  1970 *The Research Act.* Chicago: Aldine.

Deutscher, Irwin
1966 "Words and Deeds." *Social Problems* 13: 235–254.
Douglas, Jack D., ed.
1970 *Understanding Everyday Life.* Chicago: Aldine Publishing Co.
Duncan, Otis Dudley
1961 "A Socio-Economic Index for All Occupations." In Albert J. Reiss, Jr. (ed.), *Occupations and Social Status.* New York: Free Press.
Durkheim, Emile
1967 *The Rules of Sociological Method.* New York: The Free Press.
1951 *Suicide.* New York: Free Press.
Ekman, Paul
1965 "Communication Through Nonverbal Behavior: A Source of Information About an Interpersonal Relationship." Pp. 390–442 in S. Tomkins and C. Izard (eds.), *Affect, Cognition, and Personality.* New York: Springer Press.
Evans-Pritchard, E. E.
1937 *Witchcraft, Oracles and Magic Among the Azande.* London: Oxford University Press.
Freidson, Eliot
1970 *The Profession of Medicine: A Study of the Sociology of Applied Knowledge.* New York: Dodd, Mead.
Garfinkel, Harold
1952 "Perception of the Other." Ph.D. dissertation. Harvard University.
1956 "Conditions of Successful Degradation Ceremonies." *American Journal of Sociology* 61: 420–424.
1963 "A Conception of and Experiments with Trust as a Condition of Concerted Stable Actions." In O. J. Harvey (ed.), *Motivation and Social Interaction.* New York: Ronald Press.
1967 *Studies in Ethnomethodology.* Englewood Cliffs, N.J.: Prentice-Hall.
————, and Harvey Sacks
1970 "The Formal Structures of Practical Actions." In John C. McKinney and Edward A. Tiryakian (eds.), *Theoretical Sociology: Perspectives and Developments.* New York: Appleton-Century-Crofts.
Gasking, Douglas
1955 "Mathematics and the World." In Anthony Flew (ed.), *Logic and Language.* Garden City, N.Y.: Doubleday Anchor.
Girton, George
1975 "Kung Fu: Toward a Praxiological Hermeneutic of the Martial Arts." Unpublished paper. University of California at Los Angeles, Department of Sociology.
Glaser, Barney G., and Anselm L. Strauss
1967 *The Discovery of Grounded Theory: Strategies for Qualitative Research.* Chicago: Aldine.
Goffman, Erving
1959 *The Presentation of Self in Everyday Life.* Garden City, N.Y.: Doubleday Anchor.
1961 *Asylums.* Garden City, N.Y.: Doubleday Anchor.
1963 *Behavior in Public Places.* New York: Free Press.
1963 *Stigma: Notes on and Management of Spoiled Identity.* Englewood Cliffs, N.J.: Prentice-Hall.

1967 *Interaction Ritual.* Garden City, N.Y.: Doubleday Anchor.

1975 *Strategic Interaction.* Philadelphia: University of Pennsylvania Press.

Gumperz, J., and D. Hymes, eds.

1964 "The Ethnography of Communication." *American Anthropologist* 66: 127–132.

Gurwitsch, Aron

1964 *The Field of Consciousness.* Pittsburgh: Duquesne University Press.

Hall, Edward T.

1969 *The Hidden Dimension.* Garden City, N.Y.: Doubleday Anchor.

Harvey, O. J., ed.

1963 *Motivation and Social Interaction.* New York: Ronald Press.

Hays, William L.

1963 *Statistics for Psychologists.* New York: Holt, Rinehart and Winston.

Haytin, Daniel Leigh

1969 "The Methodological Validity of the Case Study in the Social Sciences." Ph.D. dissertation. University of California at Berkeley.

Heap, James Louis

1975 "Eidos, Sociology and Language: A Criticism of Free-Phantasy Variation." Paper read at the Annual Meetings of the Eastern Sociological Association, Boston.

1975 "Figuring Out Grammar: Features and Practices of Explicating Normative Order." Ph.D. dissertation. University of British Columbia.

———, and Phillip A. Roth

1973 "On Phenomenological Sociology." *American Sociological Review* 38 (June): 354–367.

Heidegger, Martin

1962 *Being and Time.* New York: Harper and Row.

Hill, R. C., and K. S. Crittenden, eds.

1968 *The Purdue Symposium on Ethnomethodology.* Monograph no. 1. Institute for the Study of Social Change. Lafayette, Ind.: Purdue University.

Hodge, Robert, et al.

1966 "Occupational Prestige in the United States: 1925–1963." In Reinhard Bendix and Seymour Martin Lipset (eds.), *Class, Status and Power.* New York: Free Press.

Holzner, Burkhart

1968 *Reality Construction in Society.* Cambridge, Mass.: Schenkman.

Horton, John ·

1966 "Order and Conflict Theories of Social Problems as Competing Ideologies." *American Sociological Review* 71 (May): 701–713.

Husserl, Edmond

1913 *Ideas.* London: George Allen and Unwin.

1970 *Cartesian Meditations.* The Hague: Martinus Nijhoff.

1970 *The Paris Lectures.* The Hague: Martinus Nijhoff.

Jacobs, Jerry

1967 "A Phenomenological Study of Suicide Notes." *Social Problems* 15 (Summer): 60–72.

1969 *The Search for Help: A Study of the Retarded Child in the Community.* New York: Brunner/Mazel.

1971 *Adolescent Suicide.* New York: Wiley Interscience.

1974   *Fun City: An Ethnographic Study of a Retirement Community.* New York: Holt, Rinehart and Winston.

1975   *Older Persons and Retirement Communities: Case Studies in Social Gerontology.* Springfield, Ill.: Charles C. Thomas.

Johnson, John

1975   *Doing Field Research.* New York: Free Press.

Jules-Rosette, Bennetta

1974   "Reflexive Ethnography, Part I: Instructions as Data: The Apostolic Case." Unpublished paper. University of California at San Diego, Department of Sociology.

Kaplan, Abraham

1943   "Content Analysis and the Theory of Signs." *Philosophy of Science* 10: 230.

Katz, Jerrold J., and P. M. Postal

1964   *An Integrated Theory of Linguistic Descriptions.* Cambridge, Mass.: M.I.T. Press.

Kuhn, Thomas S.

1970   *The Structure of Scientific Revolutions.* Chicago: University of Chicago Press.

Laing, R. D.

1967   *The Politics of Experience.* New York: Basic Books.

Lakatos, I.

1963   "Proofs and Refutations." *British Journal for the Philosophy of Science* 14: 1–26, 120–177, 221–265, 296–343.

Lemert, Edwin M.

1951   *Sociopathic Behavior.* New York: McGraw-Hill.

1962   "Paranoia and the Dynamics of Exclusion." *Sociometry* 25 (March): 1–20.

Lenneberg, E. H.

1969   "On Explaining Language." *Science* 164: 635–643.

Lofland, John

1971   *Analyzing Social Settings.* Belmont, Calif.: Wadsworth.

Luker, Kristin

1976   *Taking Chances.* Berkeley: University of California Press.

MacKay, Robert

1973   "Conceptions of Children and Models of Socialization." In Hans P. Dreitzel (ed.), *Childhood and Socialization.* New York: Macmillan.

McGee, Michael H.

1968   "Social Organization Study: Meher Baba." Unpublished research study. University of North Carolina at Chapel Hill, Department of Sociology.

McHugh, Peter

1968   *Defining the Situation.* Indianapolis: Bobbs-Merrill.

Mead, George Herbert

1934   *Mind, Self, and Society.* Chicago: University of Chicago Press.

1959   *The Philosophy of the Present.* La Salle, Ill.: Open Court Publishing Company.

Mehan, Hugh

1972   "Language Using Abilities." *Language Sciences* 22: 1–10.

————, and Houston Wood

1975   *The Reality of Ethnomethodology.* New York: Wiley Interscience.

Merleau-Ponty, Maurice

1962   *The Phenomenology of Perception.* London: Routledge and Kegan Paul.

1964   *Sense and Non-Sense.* Evanston, Ill.: Northwestern University Press.

Mills, C. Wright
    1940   "Situated Actions and Vocabularies of Motive." *American Sociological Review* 5
                (December): 904-913.
Moerman, Michael
    1964   "Who are the Lue?" *American Anthropologist* 67: 1215-1230.
Narens, Louis
    1975   "The Belief Systems of the Insane." In J. Schenkein et al. (eds.), *Topics in
                Ethnomethodology*. Berlin: Suhrkamp Publishers.
Natanson, Maurice
    1956   *The Social Dynamics of George Herbert Mead*. Washington, D.C.: Public Af-
                fairs Press.
    1962   *Literature, Philosophy, and the Social Sciences*. The Hague: Martinus Nijhoff.
National Opinion Research Center
    1947   "Jobs and Occupations: A Popular Evaluation." *Public Opinion News* 9: 3-13.
Newman, John H.
    1974   "From Space to Place: Locating a Rural Drug Program." Paper read at the
                Annual Meetings of the Pacific Sociological Association, San Jose, Calif.
Norman, Donald A.
    1969   *Memory and Attention: An Introduction to Human Information Processing*.
                New York: John Wiley and Sons.
Palmer, E. R.
    1968   *Hermeneutics*. Evanston, Ill.: Northwestern University Press.
Pannikar, Raymond
    1971   "The Ultimate Experience: The Ways of the West and the East." Unpublished
                paper. Harvard University.
Parsons, Talcott
    1949   *The Structure of Social Action*. New York: Free Press.
Pates, John L.
    1972   "Violation of Social Expectations." Unpublished paper. Harvard University.
Pirandello, Luigi
    1952   *Naked Masks: Five Plays by Luigi Pirandello*, ed. by Eric Bentley. New York:
                Dutton.
Polanyi, Michael
    1958   *Personal Knowledge*. Chicago: University of Chicago Press.
    1966   *The Tacit Dimension*. Garden City, N.Y.: Doubleday Anchor.
    1966   "The Logic of Tacit Inference." *Philosophy* 41, no. 155 (January): 1-18.
Pollner, Melvin
    1970   "On the Foundation of Mundane Reason." Ph.D. dissertation. University of
                California at Santa Barbara.
    1975   "The Very Coinage of Your Brain: The Resolution of Reality Disjunctures."
                The Philosophy of the Social Sciences 5: 411-430.
    1974   "Mundane Reasoning." *Philosophy of the Social Sciences* 4, no. 1: 35-54.
Psathas, George, ed.
    1973   *Phenomenological Sociology*. New York: John Wiley and Sons.
Riskin, Steven
    1972   "The Philosophical Grounds for Some Sociological Certainties." Paper read at
                the Pacific Sociological Association Annual Meetings, Portland.
Robbins, Thomas, et al.
    1973   "The Limits of Symbolic Realism: Problems of Empathetic Field Observation

in a Sectarian Context." *Journal for the Scientific Study of Religion* 12 (September): 259–271.

Rosenhan, D. L.
1973 "On Being Sane in Insane Places." *Science* 179, no. 4070: 250–258.

Rosenthal, Robert, et al.
1974 "Body Talk and Tone of Voice: The Language Without Words." *Psychology Today* 8: 64–68.

Sacks, Harvey
1963 "Sociological Description." *Berkeley Journal of Sociology* 8: 1–17.
1966 "The Search for Help: No One to Turn To." Ph.D. dissertation. University of California at Berkeley.
1972 "On the Analyzability of Stories by Children." In Roy Turner (ed.), *Ethnomethodology*. Baltimore: Penguin Books.
——, Emmanuel Schegloff, and Gail Jefferson
1974 "A Simplest Systematics for the Analysis of Turn Taking in Conversation." *Language* 50: 696–735.

Schatzman, L., and A. Strauss
1973 *Field Research: Strategies for a Natural Sociology*. Englewood Cliffs, N.J.: Prentice-Hall.

Schegloff, Emanuel A.
1967 "The First Five Seconds: The Order of Conversational Openings." Ph.D. dissertation. University of California at Berkeley.
1968 "Sequencing in Conversational Openings." *American Anthropologist* 70, no. 6: 1075–1095.
1972 "Notes on a Conversational Practice: Formulating Place." In David Sudnow (ed.), *Studies in Interaction*. New York: Free Press.
——, and Harvey Sacks
1973 "Opening Up Closings." *Semiotica* 8: 289–327.

Schenkein, Jim
1972 "Towards an Analysis of Natural Conversation and the Sense of Heheh." *Semiotica* 6: 344–377.

Schutz, Alfred
1944 "The Stranger." *American Journal of Sociology* 49, no. 6 (May): 499–507.
1971 *Collected Papers I: The Problem of Social Reality*. The Hague: Martinus Nijhoff.
1964 *Collected Papers II: Studies in Social Theory*. The Hague: Martinus Nijhoff.
1966 *Collected Papers III: Studies in Phenomenological Philosophy*. The Hague: Martinus Nijhoff.
1967 *The Phenomenology of the Social World*. Evanston, Ill.: Northwestern University Press.
1970 *On Phenomenology and Social Relations*. Chicago: University of Chicago Press.

Schwartz, Howard
1971 "*Mental Disorder and the Study of Subjective Experience: Some Uses of Each to Elucidate the Other*." Ph.D. dissertation, University of California at Los Angeles.
1972 "Towards a Phenomenology of Projection Errors." Paper presented at the Pacific Sociological Association Annual Meetings, Portland.
1975 "Making Ambiguity Visible: A Study in Sociolinguistics." Paper read at the Pacific Sociological Association Annual Meetings.

1976   "General Features." In J. Schenkein et al. (eds.), *Topics in Ethnomethodology*. Berlin: Suhrkamp Publishers.

Scott, Marvin B., and Stanford M. Lyman

1970   "Accounts, Deviance, and Social Order." Pp. 89–119 in Jack D. Douglas (ed.), *Deviance and Respectability: The Social Construction of Moral Meanings*. New York: Basic Books.

Siegel, Paul

1970   Occupational Prestige in the Negro Subculture." *Sociological Inquiry* 40 (Spring): 156–171.

Simmel, Georg

1902   "The Number of Members as Determining the Sociological Form of the Group." *American Journal of Sociology* 8: 1–46, 158–196.

1949   "The Sociology of Sociability." *American Journal of Sociology* 55: 254–261.

1950   *The Sociology of Georg Simmel*. Translated and edited by Kurt H. Wolff. Glencoe, Ill.: Free Press.

Skinner, B. F.

1953   *Science and Human Behavior*. New York: Macmillan.

Sommer, Robert

1969   *Personal Space: The Behavioral Basis of Design*. Englewood Cliffs, N.J.: Prentice-Hall.

Speier, Matthew

1973   *How to Observe Face-to-Face Communication*. Pacific Palisades, Calif.: Goodyear Publishing Co.

Sperling, George

1960   "The Information Available in Brief Visual Presentations." *Psychological Monographs* 74: 1–2.

Stearns, Warren A.

1953   "Cases of Probable Suicide in Young Persons Without Obvious Motivation." *Journal of the Maine Medical Association* 44: 16–23.

Stonequist, Everett V.

1937   *The Marginal Men*. New York: Scribner.

Sudnow, David

1965   "Normal Crimes." *Social Problems* 12: 255–276.

1969   *Passing On: The Social Organization of Dying*. Englewood Cliffs, N.J.: Prentice-Hall.

————, ed.

1972   *Studies in Social Interaction*. New York: Free Press.

1978   *The Ways of Hands*. Cambridge, Mass.: Harvard University Press.

Tart, Charles T.

1972   "States of Consciousness and State-Specific Sciences." *Science* 176 (June): 1203–1210.

Ten Houten, Warren, and Charles Kaplan

1973   *Science and Its Mirror Image*. New York: Harper and Row.

Theeman, Margaret

1973   "Social Configurations of the Movement "Movement": A Study in Alienation and Ecstasy." Ph.D. dissertation. Harvard University, Department of Sociology.

Thomas, .W. I.

1928   *The Child in America*. New York: Alfred A. Knopf.

————, and Florian Znaniecki
 1927   *The Polish Peasant in Europe and America: Volumes I and II*. New York: Alfred
        A. Knopf.
Webb, Eugene J., et al.
 1966   *Unobstrusive Measures: Nonreactive Research in the Social Sciences*. Chicago:
        Rand McNally.
Weber, Max
 1964   *The Theory of Social and Economic Organization*. New York: Free Press.
Wilson, Thomas P.
 1970   "Conceptions of Interaction and Forms of Sociological Explanation." *American
        Sociological Review* 35: 697–709.
 1971   "The Regress Problem and the Problem of Evidence in Ethnomethodology."
        Paper presented at the American Sociological Association Annual Meetings,
        Denver.
Wittgenstein, Ludwig
 1953   *Philosophical Investigations*. London: Basil Blackwell and Mott.
Zimmerman, Don H.
 1970   "The Practicalities of Rule Use." In Jack D. Douglas (ed.), *Understanding
        Everyday Life*. Chicago: Aldine.

Index

Index

A

Action
  and "Generalized other," 23–24
  and Intention, 330–332, 338
  Mead, George Herbert, 23–24
  Methodology, study of, 25–26
  Models, use of hypothetically to determine, 19
  Weber, Max, 18, 19, 20
  Zweckrational, 20
Actor
  Language, use of, 8
  and Observer, 28
  Point of view, 3–4, 6–8, 13, 14, 25–26, 61, 196
  Self-perception of, 296
  and Setting, 9–10, 62
  and Society (as one), 21, 371–372
  Weber, Max, 18
  See also Action; Mead, George Herbert; Member; Personal accounts; Respondent
Adato, Alan, 235
"Ad hocing," 133, 136–138, 139, 141, 258–259

  See also Bureaucracy, symbolic; Ethnomethodology; Market research
Allport, Gordon, 67–68, 73
Ambiguity, in conversation, 119
  See also Vagueness
Analysis
  "Functional," 332
  Integrating, 30–31
  of Intentions, 329–332, 360
  Philosophical, 360
  See also Analytic memos; Coding; Methodology
Analytic induction, 32
Analytic memos, 30–31
  See also Coding; Field notes; Grounded theory
Anthony, Dick, 48–49, 59
Asch, S. E., 64, 73, 288
Assumptions, endowment of, 278–280
  See also Background expectations, Disruption
Audio-visual techniques
  as Data, 81–84, 343
  Distance receptors, 82, 83
  Editing emphasis, 87, 88
  "Illustrators," 84, 102

Audio-visual techniques, *cont.*
  "Micro-displays," 84
  Physical limitations, 85
  Projective technique, 86
  Reactive measures, 89, 268–271
  Respondents as documentarians, 84–86
  Retrieval, 88–89, 270
  Sampling, 88
  Selective attention, 82–83
  Symbol system, 87–88, 213–214
  Visual anthropology, 86
  See also Conversational analysis;
    Nonobtrusive techniques
Autism, 170, 171, 175
  See also Mental retardation

B

Background expectations, 169, 214, 225,
    369, 375
  See also Case Study F; Disruption
Baker, Robert K., 102
Balance theory, 245
Ball, Sandra J., 102
Becker, Howard, 7, 32, 55, 60, 243, 245,
    317, 336
Behaviorism, 14
  See also Skinner, B. F.
Belief, 3, 267, 337, 371
  and Mental illness, 406–408
  See also Background expectancies
Bella, Robert, 48, 59
Bender, Lauretta, 176
Berger, Peter, 235
Bias, researcher
  Methodological appendixes, 58–59
  Minimizing, 27–28
  and Self-observation, 362–363
  See also Ad hocing; Bureaucracy, sym-
    bolic; Market research; Subjectivity
Bittner, Egon, 235
Bjaanes, Arne T., 397–404
Blacker, K. H., 416
Blacks, and occupational esteem, 11
Blalock, Hubert, 336
Blau, Peter, 143–144, 145, 150, 154
Blum, Alan, 235

Blumer, Herbert, 7, 24–26, 28, 33, 59,
    196
Body language, 77
  "Illustrators," 84, 102
  See also Case Study E
Boese, R., 127, 237, 238
Bowman, Peter, 176
Bureaucracy
  Efficiency, 144, 204
  Intent of organization, 144
  Unofficial change, 144, 154
  Weberian, 20, 143–144, 145, 150
Bureaucracy, symbolic
  Change, actual, 147, 148–150, 154
  Deviation and ideal form, 145
  Efficiency, 147–148
  Hierarchy of authority, 147–148
  Impersonality, 150–153
  Rules, 148–150
  Specialization, 145–147
  Worker cheating, 148–149
  See also Ad hocing

C

Case Study A, 133–142
Case Study B, 143–155
Case Study C, 156–167
Case Study D, 168–176
Case Study E
  "Abnormal behavior," 385
  Background expectancies, 385
  Body interaction, 383–384, 389, 392
  Communication, 385, 394
  Fault-finding procedures, 387, 391, 395
  Interaction, participant-observer, 382–
    383, 384–385, 387–389, 392, 394,
    395
  Interaction, social, 385, 392, 395–396
  Intersubjectivity, 386, 394
  Language, 385, 392, 395–396
  Meaning, 390, 391, 393
  Medical profile, 382–385
  Membership, 391
  Member's perspective, 386–387, 389–
    391, 395
  Methodology, 381–385

Motivation, 385
Natural language, 388
Observation, 382–393
Phenomenology, 387
Reification, 387
Rubella syndrome, 381, 382
Self-gratification, 383–384, 387, 388, 389, 390, 392, 393–394
Setting, 383, 386, 388
Subjectivity, observer's, 388, 391–392
Case Study F, 397–404
Case Study G, 405–417
Case Study H, 418–428
Castaneda, Carlos, 32, 33, 125, 130, 268, 276, 287, 387, 388
Categories, 319–322
Cavan, Ruth, 69, 74
Cavan, Sherri, 32
Character disorder, 114
Charisma, 9
Cheating: See Ad hocing; Background expectancies; Beliefs; Bureaucracy, symbolic; Conceptual laws; Market research
"Chicago school," 32
Childhood schizophrenia, 169, 170, 171
See also Mental retardation
Chomsky, Noam, 237
Churchill, Lindsey, 235
Cicourel, Aaron V., 42, 59, 127, 168, 176, 224–235, 237, 238, 252, 260, 263, 271, 309, 335
Civil inattention, 191, 194
Coding, 28–29
Analytic memos, 30
Audio-visual, 88–89
Language as, 228
Cognitive sociology
Background knowledge, 228, 232–233
Coding, 228
Indefinite triangulation, 233–234
Interpretive procedures, 230–231
Language acquisition, 225–226, 228, 230, 237, 341
Meanings, 228
Mentors, practitioners, 235
Nonpictorial, nonverbal thought, 229

and Phenomenology, 359
"Rule" application, 231
Validity, 232–233
Collective consciousness, 90, 371
Common sense
Actor's point of view, 196
Models, 210
Nature, commonality of, 197–198
Production accounts, 215–216
Reasoning, 198, 205
as Resource, 197
versus Scientific thinking, 194–196
and Sociological findings, 243, 297–300
Sociology's need for, 195–196
Suspension of, 205
Topic of study, 196–197
and Validity, 316
See also Communication; Natural attitude; Scientific attitude
Communication, 7
Children's verbal behavior, 319–320
Common scheme of, 199–200
Cross modal, 238
Face work, 193
Language, universality of, 226–227
Nonverbal, 89, 102, 231, 234
within Social structure, 186, 208
Vagueness and literalness, 258–259
See also Body language; Case Studies E, H; Natural attitude; Novice; Phenomenology, Scientific attitude
Competence
of Ideal speaker-hearer, 363
and Imitation, 397–404
and Member, 212–213, 254–255, 375, 380
and Mental illness, 412, 416
Reconsideration of, 427
and Retardates, 402–404, 427
Retrieval of, 375
See also Case Studies E, F, G, H; Member; Novice
Comstock, George A., 102
Comte, Auguste, 13, 16
Conceptual laws, 323–326, 327, 328–329, 337, 338

Conflict theory, 372–373
  See also Socialization
Consensus
  in Groups, 186
  Rejecting validity of group's, 61
  Verification of seeming contradictions,
    41
Constraints
  Anxiety, 282–283
  See also Social facts; Social structure;
    Suicide
Constructive analysis, 221–224, 237
Content analysis, 77–78
Conversation
  Ambiguity, 119
  Analysis, 119–120, 130, 326–327,
    335–336
  Competence, 427
  as Embodied activity, 265
  Formulating, 129, 216–217, 416, 421–
    422, 425–426, 428
  Improvisational nature of, 255
  and Inference, 119
  Initiating, 26–27
  versus Interviewing, 62–63
  Natural, 326–327, 341–342
  Organization of, 120–121
  Patterns, 412–414
  as Process, 29, 265
  Regulating hearing, 83, 120
  Relationships within, 421–424
  and Sexism, 88
  Side sequences, 121–122
  Turn taking, 338
  Universality of, 340–341
Conversational analysis
  Cluster, 421, 422
  "Context-free-context-sensitive" rules,
    363
  Conversational objects, 348
  Data, 335–336, 343, 345–347
  Demonstrating ambiguities, 119–122,
    130
  Dominance and deference, 352
  Excavation, 345–346
  "Hearing," 343–344
  Identification categories, 346

Induction, 347
  and Interaction, 347–348, 349
  Interruptions, 352, 363
  Listening noises, 349
  Manipulation, 345–346
  Mentors, practitioners, 235–236
  Misidentification, 346
  Natural conversation, 326–327, 341–
    342, 349
  Preinvitations, 299, 348
  Projectible utterance, 351–352
  Significance/recounting aspects, 423–
    424
  Structural organization, 341, 342, 349,
    352
  Subject matter, 341–342, 424
  Summons-answer sequences, 347
  Timing, 350–351, 364
  Turn taking, 326–327, 342, 350–351,
    352
  Utterance, 428
Cooley, John Horton, 7
Cottell scale, 172
Cressey, Donald, 32, 158, 167
Critical attitude, 313–315, 335
  See also Natural attitude; Validity
Cults, religious, study of, 48–49
Curtis, 48–49, 59

D

Data, 3
  Audio-visual techniques, 81–84
  Collection and categorizing, 28–29,
    308, 310
  Descriptive, 10
  and "Fit" with theory, 10
  Framework of, 291
  and Hypotheses, 323, 334, 336
  Macroscopic, 242
  Microscopic, 242–243
  and Phenomenologists, 6
  and Positivisits, 8, 11
  and Psychoanalysts, 6
  Subjective effect of, 232
  and Symbolic interactionists, 6–7

See also Case Studies A, B, C, D, E, F,
    G, H; Interview; Life history; Market
    research; Natural language; Partici-
    pant observation; Personal accounts;
    Phenomenology
Davis, Fred, 32
Deception
    Acquiring concept of, 23
    and Body language, 77, 102
    in Interviews, 41
    Misfit, cultural, 261–262
    Self-, 23, 362
    See also Ad hocing; Background expecta-
        tions; Mental illness; Mistakes
Defense mechanisms, 110
Definitions, 327–328
Demography, 11
Depersonalization, 24
    See also Bureaucracy
Descartes, René, 202
Deutscher, Irwin, 46, 59
Deviant, labeling of, 317–318, 336
Discrimination
    and Blacks, 11
    Manipulation, 345–346
    Sexism, 88
    See also Ad hocing; Conversational
        analysis
Disruption
    Background expectations, assumptions
        revealed, 275, 278–280
    Failure to disrupt, 285–286
    Failures in discrepancies, 279–280
    First-person experimentation, 286–287
    and Games, 274
    Moral considerations, 283–287
    Reality disjuncture, 278
    Retrieval of information, 283
    Senseless action, 276–278, 281–282
    of Social rules, 281–283
    Technical problems, 272–273, 276–
        277, 282
    See also Case Study F; Misfit, cultural;
        Troublemaker, cultural
Distance receptors, 82, 102
Doll, E. A., 176
Don Juan, 125, 268

Double bind, 413–414, 416
Douglas, Jack, 235
Duncan, Otis Dudley, 16
Durkheim, Emile, 8, 13, 14, 15, 16, 90,
    103, 126, 157, 161, 166, 167, 185,
    194–195, 196, 207, 281, 299, 332,
    338, 371, 372
Dyads, 185, 186

E

Eckman, Paul, 83, 89, 102, 103
Edgerton, Robert, 171, 176, 381
Ego, 21, 22, 356
Eidetic approach, 356–357
    Reduction, 364
    Science, 359
Ellsworth, P., 102
Emerson, Joan, 133, 142
Emerson, Robert, 32
Entitlement, 124–125
Erikson, Kai, 32
Errors
    Critical attitude, 313–315, 335
    Fear of, 308, 312
    and Hypotheses, 323
    Qualitative methodology and, 312
    Type I, 311–313, 323
    Type II, 311–313, 323, 326
Esteem, 10–12
    See also Patterns; Socioeconomic status
Ethnography
    Causal nature of social facts, 299–300
    Field studies, 32, 289–304
    and Labeling roles, 33
    Models and frameworks, 295–296,
        298–299
Ethnomethodology
    and Cognitive sociology, 234, 235
    Constructive analysis, 221–224
    "Etc." clause, 217–218
    Ethnologist as member, 223–224
    Formulations, 216–217, 219, 410–411
    Hunt-and-peck, 289–304
    Instruction, 256–259, 265
    Invariant properties, 376
    and Juries, 210–212

Ethnomethodology, *cont.*
  Member, concept of, 212–213
  Mentors, practitioners, 235
  as Methodology, 210–211, 212
  Practicality, 212–213, 214, 220
  Production accounts, 215–216
  Reflexivity, 218–221, 222–223, 224
  Single-case analysis, 290–291
  as "Theory," 224
  Validation, 297–298
  See also Examples; Member; Novice;
    Rational accountability; Setting
Examples
  Empirical status of, 292
  Leading to new aspects of social action,
    294
  Pedagogical uses, 292–293
  Perspective of observer, 295–296
  Pseudogeneralizations, representations
    of totality, 291–292, 293–294
  Source of, 294–295
  Validity of, 295
  See also Critical attitude; Data; Double
    bind; Hypotheses
Excavation, 345–346

F

Facial poses, expression
  as Indicator of emotion, response, 77, 83
  Meanings, 129
  "Micro-displays," 84
  as "Personal front," 191
  See also Audio-visual techniques; Body
    language; "Illustrators"
Farberow, Norman, 156, 160, 167
Feedback
  Constant, 31
  and Instructions, 257
  in Interview situation, 41, 45
  See also Interaction, observer-member
Feshback, Seymour, 102
Field notes
  Analytic memos, 30
  Literal nature of, 28
Filming, 81
  See also Audio-visual technique
Fletcher-Munsen effect, 82

Formal sociology
  and Conceptual laws, 324–326
  Definition of, 180–181
  and Ethnography, 289
  Methodology, 308–310, 375–376
  Models and frameworks, 295–297
  Oneself as part of study, 375–376
  Rigor in, 333–334
  See also Goffman, Erving; Misfit, cul-
    tural; Novice; Relevance; Simmel,
    Georg; Sociation; Trivia; Trou-
    blemaker, cultural
"Free floating intellectual," 184
  See also Marginal man
Freidson, Eliot, 6, 15, 243, 245
Freud, Sigmund, 21, 22, 68
Friesen, W., 102, 103
Function, and social action, 332–333
Functional mental retardation, 170
  See also Case Studies E, F, H; Mental
    retardation

G

Gaddy, Michael, 381
Games
  Disruption interpreted as, 274
  Illegitimate behavior in, 274
  See also Case Study F
Garfinkle, Harold, 51, 60, 70, 73, 74, 79,
    102, 112–113, 114, 115, 128, 129,
    133, 139, 141, 169–170, 176, 181,
    210–224, 225, 234–237, 241, 243,
    249, 252, 260–262, 271–274, 277–
    280, 282–283, 286–288, 309, 334,
    363, 374–375, 377, 381, 397, 416
Gasking, Douglas, 324, 337
"Gatekeepers," 53, 54, 55, 80
  See also Insider; Member; Novice
Gestalt, 8
Gibbs, Jack P., 157, 167
Girton, George, 265
Glaser, Barney, 26–32, 33, 256
Goffman, Erving, 141, 142, 155, 181,
    183–185, 189–194, 206, 207–208,
    225, 235, 243, 259, 295–296, 299,
    304, 309, 369–370
Goldfarb, William, 176

Goode, David, 264, 265, 381–394
Grounded theory, 27–33
  See also Novice

H

Hall, Edward T., 23, 33, 82, 102
Hatt, Paul K., 310
Hays, William L., 334
Haytin, Daniel Leigh, 73
Heap, James Louis, 114, 128–129, 235,
  359, 365, 378
Heidegger, Martin, 358
Heisenberg principle, 127–128
Heisenberg property, 108, 109, 127
Heisenberg's disease, 115
"Heisenberg's Horror," 110
Henry, Andrew, 157, 167
Hochschild, Arlie, 89, 103
Hodge, Robert, 11, 16
Holzman, Burkhart, 235
Horizontal potentials, 128
Horton, John, 334, 339
Hume, David, 166, 167
Husserl, Edmund, 202, 235, 353–356,
  359–361, 364, 365, 378, 417
Hypotheses, 3–4
  and Conceptual laws, 324–325, 327,
    328–329
  Empirical, 322–323, 327, 328
  Function of, criteria for, 322–323, 338,
    373
  and "Generalized other," 24
  Intuition, 326–327
  Statistical, 337
  Theoretical, 322–323
  Validating, 326–327, 328, 336, 339
  and *Verstehen*, 20

I

Id, 21, 22
Ideal types, 19–20, 319
Identification
  as Anthropological or linguistic concern,
    317

  as Sociological tags, 317, 319, 322
  as a Topic, 322
  See also Categories; Labeling theory;
    Misidentification
Idiographic approach, 69
"Illustrators," 84, 102
Ima, Kenji, 238, 264
Impression formation, 301–302, 303
Incorrigible proportions, 324
Indefinite triangulation, 233–234
Indexicality, 219, 224, 237
  and Disruption, 282
  and Patterns, 370
  of Work, 269
  See also Reflexivity
Inferences, indirect
  First-form, 116–119, 128
  "Indexical," 118
  Second-form, 119–123
Infinite regress, 222, 233, 238
Information and Similarities Subtest, 173
Inner dialogues, and social interaction, 22
  See also "Other, generalized"; "Self"
"In-order-to motives," 19
Insider
  Entitlement, 124–125
  Indexical ability, 118
  Knowledge of, 38, 55, 124–127, 149–
    150
  Language of, 124
  Legitimate accounts from, 125–126
  Meaning of accounts from, 47
  Patterns of, and "science," 126–127
  See also Bureaucracy, symbolic; Market
    research; Member; Novice
Intentions
  and Actual actions, 330–332, 338
  Analysis of, 329–332, 359
  See also Function; Motives
Interaction, observer-member, 8, 9, 14
  Ethnographic context, 42, 44
  Involvement, level of, 55–56, 57
  Known observer, 55–56
  Recursive nature of, 45
  Role of observer, 50–51, 57
  "Sensitizing," 39–42
  Tolerance, degree of, 48–49, 55
  Unknown observer, 53–55

Interaction, observer-member, *cont.*
   See also Bureaucracy, symbolic; Case
     Studies E, F, G; Disruption; Market
     research; Mental retardation; Observa-
     tion, participant
Interaction, social
   and Audio-visual techniques, 89
   Children and, 229–230
   in Conversation, 425–427
   and Conversational analysis, 347
   Embarrassment avoidance, 141
   Face-to-face, 191–192, 206, 332
   Functions of, 332–333
   Imitation, 397–404
   Impression formation, 301–302
   and Inner dialogues, 22
   Language and, 227, 409–410
   and Meaning, 24–25, 409–410, 412,
     416
   Misfit, cultural, 260–262
   Ontology, 192–194
   Relevance of terms in, 318–319
   and Setting, 9, 10–11, 29, 190–191,
     303–304
   and Size of group, 185–186
   and Socialization, 371–372
   Strategic, 193
   Syntactical relations, 295–296
   Troublemakers, 262–264
   Unfixed nature of, 193–194
   See also Civil inattention; Case Studies
     E, F, G; Conversation; Conversa-
     tional analysis; Goffman, Erving;
     Mentally ill, the; Process; Public
     places; Reflexivity; Sociation; Topics
     discovered
Interaction effect, 115, 129
Interactional objects, 299
Interactional syntax, 295–296
"Interactional tonus," 191
Interpretation
   Documentary method, 78–80
   and Formal sociologists, 374
   Indicators, 79
   and Intersubjectivity, 371
   and Interviewing, 41–42

of Members of audio-visual data, 85–86
Metalinguistics, 409–410, 412
Perspective, 330–332
and Process, 29
of Respondent, 62–65
and Self-observation, 362–363
and Weber, Max, 20
See also Audio-visual technique; Case
     Studies E, F, G, H; Phenomenology
Intersubjectivity
   Common scheme of communication,
     199–200, 381–382
   Reciprocity of perspectives, 200–202
   and Society, 360, 371
   Trust, 358, 360
   See also Case Studies E, H
"Interview guide," 40
Interviewing
   "Accounts," meaning of, 47, 63–65
   Combined with observation, 45–46
   Constraints, 64–66
   versus Conversation, 62–63
   Deception, 41, 47
   Ethnographic context, 42–45, 62
   Recursive nature of, 45
   Retention and retrieval of data, 43–44
   Structured, 38–39
   Unstructured, 40–42, 80
   See also Bureaucracy, symbolic; Market
     research; Personal account; Respon-
     dent
"Involvement shields," 190
I. Q., 171, 172, 173, 403
   See also Cottel scale; Kuhmann scale;
     Mental retardation; Normality; Sub-
     normality
Itard, Jean, 386, 388, 395

J

Jacobs, Jerry, 16, 45, 62, 64, 70–71, 73,
   74, 80, 89–101, 102, 117–118, 133–
   176, 283, 336, 361, 380
Jefferson, Gail, 121, 129, 236
Jones, Edward E., 338
Jules-Rosette, Bennetta, 265

K

Kaplan, Abraham, 77, 102
Kleiner, Robert, 157, 167
Knowledge
  Abstract thought, 308
  Change through, 307
  through Intersubjective trust, 358
  Retrieval of, 375
  Sight versus thought, 306–308
  See also Case Study F; Member;
    Phenomenology
Koch, Sigmund, 128
Kuhman scale, 172
  See also I. Q.
Kuhn, Thomas, 338, 373, 377

L

Labeling, 317–318, 336
  and the Mentally retarded, 403–404
  Mentors, practitioners, 32
  Theory, 32–33
Labor, division of
  and Collective consciousness, 90
  in Sociological methodology, 308
  See also Bureaucracy; Bureaucracy,
    symbolic
Laing, R. D., 407
Lakatos, I., 337
Language
  Acquisition, 225–226, 228, 230, 237,
    341
  Actor's use of, 8
  Computer, 308
  Esoteric, 229–230, 237–238
  Indexibility, 219–221
  Insider/outsider, 124–126
  Natural, 4–5, 111, 113, 125–126, 298,
    341, 371, 365
  Phenomenologist's, 114
  Structure of host natural language, 304
  as Tool, 227
  See also Case Studies, E, G; Conversa-
    tion; Conversational analysis;
    Phenomenology

Lasswell, H. D., 77
Lavell, Martin, 156, 167
Laws, Donald F., 403, 404
Learning theory, 225–226, 237
Legitimizing beliefs, 3
Lemert, Edwin, 32, 73, 74, 141, 142
Lenneberg, E. H., 237
Life histories
  Accuracy of, 72–73
  Data, collection of, 70–71
  and Goal of questioner, 66
  Idiographic approach, 69
  Nomothetic approach, 69
  Reaction against, 69
  See also Suicides
Linch, Kevin, 347
Lindesmith, Alfred, 32
Linguistics (as opposed to conversational
    analysis), 341–342
Listening noises, 348
Litman, Robert E., 160, 167
Lofland, John, 32, 41, 59, 60
Luckman, Thomas, 235
Luker, Kristin, 27, 33, 67, 73
Lyman, Stanford M., 235

M

Mannheim, Karl, 184
"Marginal man," 48, 66, 184
  See also Free floating intellectual
Market research
  Bias, 141
  Cheating, 135, 136, 137, 140
  Cost analysis, 139
  Failures, 141–142
  "Orientation period," 135–136
  "Random sampling," 136–139
  Researcher attitude, 138–139
  Respondents, nature of, 136–138
  Success of, 133–135
  See also Ad hocing; Bureaucracy, sym-
    bolic; Interviewing
Manipulation, 345–346, 359
  and Mental illness, 406–408, 412–414
Martin, Walter T., 157, 167

Marx, Karl, 77, 126, 243, 266
Maslow, A. H., 393
Matza, David, 32
Mazur, Alan, 376
McGee, Michael, 59
McHugh, Peter, 235
McKinney, J. C., 237
Mead, George Herbert, 7, 21–24, 26, 27, 238
Meaning ascription, 198
Meaning systems, 7
Meanings, 10, 13, 18
   of Accounts, 47
   and Blumer, Herbert, 23–24
   and Ethnographic contexts, 42–43, 44–45, 47–48
   Imputing, 267
   Origin of, 371–373
   and Process, 29
   and Reality, 25, 267
   Reflexivity and indexicality, 219–221
   Symbolically interpreted by sociologist, 18
   and Weber, Max, 18–19
   See also Case Studies E, G; Cognitive sociology; Conversational analysis; Facial poses, expressions; Subjectivity
Merleau-Ponty, Maurice, 358, 416
Media
   Content analysis of, 77–78
   Use of, as symbol system, 87–88
   and Violence, 102
   See also Intersubjectivity
Mehan, Hugh, 258–259, 378
Member, 15–16
   Arbitrary, of group, 61
   Child as, 225, 230
   and Competency, 212–213, 220, 257–259, 268–271, 375, 383–384, 387, 388, 389, 390, 392, 393–394, 427
   Ethnomethodologist as, 223–224
   Knowledge of, 8, 135, 183, 185, 248, 251, 375
   Knowledge unknown to, 299
   Objectivity, as observer, 53–54, 63–65
   Reality of, 258
   Sociologist as, 240, 244, 254
   Term as convenience, 236

   and Trivia, 183
   See also Actor; Case Studies E, H; Ethnomethodology; Insider; Market research; Novice; Personal accounts; Stranger
Mental deficiency, 170, 427
   See also Case Studies E, F, H; Mental retardation
Mental retardation
   Background expectancies, 169
   Causal factors, 171, 172, 175
   and Competence, 383–384, 387–390, 392, 393–394, 427
   Diagnosis, 169, 170–172, 174–175, 427
   Imitation, 397
   I. Q., 171–173, 403
   and Language acquisition, 226
   "Passing behavior," 403
   Perceptions, others' of retardate, 402
   Recoveries, 169–171, 173–175
   Rubella syndrome, 381–394
   Self-perception, 403
   Setting, 169–170, 174
   Severe and/or schizophrenia, 169, 171, 173–174
   Terminology, 170, 171
   and Time, 265
   Treatment, 171, 385, 391, 392, 395–396
   See also Case studies E, F, H; Labeling; Normality; Subnormality; Troublemakers, cultural
Mentally ill, the
   Beliefs of, 406–408, 409–410
   Communication with, 201–202, 206, 207
   and Competence, 412, 416
   Hypothetical attitude, 207
   Listening to, metalinguistically, 409–410, 412, 417
   Manipulation, 406–408
   Perception of, 405–406
   Public and private knowledge, 201–202
   Self-observation, 413–414
   Self-perception, 406–408
   and "Truth" evaluations, 406–407, 409–410, 412–414

See also Case Study G; Mental retardation; Normality; Subnormality
Methodology, 3, 6
  Blumer, Herbert, 25–26
  Developed with research, 381–394
  Limitations of, 376–377
  Mead, George Herbert, 25–26
  Methodological appendixes, 58–59
  Qualitative versus Quantitative, 6, 10–12
  Strategies, 7–11
  Weber, Max, 17–20
  See also Analytic memos; Audio-visual technique; Case Studies A, B, C, D, E, F, G, H; Coding; Cognitive sociology; Content analysis; Conversational analysis; Disruption; Eidetic approach; Errors; Ethnomethodology; Field notes; Formal sociology; Gestalt; Grounded theory; Hypotheses; Identification; Idiographic approach; Interpretation; Interviewing; Labeling; Life histories; Market research; Natural attitude; Null hypothesis; Observation; Observation, participant; Patterns; Personal accounts; Phenomenology; Reactive techniques; Reflexivity; Reification; Sociolinguistics; Subjective phenomena; Suicide notes, a study; Survey research; Symbolic interaction; Topics discovered; Unobtrusive measures; Validity
Micro-displays, 84
Mills, C. Wright, 46, 59, 282, 416
Minnesota Multiphase Personality Inventory, 46
Misfits, cultural, 260–262
  See also Troublemakers, cultural
Misidentification, 323–325, 336
  and Degradation, 346
Moerman, Michael, 336, 428
Moral commitments
  of Known observer, 55
  of Unknown observer, 54
Morals, 10, 13, 374, 375
Motives, 10, 13, 18
  and Action, 19
  as Idiom, 374

"In-order-to," 19
  Observation of, 410, 416
  and Weber, Max, 18, 19
  See also Case Study E; Function
Murray, Joseph P., 102

N

Narens, Louis, 73, 74, 207
National Opinion Research Center, 11, 12, 16
"Natural," sociologists' concern for, 168–169
  See also Mental retardation
Natural attitude
  Constitutive accents, 198
  as Constraint to sociologist, 240
  Disruption of, 277
  and Familiarity, 247, 248
  Intersubjectivity, 199–202
  as Methodology, 208
  Multiple realities, 204, 205
  Practicality, 202–203
  Suspension of doubt, 202, 205
  Time perspective, 203–204
  Transcending, 242, 260–264
  See also Mentally ill, the; Misfit, cultural; Novice; Scientific attitude; Stranger; Troublemaker, cultural
Newman, John H., 287
Nisbett, Richard E., 338
Nomothetic approach, 69
Nondiscursive reasoning, 268
Nonreactive techniques: *See* Audio-visual techniques; Unobtrusive techniques
Nonverbal abilities, 229–231
Normality
  and "Everyday life," 180–181
  and Facial expression, 191
  Inspected through disruption, 273–274, 397–404
  Redefinition of, 427
  See also Case Studies E, F, H; Labeling; Subnormality
Norman, Donald A., 60
North, C. C., 310
Notation, 3, 4
Note taking, 43–44

Novice
  Creating the reality, 257–259
  Grounded theory, constructing, 256
  Instructions, 256–259
  Learning skills, 255–256
  Membership, attaining, 254
  as Observer, 259–260
  Transcending natural attitude, 253–254
  See also Competence; Insider; Misfit, cultural; Troublemaker, cultural
Null hypothesis, 311, 334
Numbers, use of, 4–5

O

Objectivity, 5
  and Common sense, 196
  and Formal sociologists, 374
  of Member, as observer, 53–54
  and Positivisits, 6–7
  and Self-observation, 362–363
  and Troublemakers, cultural, 263–264
  See also Natural attitude; Observation, participant; Phenomenology; Scientific attitude; Subjectivity
Observation, participant
  "Accounts," significance of, 47
  Consensus, 47
  and Contradictory evidence, 46–48
  and the Insider, 125–126
  and Interviews, 45–46
  Involvement and objectivity, 48–49, 55–56, 57
  Known observer, 55–57
  Misfit, cultural, 260–262
  Morals, 54, 55, 283–287
  Multiple observers, 259–260
  in Natural setting, 8–9
  Relationship between words and deeds, 46
  Role of the observer, 50–51, 57
  Sampling and coding, 29–30
  Unknown observer, 53–54, 57
  and Weber, Max, 20
  See also Case Studies E, F, G; Disruption; Grounded theory; Interaction, observer-member; Mental retardation; Methodology; Novice; Stranger

O'Neill, John, 235
Ontology, 192–194, 206
Order theory, 371
"Other, generalized"
  Anticipation of social action, 23–24
  Talking to oneself, 238
  See also Patterns; Self
Outsider
  Entitlement, 124–125
  Language of, 124
  See also Competence; Insider; Member

P

Panikkar, Raymond, 108, 110, 128
Paranoia
  Drug-induced, as study, 291
  Nondiscursive reasoning, 268
  See also Mentally ill, the
Parkinson's Law, 147–148
Parsons, Talcott, 33, 371
Pasamanick, B., 176
Pates, John L., 287, 288
Patterns
  and Data, 334
  Finding and identifying, 192
  and Methods, 370, 412–414
  Situational improprieties, 370
  and Social order, 370–373
  and Symbolic interaction, 373–377
  See also Ethnomethodology; "Other, generalized"; Roles; Social forms; Symbolic interactionists
Perl, Fritz, 22
Personal accounts
  from Agencies, 66
  Analyzing, 61–63
  Interviews, privileges and setbacks, 62–65
  Preaccount data, 62
  Respondent as researcher, 66–67
  Strategies, 65–66, 125
  Tapes, 66
  Validity of, 63–65
  Written documents, 62, 63, 66, 67–68
  See also Actor; Insider; Interviewing; Life histories; Member; Respondent; Suicide notes, a study

Phenomena
Identification of, 299
Measuring, 335
and Phenomenology, 356–357, 359
Phenomenology
Beliefs, 355
Communication, 360
Compared to symbolic interaction, 360
Consciousness, intentional structure of, 356
and Data, 358, 360
Dealing with mentally ill, 412–414
Essence, eidos, 357
Existential nature of, 355–356
and Intersubjectivity, 376
Language of, 114, 365, 376
Mentors, practitioners of, 235
of Mistakes, 405–417
Non-Husserlian practitioners, 358
Observation, 355–356
Personal knowledge, 353
and Phenomena, 356–357, 365
and Phenomenological sociology, 358–363
Reduction, 353–355, 356, 359, 360, 364
as Structure, 245
Transcendental ego, 356
Transcendental subjectivity, 358, 364
See also Case Study E; Common sense; Conversational analysis; Natural attitude; Scientific attitude; Suicide notes
Philips, I., 176
Photo analysis, 81
See also Audio-visual techniques
Pirandello, Luigi, 14, 16, 80, 368
Pitcher, E. G., 334
Polanyi, Michael, 129, 338
Pollner, Melvin, 47, 59, 235, 288, 338, 381
Pomerantz, Anita, 235
Positivists
and Actor's point of view, 10–14
and Data, 5–6
and Science, understanding of, 334
and Self-observation, 362–363
Powell, Elwin H., 157, 167

Preinvitations, 299, 348
Prelinger, E., 334
President's Panel on Mental Retardation, 176
Process, 29, 30
Production accounts, 215–216, 219
Projective technique, 86
Psathas, George, 235
Public places
Behavior in, 190–192, 206
Random collection of "character," 259

Q

Quantitative
Data, 4, 6
Notation, 4
Questionnaires, structured nature of, 39

R

Racism, and status displays, 345–346
See also Ad hocing; Discrimination
Rational accountability
Background expectancies, 214
"Etc." clause, 217–218
and Ignorance, 213–214
Social facts, 214
Reactive measures, 89
Defining activities, 268–271
Moral considerations, 271
Practicality, 270
Reality
Constructed through meaning, 25–26
Multiple, 266–268
as Ongoing process, 268
See also Phenomenology
Reality disjuncture, 47, 288
through Disruption, 278
and Life histories, 71–73
Reflexivity, 51–52, 218–223
Indexical expressions, 219–220, 222, 223, 237, 282
Indexical particulars, 220, 221, 237, 271
and Patterns, 370
and Reasoning, 222–223
Reflexive sociology, 360

Reification
  Disruption, 271–286
  Moral considerations, 270
  Multiple realities, 204, 266–268
  Normality inspected, 273–274
  Practicality, 270
  See also Case Study F; Reactive measures
Relevance
  for Sociologist, 242–245, 312, 316
  in Terms of interaction, 318–319, 320–322
  See also Critical attitude; Topic discovered; Trivia; Validity
Replication, value of, 308, 310, 314
Respondent
  Accuracy of, 72–73
  Deceit, 41
  Ethnographic context, 42, 44, 84–86, 135
  Familiarity and rapport with, 41, 62, 65–66, 391–404
  Meanings of, as insider, 42, 47, 66
  Misfit, cultural, 260–261
  Procedure of, 47
  Relating subjective phenomena, 111–115
  as Researcher, 66–67, 84–86, 87, 88, 112–113, 114
  as Source of general information, 38
  See also Insider; Interaction, observer-member; Intersubjectivity; Interviewing; Personal account; Subjectivity
Rickels, Paul, 134–135
Riskin, Steven, 310, 323–325, 328, 337
Robbins, Thomas, 48–49, 59, 390
Roles
  and Conversation, 29
  Lack of, and social order, 229–230
  and Participant observation, 50–52, 57
  Patient-therapist, 406–410
  See also Interaction, social
Rosenham, D. L., 264
Rosenthal, Robert, 102
Roth, Julias, 32
Roth, Philip, 235, 365

Rubella syndrome, 381–382
Rubinstein, Eli A., 102
Rules
  Analysis of, 333
  Violation of, 397–403
  See also Disruption; Reality disjuncture
Ryave, Alan, 235, 294, 336, 348, 352, 403, 404, 418–428

S

Sacks, Harvey, 65, 73, 130, 216, 235, 236, 299, 304, 312, 314, 320, 321–322, 326–327, 328, 334, 335–336, 338, 363, 416, 427, 428
Sampling, 29–30
  Audio-visual, 88
  in Interviewing, 38
  See also Ad hocing; Market research
Schactel, Ernest, 102
Schatzman, L., 60
Schegloff, Emmanuel, 235, 338, 347, 364
Schenkein, Jim, 236
Scherer, W., 102
Schizophrenics
  Depersonalization, 24
  Personal space, 23
  See also Case Study G; Childhood schizophrenia; Mentally ill, the; Mental retardation; Normality; Phenomenology; Reality
Schutz, Alfred, 19, 33, 73, 126, 181, 183, 194–205, 224, 235, 240, 242, 243, 245, 247, 248, 264, 274, 277, 288, 335, 358, 378
Schwartz, Howard, 114, 122, 128, 129, 130, 248–249, 252–253, 268, 269–270, 291, 299, 304, 310, 335, 338, 346, 405–417
"Science, positive," 4–5
  and the Insider, 126–127
Scientific attitude
  and Common sense, 205, 207–208
  Definition of, 195–196
  Limitations of, 241–242, 247–248

See also Critical attitude; Natural attitude
Scott, Marvin B., 59, 235
Segal, Harvey, 339
"Self"
  "Different selves," 22
  Freud, Sigmund, 21
  Mead, George Herbert, 21-24
  Perception of, 411-412
  Presentation of, 193
  See also "Other, generalized";
    Phenomenology; Social psychology;
    Sociation; Trust violation
Self-deception, 23, 362
Self-observation, 6, 361-363
Self-report form, 112-113
"Sensitizing," 39, 43
Sensitizing concepts, 28, 43, 59
Sequin Form Board, 173
Serendipitous finding, 80-81
Setting
  and Conversation, 29
  Ethnographic context and interview, 42,
    45, 47-48
  of Events, and recounting of, 62
  Filming, as type of, 85, 89
  Gaining access to, 53-55
  Interview, as type of, 64-65
  Isolating the phenomena, 244
  Natural versus contrived, 300-303
  and Observation, 8-10
  Order of, 374
  and Social structure, 9-10
  Varied, and social interaction, 303-304
  See also Audio-visual techniques; Case
    Study E, F; Disruption; Ethnography;
    Insider; Member; Mental retardation;
    Observation; Reactive measures; Reflexivity; Reification; Unobtrusive
    measures
Sexuality, determining, 260-261
Shneidman, Edwin, 156, 160, 167
Short, James F., 157, 167
Shumsky, Marshall, 233-234
Side sequences, 121-122
  See also Conversation

Siegel, Paul, 11, 16
Signs of prohibition, 89-101
Simmel, Georg, 126, 181, 183, 184,
    185-189, 192, 206, 235, 249-250,
    369
Singer, Robert D., 102
"Situational properties," 206
Skinner, B. F., 14, 16, 55, 60
"Snowball sample," 80-81
"Sociability," 188-189, 206
Social equity
  Durkheim, Emile, 90-91
  Prohibition, 89-101
Social facts, 8, 9
  Causal nature of, 299-300, 332
  and General social patterns, 13, 185,
    186, 368
  Occupational esteem studied as, 11, 12
  and Rational accountability, 214
  Suicide as, 157
  See also Phenomenology; Social structure; Trivia
Social forms, 187, 188, 189
Socialization, 371-373
Social order
  Equilibrium, 373
  Order theory, 371
  Universality of, 370-371
"Social physics," 13, 190, 206
Social psychology, 21
  and the Self, 23
Social structure, 10, 185-187
  Children and, 229-230, 281, 373
  and Common sense reasoning, 214-218
  Communication, 186
  Consensus, 186
  "Etc." clause, 217-218
  Flexibility of, 282-283
  and Individual, 187-188
  See also Constraints; Ethnomethodology; Interaction, social; Patterns
"Social territories," 53
Sociation, 187
  See also Goffman, Erving; Lyman, Stanford; Scott, Marvin; Simmel, Georg;
    Social forms

"Society," 188
Socioeconomic status, 10–12, 16, 369
   See also Interaction, social; Methodol-
      ogy; Patterns; Sampling; Social struc-
      ture
Sociolinguistics, 227
   See also Cicourel, Aaron; Cognitive
      sociology; Conversational analysis
Sommer, Robert, 60
Space
   Personal, 206, 275
   Personal, and schizophrenics, 23
Speir, Matthew, 236, 237, 364
Sperling, George, 128
Stearns, Warren A., 74
Stereotypes as conversational items, 27
Stigma, 193
   See also Labeling
Stonequist, Everett V., 59, 184
Stranger
   Ability to "see," 249–250
   Choosing the stranger, 253
   Cultural conventions, 248–249
   Environment to study, 249–251
   Identity of, 251
   Information retrieval, 252
   Language, 124–126, 248, 252
   and Natural attitude, 249
   as Observer, 259–260, 264
   Practical nature of, 248–249, 250
   See also Competence; Insider; Member;
      Misfit, cultural; Novice; Respondent
Strauss, Anselm, 7, 26–32, 33, 60, 256
   See also Glaser, Barney; Grounded
      theory
Structural functionalism, 332
Structuralism, 12–14
Subculture, blacks, 11–12
   See also Manipulation
Subgroups, and socioeconomic status, 12
Subjective phenomena
   First-person method, 109–110
   Heisenberg property, 108, 109, 110
   Interaction effect, 115
   Language difficulties, 112–115
   Perceptions, 115
   Retrieval, 111–115

Third-person method of study, 110–123,
   129
   See also Inferences, indirect; Phenom-
      enology
Subjectivity
   of Actor, 5, 6–7, 18, 19, 263–264
   and Behaviorism, 14
   Conversation, 119
   Data and, 232
   Data removed from, 11
   Intersubjective trust, 358, 360
   and Language structure, 85
   and Mistakes, 405–417
   and Observer, 20–21, 28, 82, 114,
      169–170, 183–184, 319–322, 402
   and Phenomenologists, 6
   and Psychoanalysts, 6, 406
   Reciprocity of perspectives, 200–201
   Selective attention, 82–83
   and Weber, Max, 18, 19, 20
   See also Background expectancies; Bias,
      researcher; Case Studies E, G; Com-
      mon sense; Insider; Mentally ill, the;
      Mental retardation; Natural attitude;
      Outsider; Phenomena; Phenomenol-
      ogy; Subjective phenomena; Suicide
      notes, a study; Translation; Trivia;
      Troublemaker, cultural; Trust viola-
      tion
Subnormality
   Believing respondent, 73
   Redefining, 427
   See also Case Studies E, F, H; Mental
      deficiency; Mentally ill, the; Mental
      retardation
Sudnow, David, 235, 255, 265, 364
Suicide
   Definition, 194–195
   Life-history analysis of, 69, 70–71
   Notes, 70, 71, 78
   Patterns discerned, 71
   Rates, 13–14, 157
   Rationality, 71, 73
   as Social fact, 157
   Sociological theories, 157
   See also Durkheim, Emile; Suicide
      notes, a study

Suicide notes, a study
  Account, unsolicited, 156
  Causes, 156–157, 162
  Direct-accusation notes, 159, 160–162
  First-form notes, 159, 160–162
  Forgiveness, 161, 164, 165
  Formulations, 157–160
  Humor, 166
  Illness notes, 159, 162–163
  Isolation, 162
  "Next World," 164–166
  Notes of instruction, 159
  Rationality, 161–162
  Trust violation, 158, 159–160, 161
  Uncertainties, 165, 166–167
  Will and testament notes, 159–164
Superego, 21, 22
Survey research
  Relationship between words and deeds, 46
  See also Ad hocing; Bureaucracy, symbolic; Market research
Sutherland, Edwin, 32
Symbol system
  Knowledge through, 358
  Portraying the "outside," 213–214
  Use of media as, 87–88
Symbol system, common, in communicating subjective phenomena, 111–115
Symbolic interaction, 6–7
  "Generalized other," 23–24
  and Member's perspective, 375
  and Observation, 9, 29–30
  and Patterns, 373–377
  and Phenomenology, 360
  and Process, 29
  See also Blumer, Herbert; Mead, George Herbert; Meaning; Phenomenology; Weber, Max
Symbolic realism, 48–49
Symbolization, natural, 124
Symbolizations, cultural, 112
Symbols, actor's use of, 8
Szasz, Thomas, 416
Szurek, S. A., 176

T

Tape recording
  Interviewing, 43
  and Personal accounts, 66
Tart, Charles T., 2
Terminology, 3
Theeman, Margaret, 257–258, 265
Thematic Apperception Test, 46, 79, 85
Theory
  Abstraction, level of, 31
  Developing, 30, 32
  See also Analytic memos; Grounded theory; Hypotheses
Thomas, W. I., 15, 25, 70, 74, 236
Thought, nonverbal, 229
Thought, verbal, 107–108, 109
Time perspective, 203–204
  and the Mentally retarded, 265
Tiryakian, Edward, 235, 237
Topics discovered
  as Empirical finding, 315–317
  Exhibition of special relationships, 320
  Identification as, 322
  Methodology of choosing, 317–322
  Validating, 316
  Variables considered, 315–317
  See also Phenomena; Trivia
Transcendental ego, 356
Translation procedure, 112, 113–114, 115
Triad, 186–187, 206
Trivia
  Attitude toward, 184–185
  Formal features of, 184
  and Logic, 211–212
  as Topic, 180–181, 183–185, 243
Troublemakers, cultural, 262–264
Trust violation, 158, 159–160, 161
Tuckman, Jacob, 156, 160, 167
Turner, Roy, 236

U

Unobtrusive measures
  Body language, 77
  Content analysis, 77–78
  Documents, 78–80

Unobtrusive measures, *cont.*
  Indicators, 75–76
  Nonverbal measures, 77–78
  Serendipitous findings, 80–81
  See also Audio-visual techniques

V

Vagueness
  Accepting, 275
  in Instruction, 258–259
  as Social necessity, 222, 241
Validity
  Critical attitude, 313–315, 335
  Double binds, 413, 416
  of Models, frameworks, 295–296
  Problems of, 222, 233, 238
  of Topic discovered, 316
Values
  Lack of, and social order, 229–230
  Origin of, 7
Variables, 315–317, 335
  See also Topics discovered
Verstehen, 8, 9, 15, 16, 19, 20, 33
Victoire of Aveyron, 386, 388, 395
Videotaping, 81
  See also Audio-visual technique

W

Walter, Andrew, 207
Weber, Max, 8, 15, 16, 17–21, 26, 33, 84,
    126, 143–145, 150, 154, 195, 282,
    319
West, Candice, 88, 102, 352, 364
Whorf-Sapir hypothesis, 85
Whyte, William Foote, 32
Wieder, Larry, 235
Wilson, John, 87, 102
Wilson, Thomas, 235, 238, 338
Wood, Houston, 258–259, 265, 378
Work
  Indexical nature of, 269
  as Topic of research, 243–244
  See also Labor, division of
Wulbert, Roland, 243, 245

Z

Zetterberg, Hans, 336
Zimmerman, Don, 88, 102, 235
Znaniecki, Florian, 32, 70, 74
Zweckrational, 20